The Complete Book of
WOODWORKING

The Complete Book of WOODWORKING

Published by Landauer Publishing, LLC
3100 101st Street, Suite A, Urbandale, IA 50322   1/800-557-2144

Produced in cooperation with Publishing Solutions, LLC
James L. Knapp, President

Credits

Tom Carpenter, Director of Book Development

Mark Johanson, Book Products Development Manager, Editor

Dan Cary, Photo Production Coordinator

Chris Marshall, Editorial Coordinator

Steve Anderson, Senior Editorial Assistant

Bill Nelson, Series Design, Art Direction & Production

Mark Macemon, Lead Photographer

Ralph Karlen, Photography

Kim Bailey, Tad Saddoris, Contributing Photographers

Bruce Kieffer, Illustrator

Craig Claeys, Contributing Illustrator

Brad Classon, John Nadeau, Production Assistants

Michele Teigen, Book Development Coordinator

Shelton Design Studios, Cover Designer

ISBN 13: 978-0-9800688-7-0
ISBN 10:   0-9800688-7-8
Printed in China by C & C Offset Printing Co., Ltd.
30 29 28 27 26

Introduction

For anyone with creative instincts and a joy for working with your hands, woodworking can be a very rewarding hobby, perhaps even a lifelong passion. It's more than just a way to turn wood products into furnishings and accessories for your home. It is exercise for your compulsion to be productive. It is a refuge from the stresses of life. It is an art form that yields beautiful objects to make life more pleasant for you and your loved ones. It is an opportunity to experience the pride and satisfaction that can only come from making something yourself.

Once you've started down the woodworking path, you'll find there are many directions you can take. You may enjoy making fine furniture, or perhaps toys and gifts that you can pass along to others. You may be attracted to the design process and spend most of your shop time at the drafting table, dreaming and sketching. Or you may succumb to the lure of the workshop—for many of us, the real pleasure of woodworking is in setting up our own private spot in the world and whiling away the hours simply puttering. The choices are virtually unlimited.

The Complete Book of Woodworking is both an indispensible reference volume and a source of inspiration. In the first section, you'll find fully photographed, step-by-step instructions that show you precisely how to accomplish all of the most essential woodworking skills. Whether you're a beginner or an old hand in the shop, you'll find a wealth of tips and techniques that will make you a better woodworker.

The first chapter, *Setting Up Shop*, provides a useful glimpse into how seasoned woodworkers go about creating and furnishing their workshops. *Designing Woodworking Projects* walks you through the entire process of developing a raw idea into a complete woodworking project plan. *Introduction to Wood* explains the mysteries of wood and offers practical advice on selecting the species that's right for your project, as well as some inside information that will help you find your way around the lumberyard. The fourth chapter, *Squaring, Marking & Cutting Stock,* is a comprehensive guide that shows you how to prepare your rough wood, make layout lines and cut your project parts to size and shape. It also provides a solid introduction to the basic woodworking tools you'll use to machine wood stock.

Making Joints & Assembling Projects discusses the best wood joinery options and techniques, as well as essential clamping and gluing skills. Finally, in *Applying Finishes,* you'll receive a crash course in prepping, staining and topcoating wood.

But *The Complete Book of Woodworking* is more than just a comprehensive reference book for woodworkers. After all, what fun is it to learn new skills if you have nothing to do with them?

Toward that end, we have included plans, measured drawings, cutting lists, instructions and photographs for 40 original woodworking projects you can build to put your new skills to the test. Covering a range of skill levels, from beginner to advanced, the projects create an irresistible menu of furnishings and accessories. No matter what your tastes or needs, you're sure to find just the item you've always wanted to make.

Home Accessories includes plans for a wide variety of clever projects that will make your home more attractive, more functional and truly your own. Included are a beautiful mission-style coat tree, a country-style wall-hung cupboard, benches, boxes, picture frames and more. *Home Furnishings* features plans for bookcases, bigger benches, a dresser, a gorgeous rocking chair, and a couple of tables. All the projects are unique, buildable and beautiful.

Outdoor Projects takes you into perhaps the most popular woodworking area these days. A stunning array of projects for outdoor seating, dining and leisure will dress up any yard or deck. Most are built with dimension lumber and simple joints, making them perfect for the beginner. But you'll find a few eye-poppers that will challenge your skills, as well! Finally, *Workshop Projects* provides plans for a half-dozen helpful furnishing and accessories to make your workshop more functional and pleasant, including a pair of clever workbenches.

Because it is both a thorough guide to woodworking skills and a treasure-trove of terrific woodworking project plans, we think you'll understand why we say *The Complete Book of Woodworking* is truly complete.

IMPORTANT NOTICE

For your safety, caution and good judgement should be used when following instructions described in this book. Take into consideration your level of skill and the safety precautions related to the tools and materials shown. Neither the publisher nor any of its affiliates can assume responsibility for any damage to property or persons as a result of the misuse of the information provided. Consult your local building department for information on permits, codes, regulations and laws which may apply to your project.

Setting Up Shop . . . . page 6

Designing Woodworking
Projects . . . . . . page 16

Introduction to Wood . . . . page 34

Squaring, Marking &
Cutting Stock . . . . page 52

Making Joints &
Assembling Projects . . . . page 94

Applying Finishes . . . .
page 134

Table of Contents

Home Accessories
page 160

Home Furnishings
page 246

Outdoor Projects
page 342

Workshop Projects
page 440

A "Dream Shop" like this is fun to think about but not really a viable option for most of us. Still, by making smart tool-buying choices and using limited space efficiently, you can turn your own modest shop space into a hardworking part of your home that provides a pleasant place to retreat.

Setting Up Shop

A workshop is a defined space that, together with everything contained in it, provides the means to explore your woodworking hobby. Even if you're still at the stage where you're only thinking about learning the craft of woodworking, you probably have a space in mind already, along with some ideas about how you could customize it and furnish it to meet your needs.

Woodworking virtually demands its own space. The necessary power tools are fairly big. The materials, too, are bulky. And with each project you undertake you'll undoubtedly have a few wood scraps or pieces of hardware left over that you can't bear to throw away. And since most projects are completed over a period of days, weeks, months or even years, they'll need a place to reside. Also consider others: woodworking in action isn't always neigh-

borly—the tools are generally noisy and they generate a lot of dust, which can be a real nuisance to those who share your home. Confining the mess and noise to a dedicated area will make everyone happier.

There is no "correct" order to follow when setting up or rehabbing your workshop space. Certainly, it's always good advice to think and plan a bit before you start knocking out walls, running new wiring circuits or maxing out your credit cards at the tool store. But don't get so hung up in the planning and dreaming phase that your workshop never comes into being. Take a few chances, see what works out well for you and your family and what does not. Experiment as you plan. And don't forget that the more pleasant and comfortable your shop environment, the more likely it is that you'll spend time in it—and the more likely you'll be to finish the projects you start.

> The more pleasant and comfortable your shop environment, the more likely it is that you'll spend time in it.

The Basement Shop

The basement offers many advantages as a shop location. It's accessible yet set off from the rest of the house, and the essential house systems are right there. Drawbacks tend to be limited headroom, negligible natural light, concrete floors and overall dampness/poor ventilation.

The Garage Shop

The garage, especially one attached to the house, offers the convenience of a basement shop with fewer drawbacks. Overhead doors provide excellent access, greater headroom, lower humidity and better ventilation. The main general drawback is that garages are usually home to one or more vehicles and a host of other outdoor items. A good solution is to mount your stationary tools on casters so they can be wheeled out of the way to make room for other things.

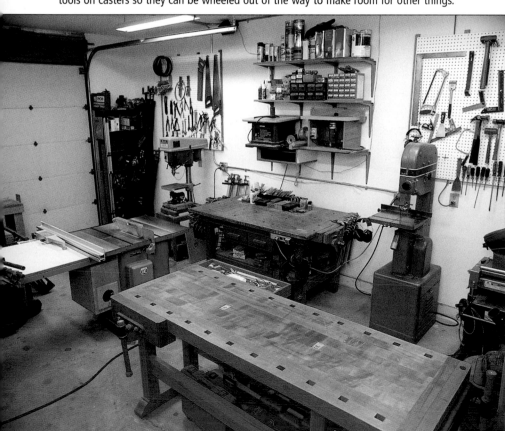

Choosing Your Space

Without a doubt, the best shop is a large, separate building, with plumbing and heat. It is divided up to include a storage area adjoining a large door to the outside, a central workspace, and a finishing room that's walled off from the rest of the shop and ventilated to the outdoors. Obviously, establishing and maintaining such a shop requires money and space that most of us don't have available. So look for realistic alternatives.

The two most common shop locations are the basement and the garage. Shops have been set up in spare rooms, attics, even in closed-in porches. When assessing potential shop areas, or considering upgrading or remodeling your current shop, keep the following factors in mind:

Space needs. You'll want to have enough space to maneuver full-size sheet goods and boards that are eight feet or longer. Ideally, this means a large enough area that you can feed large stock into a stationary tool with enough clearance on the infeed and the outfeed side.

Access. You'll need a convenient entry/exit point so you can carry materials into the shop and completed projects out of the shop.

Power. You should never run more than one tool at a time (except a tool and a shop vac or dust collector). Nevertheless, you'll need several accessible outlets.

Light. Adequate light is essential for doing careful, comfortable, accurate and safe work. You'll need good overall light (a combination of natural and artificial light sources is best) as well some movable task lighting.

Ventilation/climate control. To help exhaust dust and fumes, you need a source of fresh air and dust collection. Depending on where you live, year-round shop use likely will require a means of heating and/or cooling the shop as well as controlling humidity.

Isolation. Keep the inevitable intrusions of noise and dirt into the rest of the home to a minimum.

Mount a power strip to the base of your workbench, assembly table or workstation where you'll be using more than one power tool. Retractable extension cords provide an additional power supply and can be hung from the ceiling to stay out of your way when not in use.

An articulated desk lamp provides focused task lighting that's easy to move wherever it's needed In your shop. Incandescent lighting is the best choice for task lights that are used frequently.

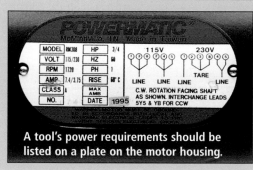

A tool's power requirements should be listed on a plate on the motor housing.

Calculate your power load

Add up the total wattage (amperage times voltage) of each tool and light on a circuit. Note: Use the wattage listed on incandescent bulbs. The wattage requirements for fluorescents needs to be increased 20% to account for the lamp ballast load. Generally, the maximum load for a 15-amp circuit using either 14-gauge or 12-gauge wire should be under 1,500 watts. A 20-amp, 12-gauge circuit should not carry more than 2,000 watts of load. Include every item in the circuit that draws power, whether you plan to run them at the same time or not. If your total wattage exceeds the ratings of the circuit supplying your shop, add an additional circuit or two.

Power & Lighting

Nearly every potential shop space will need electrical improvements. You may not need to go to pro-shop extremes, where each tool has a dedicated circuit. But avoid putting larger stationary tools (especially dust collectors) on a shared circuit. Since many larger stationary tools run on 230-volt service, it's not a bad idea to run a 230-volt circuit for future use if you're already updating the wiring.

There is a limit to the number of receptacles or fixtures you can hang on a circuit. A good rule of thumb is 8 to 10 lights or outlets per circuit. Rules and regulations are outlined in the National Electrical Code (NEC), but you should also consult your local city or county codes. Unless you have experience wiring, hire a licensed electrician for the job.

The best lighting for the shop is a balance of natural and artificial light and a balance of overall light and task light. Unfortunately, natural light is often hard to come by; many shops simply don't have windows. One way to compensate for poor lighting is simply to do some basic cleanup and some painting with a light color. The walls and ceiling are the primary reflective surfaces, but a floor covered with light-colored enamel paint or vinyl tile will also make a big difference.

At minimum, you should have 20 foot-candles of lighting at floor level, throughout the shop: figure on providing at least one-half watt of fluorescent light or 2 watts of incandescent light for each square foot of shop floor (fluorescent lights are four to six times more efficient than incandescent and cast more uniform, shadow-free light). You'll also need task lighting.

Wiring tips

■ Separate lighting circuits from receptacle circuits. If you trip a breaker with a power tool, you don't want to be left in the dark.

■ Provide full power to a centrally located workbench through a floor-mounted receptacle or via a retractable cord suspended from the ceiling.

■ Alternate the circuits from receptacle to receptacle. Or, wire each outlet of a duplex receptacle to a different circuit. That way, if you plug a power tool into one outlet and a shop vac into the other, then run both simultaneously, you'll be drawing power from two circuits, rather than one.

■ Ground-fault circuit interrupters (GFCIs) are required in garages, unfinished basements, outdoors, and locations near water.

Ventilation, Dust Collection & Climate Control

An elaborate dust collection system is the hallmark of a serious woodworker. In this shop, each stationary tool has a dedicated hose and port that tie into the central vacuum ductwork.

Ventilation. In any shop, ventilation can be problematic. The air fills with fine sawdust particles or finishing fumes very quickly. Airflow—all it takes is a window or attic fan—can clear the air, but if it carries the dust and stink into the living areas, or pulls cold air into the heated space, it isn't a remedy. An ambient air filtration system that circulates air though filters may be your best solution.

Dust collection. Accumulating sawdust is the bane of the woodworker. It conceals cutting lines, plugs up tools and presents several dangers to your safety. That's why setting up a system to remove as much sawdust as possible at the source is so critical.

Climate control. Heating a shop is important not simply for your personal comfort. Some woodworking operations—gluing and finishing are examples—are sensitive to temperature. A wide range of heating systems are available: central systems, radiant panels, in-wall space heaters, and portable space heaters fueled by wood, oil, gas, propane, kerosene, and electric, even coal and pellets. Avoid open-coil electric heaters, kerosene heaters, and open-flame heaters of any sort, because they can ignite sawdust, wood shavings, or flammable finishes in a shop. Use dehumidifiers and humidifiers to control shop humidity.

A humidity gauge lets you monitor the humidity level in your shop so you can run humidifiers and dehumidifiers as needed to keep the humidity constant for the duration of your project. Where possible, try to achieve a base humidity level that is roughly the same as the average humidity in the room where the project will end up.

Dust collection/air filtration devices improve air quality in the shop. *Single-stage dust collectors* attach to stationary power tools through a system of flexible ductwork. A motor-driven impeller draws air through the ductwork and into replaceable collection bags. *Ambient air cleaners* are fitted with filters to trap fine, airborne dust that can elude other dust collectors. Both portable and ceiling-mounted styles are available. A *shop vacuum* is handy for spot-cleaning but not designed to be the heart of a dust-collection system.

Single-stage dust collector

Portable ambient air cleaner

Ceiling-mounted ambient air cleaner

Shop vacuum

Workshop Furnishings

A shop needs flat sturdy worksurfaces and plenty of storage. Both of these needs are filled by your workshop furnishings.

Workbench. A first-class bench can be expensive, but you don't need anything elaborate. A low-cost handyman's bench from the local home center may actually be better for your needs. You can also build your own. Simple workbenches aren't difficult to make, and you'll end up with exactly what you need. You can even speed things up a bit by using some prefabricated materials, like cabinets and countertops. Bench dimensions vary by intended use, but a good all-purpose bench size is 34 in. high, 30 in. wide, and 60 in. long.

Regardless of the design of your workbench, you want it to be heavy and rigid. The starting point is the leg assembly. A commercial joiner's bench usually has a trestle-type base assembled with mortise-and-tenon joints. It will be made of hard maple or beech, maybe oak. But a massive, rigid structure can be built with nothing more exotic than 2 × 4s, glue, and drywall screws. The resulting bench may not look as handsome as a commercial unit, but it will be heavy and very strong. The time-honored way to beef up a bench is with a thick top. Manageable ways of getting a good top include buying a length of butcher-block countertop, face-gluing lengths of well-dried Douglas fir 2 × 4s, and layering several pieces of plywood, particleboard, or medium density fiberboard (MDF). Two or three coats of penetrating oil, such as tung oil or Danish oil, is the best finish for a benchtop. Never stain or paint a benchtop; the color can mar workpieces.

Vises & bench dogs. Strong and easy to operate, a bench vise is all metal, including the jaws (add wood facings to the jaws to protect your work). A sliding dog in the movable jaw, used in conjunction with a dog in the benchtop, comes in handy for clamping work on the bench surface. One great feature is the quick-

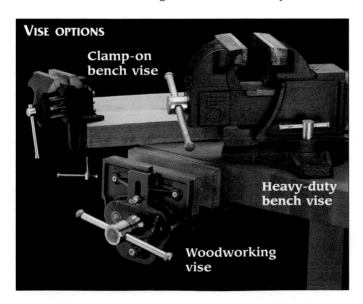

VISE OPTIONS

Clamp-on bench vise

Heavy-duty bench vise

Woodworking vise

A woodworker's workbench (purchased or shop-built) with one or two woodworking vises, bench dogs and a heavy-duty hardwood benchtop is the centerpiece of a wood shop.

A rugged set-up table made from dimension lumber and sheet goods is economical, easy to make and can accommodate most woodworking functions.

Kitchen cabinets work well in a shop. Find inexpensive or used base cabinets and attach a countertop to create a worksurface that can also be used for short term storage or a workstation.

Lumber storage

(Left) Exposed wall framing members (or ceiling joists) in garages or basements can be converted to out-of-the-way storage spots for lumber simply by attaching a scrap wood rail that spans the framing members and holds the boards in place.

(Right) A typical lumber rack is constructed from inexpensive dimension lumber. It should contain several racks for storing lumber flat, as well as a vertical cubby for storing full-size sheet good panels on-edge. The vertical supports should be tied into both the floor and the ceiling.

action lever, which allows the front jaw to be moved without all the tedious cranking.

Mount at least one vise on your bench, bolting it to the underside of the benchtop, so the top edges of the jaws are flush with the bench's top surface. Bench dogs expand the utility of your vise. Locate a row of dog holes in line with the pop-up dog on your vise. Position them about 4 in. apart.

Workbench storage. Storage can be organized under the workbench. Most straightforward is a simple shelf for tools and supplies. A built-in cabinet, with drawers and doors, does a better job of organizing the space and keeping things clean, but it blocks access to the benchtop for clamping purposes. The best compromise is a cabinet installed between the bench legs, 8 in. or so below the benchtop.

Storage furnishings. Woodworking involves a vast array of tools, equipment, accessories, supplies, and materials that make well-designed storage essential. The photos on these two pages will give you some good ideas for coping with clutter.

A rolling lumber cart makes transporting stock to the work area more convenient, but its best feature is that you can move it out of the way as needed to free up working space in a small workshop.

Perforated hardboard (pegboard) is a trademark of the organized workshop. In addition to general pegboard hooks, you can purchase whole systems of hanging devices in many sizes and configurations. Use tempered hardboard and set it into a sturdy frame to create clearance for the hook ends behind the pegboard.

Wall-mounted clamp racks protect your clamps and keep them organized and accessible. A few lengths of scrap lumber and some ingenuity are all it takes to devise your own clamp storage system. Cut notches to hold heavier bar and pipe clamps. Smaller clamps can simply be tightened onto your rack or hung from a cord.

A rolling scrap bin is handy in shops of all sizes, and can even double as an outfeed "table" if the rim of the bin is set to the proper height. Use the bin to store cutoff pieces while a project is in progress. Then, once the project is built, sort through the leftover pieces and save or discard them as you see fit. You might consider painting the bin to avoid confusing it with your trash can.

A locking cabinet is a good idea for storing your valuable hand tools and portable power tools. More than security against theft, it keeps them from being used by kids or unauthorized people. You can make a basic cabinet yourself from just a couple of sheets of plywood. For maximum efficiency, measure the height and depth of your tools first and dimension the cabinet with a suitable space in mind for each tool.

A roll-around cabinet, like this mechanic's parts cabinet, is a great shop furnishing for storing hand tools, saw blades, drill bits, hardware and other small tools that need to be kept organized. By rolling the cabinet to your work area, you'll save a lot of trips back and forth across your shop retrieving tools or putting them away again.

A metal cabinet with tight-closing, locking doors is not only a good idea for storing finishing materials and chemicals, it's also required by most fire codes for commercial workshops. Used office furnishing stores are great places to look for metal cabinets like the one shown here. Paint a clearly visible warning on the cabinet doors.

Workpiece Support

Furnish your shop with a number of convenient (and preferably portable) work supports. Adequate workpiece support is critical to making accurate, safe cuts. Most woodworkers have several different types of work supports in their shop, from manufactured, adjustable outfeed supports to saw table extensions. A few sturdy pairs of sawhorses will also come in handy. And you can use rolling caster bases for your benches or other stationary tools to set the top surfaces at a uniform height.

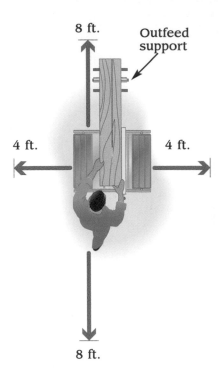

A power miter saw workstation with auxiliary tables and fences lets you support and cut longer stock without having to set up additional supporting devices first. Keeping your portable tools in one spot as much as possible also prevents them from falling out of square as readily.

Make room for sawing. Allow 4 ft. of clear space on each side of a table saw and 8 to 10 ft. in front and in back so you'll have plenty of room to work. Be sure to have adequate outfeed support in place when cutting larger stock.

"Sturdy" and "movable" are the two most important characteristics of good work support. Casters can make just about any shop furnishing into a useful work support (photo above). And you can never have too many sawhorses or portable workstations (right photo).

Tips for setting up & equipping a safe workshop

Protect hearing with ear muffs (A) expandable foam earplugs (B) or corded ear inserts (C).

Protect against dust & fumes. A particle mask (A) is for general work. A dust mask (B) has replaceable filters. A respirator (C) can be fitted with filters and cartridges.

Protect eyes. A face shield (A) is for very hazardous work. Safety goggles (B) and glasses (C) with shatterproof lenses are for general cutting and shop work.

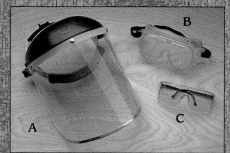

A first aid kit should contain (as a minimum) plenty of gauze and bandages, antiseptic first aid ointment, latex gloves, a cold compress, rubbing alcohol swabs, a general disinfectant such as iodine and a first aid guidebook.

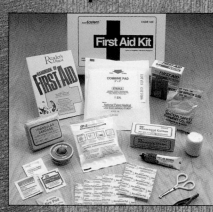

The ABC's of fire extinguishers

Fire extinguishers are rated by their ability to combat fires of varying causes. An extinguisher rated "A" is effective against trash, wood and paper fires. "B" will extinguish flammable liquid and grease fires. "C" can be used on electrical fires. For the workshop, choose a dry chemical extinguisher with an "ABC" rating.

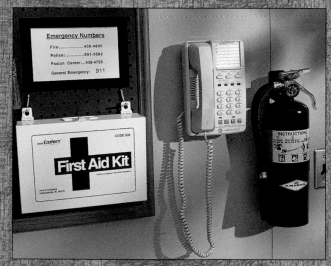

Create an emergency area
The workshop is perhaps the most accident-prone area of your home. Sharp blades, heavy objects, dangerous chemicals and flammable materials are just a few of the factors that increase the risk of accidents in the shop. While good housekeeping, respect for your tools and common sense will go a long way toward reducing the risk of accidents, you should still be prepared in the event an accident occurs. Designate part of your shop as an emergency center. Equip it with a fully stocked first aid kit, fire extinguisher and telephone with emergency numbers clearly posted.

Avoid fatigue
A lapse in concentration brought on by physical or mental fatigue is responsible for most shop accidents. A few simple precautions, like setting a cushioned floor mat at your workstations, can help reduce physical fatigue. Take plenty of breaks to stay mentally alert and never work with tools if you've consumed drugs or alcohol.

22¾"

• solid cherry
• legs tapered on 2 sides

Table top dip

32"

GERMANY

TABLE IDEAS

Designing Woodworking Projects

Decisions, decisions, decisions. That's what designing a project is all about. Whether you use an existing project plan, modify an existing plan, or develop your own plan, completing a design process is a necessary and rewarding first step before you ever start to build your project.

Most people think of project design as merely deciding the appearance, or the "look" of the finished piece, but there's much more to it than that. It's a process that takes you through all the aspects of developing your best ideas, then figuring out the best way to give those ideas form in the shape of a woodworking project. It also helps you plan thoroughly so your project will function as intended. When you're done with the design process, no decisions should be left unmade.

Essentially, you build your project using drawings, prototypes, and a lot of forethought prior to the construction stage. Think the plan through completely. It is possible to work out some details during the construction, but it's much better to anticipate and solve those problems in advance, rather than backtracking during the construction and even remaking part of what you've already built.

As you work your way through the design process, you'll want to consider goals such as: creating a piece with an overall appealing look that also fits well in its surroundings; making your style, proportions, wood, moldings and details, hardware, and finish choices all blend together; and making sure your piece will work. If it's a chair, will it be comfortable? If it's a storage cabinet, will the items fit well in the space you provide? You'll also want to consider the tools and construction techniques needed to create your project, and what different ways there may be to achieve similar results better and more efficiently.

Project design may seem like a daunting process, but it doesn't need to be. In fact, most woodworkers feel that the contrary is true. The more involved and familiar you become with the design process, the more rewarding and easier it and your construction process will become. While you don't necessarily need to follow the steps of the design process in the order given in the pages that follow, you do need to follow them in some manner. You'll probably find that you jump from step to step and go back and forth a bit. This is fine as long as you do it all, and do it thoroughly. Get in the habit of using the fundamentals of design, and your finished projects will be much more satisfying and definitely much better accomplished.

This chapter will guide you through the design process so you can make better design decisions. The process will show you how to analyze your options, and it will explain the reasons why you might choose one option over another. The end results should help ensure that you design a solid project you'll be happy with. The last part of this chapter will explain different types of drawings you can make to help you visualize your ideas, as well as a section about the process of building prototypes to help you work out your design details quickly and three-dimensionally.

> *Project design is a process that takes you through all the aspects of developing your best ideas then figuring out the best way to give those ideas form in the shape of a woodworking project.*

WOODWORKING WORKS

A successful woodworking project starts with a well-planned design. You can base your plan on a familiar furnishing, like the Mission-style rocker to the right, or come up with something completely new and completely yours, like the play table and chairs on the left.

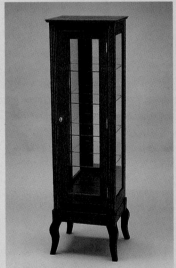

What should I build?

Deciding what to build is the point where the design process seems to always begin.

Most often, the desire to build something comes from a specific need: Maybe the need is to replace an old, worn out piece of furniture, or to build a piece of furniture to supplement the furnishings you already have. Perhaps you need an entertainment center to organize and store your audio and video equipment and accessories, or a bookcase to hold all of your books. Maybe your goal is as simple as the desire to build something. Or perhaps you want to challenge your woodworking skills by trying something different or learning something new. Sometimes even the desire to make something in a style you haven't worked in before is reason enough to get you started.

I recently built myself a new desk. My old desk got too small for all the things I wanted close at hand and the desktop was jammed with computer equipment, leaving me no room to work comfortably. My office was large enough to handle a much bigger desk. So there I was: I had a need to fill and I decided to design and build a new desk for myself. And it turned out great—mostly because I spent a lot of time with the design process.

Deciding what to build is probably the easiest part of the design process. All it takes is a little imagination and some planning. And remember that a healthy desire to explore new techniques is what makes woodworking a hobby, not a chore.

~Bruce Kieffer

The Woodworking Project Design Process

The woodworking project design process starts with a simple idea, sometimes based on a specific need. The raw idea is tossed around, mulled over and compared to other ideas, existing furnishings and design styles. Gradually, a rough concept takes shape, usually in the form of a sketch. The concept is tested by making more sketches or models and simple prototypes. The bugs are worked out. Finally, it is put down on paper in a measured, dimensioned form, along with cutting lists, shopping lists and details of some of the joinery. The end result is a hard plan that becomes the road map to building your woodworking project.

Generating project ideas

There is no single best way to come up with good ideas for woodworking projects. But there are a few places you can look to help you refine a basic concept. One of them is actual pieces of furniture, whether they're in your home, a friend's home, or a furniture store. Seeing living, breathing woodworking projects and home furnishings will give you an opportunity to scrutinize different designs and styles up close; to get an idea how the parts fit together; to analyze the small details, as well as the overall proportions; and to evaluate how well different pieces of furniture function.

Another good way to generate and refine your ideas is simply to discuss them with fellow woodworking enthusiasts. They're usually not hard to find and are more than happy to chat about their favorite pastime with anyone who will listen (See *tip box,* next page).

The local library or your own collection of books and magazines can be excellent sources to help you put a face on the project you've been imagining. You may even encounter a completed set of project plans that meets your needs to a tee. Many woodworking project plans include drawings, cutting lists, shopping lists, how-to instructions and photographs. And if what you find is close, but not exactly what you need, most likely you can modify it to suit your needs. You can save a lot of design time by using an existing plan. Just make

Evolution of a woodworking project

1 Create the design. This step is not as simple as it sounds, but for many woodworkers it is perhaps the most gratifying, if not fun, stages of the process. In it, you'll move from a raw idea to a hard plan.

2 Build a prototype. Not everyone chooses to test their plan by building a scale model or a simple prototype, but it is the best way to catch errors and make improvements before you start. Prototyping often takes place before the hard plan is finished.

3 Build the project. The more time you spend in the design phase, the more smoothly the actual construction of your project will go. You may still end up doing a little bit of "designing on the fly," but the chances of a major catastrophe are greatly reduced if the plan is solid.

Antique stores, salvage yards and furniture stores are rich with possibilities for generating ideas. Explore them. Pay attention to shapes and proportions and even joinery techniques. If you see something you like, chances are you can come up with a way to make one for yourself.

sure to work out in advance those aspects of the published plan that are new to you.

Even watching television and movies can be a productive way to generate some good ideas. This may sound a little strange, but most professional woodworkers and designers are on constant lookout for new ideas. Television and movie stylists tend to put a lot of time and effort into choosing their props, and they pay attention to style and design trends.

In reality, the things that can influence you and help you generate ideas are everywhere—you just need to look closely and you will see them.

Creating a concept sketch. Once you have a rough idea of the project in mind, it's time to get it down on paper. The initial drawings, called "concept sketches," don't need to be fancy or even drawn to scale. But getting them down on paper is the trigger to refining the design—it's also a good idea to have a representation of the idea that you can hold onto, since none of our memories are what they used to be.

As you sketch and doodle, start thinking about some of the more concrete design issues: Is there a particular style you favor (See pages 22 to 23)? Exactly how big do you want it to be? What should the proportions be (See pages 24 to 25). In short, play around with ways the project might look until you find one you like.

Share ideas with other woodworkers

One of the best sources for project ideas is other woodworkers. As a group, woodworkers love to talk about woodworking. You probably already know a lot of other woodworkers, but if not, they're easy to find. Look in the phone book to find local professional woodworkers. But don't just pop in on the professionals. Be considerate, call and ask if they would be willing to spend a little time guiding you. Phrased that way you're more likely to get advice.

You can also find woodworkers at a local woodworking club or guild. Woodworking guilds can be professional, amateur, or a combination of both. Most of the members are amateur woodworkers who joined to learn more about woodworking by attending our monthly educational meetings. You could also visit

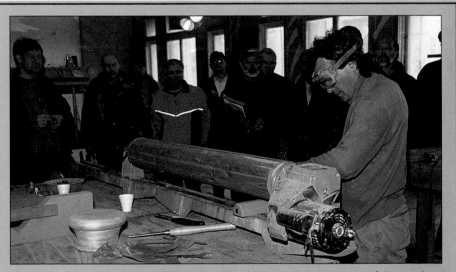

At a typical woodworker's guild meeting, like this one in Minnesota, one of the members or a special guest will give a demonstration on a new or favorite technique.

your local woodworking supply stores and see who you run into. Woodworkers are all over those places, and most of them are very eager to talk shop and give out a few of their opinions.

Practical considerations. Once you've got a fairly detailed concept sketch in hand, and a pretty good idea of where you're headed with the project, turn your attention to some of the more practical details.

One of the first "practical" decisions you'll need to make, other than the approximate size and scale, is which wood species to use. In most cases, the furniture style you choose will dictate the best wood species to use. If your goal is to reproduce a style accurately, then not just any wood will do. For example; Mission-style pieces were almost all built using quartersawn white oak. Not only would it be a shame to build a Mission-style piece using, say, knotty pine, it probably wouldn't look right. In the same respect, building a country-styled piece using teak would be a questionable choice. It isn't unheard of for professional designers to throw an odd species or two into a more traditional plan for effect, but more likely than not you'll be disappointed with the outcome if you try it.

As much as (if not more than) style, function and budget will bear on your wood species selection. Outdoor furniture, for example, must be made using rot-resistant lumber or it won't hold up to the weather.

Browse published woodworking plans in your search for project ideas. You may even stumble across a design and plan that will work for you, saving you a lot of time and energy. Since most published plans already are shop-tested, you can be fairly confident that they're accurate (but it's still a good idea to double-check as you read the plan).

Unless you're willing to shell out the money for teak or mahogany, that leaves white oak, redwood, cedar and cypress as the main options (excluding pressure-treated pine, which is perfectly suitable for projects that are not "fine woodworking"). By the same token, making a woodworking bench using a softwood would not be advisable. It wouldn't be long before the benchtop would wear out and the joints would fall apart from the stresses they'd receive. When building any kind of load bearing piece, you need to consider the strength of the wood you choose. Softwoods crush easily, and under repeated stress, the joints will weaken and fail quickly.

As for the budget issue, you should certainly factor it in. If making your spice rack out of zebrawood means your material costs would be $100 instead of $20 for maple, ask yourself if the benefit is worth the extra cost. But be sure to consider the impact, if any, the species choice will have on the longevity of the product. If the zebrawood spice rack will last 50 years and the maple only three, which one is the better bargain? The old tool-buyer's saw "Buy the best tool you can afford" can easily be applied to wood selection.

Another factor that should influence your wood species choices is the desire to match the piece you plan to build with

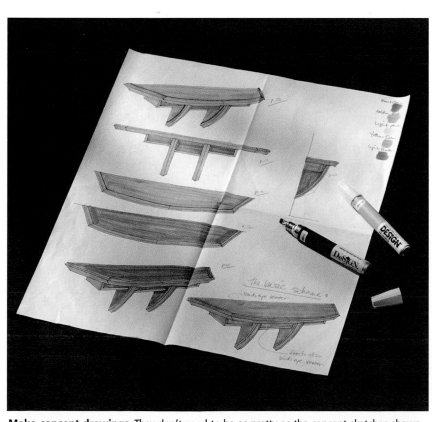

Make concept drawings. They don't need to be as pretty as the concept sketches shown above, but making a few drawings that capture the gist of the project will get the project-design ball rolling.

American Farm	**Country**	**Queen Anne**
Typical features: Elaborate "pressed" back-rest with relief design, heavily beaded turned legs and spindles, caned seats.	Typical features: Overall rustic appearance (although often achieved with complex construction methods).	Typical features: Cabriole legs, upholstered seat, curved back legs with decorative center slat, spindle-turned spreaders.

The Essentials of Style

"Style" is a bit of a double-edged sword when it comes to woodworking. Borrowing from a particular furniture style is a good way to ensure that your project design will work out, but paying too much attention to the period of a piece can limit your creativity and even cause you to lose sight of the most basic goal: creating a nice furnishing for your home. But as you work through the basic questions you need to answer when starting to develop a project plan, it is still a good idea to take style into consideration—especially if the piece you build will coexist with other furnishings of a definite style.

Another good reason to consider style is that it can help you make some initial decisions about the difficulty of the project you want to attempt. If you're a beginning woodworker, for example, you should consider some of the easier to build styles such as Mission, Shaker, country, contemporary, and modern. They tend to incorporate simple shapes with less complex construction techniques, and rely more on relative proportions to achieve their appearance than they do on complex details.

This is not to say that these styles are not for more advanced woodworkers, since some pieces made in these styles can be very complex. It's just that these styles are easy to simplify using modern woodworking techniques, thereby eliminating some or most of the complex joinery. More complex and detailed styles, such as early American, Victorian, classic, traditional, Queen Anne, and gothic, should not necessarily be ruled out from the outset. Making your piece using one of these styles may be challenging, but could also be very rewarding.

The photographs on these two pages give a good illustration of the effect style has on the appearance of a piece of furniture. By comparing and contrasting the characteristics of each of the nine chairs shown, you'll get a fair idea of which features define each particular style type. Although some of the elements are unique to chairs, look for details you find appealing and, if you're interested in tackling a period woodworking project, use the information as a starting point for investigating a little deeper into the style you like.

Folding Chairs
Typical features: Hinged legs and seat to fold flat, often slat-built, not technically a design "style" but still a good option.

Danish Modern
Typical features: Spare, open design, graceful curves, strong horizontal lines, often built with teak and dark non-wood accents.

Contemporary
Typical features: Irregular shapes, parts made from laminated sheet goods, no ornate detailing.

Windsor
Typical features: Arched back frame with spindle infills, scooped seats, splayed legs connected by spindle spreaders.

Shaker
Typical features: High backs, round or tapered legs, woven seats, simple and graceful appearance.

Mission
Typical features: Simple, square joints, narrower slats and spreaders, mortise-and-tenon joints, usually quartersawn oak.

the wood found in other furniture pieces and trim that will be in the same room. Before purchasing all your stock, get a sample of the lumber so you can see what it looks like with finish applied. Compare the sample to wood you're trying to match.

Solid wood, plywood or veneer? Will you use only solid lumber, or a combination of solid lumber and hardwood plywood, or even make your own veneered panels? Once again, this decision is most often dictated by the style you've chosen. Sleek modern styled projects almost always are built using plywood with solid wood edgings. This is because of the necessity to account for wood movement. The doors and drawers used on modern styled pieces are flat panels with small gaps between the parts. Even if you live somewhere where the

Outdoor projects require rot-resistant lumber, like the cedar being used to build the planter above. The species of wood you'll use can impact the longevity of your project.

relative humidity is constant all year long, using solid wood for these parts would be a bad idea.

Choosing hardware & finishes. Decisions about functional hidden hardware such as concealed hinges, drawer slides, and fasteners, as well as decorative exposed hardware, such as butt hinges, and door and drawer handles, need to be made as part of the design process. If you're trying to make a decision about some piece of functional hardware that's new to you, and you're not completely sure how it will work, then now's the time to make a simple prototype. Let's use a drawer slide as an example. Say you choose a new style drawer slide that you haven't used before. Staple together four boards to imitate a cabinet, and four boards to imitate a drawer (this is as sophisticated as a prototype need be). Mount the slide and see that it functions as you want it to. Doing this will also give you an idea of how forgiving the mounting tolerances will be. This is important to know since it may require you to preform the construction with a greater degree of accuracy than you're accustomed to.

Choosing your decorative hardware can be more difficult because of all the choices available. Look-

Veneer

Making your own veneered panels is a great alternative to using manufactured plywood. Using veneer allows you to apply thin solid wood edgings to particleboard cores, and then apply the veneer on top of that construction. With the edging strip under the veneer, you get the look of a solid wood panel, but

Exotic and distinctive veneer types include: (A) Zebrawood; (B) Birdseye maple; (C) African Padauk (vermillion); (D) Madrone burl; (E) Maple burl; (F) Purpleheart. All shown with oil finish.

with a stable construction like plywood provides. Plus, using veneer gives you the opportunity to really get your creative juices flowing with all the different ways you can match the veneer sheets together. Using it is an option you should consider if you're a moderately experienced woodworker and you want total control of the finished look of the project you plan to build. There are many good books available that can teach you how to make veneered panels if this technique is new to you. By veneering your own panels, you can also make "custom" sheet goods with unusual or exotic faces not found in lumber yards or building centers.

ing in hardware catalogs is a great way to start, but you should make your final decisions with an actual piece of the decorative hardware in your possession.

The time to choose a finish is also during design, not after your project is built. You want to know far in advance how the finish will look and how it will be applied. Unless you're very familiar with the finishing product you plan to use, you should test it on a large scrap of the actual project stock.

If you plan to stain your wood, you'll need to make more involved samples. You need to find out in the design stage how the stain looks on a large sample, and you need to know how easy or difficult it is to apply. Some stains are harder to apply than others. Gel stains and other thick stains tend to be more difficult to apply, and oil stains somewhat easier. When planning to use a difficult-to-apply stain, make samples of inside corner joints. Since a stained inside corner has to be wiped cross grain, that can have a huge effect on how the stain looks there. To complete your stained samples, also apply the topcoat product you plan to use. The topcoat will alter the look of the stained board in most cases.

Use sheet goods to build cabinetry. Contemporary cabinets often are made with visible reveals between the doors and cabinet box. As a result, even a little warpage will be easily noticeable. Since plywood and other sheet goods are much more stable, you're less likely to have warpage problems using them than with glued up solid wood panels.

Test hardware on working project prototypes, especially if you don't have any experience with that type of hardware. Drawer slides, especially, vary a great deal in installation method and in acceptable tolerance for error, and they can impact the required size of the drawer opening.

Test finish products on scraps of the same type of wood to be used in your project. Once you've made a selection, retest your choice on a larger scrap board to get a more accurate idea of how the finished project parts would look.

Build scale models. Although not useful for testing mass or joinery, models give you a 3-D perspective on your plan as well as a sense of part proportion.

Prototype tricky joints by cutting full-sized workpieces from inexpensive wood, then building the joint. Among other advantages, this will help you decide which is the best tool for cutting the actual project joints.

Making Prototypes

At some point during the planing process you should consider making a prototype of your project. Prototypes can, and in most cases should be, crude and quick constructions. The intention here is to build a full-sized section of a part of the construction that you're having difficulty working out in your mind or on paper. How much prototyping you need to do will depend on what it is you're building. Here are some examples: Say you plan to build a large entertainment center and you want to see how big it really will be. Cut up large pieces of cardboard for the front, top and sides, and tape them together. Now you can see how big it really is. Or, say you plan to build a table with a routed edge, but you don't know which routed profile to use. Make some large test wood pieces, rout some profiles, and see how they look. When you've narrowed down the choices, add wood pieces to approximate the table aprons and tabletop overhang.

Building any kind of seating is a *must* prototype situation. Start by sitting in a number of chairs or sofas and take measurements from them. Then prototype the seating you plan to build. I do this with 2 × 4's and particleboard. If you start with the prototype a little short, you can easily add more pieces of particleboard to raise and test a higher seat. You just have to

Standard furniture dimensions:

Dining tables

Top height: 29 to 30 in.
Place setting width:
24 in. minimum, 30 in. optimum.
Table edge to pedestal base clearance: 14 in. minimum.
Apron to floor minimum clearance: 23½ in.

Miscellaneous tables

Coffee tables: 12 to 18 in. tall.
End tables: 18 to 24 in. tall.

Desks

Depth: 30 in. deep.
Writing height: 29 in. to 30 in.
Computer keyboard stations: 25 in. to 27 in. tall.

Bedroom furniture

Dressers: 18 to 24 in. deep,
30-in. minimum height.
Night stands: 18 to 22 in.
Bed mattress height: 18 to 22 in.

Chairs

Seat height: 15 to 18 in.
Seat width: 17 to 20 in.
Seat depth: 15 to 18 in.
Arm rest (from seat): 8 to 10 in.

Build a full prototype. You don't have to use the actual wood stock or even make the parts look exactly like they will, but building a full-size, working prototype from inexpensive materials is a good idea, especially for seating projects.

Make a cardboard prototype. To get an idea of the actual footprint and mass of a larger project, rig up some pieces of cardboard to fit together in the rough project shape and dimensions. Actually position the prototype in the spot where you're planning to put your project.

be able to sit comfortably in the prototype before you build the actual chair, or chances are the real thing won't sit comfortably. If your seating will be cushioned, approximate the cushion thickness in your prototype too. Prototype

everything you think you need to, but make it a quick process so you can get on to drawing your plans and then building your project.

Scrapwood, particleboard, cardboard, sheetrock and paper are all good and cheap materials for mak-

ing prototypes. Hot glue, drywall screws, staples, nails, duct tape, masking tape, contact cement and spray adhesives are all suitable fastening materials you can use to assemble prototypes.

In addition to prototypes, many designers like to build scale models of their designs. The models serve mostly a visual purpose, since testing a $1/10$th size joint would be futile, if not impossible. Models can be made with a variety of materials, including cardboard, balsa wood, foam-core board or even construction paper. Or, you may want to resaw some of the actual stock you plan to use into thin strips, then use that to build the model. The main benefit models offer is a 3-D view of the project to give you a better sense of how the relative proportions work.

Standard furniture dimensions:

Bookcases

Depth: 12 in.
Height: 76 in. maximum.
Shelf width: 24 in. maximum width for $3/4$-in. plywood shelves; 36 in. maximum width for $3/4$-in. solid wood shelves.

Lounge seating

Seat height: 14 to 17 in.
Seat width: 24 in. minimum per person.
Seat depth: 15 to 18 in.
Arm rest height from seat): 8 to 10 in.
Seat angle tilt backwards: 3° to 5°.
Backrest tilt angle from seat: 95° to 105°.

Making Plan Drawings

To visualize and refine finer details such as overall and relative proportions, you'll need to make "scaled" working drawings. A scaled drawing is basically a shrunk-down, yet correctly proportioned drawing that shows your project's details and its dimensions. If you were drawing in ¼ scale, every real inch would equal 4 inches. The term "working" refers to the fact that you will follow these drawings closely when you build your project and use these drawings to determine the dimensions of the wood parts you need to cut.

To make professional-quality scaled working drawings you'll need an architect's scale, drafting table, T-square, 45° triangle, 30 × 60° triangle, and a compass for drawing circles. French curves are useful for drawing curved shapes. Other more specialized drafting tools are available at graphic design stores.

The architect's scale. Many scale rulers are available, but an architect's scale is the one used by most woodworkers. An architect's scale is a ruler with six sides. Although architects use these scales to draw in feet increments, the architect's scale is just as easily used to draw in inch increments, which is what most woodworkers do. The side with the number *16* marked at the left end is a full size ruler, meaning 1 inch equals 1 inch. The number *16* label means each inch is divided into sixteenths. The rest of the sides are marked with two different scales per side. One scale runs left to right, and the other runs right to left. To understand how to use an architect's scale, start by looking at the side marked on the left end with the fraction ³/₃₂. Using that side and working from left to right means that every ³/₃₂ inch equals 1 inch.

Accurate, detailed plan drawings not only create a blueprint for your woodworking project, they help you determine part sizes and get a better sense of what your project will look like when completed. An assortment of drafting tools will make drawing scaled plans much easier. A triangle, circle template and an architect's scale are shown in the photo above. For maximum benefit, draw your project from several different viewpoints.

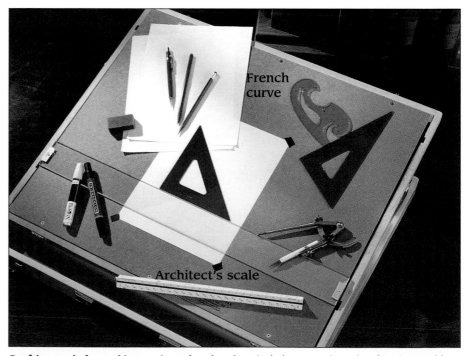

Drafting tools for making project plan drawings include a smooth worksurface (a portable drafting table is shown here), a variety of pens and pencils including a mechanical pencil, an architect's scale, a compass, a triangle or two and one or more french curves.

The architect's scale is virtually indispensible for making scale drawings of your woodworking projects. The six-sided ruler is calibrated to make automatic conversions in several different reduction scales, saving you plenty of math work.

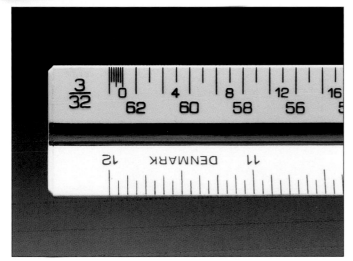 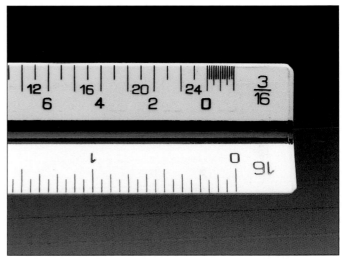

Reading an architect's scale. To understand how to use an architect's scale, start by looking at the side marked on the left end with the fraction "3/32." Using that side and working from left to right means that every 3/32 inch equals 1 inch. In this scale, the real measurement of 12 inches would equal 128 inches and those divisions are marked off with the upper row of numbers on that side. On the right end of the same side of the scale, is a fraction label that says "3/16." Working from right to left and using the lower row of numbers marked on that side offers the 3/16 inch equals 1 inch reduction scale.

In this scale, the real measurement of 12 inches would equal 128 inches and those divisions are marked off with the upper row of numbers on that side. On the right end of the same side of the scale, is a fraction label that says "3/16." Working from right to left and using the lower row of numbers marked on that side is the "3/16 inch equals 1 inch" scale. The other fraction-labeled scales work the same way. The sides with the ends labeled 1, 1½, and 3 are used for scaling at "1 inch equals 12 inches," "1½ inch equals 12 inches," and "3 inches equals 12 inches," respectively.

Drawing scaled plan views. When using an architect's scale, work using a scale on the ruler that allows you to draw the largest scaled drawings on the paper you draw on. This will make it easier for you to interrupt your drawings and see the details and proportions, since your drawings will be as large as they can be. Finding the best scale to use is done by starting with the largest dimension you need to draw. Say your project is longer than it is tall and deep. Then, length is the dimension to use to determine the scale to use. Fit the scale to your paper and allow for all the views you plan to draw on one sheet. Use your T-square to draw horizontal lines, use your triangles to draw vertical and angled lines, and use your compass to draw circles.

Start by drawing two-dimensional plan and elevation view drawings. A *plan view* can be a top or bottom view, and an *elevation view* can be a front, right side, left side or back view. Making these drawings will give you a sense of the overall proportions and help you to adjust those proportions that seem wrong. For most everything you build, you'll draw a front view, top view and one side view. For projects that have different-looking sides, you'll draw the other side view, too. The back and bottom views can be drawn too, but they're not needed very often since the details they provide are not usually that important.

When drawn properly, each view projects it's dimensions onto the other views. You can see this indicated with the lighter lines flowing from view to view. A typical three-view drawing shows a front, top, and right

Typical 2-D views

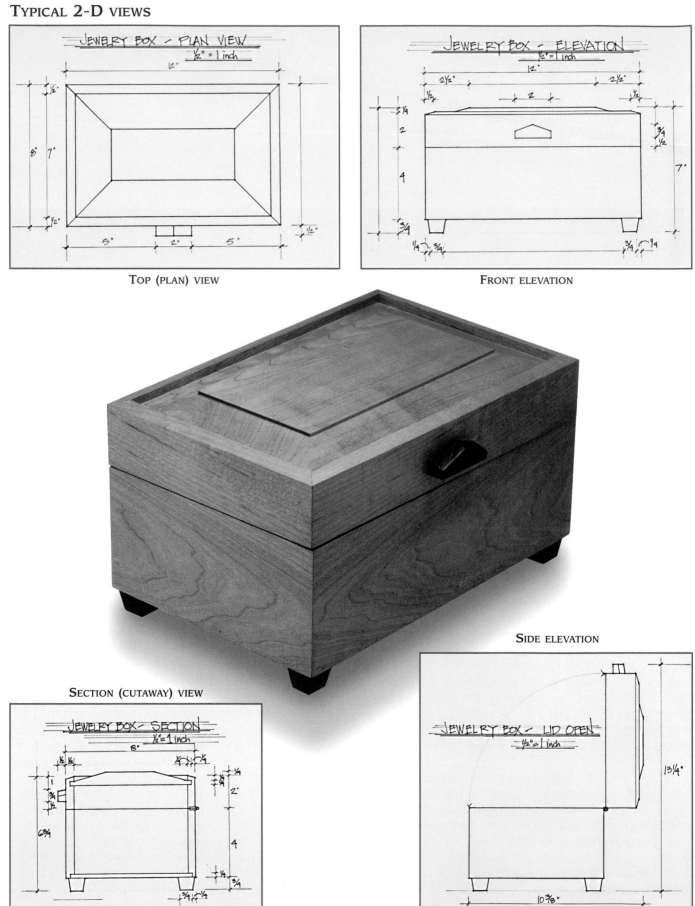

JEWELRY BOX - PLAN VIEW
½" = 1 inch

Top (plan) view

JEWELRY BOX - ELEVATION
½" = 1 inch

Front elevation

Section (cutaway) view

JEWELRY BOX - SECTION
½" = 1 inch

Side elevation

JEWELRY BOX - LID OPEN
½" = 1 inch

side view. Start by drawing your front view. Project its width dimensions upward onto the top view. Add the depth dimensions to the top view. Now, project the height dimensions of the front view over to the right view, and the depth dimensions of the top view over and down onto the right view. Make drawings showing your overall project as well as the details which can be drawn in a larger scale, closer to their actual sizes.

Isometric & perspective drawings. Making three-dimensional drawings is a great way to see how your project will look without actually building it, and to help you interpret your two-dimensional drawings.

An *isometric drawing* is an easy-to-create, three-dimensional view that combines your two-dimensional view drawings into one drawing. The dimensions used to make an isometric drawing are derived directly from your two-dimensional drawings, so everything remains "in scale" and measurable off the isometric drawing. Isometric drawings are dimensionally correct, but not visually correct since they have no foreshortening which would give them

CONSTRUCTING 2-D DRAWINGS

Concept sketches typically are made to help you visualize different ideas and treatments for your project. While not normally part of the final design package, they can be made easily with the same drafting tools used to construct final scaled project drawings.

Make vertical lines with a triangle guide resting against a straightedge that is secured to the work-surface, parallel to the horizontal lines of the drawing. A mechanical pencil makes a true, accurate line. The front view elevation is being created in the photo to the right. Most mechanical drawings start with a front view.

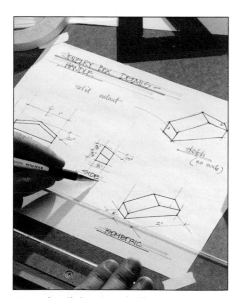

Draw detail drawings to illustrate and plan the more complicated joints and profiles in your woodworking project.

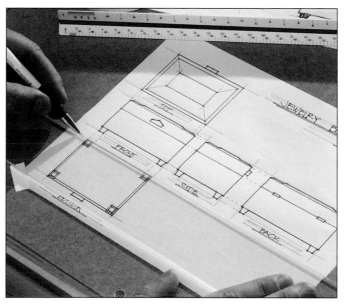

Draw multiple views to give the complete picture. Try to fit all the useful views onto a single page to create a total "snapshot" of the project. Here, top, front, side, back and bottom views are added around the front view drawing.

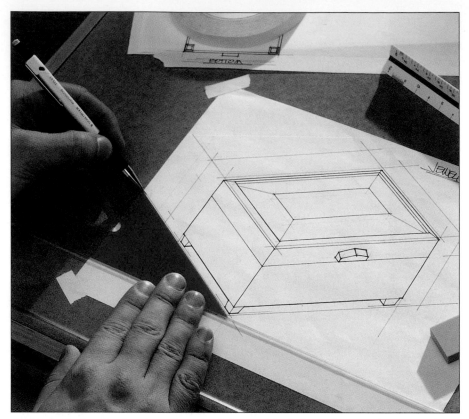

An isometric drawing is a three-dimensional sketch with all planes drawn to the same scale. Isometrics are very handy for calculating part sizes, but they are less effective at conveying the actual "look" of the project than perspective drawings (below).

Perspective drawings are made by extending the horizontal lines from the verticals and out toward "vanishing points" to give the drawing a sense of depth. They do the best job of portraying the actual appearance of the project.

the illusion of depth. The foremost point of an isometric drawing is usually one front corner of your project. This edge or line is drawn vertically and to the same height as it appears on your front view drawing. The front/top and front/bottom edge lines are drawn to the left of the corner line and drawn at 30° angles. The length of the front/top and bottom edge lines are the same as they appear on your multi-view drawing. The right side is drawn to the right of the corner line and drawn at 30° also. The drawing is completed by projecting the outside upper corner lines to each other at 30° angles to fill in the top.

A *perspective drawing* is a three-dimensional view foreshortened in such a way as to imitate the way your brain sees objects and give the illusion of depth. In other words, the drawn object looks the way you would see it in reality. A perspective drawing is created using *vanishing points.* A vanishing point is a point far off in the distance where two parallel lines converge as your eyes would see them. Just imagine a long hallway: As you look down it, all the lines converge at one point. That's the vanishing point. You could make accurately proportioned "technical" perspective drawings using your drafting tools, but the process is extremely complex. So much so that your end results are not worth the effort required to produce the drawing. Your library should have drafting technique books that explain how to produce a technical perspective view drawing if this is what you want to learn. Instead, you're probably better off making perspective sketches. They are much easier to draw, but not proportionally accurate.

Use two-point perspective, which means there are two vanishing points, when making your perspective sketches. A two-point perspective has one vanishing point to the left and one vanishing point to the right. All of the vertical

Modify finished plan drawings to suit your need, using a calculator and an architect's scale. You'll find it helpful to redraw the project, noting which parts need to be modified.

lines in the drawing are drawn 90° to the ground plane, and all of the horizontal lines are drawn from the vertical lines outward to the vanishing points. With a little practice, you'll find making these sketches pretty easy.

Cutting lists and shopping lists. Once you've completed your plan drawings, you'll have a much easier time coming up with cutting lists and shopping lists. These last two items will round out your project plan so you have all the information you need to start building.

A cutting list is simply a roster of all the project parts you'll need. It should include the name of each part, the quantity you'll need, the dimensions (thickness × width × length), and the material the part will be made from. Use the cutting list as a guide when cutting parts, but always check the dimensions against the actual workpieces you've already cut in case you made any errors.

A shopping list can be surprisingly difficult to make for woodworking projects. This is because most woodworking lumber is sold in random widths and lengths. Even if you calculate your shopping list in board feet (See page 43) you won't ever find the exact combination of boards you need to make your parts without any waste. Still, knowing how many board feet of each material you'll need lets you make a reasonably good cost estimate. When working with sheet goods, draw a cutting diagram to calculate how many sheets you'll need and help you determine how to minimize waste.

No. 3

No. 1

MATERIALS LIST

- CHERRY
    - 8 B.F. - 4/4 ROUGH
    - 4 B.F. - 3/4 S4S

- 3/8" DOWELS

Introduction to Wood

Choosing lumber for your project is as much a part of woodworking as any other step in the process. Lumber is expensive, so it pays to know what your options are before you head to the lumberyard—sometimes an economical species will serve the same function as a more costly alternative.

In addition, each wood type has natural characteristics that influence workability, appearance and durability. It's important to be aware of these factors before you build. Hardwood and softwood lumber is sold in various industry grades based on the percentage of clear (knot-free) lumber the board

WOODWORKING WORKS
One of the distinctive features of this tool chest is how the design integrates contrasting wood types. While the majority of the project is made of white oak, the drawer pulls and lid edge are walnut. Generally, the most attractive approach is to pair light and dark woods and limit the contrast to two wood types.

Woodworking Wisdom

A woodworker in Wyoming once sent me some photographs of a cigar humidor he had built from a plan of mine. It was a Honduras mahogany box with brass inlay, a gift for his father-in-law who enjoyed an occasional stogie. The accompanying cover letter said that he was especially proud of the beautiful cedar lining that he had custom-fitted to the interior. But when I got to that photo, my heart sank. This well-intentioned fellow had unfortunately lined the humidor with aromatic instead of Spanish cedar. If the humidor had been used, his father-in-law's cigar collection would have been ruined by the strong cedar smell. Instances like this illustrate an important lesson when selecting wood for a project: Be sure to consider the characteristics of the wood species you choose before you build. It can make or break a project.
~John English

must have, as well as whether or not the boards are planed at the mill or left roughsawn. You'll need to pick a lumber grade that is suitable for your project needs, tools available to you and your project budget, then sift through stacks of boards carefully—lumber within the same grade can vary widely in terms of color, figure and defects.

So how do you choose which species to use and which boards to buy? Making good lumber choices to some extent comes only by experience. You'll need to build with different species and grades of wood to know what truly works best for projects intended for different purposes. But familiarizing yourself with the various topics covered in this chapter is a good first step to buying smart.

In the pages that follow you'll become familiar with distinctions between hardwoods, softwoods and sheet goods and examine some of their different uses. Learn about figure and defects in lumber, see how mills cut logs into boards, and discover how wood reacts to changes in moisture. We'll cover how lumber is sized and sold, as well as overview the standardized lumber grading systems. Finally, the end of the chapter reveals some time-tested guidelines about where and how to shop for lumber like a pro.

Once you've read this chapter and calculated the quantity and quality of boards your project requires, you can venture more confidently off to the lumberyard to pilfer through stacks of boards. You may even save a bit of money in the process.

Anatomy of a Tree

At the very center of a tree is a small area of softer tissue called *pith.* Surrounding the pith are numerous annual rings of growth, already dead, that provide support and structure to the tree. This is the *heartwood,* the area most treasured by woodworkers because of its even density and grain pattern. Beyond the heartwood is a thinner section of still-living rings, called *sapwood,* that provide a conduit from the roots to the leaves for transporting soluble mineral salts. The outermost sapwood ring—the *cambium*—is the growth region in a living tree. Cambium contributes girth to the trunk over time, adding another new layer of sapwood each year. Between the cambium and the protective layer of bark is yet another thin region called the *phloem.* This is the conduit that brings food (made in the leaves through photosynthesis) back down to the root system.

Most mills remove all the exterior layers (bark, phloem, cambium and sapwood) from logs before milling them into boards or dimensional stock such as 2 × 4s. Today, most of the bark and sapwood is ground up and used as mulch in gardens, sold to paper mills, burned as fuel or even used as animal bedding. Occasionally you'll run across a board at the lumberyard that contains sapwood. In darker-grained varieties, like walnut or cherry, sapwood appears as a band of lightly colored, softer wood that runs lengthwise near one long edge of the board. If incorporated into a project, sapwood will become more prominent when you apply a finish unless you stain it to match the rest of the board. For this reason, sapwood is seldom used for furniture.

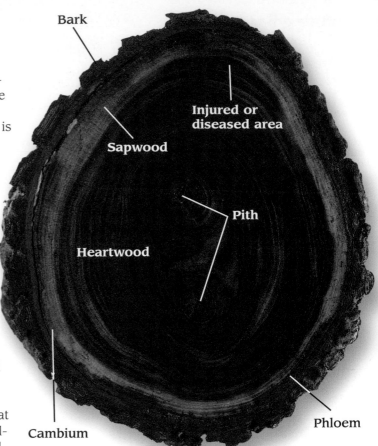

This Chinese Elm sample exhibits all the major anatomical areas of a tree: bark, phloem, cambium, sapwood, heartwood and pith. The cross-section shown here, with two pith regions, likely came from a tree whose trunk split into two major branches. Notice also the darker area, a sign that the tree experienced a period of injury or disease.

FOREST MANAGEMENT

Softwoods (also called conifers) nearly always grow at a faster rate than hardwoods, and this fact helps explain how supply and demand influence prices of both softwood and hardwood lumber. The rapid growth rate of softwoods allows for frequent replanting and harvesting—sometimes in as little as 15 years—compared to a minimum of 75 years for most common hardwoods. Shorter harvest time helps to keep softwood quantities stable and costs below that of hardwoods—a benefit to both the construction industry and to softwood supplies for woodworking.

Because softwood trees reproduce with heavy cones rather than flowers or nuts, the seeds often fall close to the parent tree. This natural adaptation enables softwoods to grow close together—a fact that can be a boon to a lumber mill. The mill's forester can plant more trees per acre. Each plant, seeking light above the canopy created by its siblings, will tend to grow straight and true. Loggers have long taken advantage of this growth pattern, replanting conifers in tightly spaced rows that yield easily milled, straight logs.

Softwood seedlings (right photo) are planted in tightly-spaced rows, then transplated in wider rows **(top photo)** until they mature into trees suitable for lumber harvest. Note the tall, straight trunks—a characteristic trait of softwood trees.

Defining Hardwoods & Softwoods

Botanically speaking, trees are categorized as either hardwoods or softwoods. Here's a simple way to distinguish the two: hardwoods are deciduous (broad leafed), generally losing their leaves in late fall and reproducing with flowers and fruits or nuts. Softwoods, on the other hand, are coniferous; they retain their needle-shaped leaves in the winter and reproduce by spreading their seed through open cones. The terms 'softwood' or 'hardwood' have nothing to do with whether the wood is physically hard or soft.

All trees have two growth spurts each year. Their spring growth produces a light-colored material between the rings, called *early-wood.* The more dense cells produced in the late summer and fall are known as *latewood,* and these constitute the darker rings that every child has counted to determine a tree's age.

Softwood trees tend to grow more rapidly than hardwoods, and they have wider bands of early-wood than most slow-growing hardwoods. Softwood trees also have larger, less dense cells in the earlywood than hardwoods. This

HARDWOOD VS. SOFTWOOD

Oak

Pine

Despite what the categories imply, the distintion between hardwoods and softwoods has to do with leaf type and is not a measure of wood hardness. Oak, a common hardwood, has broad leaves that shed in the fall, while pine, a coniferous softwood, retains its needles all winter.

helps explain why a nail can be driven into a wide-celled pine board more easily than a tight-grained oak board; the cell structure is less dense, allowing easier penetration.

Another property worth noting is that hardwood trees allow their

branches time and space to grow in almost any direction, in order to maximize leaf exposure to sunlight. The internal stresses present in the wood, resulting from the weight of these outspread branches, create interesting figure and grain patterns in the wood (See below, left). However, there is a price to pay for that beauty: highly figured wood tends to distort more readily than straight-grained boards as the stresses are released.

Three centuries ago, colonial woodworkers cut their lumber from vast tracts of virgin coniferous forest. It wasn't uncommon for them to glean white pine boards measuring 2, 3 and even 4 ft. wide, with no knots or other disfigurement. It's no surprise that much of their early furniture was built from softwood. Boards culled from today's replanted pine forests, on the other hand, have knots every 12 to 18 in. along their length (one year's growth). Because of their minimal girth at harvest, boards often contain considerable sapwood as well.

The best uses for today's softwoods

COLOR, FIGURE & GRAIN PATTERN

Part of the attraction of woodworking comes from the opportunity to work with wood displaying dramatic differences in color, figure and grain pattern. Wood color is a product of of how its tannins, gums and resins react to exposure to the air. Often, wood will continue to darken and change color over time, developing a rich patina. Figure—the surface pattern on a board—can be the result of numerous natural causes ranging from drought or freezing to prevailing winds, disease, age or insect damage. Grain display is dependent on the direction and regularity of the wood fibers relative to the center of the trunk as well as how the lumber is cut from the tree.

Massive sawmill blades make quick work of slicing a log into green lumber. Once cut, these boards will be graded, stacked, dried and possibly planed smooth on faces and edges before they're ready for sale.

TYPICAL LUMBER CUTS

Lumber is cut from logs in a number of different ways, to maximize yield or to control wood grain direction and avoid log defects. Plain-sawn boards are produced by rotating a log in quarter-turn increments and cutting around the center pith area. Quartersawing, a less efficient way to maximize board yield, nevertheless produces more dimensionally stable lumber. Quartersawn oak also displays prominent medullary rays that would not otherwise show if the boards were plainsawn. A third milling method, through-and-through cutting (not shown), involves simply slicing the log completely across, which produces a mix of plain-sawn and quartersawn lumber.

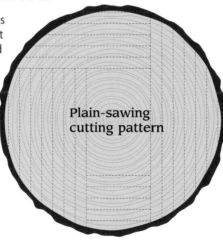

Plain-sawing cutting pattern

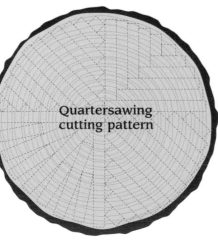

Quartersawing cutting pattern

are in applications where straight, abundant, less expensive lumber is needed. Mills cut softwoods largely into construction lumber for framing walls, floors and roofs or process it into plywood, chipboard and oriented strandboard to sheathe buildings. Of course, a percentage of this lumber also is headed for woodworkers, but premium-grade softwoods can command prices that compete with hardwoods.

Hardwoods, on the other hand, are most often sturdier, heavier, more figured and show a great variety of colors. So, it's no surprise that the more attractive, yet less available hardwoods are more costly and are the natural choice for furnituremaking, cabinetry and trim work. It also explains why hardwoods are not available in the same nominal dimensions as softwoods intended for construction purposes.

Cuts of Lumber

Mills saw lumber in a variety of ways, depending on the intended use of the boards and the species and quality of the logs. The most common cuts are plain-sawing and quartersawing. Plain-sawing (also called flat-sawing) involves cutting the log to maximize lumber without including the center pith area. The log is rotated to make successive series of cuts around the pith. Plain-sawing produces lumber most economically for both the mill. It is suitable for most construction and woodworking purposes, but since the cuts are made tangentially to the growth rings—the direction of greatest wood movement—the lumber is more prone to distortion than quartersawn lumber. (For more on wood movement, see page 40).

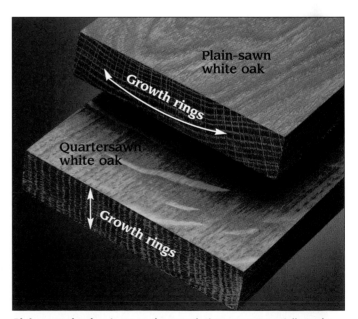

Plain-sawn white oak

Growth rings

Quartersawn white oak

Growth rings

Plain-sawn lumber is cut so the growth rings run tangentially to the board faces, producing a wider, wavy grain pattern. The growth rings on quartersawn lumber, on the other hand, run radially to the board faces, resulting in a tigher, parallel grain pattern.

LUMBER DRYING METHODS

Air-drying: Short lengths of scrap wood, called stickers, are inserted between each board in a stack to allow air to circulate all around the boards. The stacks are left to dry fully exposed to the elements, are covered up or stored in open sheds for months or even years at a time. Without stickers, green lumber will dry unevenly or attract mold and slowly decompose.

Kiln-drying: Once stickered lumber is loaded into a kiln, the kiln is closed up and heated evenly for several weeks until the moisture inside is reduced to acceptable levels. Drying time will vary depending on wood species and the grade of lumber. Kiln-drying is a faster method of producing general-purpose lumber, and kiln-dried boards are what you'll find at all discount lumber outlets and home centers.

Quartersawn lumber is made by first sawing the log along its length to create four wedges. These are then ripped so the growth rings run more or less perpendicular (radially) to the board faces. Quartersawing yields boards with close, tight, straight grain. In some hardwoods, like oak, it also exposes beautiful, translucent medullary rays that have been coveted by woodworkers for generations. The downside to quartersawing is that it produces less lumber per log than plain-sawing, making the lumber more expensive to buy. Generally, quartersawn hardwoods are more common to find than quartersawn softwoods.

Methods of Drying Lumber

When boards are first cut from a log, they are considered "green", which means they contain a high percentage of water weight and must be dried before they are suitable for most uses. Lumber is dried commercially in two ways—by air or by kiln. Air drying is simply that: the stock is stacked in such a way that the air can circulate through and around it. Small pieces of lumber, called *stickers,* are inserted between the boards at regular intervals. The stack is then left to dry for a long time, sometimes several years, until the moisture evaporates to acceptable levels. Variations on the method involve covering the top layer with plastic or canvas, turning the sides to the prevailing wind, periodically dismantling and rebuilding the stack in reverse, all in an attempt to control the drying process. If lumber is improperly dried, it may begin to mold, which leads to a sometimes desirable defect called *spalling* (See page 41).

Kiln-drying is done in a gas, electric or solar-powered oven. Kilns are expensive to operate, but they offer a precisely controllable drying environment. Some mills may be inclined to speed up the process to save money. However, rapid drying can lead to a multitude of defects, such as *case-hardening* (See page 41).

What is "green" lumber? The American Lumber Standards Committee classifies green wood as having 20% or higher moisture content, and dry lumber as 19% or less. Board moisture is measured in terms of weight, not volume.

From a woodworker's point of view, air-dried lumber is a lot cheaper, but it is less common. Most lumber, including everything you'll find at a home center, is kiln dried, because it is ready for market in a shorter time. The kiln is also a more controllable method than air-drying, especially with large volumes of lumber.

Moisture & Wood Movement

Regardless of whether boards are air- or kiln-dried once they are cut from a log, lumber will continue to seek what is known as *equilibrium moisture content* (EMC): it will absorb moisture or dry out until its moisture content matches the relative humidity in the surrounding air. A kiln-dried board will never absorb as much moisture as it initially had when it was green, but its sponge-like qualities cannot be stopped, even when a wood finish is applied.

The amount of moisture a board contains at the lumberyard is measured in percentages, which range from 6% to more than 20%. Framing lumber should be less than 18% moisture when purchased (about 14% is ideal), while stock destined for furniture or casework should be down around 6 to 8%. Moisture percentages are measured in terms of water weight vs. wood weight, not according to volume.

The only accurate way to check this is with a moisture meter (See *Evaluating Moisture Content,* below), a small electronic tool with two sharp pins that are inserted into a freshly cut surface of the wood (old cuts dry quickly and give a false reading, so a fresh cut is essential). Most fine hardwood vendors will loan you a meter to examine their stock before you buy, or you can ask them to take a reading in your presence.

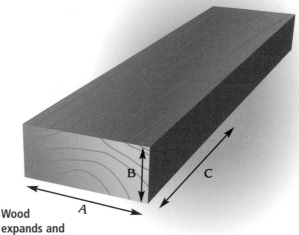

Wood expands and contracts in response to changes in moisture and temperature. Tangential movement (A) occurs parallel to the growth rings, while radial movement (B) happens across the rings. Wood moves very little along its length (C). Generally a board's tangential movement is about double its radial movement.

As wood absorbs moisture from the air, it expands, and as the moisture evaporates, it will contract. You may be surprised to learn that wood basically moves parallel to the growth rings (tangentially) and across the rings (radially), but almost never along it (longitudinally). Therefore, in a standard plain-sawn board (see *Lumber Cuts,* previous page), expansion or contraction essentially occur in just two directions: width and thickness. Movement across the width is normally about twice that in thickness. The "greener" the board, the more it will move. It is critical, when designing and building woodworking projects, to consider how these forces of expansion and contraction will affect your project; they cannot be entirely eliminated.

Lumber Distortion & Defects

Often lumber will not expand and contract uniformly, causing it to distort. Four types of distortion, caused largely by improper kiln drying, are cupping, crooking, bowing and winding. *Cupping* is where the two long edges of the board begin moving toward each other, while the middle remains flat. A cupped cross section resembles the letter C. About the only way to fix this is to rip the board into several small strips after they have attained equilibrium, joint their edges, and then reglue them, alternating the growth rings (See page 128).

Crooking is evident when a board's faces are flat but it warps from side to side. This is an easy fix: after the board reaches equilibrium, simply joint one edge of the board, then rip the second edge parallel (See page 58). Fixing both cupped and crooked boards will incur some degree of waste.

Bowing is a more difficult problem to deal with. In this case, a board cups along its length and resembles a very wide rocking chair runner. About the only solu-

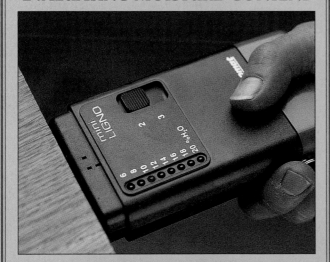

EVALUATING MOISTURE CONTENT

A moisture meter will tell you immediately the moisture content of a board. The red glowing light on this meter indicates the moisture content in this board to be 10%, an acceptable level for cutting and for project use. Calibrated moisture meters aren't cheap, but you may want to invest in one if plan to do fine furniture work or if the humidity in your shop fluctuates widely. It's also a good idea to test the moisture content of air-dried lumber if you purchase it directly from the mill. Be sure to test the wood on a fresh-cut edge or end—old edges dry quickly and will not provide an accurate reading.

tion is to support the ends and place weights on the center with the board's convex side facing up. In some instances, the board will flatten when it reaches moisture equilibrium.

Sometimes the ends of a board will twist in opposite directions. Twisting is difficult to remedy, but you may be able to flatten the faces of thicker boards by running them repeatedly over the jointer (See page 56).

Distortions can be spotted easily

LET YOUR LUMBER ACCLIMATE

Once you have purchased lumber for a project, allow it to acclimate to its new environment for a few weeks before building with it. If your shop is particularly damp, insert sticking between each board so that the air can surround it evenly on all sides.Or wrap it completely in 6 mil plastic until you need to use it, then machine and finish the lumber immediately.

at the lumberyard by simply sighting down the edges and faces of each board before you buy.

Defects like pitch pockets, spalling or loose knots are easy to spot if you look carefully. Boards with these defects are salvageable by simply cutting away the bad areas. One defect that can't always be seen until after the lumber is rip-cut is a condition called *case-hardening*. Case-hardening occurs when the outside faces of the board dry quickly while the center remains wet, causing tremendous internal stresses. Telltale signs of case-hardening are checks (small cracks), shakes (large cracks, most often radiating out from the center across the grain), and a problem referred to as honeycombing: when the board is ripped, the inside looks just like the inside of a beehive, full of tiny honeycombs. To safeguard against case-hardening, check boards along their edges and ends, paying close attention to honey-combing, the worst kind of case-hardening. If one board in a pile is affected, chances are several more from the same batch will have the same defect.

COMMON LUMBER DEFECTS

Spalling is a gray to green permanent discoloration of the wood caused by fungal growth. Be sure to keep spalled lumber dry, or the discoloration will continue and spread.

Knots are easy to cut out of clear sections of lumber. The lower the lumber grade, the higher will be the percentage of allowable knots.

COMMON LUMBER DISTORTIONS

Boards distort in four primary ways, due to how internal stresses are released when it is machined as well as how the board absorbs and releases moisture. Moisture distortion is largely a measure of how the wood was dried at the mill. Wood that bows is flat across its width but the faces curve lengthwise. A crooked board is flat across the face but curves along the edges in one direction or the other, like the rocker on a rocking chair. Cupping occurs when a board is flat along its edges but curls across its width. Twist is the condition where one or both ends of a board twist so the board faces are no longer flat.

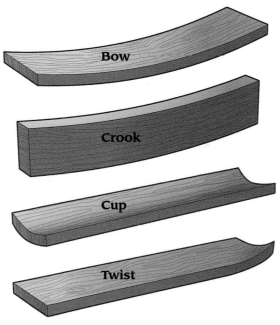

Bow

Crook

Cup

Twist

Case-hardened boards should be avoided when purchasing woodworking lumber. Case-hardening results from insufficient and hasty kiln-drying at high temperatures. The board dries too rapidly on the outside but stays wet within, creating stresses that literally cause it to pull itself apart until it reaches equilibrium.

Softwood Lumber Sizes

All construction lumber sold in the U.S. bears an industry grading stamp such as the Western Wood Products Association (WWP) stamp shown above. Nominal softwood lumber is graded similarly, but usually the stamp doesn't show. Here's how to decipher grade stamps:

12 — Identifies the mill. This can be letters or numbers.

1&BTR — This is the grade of lumber, in this case #1 Common and better, an excellent furniture grade.

WWP — The grading association that graded the board, in this case the Western Wood Products Association.

S-DRY — The condition of seasoning at the time of surfacing, in this case dry, or seasoned lumber below 19% moisture content. If the stamp read KD-15, it would denote kiln-dried lumber with a maximum of 15% moisture content. Product stamped S-GRN stands for unseasoned (green) lumber containing more than 19% moisture content.

DOUG FIR-L — Indicates the wood species, in this case, Douglas fir.

Slide your measuring tape across a 2 × 4 and you'll discover that it doesn't actually measure two inches by four inches. In fact, it will be ½-in. shy in both directions. In its rough state, when the lumber was originally ripped into studs, this same piece was in fact a true 2 × 4. But after drying, it shrank a little. Then it was surfaced (planed) on all four faces, and it shrank a little more.

When you buy standard softwood lumber at your home center, surfaced and jointed on all faces and edges, the industry sells it to you in finished dimensions, but still describes it in *nominal* dimensions—the size it was before milling.

A piece of softwood lumber with a nominal 1-in. thickness is generally referred to as a board, while nominal 2-in.-thick softwood is called framing stock (as in studs, joists and rafters), or *dimension* lumber. The chart below lists nominal and dimension lumber sizes for the stock you'll find in home centers.

Softwood lumber is graded by strength and appearance as well as moisture content. For woodworking applications, the three common grades to know are Select, Finish and Common (See the chart, below left). While boards in the Common grade categories may contain some blemishes and knots, Select and Finish grades are clear or nearly clear of defects. Be aware, however, that boards within any grade may exhibit some degree of natural distortion (cupping, bowing, twisting), so it's important to examine each board carefully by sighting along its length and width before you buy.

SOFTWOOD LUMBER GRADES

Grade	Grading criteria
B Select and BTR	Highest quality lumber with little or no defects or blemishes. Nominal sizes may be limited.
C Select	Some small defects or blemishes permissible, but still largely clear and of high quality.
D Select	One board face usually defect-free.
Superior Finish	Highest grade finish lumber with only minor defects.
Prime Finish	High quality with some defects and blemishes.
No. 1 Common	Highest grade of knotty lumber; usually available by special-order.
No. 2 Common	Pronounced knots and larger blemishes permissible.

Nominal vs. dimension softwood lumber sizes

Nominal	Finished
1 × 2	³⁄₄ × 1½
1 × 3	³⁄₄ × 2½
1 × 4	³⁄₄ × 3½
1 × 6	³⁄₄ × 5½
1 × 8	³⁄₄ × 7¼
1 × 10	³⁄₄ × 9¼
1 × 12	³⁄₄ × 11¼
Dimension lumber sizes	
2 × 2	1½ × 1½
2 × 3	1½ × 2½
2 × 4	1½ × 3½
2 × 6	1½ × 5½
2 × 8	1½ × 7¼
2 × 10	1½ × 9¼
2 × 12	1½ × 11¼

Hardwood Lumber Sizes

While nominal dimensions are widely used for selling softwoods, some retailers have extended the practice to hardwood boards as well. Your local home center probably stocks a few species of hardwoods, like oak, maple and cherry. These boards generally are planed to ¾ in. thick, jointed flat on the edges and cut to standard widths and lengths. Within the lumber industry, lumber of this sort is categorized as "S4S", which stands for Surfaced Four Sides. All of this surface preparation at the mill translates to higher prices for you, but it may make the most sense to buy S4S lumber if you don't own a thickness planer or jointer to prepare board surfaces yourself.

To find specialty or thicker hardwoods, you'll need to shop at a traditional lumberyard. A good lumberyard will offer a wide selection of hardwoods in random widths and in an assortment of thicknesses and grades (See *Hardwood Lumber Grades,* below). In addition to S4S, you'll find S2S lumber (planed smooth on two faces but the edges are rough), and roughsawn boards that are simply cut from the log, dried and shipped to the lumberyard.

Because of their diverse uses, hardwoods are offered in a much larger variety of thicknesses than standard 1× and 2× softwoods. This has led to the quartering system for determining lumber thickness, which allows you to buy hardwoods in ¼-in. thickness increments from ¼ in. on up. Most yards offer popular hardwood species in three, four, five, six, eight, ten and even twelve quarter thicknesses (which read as ¾, ⁴⁄₄, ⁵⁄₄, ⁶⁄₄, ⁸⁄₄, ¹⁰⁄₄ and ¹²⁄₄ on the label at the rack). These correspond to rough (pre-planed) thicknesses of ¾ in., 1 in., 1¼ in., 1½ in., 2 in., 2½ in. and 3 in.

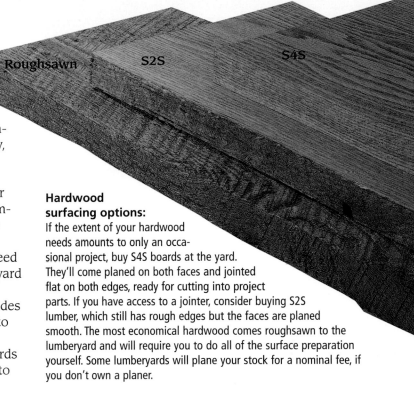

Roughsawn   S2S   S4S

Hardwood surfacing options:
If the extent of your hardwood needs amounts to only an occasional project, buy S4S boards at the yard. They'll come planed on both faces and jointed flat on both edges, ready for cutting into project parts. If you have access to a jointer, consider buying S2S lumber, which still has rough edges but the faces are planed smooth. The most economical hardwood comes roughsawn to the lumberyard and will require you to do all of the surface preparation yourself. Some lumberyards will plane your stock for a nominal fee, if you don't own a planer.

HARDWOOD LUMBER GRADES

Hardwood lumber is graded using a different classification system than softwoods. Grades are based on the percentage of clear face cuts that can be made around a board's defects (knots, splits, pitch pockets, and so forth). From highest grade (clearest) to lowest (most allowable defects), the grades are:

Grade	Percentage of clear cuts
FAS (Firsts & Seconds)	83⅓%
Select	83⅓%
No. 1 Common	66⅔%
No. 2A & 2B Common	50%
No. 3A Common	33⅓%
No. 3B Common	25%

Choose the lumber grade that best suits the needs of your project parts and your budget. It could be that a Common grade will provide all the knot-free lumber you need at a significant savings over FAS.

CALCULATING BOARD FEET

Hardwood lumber is sold at most lumberyards by the board foot, which can make calculating the amount of lumber you need a little confusing. The three boards below, for instance, all equal 2 board feet, though their physical dimensions are quite different. A board foot is actually ¹⁄₁₂ of a cubic foot of rough lumber, or 144 cubic inches. It is the equivalent of a piece of stock that is 12 in. wide, 12 in. long and 1 in. thick. But any combination of dimensions that multiplies to 144 is equivalent to one board foot.

To calculate the number of board feet a piece of lumber contains, its thickness times its width times its length (all in inches) then divide by 144. If one dimension is easier to calculate in feet rather than inches, divide by 12 instead. When calculating board feet, don't forget to build some waste into the project estimate. The pros generally count on close to 30% when they're buying S2S stock, and 40% with roughsawn lumber (mostly because they can't see the defects until after planing).

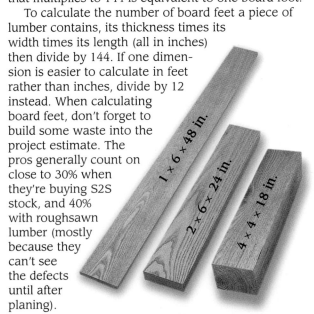

1 × 6 × 48 in.

2 × 6 × 24 in.

4 × 4 × 18 in.

Large retail lumber outlets and home centers make shopping for lumber easy. Most of the lumber you'll find is fully surfaced and ready for building. Some larger home centers even stock lumber inside where it's kept warm and dry. The downside to all of this convenience is that species options are limited, especially for hardwoods.

Buying Lumber

It's important to know your options for where to shop for wood. Chain home improvement stores generally offer a basic variety of framing lumber and nominal softwood but very little hardwood. What they do carry is often priced lower than specialty yard stock, but the grades and dimensions are limited. Here are a couple of other options to consider:

Contractor yards, where framing and finish carpenters buy their materials, usually offer a wider array of lumber options, including an assortment of millwork products and custom moldings. Often they can special-order materials that the chain stores simply can't supply. The quality of the stock here is better, and the prices reflect the quality you'll find.

Specialty yards: Most metropolitan areas have specialty yards that sell only hardwoods and veneered sheet goods. Their primary customers are commercial cabinetmakers, architectural millwork shops and professional furniture builders. While the salespeople here are used to dealing with pros, they are usually willing to take a few minutes to explain the finer points to an interested amateur. However, time is money for these folks, so they won't appreciate spending too much time on what they by necessity must consider a minor sale. The stock sold here here is normally S2S or rough-sawn, so you'll need a jointer or planer to prepare the

Reclaimed lumber

In recent years there has been a lot of talk about reclaimed lumber. Most reclaimed lumber is salvaged from the beams and timbers of old buildings, and some is recovered from the chilly depths of the Great Lakes. Such lumber was culled from virgin forests a century or more ago, and it is generally very straight-grained and true. It is also extremely seasoned; only large swings in temperature or humidity seem to affect it. Reclaimed lumber is generally a great product, and numerous mills advertise on the internet. The price may be high, however, especially for premium cuts and grades.

Buying reclaimed lumber is by no means your only source for obtaining it. Before you toss an old piece of furniture or dispose of boards and trim from a big remodeling project, consider reusing the lumber for woodworking. Sometimes all it needs is to be stripped, sanded or run through a planer. Visually inspect any reclaimed lumber carefully or check it with a metal detector before passing it through a saw or router, to be sure there are no hidden metal fasteners present.

Don't overlook "diamonds in the rough": These mahogany boards, salvaged from a discarded couch and passed through a planer, will make excellent stock for a woodworking project.

Consider buying your lumber from a local saw mill. Here you'll find a wide range of species in a host of dimensions. Most mills will sell stock to you at a fraction of the price a lumber-yard charges.

lumber further. Be aware that, when buying rough-sawn lumber, you can't tell much about the color, grain or quality of the board until after you expose it to the planer knives.

It's quite acceptable to rummage through the stock at a specialty yard, but make sure you rebuild the stacks as you found them. Longer, wider boards belong at the back of the rack. Don't mix the boards from different bins. Boards in two binds may look the same at first glance, but they may be different grades. Check the board ends to see if the yard has painted different colors there—the colors represent the grades.

Buying basics

Whether you buy from a chain store, specialty or contractor's yard or by mail, keep a few basic rules of thumb in mind when shopping for project lumber:

1. Develop a realistic shopping list. Base your list on a clear understanding of common lumber proportions and grades (See pages 42 to 43 for more on common lumber sizes and grades). Make a preliminary visit to your lumberyard, acquire a catalog, or call the city desk before leaving home to verify that the dimensions and species you need are available. Know ahead of time what compromises you can make to your cutting and shopping lists, if what you need isn't available in the right size or species.

2. Consider using less-expensive woods like poplar or pine in hidden areas of your project. Woodworkers have used "secondary" woods for centuries in fine furniture and cabinetry, saving premium lumber for prominent project parts like face frames, doors, drawer fronts and tabletops. Don't underestimate the versatility, economy and structural benefits of using sheet goods like plywood and particleboard over solid wood (See pages 46 to 47).

3. Factor in about 30% waste. As you become more practiced in estimating, you'll be able to reduce this percentage somewhat. If you are just getting started as a woodworker, buy more lumber than what you'll need for a project. Save your receipt and return what you don't use. Published plans occasionally have errors in shopping and cutting lists that will require you to have more material on hand. If you buy lumber

MAIL-ORDER LUMBER

Lumber by mail: If you don't have a specialty lumberyard nearby or need a more unusual species for your project, consider ordering lumber by mail. The range of species offered is usually quite broad, and the prices are competitive. Thumb through the back of most woodworking magazines and you'll see numerous mail-order suppliers to choose from. One drawback to buying by mail is that you'll be ordering lumber sight unseen. As a safeguard, make your first order small, so you can inspect the quality. Ask about moisture levels, too, so you can use what you order right away without needing to let it dry first.

roughsawn, you may not discover an unsightly blemish or pitch pocket until after you plane it, resulting in less usable lumber than you initially planned. And be honest about your own "fudge factor." One miscalculated cut late on a Saturday afternoon might put an end to your woodworking for the weekend if your lumberyard isn't open on Sundays.

4. Comparison shop before you buy. Once you are sure of your project requirements, check how the prices vary among suppliers. Yards may offer discounts on slightly damaged lumber or overstocks, especially at inventory time.

5. Plan for how you'll safely transport large materials home, especially sheet goods. If the yard offers delivery, take advantage of the service especially if your only other option is to tie several unwieldly sheets of plywood to the roof of the family sedan. Some yards will cut your lumber into more manageable proportions for free, or for a modest charge. If you go this route, double-check your cutting list so you can decide ahead of time what can be sized down without compromising your project needs.

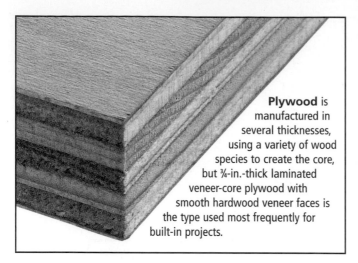

Plywood is manufactured in several thicknesses, using a variety of wood species to create the core, but ¾-in.-thick laminated veneer-core plywood with smooth hardwood veneer faces is the type used most frequently for built-in projects.

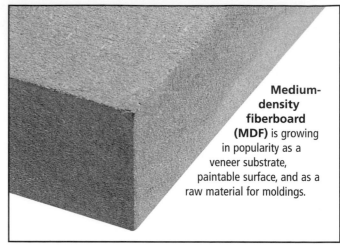

Medium-density fiberboard (MDF) is growing in popularity as a veneer substrate, paintable surface, and as a raw material for moldings.

Particleboard is used almost exclusively as a substrate for plastic laminate or veneer, especially for countertops. It is inexpensive but lacks sufficient strength to be used for shelving or structural members.

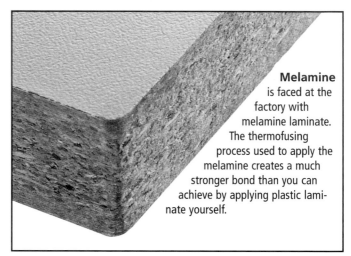

Melamine is faced at the factory with melamine laminate. The thermofusing process used to apply the melamine creates a much stronger bond than you can achieve by applying plastic laminate yourself.

Sheet Goods

The basic structural component of cabinetry is some form of sheet goods; most frequently plywood. Other commonly used sheet goods are particleboard, fiberboard, melamine panels and hardboard. These materials come in handy when you need to cover a broad project area without including seams. Sheet goods are dimensionally stable (there is no substantive wood grain to contend with) and relatively inexpensive, when compared to the price of solid lumber. You'll turn to them time and time again for different woodworking applications. Here is an overview of the options you'll find at most home centers and lumberyards:

Plywood. Plywood is fashioned from sheets of wood veneer, primarily pine and fir. By orienting the wood grain of each laminated sheet so adjacent sheets are perpendicular, the product is able to withstand greater stress than construction lumber of the same thickness. In addition, it is more dimensionally stable.

Most lumberyards stock furniture-grade plywood in several thicknesses and face veneer options (pine, red oak, birch and maple are the most common face veneers). Lumberyards can order plywood with dozens of additional veneer options.

Choosing the right plywood for your woodworking project is an important task. In addition to the various core, thickness and face veneer options, you'll also need to make a decision on the plywood grade. Basically, there are two grading systems in use today. The one most people are familiar with is administered by the APA (Engineered Wood Association, formerly the American Plywood Association). The APA grade stamps (See *Illustration*, next page) are found on sanded plywood, sheathing and structural (called performance-rated) panels. Along with grading each face of the plywood by letter (A to D) or purpose, the APA performance-rated stamp lists other information such as exposure rating, maximum allowable span, type of wood used to make the plies and the identification number of the mill where the panel was manufactured. Many hardwood-veneer sanded plywood panels are graded by the Hardwood Plywood and Veneer Association (HPVA). The HPVA grading numbers are similar to those employed by APA: they refer to a face grade (from A to E) and a back grade (from 1 to 4). Thus, a sheet of plywood that has a premium face (A) and a so-so back (3) would be referred to as A-3 by HPVA (and AC by APA).

Particleboard: Particleboard possesses several unique qualities that might make it a good choice for your next built-in project—particularly if the project includes a counter or tabletop. Particleboard is very dimensionally stable (it isn't likely to expand, contract or warp); it has a relatively smooth surface that provides a suitable substrate for laminate; it comes in a very wide range of thicknesses and panel dimensions; and it is inexpensive. But particleboard does have some drawbacks: it lacks stiffness and shear strength; it has poor screw-holding ability; it degrades when exposed to moisture; it's too coarse in the core to be shaped effectively; and it's heavy.

Medium-density fiberboard (MDF): MDF is similar to particleboard in constitution, but is denser and heavier. The smoothness and density of MDF make it a good substrate choice for veneered projects; the rougher surface of particleboard and most plywoods do not bond as cleanly with thin wood veneer. You can even laminate layers of MDF to create structural components that can be veneered or painted. MDF is also increasing in popularity as a trim molding material.

Melamine board: Melamine is fashioned with a particleboard core with one or two plastic laminate faces. Thicknesses range from ¼ to ¾ in. Stock colors at most lumber yards and building centers generally are limited to white, gray, almond and sometimes black. The panels are oversized by 1 in. (a 4 × 8 sheet is actually 49 × 97 in.) because the brittle melamine has a tendency to chip at the edges during transport. Plan to trim fresh edges.

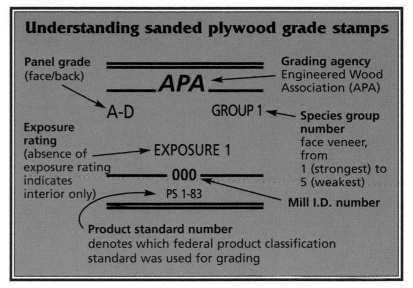

Every sheet of plywood is stamped with grading information. On lower-grade panels, such as exterior sheathing, the stamp can be found in multiple locations on both faces. Panels with one better-grade face are stamped only on the back, and panels with two better-grade faces are stamped on the edges.

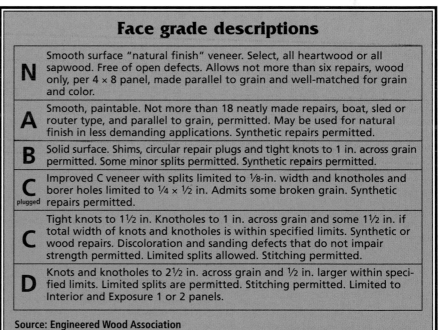

Face grade descriptions

N	Smooth surface "natural finish" veneer. Select, all heartwood or all sapwood. Free of open defects. Allows not more than six repairs, wood only, per 4 × 8 panel, made parallel to grain and well-matched for grain and color.
A	Smooth, paintable. Not more than 18 neatly made repairs, boat, sled or router type, and parallel to grain, permitted. May be used for natural finish in less demanding applications. Synthetic repairs permitted.
B	Solid surface. Shims, circular repair plugs and tight knots to 1 in. across grain permitted. Some minor splits permitted. Synthetic repairs permitted.
C plugged	Improved C veneer with splits limited to ⅛-in. width and knotholes and borer holes limited to ¼ × ½ in. Admits some broken grain. Synthetic repairs permitted.
C	Tight knots to 1½ in. Knotholes to 1 in. across grain and some 1½ in. if total width of knots and knotholes is within specified limits. Synthetic or wood repairs. Discoloration and sanding defects that do not impair strength permitted. Limited splits allowed. Stitching permitted.
D	Knots and knotholes to 2½ in. across grain and ½ in. larger within specified limits. Limited splits are permitted. Stitching permitted. Limited to Interior and Exposure 1 or 2 panels.

Source: Engineered Wood Association

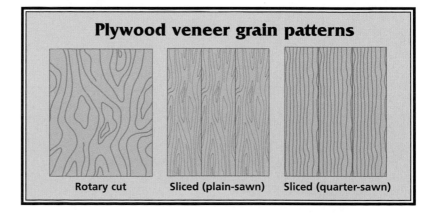

Plywood veneer grain patterns

Rotary cut   Sliced (plain-sawn)   Sliced (quarter-sawn)

A. RED OAK

Uses: Indoor furniture, trim, flooring, plywood and veneers
Sources: United States and Canada
Characteristics: Straight, wide grain pattern with larger pores. Tan to reddish pink in color. Quartersawing reveals narrow medullary rays.
Workability: Machines easily with sharp steel or carbide blades and bits. Not prone to burning when machined. Drill pilot holes first for nails or screws.
Finishing: Takes stains and clear finishes well, but pores will show through if painted unless they are filled
Price: Moderate

B. WHITE OAK

Uses: Indoor and outdoor furniture, trim, flooring, plywood and veneers
Sources: United States and Canada
Characteristics: Straight, wide grain pattern, tan with yellow to cream tints. Quartersawing reveals wide medullary rays. Naturally resistant to deterioration from UV sunlight, insects and moisture.
Workability: Machines easily with sharp steel or carbide blades and bits. Not prone to burning when machined. Drill pilot holes first for nails or screws.
Finishing: Takes stains and clear finishes like red oak, but narrower pores reduce the need for filling
Price: Moderate to expensive

C. HARD MAPLE

Uses: Indoor furniture, trim, flooring, butcher block countertops, instruments, plywoods and veneers
Sources: United States and Canada
Characteristics: Straight, wide grain with occasional bird's eye or fiddleback figure. Blonde heartwood.
Workability: Difficult to machine without carbide blades and bits. Dull blades will leave burns.
Finishing: Takes clear finishes well, but staining may produce blotches
Price: Moderate to expensive, depending on figure

D. CHERRY

Uses: Indoor furniture, cabinetry, carving, turning, plywood and veneers
Sources: United States and Canada
Characteristics: Fine grain pattern with smooth texture. Wood continues to darken as it ages and is exposed to sunlight.
Workability: Machines easily with sharp steel or carbide blades but is more prone to machine burns
Finishing: Takes stains and clear finishes well
Price: Moderate

E. WALNUT

Uses: Indoor furniture, cabinets, musical instruments, clocks, boat-building, carving
Sources: Eastern United States and Canada
Characteristics: Straight, fine grain. Moderately heavy. Color ranges from dark brown to purple or black.
Workability: Cuts and drills easily with sharp tools without burning
Finishing: Takes natural finishes beautifully
Price: Moderate

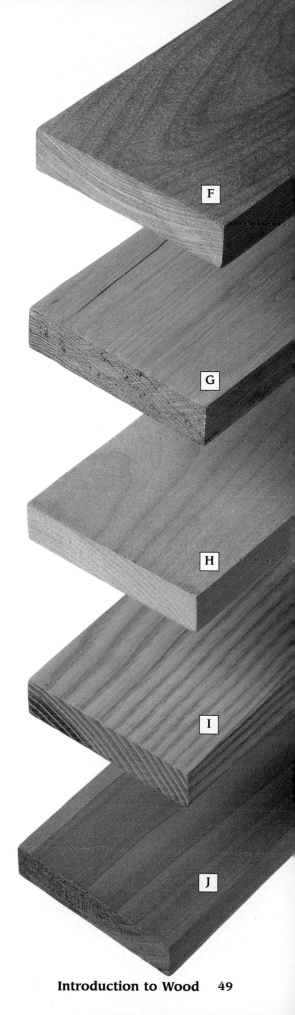

F. Birch

Uses: Kitchen utensils, toys, dowels, trim, plywood and veneers
Sources: United States and Canada
Characteristics: Straight grain with fine texture and tight pores. Medium to hard density.
Workability: Machines easily with sharp steel or carbide blades and bits. Good bending properties. Drill pilot holes first for nails or screws.
Finishing: Takes finishes well, but penetrating wood stains may produce blotching
Price: Inexpensive to moderate

G. Hickory

Uses: Sporting equipment, handles for striking tools, furniture, plywood and veneers
Sources: Southeastern United States
Characteristics: Straight to wavy grained with coarse texture. Excellent shock-resistance.
Workability: Bends well, but lumber hardness will dull steel blades and bits quickly. Resists machine burning.
Finishing: Takes stains and clear finishes well
Price: Inexpensive where regionally available

H. Aspen

Uses: A secondary wood used for drawer boxes, cleats, runners and other hidden structural furniture components. Crafts.
Sources: United States and Canada
Characteristics: Indistinguishable, tight grain pattern
Workability: Machines easily with sharp steel or carbide blades and bits. Takes routed profiles well.
Finishing: Better suited for painting than staining. Tight grain provides smooth, paintable surface.
Price: Inexpensive

I. White Ash

Uses: Furniture, boat oars, baseball bats, handles for striking tools, pool cues, veneers
Sources: United States and Canada
Characteristics: Straight, wide grain pattern with coarse texture. Hard and dense with excellent shock-resistance.
Workability: Machines easily with sharp steel or carbide blades and bits. Drill pilot holes first for nails or screws. "Green" ash often used for steam bending.
Finishing: Takes stains and clear finishes well
Price: Inexpensive

J. Poplar

Uses: Secondary wood for furniture and cabinetry, similar to aspen. Carving, veneers and pulp for paper.
Sources: United States
Characteristics: Fine-textured with straight, wide grain pattern. Tan to gray or green in color.
Workability: Machines easily with sharp steel or carbide blades and bits. Not prone to burning when machined. Drill pilot holes first for nails or screws.
Finishing: Better suited for painting than staining. Tight grain provides smooth, paintable surface.
Price: Inexpensive

A. WHITE PINE
Uses: Indoor furniture, plywood, veneers and trim, construction lumber
Sources: United States and Canada
Characteristics: Straight grain with even texture and tight pores
Workability: Machines easily with sharp steel or carbide blades and bits. Not prone to burning when machined. Lower resin content than other pines, so cutting edges stay cleaner longer.
Finishing: Stains may blotch without using a stain controller first. Takes clear finishes and paints well.
Price: Inexpensive

B. WESTERN RED CEDAR
Uses: Outdoor furniture, exterior millwork, interior and exterior siding
Sources: United States and Canada
Characteristics: Straight, variable grain pattern with coarse texture. Lower density and fairly light-weight. Saw- and sanding dust can be a respiratory irritant. Naturally resistant to deterioration from UV sunlight, insects and moisture.
Workability: Soft composition machines easily but end grain is prone to splintering and tear-out
Finishing: Takes stains and clear finishes well, but oils in wood can bleed through painted finishes unless primer is applied first
Price: Inexpensive to moderate where regionally available

C. AROMATIC CEDAR (TENNESSEE)
Uses: Naturally-occurring oils seem to repel moths, making this wood a common closet and chest lining. Also used for veneers and outdoor furniture.
Sources: Eastern United States and Canada
Characteristics: Straight to wavy grain pattern with fine texture. Red to tan in color with dramatic streaks of yellows and creams. Distinct aroma emitted when machined, and dust can be a respiratory irritant.
Workability: Machines similarly to western red cedar
Finishing: Takes stains and clear finishes well
Price: Inexpensive

D. REDWOOD
Uses: Outdoor furniture, decks and fences, siding
Source: West coast of United States
Characteristics: Straight, fine grain with few knots or blemishes. Relatively light weight. Reddish brown with cream-colored sapwood. Naturally resistant to deterioration from UV sunlight, insects and moisture.
Workability: Machines and sands easily
Finishing: Takes stains and clear finishes well
Price: Moderate to expensive and not widely available in all nominal dimensions

E. CYPRESS
Uses: Exterior siding and boat building. Interior and exterior trim, beams, flooring, cabinetry and paneling.
Source: Mississippi delta region of the United States
Characteristics: Straight, even grain pattern with low resin content. Naturally resistant to deterioration from UV sunlight, insects and moisture.
Workability: Machines and sands easily
Finishing: Takes stains and clear finishes well
Price: Inexpensive where regionally available

A. PADAUK

Uses: Indoor furniture, cabinetry, flooring, turning, veneer
Source: West Africa
Characteristics: Coarse texture, straight interlocked grain
Workability: Machines easily with sharp steel or carbide blades and bits
Finishing: Takes stains and clear finishes well
Price: Moderate to expensive

B. ZEBRAWOOD

Uses: Turning, inlay, decorative veneers, furniture and cabinetry
Source: West Africa
Characteristics: Interlocked, light and dark varigated grain pattern
Workability: Somewhat difficult to machine. Use carbide blades and bits
Finishing: Can be difficult to stain evenly
Price: Expensive

C. WENGE

Uses: Inlay, turning, decorative veneers
Source: Equatorial Africa
Characteristics: Hard, dense straight grain with coarse texture. Heavy.
Workability: Dulls steel blades and bits quickly, so carbide cutters are recommended. Drill pilot holes for screws and nails.
Finishing: Pores should be filled before finish is applied
Price: Moderate

D. HONDURAS MAHOGANY

Uses: Indoor and outdoor furniture, veneers and trim, boat-building
Sources: Central and South America
Characteristics: Straight, interlocked fine grain. Dimensionally stable.
Workability: Machines well with carbide blades and bits
Finishing: Takes stains and clear finishes well
Price: Moderate

E. PURPLEHEART

Uses: Pool cues, decorative inlay, veneers, indoor and outdoor furniture.
Sources: Central and South America
Characteristics: Straight grain with coarse texture
Workability: Gum deposits in the wood make it difficult to machine; cutting edges dull quickly
Finishing: Takes stains and clear finishes well.
Price: Moderate

F. TEAK

Uses: Boat-building, indoor and outdoor furniture, veneers, flooring
Sources: Southeast Asia, Africa, Caribbean
Characteristics: Straight grain with oily texture. Dense and hard.
Workability: High silica content will dull steel blades and bits quickly. Oily surfaces require cleaning with mineral spirits first or glue will not bond.
Finishing: Takes oil finishes well
Price: Expensive

G. ROSEWOOD

Uses: Inlays, turning, veneers, cabinetry, furniture, musical instruments
Sources: Southern India
Characteristics: Interlocked grain with medium to coarse texture
Workability: Dense structure dulls cutting edges quickly
Finishing: Takes stains and clear finishes well
Price: Expensive

Squaring, Marking & Cutting Stock

Creating parts for your woodworking project is a three-step process. First, the wood must be squared and sized for thickness. Second, the stock needs to be marked with layout and cutting lines. Finally, the boards must be cut and shaped into parts with a variety of woodworking tools.

Before embarking on the process of creating project parts, it's important to do a little planning. If you're working from a set of published plans, read it over thoughtfully. If you're building an original design, take this time to make up your own step-by-step plans. This minimizes eleventh-hour problems and enables you to order or purchase all necessary materials and have all necessary tools on hand.

Working from a cutting list is essential; if you don't have one, write one up. It organizes all parts with their correct dimensions and keeps minor parts from slipping through the cracks. Make a dimensioned drawing to work from (it doesn't have to be a Da Vinci, just clearly readable by you), and make a simple sketch. Calculate how you can most efficiently get your parts out of the rough materials with minimal waste. If any of the parts are angled, curved, or tapered, come up with a layout

WOODWORKING WORKS
Thorough stock preparation followed by careful layout and cutting of project parts will have a dramatic impact on the success of your woodworking project. This Mission-style bookcase is a fine example of the pleasing results you can expect from doing careful work.

plan so they nest into each other and consume less of the board length than if they were laid out end-to-end. Plywood parts can be cut from full or half sheets in numerous ways. Draw plywood cutting diagrams (scale rectangles of 4 × 8 sheets) and map out the parts, remembering to slightly oversize them to allow for the saw blade kerf and any cutting errors.

Grain direction is a factor to contend with when planning and laying out parts. The fibrous structure of wood makes it stronger in one direction than the other. Parts should be laid out *long grain;* that is, with the wood fibers running along the length of the part whenever possible. If a narrow part were laid out and cut with the grain pattern running across the part's width—called *short grain*—it would be weak and break easily along the grain. Curved parts should be oriented to minimize short grain. This is why the sharply curved legs on traditional tripod pedestal tables often break, and why a Windsor chair back wouldn't last 10 minutes if it were bandsawn out of a wide board instead of being steam bent or laminated out of thin strips.

In short, it is very important to temper the excitement that accompanies the feeling of cutting that first project board. Take a reasoned, thoughtful approach to this critical step, and you'll find that you make more efficient use of your materials, and you get better results.

Woodworking Wisdom

Before introducing a board to a tool or machine, always thoroughly check the wood for nails or screws. Besides the obvious damage to the machine's cutting edges, these unnoticed hazards can pose other insidious threats. The protruding barbs can severely slash your fingers or your machine (a scar that won't heal). I learned this valuable principle early in my very first (and short-lived) woodworking job. I worked for a man who had filled his spanking-new shop with spanking-new state-of-the-art German woodworking machines. He was doing a furniture repair for a previous customer and I was asked to resurface a disassembled part. I didn't have the slightest idea what it was and how it fit together, but I sure loved to operate the 36 in. planer with push-button automatic table lift and LED digital readout. Well I didn't notice the four hidden #10 screws sticking out the bottom of the board until the noise drew a crowd to marvel at the troughs plowed into the surface of the planer's precision-milled table. Needless to say, that job didn't exactly get off to a flying start.

~Kam Ghaffari

Squaring Stock

Squaring up, or milling your wood four-square, is the important initial step in turning a piece of solid wood lumber into a part for a woodworking project. It involves taking a board to the proper thickness, width, and length; and making it flat, straight, and square-edged in the process. In this section we'll take you through the wood milling process.

Almost all lumber will have some type of warpage, whether cup, bow, twist, or crook. If you buy your lumber rough-milled, it will be oversized in all dimensions, and rather shaggy from the sawmill marks. Even if you buy lumber planed on two faces you may still get a bowed or twisted board. Rough or planed, the boards must be trued flat and square or you can have all sorts of problems—from mechanical headaches to visual eyesores.

Squaring stock is typically done with a power jointer, a thickness planer, and a table saw. Jointers and planers are relatively expensive machines. But if you plan on doing woodworking as a serious hobby, particularly fine furnituremaking, consider buying a 12-in. portable planer and at least a small jointer for truing edges. They are not out of reach anymore; nowadays good new ones can be had for a few hundred dollars, and used ones for even less. Combination jointer/planer machines are also available. But lumber can also be squared using only the traditional hand-planing methods we'll show how in the pages that follow.

Squaring and sizing lumber is essentially a six-step procedure (See *Four Steps to Square Stock,* below).

1. Rough-cutting. No matter what milling methods you use, start by cutting your boards close to final dimension—but always leave them slightly oversized. Generally, allow about ¼ to ½ in. extra in width and at least 1 in. extra in length whenever possible. This provides enough material for fixing mistakes or jointing crooked edges, as well as removing accidental chip-out and corners or edges damaged or rounded in the milling process. If you have a planer that snipes, you may need to leave as much as an extra 2 in. on each end so the snipe marks can be cut off afterward. When jointing and planing rough lumber you'll usually lose between ⅛ and ¼ in. in thickness, so 4/4 lumber generally gets reduced into ¾-in.-thick boards. Long or severely warped boards may require more material to true them up. Carefully examine the ends of your boards for any hidden checking

Four steps to square stock

1. Rough cut the board to approximate size.
2. Flatten one face.
3. Straighten one edge square to the flat face.
4. Plane the board to desired thickness.

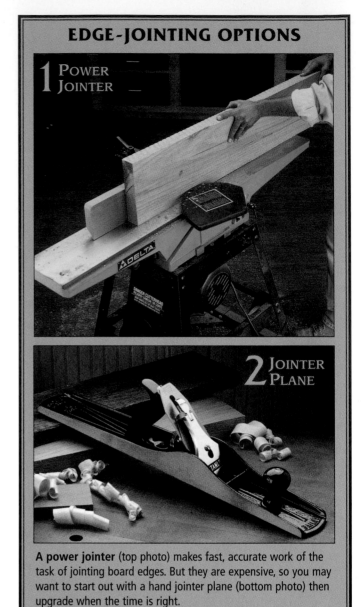

EDGE-JOINTING OPTIONS

1 POWER JOINTER

2 JOINTER PLANE

A power jointer (top photo) makes fast, accurate work of the task of jointing board edges. But they are expensive, so you may want to start out with a hand jointer plane (bottom photo) then upgrade when the time is right.

Dealing with defects: Trim off the ends of boards containing cracks or checks before you spend a lot of time milling them. Make sure the trim cut is at least an inch or two past the point where the defect terminates. You can also cut around knots to create shorter, usable boards.

SURFACE PLANING OPTIONS

1 POWER PLANER

2 BENCH PLANE

A **power planer** (top photo) can hog through a lot of stock quickly, and the benchtop models are not too expensive. But don't dismiss the hand planing option. A bench plane (bottom photo) has been the planing tool of choice for centuries.

Blade guard removed for clarity

Dealing with defects: Rip-cut cupped lumber on a table saw with the concave side facing up. In severe cupping situations, as with this board, saw the board into smaller flat pieces. Keep the board from rocking as you cut it, to reduce the chances of kickback.

and make your cuts well back from the apparent ends of the splits. You may have to sacrifice the first few inches of a board that has been stored for some time. For a few tips on salvaging usable lumber from defective stock, see the photos on the bottom of the next page.

2. Flattening. In order to make accurate, reliable rectangular parts, one face of the board must first be trued flat. The idea is to progressively plane down the high spots on an uneven board, using an assortment of tools until the surface is flat. Although it seems a little counterintuitive, the tool you don't want to use for the initial flattening of stock is the first one most people would think to use: the power planer. The problem with flattening on the power planer is that the workpiece rides on the planer bed while the cutters work on the opposite face from above. So if the face riding on the bed is not flat, the planed side won't be flat either. A jointer, on the other hand, tools the face that rides on the bed, flattening it with each pass. Hand planes, of course, can be used selectively on the board face to knock down high areas. If you have a jointer and your stock is narrower than the width of the cutterhead, use the jointer for the initial flattening of your stock.

Flattening on a power jointer: (See Step-by-step instructions, next page). A power jointer does an excellent job of flattening one side of stock (as long as the stock is within the cutting capacity of your jointer—6 in. on the most common home shop models). If you're flattening hardwood, set the cutters to remove no more than about 1/16 in. of stock per pass. If your jointer has no calibrated depth gauge, you can set the cutting depth manually: With the jointer unplugged, turn the cutterhead with a stick so all the knives are below the level of the infeed and outfeed tables. Lay a flat board or straightedge down on the outfeed table with its end protruding over the infeed table. The gap between the underside of the board and the infeed table will be your depth of cut at the current setting. Adjust the height

A good option to squaring lumber yourself is to do what many pros do: sub it out. Some large woodshops have thickness sanders (often called "timesavers") that work like planers but won't chip out the grain of figured wood. The machines are expensive to buy, so the shops often accept outside sanding work to help pay for them. Or, you may be able to use the equipment yourself for an hourly rate.

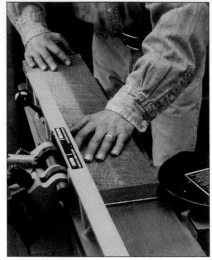

1 Place the board flat on the infeed table of the jointer. If the wood is bowed or cupped, the concave face should be down so the board does not rock. The high corners or ends will contact the cutters and get planed first. Set the depth of cut to no more than about 1/16 in. for hardwood stock; with softwoods you can take a little deeper initial cut if you like. Feed the board so the blades cut with the grain.

2 Hold the front of the board firmly down against the infeed table with your left hand and in your right hand use a push block with a trailing lip hooked around the end of the board. Don't use excessive force; unless you're flattening a thin board, let the weight of the board do most of the work.

3 Guide the wood across the jointer with even pressure, walking slowly along the side of the machine as you go. If the board is long, you can feed it with both hands and pick up the push block as the end of the board approaches the cutter. With a narrow board, don't keep your hand on the board as it passes over the cutters. Instead, walk your hands along and raise each one over the cutter and onto the wood.

Which way is with the grain?

It's common knowledge in woodworking that wood should be planed or jointed *with the grain*. But determining which way the grain runs is not as easy as it sounds. You can sometimes tell grain direction by looking at the grain lines on the board's edge. But this is not foolproof. You will know the correct feed direction, though, once you make the first pass through the jointer or planer. If the stock is being fed against the grain, you'll hear the knives tearing out little chunks of the wood and you'll know to feed the board the opposite way (one or two passes will smooth out the surface).

of the infeed table until the gap is the same thickness as the depth of cut you want to make.

Before using the jointer, read the safety tips on page 58. And here are a couple more helpful tips to keep in mind when flattening on the jointer:

- Don't worry if there are a few small patches of rough wood surface left. It will be cleaned up when it's run through the planer.
- You generally want to remove as little material as possible when jointing for flatness. You can quickly end up with a board that's too thin.
- With a moderately warped board, take a deeper cut on the first pass, then switch

The shaggy surface of rough lumber is a good gauge for flattening stock on a jointer. Joint the board in shallow passes until fresh wood is exposed on the entire face. A little roughness here and there is okay: it can be removed with a plane or a power planer.

to a shallower cut for the last pass or two to smooth the surface.

- Jointing a twisted board is tricky. Balance the board so the twist is distributed evenly along the length of the board. Try to keep the board riding on the same two or three points throughout the first pass or two until a stable, flat surface is established.

Flattening with a hand plane: Hand planing is a pleasant activity, and not at all difficult. The key is to start with a

well-tuned plane with a razor-sharp blade. For surface planing boards, longer bench planes (#5 or #6) work best because they have more surface area and can span the dips in uneven wood as you flatten the surface. It's generally easier to flatten the convex face on cupped stock.

Use the basic planing technique shown in the photos to the right for all surface planing, including flattening. Here are a few tips:

- If the wood is uneven and rocks, shim beneath it.
- Set the blade for a fairly light depth of cut and hold the plane in a firm but relaxed grip.
- Begin by leveling any noticeable high spots, then focus on overall, even planing.
- Work at a diagonal, and overlap your strokes. When you reach the end of the board, plane diagonally the other way.
- Check the surface periodically with a straightedge at several points across the board, and sight down the board face from each end to check for twist.
- As the surface becomes flattened, switch to planing down the length of the board with the grain, but keep the sole of the plane at a slight angle for a smooth, shearing cut.

3. Straightening an edge. Once the face is flattened, choose the best edge and trim it so it's perfectly

Bench planes usually have a number prefix in their name: the smaller the plane, the smaller the number. Use a No. 4 or No. 5 bench plane (also called jack planes) for flattening. For edge-jointing, use a No. 6 fore plane or a No. 7 jointer plane.

HOW TO USE A HAND PLANE

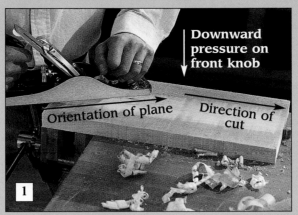

1 Downward pressure on front knob
Orientation of plane — Direction of cut

2 Downward pressure on handle

Orient the board so you're planing with the grain. Clamp the workpiece with bench dogs or clamped blocks below the surface of the wood so movement of the plane is unobstructed. Angle the body of the plane so it's at a diagonal to the direction of the cut. Begin the cut with downward pressure exerted on the front knob of the plane **(Photo 1, left)**. Then, as you near the end of the pass, lighten the pressure on the knob and exert heavier pressure on the handle at the back of the plane **(Photo 2, left)** until the pass is completed.

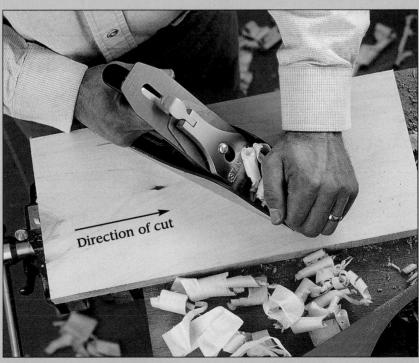

Direction of cut

Smoothing with a hand plane: Final smoothing of a surface is done using the same general techniques shown in the two photos above. For best results, use a No. 4 or smaller smoothing plane. Make sure to work with the grain direction, keeping the body of the plane diagonal to the cutting direction.

HOW TO EDGE-JOINT BOARDS

With a jointer: Set the concave edge of the board on the infeed table, with the flattened face against the fence. As you push the board across the cutterhead, hold it against the fence with both hands and exert downward pressure directly over the infeed table. When most of the board has passed over the cutters, shift downward pressure over the outfeed table. Make shallow passes until the edge is flat, smooth and square to the flat face.

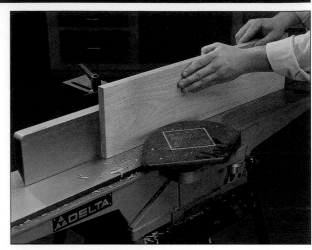

With a jointing plane: Clamp the workpiece securely in a bench vise, leaving plenty of clearance from the jaws of the vise. Start planing in the center of the board, then strike off the ends so they're even with the rest of the edge. Apply pressure on the front of the plane at the beginning of the stroke and gradually transfer the pressure to the back of the plane by the end of the stroke. Check your work regularly with a straightedge and a square.

The surfaces of rough lumber are shaggy and often embedded with grit and gravel that can wreak havoc on blades. Keep a wire brush within easy reach of your jointer and planer, and give the faces and edges of your boards a stiff brushing before you start milling.

straight and at right angles to the face. This square reference edge is known as the *face edge.* The straightening process, known as *edge-jointing,* was traditionally done with a large hand plane, but these days it is usually done on a stationary power jointer. If your board is less than 1½ in. thick, you can joint it cleanly and easily with a router and a flush-trim bit.

Edge-jointing with a jointer: Edge jointing is the most common task performed on the jointer. Set the jointer fence so it

is perpendicular to the surfaces of the infeed and outfeed tables—check this with a square. Set the cutters for a shallow cut (no more than ⅟₁₆ in.) to avoid tearout. The goal should be to create a straight, square edge while removing as little material as possible. TIP: If the grain direction is wrong and you get too much tearout, feed the other (unflattened) face of they board through the planer so you can flip the board around and joint the other edge.

Edge-jointing with a plane: If you

The name "jointer" refers to the common use of the tool to prepare the edges of boards for edge-gluing panels. In practice, you'll likely use it most often to square up rough stock.

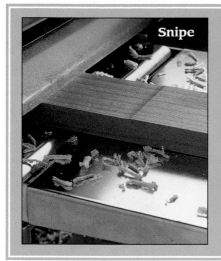
Snipe

COMMON PLANING PROBLEMS

Snipe (left photo) occurs when the infeed and outfeed planer tables are not exactly parallel. In many cases, simply making sure the tables are aligned will take care of it, but it's usually a good idea to allow for snipe by choosing raw stock that is long enough so the affected areas can be trimmed off after planing.

Tearout (right photo) is caused by feeding the board into the planer against the grain or by taking a cut that's too deep. If flopping your feed direction and decreasing the cutting depth don't stop the tearout, it's a good bet that the grain in your stock switches directions. In this case, switch to a hand plane so you can change planing directions to follow the grain.

Tearout

choose to square board edges with a hand plane, choose a No. 6 fore plane or, better yet, the longer No. 7 jointer plane—you may even be able to find a 24-in.-long No. 8 jointer plane, but these have become scarce in modern times. Set a shallow cutting depth and make sure the blade is straight (parallel to the sole). While it's not difficult to plane a straight edge, it requires a good deal of care to assure that the edge is also square to the flattened face. You can let your fingers curl under the sole of the plane and ride against the face of the wood to help stabilize the plane and keep its position constant throughout the length of the stroke.

4. Thickness planing. For this procedure a power thickness planer is a godsend. Not only will it plane the board to the proper thickness and make the second face absolutely parallel to the first, but it can machine as many boards as you need to exactly the same dimension—which is essential to properly fitting parts together for a furniture project. Plane all your parts to be brought to a common dimension at the same time. Lay them out in a pile on a table or sawhorses close to the planer with the unplaned faces up and the grain oriented properly to avoid tearout. This way you can just feed them through one at a time without having to think about which way each one goes.

NOTE: Don't feed stock that's less than 12 in. long through the planer—it won't reach the outfeed roller and will either get chewed into a mulch or the planer will spit it back out.

If you're trying to plane your stock to an exact thickness, stop planing when the stock is reduced almost to exact thickness. Run pieces of scrap through and adjust the planer setting until the scrap is the correct thickness. Then, run the actual workpieces through.

How to Operate a Power Planer

1

1 Set the table height (which establishes cutting depth) so the thickest part of the thickest board fits snugly under the infeed roller. Then remove the board and raise the table slightly (about 1/16 in.) with the table height crank.

2

2 Stand to one side and use both hands to feed the board straight into the machine. Once the infeed roller grabs the board it can slap it down hard against the table, so don't let your fingers get between the board and the table. As the board passes through the planer, walk around to the other side and support the overhanging wood as it leaves the machine. If you have to remove a lot of material, take heavier cuts at first, but finish up with a fine cut for a better finish. Once you've flattened the top face turn the board over and take at least a skim cut off the first face (if you're removing lots of material, alternate faces to even out stock removal and avoid warping).

Careful planning and layout of project parts helps ensure pleasing, professional results. It also helps you make more efficient use of your building materials.

Laying Out Parts

Whether you're working from a set of plans or concocting your own design, the quality of your workmanship depends on accurately transferring the dimensions, lines, shapes, and angles of your parts to your building materials. These precise measurements and marks provide the guidelines for sawing, drilling, and shaping operations. To prevent serious problems always check and double check each measurement before you cut.

Measuring. While some woodworkers and carpenters still prefer using a traditional folding rule, the mainstays of measuring today are the tape measure and the steel rule. *Tape measures* are quick and convenient, and portable. Their flexibility also makes them useful for measuring along curved surfaces. A *steel rule* provides more accurate measurements than a tape measure. Some 1 or 2-ft.-long rules can be fitted with a *combination square* head, increasing their versatility many times over. In critical situations when you want to make certain you're getting a precise reading (or if your tape tip is damaged) you can measure from the 1 in. mark on the tape or rule. But remember to subtract that 1 in. from your measurement at the other end.

Marking tools. For general sketching, writing, and marking in the shop an ordinary *No. 2 pencil* is indispensable. The lead is soft enough to leave a bold line without denting the wood, as harder pencil lead will. For drawing layout lines, a mechanical pencil with 0.5 mm or 0.3 mm lead will maintain a fine point without requiring you to sharpen it every five minutes. Of course, none of these pencils shows up very well on dark materials like walnut or hardboard. For these, use a soft-lead, white colored pencil instead.

Knives are handy in the shop for a multitude of uses. A sharp knife can be used as a marking tool that not only lays out precise lines for cutting joints, but also leaves a dead-accurate incision that you can register your chisel in for

Layout tools for woodworking include: **(A)** steel rule calibrated to ¹⁄₁₆ in. or higher; **(B)** sliding bevel gauge (also called a T-bevel) for measuring and transferring angles; **(C)** steel tape measure; **(D)** marking gauge; **(E)** compass for drawing circles and arcs; **(F)** combination square; **(G)** marking pencils, including a lumber pencil for marking rough stock, a regular No. 2 pencil (not shown) and a white pencil for marking darker stock; **(H)** try square; **(I)** chalkline for marking sheet goods.

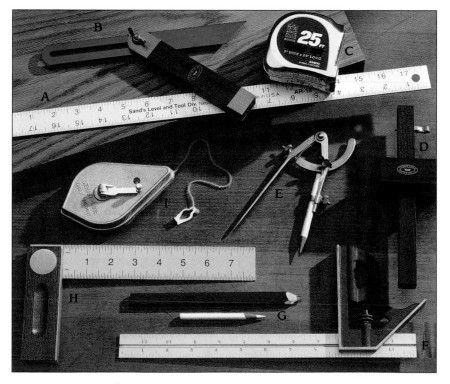

the final paring cut when doing hand work. Any kind of knife will work (pocket knife, utility knife, fine craft knife, or dedicated woodworker's marking knife) as long as it's sharp and comfortable to work with.

Drawing layout lines.

• *Straight lines.* You can draw a straight line anywhere with the aid of a steel rule or straightedge.

• *Parallel lines.* There are many tricks for drawing a line parallel to a board edge. One good method is to use a combination square: Hold your pencil against the end of the square's blade and, holding the square's head tightly against the edge of the wood with your other hand, slide the square and pencil together down the board. Marking and cutting gauges are fine woodworking tools that allow you to do this same operation one-handed. They accurately reproduce identical joint layout lines on multiple parts.

• *Perpendicular lines.* Successful woodworking depends on accurately drawn and cut 90° (right) angles. The square is the workshop tool used for laying out these lines and testing the precision of the subsequent cuts. Squares vary in

quality. Inexpensive plastic-bodied squares are available for rough work and carpentry, but are not accurate enough for furniture and cabinetmaking. Quality *try squares* (usually with steel blades and metal-faced hardwood bodies, or stocks) and *engineer's squares* (with all-steel construction) are great shop tools for setting blade angles and jointer fences, and for many other uses in addition to layout. But the most versatile jack-of-all-trades is the *combination square.* The blade is a removable, gradu-

ated steel rule. The stock has a 90° face as well as a 45° face for laying out miters. The blade slides into the tool and can be locked at any position so it can also be used to check the squareness of tiny rabbets and gauge depth and height.

• *Angled lines.* When your two workpieces meet at 90°, it's generally common practice to join them with a butt joint. But for finer work where you want a more elegant, symmetrical joint, miter the ends of the mating workpieces at 45°. To lay out miters accurately and check the finished cuts, you'll need a miter square. This can be any square with its blade permanently mounted to give you both 45° and its complimentary angle, 135°; or you can use the versatile combination square, which is equipped with a 45° face opposite its 90° face. For angles other than 90° and 45° you'll need a *bevel gauge.* This is essentially an adjustable square that can be set to any angle and locked into position. Use a protractor as a guide to set the legs of the bevel gauge, or adjust the square to match an existing angle and transfer the angle to another workpiece.

To square a line around a board, as for laying out a tenon shoulder or a making a four-sided cutoff line, start marking with the trued-up edge of the board. Press the stock of the square firmly against this edge, with the blade lying flat against the reference face at the required location. Mark a line along the blade with a pencil or knife. Then, draw square lines from the reference face across each edge. Finally, with the stock against the reference edge, square a line across the opposite face, connecting the edge lines.

To apply a marking gauge to your workpiece, extend your thumb so it backs up the cutter in the post. Tilt the tool forward slightly, and make the mark by pushing the tool. Your thumb provides forward pressure while your fingers push downward with just enough force to press the pins or blade into the wood.

Marking Curves & Circles

Laying out curved or round cutting lines accurately is mostly a matter of choosing the best marking guide or technique for the shape and size of the curve.

Curves & arcs. In order for a curve to be visually pleasing it must be *fair* (meaning smooth) and consistent without ripples or flats. To mark smooth, well proportioned curves of small to medium size, you can often use draftsmen's plastic *French curve* templates (See next page). Curves or arcs that are too large to be made with these tools can be marked using a flexible drawing guide. *Segmented flexible splines,* available from 14 in. to 48 in. long, can be found (along with French curves) at drafting supply stores. A flexible steel rule or even a thin strip of wood can be sprung to your desired curve through a series of plotted points (See photo below). Arcs and roundovers can be drawn with a standard compass (See photo, above right).

Circles. The best way to draw a perfect circle for layout depends on the size. For small circles of common diameter, a basic set of plastic circle templates is accurate and easy to use; for circles up to about 12 in. in diameter, a compass will do the job (you can get larger compasses with greater range); for larger circles (a foot or more in diameter), use a pair of *trammel points.* Woodworker's trammel points clamp onto a wooden bar. One of the points is fitted with a pencil holder, the other is a metal pin for pivoting. Measure and set the distance between the pivot point and the pencil to equal the radius of the circle. Or, you can make a simple trammel yourself with any piece of long, narrow wood scrap (See photo, lower right).

Of course, for quick-and-dirty curves and circles, a woodworker can always grab whatever is close at hand to trace around—a tin can, a roll of masking tape, a coffee mug...just about anything will do.

French Curves

A set of French Curves is used mostly for drafting and laying out scale versions of projects that feature lines of non-constant radius. Made of hard plastic or acrylic and usually sold in sets, French Curves can be used to draw many different arc shapes by tracing either the interior cutouts or the outer profiles.

A similar set of layout tools known as "ship curves" are used the same way, but have plainer, less complicated shapes.

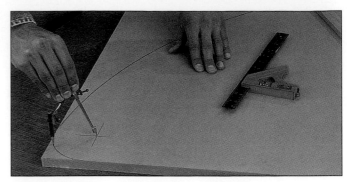

The infinitely adjustable compass

An ordinary compass is the tool of choice for marking arcs and roundovers of a defined radius and for drawing circles up to about 12 in. in diameter.

Quick & easy trammels

A homemade trammel pivots around a centerpoint (usually a finish nail) while the free end is fitted with a pencil for marking the circle. Just drive a nail through one end of the strip, then measure out from the nail toward the other end an amount equal to the radius of the circle. Mark a centerpoint for drilling a pencil guide hole at that point (usually, 3/8 in. dia.). Tack the nail at the center of the workpiece, insert the pencil into the guide hole, then make a single revolution around the nail with the pencil to draw the circle.

Laying out arcs

You don't need a fancy jig to draw a smooth arc—all it takes is a strip of hardboard and a few nails. Tack one nail at each endpoint of the arc, and tack the third nail at the apex of the arc. Cut a thin strip of hardboard a few inches longer than the length of the arc. Bend the strip between the the nails and trace along the inside edge.

Making & Using Patterns

For project parts with complex shapes, building plans often include patterns that are intended to be transferred to your stock or to material for making a template. If the pattern is actual size, you can transfer it directly to the work-piece by using carbon or transfer paper and tracing over the lines. More frequently, however, patterns are provided in a scaled down format, so they need to be enlarged. Typically, patterns are printed on scaled grid squares, with the size of the full-scale squares indicated. There are several methods for enlarging grid drawings. You can plot a grid pattern directly onto the workpiece or the template material (make sure to use the same scale noted with the drawing—if the scale is ¼ in. equals 1 in., for example, plot the grid with 1 in. squares). Once the grid pattern is laid out, draw the shape of the part, using the printed pattern as a reference. In some cases, you can enlarge the pattern to full size on a photocopier—if the scale is ¼ in. equals 1 in., for example, you'll need to enlarge the printed pattern 400%). Another option is to use an overhead projector to project the pattern onto larger paper. Patterns for large or very complex parts can be enlarged to actual size at any blue-print shop.

> *For symmetrical patterns, draw half the shape on paper, fold the paper in half along the centerline, and cut out the pattern. Or, make a half template then trace it first one way and then flipped over.*

If you're making multiple parts of the same size and shape, it's generally a good idea to create a template (See *How to Make & Use a Template,* right). Templates can be created from just about any material, including cardboard or paper. Hardboard (⅛ or ¼ in. thick) works very well, as does thin MDF (medium-density fiber-board), or quality veneer-core plywood.

Following grid drawings

Transfer grid drawings to your workpiece by plotting a scaled grid onto the stock or the template material, then recreating the pattern using the printed pattern as a reference. You may find it helpful to use a compass or flexible ruler to draw curves.

HOW TO MAKE & USE A TEMPLATE

1 Draw the full-sized shape onto template material (hardboard is shown here) then cut it out with a jig saw or coping saw. Sand or file the edges smooth, then trace the shape onto your wood stock.

2 Cut out the part, cutting just outside the layout lines. Use a wood file or sandpaper to smooth out the edges and remove waste wood up to the cutting lines.

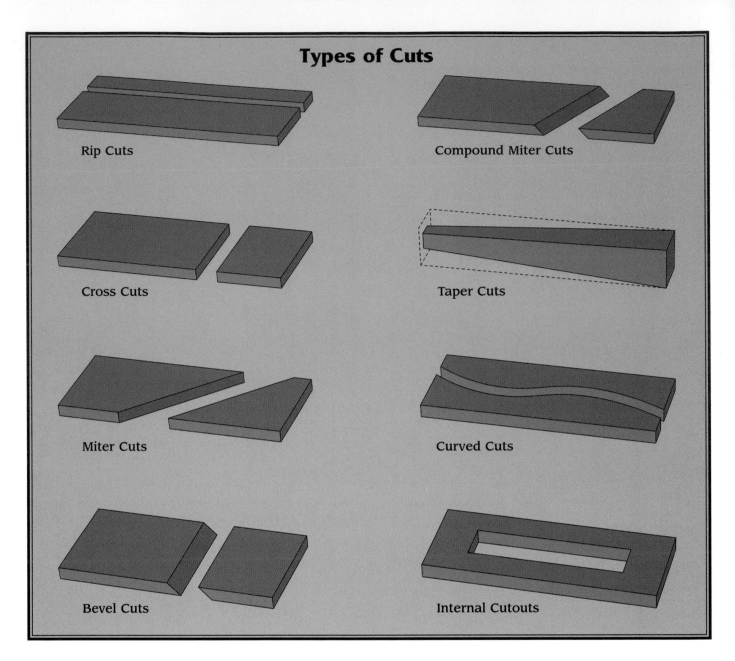

Types of Cuts

Rip Cuts

Compound Miter Cuts

Cross Cuts

Taper Cuts

Miter Cuts

Curved Cuts

Bevel Cuts

Internal Cutouts

Cutting Project Parts

Cutting parts to size usually involves making several different types of cuts with multiple tools. In this section we've described most of the standard cutting operations you're likely to encounter while woodworking. For each operation we've suggested what we believe to be the best method, as well as a few alternatives that can get the job done adequately if you don't own the suggested tool.

The essential cuts you'll make time and again are *rips cuts* (for width) and *cross cuts* (for length). As your skills advance and the complexity of the projects you undertake increases, you'll also need to make *miter* and *bevel cuts, tapers, curved cuts, pattern-following cuts, edge-profile cuts* and *resawing* stock for thickness.

All of these cuts can be made with portable hand tools. But you'll generally get faster, more accurate results with stationary sawing tools. Of these, the table saw and the power miter saw are the most versatile. A band saw and a scroll saw are also valuable additions as you develop your workshop.

> Each cutting machine excels at certain operations, performing the work more easily, safely, and accurately than other machines. Choosing the best tool for the cutting task at hand will go a long way toward ensuring good results.

The versatile jig saw (also called a saber saw) is capable of making any cut. It excels at cutting curves and making interior cutouts.

A **circular saw** and straightedge cutting guide can be used for cross cuts, rip cuts, bevel cuts and miter cuts.

A **power miter saw** is perfect for making repetitive cross cuts, including mitered or beveled cuts (bevels require a compound miter saw).

A **table saw** is the most heavily used tool in most woodshops. It can make just about any straight cut, including bevels and miters.

A **router** is used to make dadoes and rabbets as well as edge profiles. With special bits and accessories it can also be used for pattern cutting, circle cutting and many other cutting tasks.

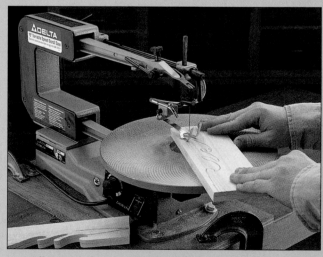

A **scroll saw** is a favorite tool for cutting intricate curves and patterns. They are not powerful but are relatively easy to manage.

Making Rip Cuts

The process of rip-cutting is often referred to as cutting parallel to or parallel with the grain. While this is true for solid wood, you'll often find yourself ripping plywood across the surface grain. So it's perhaps better to think of rip-cutting as the process of cutting stock to width.

Rip-cutting with a table saw

The table saw is certainly the most convenient and most accurate machine for ripping lumber and sheet goods. Make sure the rip fence is adjusted so it's parallel to the blade and at a right angle to the table. Squaring up the fence can be tricky with the often-flimsy fences that come with some table saws. That's why you may want to consider seriously investing in after-market calibrated fences that are sturdy, adjustable, and accurate. Many new saws now come equipped with a higher-end rip fence.

Table saws also come equipped with a number of safety features to reduce the hazards of rip cutting.

Ripping boards to width should be done after one edge has been squared (see previous section) so a flat even surface can ride against the saw fence or be used to register your straight-edge for making rip cuts with hand-held tools.

1 Start rip cuts with your left foot against the front left corner of the saw base. Feed the workpiece with your right hand, and use your left hand to keep the workpiece snug against the rip fence. Use a pushstick whenever a workpiece requires your hand to be closer than 6 in. to the blade.

2 Continue feeding the workpiece through the blade with your right hand as the end of the board approaches the front edge of the saw table. Switch to a pushstick in your right hand if necessary. Keep your left hand on the infeed side of the blade at all times.

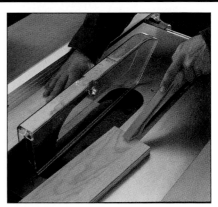

3 When the blade cuts the board in two, push the workpiece past the blade with your right hand until it clears the blade on the outfeed side. Slide the cutoff piece away from the blade with your left hand or a pushstick to prevent it from coming in contact with the blade.

In addition to the blade guard, the riving knife with antikickback pawls behind the blade prevent kickback when ripping boards.

Making rip cuts. (See photos, previous page.) Set the rip fence so the distance between its inner face and the teeth of your saw blade is equal to the width you're after for your workpiece. Use a steel rule to set the distance, rather than relying on the calibration marks on the front of the table. Once the blade is positioned correctly, lock the fence in position with the locking handle. Set the blade height so it extends no more than about ½ in. above the surface of your workpiece. Stand slightly to one side of the blade, not directly behind it so you're out of the line of fire in the event a board gets thrown back. Push the board with your right hand while guiding it firmly against the fence with your left. Maintain firm control of the workpiece throughout the cut until it is well past the blade. Then turn off the saw and walk around to the back of the machine to retrieve the board. Always make a test cut on scrap wood before cutting your stock. Measure the scrap to make sure it is exactly the right width.

One key point to remember is to never let your fingers get closer than about 6 inches from the blade. Never let your hands get directly behind the blade or they could get pulled into it in the event of kickback.

To rip a narrow board, use a push stick rather than your hand to feed the board. A featherboard clamped to the saw table will press the stock against the fence and allow you to keep your left hand away from the blade. Hold downs can be clamped to the rip fence to prevent the stock from bouncing or chattering as you feed it through the blade. Make sure featherboards and hold downs are not pressed too tightly against the stock.

Long boards

When ripping long boards, tip the back edge of the board up so it is slightly higher than the saw table. Doing this will press the leading edge of the board firmly down on the saw table. Lower the back edge of the board as the cut progresses.

Ripping sheet goods

Full sheets of plywood, particleboard and other sheet goods can be ripped effectively on a table saw if you position a sturdy table on the outfeed side of the saw, at or just below the saw table surface. But many woodworkers prefer to cut the sheets down to size with a circular saw or panel-cutting saw first.

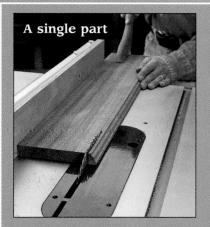
A single part

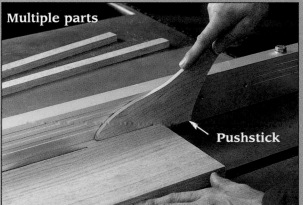
Multiple parts

Pushstick

RIPPING NARROW STRIPS

When rip-cutting a single narrow workpiece from a wider board, the narrow strip should be on the opposite side of the blade from the rip fence (left photo). This keeps the wider portion of the board between the blade and the rip fence to allow more room for your hand or a pushstick. To rip a series of narrow workpieces, set the distance between the blade and the rip fence to match the intended width of the workpieces you need. Use a narrow pushstick to guide the pieces along the rip fence (right photo).

Straightedge cutting guide

With the help of a good straightedge you can use your circular saw to make rip cuts that are nearly as accurate as those made on a table saw. You can purchase a straightedge, like the extruded aluminum model shown above, or select a piece of stock (a strip of particleboard, for example) that's straight, smooth-edged and even.

Adjustable ripping fence

Most circular saws come with an adjustable ripping fence that attaches to the foot of the saw. The fence rides along the edge of the board to guide the saw so it cuts a line parallel to the board edge. These accessories are fine for rip cuts that don't demand a high level of accuracy.

Rip-cutting with a circular saw

While it won't give you quite the precise, clean cuts of a table saw, a circular saw with the right blade can do a fairly good job of rip-cutting on non-critical work. Its portability makes it ideal for on-site construction.

Ripping a straight line with a circular saw requires the use of a cutting guide. Most saws come with an adjustable ripping fence that attaches to the base plate. This is used for ripping fairly narrow strips parallel to an edge, particularly on boards too narrow to be ripped with a straightedge guide. The accuracy of the adjustable ripping fence can be improved by screwing a wooden batten to it to extend its bearing surface. The best way to guide the saw in a rip cut is to clamp a straightedge guide to the workpiece and run

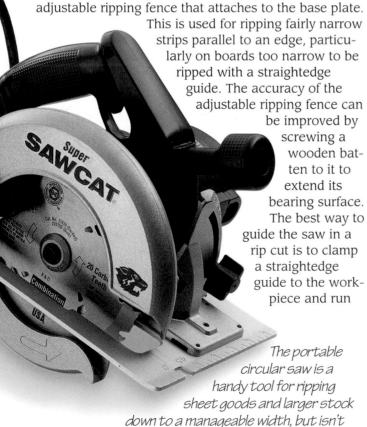

The portable circular saw is a handy tool for ripping sheet goods and larger stock down to a manageable width, but isn't well equipped for fine woodworking cuts.

the edge of the saw's base plate (foot) against it. This guide can be store-bought or shop-made, but must be long enough to overhang the workpiece on both ends.

Determining the offset. The "offset" of your saw is the distance from the edge of the foot that will ride along a straightedge to the closer edge of the cutting blade. To use the saw with a straightedge guide you'll need to know this distance. To find it, simply clamp a straightedge to a piece of scrap and make a cut, following the straightedge. Measure from the edge of the kerf to the straightedge: this is the distance your straightedge must be clamped from the cutting line on your workpiece. Or, you can make a guide with a built-in offset (See photo, next page, bottom).

TIP: When making long rip cuts, stop the cut periodically and slip wood shims into the kerf you've cut. This will prevent the kerf from closing up and causing the saw blade to be pinched in the cut (which can bog down the blade or even throw the saw).

> *The best circular rip-cutting blades have fewer, larger teeth and a thin profile that removes less material. For a 7¼ in. circular saw, use a 16-tooth antikickback blade; for a 10-in. table saw, use an 18- to 24-tooth blade.*

RIP-CUTTING WITH A BAND SAW OR JIG SAW

Both the jig saw and the band saw are quite capable of making straight cuts, but you can't expect either to produce finish cuts. While a table saw can leave a dead-accurate cut with a surface that requires only light sanding, a jig saw or band saw cut is rippled and its blade has a tendency to wander. So if you're going to do your ripping and cross cutting this way, you'll have to clean up the sawn surfaces with a hand plane or use a router with a piloted flush-cut bit.

Unlike table saw cuts, jig saw and band saw rip cuts can be made freehand, following a scribed line. This can be a real advantage when making a rip cut that is not precisely parallel to the edge of the board or perhaps even has a slight turn or curve to it. You can also make straight rip cuts with these tools if you choose, using a straightedge guide with the jig saw or a guide or fence with the band saw. Some jig saws come with an adjustable side fence, similar to that on a circular saw, for making narrow cuts parallel to an edge.

When ripping with a jig saw, choose a thicker blade (less prone to flexing) with a relatively low number of teeth per inch. The bandsaw should be fitted with a wide (½ in. or wider) skip-tooth blade.

Rip-cutting with a jig saw

One advantage to using a jig saw to make rip cuts is that it's easy to set up a straightedge and make a cut that's not parallel to the edge of the board. Be sure the guide is set to allow for the offset between the saw foot and blade.

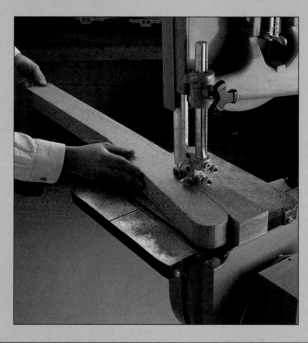

Rip-cutting with a band saw

Like jig saws, a band saw can make "rip" cuts that generally follow the grain of the wood but aren't necessarily straight or parallel to the edge of the board. You can also make "true" rip cuts that are parallel to the edge using the fence that comes with most bandsaws. The edges of the cut won't be as sharp as a table saw cut, however.

Offset cutting guides

A long straightedge guide with a built-in offset can be made with two pieces of scrap from your shop. You'll need a strip of hardboard or plywood (¼ in. works well) that's at least 12 in. wide and preferably 8 ft. long. Tack a piece of straight scrap wood (a 2 × 4 or a narrow strip of ¾ in. plywood will work) to the hardboard so the scrap is parallel with the hardboard or aligns with one of its edges. Orient the scrap and hardboard so there is an offset that is slightly longer than the distance from the edge of the saw foot to the blade. Then, simply trim off the edge of the hardboard with the saw foot riding against the scrap "fence." Clamp the guide to your workpiece so the trimmed plywood edge aligns with your cutting line.

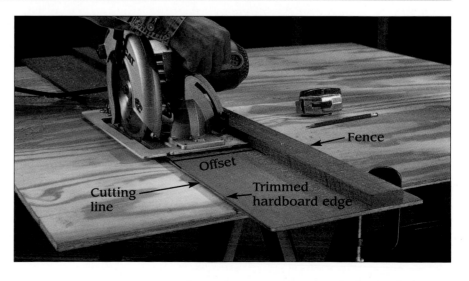

Fence

Offset

Cutting line

Trimmed hardboard edge

Making Cross Cuts

Cross-cutting, or cutting across the grain, is employed to cut your workpieces to length. Usually, crosscutting implies that you are making square cuts on the ends of your boards or project parts, although technically a crosscut could also be angled from beginning to end.

A number of woodworking tools perform cross cuts accurately, and among them are the power miter saw, table saw, circular saw and radial arm saw. A sharp crosscut hand saw also makes quick work of cutting boards square and to length, but you probably should reserve hand-sawing for rough-cutting.

Cross-cutting with a power miter saw

The power miter saw (known familiarly as the *chop saw*) is well-equipped for making fast, accurate cross cuts. Cross-cutting on a power miter saw or compound

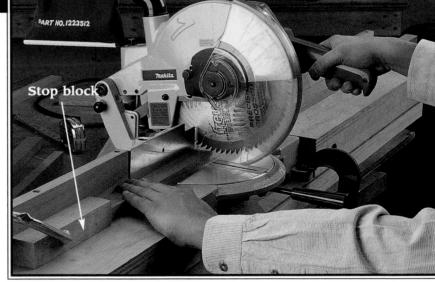

Set up a chop saw work station

A homemade table and fence greatly expands the usability of a power miter saw. The table sections should be flush with the saw table, and the fence attached to the tables should be perpendicular. The fence allows you to clamp a stop block in place for making repetitive cuts.

miter saw is done by holding the workpiece firmly against the table and fence of the saw with one hand, and slowly swinging the motor and spinning blade down with the other hand to make the cut. Theoretically, you can cut from either side of the saw, but unless you're ambidextrous it's a bit awkward from your less coordinated side. Sometimes it's helpful to clamp your workpiece to the fence or table—always do this if the piece is so short you would need to place your hand close to the blade to make the cut. Allow the blade to build to full speed before cutting, and wait until it has stopped spinning before moving your work. When cutting with a sliding compound miter saw, pull the blade and motor toward you before turning the saw on, then push it forward through the workpiece as you would with a radial arm saw.

The primary limitation to crosscutting with a power miter saw is the saw capacity. Since these machines were originally designed for cutting 2 × 4s and moldings, the size of workpieces they can handle is limited. Recently, however, models with larger blade diameters (up to 14 or 16 in.) have become available at reasonable costs. Bigger blades mean greater capacity.

Before setting up to cut your stock, test the blade to make sure it's perpendicular to the table and make a test cut on a piece of scrap.

Power miter saws tend to be quite loud, so ear plugs are recommended when operating or working around them. And, as with all power tools, wear eye protection.

> You can increase cutting capacity on your power miter saw by raising the workpiece with a plywood spacer so it's closer to the wide part of the blade.

Squaring the blade

Straight cuts start with a straight blade: or, in the case of power miter saws, a blade that's perpendicular to the saw table when set to make a 0° cut. To check if your blade is perpendicular, set a small try square with the stock on the saw table and hold the blade of the square against the body of the saw blade (make sure the square fits in a gullet area of the blade so it doesn't hit any saw teeth). Spin the saw blade and check it in several spots.

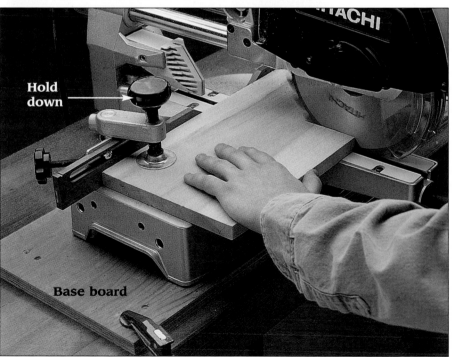

Hold down

Base board

Secure your saw, secure your work

Power miter saws are designed to be transported easily from jobsite to jobsite, so they are relatively light and can slide or bounce when in use. To keep your saw from traveling when it makes a cut, attach a base board to the saw base—the corners of most saw bases are predrilled to accept bolts. Make sure to countersink the heads of the bolts. Then, simply clamp the base board to whatever worksurface you're using. For added stability, use hold downs attached to the saw fence to apply downward pressure to the workpiece.

Cross-cutting with a table saw

A table saw has the ability to cross-cut a board so it's perfectly square and smooth. In fact, if using a good quality, sharp blade, you should be able to make end cuts that require no sanding.

Cross-cutting on the table saw is done using the saw's miter gauge to guide your stock, or with a crosscut sled. The miter gauge has a miter-slot bar that rides in one of the slots in the saw table on either side of the blade. The head of the miter gauge has a fairly small surface area, but you can increase your control and accuracy by attaching a hardwood auxiliary fence to the face of the miter gauge head. This will also help prevent tearout by backing up the workpiece as it's fed past the blade.

If the workpiece is too short to be held against the miter gauge with both hands, clamp it to the fence. **TIP:** *The spinning blade has a tendency to pull the stock toward it when the miter gauge is being used. Keep workpieces from sliding by attaching medium-fine grit sandpaper to the face of the auxiliary fence with spray adhesive.*

Since the miter gauge is small and only rides in one slot, it can wobble and is really only suitable for cutting relatively small parts. Some expensive saws have a fancy ball-bearing action sliding table with a long cross-cut fence and swing-down stops. Failing that, you can achieve a similar level of con-

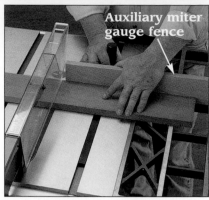

Auxiliary miter gauge fence

Miter slot bar

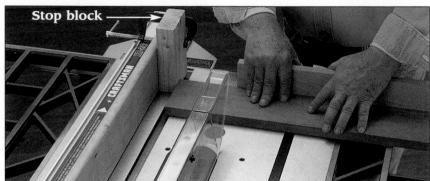

Stop block

TOP LEFT: Use a square to check the head of your table saw miter gauge: it should be at an exact right angle to the miter-slot bar.
TOP RIGHT: Attach an auxiliary fence to the miter gauge to create more bearing surface for guiding your workpiece through the saw blade.
BOTTOM: Clamp a stop block to the rip fence or auxiliary fence to register boards for cross-cutting. The stop block should be positioned well behind the saw blade.

venience, accuracy, and safety by building a simple cross-cut sled (See tip, below). If made carefully, this accessory, found in countless small professional and amateur workshops, can revolutionize your cross-cutting. It can handle wide panels and long boards as well as short pieces, and pops on and off your saw easily.

You can streamline multiple cuts of the same length by using a stop block. This is usually a squared wooden block that's clamped to an auxiliary fence on your miter gauge. Or, it can be attached to the front fence or auxiliary fence on a cross-cut sled. To use a stop block to register repetitive cuts, start by cutting one end of each board square. Then, measure, mark and cut one board to length. Use this board to set the stop distance from the blade. Once you've attached the stop, butt each board against it to cut parts of the same length.

NOTICE: It is sometimes tempting to use the rip fence as a stop, but this is extremely dangerous as it can cause the workpiece to bind and kick back.

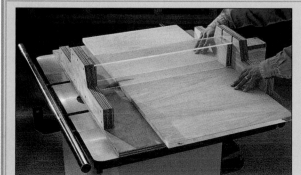

Cross-cut sled

With tracks on the underside that ride in the miter slots, a cross-cut sled supports the workpiece so it can't pivot or shift as you feed it through the blade. You can purchase a crosscut sled or build your own from plywood and acrylic, as shown here.

ABOVE: Use a speed square to guide your circular saw blade when making cross-cuts on narrower stock. With the blade of the square flat on the face of the board, press the lower flange lip against the board edge tightly and align the saw blade with your cutting line.

LEFT: Make a "T-Square" sawing guide to use when cross-cutting wider stock. Make sure the crosspiece (which is pressed against the edge of the workpiece) is square to the guide. The first time you use it, your saw will trim the crosspiece so the edge aligns with the cutting line.

Cross-cutting with a circular saw

The circular saw isn't always the first power tool that comes to mind when you think of woodworking. But beyond its many uses as a carpentry tool on the jobsite, you'll find plenty of times when it comes in handy in the wood shop as well. Circular saws are par-ticularly good cross-cutting tools. If you need to cut larger pieces of stock to rough length, it's much easier to pull out the circular saw and apply it to the work-piece than to try to wrangle heavy, awkward boards through a table saw. Use cutting guides (like those shown above) for best results.

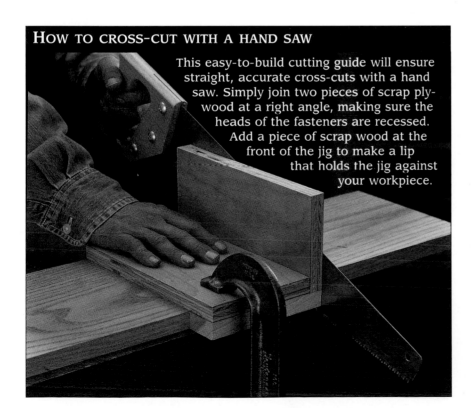

HOW TO CROSS-CUT WITH A HAND SAW

This easy-to-build cutting guide will ensure straight, accurate cross-cuts with a hand saw. Simply join two pieces of scrap ply-wood at a right angle, making sure the heads of the fasteners are recessed. Add a piece of scrap wood at the front of the jig to make a lip that holds the jig against your workpiece.

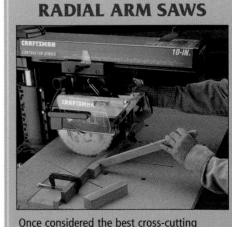

RADIAL ARM SAWS

Once considered the best cross-cutting machine, the radial-arm saw has lost its lofty designation to the cheaper and safer power miter saw. Still, there are plenty of radial arm saws in use and they do an excellent job of cross-cutting. The key to using them safely is to make sure your workpiece is held very tightly or, better yet, clamped against the saw fence.

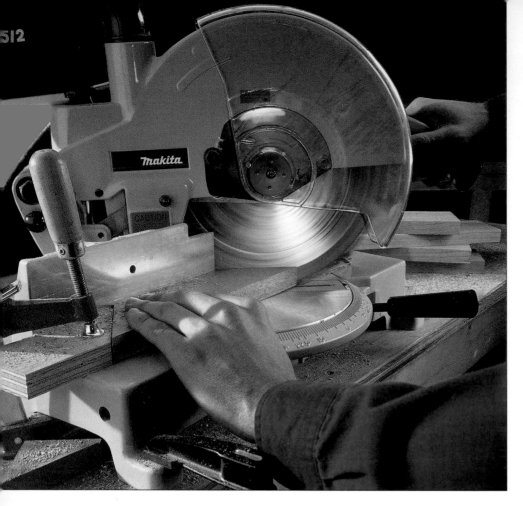

Compound miter cuts have both a bevel and a miter angle. With a compound miter saw you can cut them easily by combining the procedures for cutting miters and bevels.

360° by the number of joint angles. Then divide this by two to arrive at the cutting angle for each part.

Cutting miters with a power miter saw. A power miter saw is a convenient and accurate tool for cutting snug-fitting miters. Most saws can be angled to cut just beyond 45° both to the left and to the right, and some higher-end models have greater capacity. Typically, the saw will have a positive stop at 45°, but check the cut to be sure it is correct. Attaching a long table and fence to the saw (See page 70) makes it a little easier to use, and gives you something to attach a stop to for repetitive cuts.

If you're cutting multiple parts with miters at both ends, first cut one end of each part square. Attach a stop at the appropriate distance from the blade, and butt the square end of each part against the stop to miter one end. Then just flip the stop over and miter the other end at the same setting.

Making Angled Cuts

Angled cuts are required in just about any woodworking project of intermediate or higher difficulty, so it's worth the time to learn how to do them right. There are two basic angled cuts you'll need to know: *miter cuts* and *bevel cuts*.

Cutting miters

A miter is actually a joint in which two parts to be assembled are cut with the same angle (usually 45°). Miters are cut to make parts for projects such as picture frames, tabletop edging, face frames, and moldings. The methods for cutting them can also be used for any general shaping of angled parts.

A miter is functionally worthless unless it's dead accurate. It must be straight, square to the faces, and at the correct angle. If the angle is slightly off, the parts may match up perfectly but not form a

90° angle. It's not hard to get it right; it just requires a little patience and a few trial cuts. One point to remember is that the cutting angle required is half the joint angle; so a 90° joint requires two 45° cuts. To determine cutting angles for making multi-sided shapes such as hexagons, divide

A **compound miter saw** has become the preferred woodworking tool for making fast, accurate miter cuts. The sliding compound miter saw here costs a bit more than a compound miter saw or a simple power miter saw, but the blade travel expands the cutting capacity substantially, allowing to you to cut boards up to 12 in. wide in some cases.

Miter-cutting with a table saw

Attach an auxiliary fence to the miter gauge to support your workpiece right up to the blade. For best control when miter-cutting, set up your cuts so the cut end leads the rest of the workpiece across the table, as shown above.

Miter-cutting with a circular saw

When making miter cuts with a circular saw, a protractor-type cutting guide ensures accurate, consistent cuts.

Cutting miters with a table saw. As with other types of straight cuts, the table saw is capable of giving you very good results with miters. Mitering on the table saw is commonly done with the assistance of the miter gauge. Be aware that with the gauge angled to the blade, the workpiece tends to get pushed or pulled (depending on which way it's angled) by the action of the blade and as a result it can creep. The angled face also can cause the workpiece to pivot off the front edge of the miter gauge. To counteract these forces, use a longer auxiliary fence attached to the gauge and face it with sandpaper; a clamp or two when feasible will make things even more secure. Feed the stock slowly. A stop block can be attached to the fence for cutting multiple parts.

Using the miter gauge to make miter cuts in the table saw does have some inherent problems. First of all, the gauge needs to be accurately set and tested each time you need it. With flat stock you can cut both halves of the miter by flipping one workpiece upside down, but you may get tearout along the unsupported, lower faces. And since you can't invert shaped stock like moldings, you need to change the miter gauge setting for mating cuts, making it difficult to match the left and right halves.

Cutting miters with a circular saw. Miter cuts can be made with the circular saw by running the base against an angled guide.

The angled guide can be a standard straightedge clamped to the workpiece diagonally, or a manufactured protractor guide that can be adjusted to the desired angle and locked in place. A circular saw can't give you precise miters for critical work, but is ideal for cutting angles and notches on wide construction lumber such as joists and rafters.

Test the blade angle setting

Test the blade angle setting on your table saw: the angle indicated on the dial gauge may differ from the actual tilt.

STEP 1: To test the actual cutting angle, set the blade tilt for a 45° cut. Mark one face of a piece of scrap and cross-cut it with the workpiece held against the miter gauge.

STEP 2: Flip one of the cut edges and set the scrap pieces together to form a mitered corner. The pieces should form a 90° corner. If they don't, use a t-bevel to set the saw angle at 45°, then reset the dial indicator to 45°. Retest.

With a jig saw

The best reason to use a jig saw to cut bevels is that it is very easy to control. You also get a better view of the blade and the cutting line than with other portable saws. If your jig saw has a tilting base, set the base to the desired cutting angle and make a test cut on scrap (if the base of your saw does not tilt, choose a different tool). Make the cut, following a straightedge guide.

With a compound miter saw

Compound miter saws have blades that can be tilted to cut bevel angles up to around 45°. Most also have positive stops at common bevel settings, but always make a test cut first and measure it with a T-bevel or protractor.

With a table saw

Set up beveled rip cuts so the blade tilts away from the rip fence. This keeps the workpiece from becoming trapped between the fence and the blade. Clamp featherboards and hold downs to the saw to secure larger panels.

Cutting bevels

A bevel is an edge at an angle other than 90° to the face of a board. Bevels are often done for decorative purposes, although some can have a structural function. Cabinet or box sides can be beveled at 45° and reinforced with splines or biscuits to form long miter joints. Assembling triangles, octagons, or other multi-sided figures requires multiple precisely-cut bevels as well. Accuracy is very important on these miter-joint bevels: while a half degree doesn't seem like much error, multiply it by 16 (in the case of an octagon) and you can imagine the gap when you fit in the last piece. A chamfer can be cut like a bevel, but you make a partial, rather than a through cut.

Cutting bevels with a table saw. Bevels of any angle can be cut on the table saw simply by angling the blade. Set your cutting angle on a bevel gauge, lay the gauge on the saw table and set the blade to match the bevel angle. You can cut bevels with the grain by using the rip fence to guide your workpiece. Cross-grain bevels are cut with the miter gauge, as when making 90° cross cuts, or with a sled (See previous page). Some woodworkers maintain a separate sled for bevel-cutting because the angled blade widens the kerf in the sled so it will no longer back up a straight cut.

Cutting bevels with a circular saw. To cut a bevel with a circular saw, loosen the knob and adjust the angle of the saw base. Tighten the knob and proceed as with a standard cut, running the base against a straightedge guide. You'll need to make a new mark on the base to line up with the cut line unless your saw has a second sight line for cutting 45° bevels.

Cutting bevels with a power miter saw. A compound-miter saw can cut smooth cross-cut bevels. The saw blade usually angles to the left, although some can angle either way. An auxiliary plywood fence is recommended when bevel-cutting, and clamping your workpiece is always a good idea. If you change the miter angle as well as the blade angle you can cut angles in two planes, giving you a compound miter.

Cutting bevels with a band saw or jig saw. Cut bevels with a band saw by tilting the saw table and using the fence as a guide. With a jig saw, tilt the angle of the saw foot and cut with a straightedge guide.

TAPER JIG

Work stop

1 Set the taper scale to match the desired amount of taper (in degrees or inches per foot) and lock the hinged arm in place. Mark cutting lines for the taper on the workpiece, set the jig against the saw fence, then set the workpiece into the jig, against the work stop.

Start of taper

2 Position the fence so the start of the taper line will meet the edge of the saw blade when the jig is fed forward. With the jig well back from the blade, turn on the saw. Pressing the workpiece against the jig, grasp the jig handle and start the cut.

3 Finish the cut, removing your guide hand from the workpiece well in advance of the completion of the cut. If tapering multiple sides, reposition the workpiece to cut an adjacent face. For four-sided tapers, double the taper setting before cutting the other two faces.

TABLE LEGS *and chair legs are the most typical project parts to receive tapers. Tapered legs give the table a more refined, elegant appearance without detracting from its structural integrity.*

Cutting tapers

Tapers are straight cuts that are not parallel to the edge of the workpiece, resulting in a workpiece that is wider on one end than the other. Typically, two or four sides of the workpiece are tapered. Tapers can be cut on a band saw or table saw using either a shop-made or purchased taper jig. Adjustable tapering jigs can be set to cut tapers of various degrees of slope. Most jigs are made of metal and come with an adjustable brace that spans the "arms" of the jig to lock them in position. Scales have settings by *angle* (in degrees) or *slope* (in inches-per-foot). They can be used with a band saw or table saw (See photos, left). If you own a jointer, you can use it to cut smooth, clean tapers that require no special jigs to make.

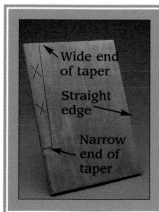

Wide end of taper

Straight edge

Narrow end of taper

SHOP-BUILT TAPER JIG

You can build a simple, single-use taper jig from a square piece of ¾ in. plywood. Cut out a section of the plywood that's the same width at the bottom and top as the narrow and wide part of the taper, respectively. Insert the workpiece into the cutout area of the jig and feed it through the blade to cut a perfect taper. Use a hold-down to keep the workpiece firmly against the table and the pocket in the jig. If you need to taper all four sides, use one of the cutoff pieces as a shim so the workpiece is square in the jig.

Squaring, Marking & Cutting Stock   77

A jig for the jig saw

Make circular cutouts with a jig saw and trammel jig. The jig shown above is created by attaching a cradle for the saw foot in one end of a strip of plywood. Cut a guide hole in the plywood for the saw blade. Tack a nail into the jig so the distance from the nail to the saw blade equals the radius of the circle you want to cut. Then, simply drive the nail through the jig and into the center of the stock. The trammel will pivot on the nail, creating a perfect circle as you cut.

Making Curved Cuts

The easiest way to cut smooth, regular curves on large project parts is to use a cutting tool that you apply to the workpiece (as opposed to one you feed the workpiece into). Jig saws and routers are both well suited for the job. Jig saws are faster to set up and easy to use, but won't yield as smooth a cut as a router. For smaller parts, use a band saw or scroll saw.

Cutting curves with a jig saw. One of the best features of the jig saw is its ability to cut curves, particularly in sheet goods. It has no workpiece size limitations, its portability makes it handy for on-site work and such tasks as rounding corners on large tabletops. Clamp the workpiece securely and feed the saw slowly to prevent the blade from deflecting. To start internal cuts, drill an entry hole with a bit slightly larger than the width of the saw blade. Circles can be cut freehand to a line, or if you want a little more exactness you can use a shop-made or commercial circle-cutting jig that pivots about a centerpoint.

Gang-cut parts for consistency and speed

When making project parts with curved lines, gang the workpieces together whenever you can. In addition to making less cutting work for you, this will ensure that the cut edges are consistent. With most saws, you can tape the workpieces together with double-edged carpet tape.

Use the scrolling feature. Scrolling jig saws feature a blade-angle adjustment knob at the top of the handle. By turning the knob, you change the blade direction—without turning the body of the saw.

Keep pressure directly above the blade. Whether you're using a top-handle saw, like the one above, or a barrel grip saw, hold the tool so your hand is forward and directly above the blade area. Take care not to force the saw: the blade will break or deflect from the cut line.

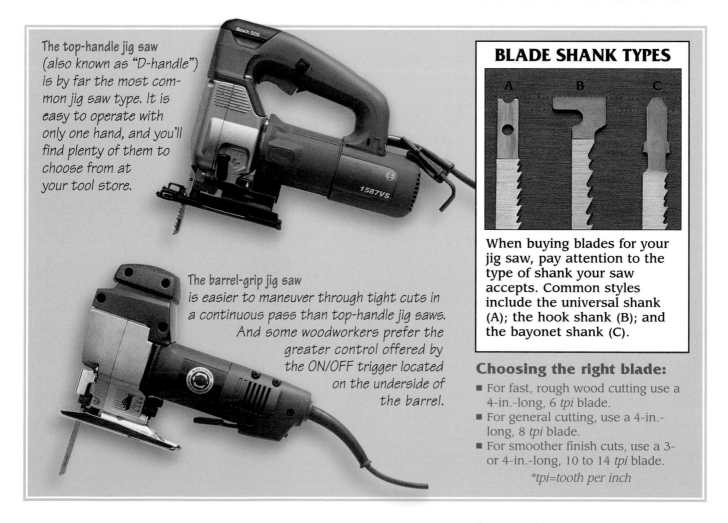

The top-handle jig saw (also known as "D-handle") is by far the most common jig saw type. It is easy to operate with only one hand, and you'll find plenty of them to choose from at your tool store.

The barrel-grip jig saw is easier to maneuver through tight cuts in a continuous pass than top-handle jig saws. And some woodworkers prefer the greater control offered by the ON/OFF trigger located on the underside of the barrel.

BLADE SHANK TYPES

When buying blades for your jig saw, pay attention to the type of shank your saw accepts. Common styles include the universal shank (A); the hook shank (B); and the bayonet shank (C).

Choosing the right blade:

- For fast, rough wood cutting use a 4-in.-long, 6 *tpi* blade.
- For general cutting, use a 4-in.-long, 8 *tpi* blade.
- For smoother finish cuts, use a 3- or 4-in.-long, 10 to 14 *tpi* blade.

*tpi=tooth per inch

Band saws do an excellent job of cutting smooth curves on workpieces that are small enough to be handled and maneuvered easily.

narrower blades can turn tighter curves, and relief cuts will keep the blade from binding if the curve is too tight. See the chart on the following page for approximate smallest-radius cutting capacity for different blade thicknesses.

- On a convex curve near an edge you can simply run your cut out to the edge of your work (through the waste) and then start again from a gentler angle.
- If you need to back the blade out of the cut, turn the saw off first, then maneuver the stock back through the kerf.
- Always hold the workpiece with both hands.
- As you complete each cut, be sure your hands are clear of the blade. At this point it's often helpful to reach around and pull the workpiece through the end of the cut from the other side of the blade.
- Set the blade guide on your band saw so it's within about ¼ in. of the top of the workpiece. If the gap is too wide, the blade will flex and wander more easily and in some cases may even break.

Cutting curves & circles with a band saw. Although it is not portable like the jig saw and can't make interior cuts, the band saw still excels at cutting curves on smaller workpieces, due to its convenience, stability, cutting capacity and speed.

The band saw's immense depth capacity means you can cut very thick workpieces. You can also stack multiple blanks with double-faced carpet tape and cut them out all at one time, yielding identical parts. When cutting thick material, feed it slowly to avoid overheating or deflecting the blade.

Circles can be (and often are) cut freehand on a bandsaw: because the tool is so easy to control, you can feed the workpiece through the blade just outside the cutting line, then sand the edge down to the cutting line. If you want more accuracy or if you need several circles, you can make a an auxiliary circle cutting table to fit onto your band saw table (See next page).

Here are a few pointers for cutting curves and circles on the bandsaw:
- Curves are usually cut freehand to a marked line. As with a jig saw,

Plenty of woodworkers prefer the band saw to the table saw for general cutting, not just for cutting curves. The band saw cuts less aggressively, which gives the operator greater control.

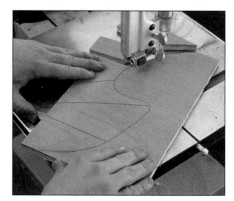

Relief for tight curves

When cutting complex shapes, make a few relief cuts through the waste area and up to the cutting line. This will make the workpiece easier to manage and the blade less likely to bind in the cut.

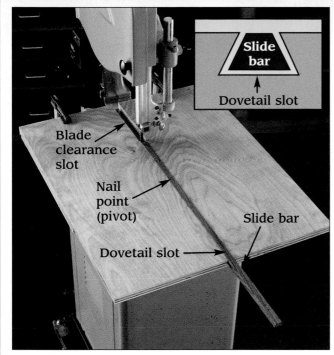

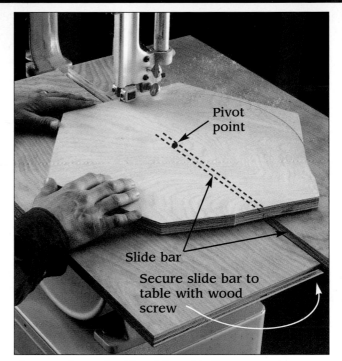

An auxiliary circle-cutting table allows you to cut smooth circles with a band saw. Start with a piece of ¾ in. plywood that's about 8 to 10 in. wider and longer than your band saw table. With a router and dovetail bit, cut a ⅜ in. deep dovetail slot in the top of the plywood, centered side to side. Bevel-rip a piece of ⅜ in. thick hardwood scrap so the edges match the profile of the dovetail slot (See the illustration above). The scrap, which will become the *slide bar,* should be roughly the same length as the dovetail slot. Insert the slide bar into the dovetail slot—It should fit snugly but slide without too much difficulty. On one end of the table, cut a slot that's wide enough and long enough to allow clearance of the band saw blade when the table is clamped to the band saw table. It's also a good idea to tack cleats to the underside of the table jig to create a recess for the band saw table. Now, drill a pilot hole and drive a ½ or ⅝ in. wire nail the same distance from one one of the slide bar as the circle radius. Set the nail head. Clamp the circle-cutting table to the band saw table then insert the slide bar until the end contacts the saw blade. Drive a small screw up through the underside of the dovetail slot to pin the slide bar in place. Drill a small starter hole at the centerpoint of the workpiece then fit it over the nail head (pivot point). You'll probably need to make a starter cut for the blade up to the edge of the cutting line. Turn the saw on and rotate the workpiece around the blade slowly to cut your circle. You'll find it helpful to trim off some of the waste on the workpiece before you cut the circle.

How tight can you cut?

Blade width	Smallest radius cut
⅛"	3⁄16"
3⁄16"	⅜"
¼"	⅝"
⅜"	1¼"
½"	3"
¾"	5"
1"	8"

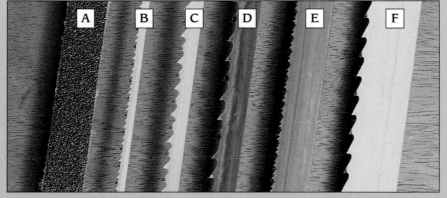

A good selection of blades for your band saw will include: (A) an abrasive belt; (B) a ⅛ in., 12 tpi blade; (C) a ¼ in., 6 tpi blade; (D) a ⅜ in., 4 tpi blade; (E) a ½ in., 18 tpi metal-cutting blade; (F) a ¾ in., 4 tpi, hook tooth blade.

Squaring, Marking & Cutting Stock   81

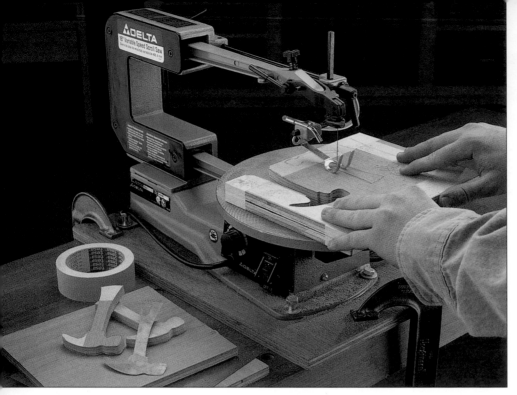

Sandwich thin stock for cleaner cuts

Thin stock, whether it's wood, plexiglas, nonferrous metal (shown here) or anything else, is hard to cut smoothly without some kind of backer board. For best results, sandwich the stock between two pieces of scrap before cutting. If cutting metal, install a jeweler's blade in the saw, set your variable speed scroll saw for around 600 strokes per minute (spm), and make your cut.

---

from hopping up and down with the force of the blade. Use two hands to guide the work, turning it as necessary to keep the cut along the waste side of the lines. Don't force-feed it; let the blade do the work. The kerf of a scroll saw blade is so fine that positive and negative shapes cut apart can be nested back together well, making possible the original jigsaw puzzle.

If you're looking to purchase a new scroll saw, consider spending a little more money to get a variable speed scroll saw. The lower-priced scroll saws typically cut at only one blade speed—about 1700 strokes per minute (spm). Better quality variable speed saws can be adjusted from 400 to 1800 spm. This allows you to use slower speed settings for harder stock.

Cutting curves with a scroll saw. The scroll saw, or true jig saw, was designed as a powered version of a hand fret saw used in its proper up-and-down cutting configuration. This machine is used in much the same way as a band saw, but is equipped with finer blades that make it possible to do very intricate work. In fact, with some ultra-fine blades you can make near-90° turns. The blade is not continuous like a band saw blade, so it can be released easily and passed through a hole in the workpiece to make internal cutouts.

The scroll saw is not used merely for working on thin craft projects; with wider, sturdier blades it can cut stock that's as much as 2 in. thick. The wide range of blades includes varieties made for cutting other materials such as metals and plastics. You can even rig up a pivot jig like

the one shown for the band saw (See previous page) to cut true circles on the scroll saw.

Scroll saw blades, particularly narrow ones, are fragile and can break easily if forced or twisted. Blades must be properly tensioned in the saw to keep them from bending in use. Most saws have a hold-down which should be adjusted to keep the workpiece

Frame saws

The category of frame saws includes the common coping saw (shown here) as well as more traditional fret saws and bow saws. Like power scroll saws, hand-powered frame saws are well-suited for making interior cutouts. First, drill a pilot hole in the waste area. Remove the blade and thread it through the pilot hole. Reattach the blade and make the cut, turning the blade in the frame as necessary so the frame clears the edges of the workpiece.

Cutting internal curves

To make internal cuts with a scroll saw, drill a starter hole in the waste area, then remove the blade and thread it through the starter hole. Reattach the blade and make the cutout.

Following a pattern

No tool can cut tight patterns and delicate fretwork with the speed and precision of scroll saw. Either attach the pattern or draw it directly onto the workpiece. Fit the saw with a narrow, skip tooth fret blade and follow the cutting lines at a slow cutting speed, making relief cuts where necessary.

SCROLL SAW BLADES

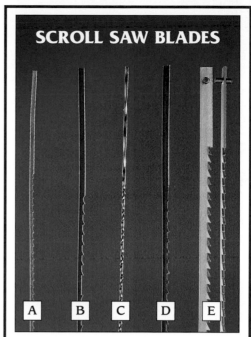

A useful selection of scroll saw blades includes: (A) #7, 12 tpi scrolling blade; (B) #7, 11.5 tpi reverse-tooth fret blade; (C) #2, 41 tpi spiral-tooth blade; (D) #9, 11.5 tpi fret blade; (E) #5, 15 tpi pinned scrolling blade (side and front views shown).

Blade Buying Tip

Look for precision-ground blades. Most inexpensive scroll saw blades are made of stamped steel. The main drawback to stamped blades is that one side is usually rougher than the other, which can cause the blade to pull toward the rough side when you cut with it. Precision-ground scroll saw blades are machined to produce two sides of equal smoothness so they're less likely to get hung up in the workpiece, and they usually last longer.

Follow these guidelines to prevent premature blade breakage:
- Keep an eye on blade tension—a blade that's too loose or too tight is the leading cause of broken blades.
- Use the best blade for the task.
- Don't try to cut a curve that's tighter than your blade can cut.
- Slow down the speed on variable speed saws if the stock is resisting the cut.
- Don't force the workpiece into the blade.
- Release blade tension when the saw is not in use.

Cut smooth circles with a router circle compass

A **circle compass** is a router accessory that attaches directly to the router base. The adjustable pivot point sets the radius of the cut. With fixed-base routers, you'll need to drill a starter hole for the router bit. Use a straight bit or a spiral upcut bit to cut the circles. In harder stock, a single-flute straight bit works better than a standard two-fluted straight bit.

Cutting circles with a router

Most handymen think of routers as primarily tools for cutting decorative profiles or perhaps an occasional dado or rabbet. But they can also be very effective tools for cutting stock to size and shape. When the right bits and techniques are used, they produce extremely clean edges that often require no sanding. The router is so versatile that you can practically run a shop with this tool alone. It can be pressed into service for (among other things) cutting, planing, shaping,

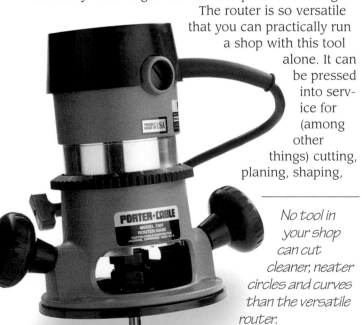

No tool in your shop can cut cleaner, neater circles and curves than the versatile router.

drilling, inlaying, and joint cutting. While certain tasks can be more conveniently done with other tools, the router excels at many jobs—and cutting smooth curves is certainly one of them. The router is difficult to use freehand, but with the aid of some cutting guides you can achieve precision results with surfaces smoother than you can get from any saw.

Accurate circles and arcs can be cut using a circle-cutting jig. There are several types commercially available, and good jigs can be made easily in the shop as well. If you need to cut a workpiece into a circular shape, a router circle compass is an excellent tool accessory to use. Simply secure the router base to the wide end of the compass, set the adjustable center pin to the desired radius of the cut, and secure the pin at the center of the circle. For best results, make the cut in several passes of increasing depth. A single-flute straight bit or a spiral upcut bit can be used to remove large amounts of waste in the cutting area, without bogging down. You'll need to use a piece of scrap plywood under your setup to prevent cutting into your worksurface, and use double-stick tape or hot glue under the disk area to keep it secure once it is cut free of the surrounding stock. It's actually quicker and creates less dust if you mark your circle on the workpiece with trammel points and cut it out to within 1/16 to 1/8 in. of the cutting line on a band saw first. Then just clean up the cut with one pass of the router.

Create a trammel-type jig to guide your router when cutting circles and arcs. After attaching the router base to the jig, measure out the radius distance from the bit and mark a drilling point (left photo). Drill a guide hole at the centerpoint, then attach the jig to your workpiece, driving a finish nail through the guide hole and into the center of the circle. Make your router cut by rotating the router on the pivot in deepening passes (right photo).

BUYING A ROUTER? CONSIDER THIS ...

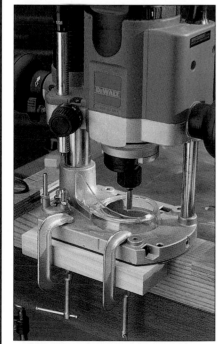

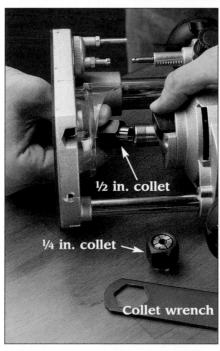

½ in. collet

¼ in. collet

Collet wrench

Plunge routers. A plunge router can be lowered into the workpiece on its steel columns, so you can start cuts or adjust the cutting depth without drilling starter holes or changing the router set up.

Collet size. More powerful routers typically have larger collets that accept bits with a ½ in. shank. The ½ in. collet can usually be removed from the spindle and replaced with a ¼ in. collet if you need to use a smaller bit.

Variable speed. Larger routers can be used to drive heavy-duty shaping bits. But the heavy duty bits generally require slower speeds (around 12,000 rpm), so the ability to adjust the speed is important.

1 Draw or trace your pattern onto a piece of thin tempered hardboard or acrylic, then cut it out (include the thickness of the router bushing in the dimensions of the pattern). We used a scroll saw to cut out the template, then smoothed down the uneven edges with a file.

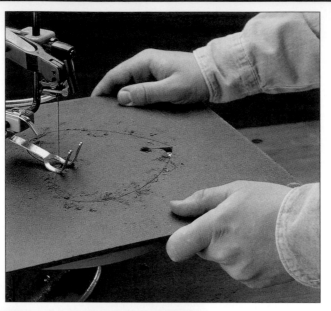

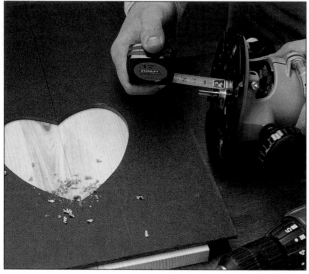

2 Install a bushing that's the same depth as the thickness of the template (See top photo, next page). Clamp or attach the template to the workpiece. Set the router cutting depth to equal the combined thickness of the template and the workpiece (with harder stock, set it to a shallower depth and cut in several passes of increasing depth).

3 Clamp the workpiece and template to your worksurface, with a scrap spacer beneath. Make sure you have room for the router base to clear the clamp. Drill a starter hole in the waste area (if using a fixed base router) then rout along the edge of the template to make the cutout.

Scrap

Template Routing

For woodworkers who frequently make projects that employ curved shapes, template routing is perhaps the most valuable router function. If you need more than one part cut to a certain shape, or even if you only need one but it must be perfectly smooth with crisp edges, make a template and cut the part or parts with your router.

A template should be made of inexpensive but sturdy material, like hardboard or MDF (medium-density fiberboard). It can also be made of quality plywood with a reliable edge surface, but that's a bit more expensive. The template material should be at least ¼ in. thick to provide enough bearing surface but needn't be any thicker than ⅜ in., so it is more easily cut out and filed, sanded and shaped than a thicker workpiece. You also don't need to worry too much if the edges get a bit out of square to the faces—the router will correct this on the final workpiece.

You can follow the template with a straight bit and a template guide bushing mounted to the router base. With this technique the bushing rides against the template and the smaller diameter bit within it makes the cut. So the template needs to be sized a little larger than the actual part to compensate for the difference in diameters between the bushing and the bit. Because of this size discrepancy,

Cutting a groove with a router requires some type of cutting guide. In template routing, you simply replace the straight cutting guide you might use for cutting a dado with a pattern that is made to conform to the size and shape of the project part you're making.

you may find it easier to use a straight bit with a pilot bearing mounted above or below the cutter. This way, you can make a template that's the exact size and shape of the planned project part.

Whether you're using guide bushings or a piloted bit, the template gets attached to the workpiece with clamps or double-stick tape (with a bottom-bearing bit the template gets attached to the underside of the workpiece) and the router is run against it to reproduce the shape.

TIP: *You can reduce mess and routing time if, before you attach the template, you cut away the excess waste from the workpiece with a band saw or jig saw. Leave only about 1/8 in. to be routed off.*

Some shapes will contain sharp corners that can't be cut with a round router bit. After you cut the template shape, square off these corners with a sharp wood chisel.

Templates are not used only for decorative items and parts. The best time to use a template often is when making structural components that need to be identical.

Bushings protect the template & guide the router bit

Universal guide bushings are held against the top surface of the router base plate with a large washer that's secured with the base plate screws. Bushings are sold in sets: choose the correct one based on the diameter of your router bit and the thickness of your template.

A piloted flush cutting bit, mounted in a router table, can follow a router template without the need for a guide bushing. The biggest advantage to this method is that you can make your template the exact size and shape of the part—you don't need to oversize it to allow for the thickness of the bushing shell. Sharp inside corners can be squared with a chisel after the router cutting is finished.

The fanciful legs and arms on this deck chair were made using a router and template (See photo, left).

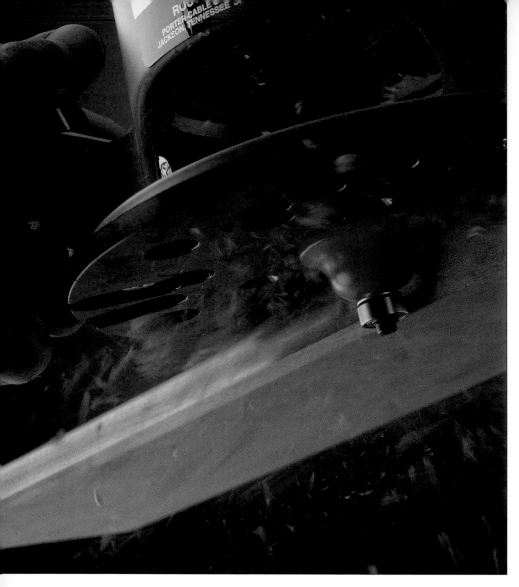

Shaping Profiles

When making project parts, you often need to shape the edge of a workpiece with a decorative profile, such as a chamfer or a roundover. This work can be done quickly, accurately, and reliably with a router. Hand tools can also be used for certain edge treatments. For a slight chamfer it may not be worth the time and effort setting up a router. A sanding block or a hand plane can knock out a straight, fairly even chamfer in no time. Similarly, a very slight rounding of sharp edges (called *breaking* or *easing* the edge, is normally done with sandpaper. Some heavy-duty freehand shaping work can be done with rasps and files, but these are more effective when you're shaping irregular contours by eye rather than trying to get consistent, even surfaces.

The router, on the other hand, can produce equally predictable results on straight, angled, or circular edges, and on inside or outside curves. One router can do the work of a whole arsenal of molding, grooving, and rabbeting planes and

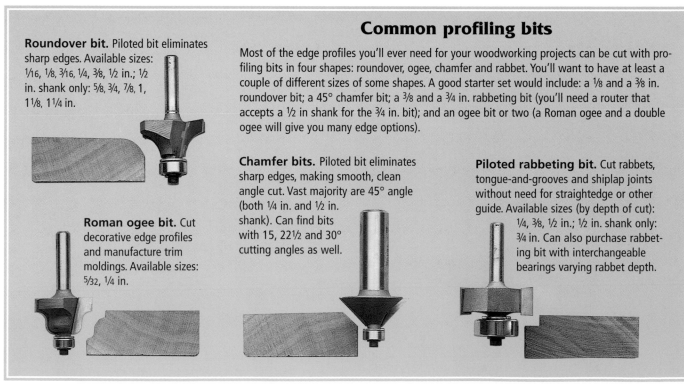

Common profiling bits

Roundover bit. Piloted bit eliminates sharp edges. Available sizes: 1/16, 1/8, 3/16, 1/4, 3/8, 1/2 in.; 1/2 in. shank only: 5/8, 3/4, 7/8, 1, 1 1/8, 1 1/4 in.

Roman ogee bit. Cut decorative edge profiles and manufacture trim moldings. Available sizes: 5/32, 1/4 in.

Most of the edge profiles you'll ever need for your woodworking projects can be cut with profiling bits in four shapes: roundover, ogee, chamfer and rabbet. You'll want to have at least a couple of different sizes of some shapes. A good starter set would include: a 1/8 and a 3/8 in. roundover bit; a 45° chamfer bit; a 3/8 and a 3/4 in. rabbeting bit (you'll need a router that accepts a 1/2 in shank for the 3/4 in. bit); and an ogee bit or two (a Roman ogee and a double ogee will give you many edge options).

Chamfer bits. Piloted bit eliminates sharp edges, making smooth, clean angle cut. Vast majority are 45° angle (both 1/4 in. and 1/2 in. shank). Can find bits with 15, 22 1/2 and 30° cutting angles as well.

Piloted rabbeting bit. Cut rabbets, tongue-and-grooves and shiplap joints without need for straightedge or other guide. Available sizes (by depth of cut): 1/4, 3/8, 1/2 in.; 1/2 in. shank only: 3/4 in. Can also purchase rabbeting bit with interchangeable bearings varying rabbet depth.

scratch stocks, as well as many tasks that can't be done with any other tool.

Routers are quick to set up, and leave a smooth, professional finish thanks to the high speed of the motor (most routers turn at anywhere from 22,000 to 25,000 rpm). Some routers have variable speed controls that permit infinite adjustment from as slow as 8,000 rpm. Different materials and techniques require different routing speeds. Although running at top speed gives the best finish for general wood and plastic laminate work, it also has a greater tendency to burn the wood than slower speeds.

Router bits. Router bits come in an astounding array of shapes and styles. Edge-forming bits generally have a pilot located below the cutter that rides against the edge of the workpiece to guide the bit, as

Router feed direction

Remembering which way to feed your router into the workpiece is one of those very important details that always seems to slip our minds. The key is to guide the tool so the bit is into the wood as you move the router: otherwise, the router will pull itself along the edge of the wood. If you're routing an outside edge, move the router in a counterclockwise direction. On inside edges, move it clockwise. Pull the tool toward your body as you work.

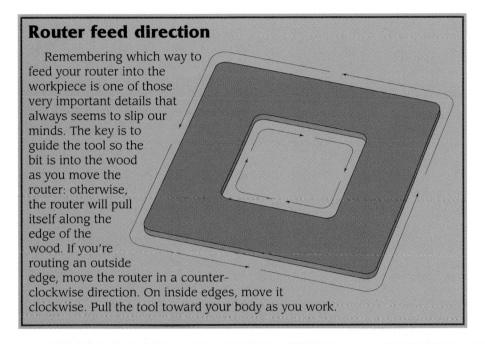

DON'T LET YOUR RABBETING BIT TURN THE CORNER

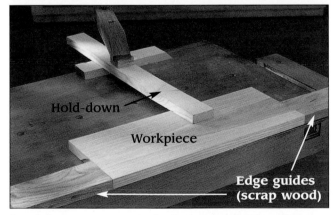

Hold-down

Workpiece

Edge guides
(scrap wood)

One of the most common mistakes beginners make when using a piloted profiling bit is failing to protect the ends of the board. Without scrap stock butted up to the ends, the bit will follow the corner, cutting too deeply into the ends of the workpiece. To prevent this from happening, simply clamp a scrap board the same thickness as the workpiece at each end. Make sure the edges of the scraps and the workpiece are flush.

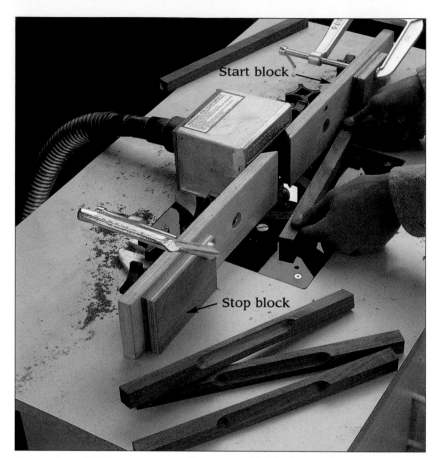

opposed to groove-forming bits that cut recesses and joints into the heart of a workpiece. Less expensive bits have integral fixed pilot tips that can generate enough friction to burn and blacken the edge of your workpiece. These bits are usually one-piece, solid high-speed steel. They are worth purchasing if you want to experiment with several shapes without spending a lot of money, or if you're cutting a particular molding only once and longevity doesn't matter. Any burn marks generated can be planed, scraped, or sanded off.

For general edge-routing in the common shapes you'll use repeatedly (flush-trim, chamfer, roundover, rabbet) you're better off buying carbide-tipped bits with ball-bearing pilots. High-speed steel dulls quickly and if overheated can lose its temper and become too soft to use (if the cutting edge turns blue, the bit has lost its temper). Tungsten carbide tips cut easily through hard materials and stay sharp much longer, especially when used on particleboard and plastic laminate. When these bits do dull, you can either replace them or get them professionally sharpened. For working with particularly delicate surfaces, like glossy laminate or solid surfacing material, you can get ball

Stopped profiles are easy to cut with a router table. The finger pull cutouts in these handles are being made by clamping a start block and a stop block to the router table fence, then feeding each workpiece between the blocks and through a cove bit.

Make your own custom molding

Create custom moldings by shaping an edge profile into a piece of stock (left photo) then ripping it on your table saw (right photo). The roman ogee bit shown here will yield a nice decorative edge for shelf-edging or dec-

orative trim. There are dozens of different profiles you can make with other router bits. Most woodworking supply stores and catalogs carry a wide selection of bits. You can even combine bits to achieve more complex profiles.

bearings with non-marring industrial plastic sleeves.

Router bits are made with varying numbers of cutting edges, or *flutes.* Single-flute bits have lots of clearance to remove chips freely. They are useful for softwoods, deeper cuts (as when making a circular cutout) or any time a fast cutting speed is more important than a smooth edge. Two-fluted bits are general-purpose bits, and leave a smooth surface on a variety of materials. Three-flute bits are available for special applications demanding an ultra-smooth finish on brittle materials.

Always use the shortest router bit you can get away with. The longer the cutting edge is, the more potentially damaging vibration and deflection the tool suffers. Try to use the largest diameter shank your router will accommodate, for similar reasons of stability. Very large diameter bits for panel raising or shaping thick materials require slower speeds and are usually labeled with maximum recommendations, sometimes as low as 10,000 rpm. At high speeds these bits can cause dangerous kickback, and they are subject to severe stress that can induce breakage. If a piece of a bit breaks off, it can be thrown out with great force. To reduce strain and get a better finish with larger bits, remove as much waste material as possible beforehand by chamfering, using a smaller-diameter bit, or by taking multiple shallow passes.

Routing technique. In general, you'll get better results if you don't try to remove all the waste in one pass. Take several shallow cuts instead, lowering the bit a little each time and finishing up with a very light cut to assure a smooth surface. NOTE: Never change the cutting depth by this by adjusting the bit shank in the collet. Always adjust the router base to set the cutting depth (plunge routers make this a little easier).

Feed direction is important when routing. Always feed the router in a direction opposite the way the bit is rotating (See page 89). And keep a firm grip on the router with both hands at all times to maintain control. Securely clamp your stock to the worksurface or use a rubberized router pad (See page 89).

As versatile as the portable router is, it can be made even more useful by mounting it upside down in a router table. It then becomes a stationary machine, a small shaper, that can be used with a variety of fences, hold-downs, and stops. On a router table, narrow stock like molding strips can be safely fed past the cutters using a featherboard as you would on a table saw. Stop blocks can be used to precisely limit cuts when creating or accommodating joinery. The large-diameter bits previously mentioned are unsafe to use freehand, but secured in a router table they can greatly extend your range of joinery and shaping choices.

Sanding profiles

An oscillating spindle sander is used to smooth out edge profiles. By stacking parts together, you can insure that the profiles match exactly, as shown above.

A belt-disc sanding station can be used to shape edges on small workpieces. In the photo above, a piece of walnut is being tapered on the end so small box feet can be trimmed off.

A belt sander is a good tool for breaking edges or making profiles on larger workpieces, like the coat rack post being tapered on the top end in the photo above.

A band saw is the most efficient tool for resawing thicker stock into thinner boards. The thin kerf of the blade wastes little wood, and the larger throat capacity allows you to saw very thick stock. Most band saws come with a fence that attaches to the saw table to be used as a guide for ripping and resawing stock. The fence is easy to use and you'll get reasonably good results. But the fence won't allow you to compensate for blade wander and grain direction, as the pivot jig shown on the bottom of this page will.

Resawing Lumber

If you have only ¾-in. lumber and need some ¼-in. parts, what do you do? It would be wasteful, messy, and time consuming to shred off ½ in. in the planer. The answer is *resawing,* or ripping a thick board into two thinner boards. Resawing is usually done on the bandsaw. The resawn lumber will still need to be planed to smooth the cut surfaces and take them to exact thickness.

It's best if the board you're resawing has flat, parallel faces, but it's essential that one edge be jointed flat and square so the board has a secure footing and is not canted to the blade. The jointed edge of your workpiece will be the lower surface that rides against the saw table during cutting. For reference, mark a cutting line down the center of the other edge, using a combination square or marking gauge.

The best blade for resawing is wide, with coarse teeth and plenty of set. Blades between ¾ and 1½ in. wide are stiff and track well in a straight line for resawing (some newer machines accept 3-in.-wide blades which track so straight you can saw your own veneer with them). If you prefer to use your standard ½ in. blade because it's on the machine and not worth changing for just one cut, be aware that you'll have to cut slower and that thinner blades have more of a tendency to bend and deflect in thick wood.

Routine resawing is generally done freehand. Steady and feed the board with a hand on each face. Feed the wood gently, letting the saw cut at its own pace. As you near the end of the board, push it through with a pushstick and also pull the cut end through from the back of the saw.

HOW TO RESAW STOCK WITH A BAND SAW & PIVOT JIG

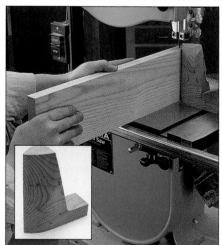

1 Make a pivot jig (inset photo) and clamp it to your saw table so the sharp edge of the jig is square to the blade. The distance from the jig to the blade should be slightly more than the resawn stock thickness. Feed the workpiece into the blade and steer it against the pivot point, following the cutting line.

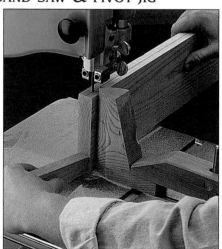

2 Continue feeding the board through the blade at a steady pace. Don't worry about a little wandering—you'll need to surface plane the board at some point anyway. As you approach the end of the cut, use a push stick to push the board through. Keep the board steady by holding it on the outfeed side.

3 Set your thickness planer and plane both faces of the workpiece to remove the saw marks created by the band saw. Plane your stock in shallow, successive passes. Measure the thickness and continue planing until the workpiece is just right.

Tips for minimizing tearout

Tearout, or *chipout*, is probably the most common problem encountered when cutting and shaping parts. It occurs when wood fibers are torn away by the action of the blade or bit, leaving ragged edges with voids. When cutting with power (or hand) saws, make it a habit to arrange your workpiece so the moving saw teeth enter the good face and exit the bad (less visible) face. It is the exit side where tearout occurs, particularly when cross-cutting. If you are using a table saw, chop saw, band saw, scroll saw, hand saw, or drill, place the good face up. Circular saws and jig saws cut on the upstroke, so cut with the good face down. Tearout also can be minimized by choosing a finer-toothed blade and keeping it sharp. Feeding the work too fast can worsen tearout.

Zero-clearance throat plate. To minimize tearout when cutting plywood across the grain directly on the saw table, replace the gaping factory throat plate with a shop-made plywood version. Insert small flathead screws under the corners and adjust them in or out to shim the plate up or down so it's flush with the table. Then position the rip fence over the plate (away from the blade path) and raise the spinning blade to cut a tight kerf.

Flatten your orbit. When using a jig saw with orbital cutting action, the path of the saw blade actually makes an abbreviated arc that increases the cutting speed, but can also increase tearout. For the cleanest possible cut, set the blade to its flattest cutting plane.

Blade orbit selection lever

Blade orbit guide

Tape the cutting line. Sheet goods covered with thin veneers, melamine or laminate are prone to tearout and chipping around the blade slot opening in the throatplate. To avoid this problem, adhere a strip of masking tape along the cutting line on the bottom of the panel before you make the cut. The tape will keep the veneer, melamine or laminate from splintering or chipping. In addition, install a sharp triple-chip, crosscut or plywood blade. Saw with the "good" (untaped) face of the panel face-up on the saw table.

Enter the better face. Tearout occurs when the blade exits, so position the workpiece so the blade enters the better face first. With circular saws, the bad face should be up, on table saws, it should be down.

Making Joints & Assembling Projects

If you've ever spent time around other woodworkers, you've heard the shop stories. Most of them are about fellow enthusiasts (never anyone present, of course!) who made unbelievable errors and wound up having to restart a project from scratch. There's the guy who built a boat in his basement and couldn't get it out past a bend in the stairs. Or the poor fellow who got so carried away with his beautiful hardwood floor that he varnished himself into a corner. Or how about—well, you get the picture.

The truth is that projects can get away from us, especially if we don't plan properly. And nowhere is planning more crucial than in the joint-making and assembly processes. Going from a benchtop full of parts to a completed piece of furniture is a big step. But sound joinery, a logical approach to assembly and a proper glue-up can make the process go without a hitch.

By the time you've cut all your project parts to size, you should already know what types of joints you'll be using, how big they'll be and how many you'll be making. If you haven't made up your mind yet how to cut the joints, it's high time to do so. There are many ways to cut most woodworking joints. Power tools are usually the first place we look since, for most of us, they are more accurate and faster to use than hand tools. Plus, we've invested a significant amount of money in our table saws and routers, so we like to use them whenever we get the chance. In fact, one of the first questions you need to ask yourself when making joinery decisions is "Can I do it with the tools I already own?" If there's a way, most of us will go with it. That's why, in the pages that follow, we've included different options for cutting the most common woodworking joints. If you don't have a table saw, we'll show you how to cut tenons for a mortise-and-tenon joint using a router. If you don't own a biscuit joiner, we demonstrate how to reinforce butt joints with dowels and an inexpensive doweling jig; or even with pocket screws or plain old wood screws.

Once you've made your parts and cut your joints, you'll be ready for that most dreaded (and for many, most exciting) part of the woodworking process: *the glue up.* We'll help you choose the best glue and clamp to use for your project and give you some valuable tips on making the process go as smoothly as possible. Because this is the part of the woodworking journey where, as they say "the rubber meets the road." Once it's done, there's really nothing left to do but the finishing touches.

> Once you've made your parts and cut your joints, you'll be ready for that most dreaded (and for many, most exciting) part of the woodworking process: the glue up.

WOODWORKING WORKS

Cutting accurate, well chosen wood joints has a great impact on the success of your project. Once the joints are cut, you'll find out in a hurry how well you did when you assemble the project. Especially with a complicated project, like the porch glider shown here, you should plan on dry-assembling all of the parts before doing the actual glue up.

Casework vs. Furnituremaking

Woodworking joinery falls into two major categories—casework and furnituremaking. Each is defined by its materials, structure and aesthetics. While there is certainly some crossover between the categories, if you're trying to determine which joints to employ for your project, making the casework/furniture distinction is a useful starting point.

Typically, sheet goods are used for casework (boxes and cabinets). Butt joints reinforced with screws, biscuits, dowels, splines or pocket screws are common, although rabbet and dado joints come in handy as well. A furnituremaker works mostly in hardwood with structures that depend on small, fitted joints, like dovetails, mortises and half-laps that need to be both strong and pleasing to the eye.

SCREWED JOINT

DOWEL JOINT

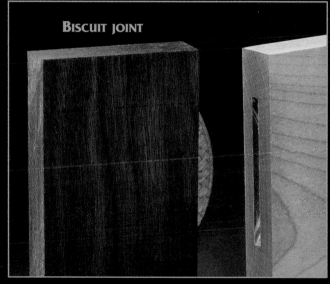

BISCUIT JOINT

RABBET JOINT

DADO JOINT

CASEWORK JOINTS

TONGUE & GROOVE JOINT

MORTISE & TENON JOINT

LAP JOINT

FINGER JOINT

HALF-BLIND DOVETAIL JOINT

DOVETAIL JOINT

FURNITUREMAKING JOINTS

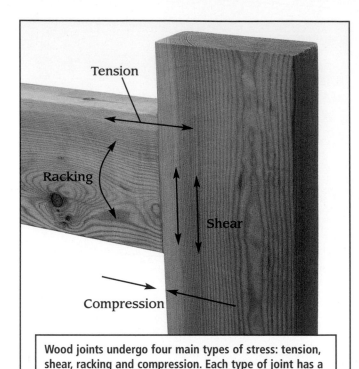

Tension

Racking

Shear

Compression

Wood joints undergo four main types of stress: tension, shear, racking and compression. Each type of joint has a different ability to resist failure by one or more stresses.

Laying Out & Cutting Joints

Successful woodworking projects depend on accurate layout and cutting of the joints. If joints aren't laid out just right, they can't be machined properly. That means that parts won't fit together as they should: they will "exceed their tolerance." In woodworking, tolerance is the amount of leeway you have in making two parts fit together. In most cases, parts should fit well enough that you have to employ a little force to bring them tightly together, but usually not so much that you have to use a hammer or mallet.

Drawing pencil lines (or, in shop parlance, *scribing*) in the right places is what layout is all about. There is an old woodshop maxim that says: "Any time a square can be used, it should be used." For example, if you're marking a line six inches from the end of a board, never assume that the end of the board was initially cut square. If it wasn't, you'll only compound the original error. So, check every board with a square, and consider this the first step in laying out any wood joint.

It is also important to scribe a cutting line for every cut you make. Even if your tool fence is set the correct distance from the blade or cutter to create similar cuts in identical pieces, you should still mark the location of the cut on the workpiece. That way, if the piece is oriented incorrectly, you'll get enough warning to avoid cutting a groove in the wrong face. Plus, if the cut wanders from the line, you'll know the tool's set-up is in need of attention.

Always make your cuts just outside the scribed line. If possible, try to actually split the line. But never cut inside the line, or the parts will fit together with too much slop and you're back to exceeding the joint's tolerance.

There are numerous measuring tools on the market that will help you gain accuracy during joint layouts (See pages 60 to 61). Among the most popular are marking gauges. They've been around for centuries and are ideal for scoring lines parallel to an edge (as when laying out tenons). Most of the traditional gauges use a steel or brass pin to score the line, but a scribing pencil is a better choice because it is more forgiving.

DOs & DON'Ts for Making Joints

■ DO make sure your stock is square, straight and parallel before a single mark is scribed (See pages 54 to 59).

■ DO size each joint correctly. A well-designed joint should be large enough to do the job, but not so large that it interferes with the aesthetics of the piece. There is no hard and fast formula for sizing the elements of a joint. See the discussion of each joint type in the pages that follow for guidelines on joint proportions.

■ DON'T forget to factor wood movement into the joint construction (See page 40).

■ DO lay out all joints with accurate marking instruments, even if you're counting on the set up of your tool to establish the cuts. Layout lines will inform you instantly if the cutting instrument is not hitting the stock in the correct position.

"Short grain" failure

■ DO pay attention to the grain direction in your wood stock. "Short grain" on highly stressed joint parts, like tenons, will cause the joint to fail quickly, as shown in the tenon above.

YES

NO

■ DON'T remove waste in an area that's more than one-half the thickness of the board (as when you're cutting a mortise).

Ways to join wood

Wood workpieces are joined in one of three primary ways, all of which can be accomplished with either a table saw and dado blade or a router and a few bits. Some boards are attached by butting faces, ends or edges together and bonding the joint with glue or mechanical fasteners like nails or screws. Other joints are made by shaping the mating parts into interlocking forms, then strengthening the union of the parts with glue. A third option is to insert a dowel or wooden peg across the joint, to lock the parts together. Which joints you choose for a project should depend largely on the look you are after, the strength you need and the tools you own.

A table saw can be used to cut many of the most useful types of wood joints, especially if it is equipped with an adjustable dado blade set.

A router, especially a plunge router like the one above, can cut just about any joint you ask it to. A straight bit used with a cutting guide can cut dadoes, rabbets, mortises, tenons and more. A piloted rabbet bit lets you cut rabbets without the need to set up a cutting guide. And specialty bits are also available for more sophisticated joints, like dovetail joints and finger joints.

Glue alone is used for some woodworking techniques, including edge-gluing boards together to form wider panels.

Interlocking joints are fashioned with parts that are cut to link together mechanically. Sometimes they are reinforced with nails or screws to reinforce the glue bond.

Pinned or pegged joints, like the mortise-and-tenon joint shown here, are strengthened with dowels, splines or wedges driven through the mating joint parts to lock them together.

A **butt joint** can be used in just about any woodworking situation. If it will undergo stress or pressure, it's a good idea to reinforce the glued butt joint with a fastener, such as a screw.

Butt Joints

Butt joints are the simplest woodworking joints to cut and build. And when used in the right applications, they are quick to assemble and plenty strong. A butt joint is formed when two workpieces are butted together face-to-face, end-to-end, edge-to-edge or any combination of these surfaces. Unlike other types of joints, the mating surfaces of a butt joint are left flat and smooth, without any additional machining. Because the mating parts do not interlock, butt joints in woodworking situations are inherently weaker than other styles and are best left for joining parts that don't need to move or support great amounts of weight.

Modern woodworking glues form incredibly strong joints—on a properly made joint, the surrounding wood fibers will break before the glue joint fails. But glue alone won't save a butt joint subjected to excessive twisting, pulling or shearing forces. If you choose to use butt joints, it's often a good idea to reinforce the joint with nails, screws or biscuits where it will be subjected to tension or racking stresses. Nails, dowels,

Reinforcement Option: Finish nails are easy fasteners to use for reinforcing butt joints. Drill a pilot hole for each nail before driving it. Set the nail head below the wood surface with a correctly-sized nail set.

Reinforcement Option: (Left) Wood screws are popular fasteners for reinforcing butt joints. They should be driven into counterbored or countersunk pilot holes.

HOW TO PLUG A COUNTERBORE

Reinforcement Option: Diagonal glue blocks can be glued beneath a butt joint for additional support. Use them with or without additional fasteners in the joint. The blocks are attached with glue only.

1 Use a counterbore bit to counterbore the pilot hole for the screw (⅜ in. is the standard counterbore diameter).

A **counterbore bit** can drill a pilot hole, shank hole and counterbore hole all at the same time.

splines, screws or bolts will strengthen a butt joint that must carry a load, preventing it from failing due to shear. Pocket screws and mechanical "knock-down" fasteners have become popular reinforcing options in recent years.

Butt joints are used for edge-gluing individual boards together to form wide panels such as tabletops, carcases, workbench and "butcher-block" surfaces and cutting boards. Edge-glued butt joints are stronger than other butt joint configurations because the boards are joined lengthwise, along the grain (called *long-grain*). Long-grain gluing provides plenty of surface area for glue along the joint, and because the wood pores run parallel to the joint instead of across it, the boards can expand and contract evenly across the grain as temperature and humidity fluctuate. Plus, long grain soaks up just enough glue to hold the joint tightly.

A **countersink bit** reams out the top of a pilot hole with a bevel that allows the screw head to be recessed.

Countersinking & counterboring

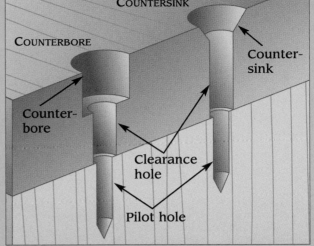

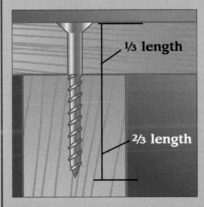

A **counterbore hole** has a cylindrical top intended to accept a wood screw plug; a **countersink hole** has a beveled top just deeply enough for the screw head to be driven below the wood surface, creating a small recess to be filled with wood putty.

The ⅔s rule

Follow the two-thirds rule: Screws should be driven through the thinner workpiece first, whenever possible. The lower two-thirds of the screw should end up in the lower board after the screw has been driven.

⅓ length

⅔ length

2 Drive the screw, then apply glue to the end of a wood plug and insert it into the counterbore hole.

Flush-cutting saw

3 Trim the plug with a chisel, flush-cut saw or rasp, then sand the plug until it's even with the wood surface.

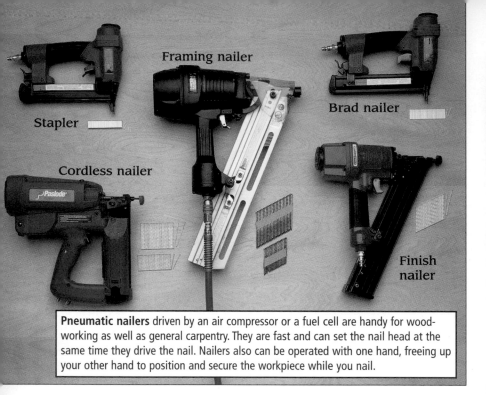

Stapler

Framing nailer

Brad nailer

Cordless nailer

Finish nailer

Pneumatic nailers driven by an air compressor or a fuel cell are handy for woodworking as well as general carpentry. They are fast and can set the nail head at the same time they drive the nail. Nailers also can be operated with one hand, freeing up your other hand to position and secure the workpiece while you nail.

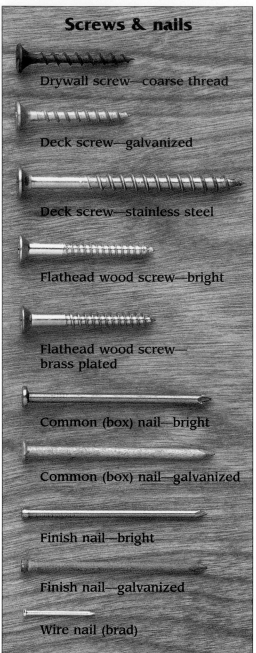

Screws & nails

Drywall screw—coarse thread

Deck screw—galvanized

Deck screw—stainless steel

Flathead wood screw—bright

Flathead wood screw—brass plated

Common (box) nail—bright

Common (box) nail—galvanized

Finish nail—bright

Finish nail—galvanized

Wire nail (brad)

Working with screws & nails

In this this day of biscuit joiners, pocket-screw jigs and fancy European knockdown fasteners, it's easy to ignore the oldest fastening devices of all: the nail and the screw. But take care not to overlook them. They are inexpensive, readily available and easy to use.

Wood screws: Many woodworking plans call for "flathead woodworking screws." These are really nothing more than the plain old bright metal screws floating around in boxes and bins in every corner of your basement. For most woodworking projects, they are the ones you want to use (in some cases, brass-plated screws are used for decorative effect, but avoid the solid brass screws: they are weaker and easier to strip out. Drywall screws and deck screws also have a place in woodworking, especially when working with sheet goods and softer stock, like pine or cedar. They have less sheer strength because of their thinner shafts, but the coarser threads give them a little extra bite. Always drill pilot holes for screws.

Nails: In woodworking, nails are used mostly to fasten trim or attach decorative hardware. They are seldom used to reinforce joinery, mostly because they don't draw the mating workpieces together and the required pounding can knock your work out of whack. The main reason they're used for trim is that they require smaller pilot holes and, when the heads are set with a nailset or pneumatic nailer, they are easy to conceal with wood putty. Bright finish nails and wire nails are used most frequently.

FACE-GLUING

Perhaps the simplest form of butt joint is not one that we typically consider to be part of the category. But *face-gluing* boards together is, by definition, a type of butt joint and it is one that every woodworker will depend on. Also called "laminating," it is a common method for joining boards into thicker blanks that are used to make project parts, such as table legs, tabletops and columns. Before gluing the boards together, run the board faces across a jointer or through a thickness planer to ensure that they are flat.

How to use a pocket hole jig

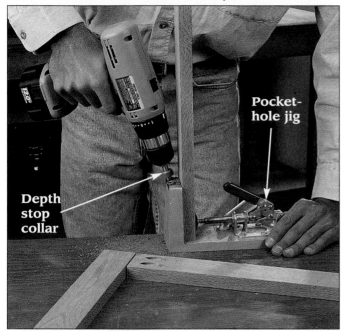

Depth stop collar

Pocket-hole jig

1 Clamp the workpiece that will contain the screw starter holes (usually the rails on a face frame, as shown above) into the pocket screw jig. The center of the jig should align with the centerline of the workpiece. Mount the step drill bit that came with the jig into a portable drill, then drill through the guide bushings and into the workpiece until the depth stop makes contact with the mouth of the guide.

Installing pocket screws

Driving pocket screws into a butt joint is a little like toenailing with a screw. Pocket-hole jigs allow you to drill pocket holes quickly and accurately for reinforcing butt joints with pocket screws. For best results, use the special drill bit, driver and screws that are usually sold along with the pocket hole jig. Pocket joints are especially handy when making face frames for cabinetry and furniture.

Pocket screws

2 Clamp the workpiece containing the starter holes to the mating workpiece, then drive pocket screws through the starter holes and into the mating workpiece. Pocket screws are sold in packets at woodworking stores. They're thinner than regular wood screws to prevent the workpieces from splitting when they're driven. Most have square-drive heads. Take care not to overdrive the screws.

Mechanical "knock-down" fasteners

Minifix-brand fittings are two-part fastening systems very similar to those used on mass-produced knockdown furnishings. The cam fits into a 15-mm hole drilled into the horizontal member and the screw assembly is fitted into an 8-mm hole in the vertical member. The screw head is inserted into the cam, and a set screw in the cam is tightened to twist the cam and draw the parts together. A decorative cap is then snapped over the cam opening.

Screw assembly

Cam

Tite Joint-brand fasteners are especially useful for joining two sheet good panels end to end, as with countertops. The heads of the fastener are mortised into adjoining panels. The mortises are connected by a groove or a guide hole that houses a threaded shaft. The sphere (the left head above) contains grip-holes so it can be spun with a scratch awl or small allen wrench to tighten the joint.

Blum-brand barrel-type two-part fasteners are used mainly to attach shelves in cabinets. The threaded nylon barrel is fitted into a 25-mm hole in the cabinet side, then the collared screw is driven into the end of the shelf so the duple-type head projects out. The head fits into the barrel, which is tightened by turning a screw-activated metal gripping plate.

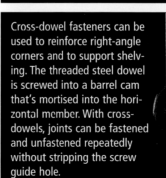

Cross-dowel fasteners can be used to reinforce right-angle corners and to support shelving. The threaded steel dowel is screwed into a barrel cam that's mortised into the horizontal member. With cross-dowels, joints can be fastened and unfastened repeatedly without stripping the screw guide hole.

Biscuit-Reinforced Butt Joints

Biscuit joiners (sometimes called *plate joiners*) are single-purpose tools designed to do just one thing: cut matching semicircular slots that accept football-shaped biscuits used to reinforce butt joints. In general, you'll find that enforcing with biscuits creates a stronger joint than using dowels or most other conventional fasteners. In addition to reinforcing joints, biscuits also give you a near-foolproof method for aligning mating parts.

Biscuits, which lock the joint together, are football-shaped disks made of compressed wood. When they come into contact with wet glue, the moisture expands them into the slots, tightening the joint. They come in several standard sizes (#0, which is ⅜ in. × 1¼ in.; #10, which is ¾ in. × 2⅛ in.; and #20, which is 1 in. × 2⅜ in.) to cover a range of joint applications.

Before making a cut with a biscuit joiner, make sure that the workpiece is secured to your worksurface. To keep the tool itself from slipping, most have an anti-slip device (either a rubber tip or a metal point) to help maintain the grip on the wood.

A biscuit joint is a reinforced butt joint used mostly in casework projects. Made with the use of a biscuit joiner (also called a plate joiner) biscuit joints are quick and easy to make. In addition to reinforcing butt joints in face frames, they are frequently employed to help align and reinforce joints when edge-gluing panels from narrower stock or butting sheet goods together to form a carcase.

HOW TO FLATTEN A BOARD ON A JOINER

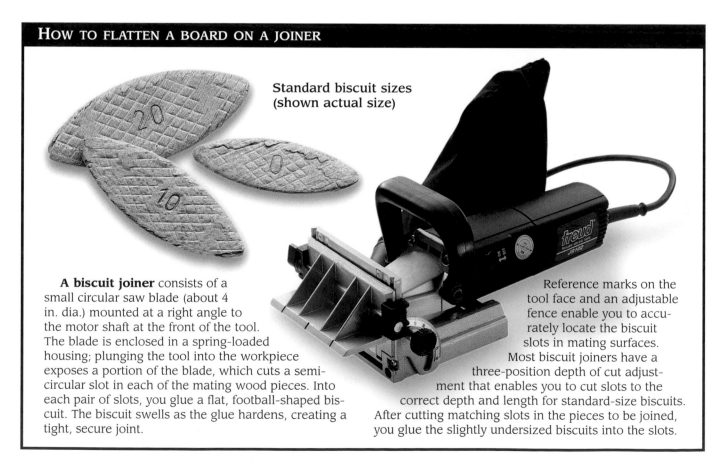

Standard biscuit sizes
(shown actual size)

A biscuit joiner consists of a small circular saw blade (about 4 in. dia.) mounted at a right angle to the motor shaft at the front of the tool. The blade is enclosed in a spring-loaded housing; plunging the tool into the workpiece exposes a portion of the blade, which cuts a semicircular slot in each of the mating wood pieces. Into each pair of slots, you glue a flat, football-shaped biscuit. The biscuit swells as the glue hardens, creating a tight, secure joint.

Reference marks on the tool face and an adjustable fence enable you to accurately locate the biscuit slots in mating surfaces. Most biscuit joiners have a three-position depth of cut adjustment that enables you to cut slots to the correct depth and length for standard-size biscuits. After cutting matching slots in the pieces to be joined, you glue the slightly undersized biscuits into the slots.

HOW TO EDGE-GLUE A PANEL WITH BISCUITS

Alternate direction of growth rings

1 Arrange the jointed boards together to get the most pleasing match of the different grain patterns. This can take some trial and error. *Tip: alternate the direction of the growth rings at the ends of the boards. This helps keep the panel from cupping.* Once you've got all the boards arranged to your satisfaction, draw a "V" across all joints in the panel. Use the legs of the "V" to maintain your alignment as you glue-up the panel.

2 Once the boards are laid out and marked, place them in position and mark the biscuit locations. Use a square to mark all mating edges to ensure that the slots align. Biscuits should be spaced about 8 to 10 in. apart, with a biscuit about 2 in. in from each end. After marking biscuit locations, cut the slots by aligning your marks with the permanent mark on the biscuit joiner.

3 Apply glue to one edge of each board to be joined, then squeeze glue into the slots. Commercial glue applicators that reach into the slots are available, or you can simply squeeze the glue in with a regular glue bottle and spread the glue with a popsicle stick. Add the biscuits to the slots on one board. If edge-gluing more than one board at a time, apply the glue and insert the biscuits in every board. Now you're ready to clamp the assembly.

HOW TO REINFORCE A RIGHT-ANGLE BUTT JOINT WITH BISCUITS

1 Lay out the position of the two mating parts using a square (note whether you're marking the top or bottom of the workpiece). Set the mating workpiece in position against the mark. Draw a perpendicular reference line on both workpieces at each biscuit location. With the workpieces clamped together and secured to your worksurface, align biscuit joiner with the reference lines and cut the slots in one workpiece.

2 With the workpieces still clamped together, cut matching slots in the other workpiece, using the reference lines to align the biscuit joiner.

3 With all the slots cut, you're ready for assembly. Apply glue in the biscuit slots and on the mating surfaces. Insert all the biscuits into the slots in one workpiece, then slip the mating workpiece into position so the parts butt together cleanly. Clamp the parts together, check for square and adjust the clamps as necessary to square up the joints.

A hidden dowel joint can be used to reinforce butt joints when assembling face frames or making furniture. The dowels strengthen the joint, and help you align the parts. For best results, use a dowel jig or dowel points for guidance when drilling the dowel holes.

Dowel-Reinforced Butt Joints

Dowel joints are reinforced butt joints that are used frequently for edge gluing and frame building—especially face frames used in cabinet construction. They increase the strength of a joint and, when used carefully, assist in the alignment of the mating workpieces. Today, they're not used as commonly as in years past due to the advent of the biscuit joiner. But for those who don't own a biscuit joiner, they're still essential to wood joinery. And unlike biscuits, dowels can be added after the joint is assembled.

Commercially produced doweling jigs, like the one shown below, are designed for making highly accurate hidden dowel joints for reinforcing butt joints or edge gluing. Dowel points (round metal spurs that fit into a dowel hole) can be used instead to transfer the exact location of the dowel hole centerpoint to the mating workpiece.

Because alignment is so important, use a drill press whenever possible. If using a portable drill, attach a right angle drilling guide.

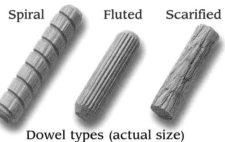

Spiral   Fluted   Scarified

Dowel types (actual size)

TOOLS FOR DRILLING GUIDES FOR DOWEL JOINTS

Dowel points

A doweling jig makes drilling accurate dowel holes a breeze. The jig is set to match the thickness of the workpieces, then fitted over each workpiece individually to guide the drill bit and ensure that the dowel holes align when the workpieces are joined. See the step-by-step instructions, next page.

Metal dowel points are inserted into dowel holes on one workpiece. When the parts are lined up and pressed together the points create drilling points on the mating workpiece.

HOW TO MAKE A DOWEL JOINT WITH A DOWELING JIG

1 To lay out the dowel joints, butt the two mating parts together, making sure the mating surfaces are flush. Mark the dowel hole locations by drawing a single line across the joint for each dowel. For best results, use at least two evenly spaced dowels at each joint.

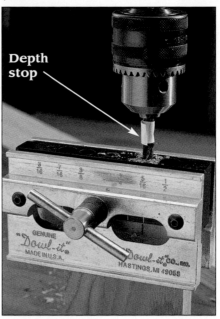

Depth stop

2 Slip the doweling jig over each mating edge. Align the mark on the jig corresponding to the diameter of the dowel hole with each location line you drew on the workpiece. Drill a dowel hole the same diameter as the dowel at each mark—use a depth stop to keep the holes of uniform depth (masking tape will suffice if you don't have a depth stop collar).

3 After drilling all the holes, apply a dab of glue into each hole. Also apply glue to the mating wood surfaces. Slide the dowels into the holes to make the joint.

4 Create all the joints, then clamp the assembly together with pipe clamps or bar clamps. Be sure to use a clamp pad between the wood and the clamp jaws so the jaws don't mar the wood. Do not overtighten the clamps.

Through dowels

One of the simplest ways to reinforce a butt joint (or a mortise-and-tenon joint, for that matter) is with *through dowels.* After the joint is assembled and the glue has dried, simply drill dowel holes through the joint, using a drill press or a portable drill with a drilling guide. Then, apply glue to the ends of pieces of doweling and drive dowels through the holes with a mallet. Tip: Bevel the leading end of each dowel first with sandpaper. Leave about ⅛ to ¼ in. of the dowel protruding past the wood surface, then trim off the ends with a flush-cutting saw or file. Sand smooth. For a decorative effect, choose dowels made from a contrasting species of wood.

DADO JOINT

RABBET JOINT

DADO/RABBET JOINT

Dado & rabbet joints interlock to add strength and increase glue surface. There are many variations of the joint, including the dado joint, the rabbet joint and the combination dado/rabbet joint.

Dado & Rabbet Joints

Dado and rabbet joints are interlocking joints used for a variety of woodworking tasks. A *dado* is a square groove that's cut across the grain of a workpiece; a *rabbet* is a square groove that's cut along the edge of a workpiece; a groove cut with the grain in the field area of a workpiece is called either a *groove* or a *plough*. By combining these cuts you can make several types of interlocking joints, including *dado joints, rabbet joints* and *dado/rabbet joints.*

Dado joints. Dado joints are used almost exclusively to joint horizontal panels or boards (usually shelves) to vertical panels or boards (usually cabinet sides). The interlocking fit, coupled with the enhanced gluing surface, makes the dado joint exceptionally strong. They can be cut with a router, straight bit and cutting guide, or on a table saw with a standard blade or, better still, a dado blade (See next page).

Rabbet joints. Rabbet joints are a better alternative to butt joints for building boxes and carcases because the joints partially interlock. You'll commonly see them, or variations of a basic rabbet joint, used in bookcase construction to conceal the ends and edges of the back and top panels. Depending upon how the joints are arranged, they can conceal most of the end grain. Creating recesses for back panels, top panels or glass panel inserts are also tasks that are commonly assigned to rabbet joints. Using a router, you can cut a rabbet with a straight bit and cutting guide, or you can cut one freehand by following the edge of the workpiece with a piloted rabbet bit. A table saw, with or without a dado blade, is another option.

Continued page 112

OPTIONS FOR CUTTING DADOES WITH A ROUTER

Straight bit and cutting guide. A router guide is needed to make a dado or plow with a straight router bit. The simplest guide is a plain, straight board clamped to the workpiece the correct distance from the cutting line.

Router edge guide. For rough work, sliding attachments that fit onto the router base may be used as a guide. Select a bit with a diameter equal to the desired width of the dado. Make the cut in multiple passes of increasing depth, moving the router left to right.

Cutting dadoes with a dado blade set

A dado blade set can be mounted on a table saw and adjusted to cut dadoes up to ⅞ in. wide. The blade sets consist of a pair of circular blades that sandwich toothed chippers. Thin plastic spacers can be inserted to fine-tune the width.

1 Set the cutting width of your dado blade by adding chippers and spacers between the two blades. Mount the set on your table saw arbor. When mounted in a table saw, dado-blade sets require a saw throat plate with an extra-wide opening.

2 Set the cutting height to the desired dado depth, then adjust the fence so the blade set will start cutting at the shoulder of the planned dado. Make a test cut first, feeding the stock through the blade slowly, with plenty of downward pressure. Use a push-block when you near the blade. Measure the dado on the scrap and adjust your setup as needed. In harder stock, it's a good idea to make the cut in multiple passes of increasing cutting depth.

CUTTING RABBETS WITH A TABLE SAW

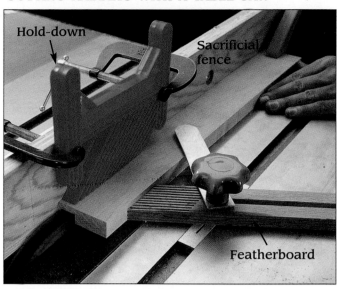

With a dado blade set. A dado blade (See photo, top left) can cut shallow rabbets in a single pass. If the rabbet is deeper than ⅜ in. or the workpiece is hardwood, make the cut in multiple passes. Attach a sacrificial wood fence to the rip fence. Set the fence position and cutting depth, then make the cut. Use a hold-down, featherboard and pushstick to guide the workpiece.

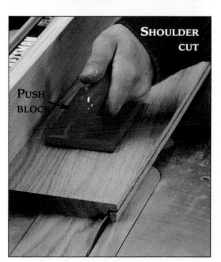

With a standard blade. Cutting rabbets with a standard-kerf saw blade involves cutting the cheeks with one saw set up, then trimming the shoulders in a second operation. When cutting, be sure that the waste piece is on the side of the blade opposite the fence and use a zero-clearance throat plate (See page 93). To make the *cheek cut,* stand the workpiece on-edge or on-end against the rip fence. Install a tall auxiliary fence for rabbeting the edges of wide workpieces. Set the distance from the rip fence to the blade so the blade cuts right at the cheek cutting line. Set the blade height so the teeth just touch the shoulder layout line. Make the cut (top photo). Adjust the saw setup and make the *shoulder cut* (bottom photo), using a push block to hold down and feed the workpiece.

Use a piloted rabbet bit to cut rabbets on the insides of frames or on the outer edges of any workpieces. Make several passes of increasing depth with the router, then square the rabbet corners with a chisel. When profiling an outside edge, clamp scrap blocks at the ends of the workpiece (See page 89).

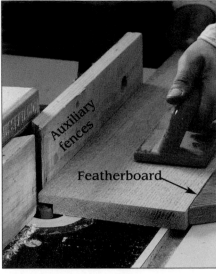

Use a router table fitted with a straight bit to cut rabbets into a board edge. You'll need to attach auxiliary fences to the table fence to create a recess for the bit. Use a featherboard to hold the workpiece securely against the fence. Set the bit height to the rabbet depth and adjust the fences to the width of the cut. Feed the workpiece through the bit with a push block or hold-down.

Dado/rabbet joints.

Dado/rabbet joints combine the enhanced gluing area of a rabbet with the interlocking characteristics of a dado or groove to form joints that are very resistant to failure from racking or shear. Dado/rabbet joints take two forms, depending on their intended purpose. One style features a rabbet with a tongue half the thickness of the workpiece that fits into a matching dado or groove. This joint is used commonly to fasten shelves to upright standards, such as bookcases. The ends of the shelves receive the rabbets, while the standards are dadoed. Another less common use of this joint is for frame and panel doors—the rabbet is cut around the four edges of the panel and the dado or groove is centered around the inside edges of the frame. The panel with the rabbet tongues faces out, which leaves a decorative reveal between the frame and the panel.

How to make dado/rabbet joints

Cut the dadoes first at the joint locations, using a straight router bit or a table saw and dado-blade set. Measure the dadoes and use the measurements as a guide for cutting rabbets with lips that fit exactly into the dadoes (in the photo above, a guide block is clamped to the router base and the rabbet cut is made with a straight bit). Make sure the rabbeted ends will not extend more than halfway into the dadoed board.

Test-fit the joint and adjust the thickness of the rabbet ledge by trimming, if needed. Apply glue to both surfaces, then assemble and clamp the joint.

Tongue & Groove Joints

Tongue-and-groove joints are a strong, easy-to-build alternative to butt or rabbet-and-dado joints. These centered-tongue joints find their way into a variety of different panel and carcase applications. Tongue-and-groove joints are often used to form cabinet back panels, and the pieces are assembled without glue. They are also useful for aligning boards when edge-gluing a panel. Cutting tongue-and-groove joints is a three-step process. You'll first cut the groove or dado along the edge, end or face of one workpiece, then make two identical rabbets along the edge or end of the mating workpiece to form the tongue. It doesn't matter whether you cut the slot first and then the tongue or the other way around.

Tongue-and-groove joints are fashioned by cutting a centered tongue in the edge or end of one board that fits into a centered dado or groove on the mating workpiece. By centering the tongue and fitting it into a centered dado or groove, the shoulders on the tongue side of the joint completely hide the slot made by the dado or groove—a real advantage for concealing the slot-side of the joint.

HOW TO MAKE A TONGUE-AND-GROOVE JOINT

1 Cut a groove in the edge of one mating board, using a dado blade or by making multiple passes over a single blade. The groove should be one-third the thickness of the workpiece.

2 On the uncut mating board, remove the waste wood on one side of the tongue area. Any rabbet-cutting technique may be used with either a standard blade or a dado blade.

3 Flip the workpiece and remove the waste on the other side of the tongue.

4 Apply wood glue in the groove, then insert the tongue. The tongue should fit fully in the groove.

The mortise-and-tenon joint is regarded by many woodworkers as the toughest type of joinery you can use in a furniture project. Making them takes some patience and practice, but the end result will make the effort worthwhile.

Mortise & Tenon Joints

Mortise-and-tenon joints are traditional joints for fine furnituremaking. With modern quick-fastening options like wood biscuits and pocket screws increasing in popularity, you won't find mortise-and-tenon joints in most mass-produced pieces of furniture or cabinets these days, or even in many one-of-a-kind woodworking projects. But whenever strength and stress resistance are critical and quality is a concern, you'll likely find a mortise-and-tenon joint.

Mortise-and-tenon joints take full advantage of those factors that contribute most to joint strength: namely, large gluing surface area and parts that interlock. Tenons have from two to four cheeks and shoulders, and all of these cheek and shoulder faces contribute surfaces for glue. As a rule of thumb, tenons are usually one-third the thickness of the workpiece and up to 3 in. long. These proportions maximize the shear strength of the tenon without compromising the strength of the mortise walls on the mating workpiece. A properly constructed mortise-and-tenon interlocks snugly without binding, just loose enough to permit a thin, even glue bond along the full joint.

HOW TO CUT A MORTISE WITH A DRILL & CHISEL

1 In your drill press, install a brad-point bit or Forstner bit with a diameter equal to the planned thickness of the mortise. Set the depth stop on the drill press to equal the depth of the mortise. Align the bit with the layout lines at one end of the mortise. Bore one hole at a time. Once a hole is bored, move the workpiece so the next hole will be next to, or slightly overlapping, the first hole. Continue drilling until you reach the other end of the outline. Clamp the workpiece to the drill press table before drilling each hole.

2 Use sharp wood chisels to remove the remaining waste wood and to clean and square up the mortise walls. To avoid splitting the wood, start with a narrow chisel, equal to the width of the mortise, and square one end of the mortise. Keep the flat face of the chisel against the mortise wall as you work. Then, use a wider chisel to clean out the length of the mortise. Let the chisel enter the mortise at an angle to help you control the cut, paring away the waste as you work. Finish the cut by chiseling straight up and down to clean the walls all the way to the mortise floor, or bottom. For square tenons, square off the ends of the mortises with a chisel. Some woodworkers prefer to round-over the ends of the tenons to fit the mortises.

Cutting mortise-and-tenon joints.
You'll find a variety of techniques to choose from for cutting mortise-and-tenon joints. The most common (mainly because it requires no special tool or jigs) is to "hog out" the waste wood in the mortise area on your drill press, then square off the walls with wood chisels. The tenons typically are cut on a table saw with a simple, shop-built jig. But you can also cut mortises and tenons with a router or, better, a router table. And there are also special mortising attachments you can buy for your drill press, and even stand-alone mortising machines for the serious or professional woodworker.

The process for cutting tenons on a table saw is straightforward, simple and possible with either a standard saw blade or a dado blade. Which blade you choose depends mainly on the number of tenons you need to cut and the proportions of the workpiece.

Cheek and shoulder cuts can be made with a standard saw blade in two ways: First, you can cut the tenon with the workpiece face lying on the saw table by making multiple, side-by-side shallow

HOW TO CUT A MORTISE WITH A ROUTER TABLE

1 Install a straight bit in your router table. The bit diameter should match the planned thickness of the mortise. Set the bit cutting depth to the depth of the mortise. Mark start and end points for the mortise on the face of your workpiece. Place some tape on the router table and mark the edges of the router bit for alignment.

2 Hold the workpiece against the fence with one end resting on the table and the other end tipped up over the bit. Position the workpiece so when it is lowered, the bit will contact it in the mortise area. Turn on the router, then lower the workpiece onto the bit until it is flat on the table. Feed it through the bit until the reference line on the board face closer to you lines up with the bit alignment mark closer to you.

3 Feed the workpiece in the opposite direction until the alignment marks farther from you are lined up, ending the cut. Move the workpiece back so the bit is centered in the mortise, then carefully tip it back up, clear of the bit.

HOW TO CUT A MORTISES WITH A PLUNGE ROUTER

1 Lay out an outline for the mortise on the workpiece. Fit a straight bit into your plunge router, then attach a guide block to the router base so the bit will be centered over the mortise when the guide is pressed against it. Also clamp stop blocks at each end of the cut. Set the depth setting on the router so the bit will plunge to the mortise depth.

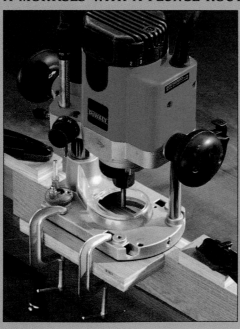

2 With the workpiece secured, plunge the bit into the wood and make the mortise cut. Shut off the router and let the bit come to a stop, then remove it from the mortise.

Shop-built tenoning jig

**OVERALL SIZE:
12 IN. × 12 IN.**

Clamping area

Five wood screws in a cross pattern can be withdrawn to adjust the jig to fit a taller or shorter fence

Distance equals height of saw fence

This classic tenoning jig is intended to be used with a table saw. The critical points in making one for yourself are to get the vertical and horizontal members exactly square to one another and to make sure the distance between the bottoms of the two members is equal to the height of your table saw fence.

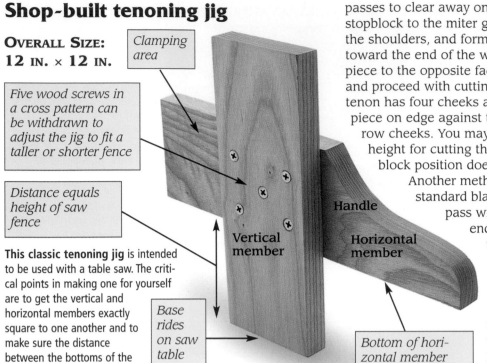

Handle

Vertical member

Horizontal member

Base rides on saw table

Bottom of horizontal member rides on saw fence

passes to clear away one cheek at a time. Clamp a stopblock to the miter gauge to start the cheek cuts at the shoulders, and form each cheek by working toward the end of the workpiece. Then, flip the workpiece to the opposite face, cut the second shoulder and proceed with cutting the second cheek. If the tenon has four cheeks and shoulders, stand the workpiece on edge against the miter gauge to cut the narrow cheeks. You may need to change the blade height for cutting the narrow cheeks, but the stopblock position doesn't change.

Another method for cutting tenons with a standard blade is to cut each cheek in one pass with the workpiece standing on-end against the tenoning jig. Set the blade height so the tips of the teeth cut to the shoulder line, and be sure to account for the thickness of the blade when setting up the cuts. Set the blade so it cuts on the waste side of the tenon layout line to keep from cutting into the tenon. If the tenon has four shoulders and cheeks, cut the narrow edges by clamping the workpiece on-end

HOW TO CUT TENONS WITH A TENONING JIG

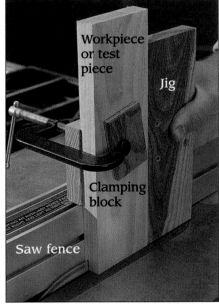

Workpiece or test piece

Jig

Clamping block

Saw fence

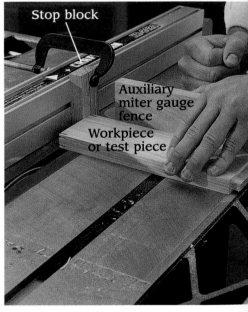

Stop block

Auxiliary miter gauge fence

Workpiece or test piece

1 Make the cheek cuts first. Clamp the workpiece to a tenoning jig (See above) so it's snug against the face of the vertical support and the front edge of the horizontal support. Set the saw fence so the distance to the opposite face of the blade equals the amount of waste being removed. Raise the blade to the depth of the tenon. Rest the jig on the fence and feed the workpiece through the blade. Flip the workpiece, reclamp, and make the cheek cut on the other face.

2 Clamp the workpiece at a right angle to the jig, with the edge flat against the horizontal member and the face of the workpiece pressed against the front edge of the vertical member. Reset the saw fence if the amount of waste being removed is different from the first cheek cuts. Make sure that everything is held securely in place, and guide the jig and workpiece through the blade. Flip and reclamp the workpiece to cut the other short cheek.

3 Make the shoulder cuts using a miter gauge as a guide. Attach an auxiliary fence to the miter gauge and clamp a stop block to the saw fence as an alignment guide. Adjust the fence so the workpiece, when butted against the stop block, slides forward and meets the blade at the base of the tenon cheek. Raise the blade above the table high enough to cut the shoulders. Cut the shoulders on each face, then reset the blade height, if necessary, and cut the tenon ends.

Use a dado blade. An adjustable dado blade set to maximum cutting width makes quick work of removing waste wood to create tenons. The technique is very similar to using a standard blade in your table saw (See previous page).

Use a router table. Install a large straight bit in the router and clamp your workpiece to the router table miter gauge. Set the cutting height to equal to the amount of waste being removed, then feed each face across the bit, using the fence as a guide. Reset the fence to make slightly overlapping cuts from the shoulder until you reach the end of the workpiece.

to a miter gauge outfitted with a tall auxiliary fence. Once you've cut all the cheeks, trim away the remaining waste by cutting the shoulders with the workpiece face-down or on-edge against the miter gauge. Reset the blade height carefully so you trim just to the saw kerfs cut for the cheeks. Use a stopblock clamped to the miter gauge to index the shoulder cuts.

A dado blade will cut tenon cheeks and shoulders more quickly because it removes more material with each pass. Use the same multiple-pass technique as you would with a single blade to cut tenons with the workpiece flat on the saw table. Use a stopblock to establish the shoulder cuts, and make these cuts first. You can also stand the workpiece on end to cut a cheek and shoulder in one pass with a dado blade, but your depth of cut may be limited if you are using an 8-in.-dia. dado blade in your 10-in. table saw.

Tenoning tip: Smooth the tenon cheeks with a sharp wood chisel to ensure a clean fit into the mortise. Take care not to remove too much wood—the tenon should still fit snugly.

Tenoning option: Since you can't fit a square tenon into a round mortise, pare the ends of the tenon with a chisel, rather than trying to square off the faces of the mortise. Pare a little at a time and test the fit frequently as you work.

Making Joints & Assembling Projects 117

CORNER HALF LAP   **"T" HALF LAP**   **CROSS LAP**

Lap joints are, in essence, extra-wide rabbet and dado joints. They're used primarily in furnituremaking and frame-making, where the extra gluing surface in the sturdy interlocking joints greatly increases the strength of any project.

Lap Joints

Lap joints combine the interlocking characteristics of rabbets and dadoes in a number of different configurations to join two boards face to face. Lap joints are a better alternative to butt joints for frame construction, because laps offer much more gluing area and the pieces actually interlock mechanically. Usually, the thickness of both parts of a lap joint are equal, and the pieces fit together so that both faces of each joint part line up with one another. In order to do this, the overlapping dadoes or rabbet tongues are as large as the mating piece is wide.

Three of the more common lap joint types are the *corner half lap, "T" half la*p and *cross lap.* Corner half laps consist of two wide rabbets cut across the faces of two workpieces at the ends. The cheek portion of each rabbet matches the width of the opposite workpiece.

"T" half laps fasten the end of one board with a wide rabbet to the midsection of another board that's fitted with a matching dado. Cross laps are half-lap joints where both members are dadoed and the joint is not at the end of either part. All three types are made by cutting a wide dado into each joint member—either on the face or edge—then interlocking the dadoes.

Cutting lap joints. Aside from their larger size, the rabbets and dadoes that form lap joints are cut just like any other rabbet or dado. Whatever blade you choose, you'll need to make multiple passes to cut these rabbets and dadoes. For most efficient cutting, it makes sense to use a dado blade so you can remove more material with each pass. A dado blade is also the right choice for long or unwieldy workpieces. In these instances, cut the rabbets or dadoes in multiple passes with the workpiece lying facedown on the saw table.

COMMON USES FOR LAP JOINTS

Chairs and benches. Lap joints are very often used to join the arms and/or spreaders of a chair base to the legs. The fitted nature of the joint provides good resistance to downward stress.

Frames. Picture frames, frame-and-panel frames or any time you're joining workpieces on the flat and you want the faces to be flush is a good time to use lap joints.

OPTIONS FOR CUTTING NOTCHES (DADOES)

Use a dado blade. A dado blade set (See page 111) installed in your table saw is the fastest tool for cutting notches in stock to create lap joints. Set the dado blade to its maximum cutting width and set the cutting height to equal the depth of the notch. Attach a sacrificial wood fence to the miter gauge for your table saw. Hold or clamp the workpiece securely against the fence so the area to be notched is clear of the miter gauge. Cut through the stock and the fence in several passes.

Use a router. Mount a straight bit in your router and set the cutting depth to equal the depth of the notch. Clamp stop block guides to the workpiece at each end of the notch. The guides should be positioned so their distance from the end cutting lines is the same as the router set-back (the distance from the bit to the edge of the base). Remove the waste wood with the router, working between the stop blocks (the central area of the notch is routed freehand).

HOW TO CUT TONGUES (RABBETS) WITH A TABLE SAW

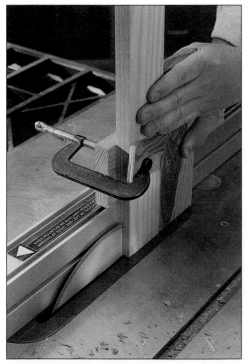

1 Cut the tongue portion of the lap joint on your table saw, using a tenoning jig (See page 116) to support and guide the workpiece. Set up the saw as if you're cutting a deep rabbet, and begin by making the cheek cuts.

2 Cut the shoulders of the tongues on a table saw, using the miter gauge to feed each workpiece past the blade. Clamp a relief block to the fence and measure out from its position to the blade to set up the cut.

Making Joints & Assembling Projects 119

Finger joints generally are selected for their visual appeal as much as their strength. With the help of a simple jig, you'll find that cutting them on your table saw is a surprisingly easy task.

Finger Joints

Finger joints (sometimes called *box joints*) typically are made on a table saw with a dado-blade set and a jig—an auxiliary board screwed or clamped to the miter gauge. When joining parts of equal thickness, a finger joint is a good choice because it's strong and effective. Like a dovetail, the finger joint is visible after it's assembled—a plus if you like to show off your handiwork (and what woodworker doesn't?). Unlike dovetail pins, finger joint pins are straight, so it's an easier joint to make than a dovetail, although it's not as strong.

To make accurate finger joints, first rip-cut and crosscut the parts to size. Cut some test slots in waste pieces with the dado blade and check the fit of an actual workpiece in the slot. The workpiece should fit snugly, but not so tightly that you need a mallet to pound it together.

HOW TO MAKE A JIG FOR CUTTING FINGER JOINTS

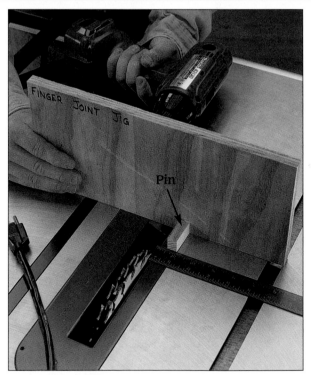

Install a dado-blade set and throat plate in your table saw (See page 111). Set the cutting width of the dado set to equal the thickness of the finger pins to be cut. Raise the blade set to cut the full depth of the pins. Clamp an auxiliary fence board to your table saw miter gauge. The board should be about 6 in. wide and at least 18 in. long. Make a pass of the auxiliary fence over the blade (left photo), then cut a strip of hardwood to use as a pin to fit in the slot. Glue the pin into the fence slot. Reset the auxiliary fence by moving it a distance equal to the thickness of one pin to the outside edge of the blade set. Reclamp or screw the fence to the miter gauge (right photo).

How to make a finger joint on the table saw

1 Make a jig for cutting finger joint (See previous page). With the pin spacer inserted in the fence slot and the fence in position, butt the first workpiece against the strip and make the first pass. You can hold the workpiece in place by hand, or clamp it to make the cut. After the workpiece and fence clear the blade, shut off the saw and back the workpiece off.

2 Reposition the workpiece by placing the slot you just cut over the pin space, then make the next cut. Continue in this manner until all the joints in that board are cut. Flip the board end-over-end and cut the fingers on the other end of the board the same way.

3 To cut the joints in the mating boards, fit the last notch you cut in the first piece over the pin, then butt the mating piece against the first piece, creating a one-notch offset. Make the first pass on the mating piece. Now remove the first piece, butt the notch in the mating piece against the pin and make the second pass. Continue until all the joints are cut in one end, then flip the board end-for-end and repeat.

4 When all the joints are cut, the pieces are ready for assembly. Glue and clamp the mating boards together to form the joint.

Dovetail joints are instantly recognizable to woodworkers and non-woodworker alike. They are exceptionally strong and add a sense of fine craftsmanship to any project (when executed correctly).

Hand-Cut Dovetail Joints

The hand-cut dovetail joint is perhaps the most famous, and intimidating, woodworking joint. As with any other woodworking skill, mastering the art of the dovetail is mostly a matter of practice. But with these joints, visualization also helps. For many first-timers, the biggest hurdle to get past is simply studying the way dovetail joints fit together until they make sense.

Dovetail joints require a fair amount of planning and a good layout drawing. As you lay out the joint, keep a few basic principles in mind:

- The dovetail joint has two parts: the *pin* and the *tail*—always begin making dovetails by cutting the pins first.
- For joint strength and integrity, the joint should begin and end with a half-pin.
- The angle of the pin should not be steeper than 80° (a 1:6 ratio of slope to pin depth).
- The pin-and-tail spacing doesn't need to be exact: the tails can be up to three times as wide as the pins. In fact, the pin and tail sizes can even vary within a joint, which creates an interesting look that's unique to hand-cut dovetails.

MAKING HAND-CUT DOVETAIL JOINTS

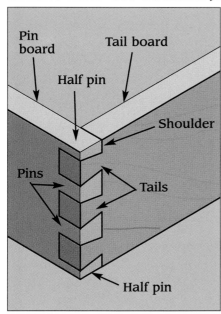

Pin board

Tail board

Half pin

Shoulder

Pins

Tails

Half pin

Dovetail saw

Pin board

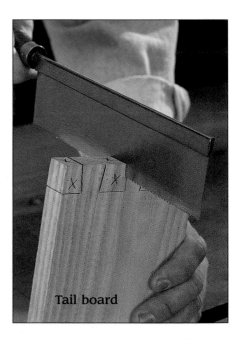

Tail board

Hand-cut dovetails aren't for beginning woodworkers. In fact, there are many highly experienced woodworkers who have never made a dovetail joint and don't ever intend to. The decision to include them in a woodworking project is almost always based more on appearance than on structural strength (although dovetails are as strong as any joint around),

The real trick to making hand-cut dovetails is in understanding how they fit together. Study the drawing above, as well as the photos on this page. If you have an old drawer box made with dovetail joints, study it too; perhaps even pull it apart. Identify the pins and tails, the half-pins and shoulders.

Hand-cut dovetails must be laid out on the workpieces. You'll need a sliding T-bevel or flanged dovetail jig. The pin shoulders are cut with a dovetail saw or miter saw, then the waste between pins is chopped out with a chisel. The pin board is used to create layout lines for the tails. Once marked, the tails are also cut out with a dovetail saw and chisel. If you cut the dovetails accurately, the fit should be tight enough that the joint stays together without glue.

Half-Blind Dovetail Joints

Unlike hand-cut dovetail joints, the primary benefit of the half-blind dovetail is structural, not aesthetic. Their main use is in drawer construction, and it's still not uncommon to find production furniture with machined half-blind dovetail drawer joinery. In this joint, the ends of the tails are hidden when viewed from the pin board front. Consequently, you get the structural integrity of a dovetail joint and its ability to resist the outward pressure caused by pulling on the drawer box, yet the drawer front has a solid appearance, unmarred by any signs of the joinery.

Half-blind dovetail joints can be cut using a chisel, dovetail saw and a Forstner bit to remove waste wood. But the easier way is to use a commercial dovetail jig. Relatively inexpensive template jigs allow you to cut both mating pieces at the same time, using a router and a dovetailing bit. When using any commercial jig, be sure to read the instructions carefully before you start, and always make some practice cuts on scrap before machining your valuable stock.

Half-blind dovetail joints are used mostly in drawer construction because the ends of the tails are hidden, leaving the drawer front solid.

Making a half-blind dovetail joint with a router & dovetail jig

Adjustable dovetail jigs give anyone with a router the power to make perfect dovetails of several varieties, including the half-blind dovetail joint. The jig shown here is used with a dovetailing router bit and template collar (inset photo). Both mating workpieces are inserted into the jig, perpendicular to one another, and are milled at the same time. One of the boards must be offset from the other

Dovetailing bit with template collar

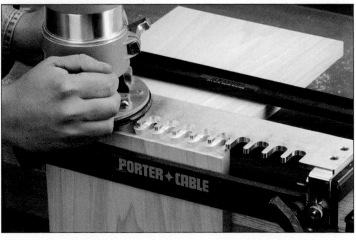

so the joint will start and finish with a partial—ideally, a half pin (See illustration, previous page). Once the mating boards are secured in the jig (photo, top right), the dovetailing router bit is fed into the joint, with the template collar riding against the guide (photo, bottom right). Once the boards are removed from the jig, no further milling is required. Simply apply glue to the pins and tails, join the parts together and clamp until the glue sets, making sure the joint is square.

White glue · Yellow glue · Liquid hide glue · Contact cement · Polyurethane glue · Liquid Nails for Projects & Construction / construction adhesive · Two-part epoxy / PC•7 · Hot glue

Guide to glues

White glue: Used on wood, paper or cloth. Interior use only. Dries in several hours and has a moderately strong bond. Poor resistance to water and heat. Emits no harmful odors. Cleans up with soap and water.

Yellow glue: Used on wood, paper or cloth. Interior use only. Dries faster than white glue and has a slightly stronger bond. Moderate resistance to water and heat. Emits no harmful odors. Cleans up with soap and water.

Liquid hide glue: Ideal for fine wood furniture or musical instruments. Interior use only. Sets slowly. Has good bond and is resistant to solvents and wood finishes. An eye irritant. Will clean up with soap and water.

Polyurethane glue: Used to bond a variety of materials including wood, metal and ceramics. Sets quickly and produces a strong bond. Waterproof.

Construction adhesive: Used with sheet goods and framing lumber. Dries in 24 hours, has a good bond.

Contact cement: Joins laminates, veneers, cloth, paper, leather, and other materials. Sets instantly and dries in under an hour. Produces a bond that is not suitable for structural applications.

Hot glue: Joins wood, plastics, glass and other materials. Sets within 60 seconds. Strength is generally low, but depends on type of glue stick. Good resistance to moisture, fair to heat. Heat will loosen bond.

Two-part epoxy: Joins wood, metal, masonry, glass, fiberglass and other materials. Provides the strongest bond of any adhesive. Bond has excellent resistance to moisture and heat. Drying time varies.

Woodworking Glue Options

Glue forms a much stronger bond between two wooden parts than screws or nails. These mechanical fasteners definitely have their place, but they can split the wood when they are driven, work loose over the years, or rust and deteriorate. Glue, on the other hand, flows into the top layers of cells under clamping pressure, becoming part of both members of a joint.

A few decades ago, woodworking glue completed its evolution from a variety of animal-based products to one very reliable option—aliphatic resin (yellow) glue. Yellow wood glue has been shop tested since

about 1960, with few changes. It is thick enough that you have time to work with it before it begins to run, yet thin enough to be spread evenly. It can be used in a wide range of temperatures, and can even survive occasional freezing—a real plus if you accidentally leave it in an unheated garage. It has a set time that leaves you a small window (a few minutes in hot, dry weather, and a little longer at other times) to reposition parts before they set. This is called "open time." But one of its most endearing qualities is the fact that aliphatic resin glue is relatively easy to clean up, as long as you catch it in time.

Some traditional craftsmen still use animal-based hide glues in certain situations, but these take a long time to mix and cure, are somewhat temperamental and are not very good at gap filling. However, they usually don't require clamping, so they do have some usability in specialty applications.

For a long time, weather resistant aliphatic resin glues were the only option for exterior wood glue. Recently, however, we've been offered new choices: polyurethane-based glues and epoxies.

For special applications, such as the installation of plastic laminates, there are contact adhesives. These used to be a big health concern. But most state and federal regulations now require professional shops to use water-based contact adhesives. These products are brushed, rolled or sprayed onto both surfaces and allowed to dry. They then bond immediately on contact when the parts are brought together: you have to get it right the first time, as they don't allow repositioning.

Glue squeeze-out should be minimal and uniform when clamp pressure is applied. Too much squeeze-out is messy to clean, and can indicate too much clamping pressure. Spots along the joint line with no squeeze-out indicate that an insufficient amount of glue has been applied. Unclamp and reglue the joint.

A glue roller is used to apply an extremely even coating of glue on large, broad surfaces, such as when applying veneer. Once the hopper is loaded with glue, it will dispense glue over the roller at an even rate when the surface is rolled.

A special glue tool for biscuits can be slipped into a biscuit slot to deliver glue with no spillage or mess.

A glue brush will deliver just the right amount of glue to tight working spots. These disposable brushes more than make up for their low cost in savings on the clean-up side.

A disposable foam paint brush is a perfect tool for spreading even layers of contact adhesive on smaller project parts. For larger parts, like countertops, use a low-nap paint roller sleeve.

Making Joints & Assembling Projects 125

A damp rag will remove glue squeeze-out before it gets a chance to penetrate into the wood pores, which reduces the wood's ability to absorb stain or topcoat products. The only downside is that it will raise the wood grain and require light sanding when dry.

An old wood chisel can be used to scrape congealed glue squeeze-out from edge-glued joints, or from any flat surface. Keep the beveled edge of the chisel down to avoid marring the wood. Make certain the chisel edge is free of nicks.

A sharp floor scraper will make quick, neat work of removing dried glue from joints. Don't get too aggressive, though. You'll likely need to sand the area before finishing to get even finish results.

Working with polyurethane glue

Poly glue requires moisture to cure, and as it cures, the squeeze-out forms an expanding sticky foam that is difficult to remove from almost everything it touches, including your skin. Wear disposable gloves, and wipe up spills immediately from clothing, tools and skin with a rag and mineral spirits or acetone.

Warning: Polyurethane glue can cause immediate and residual lung damage. This product should only be used with excellent ventilation. Asthmatics and people with chronic lung conditions should not use this product.

1 Moisten one joint surface with a clean, damp rag or sponge, and brush glue onto the other joint surface.

2 Since the glue expands as it cures, clamp the joint parts together right away, or the glue will force the joint apart.

3 Allow the glue to fully cure, remove the clamps and slice off the hardened foam with a sharp chisel.

Corner clamp

Strap (web) clamp

C-clamps

Pipe clamp

Quick clamp

Woodscrew

USEFUL WOODWORKING CLAMPS

The glue-up is a critical moment in the development of a woodworking project. Prepare for it by making sure all the mating surfaces are clean and ready to accept the glue. Also be sure to have more than enough glue on hand, protect your worksurface with wax paper (which won't bond with the project parts) and have plenty of clamps and clamp pads at the ready.

TIPS FOR CLAMPING PANELS

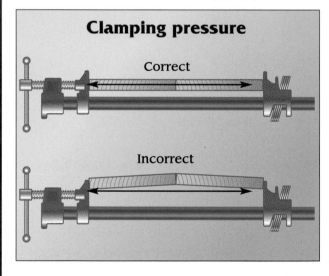

Clamping pressure

Correct

Incorrect

Position your workpieces between the clamp jaws so that the center of the glue joint lines up with the handscrew in the head of the clamp. Otherwise, the jaws can force the workpiece to bow away from the clamp.

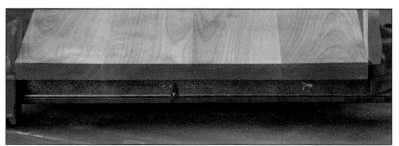

Alternate the grain direction of boards in a glued-up panel. This will help equalize the cupping pressure created as the wood expands and contracts, keeping your panel from warping.

Working with Clamps

If you've ever thought that the only adequate clamps are large pipe clamps fitted with ¾-in. diameter black gas pipe, as many of us have, you've missed out. There is a whole universe of clamps at the modern woodworker's disposal—so much so that for just about any clamping job you're likely to encounter you can probably find a specialty clamp that's just right for the task. While many of these are highly useful, it isn't necessary that you go out and buy every new clamp that pops up on the market. The bottom line is that any clamp that closes the joint tightly is all you really need.

A good rule of thumb when it comes to clamping is to choose the smallest one that will allow you to close the joint. For example, you can use spring-loaded hand clamps to assemble small parts, thin bar clamps on drawers and bentwood laminations, or big pipe clamps on casework projects. Spring-loaded clamps are ideal for small assemblies because they can be used with one hand and moved easily from place to place along a glue line. A good selection of clamps for a modest shop would include a dozen or so of the 3-in. (jaw opening) spring clamps, and perhaps four or six of the smaller 1-in. size.

Bar clamps are lighter in weight than pipe clamps and can be positioned with one hand, but you'll need a second hand to tighten them. They exert a fair amount of force, but it's hard to over-tighten them because of the nature of their round grip. They are ideal for medium-sized assemblies like drawers, single joints (like a mortise and tenon) and other spots where a pipe clamp is overkill. Four bar clamps in the 30-in. range would be a good place to start your own collection.

Pipe clamps consist of cast iron fittings that are made to fit ½-in., ¾-in. and 1-in. inside-diameter threaded pipe. The ¾-in. size in by far the most popular because the ½-in. version tends to bow a little under stress (especially when the pipe is over 2-ft. long), and the 1-in. size is a little cumbersome. Pressure is applied by means of a T-shaped

Use attachable pads for hands-free clamping

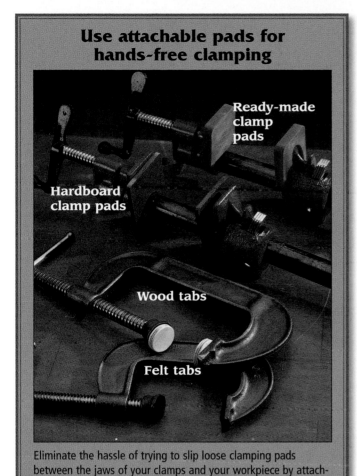

Ready-made clamp pads

Hardboard clamp pads

Wood tabs

Felt tabs

Eliminate the hassle of trying to slip loose clamping pads between the jaws of your clamps and your workpiece by attaching pads directly to your clamps or clamp jaws. Hot-glue tabs of wood or felt to C-clamp jaws. Slip ready-made clamp pads on the heads of your bar clamps, or make your own bar-clamp pads by drilling 1-in.-dia. holes in pieces of scrap hardboard.

Alternate clamping pressure. When edge-gluing boards to make glued-up panels, alternate your clamps above and below the workpiece to distribute clamping pressure evenly along all the joints. It's a good idea to clamp wood cauls across the joints as well when you are not reinforcing the panel with wood biscuits. Cauls keep the boards aligned.

Use tape for light-duty clamping. Electrical tape, shown above, has adequate holding power for low-pressure clamping chores but will not leave residue or lift splinters when you remove it.

handle that allows you to exert an enormous amount of torque. Both black and galvanized pipe are strong enough to build pipe clamps, but the zinc on galvanized pipe tends to crumble a bit under stress and that can allow the fitting to slip. Either way, thoroughly clean any pipe you buy because it is coated with grease or oil to prevent rust. This oily residue can play havoc with the finishing process on wood surfaces. Start with four 3-ft.-long and four 5-ft.-long pipe clamps. It's a good idea to use plastic pads on your bar and pipe clamps to prevent denting the wood.

A few other clamps to start your collection include: a strap clamp or two for clamping irregularly-shaped pieces, a few clamping wood screws and several C-clamps.

Fixed clamp heads meet in middle

Shop-built clamp extender

Two ways to extend the reach of your pipe clamps. For those occasions when you get caught short during glue-up, here are two clever ways to get more reach out of your pipe clamps. If you have two clamps that are both too short, arrange the fixed heads so they meet in the middle: the clamping pressure will hold them together. Or, you can build a clamp extender like the one above from scrap wood.

Assembling Projects

The final element in successful project assembly is to have a logical plan. Even though assembly takes place toward the end of the project, you must give it some thought as early as the design phase. Some workpieces will be in the way if they are installed too early, while others won't fit in a confined space if they are brought to the assembly too late.

As you make a list of the order in which parts can be assembled, keep some tried and true guidelines in mind. You need to build the project in such a way that, as each piece is added, you are erecting a stable structure that can stand on its own and bear the weight of each new, added part. Such a structure will free your hands to work, rather than force you to constantly balance various elements.

A pair of 2 × 4s stretched across a couple of sawhorses is a much better support than a workbench. Such an arrangement allows you clear access to all of the project, including the bottom. It also provides better access for sanding and finishing.

Large cabinet and furniture jobs are usually constructed in several parts and assembled on site. This process, known as staging, means that a woodworker can move a big job around the shop or transport it to the site by himself. Sometimes this breakdown is necessary to get a project through doors, up stairs or even into the back of a vehicle. Plan your large project so that it has logical break points: for example, a bookcase could be made with an 18-in. deep base unit with solid doors, and a 12-in. deep upper unit with glass doors. When the two are installed, the joint could be disguised with a molding.

In casework, it is generally most logical to begin by assembling the sides of a cabinet to the bottom (and top, if there is one), then installing the back. After that comes the face frame, and finally the drawers and doors. Before any of these parts are assembled, drill the sides for shelf supports and apply finish to the inside faces of all panels. It can be difficult to get a drill or a paintbrush into a confined space after assembly.

The elements in a case must must be square to one another. By establishing a core structure that is square and plumb, you can use it throughout the assembly process as a reference when installing the ensuing parts.

Dry-fit all parts before gluing them in place. The importance of this can't be over-stressed. It's better to discover a problem right away than to continue working through it and compound the error. Not only do you need to dry-fit the

PROJECT ASSEMBLY TIPS

Label the parts. Once you've dry-fit your project to your satisfaction, label the parts before disassembling, especially on projects that have a lot of similar pieces. Instead of writing on the parts, tack a little tape on each piece.

Use spacers. Borrow a trick from the deckbuilding trades and use spacers to maintain even spacing between slats or any other parts that should have a uniform reveal.

In furniture building, try to build from the inside out. For example, assemble a table by constructing the apron first, then attaching the legs. Follow this with bracing or rungs, then install the top. Finish up with any decorative elements.

part you will glue next, but you must also fit the parts that will be installed after it, if possible. A good way to do this is to use clamps to hold each part in place while you fit the next part. Doing such a dry fit will throw a spotlight on any assembly sequence problems. For example, if you clamp two parts together and can't install the third (perhaps because the groove it fits in is no longer accessible), you've just discovered that the assembly sequence must change. If you hadn't done a dry-fit, the first two parts would already be glued together and it would be too late to make changes.

In furniture building, try to build from the inside out. For example, begin building a table by constructing the apron, then attach the legs. Follow this with bracing or rungs, then install the top. Finish up with any decorative elements.

Take advantage of the assembly process to cut down on the amount of preparation required before finishing. Sand as many parts as possible before they are installed—that is, when they are most accessible. In many cases, you can even stain and finish most of the parts before you glue them into place. Just be sure that you don't apply finish on areas that will receive glue, such as tenons (use masking tape to protect those areas).

A good tip for the glue-up is to score a small V-groove around the edge of glue joints before assembling them. This groove, cut freehand with a utility knife, should be just out of sight. It will trap excess glue squeeze-out.

Practice staging. Build larger projects in components that can be assembled on site. Called staging, this practice can be helpful even for smaller projects. Sometimes it's easier to conceive of a project as several smaller assemblies.

Drill adjustable shelf holes before assembling casework projects. Once the project is together you'll find it's much harder to gain access with a drill. In the photo above, the project is also being held together with bar clamps during the assembly process—a good way to make sure the parts stay square.

Making Joints & Assembling Projects   131

Brace yourself. It's much easier to assemble projects when they are stable and positioned close to their intended orientation to the ground. For example, in the photo above a brace is clamped to an adirondack chair seat, holding it at the same angle it will rest once the legs are attached. This makes attaching the legs a much simpler procedure.

Attach the face frame last. When building casework, it is most important to get the carcase assembled so it is exactly square. Once the carcase is together and squared up, you can fit the face frame over it, making slight adjustments as needed.

Assembling drawers & doors

Drawer assembly requires a little thought, too. Assemble the sides to the front, slide the bottom in place, and then attach the back. In most cases, it's a good idea to trim the back so it is ½-in. smaller in height than the sides or front: this means that it can sit on top of the bottom panel—a real plus when a drawer bottom needs replacing. Then you won't have to disassemble an entire glued-up drawer to replace the one part that always seems to wear out. To secure the drawer back, make the bottom panel a little longer and attach it to the bottom edge of the back with brads or pins. In drawer building, some parts shouldn't even get cut or milled until other parts are installed. For example, a drawer opening should be established and built before you begin measuring stock to build the drawer. And glass lite panels should never be cut until the frame that will hold them is completely assembled.

To assemble a door with a floating panel insert, attach the sides of the frame (the stiles) to the top rail with glue and clamps. Then, slide the panel into its grooves (don't glue it in place as it needs to move a little to deal with changes in humidity). Glue and clamp the bottom rail in place. Always finish floating panels before installing them: if you don't, there will be an unfinished line down each edge when the panel shrinks.

Mask off parts that will receive glue when pre-finishing the project parts. The finishing products will prevent the glue from penetrating into the mating parts of the joint, and the joint will fail.

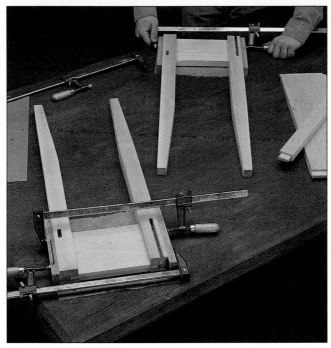

Assemble in subassemblies. Identify logical organizations of related project parts and join them into subassemblies. Then, treat the subassemblies as separate parts when you assemble the project into its finished form.

Work at a comfortable height. Most workbenches are too high for assembling anything other than the smallest projects. This can cause back strain and can make it difficult to see the parts well. A pair of sawhorses really come in handy as an assembly stage.

Finish first. There are several good reasons to apply finishing products to the parts before assembling them: access is better; you can paint or topcoat all parts in a horizontal position to eliminate dripping; on exterior projects, you can get paint or protective topcoating on the ends and edges of parts that will be concealed after assembly.

Check and check again. Getting your project square is crucial to success. An easy way to check a carcase for square is to measure the diagonals (the distances between opposite corners). If the distances are not the same, adjust your clamping pressure and shift the parts until the diagonals match.

Applying Finishes

Applying finish to a project serves several purposes: It provides a protective coating to the wood, making it more resistant to the effects of sunlight, stains, dings and moisture damage. It also helps wood maintain a more even level of moisture equilibrium; finished wood will expand and contract less dramatically with changes in humidity and temperature. But the really satisfying part of finishing is how it accentuates the depth, luster and beauty of wood. It's here that the wood you've patiently cut and shaped comes to life.

Many, many finish options are available to you, and picking a suitable one for your project may seem like a real dilemma. Then comes the fear of practicing bad technique and ruining all of your hard work anyway.

Although it might feel like much is at stake when it comes to finishing, take heart. Once you know your product options and a few time-honored finishing techniques, finishing will become much more reliable, easy and enjoyable. We'll cover these bases in the pages to follow.

Before you begin any finishing task, here are few general introductory tips to keep in mind: First, work in an orderly and logical manner (See *Five Steps to Wood Finishing,* upper right) in a clean, dry and warm environment. Finishing products perform best when applied between 65 to 75° F. Both the finish and the

project should be at room temperature for best results.

Second, follow product application instructions carefully, especially suggested drying times. Shortening the drying time causes all sorts of problems. Some finishes will take even longer to dry in cold or damp environments, so be patient between coats.

Third, practice on samples. Apply the stain and top-coat you've chosen to actual cut-offs from your project lumber. This way you'll know exactly how the finish influences the color and grain pattern of the wood. The larger your samples are, the better.

Finally, work safety. Most finishes are hazardous. They may be flammable, toxic if swallowed, harmful to breathe or a skin irritant. Wear gloves, protective clothing, a respirator approved for fumes and safety glasses.

> ## Five steps to wood finishing:
> 1 **Smooth and level wood surfaces.**
> 2 **Color the wood with stain.**
> 3 **Fill the pores.**
> 4 **Apply a finish, sanding between coats.**
> 5 **Rub out the finish.**

Smoothing Wood Surfaces

Careful surface preparation is critical to producing a professional-looking wood finish. In a nutshell, it involves leveling and smoothing wood surfaces so that finishing materials spread evenly. It removes blade and bit marks as well as burns left from the machining process, which otherwise would show through the finish. Surface prep also corrects minor defects like small dents, gouges and scratches.

There are two categories of tools used for smoothing wood surfaces: Cutting tools such as hand planes and scrapers or abrasives like sandpaper. Abrasives are used more often by beginners because the products are inexpensive and don't require sharpening or tuning in order to work properly. Planes

Surface preparation tools include putty knives, an assortment of abrasives (sanding sponges, pads and paper of various grits), random-orbit or other motorized sanders and flexible metal cabinet scrapers.

THREE-STEP SANDING TECHNIQUE

Start sanding diagonally at roughly a 35-45° angle to the grain with 80- or 100-grit sandpaper (A). This levels the wood surface more efficiently than sanding with the grain. Once you've sanded the entire surface, switch to the opposite angle and repeat (B). Finish leveling the surface by sanding with the grain (C). Switch to 150-grit sandpaper and sand with the grain until all the scratches from the previous grit are gone. Remove any remaining scratches with 220-grit paper, sanding with the grain.

DUST-FREE SMOOTHING OPTION

Cabinet scrapers are pieces of spring steel that are held on-edge and pulled or pushed across boards to scrape the wood surface smooth. To accomplish this purpose, the steel edges are first filed square, then turned over with a burnishing tool to produce a fine burr. A scraper is held with both hands, flexed slightly and either pulled or pushed along the surface of a board with the tool held at an angle to the wood. The burr peels off delicate shavings of wood, producing a silky-smooth surface that is ready for finishing. Cabinet scrapers are excellent surface prep tools, and they're a cleaner alternative to abrasives, which produce plenty of dust. But maintaining and using scrapers effectively takes practice. Abrasives are a better choice for beginners—they're easy to use, inexpensive and maintenance free.

and scrapers, the choice of many professionals, shave, rather than abrade wood surfaces. Many professional finishers will argue that these tools produce the smoothest surfaces for finishes. However, both hand planes and scrapers must be kept extremely sharp to work properly, which is a skill in itself.

If you are just beginning your woodworking hobby, turn to abrasives instead for surface preparation. Abrasives are available in flat sandpaper sheets, discs, rolls, cushioned blocks and cords and can be used by hand or machine to level and smooth wood surfaces. Three different types, designated by the type of abrasive, are used in finishing. Garnet, a natural mineral, is used for hand-sanding applications and is available only in sheets. Aluminum oxide, a synthetic abrasive, is available in a wider variety of styles and is used for hand- or machine sanding. It's tougher and longer-lasting than garnet because the abrasive particles break as you use them, exposing fresh cutting edges. Silicon carbide, another synthetic abrasive, is even tougher than aluminum oxide. You'll find it most commonly sold as black or gray-colored wet/dry sandpaper in grits above 150. It is used in conjunction with a lubricant, typically water, to smooth away minor surface irregularities between coats of finish.

Basic sanding technique

You may be surprised to learn that it's possible to over-sand or sand to too fine a grit, which actually seals the pores of the wood so finishes won't penetrate properly. The other end of the spectrum is not sanding evenly or to a grit fine enough to remove all surface irregularities and scratches—the result of impatience.

Whether you sand by hand or with a machine, the goal is the same. First, level the surface and remove machining marks with coarse-grit paper (80- or 100-grit is a good place to start). Then switch to 150- and finally 220-grit paper until the surface is smooth and free of scratches. In most cases, 220-grit is as fine a paper as you'll need to use. Finer grits produce only subtle improvements in surface smoothness and require more sanding time and effort. Adopt the three-step sanding technique illustrated on this page to make sanding an efficient and methodical process.

Try to accomplish your surface preparation while you build. Sanding is more problematic once the project is assembled, because the surfaces of some parts will be rendered inaccessible by other project parts.

Once your project surfaces are leveled and smooth, thoroughly remove all dust, dirt and sanding debris from the wood pores by wiping with mineral spirits, vacuuming or blowing with compressed air. Then apply the final topcoat as soon as possible. If your project sits in the shop for several days or weeks after sanding, the raw wood will attract dust and dirt, which will contaminate the finish.

Despite your best sanding efforts, it's easy to miss subtle scratches that will show up clearly once you apply a finish. Avoid this problem by positioning a desk light directly behind your workpiece and at the same level after sanding. From the opposite side, view across the worksurface—any shadows the light produces indicate areas that need more sanding. You can also wipe the wood with mineral spirits, which will highlight scratches and imperfections in the wood without raising the grain. Touch up missed areas with more sanding and check the surface again.

STEAMING OUT DENTS

Some dents and dings are too deep to sand away but too shallow to fill with putty. One solution to try is to place a clean, water-dampened (not wet) rag over the trouble spot, then rub with a hot iron to steam the wood. Steam will penetrate and swell the wood fibers to remove or minimize the defect. Be sure to sand the spot once it dries—steam will raise the wood grain.

Filling dents & holes

To conceal more severe dents and cover holes left by nail or screw heads, one option is to fill the recess with wood putty before applying your finish. Wood putty is sold in oil-, water- and solvent-based forms resembling pre-mixed paste or dough (it's sometimes called wood dough). You can even buy it in powdered form and mix up only what you need. Water-based putty is most common and generally the easiest to use.

The trick to puttying is to apply it exactly where you want it; once it penetrates open pores, it's difficult to remove and will be visible when a finish is applied. Also, wood putty seldom absorbs wood stain like wood, and the contrast may be quite dramatic (See tint box, below). To minimize the contrast and hide filled areas, use a putty that closely matches the finished color of the wood with stain applied. Try the putty and stain combination on project scraps first, to test the results. If the recesses are small enough, you may even want to apply finish first, then do your puttying.

Tinted vs. untinted wood putty

Untinted wood putty stained with rest of project

Tinted wood putty applied to project after staining

The best method to conceal nail and screw heads with wood putty has been debated for generations. Try filling holes with putty tinted to match the finished color of the surrounding wood, rather than applying untinted putty first, then staining. Untinted putty may absorb more stain than the surrounding wood, making the repairs conspicuous.

Fill nail or screw holes, knots and other surface defects with wood putty. Apply the putty until its surface is slightly higher than the surrounding wood. Allow the putty to dry thoroughly, then sand it flat.

Pigment stains   Dye stains

All stains are designed to color wood, but how well they perform on your project depends on which category of stain you use. Pigment stains, the most common variety you'll find in home centers and hardware stores, are best suited for woods like oak, ash and walnut, with large pores and open grain that trap the stain pigment. Dye stains are sold premixed or as concentrated dye powder that you mix with water or alcohol. They are better suited for tight-grained woods like maple, which cannot trap pigment as well. When it comes to identifying stain categories, product labels can be confusing, so test a stain on scrap before committing it to your project.

APPLYING WOOD STAINS

1 To apply stain, first mix it thoroughly, especially if it's pigment-based, to suspend the pigment particles. Be sure your project surface is clean and dry with no traces of glue (glue will not absorb stain). Wipe stain over the entire surface with a lint-free cloth, or apply it with a brush.

2 Allow the stain to penetrate into the wood for a minute or two (see the instructions on the container), then wipe away the excess. For a darker wood tone, repeat the application procedure before the stain dries.

Applying Wood Stains

Stains are liquids that color wood without hiding the grain or figure. A host of products are sold under the blanket term "stains," but stains can be divided into two groups—pigment stains and dye stains—because each type has different application characteristics.

Pigment stains. Pigment stains are the most common type of stain available and are composed of three main ingredients: a dry colored powder, a thinner (or *carrier*) that suspends the powder and a *binder,* which is a resin that envelopes the pigment and sticks it to the wood surface. Colored pigments are either mined from the earth or synthetic. Thinner is a liquid that's compatible with the binder and can be solvent- or water-based The binder generally is linseed oil, varnish or acrylic.

Dye stains. Most pigment particles are large enough to be seen with a magnifying glass. Dye, on the other hand, is a powder with particles thousands of times smaller than pigments. Once dissolved in a carrier like water, alcohol or mineral spirits, dyes will not come out of solution and settle out as pigments will, and they need no binding agent. Dye stains are available through woodworking stores or catalogs and come pre-mixed or as powders or concentrates that you mix with a solvent.

Pigment and dye stains color wood differently. Pigment stains are best suited for open-grained woods with large pores, such as oak, ash, walnut and mahogany. The pores trap the pigment, and it colors them darker than the flat grain in between. Close-grained, dense woods like hard maple are difficult to stain with pigments because nothing traps the pigment particles.

Dye stain, on the other hand, colors even hard, dense woods like maple much better, because the dye solution easily penetrates the wood fibers. Some manufacturers

Pigment and dye stains color wood differently. Notice in the pigment-stained sample (left) how the porous wood grain is darker than the surrounding flat grain. The contrast between the pores and flat grain is more subtle in the dye-stained sample (right), because the dye penetrates the porous and flat-grained areas evenly.

combine both dye and pigment components in their stains to provide benefits of both stain categories. Dye stains are usually indicated as such on the label or are sold as "NGR" (non-grain-raising) stains. If the product label does not specify, the stain likely is pigment-based or a combination of pigment and dye.

Staining technique

The goal of staining is to produce an even color across the wood. Whether you use pigments or dyes, apply them the same way. Quickly wipe or brush stain over the entire wood surface, then wipe off the excess with a clean, lint-free rag. The amount of *open time* (the period of time before the stain starts to dry) you have to work with the stain is important. Oil-based products evaporate more slowly than water- or alcohol-based stains, allowing you ample time to apply and then wipe off the stain evenly. For this reason, they're easier for the beginning finisher to control.

As long as the stain is still wet, you have several options if the color you're getting is not the color you want. To lighten a stain, wipe the wood surface with the same solvent that's listed on the label for "Clean-up" (often it's mineral spirits). If the color is still too dark, scrub the surface lightly with a fine, synthetic pad and more solvent. To darken a stain, wipe a darker-colored stain over the surface. If you're using a dye that you've mixed from concentrate, make a stronger dye solution by adding more dye to darken the color.

To change stain color, apply a different-colored stain over the first coat of stain while it's still wet.

Controlling stain penetration

The number one problem with staining is a condition known as *blotching*. Certain woods, especially softwoods like pine and some hardwoods like cherry, poplar and soft maple will stain unevenly, due to variations in density at the wood surface. There are two

Stain controllers

Stain controllers, sold under a variety of product names, are actually thinned finishes intended to minimize the blotching effects of stain on raw wood. Apply stain controller first, then stain the wood while the controller is still wet.

EFFECT OF STAIN CONTROLLERS

Liquid stain applied over untreated pine veneer looks blotchy and dark. Blotchiness is the result of uneven stain penetration on woods that lack an even surface grain density.

Liquid stain applied over pine veneer treated with a wash coat of stain controller has more even color penetration and is lighter in tone.

Gel stain applied over untreated pine veneer also provides more even color penetration, since gel stains do not penetrate wood surfaces as deeply as liquid stains.

solutions to this problem. First, use a gel stain. Gel stains are thick pigment stains that contain less solvent to limit the depth of stain penetration.

The second remedy for avoiding blotching is to use a stain controller (also known as *wood conditioner*) before applying the stain. Stain controllers absorb into into and seal the surface of the wood, which evens out stain absorption.

When choosing a stain controller, it's important to match the type of controller to the stain you are using—oil-based controllers work best with oil-based stains, while water-based controllers are intended for water-based stains. You can also thin a topcoat (shellac, varnish or lacquer) with its solvent to a 50/50 concentration to serve as a wood conditioner.

Applying stain controller is easy. Wipe or brush oil-based controllers generously onto the wood surface, wipe off the excess after 15 minutes, then immediately apply the stain. If you use a shellac or lacquer-based controller, it should dry for at least one hour before applying the stain. The stain should not be alcohol- or lacquer-based or it will re-dissolve the conditioner. Regardless of the conditioner you choose, it's a good idea to try the conditioner and stain together first on scrap. For particularly blotchy woods, you can also use a stain controller followed by a gel stain.

Filling Wood Pores

One finishing decision you may want to make, depending on the wood species, is how to treat the wood pores. Woods like oak, ash, mahogany and walnut have deep, open pores that will be visible after a topcoat is applied unless you fill them first. You don't have to fill the pores, and leaving them open in the finishing process produces an open-pored finish. Open-pored finishes have a more natural, less elegant look

Apply paste wood filler if you want to create a smooth finish on your project without the pores showing through. Spread the filler over project surfaces with a brush and remove the excess with a scraper. Depending on the product, you can fill pores before or after staining.

that many woodworkers prefer. If you want a glass-smooth, closed-pore finish, where the pores do not show through, you could lay on multiple coats of a finish like varnish to fill the pores. A better method is to use paste wood filler. It's available in water- or oil-based formulas, in "natural" or colored tints. The consistency of products called "wood fillers" may vary, and some actually are wood putty, not wood filler. (For more on wood putty, see page 137). You'll know you've got a true wood filler if it flows like thick glue. "Natural" wood filler generally is an off-white color intended to downplay the pores, blending them in with the surrounding wood. Natural fillers are best suited

THE EFFECT OF WOOD FILLERS ON GRAIN COLOR

No filler: This sample of mahogany plywood was simply stained and topcoated with varnish. No wood filler was used. Depending on how porous the wood is, pores may show through as dimples in the finish.

"Natural" filler: When wood pores are filled with "natural" tinted wood filler, the effect lightens the wood tone overall and evens out the contrast between porous areas and the surrounding flat grain.

Dark filler: Dark wood filler accentuates the wood pores and creates a contrast quite different from the unfilled sample at far left. Dark wood fillers are best suited for darker woods like walnut, cherry or oak.

for blonde woods like ash. Colored fillers are made with pigment and they're used to highlight the pores for more dramatic texture.

Applying wood fillers

When and how you apply wood fillers depends on the type of filler. Water-based filler is best applied to bare wood, allowed to dry and then sanded off. It can then be colored with alcohol or NGR dye stains. Oil-based filler can be applied to bare or stained wood. Once applied, however, it will not take stain, so it's important to select the filler color carefully to achieve the effect you want if you apply filler after stain.

To apply water-based filler, brush it liberally onto the wood surface, pumping the brush to help force the filler into the pores. Remove the excess with a rubber squeegee or piece of cardboard, drawing the tool diagonally across the wood grain to keep from pulling the filler out of the pores. Let the filler dry for at least one day. Using 220-grit sandpaper, sand the excess filler until the wood surface is clean but the pores are still

> Wood filler serves two purposes: It levels the wood pores for finish and either accentuates or blends them with the surrounding grain.

filled. Once you've sanded, the wood surface may look chalky, but this will disappear as soon as you apply stain or a clear topcoat. Any finish can be applied over a water-based filler.

If you plan to use an oil-based filler over stained wood, protect the stain color with a sealer coat before applying filler. Use shellac or varnish cut 50/50 with thinner as the seal coat, and let the sealer dry. Lightly sand with 400-grit sandpaper, then brush the filler liberally onto the wood and immediately remove as much of the excess as you can with a rubber squeegee. Wait until the filler hazes over (usually about 15 minutes). Using a piece of burlap, terry cloth or cotton, wipe away the haze, working across the grain. When the wood is clean (the filler should remain in the pores), let the surface dry for at least two days, and longer if you are working in cool conditions. Lightly sand the dried filler with 400-grit paper before applying a clear finish. Shellac, varnish and lacquer can be applied over an oil-based filler, but some water-based finishes may not adhere properly. If in doubt, seal the filler with a coat of de-waxed shellac before applying finish.

HOW TO APPLY WOOD FILLER

1 Brush a heavy coat of wood filler onto the wood surface, pressing the filler into the pores. Work quickly.

2 Remove excess filler before it dries by dragging a rubber squeegee, plastic wallboard knife or piece of stiff cardboard across the surface, diagonally to the wood grain. For oil-based fillers, wipe the surface clean with a coarse cloth, such as burlap.

3 Allow the surface to dry thoroughly. Lightly sand away the remaining filler, being careful not to sand so much that you remove filler from the wood pores. Then, depending on the filler type, apply stain and/or a clear finish.

Choosing Finishes

Walk down the finishing products aisle of your local home center and you'll find no shortage of options. Twenty years ago there were far fewer wood finishes available to consumers. But since woodworking continues to be one of the fastest growing hobbies, finish manufacturers are ever reformulating and repackaging their products to be more versatile, durable and easier for home woodworkers to apply. You'll find oil-based and water-based finishes; products that brush on, wipe on or spray on. Some contain a stain component and claim to be "all in one." But all of these products are intended for topcoating wood. How do you choose one over the next?

It's helpful to first break finishes into some manageable categories and examine their characteristics. You'll see that different finishes offer varying degrees of protection, durability and ease of application. Plus, they produce different visual effects once applied. So, choosing a finish is about trade-offs. Pick the finish that best suits the needs of each project you build.

The moment of truth: A carefully chosen wood finish not only protects your project, it also can have a transformational quality; what was an assembly of wood parts now magically becomes a piece of furniture. Finish brings out the unique character, luster and depth of wood.

'True' oils

Numerous products are hyped as "oil" finishes, but they're usually a mixture of oil, varnish and other solvents. The "true" finishing oils are a small group consisting of three main types: boiled linseed oil, pure tung oil and mineral oil (often called butcher block or salad bowl oil). Linseed and tung oil will form a solid film when exposed to air; mineral oil will not. This drying quality makes tung and linseed oil finishes more resistant to moisture and abrasion, but they're not nearly as durable as varnishes. Since mineral oil doesn't dry, it can leave an oily film if applied too heavily, but it won't crack or peel and is a safe alternative for wood that comes in contact with food.

True oils are inexpensive, easy to apply with a rag or brush and are great for adding depth and luster to wood. Oiled finishes are a snap to repair, too; just wipe with more oil to make minor scratches disappear. True oils do not dry as hard as other finishes, and they are soft and gummy if you try to build them to a thick finish. They also require some maintenance. Plan to reapply oiled finishes annually or when the wood looks dry.

Varnish

'Varnish' is an inexact term and has meant different things over time. By today's standards, varnish refers to finishes that are made from hard, durable synthetic

resins like alkyd, phenolic and urethane. These resins are heated with tung and linseed oils as well as other semi-drying oils like safflower and soya to produce a product that is much more durable than oil alone. Hybrid, water-based versions are blended with acrylic instead of oil. Varnishes dominate the consumer-grade finish market.

There are two general groupings of varnish, depending on the percentage of oil in the finish. "Long-oil" varnishes, which contain more oil, are soft and flexible. They're sold as marine varnishes, spar varnishes and exterior varnishes, because the film they form is better suited to expand and contract with the wood. "Short-oil" varnishes dry to a harder, less elastic film. Though either type can be used for interior applications, short-oils polish better.

Varnishes are typically applied with a brush, though highly thinned and gell versions can be applied with a rag or even sprayed.

Oil/varnish blends

Oil/varnish blends are mixtures of oil with a small amount of varnish. The resulting products have some of the qualities of true oils (like ease of wiping) but are enhanced to an extent by the protective qualities of varnish. Unlike varnish, which is formed from the chemical reaction between oil and resin, think of oil/varnish blends as varnish thinned with a lot of oil.

Oil/varnish blend finishes are less glossy than varnish finishes, and they lack the full degree of moisture and scratch protection offered by varnish. Watco ™, Danish oil, Teak oil, Nordic oils and a host of the other finishes sold as oil finishes fall into this category.

Lacquer

The term "lacquer" refers to a fast-drying, glossy, hard finish containing flammable solvents. It is still considered by many professionals to be the best all-around finish for wood as it imparts depth and richness, has moderate to excellent durability (depending on the type used) and rubs out well.

Nitrocellulose lacquers are the most common lacquer you'll find—if the label on the can says lacquer, it's this type. Lacquer is one of the hardest finishes for beginners to apply successfully. It's best applied with specialized spray equipment in a fire-proof spray booth and is difficult to brush. Aerosol lacquer is easier to use, although it's an expensive route to take for large objects.

Shellac

While you might think of shellac as a canned liquid, it actually refers to a natural resin derived from the secretions of an insect that feeds off trees indigenous to India and Thailand. The secretion, gathered in cocoon form, is refined into dry flakes which are then dissolved in alcohol to make the shellac solution that winds up in cans at the store. The pre-mixed variety is available in orange (amber) and clear (which is shellac that's been bleached). Shellac is also sold in flake form that you can mix yourself with denatured alcohol. Shellac flakes come in a wider range of colors and wax content than the pre-mixed variety. The more wax shellac contains, the less resistant it will be to water. If you use shellac as a sanding sealer before applying a topcoat (See page 148), the wax it contains may keep some finishes from bonding to it.

Shellac has been a popular wood finish for almost two centuries. It dries rapidly, is non-toxic once it dries and is easy to touch up later. The downside to shellac finishes is that they can be damaged by alcohol, strong household cleaners and excessive heat. Shellac can be wiped on or brushed, and you'll get the best results when you apply multiple, thin coats. Because the finish

dries rapidly, you can apply two or three thin coats easily in a day. Use a 2-lb. cut of shellac when wiping or brushing (See *Mixing Shellac*, below).

Once mixed, shellac has a shelf life of about six months or so (when mixed fresh) to three years for the pre-mixed varieties. Always try to use the freshest solution possible; the longer it sits mixed, the more time it will take for shellac to dry to a hard film.

Which finish is best?

No single finish excels in all areas, and choosing the right one for your project can be a bit perplexing. The best general-purpose finish is oil-based polyurethane. It's easy to apply, looks good, resists wear and tear and requires no maintenance. But don't shy away from trying other finish options, too. To help you choose, consider the following kinds of questions:

1. How will the project be used? Outdoor projects require a finish that performs differently than the topcoat on an end table or salad bowl. Think carefully about how your project will be used and what demands that use places on your finish.

On projects that won't be subjected to feisty two-year-olds or excessive sun or moisture, consider using lacquer, shellac, oil, or oil-varnish blends. You may want to simply wipe on a couple coats of paste furniture wax and leave your finish at that. All of these finishes are easy to repair if they get scratched. Be aware that paste wax, oils, shellac, lacquer and some water-based finishes can be damaged if exposed to water for extended periods of time. Shellac is also not resistant to alkalis like ammonia, and lacquer will break down in the presence of alcohols.

There is no "best" finish for items that come in contact with food. Mineral oil (also sold as "salad bowl oil") will not go rancid and is a great choice for treating cutting boards. A good option for food baskets and bowls is several coats of de-waxed shellac. It seals the

MIXING SHELLAC

Mixing a ratio of dry shellac flakes with denatured alcohol is called *cutting*. Different cuts are required for accomplishing specific finishing tasks. The most common cut, when shellac is used as a topcoat, is called a 2-lb. cut. Technically, this means 2 pounds of shellac flakes dissolved in a gallon of denatured alcohol. For practicality's sake, and to keep your mixture fresh, dissolve 4 oz. (by weight of dry shellac) to 1 pint of alcohol for a 2-lb. cut. Store-bought pre-mixed shellac in a can is typically sold as a 3-lb. cut, which should be reduced first to a 2-lb cut by adding 1 qt. of mixed shellac to ¾ pint of denatured alcohol. Refer to the can or flake container for mixing other cuts.

wood against water and can be wiped clean with a damp cloth. Shellac is an excellent finish for toys that children may put in their mouths. Some water-based varnishes are also child-safe; check the label carefully.

Actually, all wood finishes are non-toxic when fully cured, despite what you may have read or heard. Once the solvents evaporate from the finish, the cured film is safe enough for contact with food. This does not mean that the finish itself is safe to gobble up. It means that additives such as driers or plasticizers are encapsulated enough so that they do not migrate into what you're eating.

The best finish for outdoor projects is oil-based marine spar varnish. This tung oil/phenolic resin varnish holds up well to the elements, and it expands and contracts somewhat as the wood moves. Harsh conditions like direct sunlight may require sanding and recoating the project every few years. Specialized marine varnishes for boats have additives that make them even more resistant to sunlight and moisture, but they may be triple the cost of commonly available spar varnishes. For naturally weather-resistant woods like cedar, white oak, redwood and teak, you may want to forego a finish altogether and let the wood "weather".

2. How do you want the wood to look? For natural-looking, "close-to-the-wood" finishes, wipe on several coats of tung or linseed oil or use an oil-varnish blend. However, any finish—shellac, lacquer or varnish—can produce this effect as long as you don't build up the finish beyond several coats. Also, thin the finish with its appropriate solvent and it will flow more evenly into the pores.

For an elegant, glass-smooth finish that accentuates depth and luster, choose a hard, film-forming finish like shellac, lacquer or varnish. Be sure to fill the pores first (See *Filling Pores*, page 140). As a general rule, oils and oil-based varnishes build luster best, followed by solvent-based lacquers and shellac.

The color and penetration of the finish may be an issue worth considering. Some varnishes and orange shellac may impart an amber color that's too dark for woods you may want to keep as light as possible, like maple or birch. Water-based polyurethane tends to lay on wood surfaces rather than penetrate in, which has the effect of keeping the wood tone lighter, but the wood may end up looking dull and cold instead.

3. How clean, warm and dry is your shop? If your finishing environment is cold or filled with dust, fast-drying finishes like spray-on lacquer and shellac are good choices. Dust falling into the finish does not pose as great a problem as slow-drying finishes like oil-based varnish. Shellac and lacquer are the least temperamental when it comes to curing in cold temperatures, and they can be modified with additives (retarders) for use in hot and humid conditions as well.

CHOOSING FINISHES

Outdoor projects, like this occasional table, are subject to the damaging effects of UV sunlight and moisture. Use a marine or exterior varnish for wood on outdoor projects that requires a clear finish. The varnish film is flexible enough to move with the wood as it expands and contracts.

Cutting boards, salad bowls and other projects that come in contact with food are good candidates for a coat of non-drying, non-toxic mineral oil. Reapply oil more frequently if the project is subject to frequent washings.

Desks, tables and other furniture that may get scuffed, scratched or moved frequently need a durable finish that still enhances the beauty of the wood. Interior varnish or shellac work well here.

Applying Finish Topcoats

There are three primary techniques for applying a wood finish: brushing, wiping and spraying. We'll cover the basics of each of these application methods on the pages to follow. Choosing an application method is fairly straightforward. If you want to build up a thicker finish that fills the wood pores, or if you have a large project to finish, apply finish with a brush. Wipe on the topcoat if what you're after is a thinner, more natural finish or if the project has many small, confined areas that are hard to reach with a brush. Spray-on finishes, like aerosol varnishes and lacquers are an excellent choice for finishing irregularly shaped or small objects that are difficult to hold and finish at the same time.

Tools for applying finishes include natural and synthetic bristle brushes, foam brushes, short-nap foam pads, and clean, lint-free rags or paper towels.

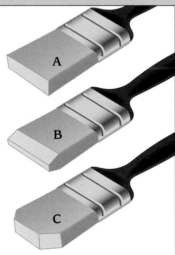
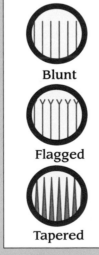

BRISTLE PROFILES

A

B

C

BRISTLE TIPS

Blunt

Flagged

Tapered

Bristle profile and tip shape determine brush performance to a large extent. *Flat profiles* (A) are a bad choice for applying clear finishes because they leave large ridges. Save these brushes for applying stains and paints. Chisel-tip brushes have shorter bristles on the outside and longer bristles in the center. Chiseled bristles are available in *rectangular* (B) or *round* (C) profiles. The chisel tip does a better job of laying down a smooth finish than flat profiles. Bristle tips can be blunt, flagged (bristles have splits at the ends), tapered or a combination of several shapes. Blunt tips, a sign of a cheap brush, tend to leave brush lines in the finish. Better brushes have flagged or tapered tips, which lay down fine, smooth finishes, regardless of brush size.

Tools you'll need

Applying finishes requires a minimal number of tools to produce good results. You'll need bristle and foam brushes, synthetic foam pads and lint-free rags. All are relatively inexpensive and easy to find.

Bristle brushes. Brushes come with either natural or synthetic bristles in a number of shapes and profiles (See *illustrations,* left). Natural bristle brushes are commonly made from Chinese hog hair (China bristle) and are made for use with oils and oil-based varnishes, shellacs and lacquers. Synthetic bristles are made from nylon or polyester and are best suited for applying water-based finishes and paint. It's a good idea to have an assortment of natural and synthetic bristle brushes on hand. If you plan to do a great deal of finishing, buy good-quality brushes, and expect to pay between $10 and $30 per brush. Clean them promptly after each use and they'll last for years. The extra performance and life you'll get out of professional brushes is well worth the cost, and they won't drop bristles in the middle of your finish like cheaper brushes will.

Rags and cloths. Any natural, clean and absorbent material works well for applying stains, but when it comes to finishes, the cloth should be as lint-free as possible. Non-textured paper towels work well, as do old cotton garments like T-shirts.

Foam pads and brushes. Short-nap painting pads and disposable foam brushes work surprisingly well for applying varnishes and water-based finishes. Plus, they're cheap enough to discard once you're through.

Brush finish off the end

Start here and brush to the opposite end

1 Starting about 3 in. in from one end of your workpiece, brush the finish toward the end and off. If you start at the end and brush inward instead, you're liable to get drips along the end.

2 Once you've finished the end of the workpiece, topcoat the rest of the surface. Begin each brush stroke where you started in Step 1, and work to the opposite end, overlapping your brush strokes.

Brushing on a finish

When brushing a finish, try to apply the finish to horizontal surfaces whenever possible, even if it means waiting for some surfaces to dry, then tipping the project on its side to change vertical surfaces to horizontals. If you must apply finish vertically, brush the finish on

CONDITIONING A BRUSH

Before applying a finish, condition the brush by dipping the bristles all the way up to the ferrule (the metal band) in the thinner for the finish you'll be using. Use water for water-base finishes, mineral spirits for oil based varnishes and alcohol for shellac. Remove excess thinner from the bristles with a rag. Conditioning makes the brush easier to clean later.

crosswise, rather than up and down, to minimize drips. Start each new brush stroke by overlapping the wet edges of the previous brush stroke.

Before beginning brushing, make sure the brush is clean by whacking it against your palm or the edge of a table to dislodge any debris or loose bristles. Then condition the brush (See *Conditioning a Brush,* left). It's also a good idea to pour the finish from its original container through a medium mesh or paper strainer into a smaller can to remove any bits of debris that you'll likely brush into the finish.

Dip the brush into the finish halfway up the bristles (never further), bring the brush out of the liquid, press it against the side of the can and let the excess finish drain out. Never scrape the bristles across the lip of the can or you'll introduce air bubbles into the finish. Then brush on the finish following the technique outlined at the top of this page.

Once you've finished an area, smooth away ridges in the finish (called *tipping off*). First, scrape any excess finish from your brush, then lightly drag the tips of the bristles across the finish to smooth it out.

Don't tip off quick-drying finishes like shellacs and lacquers; just get the finish down as smoothly as possible and leave it alone.

To brush a finish using a foam brush or pad, dip the applicator into the finish, let it absorb finish for several seconds, then scrape away the excess. Apply the finish with even strokes, then tip off the finish as you would with a brush.

Avoiding bubbles

Bubbles in the finish are a common problem when brushing on some finishes, especially varnish. Bubbles generally are caused by using the wrong kind of brush (such as a flat, blunt-tipped synthetic bristle brush with oil-based varnish) or applying too thick a finish. To thin the finish, add an ounce or two of thinner per pint of finish. If that doesn't solve the problem, try switching to a china bristle brush. If you still get bubbles, make sure that the finish, the project and the room are all at an ambient temperature of at least 65° F. If all else fails, buy a fresh batch of finish.

Tack cloths

A perfectly clean wood surface is critical to successfully applying wood finishes. Even tiny amounts of dust or grit will be visible on an otherwise smooth finish. The best way to thoroughly clean a wood surface before and during the application of a finish is with a tack cloth. Tack cloths draw fine particles up out of the pores of the wood without leaving any residue behind. You can buy or make them yourself.

Pre-made
tack cloth

Ingredients for
shop-made tack cloths

Tack cloth options. Tack cloths are sold premade and prepackaged at most woodworking stores. You can also make your own by blending small amounts of boiled linseed oil and varnish, then soaking a piece of cheese cloth in the mixture and wringing it out thoroughly. Store tack cloths in a sealed jar for reuse.

Sand between coats of finish with 320- or 400-grit sandpaper to smooth out wood grain that may have been raised by the moisture in the product (especially if using a water-based finish) and to eliminate slight imperfections in the finish. Then wipe the surface thoroughly with a tack cloth to remove all traces of grit before recoating with finish.

Sanding between coats

Sanding between coats of finish is necessary to improve the adhesion of oil-based varnishes and polyurethanes. It also removes slight imperfections in the finish. Use 320- or 400-grit sandpaper and lightly sand all surfaces. You can also abrade the surface with #0000 steel wool. Then remove the dust with a tack cloth. In a pinch, you also can use a piece of cloth sprinkled with varnish.

With lacquer, shellac and some water-based finishes, sanding between coats is only necessary to remove dust nibs or other problems. These finishes dissolve into the previous coat, so there's no need to do this between every coat to promote adhesion.

Applying sanding sealers

If you are finishing particularly oily woods like teak or applying a finish over oil-based stain, you may want to consider brushing on a coat of sanding sealer before applying the finish. Sanding sealer actually is a good first step to prepare any wood for a finish, because it locks in wood fibers so they're easy to sand off when the sealer dries.

You can buy sanding sealer premixed, but it's actually just thinned varnish with a few additives that make the sealer easier to sand. Another sealer option is to brush on a coat of de-waxed shellac. Shellac is a particularly good sealer for woods treated with oil-based or dye stains. Or you can mix up a brew of sanding sealer in the shop by blending a 50/50 mix of oil-based varnish and mineral spirits.

Brush on sealer just as you would a finish, allow it to dry and sand lightly, then apply the final finish coats.

Sanding sealer accomplishes just what its name implies: it seals wood fibers, oils and stains to prepare a surface for sanding. Premixed sanding sealers, de-waxed shellac or a mixture of equal parts varnish and mineral spirits (above photo) all make good sealer coats. Apply sanding sealer with a brush (right photo) just as you would other brushed finishes.

Tips for working with water-based finishes

Water-based finishes, made of combinations of urethane, alkyd and acrylic, are a relatively new category of wood finishes available to woodworkers. They're friendlier to use, from a health standpoint, because the flammable and polluting solvents have been partly replaced by water. Water-based finishes produce fewer fumes when applied, due to lower amounts of solvent, and they clean up easily with soap and water.

Applying a water-based finish isn't much different than applying other finishes with an oil base, but there are a few unique characteristics you should take into account. Since water-based finishes have a lower solvent content, they won't dissolve bits of dried finish that may exist in the can. For this reason, it's important to strain what you plan to use before you brush it on, or the brush will carry bits of debris onto the project.

Water-based finishes also raise wood grain, resulting in a rougher finish texture. There are several ways to avoid unwanted grain raising. You can deliberately raise the grain by wiping the wood with distilled water first, then re-sand it with the last grit in your sanding sequence (220-grit is sufficient). Then apply the finish.

Another good preventive measure for avoiding raised grain is to seal the wood with a coat of de-waxed shellac before applying the first coat of finish.

Strain water-based finishes through a medium mesh or paper filter to remove bits of dried finish that may be present in the can. It's a good idea to strain out only as much finish as you plan to use. Pour what you don't use through a clean strainer back into the original can.

Raise the grain first with distilled water. Wipe project surfaces down using a sponge or rag damped with distilled water and allow the wood to dry. Then sand with 220-grit paper. By deliberately raising the grain and knocking it off, you'll reduce the amount of grain-raising produced by the first finish coat of water-based finish.

Apply a sealer coat of de-waxed shellac: Shellac will seal the wood pores and minimize water absorption. Lightly sand the sealer once it dries to smooth the surface, then topcoat with finish as usual.

When wiping on a finish, use a clean, lint-free rag or paper towel and apply the finish in smooth, even swipes. A desk light positioned behind your work makes it easier to spot and touch up areas you might have missed.

Wiping on a finish

Any finish can be wiped on, but the easiest ones to apply this way are true oils, oil/varnish blends and thinned varnishes. Oil finishes are the easiest, because you simply wipe the finish onto the wood, allow it to soak in for a few minutes, then wipe off the excess. Varnishes are a little more tricky to wipe on, but because they dry harder than oil, they provide more protection.

To wipe on varnish, use a product made specifically for wiping, an oil-varnish blend or just make your own (See *Mixing Your Own Oil/Varnish Blend*, bottom left). Using a piece of cloth or a non-textured paper towel, wipe the varnish on in smooth, even strokes. Overlap each stroke by about 1 in.

Regardless of what finish you choose to wipe on, it helps to work with a light illuminating your project from behind so you can watch for spots you might miss. Also, avoid the temptation to spread the finish on thickly; a thick layer will take much longer to dry.

Mixing your own oil/varnish blend

Many finishers prefer to make their own wiping blends so they know what's in it and can tweak the mixture to suit individual preference. A good general recipe to follow is to mix ⅓ varnish (pick your favorite), ⅓ linseed or tung oil and ⅓ turpentine or mineral spirits. Reduce the amount of oil in the mixture for a quicker-drying finish, or substitute naptha for the turpentine.

Spraying on a finish

Spray-on, aerosol varnishes and lacquers are a good alternative to choose for topcoating intricate or odd-shaped objects that would be tough to hold securely and brush or wipe. Apply thin, even coats of finish to avoid sags and drips.

It's a good idea to wear a respirator approved for fumes, especially when spraying lacquer. Be sure to work in a well-ventilated area as well.

Spray-on finishes are convenient products for topcoating odd-shaped items, like drawer pulls. Nails or screws driven through a piece of scrap provide an easy way to hold these kinds of objects so you can spray them from all sides without touching them.

FLAT SHEEN

Rubbing a finish to a flat sheen involves sanding the surface with 600-grit silicon-carbide sandpaper, lubricated with mineral spirits. Sand edges and corners gently to avoid cutting through the finish.

SATIN SHEEN

Raise the finish to a satin luster by rubbing it with oil soap or thinned furniture paste wax and #0000 steel wool.

GLOSS SHEEN

Switch to automotive rubbing compound, pumice powder or rottenstone and a soft cloth to rub the finish out to a gloss sheen.

Rubbing out a finish

Many woodworkers aren't aware that the final coat of a number of different finishes can be improved by rubbing it out. Rubbing, which amounts to buffing with finer and finer abrasives, removes bits of dust and debris, levels the finish and establishes the sheen you're after. Only hard finishes like shellac, oil-based varnishes and lacquer can be rubbed out; oils and oil/varnish blends cannot be rubbed. The rubbing process is easier to do when the finish is fully hardened, so allow lacquers and shellac to cure for a full week and give oil-based varnishes two weeks. Allow more curing time if you work in humid conditions.

> *Rubbing, the process of buffing a finish with finer and finer abrasives, allows you to adjust the amount of sheen the finish displays.*

To rub out a finish, start by sanding with 600-grit wet/dry silicon-carbide paper, using mineral spirits or soapy water as a lubricant. Then wipe off the residue, and rub the finish with #0000 steel wool. Start with short, choppy strokes near the edges, then rub the surface in long, even strokes. The effect of this rubbing will produce a flat sheen.

To increase the gloss to a satin sheen, use Murphy Oil Soap ™ or furniture paste wax thinned 50% with mineral spirits, and rub with #0000 steel wool. For a gloss sheen, rub the finish with automotive rubbing compound, 4F pumice or rottenstone, a polishing powder available at paint and hardware stores.

Protect your new finish by applying a coat of furniture paste wax. Allow it to dry to a haze, then buff away the residue with a clean, soft cloth.

For added protection, wax the new finish. To apply the wax, wrap a golf-ball-sized lump with cheesecloth (See inset photo) and rub the cheesecloth ball over the finish. When the wax dries, buff off the haze.

GLOSSARY

Air-drying: A method of seasoning lumber in which covered stacks of stickered wood are permitted to dry slowly and naturally outdoors in the open air. Air-dried lumber generally reaches equilibrium at about 12% moisture content. See also: *Kiln drying.*

Apron: The structural rail under the top of a table, the seat of a chair or along the base of a cabinet.

Arts-and-Crafts Movement: An intellectual movement in England and America at the turn of the last century that sought to revive interest in simplicity and hand craftsmanship in the decorative arts as a reaction to the ostentation and the tasteless mass production of the time. See also: *Mission style.*

Bench planes: The wide range of general-purpose hand planes (jack, jointer, etc.) used for all the standard planing tasks: flattening, squaring and smoothing.

Bevel: An edge or end of a workpiece that meets the face at an angle other than 90°. Also refers to cutting such a surface.

Birdseye figure: Wood figure characterized by a pattern of tiny swirly dots, or eyes, caused by distortion of the wood fibers. Common in maple.

Biscuit joining (plate joining)**:** A method of joinery in which compressed wood "biscuits" are fitted into slots cut in mating parts. Biscuit joinery both reinforces the joint and keeps it aligned during assembly.

Blind: A term that refers to a cut or joint that is hidden; it does not extend to an exterior surface.

Block plane: A small variation of the bench plane adapted for one-handed use. Its blade is mounted with the bevel up rather than down, as with a standard bench plane.

Board foot: A unit of lumber measurement, equivalent in volume to a piece of wood 12 in. wide by 12 in. long by 1 in. thick (1 square foot of a 1-in.-thick board).

Bookmatch: A decorative veneering pattern formed by arranging the veneer sheets side by side in the order they come off the flitch, alternating the top and bottom faces of the sheets. Since the grain varies so little from one thin sheet to the next in a flitch, this creates a series of mirrored images.

Bow: A type of lengthwise warpage in which the faces of a board are not flat but curved.

Box joint: See: *Finger joint.*

Break or ease an edge: To slightly round over the sharp machined edge of a workpiece.

Burl: A rounded outgrowth on the trunk of a tree. When sliced it reveals densely swirled grain and yields highly figured veneers.

Butt joint: A simple joint in which the flat surfaces (edges, ends, faces) of two workpieces are butted firmly against each other and glued. When end grain is involved a butt joint usually is reinforced with screws, biscuits or dowels.

Cabriole leg: A carved, tapered leg style from the 18th century that curves outward near the top and inward near the bottom, and incorporates a simple or complex foot.

Carcase: The basic box structure of a cabinet or drawer.

Caul: A length of wood used to distribute clamping pressure along a glue joint during assembly and to protect the work from the clamp jaws.

Chamfer: A bevel (usually 45°) cut along the edge or end of a workpiece but not cut clear through the edge. Also refers to cutting such a bevel.

Chatter: In hand or power planing as well as routing, a vibration of the tool or the workpiece that causes the blade or bit to cut unevenly.

Check: A lengthwise crack across the growth rings of a board, most commonly found at the ends, that results from uneven drying.

Chuck: A device on the end of a drill that holds the bits with adjustable jaws.

Clear: A lumber grading term that denotes a board's face that is free of knots or other defects.

Climb cutting: Operating a router so that the feed direction is with, rather than against, the torque direction of the turning bit. This is not recommended, as it can result in loss of control, damage and safety hazards.

Collet: The sleeve on the end of a router's shaft that holds the bits. Collets come in ¼- and ½-in. sizes to accommodate different size bits.

Compound angle: A surface angled in more than one plane relative to the other surfaces of a squared board.

Counterbore: A hole drilled to permit the head of a screw or bolt to sit below the surface.

Countersink: A tapered shape cut into the top of a hole to permit a screw's head to sit flush with the surface. Also refers to the tool used to make such a cut.

Cove: A concave edge treatment, or a molding with such shape.

Crook: A type of lengthwise warpage in which a board is flat but its edges are curved.

Crosscut: To cut across the grain of a solid wood board, or to cut a part to length.

Cup: Curved warpage across a board's width.

Cure: To harden or set as a result of chemical or physical change.

Curly figure (fiddleback, tiger figure): A visual pattern of undulating corrugations across the surface of a piece of wood resulting from wavy grain.

Cutting list: A complete list of all parts needed for a project, along with quantities and dimensions (usually final dimensions).

Dado: A groove cut across the grain of a workpiece. Also refers to cutting such a groove.

Dovetail joint: A joint that uses interlocking, angled tabs, called pins and tails, to mechanically hold the mating parts together.

Drying oil: An organic oil, such as boiled linseed or tung oil, that hardens when exposed to the air. Drying oils are penetrating, rather than surface, finishes.

Dye: A finely ground compound dissolved in a medium and used to impart color. Dyes are transparent and penetrate into the wood to truly change its color. See also: *Stain.*

Edge: Either of the two opposite narrower surfaces of a board, adjacent to the faces and parallel to grain direction (on sheet goods it can refer to all four of the narrower surfaces of exposed core).

End: Either of the two cross-grain surfaces of a board.

End grain: The wood surface exposed after cutting directly across the direction of the wood grain.

Equilibrium moisture content (EMC): The moisture content that wood eventually attains in a given environment when it comes to a balance with the surrounding temperature and humidity.

Face: Either of the two broad, flat sides or surfaces of a wooden board or plywood panel (as opposed to the edges and ends).

Fair curve: A smooth, consistent curve without ripples or flats.

Featherboard (fingerboard): A clamping aid with angled "fingers," usually made of wood, used to keep a workpiece tight against a power tool's fence or table during machining. A featherboard permits a workpiece to move in only one direction to prevent kickback.

Figure: The distinctive pattern that appears on a board face as a result of natural tree growth. Figure is also influenced by external factors, such as drought or disease. Figure can include such features as curly or swirly grain, color variation and medullary rays.

Finger joint (box joint): A machine-made corner joint, commonly found on boxes and drawers, that involves cutting multiple, identical slots and "fingers" into the ends of the two mating boards. Numerous glue surfaces give the joint great strength.

Finish: A term used to describe any of various final treatments to wood that protect it and enhance its appearance.

Flitch: A stack of sequentially-cut veneer sheets.

Frame-and-panel: A construction method for building solid-wood cabinet sides and doors, developed to accommodate seasonal wood movement. A panel is captured, but not glued, within a groove in the surrounding frame.

Glue-starved joint: When too little glue is used in assembly it gets sucked into the pores of the wood and forms a weak bond.

Green wood: Freshly cut, unseasoned wood. Green moisture content can range from 30% to well over 100% depending on species.

Grit: A grading system for the size of crushed minerals used in sandpapers, in which the mineral grains are passed through a series of precisely woven mesh screens. Grit refers to the number of openings per linear inch in the finest screen through which the given particles will pass.

Hardboard: A general term referring to any manufactured board composed of wood fibers bonded by heat and pressure. Specifically, hardboard usually denotes ⅛- in. or ¼-in. high-density boards, either plain or tempered (impregnated with a hard resin to improve strength and water resistance). See also: *Medium-density fiberboard.*

Hardwood: Wood cut from broad-leaved trees. Although these woods tend to be more dense than softwoods, this is not always the case and the term is not a designation of actual wood hardness. See also: *Softwood.*

Heartwood: Generally a darker color than the sapwood of a tree, heartwood forms the interior bulk of a mature tree. Denser than sapwood, heartwood typically is used for lumber. See also: *Sapwood.*

Hide glue: A natural, protein-based glue made from animal skins and hooves. Available in pre-mixed form or as dry granules that are dissolved in water, hide glue bonds can be broken later when soaked in water.

Highboy: A decorative 18th-century chest-on-chest furniture style; typically the lower chest is elevated on long legs.

Honing: The process of producing the final sharp cutting edge on a blade or cutting tool by rubbing it on or with an abrasive stone or leather strop.

Jack plane: A general-purpose mid-sized bench plane about 14 to 15 in. long.

Jig: A device that holds or guides a tool or workpiece during an operation to simplify the operation, make it repeatable and improve its accuracy.

Joinery: The craft and techniques involved in permanently attaching wooden parts to one another. The range of traditional joint-cutting techniques was developed before the advent of composite materials and strong glues, to create interlocking mechanical components that securely unite parts.

Jointer plane: The longest size of bench plane (about 22 to 24 in. long) used for flattening long edges and large surfaces.

Kerf: The slot of material, usually about ⅛ in. wide, removed by the thickness of a saw blade.

Kickback: The action of a workpiece or power tool being thrown backward when the blade is pinched by the workpiece during a cut.

Kiln drying: A rapid method of seasoning lumber in a special oven, with moisture, air and temperature carefully controlled. Kiln-dried lumber should have a moisture content below 10%. See also: *Air-drying.*

Knot: The base of a fallen branch that has been overgrown by the expanding tree.

Lacquer: A hard synthetic surface finish that dries quickly, primarily by solvent evaporation, and is best applied by spraying.

Lamination: The process of uniting layers of material with an adhesive. Wood can be laminated to wood or other materials, like veneer or plastic laminate.

Lay out: To mark a workpiece for machining into project parts.

Long grain: Grain parallel to the long axis of a workpiece. See also: *Short grain.*

Lumber grading: Hardwood lumber is graded according to the percentage of usable, clear wood in a board. In descending order of quality the grades are: Firsts and Seconds (FAS), Selects, No. 1 Common, No. 2 Common, No. 3A Common and No. 3B Common.

Lumber-core plywood: Plywood with a thick central core of solid wood strips sandwiched between outer layers of veneer.

Marquetry: The art of applying decorative inlays in wood using veneers, shells, metals, or other fine materials.

Medium-density fiberboard (MDF): Smooth, heavy, fine-grained hardboard available in various thicknesses for furniture and cabinetry.

Medullary rays: Ribbon-like bands of cells that radiate from the center pith of a tree outward to the bark. They show up as flecks or streaks on quartersawn wood.

Mineral spirits: A petroleum-based solvent that is commonly used as a modern substitute for turpentine to thin and clean up paints and varnishes.

Mission style: An offshoot of the Arts-and-Crafts Movement in the early 1900s that appropriated the style of the crude handmade furniture of the old Spanish missions in the American Southwest. It is characterized by heavy, square shapes in dark-stained quartersawn oak, often with simple, prominent joinery, combined with dark leather upholstery and large hammered nailheads.

Miter: A joint formed by two parts cut with the same angle (usually 45°). Also describes cutting such an angle or joint.

Mortise: See *Mortise-and-tenon joinery.*

Mortise-and-tenon joinery: A method of joinery in which a tenon, or rectangular tab on the end of one part fits into a mortise, or matching recess on the mating part.

Particleboard: Any of several types of manufactured board composed of wood chips or flakes bonded together with a resin.

Pigment: A colored powder that is suspended, rather than dissolved, in the medium used to apply it. Pigment particles are opaque and sit on the surface of the material they are applied to. Pigments are used in paints and stains. See also: *Stain, Dye.*

Pilot hole: A preliminary hole drilled for screwing into wood. It is usually slightly smaller than the diameter of the screw threads.

Pitch pockets: Openings in the wood grain, commonly found in Douglas fir, pine and spruce, that ooze pitch, a sticky resin. If a board with exposed pitch pockets must be used, the pitch should be cleaned off with mineral spirits or lacquer thinner and the pockets sealed with shellac to keep the pitch from bleeding through the finish.

Pith: The soft, spongy wood that forms the narrow central core of a tree.

Plain-sawn lumber: Lumber cut at a tangent to the annual rings, so the rings meet the board faces at angles less than 45°. Wood cut this way swells and shrinks more dramatically across its width than quartersawn lumber. See also: *Quartersawn lumber.*

Plan view: A scale drawing showing the top view of an object. See also: *Front view, Section view.*

Plunge cut: A cut started by plunging into the face of a workpiece rather than starting at an edge.

Plywood: Composite board typically manufactured with an odd number of veneers (or plies) stacked and glued together with grain directions alternating perpendicularly. Can also have an interior core of solid wood. See also: *Lumber-core plywood.*

Pushstick: A shop aid, usually cut from wood scrap, used to push stock past a machine's blade in order to keep hands clear of the blade.

Quartersawn lumber (vertical grain, radial cut): Lumber prepared by first sawing the log in quarters, then into boards. Wood cut in this way shows growth rings approaching 90° to the board faces. It shrinks and swells minimally in width and warps less than plain-sawn lumber. See also: *Plain-sawn lumber.*

Quilted figure: A type of figure in wood that gives the impression of an overall pattern of raised swells.

Rabbet: A stepped cutout along the edge or end of a workpiece, often cut as part of a joint.

Radial shrinkage: Wood shrinkage perpendicular to the growth rings, in the direction of lines radiating out from the center of the tree (across the width of quartersawn lumber and the thickness of plain-sawn lumber). Always less than tangential shrinkage. See also: *Tangential shrinkage.*

Rail: A horizontal frame member in frame-and-panel construction. See also: *Stile.*

Raised grain: A roughened surface condition of a previously smoothed workpiece, usually caused by wetting and drying, in which the wood fibers have swollen and raised above the surface.

Resaw: To rip a thick board into thinner boards.

Resin: Any of several types of natural or synthetic organic polymers that form the hard substance in a cured finish.

Rift-sawn lumber: Similar to quartersawing, but log quarters are sawn into boards at approximately 45° to the annual growth rings. Rift-sawing oak produces a pronounced ray fleck without the elongation characteristic of true radial-cut quartersawing. See also: *Quartersawn lumber.*

Right angle: A 90° angle.

Rip: To cut parallel to the grain of a workpiece. With sheet goods, ripping commonly means cutting to width.

Rough-sawn lumber: Generally refers to hardwood lumber coarsely sawn to approximate standard dimensions and sold as it comes from the sawmill with sawtooth-marked surfaces.

Rubbing out: The final process of leveling imperfections, smoothing the surface and establishing a consistent sheen in a cured finish. Rubbing out is done with mild abrasives.

Sanding sealer: A preliminary priming, filling, and sealing coat applied prior to the final finish.

Sapwood: The newer, outermost layer of wood in a tree. It is living material that conducts the sap upward to the leaves and is usually lighter in color than the heartwood. See also: *Heartwood.*

Scribe: To mark with a pointed instrument (such as an awl). Also refers to marking and shaping the edge of a workpiece so it fits perfectly against a wall or other irregular surface.

Scrub plane: A term used rather loosely to mean a medium-sized bench plane, about 8 to 10 in. long, with a blade ground to a convex curve. It is used crosswise or diagonally to the grain to remove large amounts of wood quickly.

Seasoning: The process of reducing the moisture content of wood from the green state to a level appropriate for construction.

Section view: A scale drawing showing the project partially cut away, usually as viewed from the left or right. Section views are intended to reveal project details that otherwise would be hidden by other parts.

Sheet goods: Composite board products made up of wood strips, veneers, flakes, fragments or fibers, manufactured in standard thicknesses and dimensions. Examples are plywood, particleboard and medium-density fiberboard (MDF).

Shellac: A transparent, alcohol-soluble surface finish made from resin produced by the Oriental lac bug. It is available in a variety of natural shades, from almost clear to reddish-brown. The finish is easily repaired if damaged.

Short grain: Grain oriented across a narrow axis of a workpiece. Since wood fibers tend to cleave along the grain, areas with this configuration are fragile. See also: *Long grain.*

Show side, or face: The better-looking surface of a project part.

Smooth planes: The smallest bench planes, typically ranging from 9½ in. to 10½ in. long as well as the less common smaller sizes used for final smoothing of a surface already leveled with a larger plane.

Snipe: A power jointing or planing fault in which the first or last 2 in. or so of a board is cut slightly deeper than the rest of the board. On a jointer, snipe occurs at the end of a board if the outfeed table is set too low. Planers typically produce snipe at the front and back of a board if the lower table rollers are set too high.

Softwood: Wood cut from coniferous trees. This term does not denote the actual hardness of the wood. See also: *Hardwood.*

Solvent: Any liquid that is used to dissolve another substance. Some common solvents are alcohol, mineral spirits and water.

Spalted wood: Partially decayed wood in which the white rot is accompanied by attractive brown or black outlines; most often found in maple.

Spline: A strip of wood that fits into grooves cut in mating parts to reinforce a simple joint; usually used in miters.

Squaring up: To plane a piece of lumber flat and straight, with parallel faces and all adjacent surfaces at right angles to each other. Also called milling four-square.

Square: Adjoining surfaces that meet at a right angle. Also refers to any number of hand tools that test for square.

Stack lamination: A technique for building up blanks of wood for carving and sculpture by face-gluing boards or blocks together with staggered joints.

Stain: A finishing product used to color wood without hiding it, as paint does. Traditional chemical stains react with the wood to produce the color change, but modern commercial stains are largely pigment-based so they tend to be more opaque than dyes. See also: *Pigment, Dye.*

Stickers: Strips of wood inserted between boards in a stack to permit air circulation for drying or storage.

Stile: A vertical frame member in frame-and-panel construction. See also: *Rail.*

Substrate: Material (as wood or sheet goods) that serves as a core for a coating or covering, especially by lamination.

Surfaced lumber: Lumber planed on faces but not taken to a specific thickness. Lumber purchased pre-surfaced is designated as S2S (surfaced on two faces) or S4S (surfaced on two faces and two edges) and is usually planed and cut to standard dimensions.

Tangential shrinkage: Wood shrinkage tangent to the growth rings (across the width of plain-sawn lumber and the thickness of quartersawn lumber). Always greater than radial shrinkage; higher figures indicate less stable wood (prone to greater seasonal expansion and contraction). See also: *Radial shrinkage.*

Tanin: A substance naturally present in varying amounts in most woods. It reacts with certain chemicals to cause color changes in the wood. Iron, for example, can react with the tanin in oak to cause dark stains.

Tearout (chipout, splintering): A cutting or shaping defect in which fibers or chips of wood are torn away below the plane of cut by the action of the moving cutting edge opposing the direction of the wood grain.

Template: A solid pattern of a given shape used to aid in accurately reproducing the shape.

Tenon: See *Mortise-and-tenon joinery.*

Thicknessed lumber: Lumber planed to an exact thickness.

Thinner: Any solvent used to dilute or reduce the consistency of a finish. Each finish has its own compatible thinner.

Through-and-through sawing: The simplest and most efficient method of sawing a log, in which slabs are simply through-cut to the required thickness one after another across the width of the log. See also: *Plain-sawn lumber, Quartersawn lumber.*

Twist: Uneven warpage along the length of a board that causes each end to twist or wind in opposite directions.

Varnish: A clear, durable, slow-drying surface finish made by combining resins (such as alkyd or urethane) with a drying oil, and thinning with mineral spirits.

Veneer: Wood sliced, peeled, or sawn into sheets of $1/16$ in. or less in thickness. Standard commercial veneers are $1/28$ in. to $1/32$ in. thick. Also refers to laminating such material to a substrate, like medium-density fiberboard.

Waney edge: The uneven, natural edge on a board, sometimes with bark still attached. Standard kiln-dried lumber usually is ripped straight, so the waney edges are removed.

Warp: Any distortion in a piece of lumber from a straight, flat plane. See also: *Bow, Crook, Cup,* and *Twist.*

Wind: See *Twist.*

Projects

Page 170

Page 162

Page 238

Page 218

Page 174

Page 210

Page 182

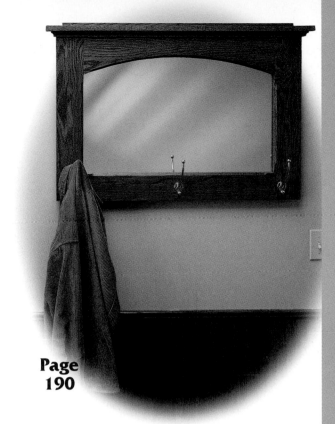

Page 190

Page 234

Page 204

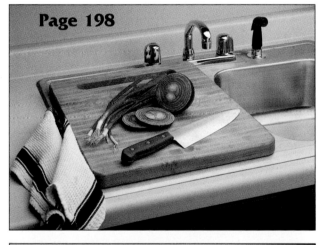

Page 198

Page 226

Mantel Clock

The mantel clock is one of the oldest clock types, sized to fit neatly on a hearth. But you don't need a fireplace for an excuse to build this heirloom-quality project. Its compact size will be equally attractive on a bookshelf or side table. Made of cherry, our design features a split-frame glass panel to highlight the brass pendulum and clock face as well as an elegant crown and base that you can make easily with a router.

Vital Statistics: Mantel Clock

TYPE: Clock

OVERALL SIZE: 10½W by 16⅞H by 5¼D

MATERIAL: Cherry, cherry plywood, glass

JOINERY: Rabbets, dowel-reinforced butt joints

CONSTRUCTION DETAILS:
- Crown and base profiles are routed onto the ends and edges of individual parts, which are then laminated together
- Face frame chamfered on the inside and outside edges
- Glass held in place with removable retainer frame
- Hole cut in back panel for easy access to clock movement
- Clockwork kit installed in case

FINISH: Satin tung oil

Building time

 PREPARING STOCK
2-3 hours

 LAYOUT
2-3 hours

 CUTTING PARTS
3-4 hours

 ASSEMBLY
3-4 hours

 FINISHING
2-3 hours

TOTAL: 12-17 hours

Tools you'll use

- Jointer
- Planer
- Table saw
- Router table with 45° piloted chamfer bit, ½-in. roundover bit, ¼-in. cove and bead bit
- Jig saw
- Drill/driver
- Doweling jig
- Clamps

Shopping list

- ☐ (2) ½ × 6 in. × 8 ft. cherry
- ☐ (1) ¾ × 6 × 12 in. cherry
- ☐ (1) ¼ in. × 2 ft. × 2 ft. cherry plywood
- ☐ (1) ³⁄₃₂ × 6¼ × 13 in. glass
- ☐ ¼-in. dowel
- ☐ #6 × ½ in. panhead screws with washers
- ☐ #4 × ¾ in. brass flathead wood screws
- ☐ 6 × 6-in. brass clock face, battery-powered quartz movement, brass pendulum
- ☐ Wood glue
- ☐ Finishing materials

Mantel Clock

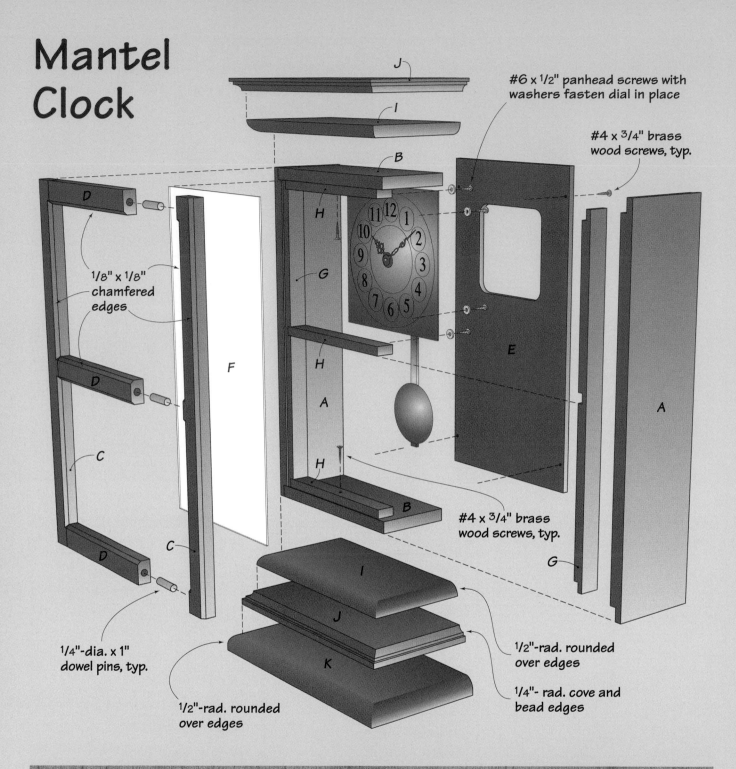

J

#6 x 1/2" panhead screws with washers fasten dial in place

#4 x 3/4" brass wood screws, typ.

I

B

D

1/8" x 1/8" chamfered edges

H

H

12 11 10 9 8 7 6 5 4 3 2 1

F

D

G

C

A

E

A

H

G

B

#4 x 3/4" brass wood screws, typ.

1/4"-dia. x 1" dowel pins, typ.

C

I

1/2"-rad. rounded over edges

J

1/4"- rad. cove and bead edges

K

1/2"-rad. rounded over edges

Mantel Clock Cutting List

Part	No.	Size	Material	Part	No.	Size	Material
A. Carcase sides	2	1/2 × 3 1/4 × 14 1/8 in.	Cherry	**G.** Retainer stiles	2	3/8 × 3/4 × 13 1/8 in.	Cherry
B. Carcase top, bottom	2	1/2 × 3 × 7 in.	"	**H.** Retainer rails	3	3/8 × 3/4 × 6 1/8 in.	"
C. Frame stiles	2	1/2 × 7/8 × 14 1/8 in.	"	**I.** Roundover top, bottom	2	1/2 × 4 1/4 × 8 1/2 in.	"
D. Frame rails	2	1/2 × 7/8 × 5 3/4	"	**J.** Cove top, bottom	2	1/2 × 4 3/4 × 9 1/2 in.	"
E. Back	1	1/4 × 7 1/4 × 14 1/8	Cherry plywood	**K.** Roundover base	1	3/4 × 5 1/4 × 10 1/2 in.	"
F. Glass	1	3/32 × 6 7/16 × 13 1/16 in.					

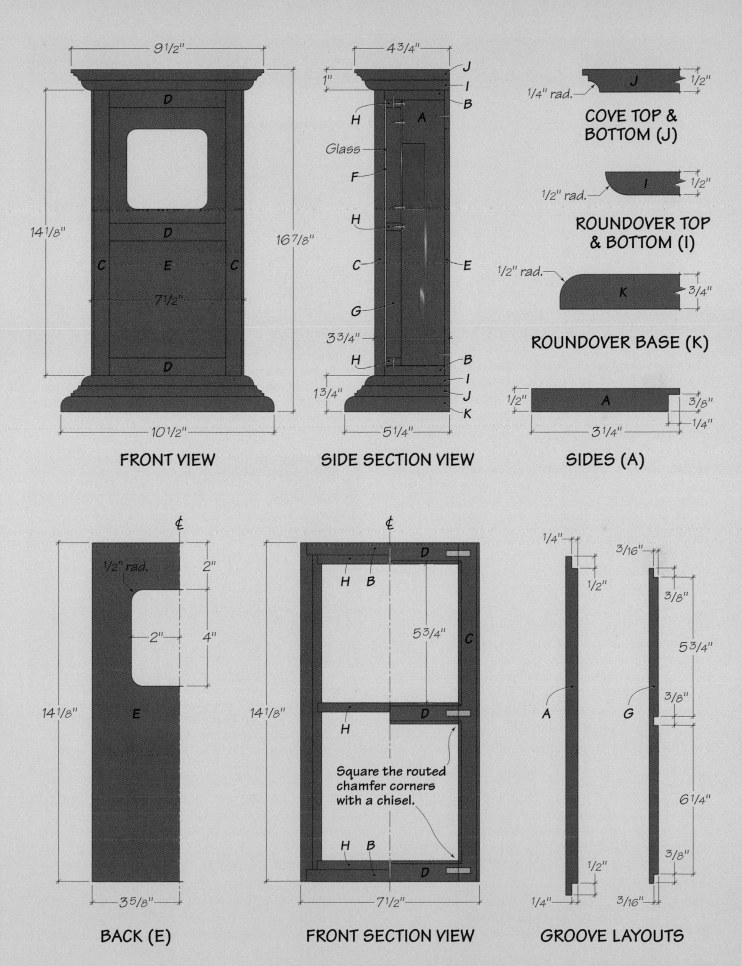

FRONT VIEW

9 1/2"

14 1/8"

16 7/8"

D

D

C   E   C

7 1/2"

D

10 1/2"

SIDE SECTION VIEW

4 3/4"

1"

J

I

B

H   A

Glass

F

H

C   E

G

3 3/4"

H   B

I

J

K

1 3/4"

5 1/4"

SIDES (A)

1/4" rad.

J   1/2"

COVE TOP & BOTTOM (J)

1/2" rad.

I   1/2"

ROUNDOVER TOP & BOTTOM (I)

1/2" rad.

K   3/4"

ROUNDOVER BASE (K)

1/2"

A   3/8"

1/4"

3 1/4"

BACK (E)

¢

1/2" rad.

2"

2"   4"

14 1/8"

E

3 5/8"

FRONT SECTION VIEW

¢

D

H   B

5 3/4"   C

D

H

Square the routed chamfer corners with a chisel.

14 1/8"

H   B

D

7 1/2"

GROOVE LAYOUTS

1/4"

1/2"

3/16"

3/8"

5 3/4"

3/8"

A   G

3/8"

6 1/4"

1/2"   3/8"

1/4"   3/16"

MAKE THE CARCASE

1 Cut the carcase parts: Rip and crosscut the carcase sides, top and bottom to size from ½-in. stock, according to the *Cutting List* dimensions.

2 Rout rabbets into the ends of the sides for the carcase top and bottom pieces. Cut these rabbets on the table saw using a dado blade. Set your dado blade to ½ in. wide, and raise it to a height of ¼ in. Cut a ½-in.-wide rabbet into each end of both side pieces.

3 Cut the back panel rabbets. First, install a sacrificial fence on your saw's rip fence to keep the dado blade from damaging the metal fence. Raise the dado blade so it cuts into the wooden sacrificial fence to a height of ⅜ in. so only ¼ in. of the blade protrudes out from the saw fence. Lay each side piece with the end rabbets face-down on the saw table, and cut a rabbet into one long edge of each (**See Photo A**).

4 Glue up the carcase: Dry-fit the carcase top and bottom pieces into their rabbets in the sides. Be sure the top and bottom fit fully into their rabbets, or the crown and base assemblies will not fit properly later. Sand the faces of the parts smooth now, while they're still accessible. Spread glue into the rabbets, and clamp up the top, bottom and sides. Adjust the clamps until the carcase is square.

5 Make the back: Rip and crosscut ¼-in. cherry plywood for the back panel. Then, lay out and cut the center access hole, using the *Back* drawingas a guide. Cut out the access hole with a jig saw. Drill a ½-in.-dia. pilot hole at each corner of the cutout area first, to make turning the jig saw easier as you cut.

BUILD THE FACE FRAME

6 Cut the stiles and rails to size: Rip and crosscut

PHOTO A: Cut rabbets across the ends and along one long edge of each side piece using a dado blade on the table saw. These rabbets form recesses for the carcase top and bottom, as well as the plywood back panel. Attach a sacrificial wood fence to your saw fence to protect the metal fence from the dado blade.

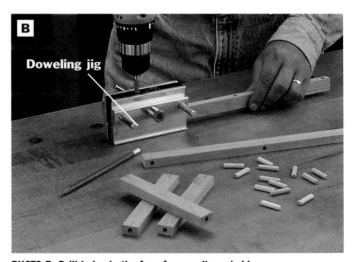

PHOTO B: Drill holes in the face frame rails and sides so you can assemble these parts with dowels. A doweling jig ensures that the holes are positioned precisely across each joint and keeps the drill bit straight in relation to the workpiece.

the two face frame stiles and three rails from ½-in. stock. Lay the face frame parts into position on the clock carcase and be sure that the overall face frame fits flush with the outside edges of the carcase.

7 Drill the face frame dowel joints: Measure and mark for dowel holes on the rails and stiles. The center rail should be centered on the length of the stiles. Then clamp each face frame part in a doweling jig and drill ½-in.-deep dowel holes, centered across the

PHOTO C: Square off the inside chamfered corners of the face frame with a chisel. Lay out these corners first with a pencil and square, then pare up to your layout lines.

PHOTO D: Rout the roundover and cove and bead profiles into the ends and along one edge of the base and crown parts. Mill the end grain first, then rout the long grain; otherwise the bit could tear out the corners of your finished edges.

thickness of the parts (See Photo B). Use a ¼-in.-dia. drill bit for boring these holes, and mark your drill bit with masking tape to keep from accidentally drilling the holes too deeply.

8 Glue up the face frame: Cut six 1-in.-long dowels, and spread an even coating of glue onto each dowel. Insert the dowels into the face frame parts, and clamp the face frame to hold the dowel joints tightly closed until the glue dries.

9 Rout the face frame chamfers: Install a 45° piloted chamfer bit in your router, and adjust the bit depth to ⅛ in. Set the face frame on a non-slip router pad, and rout counterclockwise around the inside edges of the face frame openings. Work carefully, keeping the router base held firmly against the face frame as you go. Use a pencil and combination square to square off the corners where the router bit couldn't reach, and pare chamfers into the face frame corners with a sharp chisel to square them off (See Photo C). Then, cut long chamfers along the outside edges of the face frame with the router at the same bit setting as you used for the inside chamfers. Be careful not to chamfer the ends of the face frame; they should butt flush against the crown and base.

ASSEMBLE THE CROWN & BASE
To avoid milling tiny molding and attaching it to the clock, or using wide manufactured crown molding instead, we simply routed profiles into larger blanks of cherry stock for the crown and base, then laminated these parts together. The crown is composed of

two parts—one with a roundover profile and one with a cove and bead profile. The base is made of three pieces: two roundovers sandwiching a layer with a cove and bead profile.

10 Make the roundover parts: Rip and crosscut the roundover top, bottom and base to size. Note that the base is made of ¾-in. stock, while the other roundover parts are ½ in. thick. Set up a piloted ½-in. roundover bit in the router table, and rout the profiles in two passes of increasing depth, to minimize burn marks

PHOTO E: Glue up the crown and base first, then glue these completed assemblies to the clock carcase. Glue alone will bond these parts sufficiently, so no additional fasteners are needed.

PHOTO F: Cut rabbets and dadoes into the retainer stiles for the retainer rails. Make these cuts on the table saw with a dado blade, and hold the parts against the miter gauge. We installed an auxiliary fence on the miter gauge to keep the dado blade from tearing out the grain on the retainer stiles.

PHOTO G: Install the glass and retainer frame with a pair of brass wood screws—one through the retainer top rail and one through the bottom rail. Countersink these screws.

left on the workpieces. Rout the ends of these work-pieces first, which are more likely to chip when the bit exits the workpiece. You'll clean up these corners when you rout the long edge of each part. Once the routing is complete, sand the parts smooth.

⓫ Make the cove and bead parts: Rip and crosscut the cove and bead top and bottom to size. Use the

same router techniques for milling the profiles that you used in Step 10, routing the ends first, then the edges (**See Photo D**). Sand these parts smooth and to remove all burn marks.

⓬ Glue up the crown and base: Spread glue over the mating surfaces of the crown parts and clamp them together. Be sure the back edges are flush and the cove and bead pieces overhang the roundover piece evenly. Glue and clamp the base parts together simi-larly with the bottom cove and bead piece sandwiched between the roundover bottom and roundover base. For more clarification on the orientation of these parts, see *Side Section View*.

⓭ Install the crown and base on the carcase: Spread an even layer of wood glue over the top and bottom ends of the carcase, and set the crown and base in position. Use spring clamps to hold the parts together and keep them from shifting while the glue dries (**See Photo E**).

INSTALL THE RETAINER & GLASS
The glass is held in place in the clock case with a stile-and-rail retainer frame and a couple of screws. This way, the glass remains removable, should it ever need replacing.

⓮ Cut the retainer parts: Surface plane ½-in. cherry stock down to ⅜ in. thick for the retainer parts. Rip and crosscut the two glass retainer stiles and three retainer rails to size.

⓯ Mill rabbets and dadoes into the retainer stiles for the rails. Notice in the *Groove Layouts* drawing, that the retainer stiles are rabbeted on the ends and dadoed across the middle to house the retainer rails. Make these cuts on the table saw with a dado blade set to a width of ⅜ in. and raised ³⁄₁₆ in. above the saw table. Mark the rabbet and dado locations on each of the stiles, and cut the dadoes and rabbets carefully with the stiles held against the miter gauge (**See Photo F**). Sand the retainer parts smooth.

⓰ Assemble the retainer and install the glass: Dry-fit the retainer rails and stiles together, then glue and clamp the parts. Be sure the retainer frame is flat as well as square. Once the glue dries, set the glass in place in the clock case, drill countersunk pilot holes through the top and bottom retainer rails, and fasten the retainer and glass in place with two #4 × ¾-in. brass wood screws (**See Photo G**).

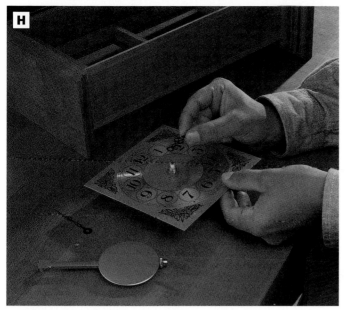

PHOTO H: Attach the quartz clock movement and hands to the clock face, according to the kitmaker's instructions.

PHOTO I: Fasten the brass clock face to the top portion of the retainer frame with six panhead sheet metal screws and washers. Pushpins serve as a handy way to hold the clock face in place as you adjust it, prior to installing screws and washers.

ASSEMBLE & MOUNT THE CLOCKWORK

17 Follow the instructions that come with your clock works to install the quartz movement and hands on the brass clock face (**See Photo H**).

18 Mount the clock face: Set the clock face into place on the top retainer frame opening inside the clock carcase. Shift the face up and down, right and left until it is positioned evenly within the retainer frame. Hold the brass face in place temporarily with pushpins while you install it with #6 × ½-in. panhead machine screws and washers. Drill pilot holes for these screws to keep them from splitting the retainer parts (**See Photo I**).

FINISHING TOUCHES

19 Prepare the clock for finishing: Disassemble the clockwork, and remove the retainer and glass from the clock carcase. Sand any remaining rough edges and surfaces smooth with 220-grit sandpaper.

20 Apply the finish. We used wipe-on tung oil to enrich the natural wood tones and grain of the cherry. After each coat, rub down the surfaces of all the wood parts with #0000 steel wool, which "burnishes" the finish and removes any surface irregularities.

21 Assemble the clock: Reinstall the glass, retainer and clock face. Fasten the back panel into its rabbets in the carcase back with four #4 × ¾-in. brass flat-head wood screws (**See Photo J**). Drill countersunk pilot holes for the screws.

PHOTO J: Apply your finish of choice to all of the wood clock surfaces, then install the clock back with brass flathead wood screws, driven through the back and into the rabbets in the carcase back.

Arts & Crafts Bookstand

Need a gift idea for a college student you know? You'll be the wise gift giver when you present this Arts-and-Crafts inspired desktop book rack. Made of red oak and decorated with authentic wedge-pinned through tenons, this useful project takes up little more desktop than a legal notepad and keeps important books within arm's reach.

Arts & Crafts Bookstand: Step-by-step

PHOTO A: Lay out and cut the two sides, back and shelf pieces to shape. Since the back and shelf parts are identical, clamp them together and gang-cut both with a jig saw.

MAKE THE SIDES, BACK & SHELF

❶ Crosscut workpieces for the sides, back and shelf, sized according to the *Cutting List*.

❷ Lay out and cut the sides to shape: Make a full-size paper grid drawing of the sides, according to the *Side Layout* drawing. Cut out the paper shape and use it as a template for drawing the sides onto the side workpieces. Cut out the sides with a jig saw.

❸ Rip-cut the back and shelf to width. Mark and cut the through tenons on the ends of the back and shelf pieces. Refer to the *Tenon Layout* drawing to mark the shape of the tenons and wedge holes on the ends of the back and shelves. Cut the through tenons to shape **(See Photo A).**

Arts & Crafts Bookstand

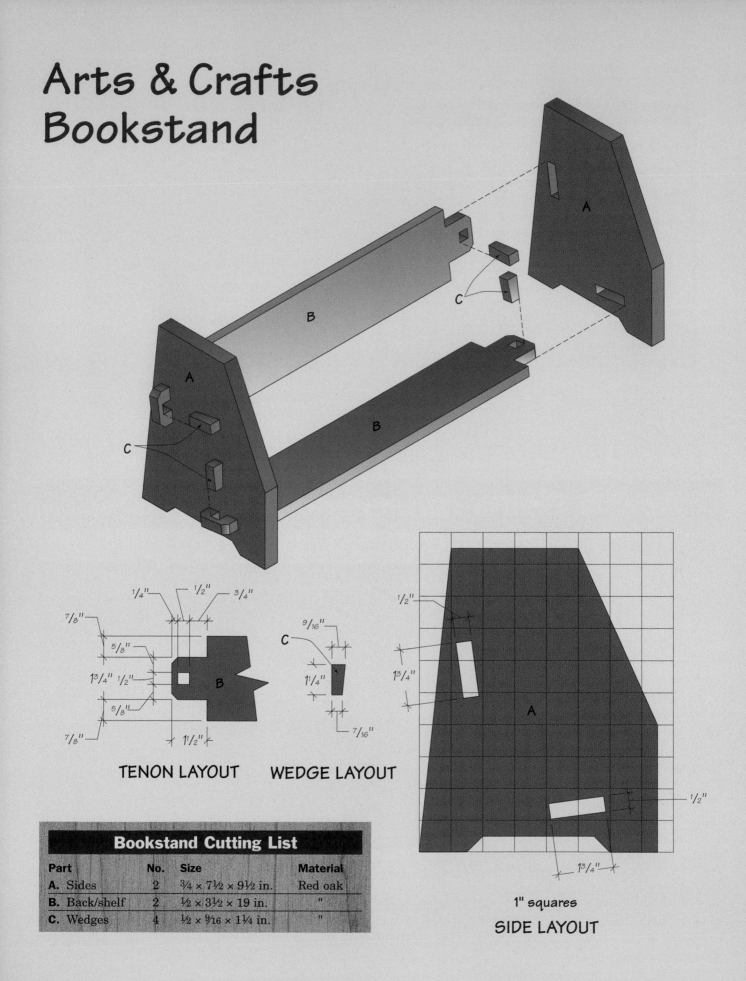

TENON LAYOUT

WEDGE LAYOUT

1" squares

SIDE LAYOUT

Bookstand Cutting List			
Part	**No.**	**Size**	**Material**
A. Sides	2	¾ × 7½ × 9½ in.	Red oak
B. Back/shelf	2	½ × 3½ × 19 in.	"
C. Wedges	4	½ × ⁹⁄₁₆ × 1¼ in.	"

PHOTO B: Drill out the centers of the wedge holes in the tenons with a ½-in. bit. Use the same bit for boring holes in the ends of the mortises in the sides. If you align the parts carefully and clamp them together, it's possible to drill through both parts at once.

PHOTO C: Clean out the remaining waste from the mortises in the sides with a jig saw. Square up the wedge holes and the ends of the mortises with a sharp chisel and a file.

PHOTO D: Lay out and cut four tenon wedges from ½-in.-thick stock. Cut the wedges a little wider than necessary so you can sand them as needed for a good fit in the wedge holes.

PHOTO E: Assemble the sides, back and shelf with clamps, then glue and insert the wedges into the wedge holes. Tap the wedges snug with a wood mallet. Wipe away excess glue before it dries.

CUT THE WEDGE HOLES & MORTISES

4 Drill out the waste from the four tenon wedge holes with a sharp ½-in.-dia. brad point bit.

5 Cut out the mortises in the sides for the back and shelf tenons. First bore ½-in.-dia holes at the ends of each mortise **(See Photo B).** Then saw out the rest of the waste in between the holes. Square up the wedge holes and the mortises with a sharp ½-in. chisel, then clean up the cut-outs with a narrow file **(See Photo C).**

ASSEMBLE & FINISH THE BOOK RACK

6 Make the wedges: Refer to the *Wedge Layout* drawing for marking the wedge shapes on a strip of ½-in.-thick stock. NOTE: *Lay out the wedges so the grain runs lengthwise.* Cut out the wedges with a jig saw so they are slightly wider than your layout lines **(See Photo D).**

7 Dry-fit the book rack together. The tenons should seat fully into the mortises when you interlock the parts. Adjust the fit of the mortises and tenons by sanding the tenons a little at a time. Aim for a snug, but not forced, fit of the tenons in the mortises.

8 Dry-fit the wedges into their holes in the tenons with the angled edges of the wedges facing the book rack sides. The wedges should overhang the tenons evenly when fully inserted. Sand the wedges until they fit properly.

9 Disassemble the book rack and sand all the parts smooth. Reassemble, this time gluing the wedges into the tenons **(See Photo E).** Wipe off excess glue immediately with a damp rag.

10 Wipe or brush on your choice of stain, followed by a clear topcoat. We wiped on two coats of Danish oil.

Firewood Box

You'll always be ready to prepare a cozy fire if you store your firewood next to the hearth in this rustic firewood box. Made of cedar, our design features a covered bin for storing the firewood and a narrower compartment for kindling.

Firewood Box: Step-by-step

MAKE THE BOTTOM, SIDES, DIVIDER & FRONT PANEL

❶ Crosscut the bottom, side/divider and front slats to length.

❷ Cut the six side corner boards (both front and rear) as well as the front corner boards and skids to length.

❸ Assemble the sides. Despite the fact that the sides eventually will be trimmed at an angle from front to back, build them as rectangular panels first, with six slats and a front and rear-side corner board. Arrange the parts so the rear-side corner board is flush with the back ends of the slats and the front edge of the front-side corner board extends ⅞ in. beyond the

PHOTO A: Assemble the bottom, sides, divider and front panel. Join the slats to corner boards or skids with 1¼-in. deck screws. You may find it helpful to clamp the slats together to keep them aligned when driving the screws.

front ends of the slats. Secure the parts with countersunk 1¼-in. deck screws, driving the screws through the slats and into the corner boards.

❹ Build the divider: Join six divider slats to the front and rear-side corner boards with 1¼-in. deck

Firewood Box

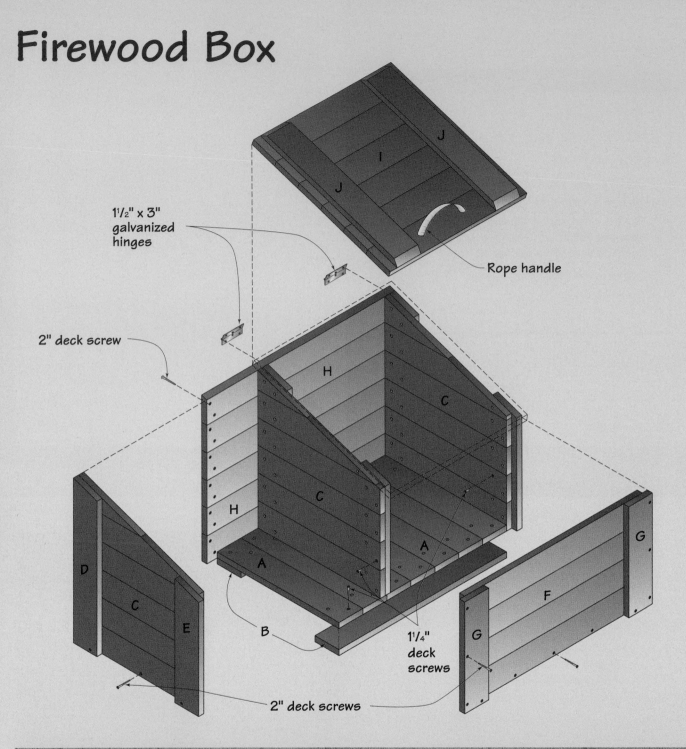

1½" x 3" galvanized hinges

Rope handle

2" deck screw

1¼" deck screws

2" deck screws

Firewood Box Cutting List

Part	No.	Size	Material	Part	No.	Size	Material
A. Bottom slats	7	⅞ × 3½ × 17¾ in.	Cedar	**F.** Front slats	4	⅞ × 3½ × 26¼ in.	Cedar
B. Skids	2	⅞ × 3½ × 24½ in.	"	**G.** Front corner boards	2	⅞ × 3½ × 14 in.	"
C. Side/divider slats	18	⅞ × 3½ × 17¾ in.	"	**H.** Back slats	6	⅞ × 3½ × 28 in.	"
D. Side corner boards (rear)	3	⅞ × 3½ × 21 in.	"	**I.** Lid slats	6	⅞ × 3½ × 20¼ in.	"
E. Side corner boards (front)	3	⅞ × 3½ × 16 in.	"	**J.** Lid battens	2	⅞ × 3½ × 21 in.	

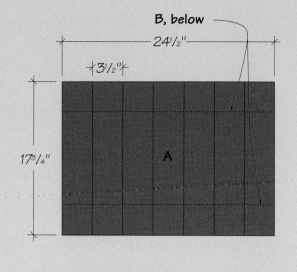

BOTTOM - SLAT LAYOUT

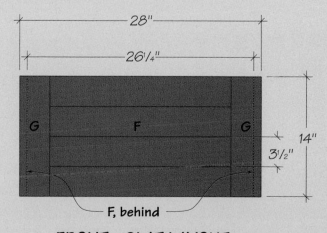

LID - SLAT LAYOUT

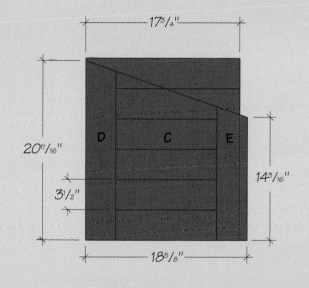

SIDE - SLAT LAYOUT

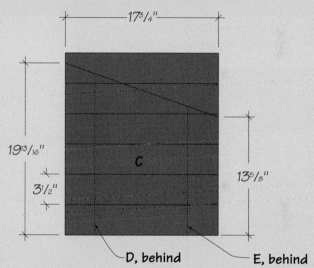

INTERIOR DIVIDER - SLAT LAYOUT

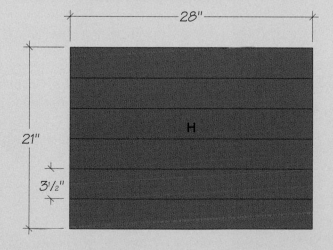

BACK - SLAT LAYOUT

FRONT - SLAT LAYOUT

PHOTO B: Mark the side panels and divider with a cutting line for the top angled profile, then clamp a straightedge to guide your saw and cut the side panels to shape.

PHOTO C: Hold the partially assembled firewood box square by tacking a temporary brace diagonally across the front of the project. Insert and tack a 6-in. spacer between the divider and the closer side as well.

screws. The outside edges of the corner boards should align with the ends of the slats.

5 Make the front: Arrange the front slats and front corner boards so the outside edges of the corner boards extend ⅞ in. beyond the ends of the slats on both sides. These corner boards will overlap the front corner boards on the side panels when the project is assembled. Screw the parts together, driving the deck screws through the front slats and into the front corner boards.

6 Assemble the bottom: Fasten the seven bottom slats to the two skids with deck screws so the slats are flush with the ends and outside edges of the skids (**See Photo A**).

7 Trim the sides and divider to shape: Lay out the angled profile that forms the shape of the top of each side and the divider, according to the slat layout drawings for these parts. Cut the angles with a circular saw or jig saw guided against a straightedge (**See Photo B**).

BUILD THE FIREWOOD BOX

8 Assemble the sides, divider and bottom: Clamp the sides to the bottom so the bottom edge of each side is flush with the bottom of each skid. Drive 2-in. deck screws through the sides and into the bottom. Install the divider so the divider slats are spaced 6 in. from the slats of one of the sides. Drive 2-in. deck screws up through the bottom and into the divider to attach the parts. Hold the sides and divider square to the bottom by nailing a temporary brace diagonally across the front of the project to the sides and divider. Tack a 6-in.-long spacer between the divider and closer side as well (**See Photo C**).

PHOTO D: After you've installed the first five back slats with screws, set the top back slat in place and mark the angle formed by the sides onto the back slat with a straightedge.

PHOTO E: Bevel-rip the top back slat along its full length with the saw set to the angle you marked in Step 11. Since the slat is narrow and the cut is right along the board's edge, hold it steady by tacking the slat to a couple of scraps, and clamp the scraps to your workbench. You may also need to clamp a board of the same thickness as the slat next to the slat to provide more support for the saw base. Be sure to allow an inch or so of space between this board and the slat to provide clear space for the strip of wood you are cutting free.

INSTALL THE BACK & FRONT

9 Cut the six back slats to length.

10 Attach five back slats to the firewood box assembly: Starting from the bottom of the project and working up, drive pairs of 2-in. deck screws through each back slat and into the sides. Offset the screw pattern. The bottom slat should be flush with the bottoms of the skids. Drive a single screw through each slat and into the divider.

11 Set the top back slat in place and mark the angles of the sides onto the slat ends **(See Photo D)**.

12 Bevel-cut the top edge of the top back slat. We nailed the slat temporarily to a couple of scraps clamped to the workbench to hold the clamp securely while making the cut **(See Photo E)**.

PHOTO F: Position the top back slat so its beveled edge matches the angles of the sides, and secure the slat to the firewood box with 2-in. deck screws.

PHOTO G: Remove the temporary brace and install the front panel with screws. Drive countersunk deck screws through the front corner boards into the sides as well as through the bottom slat into the firewood box bottom.

PHOTO H: Clamp the six lid slats together so their ends align. Position the lid battens beneath the slat assembly, inset 1 in. from the ends of the slats. Fasten the parts with countersunk 1¼-in. deck screws driven down through the slats and into the battens.

⑬ Attach the top back slat to the sides and divider with 2-in. deck screws **(See Photo F)**.

⑭ Remove the temporary brace and spacer.

⑮ Set the front panel onto the front of the project so the bottom of the panel is flush with the bottom of the front skid. Fasten the front to the side slats, divider and bottom with 2-in. deck screws **(See Photo G)**.

⑯ Bevel the top ends of the front corner boards to match the slope of the sides: Use a rasp, block plane or coarse file to shave down the front corner boards. Doing so will allow the lid to close fully over the firewood compartment.

BUILD THE LID
⑰ Crosscut the eight lid slats and two lid battens to length.

⑱ Arrange the lid slats on the battens so the ends of the slats are aligned and the battens are inset 1 in. from the slat ends. Hold the slats together with clamps. Drive 1¼-in. deck screws through the slats and into the battens. Stagger the screw pattern, installing a pair of screws at each batten location on the slats **(See Photo H)**.

FINISHING TOUCHES
⑲ Sand the project smooth and ease the edges and corners to keep the cedar from splintering.

⑳ Apply your choice of finish. We topcoated all surfaces of the project with two coats of clear deck sealer to preserve the rich cedar wood tone **(See Photo I)**. You could also leave the project unfinished, but the cedar eventually will turn a gray color if exposed to direct sunlight or moisture. Cedar also takes wood stain well, if you wish to match the project to other woodwork in the room.

㉑ Fashion a rope pull for the lid: Drill a pair of ½-in.-dia. holes about 6 in. apart through the front lid slat. Thread a length of ½-in.-dia. braided rope down through these holes in the lid, and knot the ends of the rope to form a lid pull.

㉒ Attach the lid: Set the lid in place over the firewood compartment so the ends of the lid are flush with a side, the divider and the back slats. Lay out locations on the lid and top back slat for a pair of hinges. We positioned the hinges even with the lid battens, with the hinge knuckles facing outward. Drill pilot holes for the hinge screws, and screw the hinges in place **(See Photo J).**

PHOTO I (Optional): Topcoat the project with clear or tinted deck sealer. Brush on a coat of wood stain, if you prefer. It isn't necessary to apply finish to the project if it will be located inside and out of direct sunlight. Finish will enhance the wood tones and grain.

PHOTO J: Attach the lid to the project with a couple of 3-in. galvanized butt hinges. Position the lid so it covers the firewood compartment but not the kindling compartment.

Country Wall Cabinet

Here's an attractive kitchen accent piece that includes a convenient towel rack. Built from pine and beadboard plywood, this cabinet conjures up images of country stores and farm kitchens of yesteryear. Finally, a place to display that art glass or cookie jar collection!

Vital Statistics

TYPE: Wall-mounted open cabinet

OVERALL SIZE: 32L by 29W by 9¼D

MATERIAL: Pine, beadboard plywood

JOINERY: Butt joints reinforced with glue and nails

CONSTRUCTION DETAILS:
· Cove molding miter-cut to fit around cabinet top
· Towel rod secured with a finish nail on each end

FINISH: Stain, varnish

BUILDING TIME: 4-5 hours

Shopping List

☐ (1) 1 × 4 in. × 6 ft. pine

☐ (1) 1 × 8 in. × 10 ft. pine

☐ (1) 1 × 10 in. × 4 ft. pine

☐ (1) ¾ × 1⅛ in. × 4 ft. pine
cove molding

☐ (1) 1 in. dia. × 2 ft. dowel

☐ (1) ¼ in. × 4 ft. × 4 ft. pine
beadboard plywood

☐ ¾ in. brads

☐ Finish nails (1½, 2 in.)

☐ Wood glue

☐ Finishing materials

Country Wall Cabinet: Step-by-step

MAKE THE SIDES, APRON & BOTTOM TRIM

❶ Crosscut two 31¼-in. boards for the cabinet sides.

❷ Crosscut two 24-in. lengths from the pine 1 × 4 to make the apron and bottom trim. Rip-cut the bottom trim piece to a width of 2½ in.

❸ Draw the curved profiles on the cabinet sides: Make a full-size paper template of the curved profile shown on the *Side Section* drawing. Position the template on

PHOTO A: Create a full-size paper template to draw the curved profiles on the bottoms of the cabinet side panels. Tape the template to each side workpiece and draw the curves.

Country Wall Cabinet

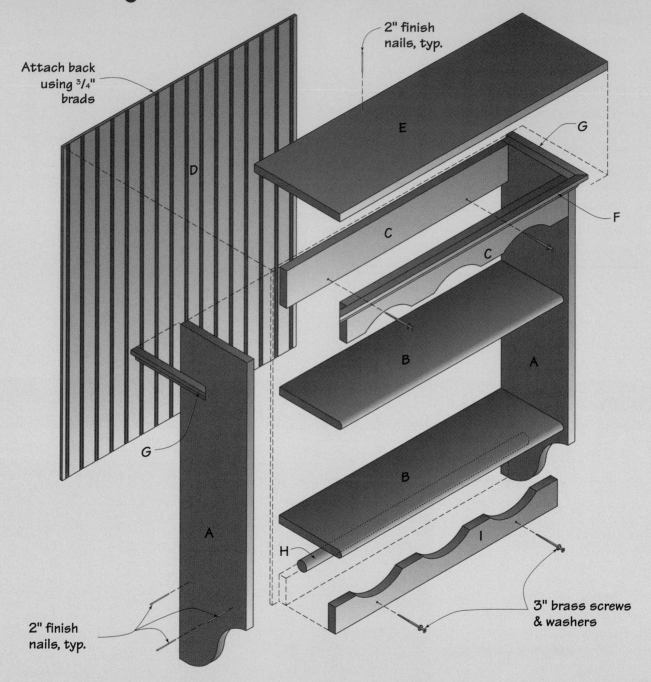

Attach back using ³/₄" brads

2" finish nails, typ.

2" finish nails, typ.

3" brass screws & washers

D

E

G

F

C

C

B

A

B

A

G

H

I

Country Cabinet Cutting List

Part	No.	Size	Material	Part	No.	Size	Material
A. Sides	2	³/₄ × 7¼ × 31¼ in.	Pine	**F.** Front molding	1	³/₄ × 1⅛ × 27 in.	Pine cove molding
B. Shelf	2	³/₄ × 7¼ × 24 in.	"	**G.** Side molding	2	³/₄ × 1⅛ × 8¼ in.	"
C. Nailer/apron	2	³/₄ × 3½ × 24 in.	"	**H.** Towel rod	1	1 in. dia. × 24 in.	Dowel
D. Back	1	¼ × 25½ × 31¼ in.	Beadboard plywood	**I.** Bottom trim	1	³/₄ × 2½ × 24 in.	Pine
E. Top	1	³/₄ × 9¼ × 29 in.	Pine				

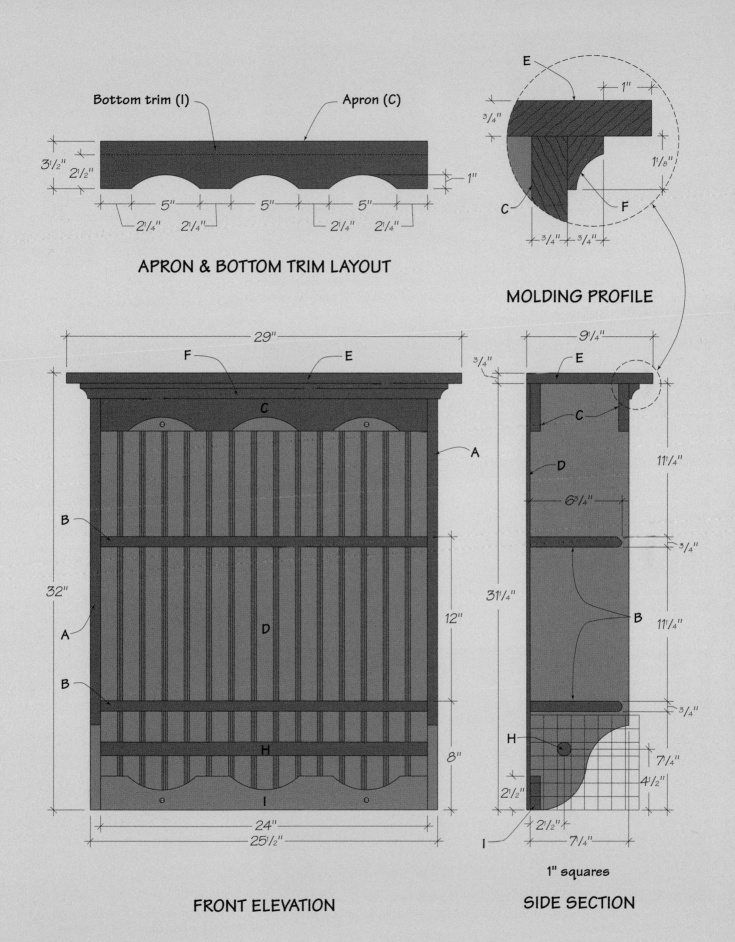

Bottom trim (I)   Apron (C)

$3\frac{1}{2}$" $2\frac{1}{2}$"

5"   5"   5"   1"

$2\frac{1}{4}$" $2\frac{1}{4}$" $2\frac{1}{4}$" $2\frac{1}{4}$"

APRON & BOTTOM TRIM LAYOUT

E

1"

$\frac{3}{4}$"

$1\frac{1}{8}$"

C   F

$\frac{3}{4}$" $\frac{3}{4}$"

MOLDING PROFILE

29"

F   E

C

A

B

32"

A

B

D

H

I

24"

$25\frac{1}{2}$"

12"

8"

FRONT ELEVATION

$9\frac{1}{4}$"

$\frac{3}{4}$"

E

C

D

$6\frac{3}{4}$"

$11\frac{1}{4}$"

$\frac{3}{4}$"

$31\frac{1}{4}$"

B

$11\frac{1}{4}$"

$\frac{3}{4}$"

H

$7\frac{1}{4}$"

$4\frac{1}{2}$"

$2\frac{1}{2}$"

I

$2\frac{1}{2}$"

$7\frac{1}{4}$"

1" squares

SIDE SECTION

PHOTO B: Lay out the arches on the apron and bottom trim pieces. A one-gallon paint can serves as a good template to draw the curves.

PHOTO C: Cut the curved profiles in the sides, apron and bottom trim pieces with a jig saw.

PHOTO D: Glue and clamp the top and bottom shelves to one of the cabinet sides. Reinforce the joints with 2-in. finish nails.

each side panel, and draw the curves **(See Photo A).**

❹ Lay out the arches on the apron and bottom trim pieces: See the *Apron & Bottom Trim Layout* drawing for marking the three arch positions on both parts. You could use a compass to draw the curves, but we found that a gallon-size paint can makes an easy template. Set the can in position on your layout marks, and draw the curves **(See Photo B).**

❺ Cut the curved profiles in the sides, apron and bottom trim pieces with a jig saw. Clamp each part to your worksurface to hold it steady while you make the cuts **(See Photo C).**

❻ Smooth the curved cuts and remove any saw marks with a file.

❼ Sand the sides, apron and bottom trim workpieces smooth with 150-grit sandpaper. It's easier to sand these parts now while all surfaces are accessible than after you begin assembly.

MAKE THE SHELVES, NAILER & TOP

❽ Lay out and crosscut two 24-in. shelves from pine 1 × 8.

❾ Cut the cabinet top to size from pine 1 × 10.

❿ Crosscut a 24-in. length of pine 1 × 4 to form the cabinet nailer.

⓫ Sand the shelves, nailer and top panel smooth.

ASSEMBLE THE SIDES & SHELVES

⓬ Lay out and assemble the shelves on the cabinet sides: Note in the *Front Elevation* drawing, that the bottom shelf is located 8 in. up from the bottom ends of the sides, and the top shelf is spaced 12 in. from the bottom shelf. Mark these positions, then attach the top and bottom shelves to one of the cabinet sides. Spread glue on one end of the top shelf and clamp it to one cabinet side so it aligns with the top shelf reference lines. Drive three 2-in. finish nails through the side and into the end of the top shelf to fasten the parts together **(See Photo D)**. Repeat this process to attach the bottom shelf to the same side.

⓭ Install the other cabinet side: Spread glue on the other ends of the two shelves and clamp the remaining cabinet side in place, so the shelves align with their respective shelf reference marks **(See Photo E)**.

INSTALL THE NAILER, APRON & BOTTOM TRIM

⓮ Fasten the nailer between the cabinet sides with glue and 2-in. nails. Position the nailer so it is flush with the top ends and back edges of the cabinet sides (See the *Side Section View* drawing).

⓯ Glue and nail the bottom trim piece in place between the cabinet sides. Position the bottom trim so the scallop profiles face the top of the project and the workpiece is flush with the back edges and bottom ends of the sides.

⓰ Install the apron: Spread glue on the ends of the apron, slip it in place between the cabinet sides flush with the top ends and front edges of the sides. Fasten the parts with nails driven through the cabinet sides **(See Photo F)**.

⓱ Recess the nailheads that secure the shelves, nailer, bottom trim and apron with a nailset.

PHOTO E: Spread glue on the free ends of the shelves, clamp the second cabinet side in place and fasten the parts with more 2-in. finish nails.

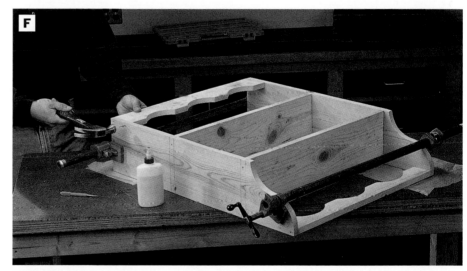

PHOTO F: Install the nailer, apron and bottom trim piece with glue and 2-in. finish nails. Recess all the nailheads with a nailset.

PHOTO G: Using wire brads, attach the beadboard back panel to the back edges of the cabinet sides and shelves as well as to the nailer and bottom trim piece. Set the heads of the brads.

Country Wall Cabinet 187

PHOTO H: Position the top on the cabinet so it is flush with the cabinet back and overhangs evenly on the sides and front. Glue, clamp and nail the top in place. Set the nailheads.

PHOTO I: Cut the front and side molding pieces to length. Form 45° mitered corners where the molding wraps around the front of the cabinet by cutting the ends of the molding in a miter box.

PHOTO J: Fasten the front and side molding pieces to the cabinet with glue and 1½-in. finish nails. Drive the nails at an angle up and into the cabinet top.

INSTALL THE BACK, TOP & COVE MOLDING

18 Lay out and cut the beadboard back panel to size with a circular saw or jig saw. Try to position the long cuts for sizing the panel to width so they split the beaded pattern evenly. Otherwise, the panel will look out of balance once it's installed in the project.

19 Fasten the back panel to the back edges of the shelves and sides as well as to the nailer and bottom trim with ¾-in. brads. Set the brad heads **(See Photo G)**.

20 Install the top: Set the top panel in place on the cabinet so it is flush with the back face of the back panel and overhangs the cabinet sides and front evenly. Mark the cabinet position on the top. Spread glue on the mating parts, and clamp the top in place. Secure the top to the cabinet with 2-in. finish nails **(See Photo H)**.

㉑ Install the cove molding: Cross-cut the front and two side molding pieces to length. Mark the ends of the front molding piece with 45° miters. Mark the front ends of the side molding pieces with 45° miters as well. Cut the miters using a miter box or a hand saw **(See Photo I).**

㉒ Dry-fit the molding strips in place around the cabinet and beneath the top. Adjust the fit of the mitered ends by lightly filing or sanding them a little at a time until the joints close.

㉓ Fasten the cove molding to the cabinet with glue and 1½-in. finish nails **(See Photo J).**

INSTALL THE TOWEL ROD

㉔ Cut the towel rod dowel to length. Mark the towel rod locations on the outer faces of the cabinet sides (See the *Side Section* drawing).

㉕ Position the dowel between the sides so it is centered on its reference marks. Drill a pilot hole at your towel rod reference marks and into the ends of the rod. Pin the towel rod in place with a 2-in. finish nail driven into each pilot hole **(See Photo K).**

FINISHING TOUCHES

㉖ Fill nailhead recesses with wood putty and sand smooth.

㉗ If you plan to stain your wall cabinet, brush on a coat of wood conditioner first. Wood conditioner will help the stain penetrate more evenly on softwoods like pine **(See Photo L).**

㉘ Apply your choice of stain, followed by two or three coats of varnish **(See Photo M).**

PHOTO K: Cut the towel rod to fit between the cabinet sides and mark its position. Install the rod with a 2-in. finish nail driven through the cabinet sides and into each end of the dowel. Drill pilot holes for the nails first to keep from splitting the dowel.

PHOTO L (Optional): If you plan to stain the project, it's a good idea to brush on a coat of wood conditioner first. Stain tends to penetrate softwoods like pine unevenly, resulting in a blotchy appearance. Wood conditioner will make the stain penetrate more evenly.

PHOTO M: Brush or wipe on a coat of stain while the wood conditioner is still wet. Allow the stain a few minutes to penetrate into the wood, then wipe off the excess with a clean rag. When the stain dries, apply a clear topcoat.

Tavern Mirror

This tavern-style entry hall mirror makes a dramatic statement to anyone who visits your home. Beyond simply offering practical conveniences, like somewhere to hang a coat and take a moment to fix your hair, it conveys a sense of warmth and welcome. If you're looking for a highly useful woodworking project with low materials cost and high visibility, this tavern mirror is the project for you.

Vital Statistics: Tavern Mirror

TYPE: Entry mirror/coatrack

OVERALL SIZE: 39W by 26H

MATERIAL: Red oak

JOINERY: Dowel joints throughout

CONSTRUCTION DETAILS:

- Arc on top rail and decorative chamfers on inside edges of rails and stiles
- Coved profile on top cap
- Three brass coat hooks
- ¼-in.-thick mirrored glass
- Mounts to wall with screws and lower hanging strip

FINISHING OPTIONS: Use clear topcoat only for more contemporary settings or use medium to dark wood stain for a more traditional wood tone.

Building time

PREPARING STOCK
1-2 hours

LAYOUT
1-2 hours

CUTTING PARTS
3-4 hours

ASSEMBLY
1-2 hours

FINISHING
1-2 hours

TOTAL: 7-12 hours

Tools you'll use

- Router with chamfer and cove bits
- Table saw
- C-clamps
- 42 in. or longer bar or pipe clamps (2)
- Band saw or jig saw
- Combination square
- Doweling jig
- Drill/driver
- Miter saw
- Electronic stud finder

Shopping list

- ☐ (2) ¾ × 6 in. × 8 ft. red oak boards (clear)
- ☐ (1) ¼ × 19 × 30 in. piece of mirrored glass
- ☐ (1) ⅜-in.-dia. wood dowel
- ☐ #6 × 1¼, #6 × 2 in. flat-head wood screws
- ☐ Wood glue
- ☐ Finishing materials
- ☐ Wall anchors
- ☐ Brass coat hooks

Tavern Mirror

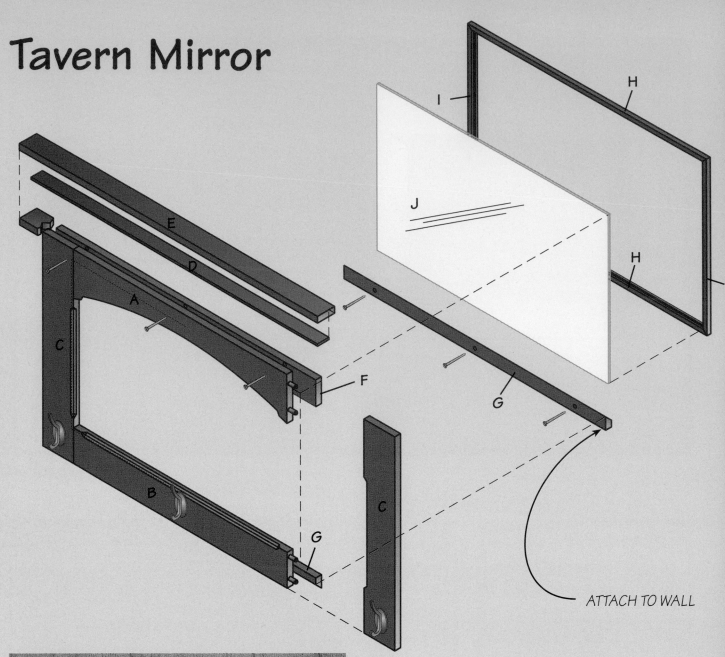

ATTACH TO WALL

Tavern Mirror Cutting List			
Part	**No.**	**Size**	**Material**
A. Top rail	1	¾ × 5½ × 28 in.	Red oak
B. Lower rail	1	¾ × 4 × 28 in.	"
C. Stiles	2	¾ × 4 × 24 in.	"
D. Coved cap	1	¾ × 1½ × 37½ in.	"
E. Cap strip	1	¾ × 2¼ × 39 in.	"
F. Hang strip (top)	1	¾ × 3 × 34 in.	"
G. Hang strip (lower)	2	¾ × 1½ × 34 in.	"
H. Retainers (top/bottom)	2	½ × ¾ × 31 in.	"
I. Retainers (side)	2	½ × ¾ × 20 in.	"
J. Mirror	1	¼ × 19 × 30 in.	Mirrored glass

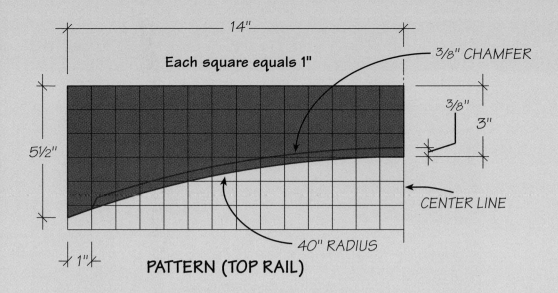

14"

Each square equals 1"

3/8" CHAMFER

3/8"

3"

5½"

CENTER LINE

40" RADIUS

1"

PATTERN (TOP RAIL)

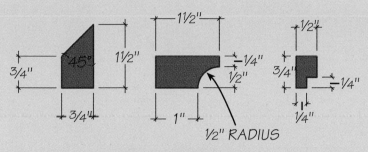

1½"

45°

1½"

3/4"

3/4"

1½"

¼"

½"

1"

½" RADIUS

½"

3/4"

¼"

¼"

¼"

DETAILS

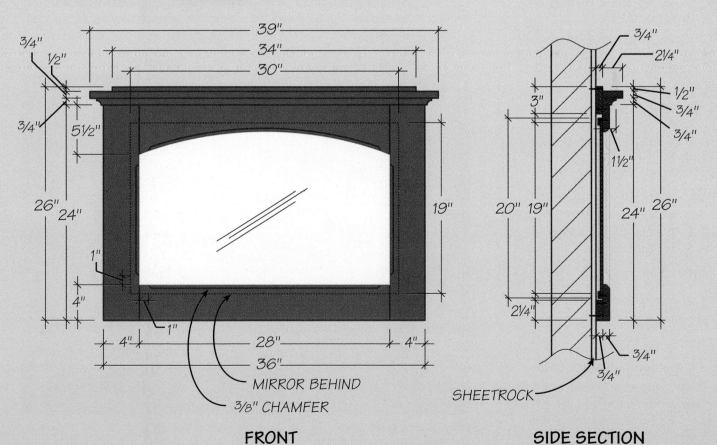

3/4"

½"

3/4"

39"

34"

30"

3/4"

2¼"

½"

3/4"

3/4"

5½"

3"

26"

24"

19"

20"

19"

1½"

24"

26"

1"

4"

2¼"

1"

4"

28"

4"

3/4"

36"

3/4"

MIRROR BEHIND

SHEETROCK

3/8" CHAMFER

FRONT

SIDE SECTION

PHOTO A: Make decorative stopped chamfer cuts on the inside edges of the rails and stiles. Use a router and piloted chamfer bit to make the cuts. Clamp stopblocks to the rails and stiles to start and stop the router at the proper points.

MAKE THE FRAME

The rails and stiles that make up the mirror frame are shaped and profiled prior to assembly.

❶ Rip-cut and cross-cut the rails and stiles to size from ¾-in. stock.

❷ Enlarge the half-pattern for the top rail curve (See *Grid drawing*) to full size. Transfer it to ¼-in. scrap hardboard and cut out the shape. Use this half-template to trace the arc onto the top rail, starting at one end and flipping it over to complete the other half of the shape.

❸ Cut out the shape with a band saw, jig saw or scroll saw. Smooth the sawn edge with sandpaper or a file.

❹ Install a piloted chamfer bit in your router and adjust the cutter height to give a ⅜-in.-deep chamfer (See *Sidebar article,* next page). Rout chamfers along the inside front edges of all the rails and stiles, starting and stopping the cuts at the points shown in the *Front* diagram (**See Photo A**).

❺ Lay out and drill holes for dowel joints in the rails and stiles using a doweling jig. Biscuit joints may be substituted for dowel joints if you prefer.

PHOTO B: Glue up the joints in the rails and stiles and assemble the mirror frame. Clamp, using scrapwood blocks to protect the wood. You can use either dowels or biscuits to help align and reinforce the joint.

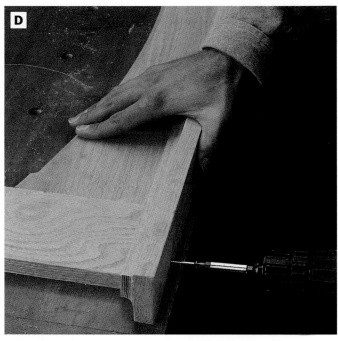

PHOTO C: Rout a coved profile around the front edge and the ends of the cove cap. The workpiece should be at least 3 in. wide to support the router base. Rip it to width after the profiles are cut.

PHOTO D: Attach the two-piece cap assembly to the top of the mirror frame with wood screws and glue.

ROUTER WITH CHAMFER BIT

An easy way to get a consistent chamfer along the edge of a board is to use a router and a piloted chamfer bit. Typical chamfer bits have a 45° angle. Set the router base on the face of the board and run the free-spinning pilot bearing against the board's edge. The distance the cutter protrudes past the router's subbase determines the depth of the chamfer. Adjust the height as close as possible to your desired depth, then make some practice cuts and adjust up or down as needed.

ROUTER WITH COVE BIT

A cove bit is the opposite of a roundover bit: it scoops out a cove, or concave arc, into the edge of a board. Like a roundover bit, cove bits are available with cutters of different radii. As with the chamfer bit, adjust the cutter height to make your desired cut, and run the pilot bearing against the board's edge. Orient the router so the direction of the bit rotation feeds the cutters toward and into the oncoming wood.

6 Apply glue to the mating frame piece ends and to the ends of ⅜ in. hardwood dowels, then clamp the frame assembly together with bar or pipe clamps **(See Photo B)**. Make sure the outer edges of the parts are flush.

MAKE THE CAP PIECES

The cap for the mirror frame is a two-piece assembly that spans across the top of the entire frame. The lower cap piece is shaped with a decorative cove, using a router and cove bit.

7 Rip-cut and cross-cut the cap strip to size. Rip-cut the coved cap to 3 in. wide (slightly oversized to leave bearing surface for the router foot), and cross-cut it to 37½ in.

8 Install a piloted ½-in. cove bit in your router (See *Sidebar article, left*). Adjust the cutter height and cut a ½-in.-deep cove **(See Photo C)**. Rout the ends of the

PHOTO E: Miter-cut the retainers to length to form a frame around your mirror. We used a power miter saw to make the miter cuts.

PHOTO F: Center the mirror over the back of the frame opening, then frame it with the retainers to hold it in place.

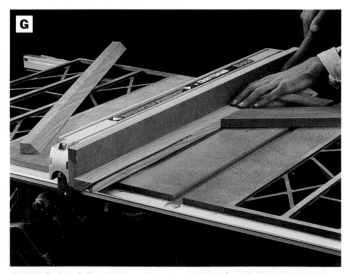

PHOTO G: Bevel-rip a 45° angle on one edge of each lower hang strip, using your table saw and a pushstick and featherboard.

coved cap, as well as the front edge, for a three-sided profile. Rip-cut the coved cap to 1½ in. wide.

❾ Finish-sand the surfaces of the cap boards, as well as the rails and stiles. Ease all sharp edges with sandpaper.

ATTACH THE CAP PIECES

❿ Glue and clamp the coved cap to the cap strip, making sure the back edges are aligned and the cap strip overhangs the ends of the coved cap by an equal amount on each end.

⓫ Set the cap assembly onto the top rail, flush with the back edge and centered along the length, from end to end. Attach the assembly to the top of the mirror frame with #6 × 2-in. flathead wood screws driven into countersunk pilot holes **(See Photo D).** Use four evenly spaced screws.

INSTALL THE MIRROR

The mirror is held in place with a retainer frame made from ½-in.-thick stock. The retainers are rabbeted on the inside edges to create a reveal for the mirror, then they're screwed to the back of the mirror frame. The ¼-in.-thick mirrored glass can be purchased cut-to-size from any glass store or most hardware stores.

⓬ On the edge of two ¾-in. oak boards at least 54 in. long, cut a ¼- × ¼-in. rabbet groove (make multiple passes on your table saw with the blade height set at ¼ in., using a rip fence and pushstick). Plane the boards down to a thickness of ½ in., being sure to remove the stock from the non-rabbeted face. Cross-cut the retainer frame pieces from these strips, making each piece an inch or two longer than called for in the *Cutting list.*

⓭ Miter-cut the retainers to form a frame for your mirror **(See Photo E).**

⓮ Touch up any rough spots on the front of the mirror frame with sandpaper. Because it's important to finish all of the wood surfaces, we stained and top-coated all frame pieces before installing the mirror. We used a dark walnut-colored stain and tung oil topcoat. Let the finish dry fully before installing the mirror.

⑮ With the mirror frame face-down on a flat surface, center the mirror over the frame opening. Drill countersunk pilot holes for #6 × 1 in. wood screws in the retainer frame pieces, then arrange the retainer frame pieces around the mirror. Secure the mirror by driving screws through the retainers and into the back of the mirror frame (**See Photo F**).

HANG THE MIRROR

The mirror is attached to a wall using a hang strip on top that is screwed to the wall framing members. A beveled hang strip mounted to the bottom of the mirror frame, on the back side, slips over another beveled strip that's mounted to the wall (the standard technique used to hang wall cabinets).

⑯ Cut the hang strips to size. The two lower hang strips are bevel-ripped at a 45° angle along one edge (**See Photo G**). Apply a finish to the top hang strip, then attach it and one of the lower strips to the back of the frame with #6 × 1¼-in. wood screws (**See Photo H**). The top strip should protrude above the top of the frame cap by ½ in. to allow room for driving screws through the strip and into the wall. The bevel on the bottom strip should be facing downward so that its bevel will interlock with the lower strip mounted on the wall. Situate the lower strips such that the other strip (mounted to the wall) will be flush with the bottom edge of the frame.

⑰ Screw the lower wall-mounted hang strip to the wall. Make sure it's level and at the correct height so the center of the mirror is at eye level. Drive screws through the hang strip and into wall framing member locations.

⑱ Before mounting the mirror to the wall, drill pilot holes and screw the coat hooks into the lower frame rail. Take care to position the hooks so they're evenly spaced and aligned horizontally.

⑲ Drill three evenly spaced countersunk pilot holes into the exposed front edge of the top hang strip. Set the mirror frame onto the lower hang strip mounted on the wall (**See Photo I**), then mark the wall anchor locations for screws to affix the upper hang strip. Take the frame down and install wall anchors at the screw locations. Set the mirror back onto the wall strip and attach the top hang strip to the wall. If you're concerned that the screwheads will be visible, cover them with wood putty or use brass screws.

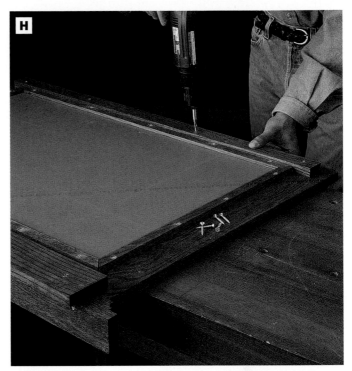

PHOTO H: Attach the top and bottom hang strips to the back of the mirror frame with wood screws driven into counterbored pilot holes.

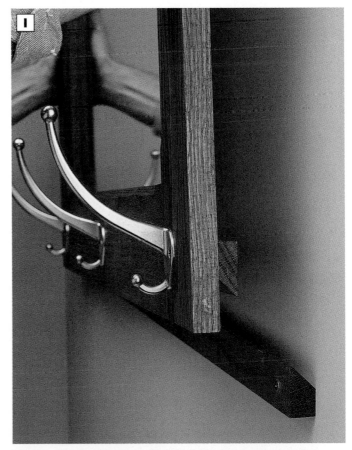

PHOTO I: Attach one lower hang strip to the wall, bevel up, at the desired height of the bottom of the mirror. Use 2 in. or longer screws driven at wall framing member locations. Set the mirror on the strip and mark drilling locations for attaching the top hang strip.

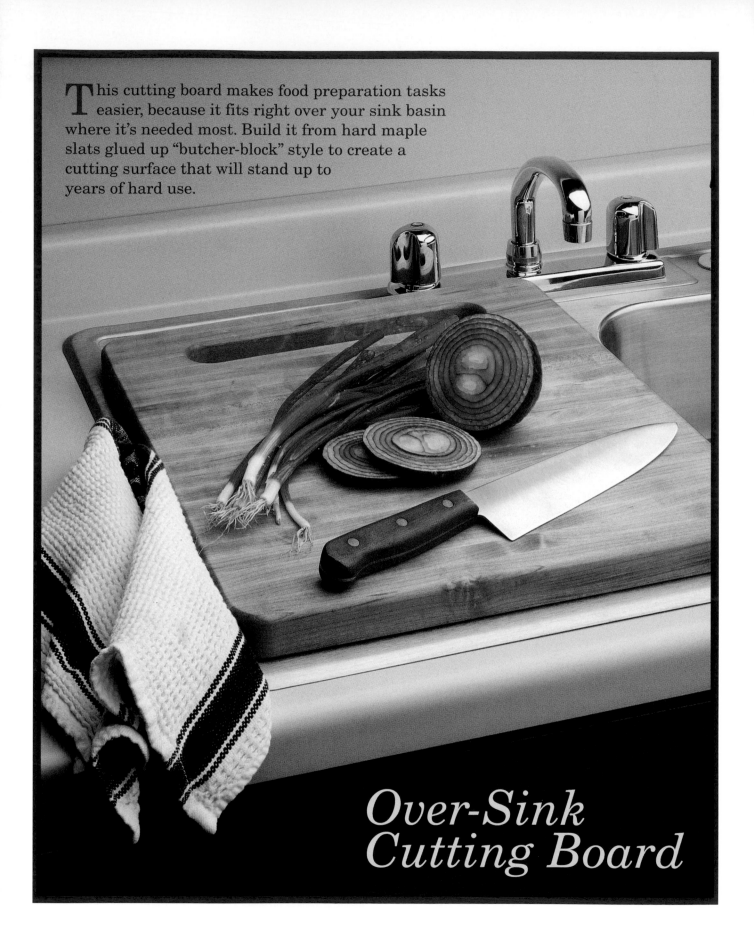

This cutting board makes food preparation tasks easier, because it fits right over your sink basin where it's needed most. Build it from hard maple slats glued up "butcher-block" style to create a cutting surface that will stand up to years of hard use.

Over-Sink Cutting Board

Vital Statistics: Over-Sink Cutting Board

TYPE: Cutting board

OVERALL SIZE: 15¼W by 1¼H by 17½L (You may need to modify overall length and width to accommodate the dimensions of your sink)

MATERIAL: Hard maple

JOINERY: Face-glued butt joints, screwed butt joints

CONSTRUCTION DETAILS:
- Board slats are oriented edge grain up, "butcher-block" style, to reduce wood movement and provide a more durable cutting surface
- Handle cutout and board edges rounded over
- Feet must be cut to fit your sink basin, then attached with screws beneath the cutting board

FINISH: Butcher block or mineral oil

Building time

 PREPARING STOCK
2 hours

 LAYOUT
1 hour

 CUTTING PARTS
3-4 hours

 ASSEMBLY
1 hour

 FINISHING
1 hour

TOTAL: 8-9 hours

Tools you'll use

- Planer
- Jointer
- Table saw
- Clamps
- Router with ¼-in. piloted roundover bit
- Drill/driver or drill press
- Jig saw
- Files and rasps
- Belt sander

Shopping list

- ☐ (1) 4/4 hard maple, about 8 board ft.
- ☐ #8 × 1½-in. stainless-steel flathead wood screws
- ☐ Polyurethane glue
- ☐ Two-part epoxy
- ☐ Finishing materials

Over-Sink Cutting Board

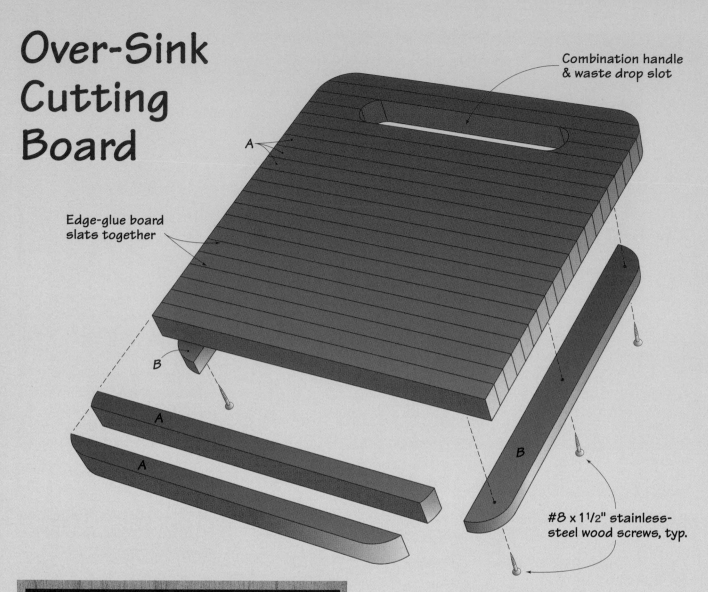

Combination handle & waste drop slot

Edge-glue board slats together

A

B

A

A

B

#8 x 1¹/2" stainless-steel wood screws, typ.

Over-Sink Cutting Board Cutting List

Part	No.	Size	Material
A. Board slats	23	¾ × 1¼ × 15¾* in.	Hard maple
B. Feet	2	¾ × 1½ × 16* in.	"

* Length will vary, depending on sink dimensions

Adjust overall dimensions & feet locations so cutting board fits your sink

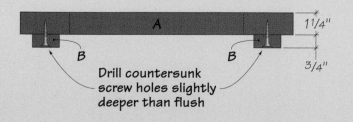

A

B   B

1¹/4"

3/4"

Drill countersunk screw holes slightly deeper than flush

END VIEW

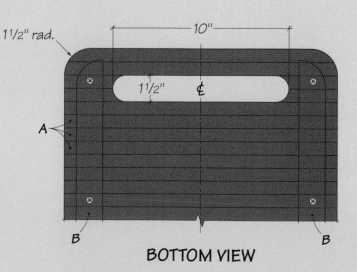

1¹/2" rad.

10"

1¹/2"

₵

A

B   B

BOTTOM VIEW

PHOTO A: Crosscut the maple stock to 15¾-in. blanks, then rip the blanks into 1¼-in.-wide slats on the table saw. You'll need to make 23 of these slats for the cutting board.

MAKE THE BOARD SLATS

❶ Plane the 4/4 maple stock to ¾ in. thick. Then joint one long edge smooth and flat. When planing hard maple, remove no more than 1/32 in. with each pass to keep from prematurely dulling the planer knives.

❷ Cut the slats to length and width. First crosscut the maple into 15¾-in.-long blanks. Then set your table saw's fence 1¼-in. from the blade. With the jointed edge of the boards against the fence, rip-cut each blank into slats (See Photo A). Cut 23 slats in all.

GLUE UP THE SLATS

❸ When gluing up this cutting board, you could glue and clamp all the joints at once, but it would be difficult to tighten the clamps without the slats sliding out of alignment with one another in the process. A better method is to glue up half the slats in one assembly, glue up the other half in a second assembly, then join the halves with one final glue joint when the halves are dry. You'll also be able to run these narrower glued-up assemblies through a power planer to smooth them.

❹ Glue up 12 slats: Place a sheet of wax paper on a flat workbench to protect the bench from glue squeeze-out. Apply an even coat-

PHOTO B: Glue and clamp the slats into groups of 12 and 11, then join these two subassemblies together to form the full cutting board blank. Subassemblies make final clamp-up easier.

ing of moisture-resistant wood glue to the mating faces of each slat, and clamp up the assembly. You could also use polyurethane glue for even more water resistance, but be sure to dampen one surface of each glue joint with water first, before applying the glue. (Polyurethane glue requires moisture in order to set up.) Alternate clamps above and below the slats to distribute clamping pressure evenly over the width of the assembly. Tighten the clamps just enough to close the glue joints. Use a mallet to tap the slats flat if they shift out of alignment.

PHOTO C: Trim the ends of the board on the table saw to even up the slats and establish the final length of the cutting board. Ours was 15½ in., but yours might vary, depending on your sink.

PHOTO D: Mark for the 1½-in. radius corners, and cut the corners to shape with a jig saw. Then smooth all of the edges with a belt sander.

5 Glue up the remaining 11 slats as you did in Step 4. Both slat glue-ups can occur at the same time if you have enough clamps.

6 Plane both faces of each slat assembly to even out the edges of the slats and remove all glue squeeze-out. Be sure to plane both assemblies at the same planer thickness settings to achieve two panels that are the same final thickness. A few shallow passes on each face should be all you'll need to produce flat, smooth faces.

7 Glue and clamp the two slat subassemblies together to form the full cutting board blank (**See Photo B**).

8 Trim the ends of the board on the table saw to cut the blank to final length (**See Photo C**). Let the final cutting board length be determined by the size of your sink. The board should completely overlap the sink opening and rest fully on the sink rim.

9 Round the corners of the board to shape: Use a compass to draw the 1½-in. radius on each corner, and trim the corners to rough shape with a jig saw. Then finish the arcs with a belt sander (**See Photo D**). Belt-sand the edges, ends, and faces of the board now, to remove any remaining saw and planer marks.

10 Cut out the handle: Lay out the proportions and location of the handle, using the *Bottom View* drawing as a guide. At the drill press, bore out the ends of the handle with a 1½-in. bit. Then use a jig saw to cut the straight lines that connect the large holes and complete the handle (**See Photo E**). If you don't have a drill press, you could also drill an entry hole for the jig saw blade and make the complete handle cutout with the jig saw instead.

11 Smooth the board edges: Round over the edges of the handle cutout and the top and bottom edges of the board with a router and ¼-in. piloted roundover bit.

INSTALL THE FEET

12 Make and install the feet: Rip and crosscut two lengths of maple for the feet, with the lengths sized according to the inside opening of your sink basin. Carefully mark the foot locations on the cutting board, so the feet run perpendicular to the slats and are flush with the sink basin walls. TIP: *Use short strips of double-sided carpet tape to hold the feet in place when you are determining their final placement on the cutting board. This way, you can shift the foot positions as needed to achieve the best fit on the sink before installing with screws.* Drill countersunk pilot holes through the feet and into the board, and install the feet with two-part epoxy and 1½-in. stainless-steel or brass wood screws **(See Photo F).**

FINISHING TOUCHES

13 Rub several coats of a food-safe finish, like butcher block or mineral oil, on all exposed surfaces of the cutting board. Pay special attention to end-grain areas, such as around the handle and on the board ends; these spots are especially susceptible to water absorption and damage. Once it dries, a food-safe finish will not seal the board entirely. For that reason, never submerse the board in water, and wipe the board dry after washing it clean. Do not clean in a dishwasher.

PHOTO E: Make the handle cutout by first drilling the curved ends with a 1½-in. bit or hole saw. Cut out the remaining waste with a jig saw, and clean up the edges with a file.

PHOTO F: Cut the feet to size and shape. Then set the cutting board in place on your sink to determine the best positions for the feet. Mark the locations of the feet on the board. Attach the feet with stainless-steel flathead wood screws and two-part epoxy.

Two-Step Stool

Those top-shelf items will always be within easy reach if you keep this step stool near the kitchen or pantry. The steps are made with premilled oak stair treads, so they're strong as well as attractive, and the 17 × 18-in. stool base will keep you sure-footed even with both feet on the top step.

Vital Statistics

TYPE: Two-step stool

OVERALL SIZE: 18L by 15H by 17D

MATERIAL: Birch plywood, oak stair tread

JOINERY: Butt joints reinforced with glue and screws

CONSTRUCTION DETAILS:
- Sides joined to stretchers with screws to strengthen the stool and to keep it from racking
- Handle cut-out in top step made by drilling out the ends of the cut-out with a spade bit, then removing the waste between the holes with a jig saw
- Sides are made of plywood to eliminate the need for gluing up solid-wood panels

FINISH: Primer and paint; varnish

BUILDING TIME: 3-4 hours

Shopping List

- [ ] (1) ¾ in. × 2 × 4 ft. birch plywood
- [ ] (1) 1 × 12 × 36 in. bull-nosed oak stair tread
- [ ] #8 × 2 in. flathead wood screws
- [ ] 2 in. finish nails
- [ ] Wood glue
- [ ] Finishing materials

Two-Step Stool: Step-by-step

MAKE THE STRETCHERS

❶ Lay out and cut the back stretchers: Rip two 2-in.-wide, 2-ft.-long strips from the plywood sheet. Make these rip-cuts with your saw guided against a straightedge. Then crosscut the strips into 15-in.-long stretchers.

❷ Lay out and cut the front stretchers: The stretcher beneath the front edge of each step receives a decorative angled cutout along the bottom edge. Since these stretchers are only 2 in. wide, it wouldn't be safe or easy to make the angled cutouts after ripping

PHOTO A: Gang-cut the stool sides to shape, following the cutting lines you drew on the top workpiece. Use a stiff, fine-toothed blade in the jig saw to produce accurate, smooth cuts. Guide the saw against a clamped straightedge for best results.

Two-Step Stool

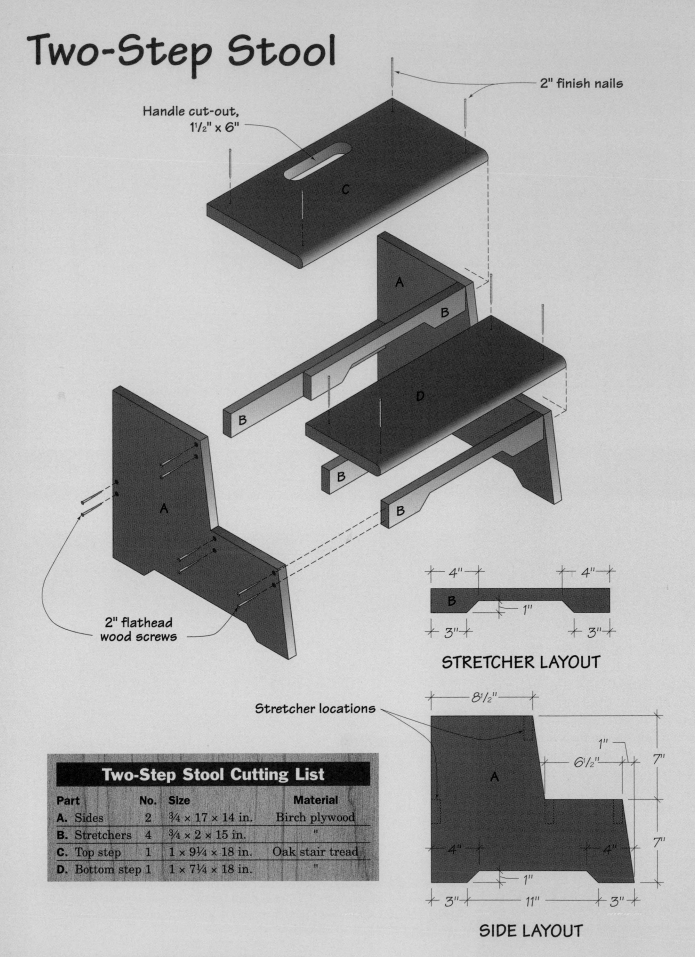

Handle cut-out, 1½" x 6"

2" finish nails

2" flathead wood screws

STRETCHER LAYOUT

4"   4"

B

1"

3"   3"

Stretcher locations

SIDE LAYOUT

8½"

1"

6½"

7"

A

4"   4"

1"

7"

3"   11"   3"

Two-Step Stool Cutting List			
Part	**No.**	**Size**	**Material**
A. Sides	2	¾ × 17 × 14 in.	Birch plywood
B. Stretchers	4	¾ × 2 × 15 in.	"
C. Top step	1	1 × 9¼ × 18 in.	Oak stair tread
D. Bottom step	1	1 × 7¼ × 18 in.	"

and crosscutting the stretchers to size. Instead, make the two stretchers one at a time, laying out and cutting the angled profile into the large sheet of plywood first, then cutting the stretcher free. For each stretcher, draw the angled cutout along the end of the plywood sheet, using the *Stretcher Layout* drawing as a guide. Cut out the profile with a jig saw. Then measure and mark the length and width of the stretcher around the cut-out, and rip and crosscut the stretcher to size.

MAKE THE SIDES

❸ Rip and crosscut two plywood pieces for the stool sides.

❹ Draw the sides: Since the proportions of both side panels match, you can draw the shape of a side onto one board, stack the boards on top of one another and cut them both to size at one time. Use the *Side Layout* drawing as a guide for laying out the profile.

❺ Cut out the sides. Clamp the plywood together so the leg shapes are in the same arrangement. Cut both sides to shape with a jig saw **(See Photo A).**

ASSEMBLE THE SIDES & STRETCHERS

❻ Mark the positions of the stretchers on the side panels: The top edge of the back stretcher is 7 in. up from the bottom of each side. The stretchers with profiles should align with the top front edges of the steps. The remaining stretcher supports the back edge of the bottom step.

❼ Fasten the sides and stretchers together: Spread glue on the ends of the stretchers and within the stretcher locations on the sides.

PHOTO B: Glue and clamp the stretchers in place between the stool sides. Fasten the parts with countersunk flathead wood screws.

PHOTO C: Conceal the screwheads and any voids in the plywood with wood putty, spreading the putty with a putty knife. Once the putty dries, sand away the excess.

PHOTO D: Measure, mark and rip-cut both oak steps to width. Be sure to clamp the workpieces securely to your worksurface when making the cuts.

PHOTO E: Remove the waste within the handle cut-out area on the top step. We drilled out the rounded ends of the cut-out first with a 1½-in.-dia. spade bit, then cut away the rest of the waste with a jig saw.

Clamp the stretchers in place between the sides. Drill pairs of countersunk pilot holes through the sides and into the stretchers, then drive 2-in. flathead wood screws to secure the parts (**See Photo B**).

FINISH THE STOOL BASE

8 Fill the holes left by the screwheads with wood putty (**See Photo C**). Fill any voids in the edges of the plywood parts with putty as well.

9 Sand the exposed surfaces of the stool base with 150-grit sandpaper to smooth the puttied areas and ease the edges.

10 Prime and paint the stool base, but leave the top edges of the sides and stretchers bare for glue in areas that will be covered by the oak stair treads.

MAKE THE STAIR TREADS

11 Cut the 36-in. length of oak stair tread in half to make the 18-in.-long stool steps.

12 Rip-cut the top and bottom steps to width: Mark the top step to a width of 9¼ in. and the bottom step to 7¼ in. Lay out these cuts so you'll trim off the edge opposite the bull-nosed (rounded-over) edge. Clamp each step to your work surface, and guide the saw against a straightedge when ripping the steps to width (**See Photo D**).

13 Lay out and cut the handle cut-out in the top step: The handle cut-out is 6 in. long and 1½ in. wide, with rounded ends. Position the cut-out so it is centered on the length of the top step and inset 1 in. from the back edge. There are several ways to remove the waste from the cut-out: You could drill a small pilot hole within the waste area for starting the saw blade, and cut away all of the waste with a jig saw. However, the tight end radii would be difficult to cut without needing plenty of sanding afterward. A better option is to drill out the curved ends of the cut-out with a 1½-in. spade bit, then remove the remaining waste with a jig saw **(See Photo E).** The second method ensures that the rounded ends of the cut-out will be uniform and smooth. Once you've removed the waste, file and sand the edges of the cut-out smooth.

INSTALL THE STEPS

14 Position the oak steps on the stool base and mark the overhang on the ends. The back edge of the top step should align with the back edge of the stool. The bottom step should seat fully on the lower flat surface on the stool sides. Both steps overhang the stool base by ¾ in. on each side. Clamp the steps in place on the stool base.

15 Fasten the steps to the stool base. Drill pilot holes for 2-in. finish nails, positioning the nails so the steps will attach to both the stool sides and stretchers **(See Photo F).** Remove the clamps and spread glue on the mating surfaces of the parts. Re-clamp the steps on the stool base and nail the steps in place. Recess the nailheads **(See Photo G).**

FINISH THE STEPS

16 Fill holes left by the nailheads in the steps with tinted wood putty. Sand the putty and the steps smooth and ease any other sharp edges.

17 Apply several coats of a clear finish, like polyurethane, to all exposed surfaces of the steps.

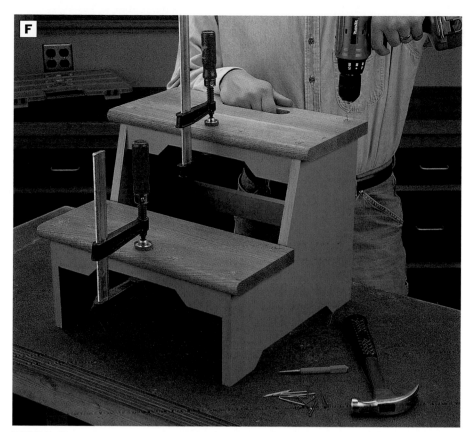

PHOTO F: Clamp the steps in place on the stool base. Drill pilot holes through the steps and into the stretchers and sides for attaching the parts with 2-in. finish nails.

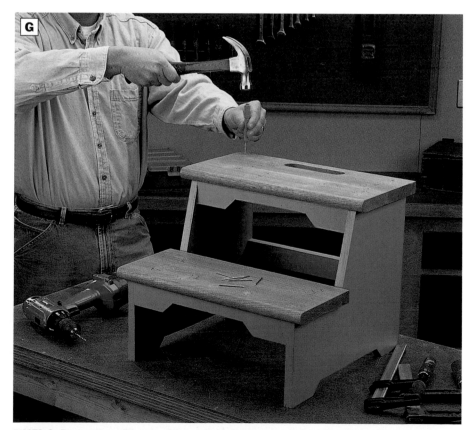

PHOTO G: Recess the nailheads with a nailset. Conceal the holes with wood putty tinted to match the oak steps.

Magazine Rack

Confine the clutter of reading materials into one neat package with this compact and highly attractive magazine rack. Built from solid cherry, this rack design accomplishes an airy, modern feeling without sacrificing the look of fine furniture. And with careful cutting, you can build it from only two cherry boards.

Vital Statistics: Magazine Rack

TYPE: Magazine rack

OVERALL SIZE: 12W by 14H by 12D

MATERIAL: Cherry

JOINERY: Hidden dowel joints

CONSTRUCTION DETAILS:
· Generously spaced slats for contemporary appearance
· Smooth handle profile for comfortable carrying
· Divided compartment promotes organization
· Makes efficient use of materials

FINISHING OPTIONS: Brush on a clear topcoat such as Danish oil (shown). Could leave unfinished to allow tannins in the cherry wood to react with the air and darken the wood naturally.

Building time

PREPARING STOCK
1-2 hour

LAYOUT
2-4 hours

CUTTING PARTS
3-5 hours

ASSEMBLY
1-2 hours

FINISHING
1-2 hours

TOTAL: 8-15 hours

Tools you'll use

· Jointer
· Table saw
· Planer
· Router with piloted ⅛-in. roundover bit
· Metal rule
· 18-in. or longer bar or pipe clamps (6)
· Jig saw, band saw or scroll saw
· Miter saw (power or hand)
· Portable drill guide
· Doweling jig
· Metal dowel points
· Mallet
· Drill/driver

Shopping list

☐ (1) 4/4 × 4+ in. × 8 ft. cherry board

☐ (1) ¾ × 4 in. × 8 ft. cherry board

☐ ¼-in.-dia. hardwood doweling

☐ Wood glue

☐ Finishing materials

Magazine Rack

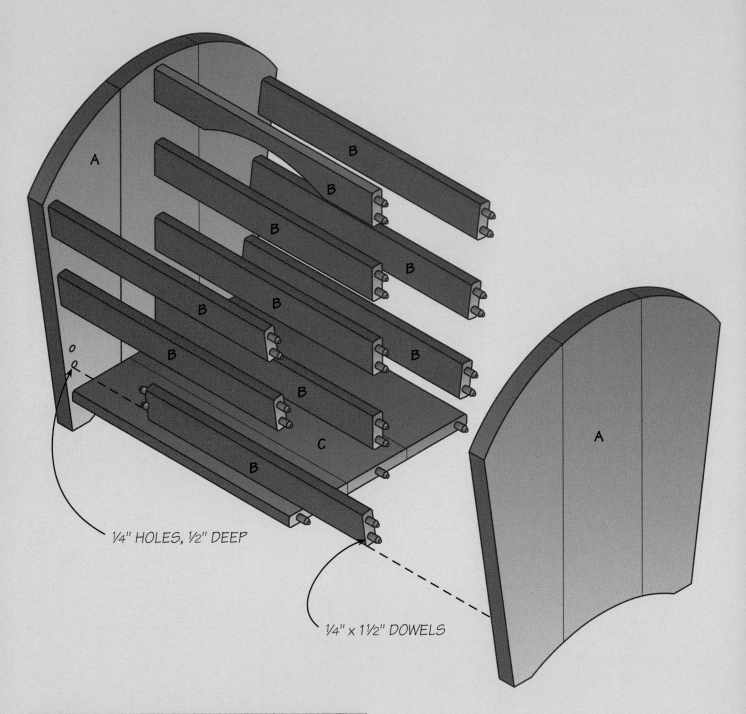

1/4" HOLES, 1/2" DEEP

1/4" x 1 1/2" DOWELS

Part	No.	Size	Material
Magazine Rack Cutting List			
A. Sides	2	3/4 × 12 × 14 in.	Cherry
B. Slats/handle	10	1/2 × 1 1/2 × 11 in.	"
C. Bottom	1	1/2 × 9 × 11 in.	"

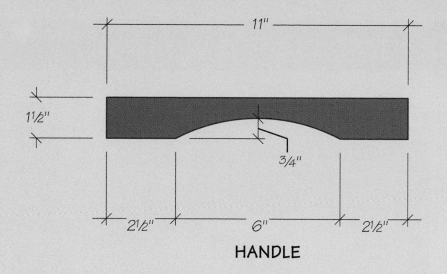

HANDLE

¼" HOLES, ½" DEEP IN ENDS AND
1¹⁄₁₆" DEEP IN RAILS, HANDLE & BOTTOM

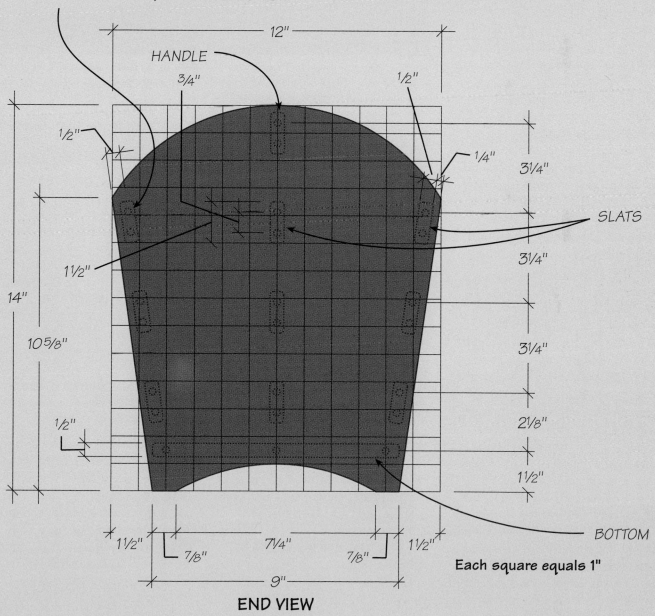

END VIEW

Each square equals 1"

PHOTO A: Edge-glue panels for the sides and the bottom. As you tighten the clamps, the glue will cause the joints to slide out of alignment, so adjust them as well as you can to keep them lined up. Be sure to use clamping pads to protect the wood.

PHOTO B: Drill small locator holes through the side template, at the centerpoints shown for each dowel location. Use scrap plywood underneath to prevent drill bit tear-out.

CUT THE PARTS TO SIZE

The parts for this magazine rack can all be cut from two 8-ft.-long cherry boards. We edge-glued three strips of ¾-in.(after planing) cherry to make the side panels. The ½-in.-thick bottom panel is also made from edge-glued cherry.

❶ Plane an 8-ft.-long, ¾ cherry board that's at least 4¼ in. wide to ¾ in. thick. Joint one edge of the board, then rip-cut it to 4⅛ in. wide (4¹⁄₁₆ in. is okay). Cross-cut six 15-in.-long sections, and edge-glue them into two panels that are roughly 12 × 15 in. **(See Photo A).** For a good glue joint, joint both edges of the middle board in each glue-up.

❷ Plane a ¾ × 4 in. × 8 ft. board down to ½ in. thick. Rip-cut a 3-ft.-long section from one end of the board, joint one edge, then rip-cut to 3⅛ in. wide. Cut the board into three 12-in.-long sections. Arrange the boards into a panel roughly 9 × 12 in. (joint both edges of the middle board) and glue up the panel to make the bottom of the magazine rack.

❸ On the remaining 5-ft. section of ½-in. stock, joint one edge, then rip-cut the jointed side to 1½ in. wide. Rip-cut the waste strip to 1½ in. wide as well, making sure to run the freshly cut edge against your table saw fence. Install a ⅛-in.-radius roundover bit in your router and ease all the edges of both strips. Reserve the strips to cut the rails and the handle.

CUT THE PARTS TO SHAPE

❹ Enlarge the *Grid Drawing* to full size by photocopying or by drawing a grid to scale and plotting out the pattern using the drawing as a reference. Secure the full-size drawing to a piece of ¼-in.-thick hardboard or plywood (we used spray adhesive). Cut out the shape along the lines with a band saw, scroll saw or jig saw to create a template. Smooth the sawn edges.

5 Place the template on a piece of scrap plywood to serve as a drilling backup board. Drill small holes (about the diameter of your awl or centerpunch) through the template at the dowel hole center-points shown on the *Grid Drawing* (**See Photo B**).

6 Cross-cut one end of each glued-up panel for the sides so the end is straight and square to the sides of the panel. Lay the template on each glued-up panel with its bottom edge flush with the squared end. Trace around the template to transfer the cutting shape. Use an awl or centerpunch to mark the dowel-hole centers through the locator holes in the template (**See Photo C**).

7 Cut out the shapes of the sides using a jig saw, band saw or scroll saw. Cut carefully along the waste sides of the lines (**See Photo D**). Sand the edges smooth.

8 Drill ¼-in.-dia. × ½-in.-deep dowel holes at the dowel-hole centers marked on each side panel. Use a portable drill guide and a bit stop (**See Photo E**).

9 Cross-cut the strips of ½ × 1½ in. stock into 10, 11-in.-long strips (**See Photo F**) to make the nine rails and the handle. We used a power miter saw with a stopblock set at 11 in. to speed up the cutting and ensure uniform lengths.

10 Choose one piece for the handle and draw a contour line for making the handle cutout. The arched cutout starts 2½ in. from each end and is ¾ high at the center (See *Detail Drawing*). Cut out the arc along the contour line and smooth the cut with a sander or file.

PHOTO C: Center the template on each side panel and outline the shape. Poke an awl or center-punch through the template holes to mark centerpoints for the dowel holes.

PHOTO D: Cut out the end shapes. We used a jig saw, but you could use a band saw or scroll saw instead. Cut along the waste sides of the cutting lines, then smooth the cuts with a file or by sanding with medium-grit sandpaper.

PHOTO E: Drill ½-in-deep dowel holes at the dowel hole centers you marked on each of the two sides with the hardboard template. Use a drill guide to ensure straight holes.

Stopblock

PHOTO F: Clamp a stopblock to the fence of a power miter saw, 11 in. from the edge of the blade, to make uniform cross-cuts when cutting the rails and handle pieces to length.

ASSEMBLE THE MAGAZINE RACK

Assembling the magazine rack can get tricky, since it involves 46 dowel pins (and 92 dowel holes). On the plus side, the scale of the project makes it easy to handle, so assembling the rack before the glue sets should be no problem.

⓫ Start with the bottom panel and drill three ¼-in.-dia. × 1¹⁄₁₆-in.-deep dowel holes in each end. The holes should align with the dowel holes you drilled into the bottoms of the side panels, using the template. To ensure that the holes do align, insert metal dowel points into the holes in the side panels, set the bottom panel in the correct position against the side panel, and press the two workpieces together. The pointed spur at the end of each dowel point will make a clear center-point for a corresponding dowel

PHOTO G: Use a doweling jig to drill centered dowel holes in the ends of the rails and handle. Clamp rails together edge-to-edge to provide more surface area for the jig.

PHOTO H: Glue the dowels in the ends of the handle, the slats, and the bottom into the corresponding dowel holes in one side panel. Then immediately glue dowels into the other end panel and set it onto the upright ends of the parts. Align the dowels into their holes and press the assembly together.

hole in the end of the bottom panel. Use a drill press or a drilling guide to bore the dowel holes. If you use a drilling guide, sandwich each workpiece between scrap boards to provide more support for the guide.

⑫ Drill two ¼-in.-dia. × 1¹⁄₁₆-in.-deep dowel holes in the end of each slat and in each end of the handle. Use a doweling jig to center the holes. Clamp a few parts at a time into your bench vise, aligning the ends straight across. This provides more bearing surface for the jig **(See Photo G)**.

⑬ Sand all the parts to 220-grit. Ease all sharp edges except for the ends of the rails and handles.

⑭ Apply glue and lightly tap ¼ × 1½-in. lengths of hardwood doweling into the dowel holes in one end of each cross member (the slats, the bottom and the handle).

⑮ Lay one side of the magazine rack on a worksurface so the dowel holes are facing up. Glue the joints and insert the cross members **(See Photo H)**.

⑯ Immediately glue and tap dowels into the holes in the other side panel. Then lay that panel on top of the exposed ends of the cross members, aligning the dowels with the corresponding dowel holes. Once the dowels are aligned, seat them by pressing against the cross members. Clamp the project across its ends, using cauls to spread the clamping pressure **(See Photo I)**.

⑰ Touch up any rough surfaces or edges with 220-grit sandpaper. Apply the finish. We brushed on three coats of clear, Danish oil **(See Photo J)**.

PHOTO I: Clamp up the rack assembly, using wood cauls to distribute pressure evenly. Use three pairs of bar or pipe clamps.

PHOTO J: Because of all the flat, narrow surfaces that are easy to access, a brush-on finish is a good choice for this magazine rack. We used three coats of Danish oil for an even, satiny finish.

Coat Tree

Mission and Arts-and-Crafts styles are enjoying a resurgence in popularity, mostly because of the simplicity and elegance of these designs. Quartersawn white oak, which was widely used in Mission furniture, is a natural choice for our coat tree. The tapered top and decorative corbels on the feet add to its sleek appearance, which sets it apart from other coat tree styles that can look clumsy and bottom-heavy. We chose to accentuate this traditional reproduction with antique brass-finished coat hooks to give the coat tree a truly vintage look.

Vital Statistics: Coat Tree

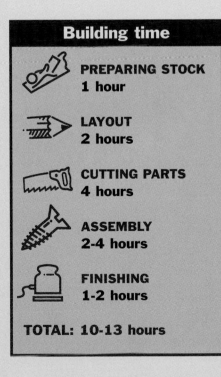

TYPE: Coat tree

OVERALL SIZE: 24W by 24D by 72H

MATERIAL: White oak

JOINERY: Half-lap and butt joints reinforced with screws

CONSTRUCTION DETAILS:
· Tapered and chamfered post top
· Decorative corbels reinforce the post/base connection
· Broad footprint design for stability

FINISHING OPTIONS: Use a medium to dark walnut stain finish for a more traditional wood tone, or topcoat with a clear varnish for a more contemporary look

Building time

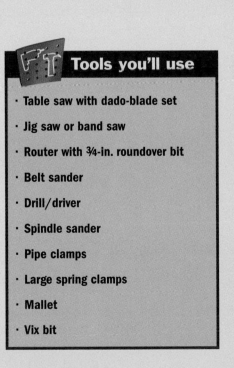

PREPARING STOCK
1 hour

LAYOUT
2 hours

CUTTING PARTS
4 hours

ASSEMBLY
2-4 hours

FINISHING
1-2 hours

TOTAL: 10-13 hours

Tools you'll use

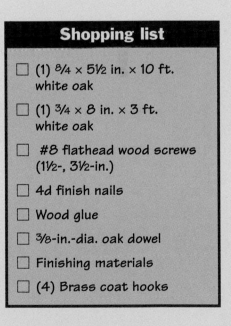

· Table saw with dado-blade set
· Jig saw or band saw
· Router with ¾-in. roundover bit
· Belt sander
· Drill/driver
· Spindle sander
· Pipe clamps
· Large spring clamps
· Mallet
· Vix bit

Shopping list

☐ (1) 8/4 × 5½ in. × 10 ft. white oak

☐ (1) ¾ × 8 in. × 3 ft. white oak

☐ #8 flathead wood screws (1½-, 3½-in.)

☐ 4d finish nails

☐ Wood glue

☐ ⅜-in.-dia. oak dowel

☐ Finishing materials

☐ (4) Brass coat hooks

Coat Tree

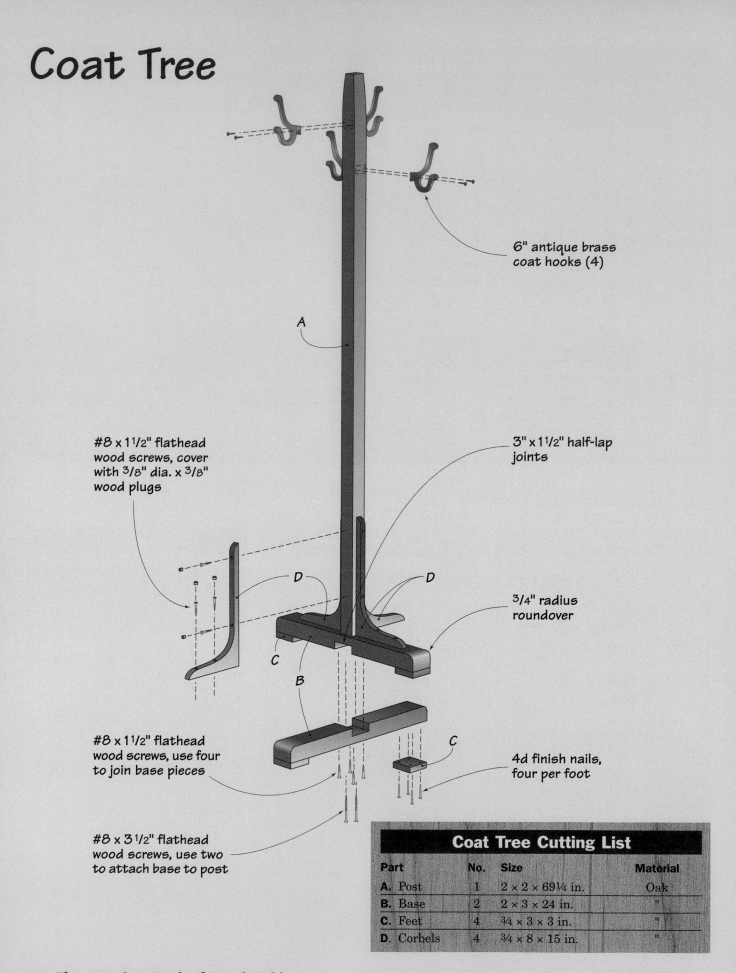

6" antique brass coat hooks (4)

A

#8 x 1¹/₂" flathead wood screws, cover with ³/₈" dia. x ³/₈" wood plugs

3" x 1¹/₂" half-lap joints

D

D

³/₄" radius roundover

C

B

#8 x 1¹/₂" flathead wood screws, use four to join base pieces

C

4d finish nails, four per foot

#8 x 3¹/₂" flathead wood screws, use two to attach base to post

Coat Tree Cutting List

Part	No.	Size	Material
A. Post	1	2 × 2 × 69¹/₄ in.	Oak
B. Base	2	2 × 3 × 24 in.	"
C. Feet	4	³/₄ × 3 × 3 in.	"
D. Corbels	4	³/₄ × 8 × 15 in.	"

Grid squares are 1" x 1"

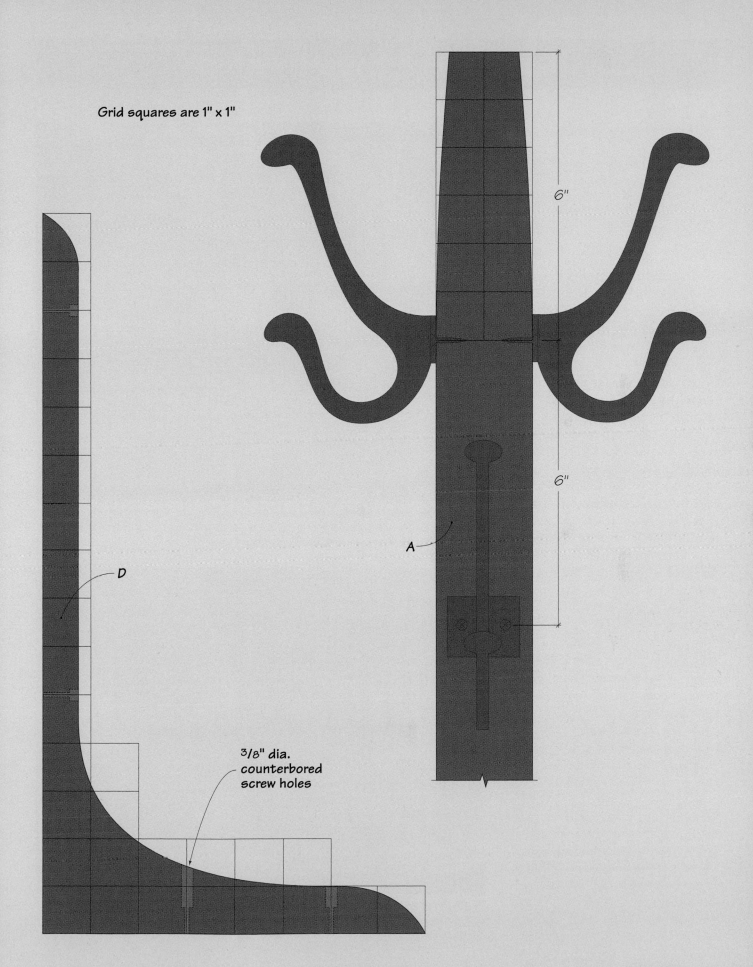

6"

6"

A

D

3/8" dia.
counterbored
screw holes

PHOTO A: Mark the post top taper lines using a full-size grid pattern, then belt-sand the post top to shape with a medium-grit sanding belt. You may need to redraw lines on each face after sanding it to reestablish the taper contour for sanding adjacent faces.

BUILD THE POST

We selected a piece of solid ¾-thick quartersawn white oak for the coat tree post and base members to give these pieces a consistent grain pattern on all four sides (quartersawn oak was widely used for Mission-style furniture). If quartersawn stock of this thickness isn't available at your local lumberyard, you could laminate several pieces of thinner oak stock together to create the coat tree parts, but keep in mind that the sides of the parts will have visible lamination lines.

❶ Edge-joint and rip the oak stock for the coat tree post to 2 in. by 2 in. Then crosscut it to a length of 69¼ in.

❷ Enlarge the grid pattern to use as a template for shaping the tapered post top. This can be done by drawing a grid with 1-in. squares and then tracing the post top shape onto your grid or by enlarging the pattern shown here on a photocopier.

❸ Transfer the grid pattern taper to all four faces of the post top and mark the square outline on the end of the post where all four tapered sides should meet. Also mark the base line on each face of the post where the taper begins.

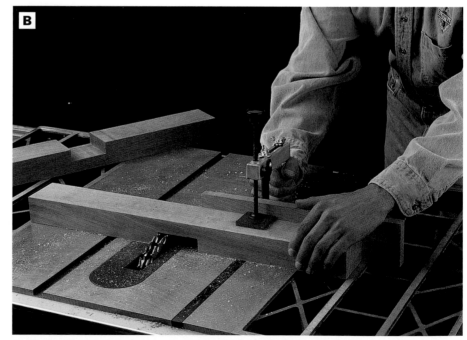

PHOTO B: Cut half-lap joints into the centers of the base pieces with a dado-blade set. Make multiple passes to cut the 3-in.-wide dadoes, using a miter gauge with a hold-down clamp to guide the stock.

4 Shape the tapers using a belt sander and medium-grit sanding belt, starting at the base line of each taper and working toward the post end **(See Photo A).** Form the tapered profile one side at a time, checking your layout lines frequently. Keep your grid template handy—you'll need to redraw your layout lines in order to shape each adjacent face of the post as you go.

CONSTRUCT THE BASE

5 Rip-cut the two coat tree base pieces from ¾ oak stock and cross-cut them each to 24 in. long.

6 Mark a 3-in.-wide by 1-in.-deep dado, centered across the face of each base member. Once cut, these dadoes will interlock and create a half-lap joint. Install a dado-blade set in your table saw. Set the cutter width to ¾ in. or more and height to 1 in. Cut the dadoes in several passes **(See Photo B).** Test the fit of the half-lap joint; the dadoes should fully interlock. NOTE: *If you don't have a dado-blade set, you could also cut these dadoes with a router and straight bit, guiding the router along a straightedge clamped to the workpiece. If you use this method, plow out the dadoes in several passes of increasing depth until you reach the final 1 in. depth. Otherwise, you could over-heat or even break your bit. A set of mortising chisels will also do the trick.*

7 Designate a top and bottom base member (once assembled, the dado will face down on the top base member and up on the bot-tom base member). Set the two base members side by side and clamp them between two pieces of scrap that are the same height and length as the bases. Install a

Roundover bit

PHOTO C: Gang-rout roundovers on the ends of the base members. We used a ¾-in.-roundover bit (See inset photo). Clamp scrap boards of the same height and length outside the base members to prevent the router bit from chipping or following the corners.

PHOTO D: Attach the post to the base with glue and two counterbored #8 × 3½-in. flathead wood screws. Secure the base in your bench vise with the post centered on the base. Make sure the post is centered on the middle of the base assembly.

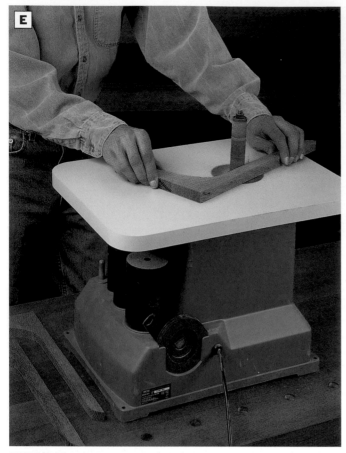

PHOTO E: After sawing the corbels to rough shape with a jig saw or band saw, smooth the edges and refine the shape. An oscillating spindle sander makes this task quick and easy.

Corbels

PHOTO F: Attach the corbels to the post with glue and #8 × 1½-in. flathead screws, driven into counterbored pilot holes.

¾-in. roundover bit in your router and rout across the top corners of the base and scrap assembly (**See Photo C**). The scrap pieces will keep the router bit from chipping the corners of the base members.

❽ Cut four 3 × 3-in. coat tree feet from ¾-in.-thick oak stock. Use glue and four 4d finish nails per foot to attach the feet to the bottom ends of the base pieces. TIP: *Drill a pilot hole for the nails first with a ¹⁄₁₆-in. drill bit. Doing so will help sink the nails more easily into the hard oak.* Set the nailheads below the surface with a nailset, to keep the feet from scratching floors or snagging carpet later on.

ATTACH THE POST TO THE BASE

❾ Apply glue to the half-laps of the base members and fasten the base together using four #8 × 1½-in. flathead screws. Drill counterbored pilot holes before you drive in the screws.

❿ Set the post onto the base assembly so it is centered and the faces are parallel to the edges of the base members. Drill two countersunk pilot holes up

through the base and into the post. Attach the post with glue and 3½-in. wood screws (**See Photo D**).

BUILD THE CORBELS

The corbels add lateral stability to the coat tree post and give the coat tree some decorative flair. Without them, the weight of coats on the tree could pull the post loose from the base.

⓫ Cut blanks out of ¾-in.-thick oak stock for the four corbels. Transfer the corbel grid pattern drawing to one of the blanks.

⓬ Cut out the corbel along the waste side of the cutting line with a band saw or jig saw, and smooth the cut edges. We used an oscillating spindle sander (**See Photo E**), but a flexible sanding pad, cabinet scraper or file would also do the trick.

⓭ Use the finished corbel as a pattern for tracing cutting lines on the three remaining blanks. Follow the same procedure for cutting and sanding the corbels to produce four identical parts.

14 Draw reference lines along the centers of the base members and along each face of the post. Center a corbel along the reference lines for each side of the coat tree and clamp them in place. Drill four counterbored pilot holes in each corbel, according to the locations shown on the pattern. Remove the clamps, apply glue to the corbels, and screw them in place with #8 × 1½-in. flathead wood screws **(See Photo F)**.

FINISHING TOUCHES

15 Plug the counterbore holes in the corbels with ⅜-in.-dia. white oak plugs. NOTE: *You may want to make your own plugs on the drill press with a plug cutter in scrap white oak stock, since white oak plugs may be difficult to find. Cut the plugs from face grain, rather than end grain, to help hide the plugs. Or you could cut the plugs from walnut, for a contrasting appearance. Walnut was often used to conceal screws in Mission furniture.* Cut the plugs ¼ in. or so longer than necessary. Apply glue to the holes and the plugs, and tap the plugs in with a mallet. When the glue has dried, trim the plugs flush with a flexible Japanese hand saw or tenoning saw, then sand the plug ends smooth.

16 Ease all sharp edges of the coat tree, and finish-sand the wood with progressively finer sandpaper, up to 180-grit.

17 Apply the stain and protective coating of your choice according to the instructions on the container. We brushed on a walnut oil stain, let it dry, then followed with three coats of satin, oil-based polyurethane varnish **(See Photo G)**. It's a good idea to rub between coats of varnish with 0000-grade steel wool to ensure a smooth finish.

18 Install the coat hooks in pairs on opposing faces of the post at 6 in., then 12 in. from the post top **(See Photo H)**. We chose hooks with an antique finish to enhance the coat tree's vintage styling. *Tip: Use a vix bit for drilling perfectly centered holes for screws used in hinges and other metal hardware, like these coat tree hooks. A guide centers the bit over the screw area. Plunge the bit forward and the spring-loaded drill bit inside drills the hole. The bit then retracts up and out of the way.*

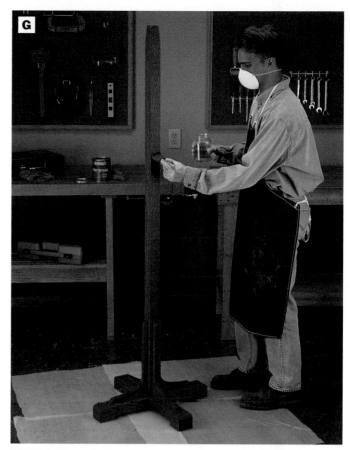

PHOTO G: We used a brush-on walnut oil stain to tint the oak, then topcoated with three coats of satin, oil-based polyurethane varnish.

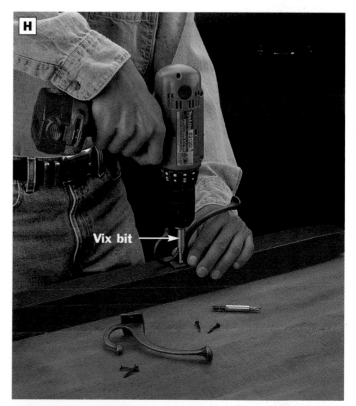

PHOTO H: Use a vix bit to drill holes that are perfectly aligned with the guide holes in the hooks.

Coat Tree **225**

Tambour Breadbox

Atraditional gift that was beginning to lose favor, the breadbox has enjoyed a huge revival recently thanks to the incredible popularity of bread machines. Whether your bread comes from a machine or the corner bakery, you'll have ample storage for all your loaves in this classic breadbox. Our design features an attractive, easy-to-build tambour door and a storage drawer on top for bread knives.

Vital Statistics: Tambour Breadbox

TYPE: Breadbox

OVERALL SIZE: 14½D by 18W by 16½H

MATERIAL: Red oak

JOINERY: Dadoes, rabbets and butt joints

CONSTRUCTION DETAILS:
- Tambour door staves glued and pressed to cotton fabric
- Door slides in grooves that are routed with a plywood template and ⅜-in. router guide bushing
- Drawer face is flush-fit to the drawer support and sides
- Drawer box assembled with interlocking rabbet-and-dado joints
- Drawer support fits into stopped dadoes in sides

FINISH: Wood stain and satin polyurethane varnish

Building time

 PREPARING STOCK
2 hours

 LAYOUT
4 hours

 CUTTING PARTS
4-6 hours

 ASSEMBLY
3 hours

 FINISHING
2 hours

TOTAL: 15-17 hours

Tools you'll use

- Table saw
- Drill/driver
- Drill press
- Power miter saw (optional)
- Clamps
- Router table with ⅜-in. roundover bit, ⅜-in. guide bushing, ¼-, ½-, and ¾-in. straight bits
- Dado blade
- Carpenter's square
- J-roller
- ⅜-in. counterbore bit
- ⅜-in. plug cutter

Shopping list

- ☐ (2) ¾ × 8 in. × 8 ft. red oak
- ☐ (1) ¾ × 6 in. × 4 ft. red oak
- ☐ (1) ½ × 4 in. × 4 ft. red oak
- ☐ (1) ½ in. × 2 ft. × 2 ft. oak plywood
- ☐ (1) ¼ × 8 × 16 in. oak plywood
- ☐ #8 × 1½-in. flathead wood screws
- ☐ (1) 2 × 2 ft. heavy cotton fabric
- ☐ (3) ½-in.-dia. brass knobs
- ☐ Wood glue
- ☐ Finishing materials

Tambour Breadbox

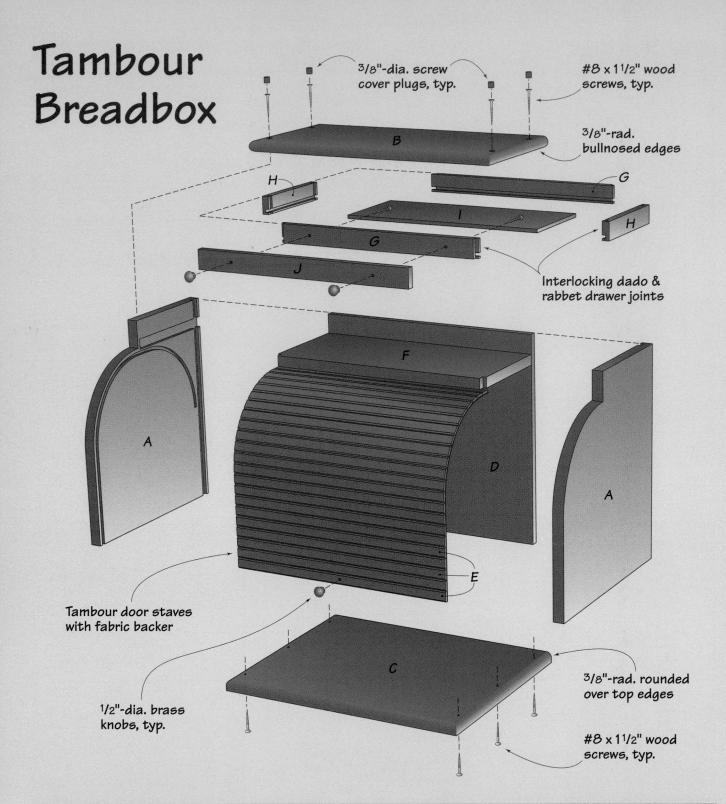

3/8"-dia. screw cover plugs, typ.

#8 x 1 1/2" wood screws, typ.

3/8"-rad. bullnosed edges

Interlocking dado & rabbet drawer joints

Tambour door staves with fabric backer

1/2"-dia. brass knobs, typ.

3/8"-rad. rounded over top edges

#8 x 1 1/2" wood screws, typ.

Tambour Breadbox Cutting List

Part	No.	Size	Material	Part	No.	Size	Material
A. Sides	2	3/4 × 14 × 15 in.	Red oak	**F.** Drawer support	1	3/4 × 7 1/4 × 16 in.	Red oak
B. Top	1	3/4 × 8 1/2 × 18 in.	"	**G.** Drawer front, back	2	1/2 × 1 5/16 × 14 7/8 in.	"
C. Bottom	1	3/4 × 14 1/2 × 18 in.	"	**H.** Drawer sides	2	1/2 × 1 5/16 × 6 3/4 in.	"
D. Back	1	1/2 × 16 × 15 in.	Oak plywood	**I.** Drawer bottom	1	1/4 × 6 1/4 × 14 7/8 in.	Oak plywood
E. Tambour staves	23	3/16 × 3/4 × 15 15/16 in.	Red oak	**J.** Drawer face	1	1/2 × 1 5/16 × 15 3/8 in.	Red oak

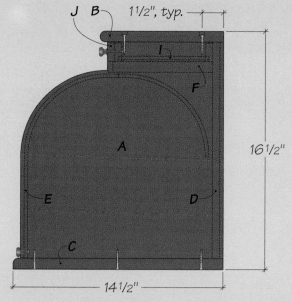

J B 1½", typ.

I

F

16½"

A

E D

C

14½"

SIDE VIEW

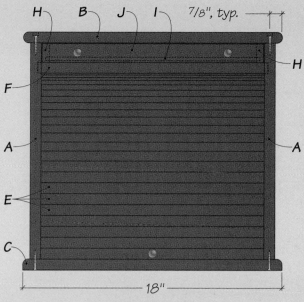

H B J I 7/8", typ.

F

H

A A

E

C

18"

FRONT VIEW

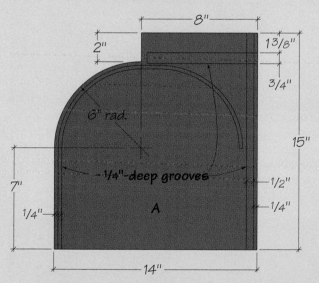

8" 1⅜"

2"

3/4"

6" rad.

15"

¼"-deep grooves 1/2"

7" 1/4"

¼"

A

14"

DETAIL: SIDES

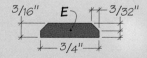

3/16" E 3/32"

3/4"

DETAIL: TAMBOUR STAVES

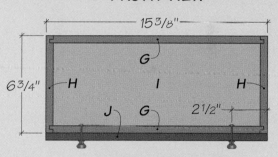

15⅜"

G

6¾" H I H

J G 2½"

TOP VIEW DRAWER

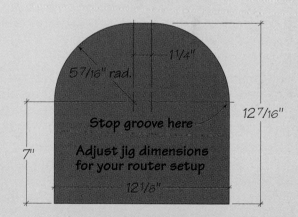

1¼"

5⁷/₁₆" rad.

Stop groove here

12⁷/₁₆"

Adjust jig dimensions
for your router setup

7"

12⅛"

**TAMBOUR GROOVE
ROUTER TEMPLATE**

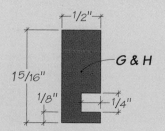

1/2"

G & H

15/16"

1/8" 1/4"

**DETAIL: DRAWER
BOTTOM DADOES**

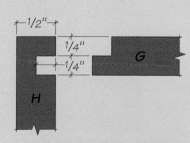

1/2"

1/4"

1/4" G

H

**DETAIL: DRAWER
CORNER JOINTS**

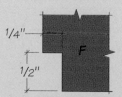

1/4" F

1/2"

**DETAIL: DRAWER SUPPORT
NOTCHED CORNERS**

BUILD THE SIDES

❶ Make blanks for the sides: Crosscut one of the 1 × 8 oak boards into four 15-in. lengths, and flatten the edges on a jointer. Edge-glue and clamp the boards in pairs to form two blanks for the sides. Then rip the blanks to a final width of 14 in.

❷ Cut the sides to shape: Use the *Detail: Sides* drawing to lay out the shape of the sides on one of the two blanks. Trace this shape onto the second blank and cut to shape. Sand all the cut edges.

❸ Rout grooves in the sides for the back and drawer support: Cut both grooves with straight bits in the router table. The ¼-in.-deep groove for the back panel is inset ¼ in. from the back edge of the sides and runs top to bottom. Mill this groove first with a ½-in. straight bit. The ¼-in.-deep shelf support dadoes are located 1⅜ in. in from the top end of the sides. They stop ½ in. from the front edge of the sides and intersect the groove for the back. Set up stopblocks on your router table to limit the length of these shelf support dadoes, then rout them into both side panels with a ¾-in. straight bit. Square up the front end of the shelf support dadoes with a sharp chisel.

❹ Mill the tracks for the tambour door in the sides. To make these cuts accurately, build the *Tambour Groove Router Template* from ¾-in. scrap, and sand it smooth. Mark the jig where the tambour track needs to stop. Install a ⅜-in.-dia. bushing and ¼-in. straight bit in your router. Align the flat edge of the jig with the bottom of the side panel, and so the router bit will cut the track groove ¼ in. in from the front curved edge of the side. Clamp the jig in place. Plow the track in two passes of increasing depth to a final depth of ¼ in. **(See Photo A).** Be sure to stop the track groove cuts as indicated on your jig. Set up and clamp the jig on the other side panel, and rout a matching track.

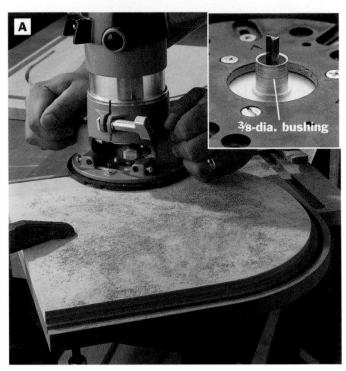

⅜-dia. bushing

PHOTO A: After the router template has been secured to the sides, begin milling the tracks for the tambour door. Install a ⅜-in. bushing and ¼-in. straight bit on your router (See inset photo) to make these cuts. Be sure to mark the template so you know where the tracks should end. Rout the tracks in two passes.

PHOTO B: Glue and install the back and drawer support into their grooves in the sides. Clamp up this assembly to hold the joints closed until the glue dries.

PHOTO C: Attach the top and bottom to the carcase so they overhang the sides evenly. The bottom gets attached only with countersunk screws for now—it will need to be removed to install the tambour door. The top is attached with glue as well as countersunk screws. Cover the screw heads with ⅜-in. oak plugs, then trim and sand the plugs flush.

PHOTO D: After chamfering both long edges of a ¾-in.-thick oak blank, set your table saw fence ³⁄₁₆ in. from the blade and rip-cut the chamfered staves from the blank. Use a pushstick when feeding the blank through the blade to keep your fingers clear. Repeat this process until you've cut 23 staves.

MAKE THE REMAINING CARCASE PARTS

5 Build the top and bottom: Make a blank for the bottom by edge-gluing two lengths of 1 × 8 stock together, and form another blank for the top from edge-glued 1 × 6. Rip the top and bottom to final width, and sand the edges and ends smooth. Ease the ends and one long edge around one face of both parts with a ⅜-in. roundover bit in the router table.

6 Rip and crosscut the plywood back panel to size, according to the *Cutting List* dimensions.

7 Prepare the drawer support. First, rip and cross-cut the drawer support to size, then trim away the front corners of the drawer support with a band saw so it will sit flush with the front of the sides and fit around and into the stopped grooves (See *Detail: Drawer Support Notched Corners*).

ASSEMBLE THE CARCASE

8 Glue and fasten the carcase parts together. First, dry-assemble the back and drawer support in the sides to test the fit. Then glue these parts into their grooves, clamp up the assembly and check for square (**See Photo B**). When the glue dries, attach the top to the sides. Be sure the bullnosed edge of the top faces up and forward and the flat edge is flush with the back of the sides. The top should overhang the sides evenly. Mark the top for four screws, then glue and fasten it in place with counterbored, 1½-in. wood

screws. Set the carcase on the bottom panel, with the bullnosed edge facing up and forward. Attach the bottom to the sides temporarily with countersunk wood screws; you'll need to remove it to install the door.

9 Cover the counterbored screw heads in the top with ⅜-in.-dia. oak plugs (**See Photo C**). Then trim and sand the plugs flush.

BUILD THE TAMBOUR DOOR

The tambour door consists of 23 staves butted edge to edge and glued to a sheet of cotton material, which provides a rugged but flexible backing for the door to bend. To mill the thin staves efficiently and safely, you'll chamfer the top and bottom edges of an oak blank and rip-cut one stave at a time from the blank, chamfering again before ripping the next stave. Or you could buy premilled tambour instead of making it (See *Prefabricated Tambour*, next page).

10 Make the staves. Begin by chucking a 45° piloted chamfering bit in your router table and set the bit height to ³⁄₃₂ in. Crosscut a ¾-in.-thick blank of oak stock to 15¹⁵⁄₁₆ in. long. Set the fence on your table saw ³⁄₁₆ in. from the blade. Mill each stave by chamfering both the top and bottom edges of the blank, then slicing the chamfered edges off on the table saw (**See Photo D**). Plane away any saw marks left on the cut edges of the blank, and repeat the chamfering and ripping process until you've made 23 staves.

PHOTO E: Cradle the staves in the crook of a carpenter's square clamped to a sheet of hardboard. Hold the staves together with strips of wide masking tape to prepare for glue-up.

PHOTO F: Attach cloth to the backside of the door with white glue, wetting the cloth slightly with a sponge to draw the glue into the cloth. Then use a J-roller to smooth out any wrinkles or bubbles. Press the cloth flat by setting heavy objects such as bricks or a bucket of water on top of the staves with a layer of wax paper beneath.

PHOTO G: Trim the ends of the cloth back about ⅜ in. from the ends of the staves. This way, the bare ends of the staves will slide more easily in their tracks.

11 Assemble the staves: Butt the staves tightly together, chamfered-face up, against the inside of a carpenter's square clamped to a piece of hardboard. The carpenter's square will help align the ends of the staves. Once the staves are aligned, hold the outermost stave in place with scrap blocks and spring clamps. Temporarily join the staves with three strips of wide masking tape **(See Photo E)**.

12 Cut a piece of cotton fabric (about the weight of denim) large enough to cover the width of all the staves and about ¼-in. short of the ends. Wash and dry the cloth before you cut it to size to minimize shrinkage later.

13 Glue the staves to the cloth. Flip the stave assembly over in the carpenter's square jig so the chamfered edges face down, and spread a thin, even coating of white glue over all of the stave backs. Lay the cloth on the staves and dampen the back with a wet sponge. Press the cloth into the glue and smooth any wrinkles with a J-roller **(See Photo F)**. Cover the cloth with waxed paper. Place weights (bricks, cement pavers, a bucket of water) on the waxed paper and let the glue dry overnight.

14 Fit the door in the door tracks. Trim excess cloth from the ends of the staves with a straightedge and a utility knife **(See Photo G)**. Remove enough cloth so about ⅜ in. of ends of the staves are bare. Unscrew

Prefabricated tambour

If you'd rather not build tambour, you can purchase it in numerous species and in a huge variety of stave dimensions and designs from woodworking supply catalogs. The most common form is a canvas-backed tambour sheet, but it is also sold as a series of staves with a sheet of paper glued to the front face. After attaching the staves to a cloth backing, you sand the paper off to expose the staves. Some manufacturers even offer tambour that requires no backing: the edges of the individual staves are profiled so that they interlock with each other, in effect forming a series of long hinges. There are even tambour sheets with the staves held together by strings, much in the way that window blinds are constructed. Do not mill any parts for your project until you have the tambour in hand.

PHOTO H: A frame clamp is a convenient way to glue up the drawer, because it keeps the assembly square. Glue the corner joints only. Leave the bottom floating in its dadoes to allow for wood movement.

PHOTO I: After the finish has been applied, install two brass pulls on the drawer and one to the bottom door stave. You'll need to buy 1¼-in.-long machine screws for the drawer knobs and a ⅜-in.-long machine screw for the knob on the tambour door.

the bottom from the breadbox carcase and slide the door into its grooves. Sand the bare ends of the staves as needed until the door slides easily along the full tracks but still holds position at any point along the tracks. Then remove the door for finishing.

MAKE THE DRAWER

15 Machine the drawer parts: Rip and crosscut the drawer face, front, back and sides from ½-in.-thick oak stock. Plow a ¼-in.-wide, ¼-in.-deep groove across the width of the inside face of the drawer sides, ¼-in. in from each end (See *Detail: Drawer Corner Joints*). Make these cuts on the table saw with a dado blade or on the router table with a ¼-in. straight bit. Using the same cutter, mill ¼-in.-deep dadoes in the drawer sides, front and back, ⅛-in. from the bottom edge and along its length for the drawer bottom. Finally, cut ¼ × ¼-in. rabbets into the ends of the outside face (the face opposite the drawer bottom dadoes) of the drawer front and back. These rabbets form tongues that fit into the short dadoes in the drawer sides.

16 Assemble the drawer: Dry-fit the sides to the front and back with the drawer bottom in its grooves, and make any necessary adjustments. The dadoes and rabbets form strong interlocking joints at the drawer corners. Disassemble the drawer, glue up the corner joints, slip the drawer bottom into its grooves (without glue) and assemble the drawer box. Use a frame clamp or other small bar clamps to hold the joints closed until the glue dries (**See Photo H**).

17 Install the drawer face: Attach the drawer face to the drawer front with glue. Hold the drawer face in position with spring clamps. Drill pilot holes through the drawer face and drawer front, and screw on the two drawer knobs 2½ in. from each end of the drawer. You'll need 1¼-in.-long machine screws for securing these knobs.

FINISHING TOUCHES

18 Sand and finish the breadbox: Remove the drawer and knobs, and sand the surfaces of all of the breadbox parts with 220-grit sandpaper. Remove any residual dust with a tack cloth. Apply the stain of your choice (or one to match your existing cabinetry). Finish all surfaces (inside and out) with three coats of clear polyurethane varnish. NOTE: *There's no need to varnish the tambour cloth.*

19 Slide the door into its tracks, and screw the breadbox bottom back on the carcase.

20 Install the tambour door knob: Drill a centered pilot hole through the bottom stave. You'll need a ⅜-in.-long machine screw to fasten the knob on the stave (**See Photo I**).

Lapped Picture Frames

Add the crowning touch to a cherished family photo when you display it in a picture frame you've built yourself. This frame design features half-lap joints in the corners—a simple and attractive way to join the four frame pieces together. Build the frame from one wood type or combine a couple of contrasting species, like walnut and maple. You could even build a frame from plywood or particleboard and paint it. The choice is up to you.

Lapped Picture Frames: Step-by-step

PHOTO A: Gang-rout the half lap joints in the short frame pieces, then the long frame pieces. Clamp pairs of frame pieces between two scraps to back up the router cuts, and guide the router against a straightedge. Mill the half laps in two router passes.

MAKE THE LONG & SHORT FRAME PIECES

❶ Crosscut the short and long frame pieces to length.

❷ Rout the half laps: Since the half-lap depth and width matches on all four frame members, it's possible to gang-rout like-frame pieces using a simple router setup. Cut the short frame half-laps first. Install a ¾-in. straight bit in your router, and set the cutting depth to ⅜ in. Lay out the 1½-in.-wide lap joints across both short frames with the ends of the parts aligned. Then clamp the short frame pieces together between two ¾-in.-thick scrap strips. The scraps will serve as backers to keep the router bit from tearing out the wood as it exits the half-lap cuts. Clamp a straight-edged piece of scrap over the short frame assembly, positioned so the router bit will cut along one set of half-lap layout lines. Mill half the lap

joint area, cutting across both the scrap and the short frame workpieces in one pass. Loosen the clamps, reposition the short frames to align the router for cutting away the remaining waste, reclamp and make another pass to complete one set of lap cuts. Turn the frame workpieces end-for-end in the router setup to rout half laps on the other ends of the parts (**See Photo A**).

Lapped Picture Frames

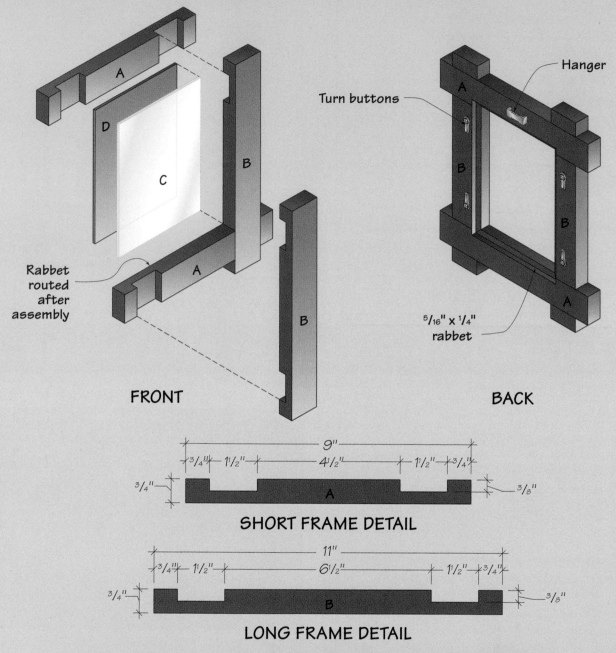

FRONT

Rabbet routed after assembly

Turn buttons

Hanger

5/16" x 1/4" rabbet

BACK

SHORT FRAME DETAIL

9"

3/4" · 1 1/2" · 4 1/2" · 1 1/2" · 3/4"

3/4"

3/8"

A

LONG FRAME DETAIL

11"

3/4" · 1 1/2" · 6 1/2" · 1 1/2" · 3/4"

3/4"

3/8"

B

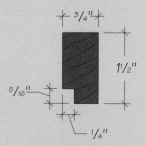

3/4"

1 1/2"

5/16"

1/4"

RABBET DETAIL

Lapped Picture Frames Cutting List

Part	No.	Size	Material
A. Short frames	2	3/4 × 1 1/2 × 9 in.	Any wood
B. Long frames	2	3/4 × 1 1/2 × 11 in.	"
C. Glass	1	1/8 × 5 × 7 in.	
D. Backer	1	1/8 × 5 × 7 in.	Hardboard

❸ Rout the half-lap joints on the long frame pieces using the same router setup and procedure as you used in Step 2.

ASSEMBLE THE FRAME

❹ Dry-assemble the long and short frame pieces to check the fit of the lap joints. Sand the routed areas slightly wider or deeper to improve the fit.

❺ Spread glue into the routed areas, and clamp the frame parts together **(See Photo B).**

❻ Rout a rabbeted recess around the inside back edges of the frame for housing the glass, photo and backer. Use a piloted ¼-in. rabbeting bit set to a depth of ⁵⁄₁₆ to mill this rabbet **(See Photo C).**

❼ Square up the corners of the back rabbet with a sharp chisel.

FINISHING TOUCHES

❽ Sand the frame with 150-, then 220-grit sandpaper, and apply your choice of finish.

❾ Fasten four turnbuttons around the rabbeted area on the back of the frame to hold the glass, photo and backer in place.

❿ Insert the glass, photo and backer in the frame, and swivel the turnbuttons into position.

⓫ Carefully tack a sawtooth picture hanger to the top short frame piece on the frame back **(See Photo D).** You may want to remove the glass, photo and backer first.

PHOTO B: Spread glue in the lap-joint cut-outs and clamp the frame pieces together.

PHOTO C: Rout a ¼-in.-wide, ⁵⁄₁₆-in.-deep rabbet around the inside back edge of the frame for the glass, photo and backer. Square up the corners of the rabbet with a chisel.

Building other frame sizes

The picture frame depicted in the technical drawings, these photos and in the *Cutting List* is sized for a 5 × 7-in. photograph. If you'd like to make similar frames for other popular photo sizes, build according to the part dimensions listed below:

For 4 × 6-in. photographs:
Short frame pieces: ¾ × 1½ × 8 in.
Long frame pieces: ¾ × 1½ × 10 in.
Glass, backer: ⅛ × 4 × 6 in.

For 8 × 10-in. photographs:
Short frame pieces: ¾ × 1½ × 12 in.
Long frame pieces: ¾ × 1½ × 14 in.
Glass, backer: ⅛ × 8 × 10 in.

PHOTO D: Install turnbuttons and a sawtooth picture hanger on the back of the frame.

Lapped Picture Frames 237

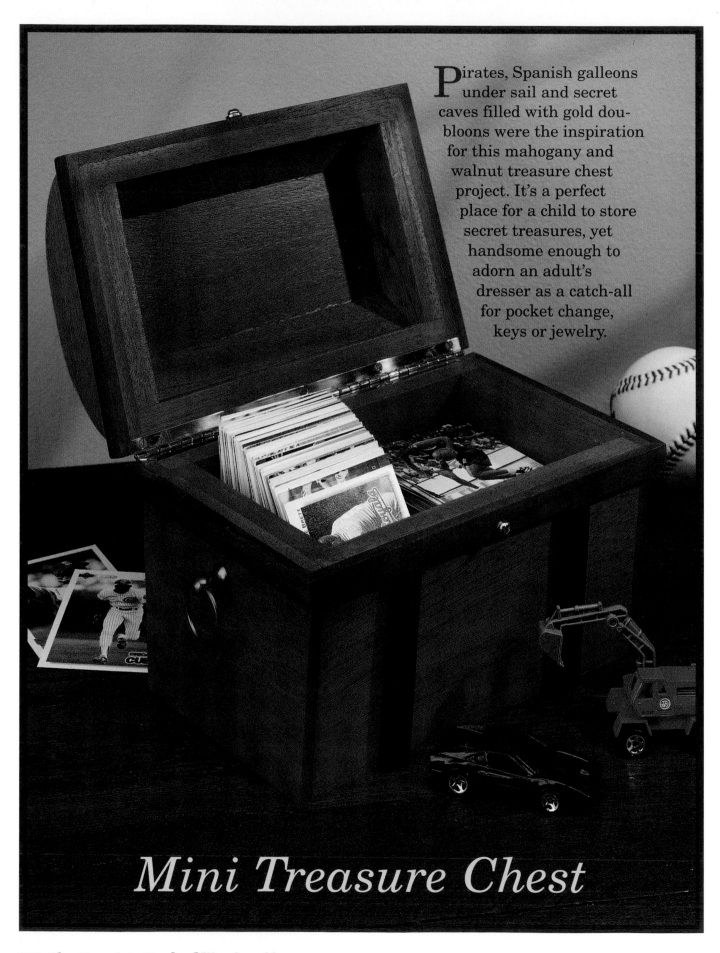

Pirates, Spanish galleons under sail and secret caves filled with gold doubloons were the inspiration for this mahogany and walnut treasure chest project. It's a perfect place for a child to store secret treasures, yet handsome enough to adorn an adult's dresser as a catch-all for pocket change, keys or jewelry.

Mini Treasure Chest

Vital Statistics: Mini Treasure Chest

TYPE: Jewelry/valet chest

OVERALL SIZE: 5½W by 6¼H by 8L

MATERIAL: Honduras mahogany, walnut

JOINERY: Butt, dado joints

CONSTRUCTION DETAILS:

· Lid arch formed by a seven-piece glue-up that is hand-planed to shape
· Box front and back tapers are hand-planed to shape
· Curved walnut lid strapping is drawn onto flat stock with a compass, then cut to shape on the band saw
· Bottom floats In grooves in the box front, back and ends
· Lid attached to box with brass piano hinge

FINISH: Spray-on satin lacquer

Building time

 PREPARING STOCK
2 hours

 LAYOUT
1-2 hours

 CUTTING PARTS
4-5 hours

 ASSEMBLY
2 hours

 FINISHING
1 hour

TOTAL: 10-12 hours

Tools you'll use

· Table saw
· Dado blade (optional)
· Router and ¼-in. straight bit (optional)
· Band saw
· Back saw
· Clamps
· Hand plane
· Belt sander
· Drum sander
· Drill/driver
· Chisel

Shopping list

☐ (1) ⁴/₄ × 8 in. × 6 ft. Honduras mahogany

☐ (1) ½ × 4 in. × 2 ft. walnut

☐ (1) ⅝ × 8-in. brass piano hinge

☐ (1) 1-in. brass hook latch, mounting screws

☐ (2) 1-in.-dia. ring pulls

☐ Wood glue

☐ Spray adhesive

☐ Finishing materials

Mini Treasure Chest

45° mitered ends, typ.

Hinge mortise

1" brass hook latch

5/8" x 8" brass piano hinge

1/4" x 1/8"-deep rabbets, typ.

1"-dia. brass ring pulls, typ

Mini Treasure Chest Cutting List

Part	No.	Size	Material	Part	No.	Size	Material
A. Chest ends	2	¼ × 6 × 5 in.	Mahogany	**G.** Bottom	1	¼ × 4¼ × 6¾ in.	Mahogany
B. End build-ups	2	½ × 5¼ × 4 in.	"	**H.** Trim front, back	4	¼ × ½ × 8½ in.	Walnut
C. Lid front, back	2	¾ × 1¼ × 7½ in.	"	**I.** Trim ends	4	¼ × ½ × 5½ in.	"
D. Lid top	1	¼ × 4½ × 7½ in.	"	**J.** Lid strapping	2	½ × 1¾ × 5½ in.	"
E. Fillets	2	¾ × ¾ × 6½ in.	"	**K.** Box strapping	4	¼ × ½ × 3½ in.	"
F. Box front, back	2	½ × 4 × 7½ in.	"				

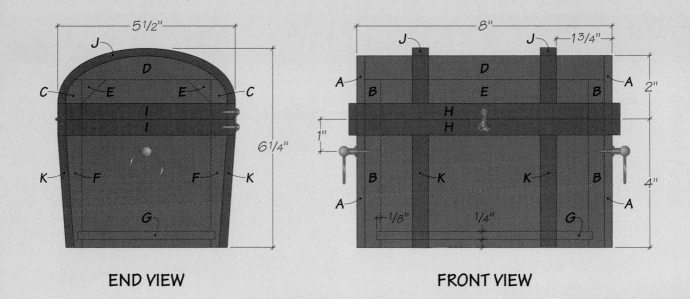

END VIEW

FRONT VIEW

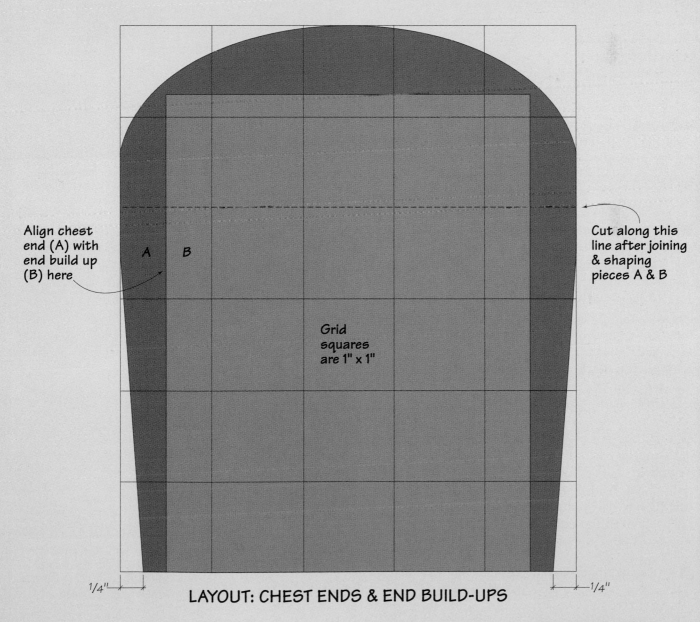

Align chest
end (A) with
end build up
(B) here

Cut along this
line after joining
& shaping
pieces A & B

A B

Grid
squares
are 1" x 1"

1/4"

1/4"

LAYOUT: CHEST ENDS & END BUILD-UPS

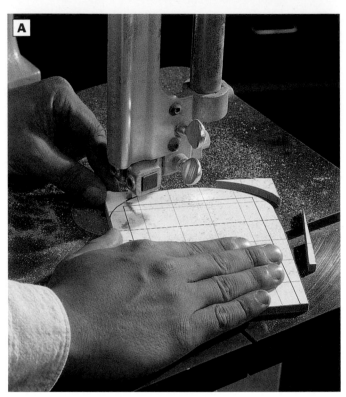

PHOTO A: Stick paper templates to the chest end workpieces with spray adhesive, and cut out the parts on the band saw. Leave the patterns in place temporarily, to mark the end build-up locations.

PREPARE THE MAHOGANY STOCK

This project is made mostly of mahogany in several thicknesses—¾ in., ½ in. and ¼ in. Most lumberyards will not stock mahogany milled to these specific thicknesses, so you'll have to start from a thicker 4/4 (about 1-in.-thick) board. Before you begin the project, take time to evaluate how you will size down your 4/4 mahogany to produce stock with the correct thickness for all of the treasure chest parts. To make most efficient use of your mahogany, resaw the stock on the band saw if you have one, then plane the resulting thinner boards to the thicknesses you need. This way, you'll waste only a fraction of the mahogany as opposed to just planing down the stock.

MAKE THE LID & BOX ENDS

❶ Cut the chest ends to shape: Make two full-size patterns of the chest ends (See *Layout: Chest Ends & End Build-Ups* drawing) and mount these to ¼-in. thick mahogany stock with spray adhesive. Band-saw the two chest ends to shape, cutting along the outside pattern layout lines only **(See Photo A)**. Score along the pattern layout lines that mark the locations of the end build ups with a utility knife and straightedge. Mark the line that will separate the lid ends from the box ends on these parts as well. Then peel off the paper patterns.

❷ Make the end build-ups. Rip and crosscut the two end build-up pieces from ½-in. stock. Cut a ¼-in.-wide, ⅛-in.-deep groove across the inside face of each build-up, ¼ in. up from the bottom edges of the parts. These grooves will house the chest bottom. Cut the two grooves on the table saw with a dado blade or on the router table with a ¼-in. straight bit.

❸ Attach the build-ups to the chest ends: Spread glue on the undadoed faces of the build-ups, align

Wood blade guide

PHOTO B: Glue the end build-ups to the chest ends, then clamp a wood blade guide to mark the location of the cutting line that separates the chest ends into the lid and box ends. Saw through the chest ends and build-ups with a back saw held against the wood blade guide.

them with the score marks on the chest ends, and clamp up the assemblies. The bottom edges of the parts should be held flush.

❹ Cut through the chest end/build-up assemblies to separate the lid and box ends. A good way to do this is to clamp a block of wood along the lid/box separation line and use it as a blade guide for cutting through the parts with a back saw. Cut through the parts to produce two lid ends and two box ends **(See Photo B).**

BUILD THE LID

The arched chest lid is actually a combination of seven parts: the lid front, back, top, fillets and ends. You'll glue the parts together first, then trim off the square top front and back edges on the table saw and shape the arch with a hand plane and belt sander.

❺ Cut the lid parts to size on the table saw: Rip and crosscut the lid top from ¾-in. stock. Bevel-rip, then crosscut the two lid fillets to size from ¾-in. stock as well. Cut the ½-in.-thick lid front and back pieces. For all of these parts, the grain should run lengthwise, to make planing easier.

❻ Glue the lid parts together. Assemble the parts so the lid front, back and top fit around the build-ups on the lid ends. Spread glue on the square edges of the fillets, and clamp them into the inside corners of the lid **(See Photo C).**

❼ Shape the top of the lid to conform with the lid end arcs. First, tilt your table saw blade to 45° and trim the long, square corners off the top of the lid before you begin planing. Doing so reduces

PHOTO C: Glue up the lid top, front, back and ends first, then reinforce the lid glue joints by attaching fillets to the long inside corners of the lid. Attach the fillets with glue and hold them in place with spring clamps.

PHOTO D: Trim off the long top corners of the lid on the table saw, with the blade tilted to 45°. Secure the lid in a bench vise and plane it to shape using the arcs on the lid ends as guides. Shave off the waste in long shallow passes with a sharp smoothing plane.

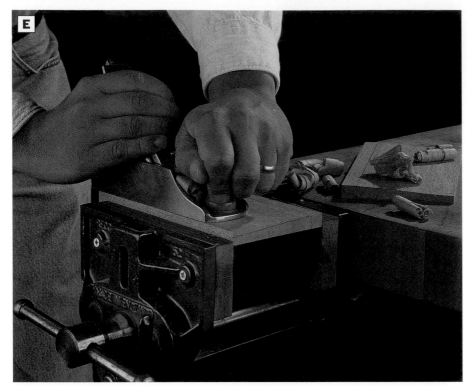

PHOTO E: Form tapers on the outside faces of the box front and back with a hand plane. Mark the profiles of the tapers on the ends of each workpiece. Remove the waste with a hand plane down to your layout lines, and sand the tapered areas smooth.

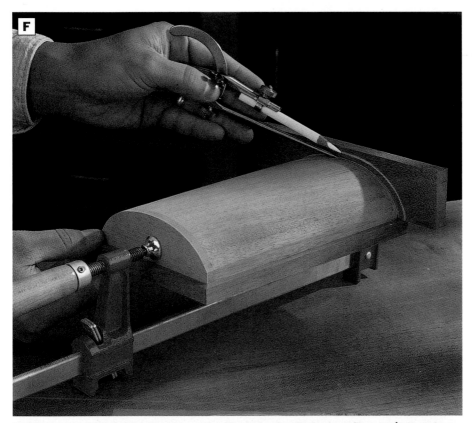

PHOTO F: Lay out the bottom lid strap cutting line by tracing the arch profile onto ½-in. walnut stock with a white colored pencil. Then scribe the top lid strap cutting line. Set the compass so the strapping will be ¼ in. thick. Draw layout lines all the way over the lid arch so the strapping will butt against the front and back walnut trim molding once it is cut and installed.

the amount of hand-planing you'll have to do. Clamp the lid in a bench vise, and plane the top, front and back of the lid until it conforms to the arched profiles of the lid ends. This process goes rather quickly and is easy to do on the soft mahogany. Work in long, smooth passes, planing with the grain (**See Photo D**). Stop planing when you are within about ¹⁄₁₆ in. of the lid end profiles, then finish shaping the lid with a belt sander and 150-grit paper.

ASSEMBLE THE BOX

The ends of the treasure chest box are wider at the top than at the bottom. You'll need to plane a taper into the box front and back pieces so they match the shape of the box ends, once the box is assembled. These workpieces are too thin and wide to form the tapers safely on the table saw or band saw, so you'll need to make them with a hand plane and sander instead.

8 Make the box front and back: Rip and crosscut these parts to size from ½-in. stock. Then refer to the *Layout: Chest Ends & End Build-ups* drawing to mark both ends of the chest front and back workpieces for planing the tapered faces. Secure each workpiece in your bench vise, and follow the layout lines to shape the tapers with a hand plane (**See Photo E**). Once you've planed the tapers, flatten the planed surfaces with a belt sander. Then cut or rout ¼-in.-wide, ⅛-in.-deep grooves across the bottom inside faces of the chest front and back for the bottom panel. The grooves run the full length of these parts.

9 Cut the ¼-in.-thick bottom panel to the size.

10 Glue and clamp the box together: Dry-assemble the box front and back between the box ends and against the build-ups. Fit the bottom panel into its grooves as well. Disassemble the parts, and sand the inside faces of the parts smooth. Then, spread glue on the ends of the front and back pieces as well as the ends of the build-ups, and clamp the box together with the bottom in place.

ADD THE DECORATIVE TRIM

11 Rip-cut two sticks of walnut for the straight trim pieces: Set the table saw fence ¼ in. from the blade, and rip three 2-ft. lengths for trim stock.

12 Cut the trim pieces to length: Crosscut the four front and back trim pieces as well as the four end pieces. Miter-cut the ends of these parts to 45°. Crosscut the four box straps to length. Sand the trim pieces smooth.

13 Install the straight trim. Glue and clamp the front and back trim and the box strapping to the lid and box. There's no need for nails.

14 Make the lid strapping. First, cut two 2 × 8-in. pieces of walnut to size. Clamp each walnut blank to the ends of the lid, and draw the lid profile on the walnut. Then, set a compass with a white colored pencil to ¼ in. and scribe around the lid onto the walnut to form the outer lid strapping cutting line **(See Photo F)**. Cut out the lid strapping just outside your layout lines on the band saw or scroll saw. Sand the lid strapping on the drum sander until the pieces conform tightly to the lid curvature.

15 Glue the lid strapping in place on the lid.

FINISHING TOUCHES

16 Install the hinge. Start by paring a shallow mortise for the hinge into the back walnut trim of the lid and box with a sharp chisel. Drill tiny pilot holes for the hinge screws first, then attach the hinge to the box and lid.

17 Apply the finish. We decided to leave the mahogany and walnut wood tones natural, rather than wiping on a wood stain. Spray on three light coats of aerosol lacquer, available at craft stores. Buff between coats of finish with #0000 steel wool or 320-grit sandpaper to remove any grit and "burnish" the surface smooth.

18 Install the brass hook latch and ring pulls. Drill a pilot hole in the front lid and box trim for fastening the lid catch, and screw the catch in place. If you prefer, you could purchase and install a keyed jewelry box lock instead. For added charm, we attached a couple of decorative brass ring pulls on each end of the chest **(See Photo G).**

PHOTO G: Attach the brass hook latch and ring pulls to the chest. Be sure to drill pilot holes for the hook latch screws to keep them from splitting the front walnut trim pieces.

Mini Treasure Chest 245

Page 276

Page 330

Page 266

Page 288

Page 322

Page 248

Page 296

Page 280

Page 258

Page 252

HOME FURNISHINGS

Five-Board Bench

Bring a classic piece of Colonial Americana into your home when you build this five-board bench project. True to its name, this bench consists of only five parts that you can cut and assemble in just a few hours. Our design seats two adults or three children comfortably.

Vital Statistics

TYPE: Five-board bench

OVERALL SIZE: 48L by 18H by 11¼D

MATERIAL: Pine

JOINERY: Butt joints reinforced with glue and screws

CONSTRUCTION DETAILS:
· Stretchers recess into notches cut in legs
· Matching pairs of stretchers and legs allow for gang-cutting parts to speed construction

FINISH: Primer and paint

BUILDING TIME: 2-3 hours

Shopping List

☐ (1) 1 × 12 in. × 8 ft. pine
☐ (1) 1 × 12 in. × 4 ft. pine
☐ #8 × 2 in. flathead wood screws
☐ ⅜ in. dia. wood plugs (optional)
☐ Wood glue
☐ Finishing materials

Five-Board Bench: Step-by-step

LAY OUT THE PARTS

❶ Measure and cut workpieces for making the legs and stretchers: Cut a 35-in. length of the long pine board for the legs and a 47-in.-long piece for the stretchers. Rip the leg piece to 10¼ in. wide and crosscut into two 17¼-in. lengths. Rip the two 4½-in.-wide stretchers from the 47-in. workpiece.

❷ Lay out the legs: First, measure and mark the two ¾-in.-deep, 4½-in.-long stretcher notches along the top outside edges of each leg. Then draw the V-shaped cutout on the bottom of each leg to form the bench feet. Start the V-shape 3 in. up from the bottom of the legs, centered on the width of each leg. Make reference marks 2½ in. in from the edges of the legs along the bottom to mark for the bench feet. Connect the V-cutout reference marks with a straightedge (**See Photo A**).

❸ Draw the tapered ends on the stretchers. Refer to the *Stretcher End Layout* to measure and mark your cutting lines.

CUT THE PARTS

❹ Trim the ends of each stretcher with a jig saw to form the tapers on the ends of these parts.

PHOTO A: Lay out the stretcher notches as well as the V-shaped leg cut-outs with a straightedge.

❺ Cut the legs to shape. You could cut out the leg details one leg at a time, but most jig saw blades are long enough to allow you to gang-cut both legs at once. To do this, stack the legs on top of one another and in the same orientation. Clamp the assembly to your bench so the stretcher notch areas overhang the bench. Cut along your layout lines to form the two stretcher notches in both legs. Cut slowly and carefully to keep the jig saw blade from bending and veering off course as you cut. Once the stretcher notches are cut, unclamp the legs, turn them around on the bench so the V-notch areas overhang, reclamp and make the remaining cuts (**See Photo B**).

Five-Board Bench

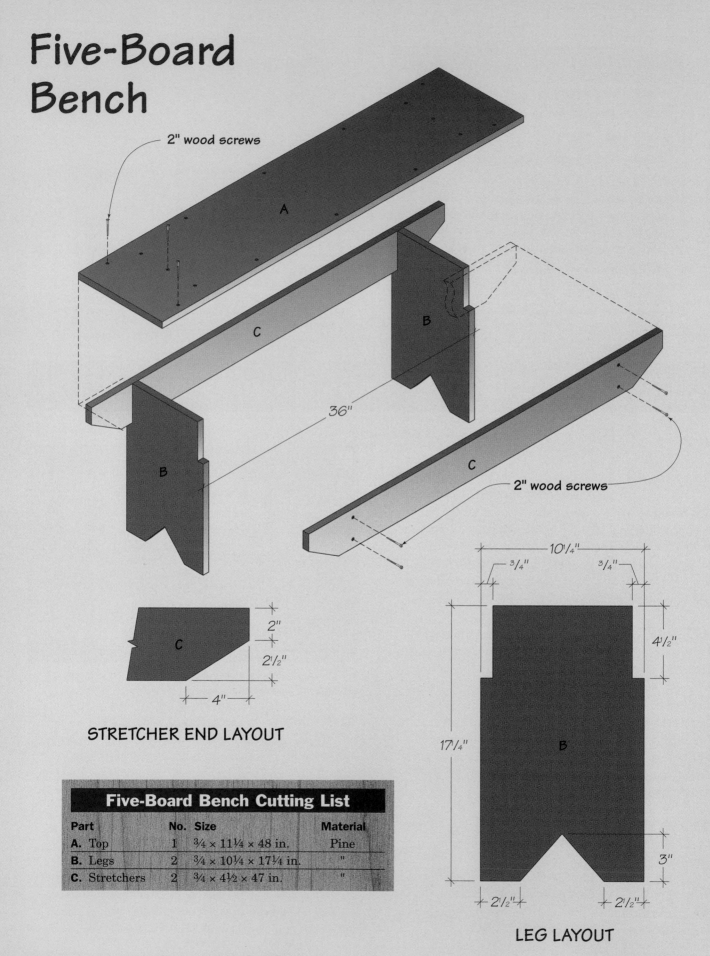

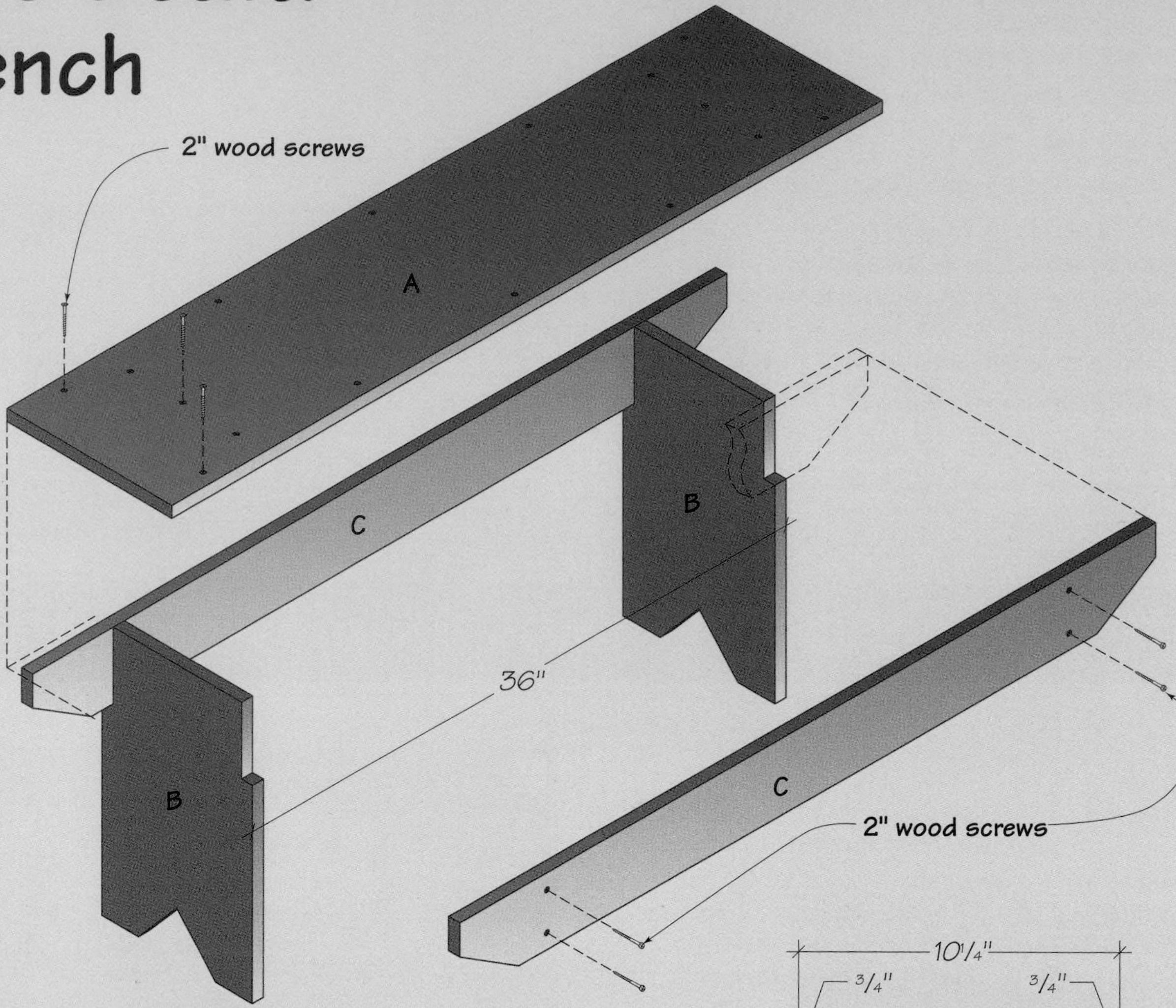
2" wood screws
A
C
B
36"
B
C
2" wood screws

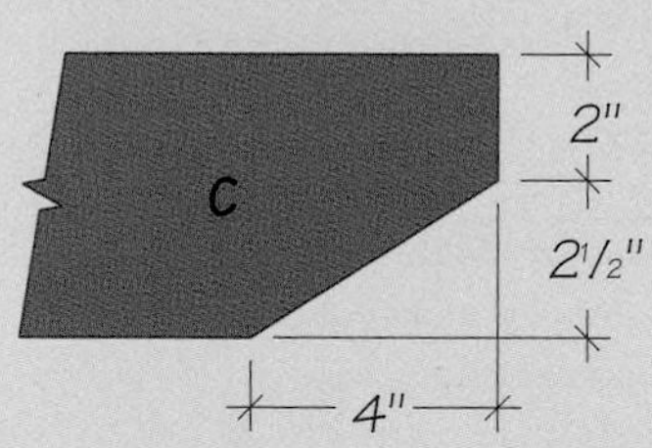
C
2"
2 1/2"
4"

STRETCHER END LAYOUT

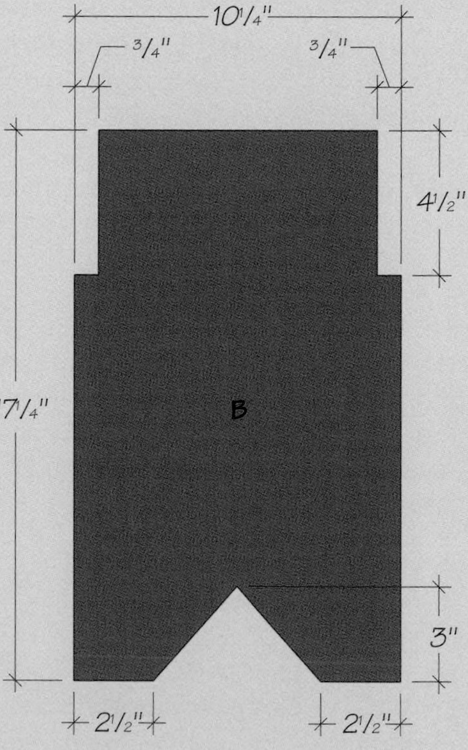
10 1/4"
3/4"
3/4"
4 1/2"
17 1/4"
B
3"
2 1/2"
2 1/2"

LEG LAYOUT

Five-Board Bench Cutting List

Part	No.	Size	Material
A. Top	1	¾ × 11¼ × 48 in.	Pine
B. Legs	2	¾ × 10¼ × 17¼ in.	"
C. Stretchers	2	¾ × 4½ × 47 in.	"

Assemble the bench

6 Attach the stretchers to the legs: Draw a reference line across the width of each stretcher, 5⅞ in. from the ends to mark the leg locations. Spread glue in the stretcher notches on the legs. Clamp the legs in place between the stretchers so the legs are centered on the stretcher reference lines you just drew. Drill pairs of countersunk pilot holes through the stretchers and into the legs, and fasten the parts with #8 × 2-in. flat-head wood screws.

7 Install the bench top: Lay the bench top on the stretcher/leg assembly so it overhangs evenly all around, and mark this position on the bottom face of the bench top. (If you've measured and cut accurately, the overhang should be ½ in.) Remove the bench top, spread glue along the top edges of the stretchers and clamp the bench top in position. Attach the top by driving countersunk screws into the legs and stretchers (three screws per leg and five screws per stretcher, spaced evenly) **(See Photo C).**

Finishing touches

8 Fill the holes left by the screwheads. Since we painted our bench, we used wood putty to conceal the screws. You could also install wood plugs, which look more natural on a bench that will be stained and/or varnished.

9 Sand all surfaces of the bench smooth with up to 150-grit sandpaper. Apply your topcoat of choice. We brushed on a coat of primer followed by several coats of paint.

PHOTO B: Clamp the leg blanks one on top of the other so you can cut them both at once with a jig saw.

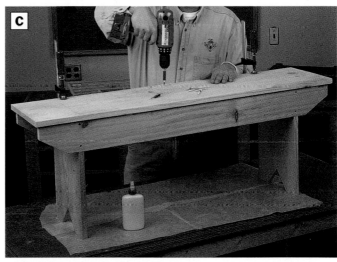

PHOTO C: Assemble the bench parts with glue and 2-in. flathead wood screws, driven into countersunk pilot holes.

Five-board benches

Five-board benches have been an American furniture mainstay since Colonial times. Their utilitarian styling and simple construction have made them common fixtures in barns, workshops and even around long dinner tables. You'll find five-board benches made of just about any available wood and in all lengths and heights, but usually they're constructed from pine and painted. The splayed legs typically are scalloped or notched to create feet. Many shorter benches also have handle cut-outs in the top. If you decide to build a five-board bench for outdoor use, it's a good idea to construct it from a naturally weather-resistant wood like cedar or white oak instead of pine.

Basic Bookcase

Good-quality prefabricated bookcases are tough to come by for less than $100. Spend a fraction of that amount on materials for this project, and you can construct a bookcase that will last for years. Our low-standing bookcase is just the right height for kids, but it's also a sturdy and practical addition to any room in the house. Build it from one sheet of paint-grade plywood in an afternoon.

Basic Bookcase: Step-by-step

PHOTO A: Lay out the bookcase parts on the plywood sheet, then rip and crosscut them to size. We arranged the shelves end-to-end on the plywood so we could rip one long strip, then crosscut the strip twice to form the three shelves.

CUT THE PARTS

❶ Rip and crosscut the bookcase back and top to size.

❷ Rip a 10-in.-wide, 62⅝-in. strip of plywood, then crosscut the strip in half to form the two bookcase sides.

❸ Lay out the three shelves end-for-end along one long edge of the plywood sheet, then cut off this strip of shelving. Crosscut the strip along your reference lines to divide it into three shelves (**See Photo A**).

Basic Bookcase

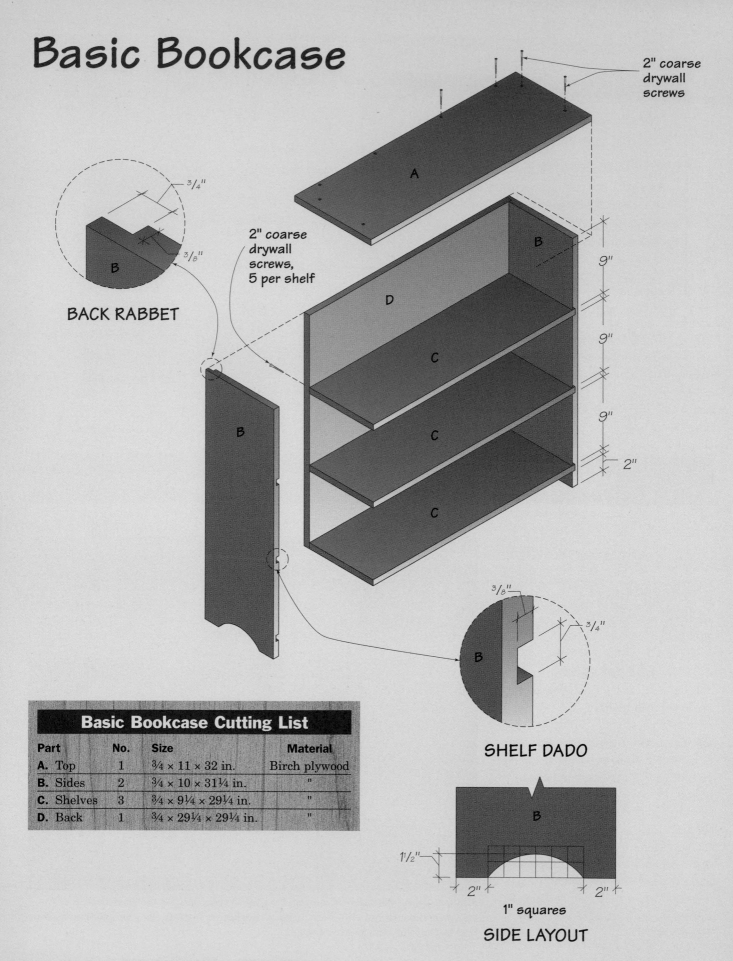

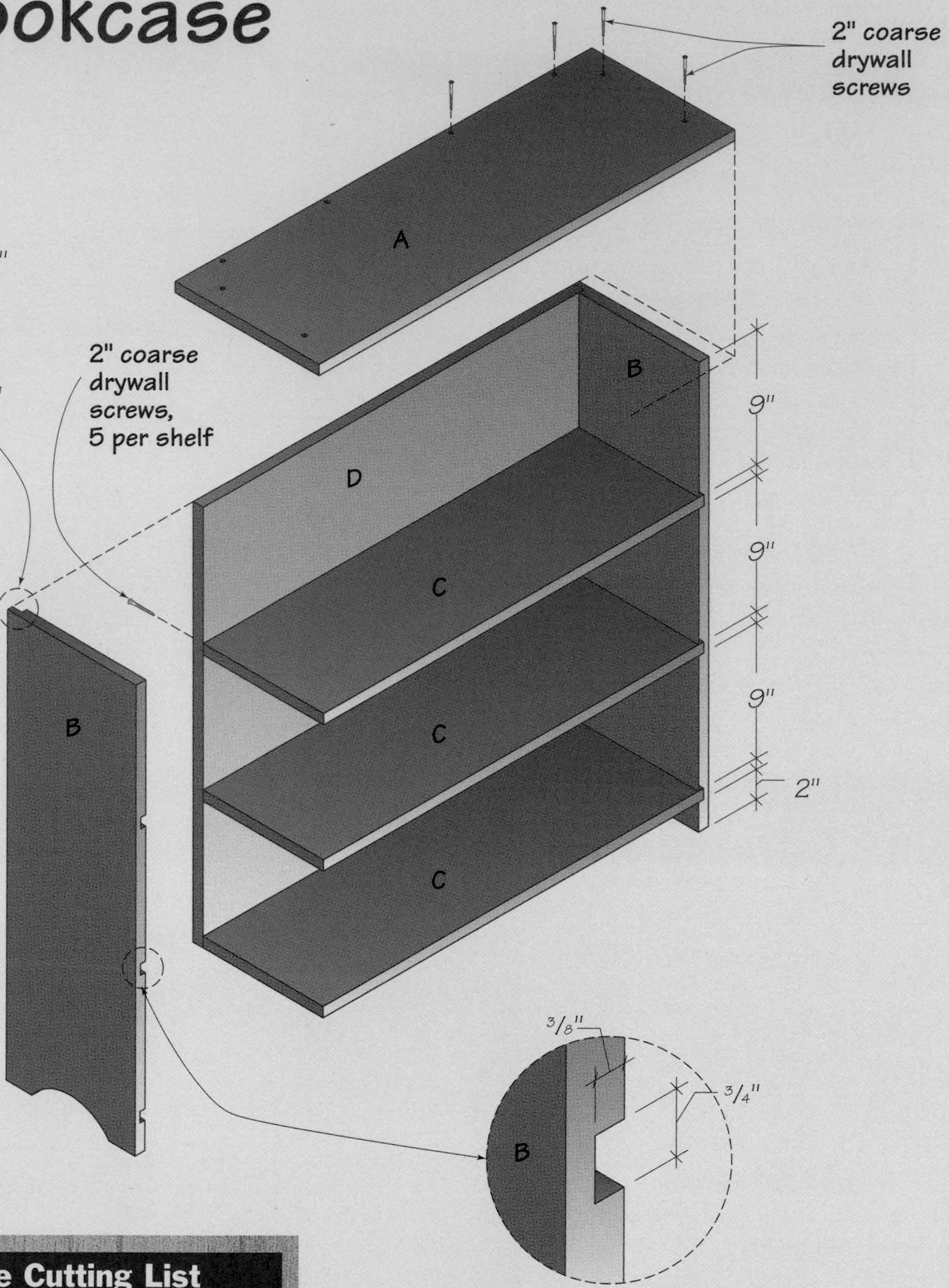
2" coarse
drywall
screws
A
2" coarse
drywall
screws,
5 per shelf
D
B
C
C
C
B
9"
9"
9"
2"
3/8"
3/4"
B

SHELF DADO

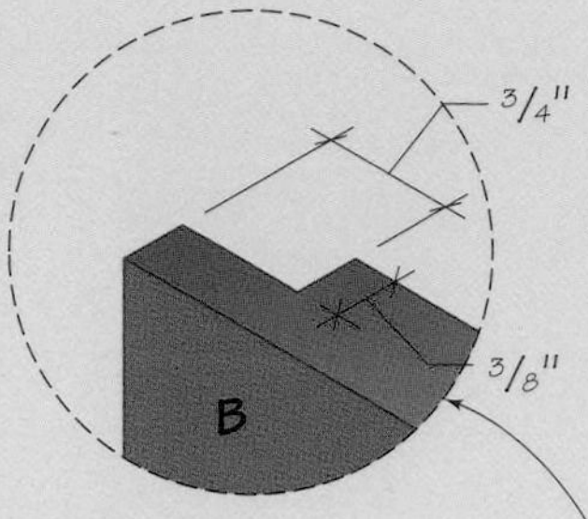
3/4"
3/8"
B

BACK RABBET

Basic Bookcase Cutting List			
Part	**No.**	**Size**	**Material**
A. Top	1	¾ × 11 × 32 in.	Birch plywood
B. Sides	2	¾ × 10 × 31¼ in.	"
C. Shelves	3	¾ × 9¼ × 29¼ in.	"
D. Back	1	¾ × 29¼ × 29¼ in.	"

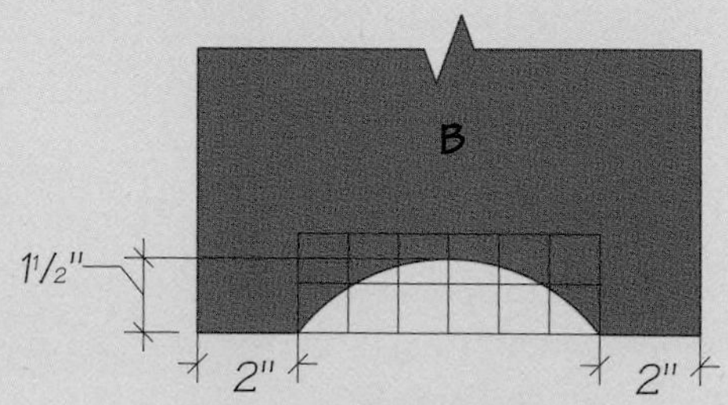
B
1½"
2"
2"

1" squares

SIDE LAYOUT

MAKE THE SIDES

4 Draw and cut the arched profiles along the bottom edges of the side panels: Lay out the arches, following the *Side Layout* grid drawing. Make these curved cuts with a jig saw, and smooth the cut edges with a file and sandpaper.

5 Rout the shelf dadoes in the sides. To set up for this milling operation, clamp the side panels together side by side, so the parts are aligned and configured with the arched ends next to one another. Refer to the *Exploded View* drawing to mark the shelf dado locations across both side panels. Rout each shelf dado with a ¾-in.-dia. straight bit set to a depth of ⅜ in. Guide the router base against a straightedge clamped across the workpieces, and gang-rout the dadoes across both side panels (**See Photo B**).

6 Mill rabbets along the inside back edge of each side panel for the bookcase back. Use the same router bit and depth setting as for the shelf dadoes (See the *Back Rabbet* detail drawing). Clamp a straightedge lengthwise along each side panel to guide the router base while you cut each rabbet (**See Photo C**).

ASSEMBLE THE BOOKCASE

7 Dry-fit the shelves and back panel in the bookcase sides to be sure the parts fit in the dado and rabbet grooves. NOTE: *Some plywood is slightly thicker than ¾ in., so the shelves may fit tightly in the dado grooves. If this is true for your plywood, widen the dadoes slightly with a file until the shelves fit without force.*

PHOTO B: Clamp the sides together side by side, lay out the shelf dado locations and gang-rout the dadoes across both sides. Clamp a straightedge across the side workpieces to guide the router cuts.

PHOTO C: Rout ¾-in.-wide, ⅜-in.-deep rabbets along the inside back edge of each side panel for the bookcase back. Clamp each side panel to your bench to hold it securely as you rout the rabbet, and guide the router base against a straightedge.

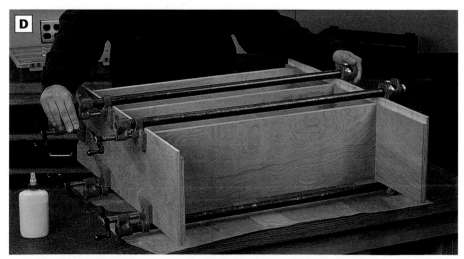

PHOTO D: Glue and clamp the shelves into their dadoes in the bookcase sides. Keep the shelves flush with the front edges of the sides so they don't obstruct the back rabbets.

PHOTO E: Install the back on the bookcase with glue and screws driven into the back edges of the shelves. Mark the shelf locations on the back first, so you can drive the screws accurately.

PHOTO F: Position the top panel on the bookcase and fasten it with 2-in. drywall screws driven into countersunk pilot holes.

8 Assemble the shelves and sides: Spread glue in the dadoes, set the shelves in place and clamp up the parts. Be sure the shelves are flush with the front edges of the bookcase sides (**See Photo D**).

9 Install the back. First, mark shelf centerlines across the back panel for installing screws. Then spread glue in the rabbets and set the back in place so the top edges of the sides and back are flush. Drive countersunk 2-in. drywall screws through the back and into the shelves along your pencil reference lines (**See Photo E**).

10 Attach the top: Set the top in place on the bookcase so the back edge is flush with the bookcase back. The ends and front should overhang evenly. Mark centerlines on the top for driving screws into the sides and back. Drill countersunk pilot holes along these lines. Fasten the top in place with 2-in. drywall screws (**See Photo F**).

FINISHING TOUCHES

11 Fill the screwhead recesses, gaps around the shelf dadoes and any voids in the plywood with wood putty (**See Photo G**).

12 Sand the puttied areas and all project surfaces smooth with 150-grit sandpaper.

13 Finish the bookshelf by rolling or brushing on a coat of primer followed by two coats of paint (**See Photo H**).

PHOTO G: Conceal the screwheads and any voids or gaps in the plywood with wood putty. Sand the putty smooth when it dries.

PHOTO H: Roll or brush on a coat of primer to all exposed surfaces, followed by two coats of paint.

Stiffening long shelves

The main factor that determines the width of a bookcase is the load-bearing capacity of the shelves. A ¾-in.-thick plywood shelf can span about 30 in. without additional support before it begins to sag. If you decide to modify this bookcase project and build it with longer shelves, stiffen each shelf by gluing and nailing a 1½-in.-wide strip of solid wood or plywood along the front edge. You could also double-up the thickness of the shelves by gluing on another layer of ¾-in.-thick plywood. A third, but more involved alternative would be to add a vertical divider at the middle of each shelf.

Tile-Top Coffee Table

High durability and a fresh look are two of the best reasons for choosing to build a table with a ceramic tile tabletop. An increasingly popular design element, tile adds new textures and colors to wood furnishings. When combined with a strong, simple birch table base, the effect is quite stunning—as you can see.

Vital Statistics: Tile-Top Coffee Table

TYPE: Coffee table

OVERALL SIZE: 49½L by 15H by 25½D

MATERIAL: Birch with ceramic tile top

JOINERY: Rabbet joints and butt joints reinforced with glue and screws

CONSTRUCTION DETAILS:
- Tabletop is made of 32 ceramic floor tiles applied to an MDF substrate
- Rabbets cut in leg tops create ledges for the aprons
- Hardwood cleats provide support for tabletop
- Counterbores filled with wood plugs

FINISHING OPTIONS: Clear coat for casual, contemporary look enhanced by tiles; alternately, birch can be stained to take on on the characteristics of most other wood species.

Building time

 PREPARING STOCK
2 hours

 LAYOUT
2 hours

 CUTTING PARTS
3-5 hours

 ASSEMBLY
2-4 hours

 FINISHING
2-4 hours

TOTAL: 11-17 hours

Tools you'll use

- Table saw
- Jointer
- Surface planer
- Cross-cutting saw
- Flush-cutting saw
- Tape measure
- 36-in. or longer bar or pipe clamps (6)
- Wood mallet
- Combination square
- Drill/driver
- Counterbore/countersink bit
- Dado-blade set
- Notched trowel
- Grout float

Shopping list

- ☐ (1) 4 × 4 in. × 6 ft. solid birch
- ☐ (2) ¾ or 4/4 × 4 in. × 8 ft. birch
- ☐ (2) 1½ × 1½ in. × 8 ft. inexpensive hardwood
- ☐ (1) ¾ × 24 × 48 in. MDF particleboard
- ☐ (32) 6 × 6 ceramic floor tiles
- ☐ Tile adhesive and grout (latex additive optional)
- ☐ Wood glue
- ☐ #10 × 2-in. wood screws
- ☐ ⅜ × ⅜ wood plugs
- ☐ Finishing materials

Tile-Top Coffee Table

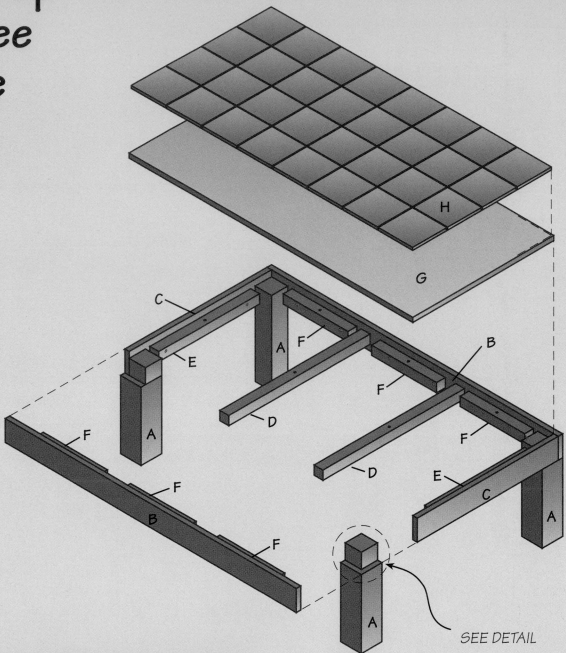

SEE DETAIL

Coffee Table Cutting List			
Part	**No.**	**Size**	**Material**
A. Legs	4	3½ × 3½ × 14 in.	Birch
B. Side Rails	2	¾ × 3½ × 49½ in.	"
C. End Rails	2	¾ × 3½ × 24 in.	"
D. Cleats (middle)	2	1½ × 1½ × 24 in.	Hardwood
E. Cleats (end)	2	1½ × 1½ × 17 in.	"
F. Cleats (side)	6	1½ × 1½ × 11 in.	"
G. Sub-top	1	¾ × 24 × 48 in.	MDF
H. Tiles	32	¼ × 6 × 6 in.	Ceramic

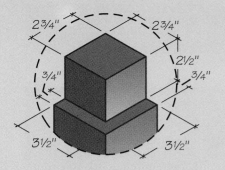

**DETAIL
(TOP OF LEG)**

2¾" 2¾"

¾" 2½" ¾"

3½" 3½"

TOP VIEW

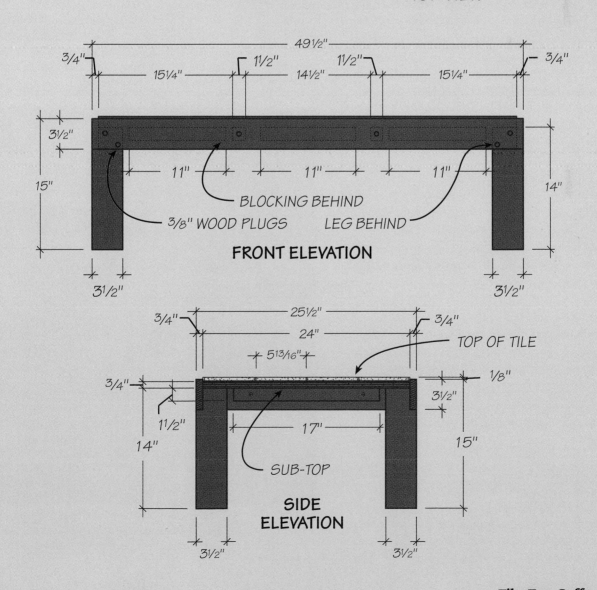

49½"

¾" 1½" 1½" ¾"

15¼" 14½" 15¼"

3½"

15

11" 11" 11"

14"

BLOCKING BEHIND

3/8" WOOD PLUGS *LEG BEHIND*

FRONT ELEVATION

3½" 3½"

25½"

¾" 24" ¾"

5¹³/₁₆" *TOP OF TILE*

¾" 1/8"

3½"

1½" 17" 15"

14"

SUB-TOP

**SIDE
ELEVATION**

3½" 3½"

PHOTO A: Make rabbet cuts in the tops of two adjoining faces of each leg to create ledges for the rails. We used a dado-blade set. Feed the stock with the miter gauge to assure a square cut.

NOTE: *Because the actual dimensions of tile can vary significantly among styles and manufacturers, we strongly recommend that you purchase the tile for your table before you begin building the table base. A nominal 6 × 6 tile you may find can be anywhere from 5½ to a full 6 in. square. Rather than cutting the tiles to fit, purchase the style and color you like and dry-lay the tiles to the approximate size of the coffee tabletop (24 × 48 in. if you build it as shown here). Measure the width and length of the dry-lay, and base the size of your aprons and substrate on that dimension (don't forget to allow about 1/16 to 1/8 in. between tiles for grout joints if your tiles don't have nibs that set the grout joint automatically).*

MAKE THE LEGS

The legs for this coffee table were made from solid 4-in.-thick birch stock. If you're unable to find wood of that thickness, or if you choose to build the coffee table with a different wood species that's not available in such beefy dimensions, simply laminate thinner strips to make the leg stock.

❶ Joint and plane the leg stock to 3½ in. thick. Ideally, use a workpiece that's at least 58 in. long. To prepare the stock, run two adjoining faces through your jointer to create flat, smooth faces, then rip-cut the stock so it's square and slightly thicker than 3½ in. Reduce the stock to 3½ in. square using a planer or jointer. Cross-cut four lengths to 14 in. long to make the legs.

❷ The legs are rabbeted on the top, outside faces to create ledges for the rails. Lay out the shoulders of the rabbets by drawing square lines on adjoining faces, 2½ in. down from the top of each leg. If you've laminated the legs, mark the cuts so the grain is consistent on each side (i.e., the faces of both legs on a

PHOTO B: Attach the side and end rails to the legs with two screws per joint. Stagger the screws as shown to keep screws on adjoining sides from interfering with each other. The screw hole counterbores will be plugged with wood plugs.

particular side should be either edge grain or face grain when viewed from straight on).

❸ We used a dado-blade set mounted in a table saw to remove the stock in the rabbet areas. A band saw can also be used or even a hand saw if you've got some time to kill. Set the dado-blade set for its widest cut, and adjust the cutting height to ¾ in. Use a miter gauge to guide each work-piece across the dado set, starting at the end and working your way toward the shoulder line (**See Photo A**).

MAKE THE RAILS & ASSEMBLE THE TABLE BASE

❹ Cut the end rails and side rails to finished size.

❺ Lay two legs down on a work-surface, about 4 ft. apart, with the rabbeted sides facing up and out. Place a side rail on top of the legs in the rabbeted recess. Adjust the legs so the outside corners are flush with the ends of the rail and the lower edge of the rail is tight up against the shoulders of the rabbets. Clamp the rail into position and drill two counterbored pilot holes through the rail into each leg. The counterbore should be ⅜-in.-dia. × ⅜-in.-deep to accept a standard-sized wood plug. Apply glue to the mating surfaces, then drive #10 × 2-in. flathead wood screws into the counterbored pilot holes to attach the rails to the legs. Repeat the procedure for the other side rail and the other two legs, creating two side-rail assemblies.

❻ Stand the two sides upright and attach the end rails between the side-rail assemblies (**See Photo B**). Make sure the ends of the end rails are tight against the

PHOTO C: Attach cleats to the rails with glue and screws. Drill countersunk pilot holes in the bottoms of the cleats (for attaching the sub-top) before installing them.

PHOTO D: Drive 2-in. screws through the cleats and into the underside of the sub-top. If your drill/driver has a clutch, set it to a low setting to help avoid overdriving the screws.

inside faces of the side rails.

❼ The substrate for the tiled tabletop (we're calling it the "sub-top") will rest on top of the legs, at a point 1 in. down from the top edges of the rails. To support the weight of the substrate and tile, we added cleats that are installed with their tops flush to the tops of

the legs. To mark the cleat loca-tions, draw reference lines all around the inside faces of the rails, 1 in. down from the top.

❽ Cut the 10 cleats to length from 1½ × 1½-in. stock (any hard-wood will do). Drill two evenly spaced, countersunk screw holes into one face of each cleat for the

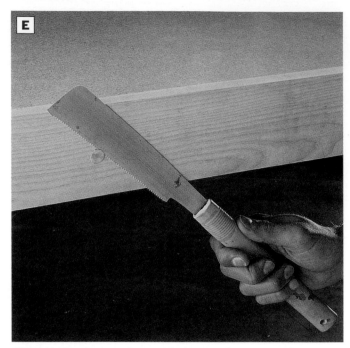

PHOTO E: Plug the screw holes with plugs cut from scraps of the same wood used to make the table base (if you have a plug cutter). When the glue is dry, trim the ends of the plugs with a flush-cutting saw, like this Japanese saw.

PHOTO F: Finish-sand the table base and apply the finish you've chosen. We simply topcoated the wood with three coats of clear Danish oil, preserving the natural color of the wood.

screws that will be used to attach the substrate.

9 Attach the cleats at the locations shown in the *Grid patterns* using glue and 2-in. screws driven into countersunk pilot holes. Make sure the tops of the cleats are aligned with the reference lines **(See Photo C).** The middle cleats are attached with screws driven through counterbored pilot holes in the outside faces of the aprons, and into the ends of the cleats.

10 Cut the sub-top to size from ¾-in. particleboard or plywood. We used MDF (medium-density fiberboard) particleboard, which is a superior substrate material to either plywood or ordinary oriented-strand particleboard.

11 Spread glue on the top surfaces of the cleats. Drop the top in and flip the whole table upside down onto blocking. Drive 2-in.

screws through the cleats and into the sub-top **(See Photo D).**

12 Plug the screw counterbore holes. Birch plugs in the standard ⅜ × ⅜-in. size are fairly easy to find. For a better match, cut your own plugs from scrap pieces of your stock, using a plug cutter mounted in your drill press. Apply glue to the ends of the plugs and tap them in with a wood mallet. Trim the ends of the plugs flush with the rails using a flush-cutting hand saw **(See Photo E).**

13 Sand the table base with 150-, then 180-grit sandpaper and ease all sharp edges and corners. Apply your finish of choice to the rails and legs (but not the sub-top). We applied a clear Danish oil finish **(See Photo F).**

INSTALL THE TILES
14 Tape off the top edges of the rails with masking tape to protect the wood from the tile adhesive.

15 Apply tile adhesive to the sub-top. It can be a thinset mortar or mastic. Spread it evenly across the entire surface with a notched trowel **(See Photo G).**

16 Set the tiles in the adhesive **(See Photo H).** Don't use too much top pressure when setting the tiles—you could squeeze out all the adhesive from beneath the tiles and ruin the bond. If your tiles are not self-spacing, try to keep even gaps of ¹⁄₁₆ to ⅛ in. on all sides of each tile.

17 When the adhesive is fully set (see manufacturer's recommendations), grout the tiles. Choose a grout color that complements the tile color. *TIP: For added resistance to cracking, add latex grout additive to dry grout mix instead of water.* Spread the grout diagonally across the joints with a rubber grout float. Fill all the gaps to the top **(See Photo I).** When the grout has begun to set up, wipe

PHOTO G: Apply a medium-thick layer of tile adhesive (dry-set mortar or mastic) to the surface of the sub-top, using a notched trowel. Protect the finished wood with tape.

PHOTO H: Set the tiles into the bed of adhesive, spacing them evenly so the gaps are consistent. Press down lightly on each tile to seat it into the adhesive, but take care not to apply too much pressure. Leave a gap of about ⅛ in. between the tiles and the tops of the rail boards. Try to get the tiles positioned correctly on the first try, minimizing the need to move and adjust them.

PHOTO I: Spread grout into the joints between tiles (and around the border of the tiled top), using a grout float. Always wear rubber gloves when working with grout. Use a latex additive in the grout to help keep it from crumbling and to improve the bond with the tiles.

PHOTO J: Before the grout dries completely, wipe off the excess from the surfaces of the tile, using a damp sponge. After the grout is dried, buff the tile with a soft cloth to give it a glossy sheen.

the excess from the surfaces of the tiles with a damp sponge **(See Photo J).** Continue until the tiles are clean—grout can be very hard to clean off once it dries. Work diagonally across the joints, being careful not to remove grout from between the joints.

18 Remove the masking tape from the wood, pulling it up slowly.

Changing Table / Dresser

Y ou'll be the toast of the baby shower when you produce this striking and efficient baby changing table for your loved one. Clean lines and contemporary styling create a little design flair that will enhance baby's room. And the easy-clean plastic laminate surfaces will be much appreciated by the new parents. NOTE: if you're giving this changing table as a gift, the new parents will also appreciate it if you throw in a changing pad to go with it. When baby no longer needs the changing table, it can be easily converted to a dresser or linen cabinet for bedrooms and bathrooms.

Vital Statistics: Changing Table/Dresser

TYPE: Changing table with storage

OVERALL SIZE: 40L × 20W × 32H

MATERIAL: Maple or birch plywood, solid mahogany or birch, particleboard, plastic laminate

JOINERY: Biscuit joints, pocket screws, tongue-and-groove drawer joint

CONSTRUCTION DETAILS:

· Top surface, door and drawer fronts covered with easy-to-clean plastic laminate
· Cabinet sides and front rails/legs taper outward.
· Left side has free-floating drawers, right side has interior cabinet with adjustable shelves.
· Tabletop mounts with corner braces.

FINISH: Satin polyurethane on maple parts

Building time

PREPARING STOCK
2-4 hours

LAYOUT
2-4 hours

CUTTING PARTS
2-4 hours

ASSEMBLY
6-8 hours

FINISHING
4-6

TOTAL: 16-26 hours

Tools you'll use

· Table saw
· Corner-beading bit
· Drum sander
· Circular saw
· Jig saw
· Square
· Router and router table
· Dado blade set
· Flush-trim bit
· Small level
· Straightedge
· Laminate trimmer (router)
· Straightedge guide
· J-roller
· Band saw (optional
· Laminate file
· Biscuit joiner
· ¼-in-radius roundover bit
· Bar or pipe clamps
· Belt sander
· Drill/driver
· Pocket screw drilling jig

Shopping list

- ☐ (1) ½ in. × 4 ft. × 4 ft. maple plywood
- ☐ (1) ¾ in. × 4 ft. × 8 ft. maple plywood
- ☐ (1) ¾ in. × 4 ft. × 8 ft. particleboard
- ☐ ¾ × 4 × 40 in. maple
- ☐ 1⁄32 in. × 4 ft. × 4 ft. laminate
- ☐ (1) maple edge banding (8 ft.)
- ☐ (2) European face-frame hinges
- ☐ (4) 1¼ in. door/drawer knobs
- ☐ (6) 16 in. low-profile drawer slides
- ☐ (6) 3 in. drawer slide mounting sockets
- ☐ (8) 1¼ in. shelf supports
- ☐ (4) 9½ in. corner braces
- ☐ 1¼ in. pocket screws
- ☐ #20 biscuits
- ☐ Wood glue, finishing materials

Changing Table

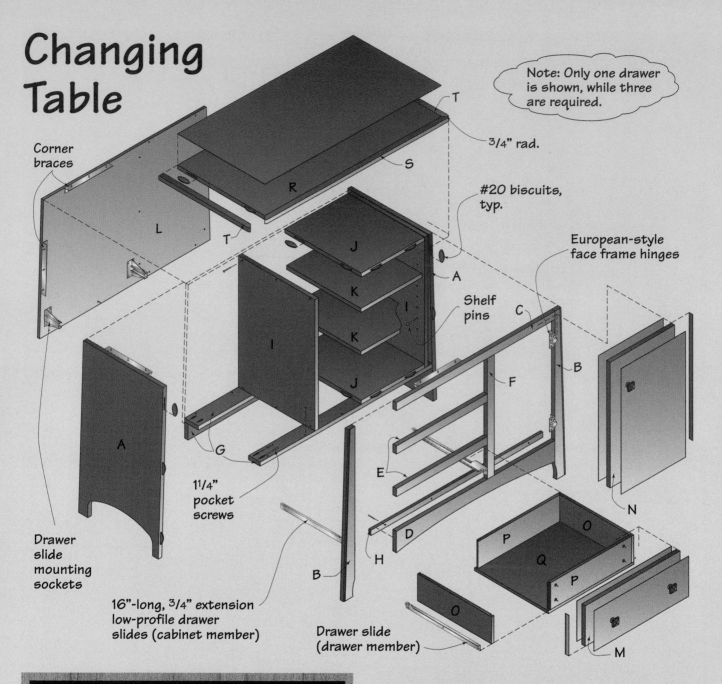

Corner braces

Note: Only one drawer is shown, while three are required.

³/4" rad.

#20 biscuits, typ.

European-style face frame hinges

Shelf pins

Drawer slide mounting sockets

1¹/4" pocket screws

16"-long, ³/4" extension low-profile drawer slides (cabinet member)

Drawer slide (drawer member)

Cabinet Cutting List

Part	No.	Size	Material
A. End panel	2	³/4 × 17⁷/16 × 31¼ in.	Maple plywood
B. Stiles	2	³/4 × 2½ × 31¼ in.	Solid maple
C. Top rail	1	³/4 × 1½ × 34 in.	"
D. Bottom rail	1	³/4 × 4 × 34 in.	"
E. Drawer rail	2	³/4 × 1½ × 19½ in.	"
F. Divider	1	³/4 × 1½ × 22¼ in.	"
G. Blocking	3	³/4 × 3 × 37 in.	Maple plywood
H. Front cleat	1	³/4 × 1 × 37 in.	Solid maple
I. Side panels	2	³/4 × 16⁷/16 × 24½ in.	Maple plywood
J. Fixed shelf	2	³/4 × 16⁷/16 × 13³/8 in.	"
K. Adj. shelf	2	³/4 × 16 × 13¹/8 in.	"
L. Back panel	1	½ × 37¹/8 × 25½ in.	"

Drawers/Door Cutting List

Part	No.	Size	Material
M. Drawer core	3	³/4 × 7⁷/16 × 20⁷/16 in.	Particleboard
N. Door core	1	³/4 × 13¹⁵/16 × 23⁷/16 in.	"
O. Side	6	½ × 5 × 16 in.	Maple plywood
P. Front/back	6	½ × 5 × 17¹⁵/16 in.	"
Q. Bottom	3	½ × 16 × 18⁷/16 in.	"

Top Cutting List

Part	No.	Size	Material
R. Top panel	1	³/4 × 19 × 38 in.	Particleboard
S. Front edge	1	1³/16 × 1 × 40 in.	Solid maple
T. Side edge	2	1³/16 × 1 × 20 in.	"

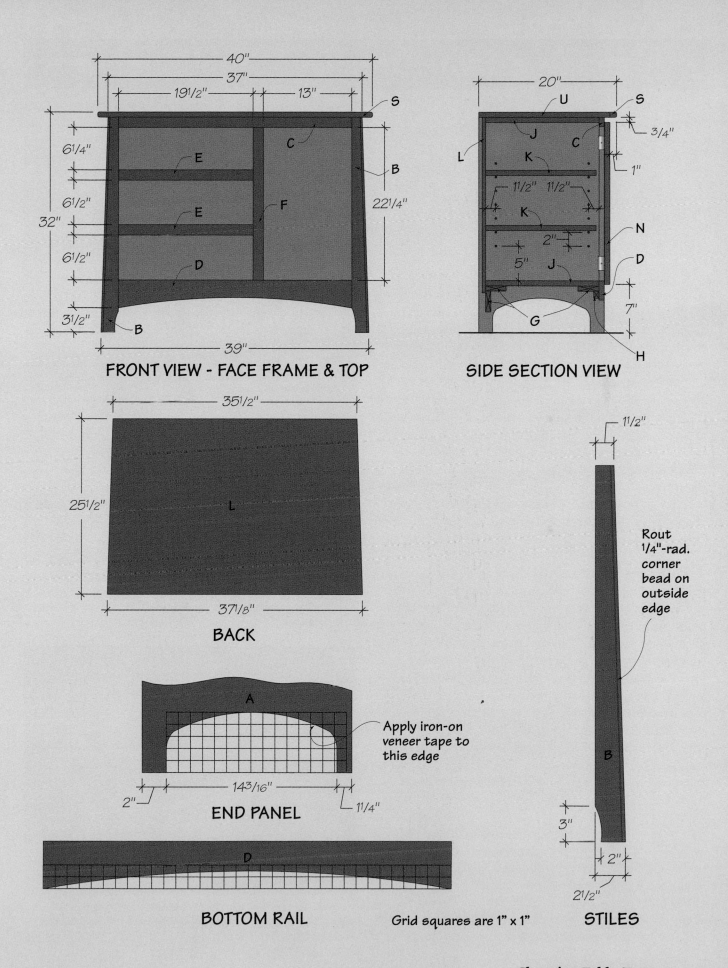

FRONT VIEW - FACE FRAME & TOP

40"
37"
19 1/2"
13"
S
C
6 1/4"
E
B
6 1/2"
E
F
22 1/4"
32"
6 1/2"
D
3 1/2"
B
39"

SIDE SECTION VIEW

20"
U
S
J
C
3/4"
L
1"
K
1 1/2"   1 1/2"
K
N
2"
5"
J
D
7"
G
H

BACK

35 1/2"
L
25 1/2"
37 1/8"

END PANEL

A
Apply iron-on veneer tape to this edge
2"
14 3/16"
1 1/4"

BOTTOM RAIL

D

Grid squares are 1" x 1"

STILES

1 1/2"
Rout 1/4"-rad. corner bead on outside edge
B
3"
2"
2 1/2"

Changing Table/Dresser 269

BUILD THE CARCASE

1 Cut the two end panels to size from ¾-in. birch or maple plywood. Since the ends will angle outward slightly, their top and bottom edges will need to be cut at a bit of an angle to be parallel to the floor. Set your table saw blade at a 2° angle and lower it so it just barely protrudes from the table. Attach an auxiliary plywood or particleboard fence to your rip fence with clamps or double-stick tape. Using scrap pieces of plywood (preferably from the same plywood sheet) to test the cut, adjust the rip fence and the blade height so the blade cuts into the auxiliary fence at just the right point to cut a bevel on the plywood edge without reducing its overall length. Bevel both ends of each finished end with this setup, making sure the bevels are parallel.

2 Using the drawing of the lower cutout on the end panel as a guide, make a template from ¼ in. hardboard. Cut out the shape and smooth the edges of the template with a drum sander. Label the front and back leg sections of the template, as they differ in width to allow for the added thickness of the face frame in front. Trace the template shapes onto the outside faces of the end panels, making sure the beveled top and bottom edges are aligned correctly **(See Photo A)**. Cut close to the lines with a jig saw; then clamp, nail or double-stick tape the template to each end panel, in succession. Trim the end panels flush to the template outlines using a router and a flush-trim (pattern-cutting) bit.

3 Cut the cabinet face frame parts, including the stiles, top rail, bottom rail, drawer rails and divider from solid birch. Also cut the birch front cleat to size. Taper the outside edges of the stiles from 2½ in. wide at the bottoms to 1½ in. wide at the top. We used a straightedge template and flush-trim bit mounted in a router table to cut the tapers. You could also use a

PHOTO A: Make a hardboard template of the cutout shape for the bottoms of the end panels. Trace the shape onto the lower portions of each end panel (make sure the beveled bottom edge is facing in the correct direction).

PHOTO B: Glue the face frame joints and clamp the parts together, making sure all faces are flush. Drive pocket screws to hold the face frame parts together.

PHOTO C: Attach the blocking to the inside of the cabinet with pocket screws. Mount the blocking so its lower faces ride on lines drawn 6 in. up from the bottom edges of the end panels.

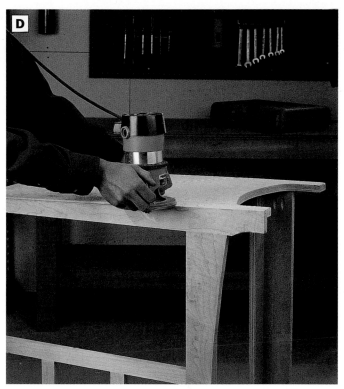

PHOTO D: To create a decorative bead on the outer corners of the cabinet, rout a corner bead along the front outside edge of each stile.

taper-cutting jig and a table saw. Using the measurements and a French curve or flexible spline curve as references, draw the decorative cutout on the bottom inside edge of each stile. Make the cuts with a band saw or jig saw and sand the edges smooth with a drum sander.

❹ Draw the arc on the bottom edge of the bottom rail using a flexible strip of thin scrap wood to form the arc. Cut the arc with a band saw or jig saw and smooth the cut edges with a drum sander.

❺ Lay out the joints on the face frame parts, and drill pocket screw holes on the inside surfaces of all the rails and the center divider. Machine for two pocket screws at each joint.

❻ Assemble the face frame using glue and pocket screws **(See Photo B)**. Hold the parts together with clamps while you insert the screws. Wipe up excess glue squeeze-out with a damp cloth.

❼ The end panels get attached to the face frame by biscuit-joining the front edges of the panels to the stiles. Butt the parts together, then mark out and cut slots for #20 biscuits in the joint area. Glue biscuits into the backs of the stiles, spread glue on the edges

of the end panels, and clamp the end panels to the face frame with padded bar or pipe clamps. Make sure the top and bottom edges are all flush, and that the joints are square (you can use a combination square, or measure across the front and the back of the assembly—the distances should be equal). Wipe up glue squeeze-out.

❽ Use glue and countersunk screws to attach the front cleat to the inside face of the bottom rail, 1½ in. below the top edge of the rail.

❾ Cut the three blocking strips to size from ¾-in. plywood. On the inside face of each end panel, measure up and make marks 6 in. from the bottom edge, at the front and back of each. Use a straightedge to draw a line connecting the two points, creating a reference line across each end panel. This is the height at which the blocking will be mounted. Machine for pocket screws at both ends of each blocking strip. Attach the front blocking with countersunk screws driven down into the front cleat, and with pocket screws driven into the end panels. The lower face of the blocking should ride against the lines on the end panels. Using glue and clamps and/or screws, make an "L" with the two remaining blocking strips in the configuration shown in the *Side Section View*. Fasten

PHOTO E: Use a square and a straightedge to draw a line down the right side of the back panel. The line should be perpendicular to the top and bottom edges and it should cut off the angled edge. This will create a reference for attaching the internal cabinet to the back panel.

PHOTO F: Cut biscuit joints for attaching the top and bottom front edges of the internal cabinet to the inside of the face frame.

the "L" to the end panels with pocket screws, aligning the lower face of the top member with the lines drawn on the end panels (**See Photo C**). The back edge of the "L" should be inset 1 in. from the back edges of the end panels to allow room for the cabinet back. Because the internal cabinet structure will rest on the blocking, the upper face of the cabinet bottom should be flush with the top edge of the bottom rail.

❿ With a corner-beading bit mounted in your router, rout a decorative corner bead profile along the front outside corner of each stile (**See Photo D**).

CONSTRUCT THE INTERNAL CABINET

To simplify assembly of the changing table, we designed it as essentially a cabinet within a cabinet. The internal cabinet structure is squared up and assembled separately, then mounted inside the larger cabinet carcase.

⓫ Cut the side panels, fixed shelves and adjustable shelves to size from ¾-in. plywood. Also cut the back panel from ¾-in. plywood. The back panel will be angled on both ends to fit between the angled ends of the cabinet. Lay out the angled lines with a straightedge, according to the cutting diagram labeled *Back*. Make the cuts with a circular saw and a straightedge guide. Then, use a square and a straightedge to square a line down from the top right corner of the back (**See Photo E**). This will give you a reference for positioning the internal cabinet against the back panel.

⓬ Cut slots for #20 biscuits used to assemble the internal cabinet (the top and bottom will be captured between the sides). Then, drill ¼-in.-dia. shelf pin holes in the sides (make sure the holes are even and are sized to fit your shelf pins). Use a drill press or a portable drill with a right-angle drilling guide.

⓭ Glue and clamp up the internal cabinet, reinforcing the joints with biscuits. Adjust the clamps as needed to square up the cabinet. Clean up glue squeeze-out.

⓮ Attach the back panel to the internal cabinet with countersunk screws, following the reference line drawn on the inside face of the back panel. The back panel can help ensure the cabinet is squared correctly. The back panel will overhang the internal cabinet by 1 in. at the bottom.

⓯ Apply iron-on veneer tape to the front edges of the

adjustable shelves, and trim off excess with a hand edging trimmer or a sharp chisel.

JOIN THE INTERNAL & MAIN CABINETS

16 Lay out and cut slots for #20 biscuits to join the top front edge of the internal cabinet to the inside face of the top rail, and the bottom front edge of the interior cabinet to the inside face of the bottom rail (**See Photo F**). Glue biscuits into the slots in the face frame, and dry fit the assembly. The back panel should fit snugly in between the end panels.

17 Disassemble the construction and apply glue to the front edges of the internal cabinet. Clamp the internal cabinet to the face frame with bar or pipe clamps. Use wood cauls to spread the clamping pressure. Using the screws provided with the hardware, attach metal corner braces at the left end/back panel joint, as well as along the top edges of the end panels, the back, and the top rail in the drawer section of the cabinet (**See Photo G**).

BUILD & HANG THE DOORS & DRAWERS

18 Cut the drawer sides, fronts/backs and bottoms to size from ½-in. plywood. The drawers will be constructed with tongue-and-groove drawer joints. Install a dado blade set adjusted to ¼ in. in your table saw, and cut ¼ × ¼-in. grooves in the drawer sides ¼ in. from each end (**See Photo H**). Then, cut matching tongues in the drawer fronts and backs by cutting ¼ × ¼-in. rabbets in the end of each board (**See Photo I**).

19 Finish-sand the interior faces of the drawer parts. Spread glue on the mating parts and clamp the drawer sides to the fronts and backs with bar or quick-action clamps. Make sure the boxes are square during assembly. Wipe up any glue squeeze-out with a damp rag.

20 Attach the drawer bottoms with 1 in. countersunk screws (**See Photo J**), making sure the edges of drawer and bottom are flush all around.

21 Mount the drawer slides to the face frame, according to the manufacturer's directions. Use mounting sockets to attach the back end of each slide to the cabinet back so the slide is level. Attach the mating drawer slide members to the drawers and make sure they operate properly. The slides should be mounted so each drawer hangs in its face frame opening with ½ in. above and ½ in. below.

PHOTO G: Glue the internal cabinet to the inside of the face frame with biscuit joints, using wood cauls to spread the clamping pressure. Through a metal corner brace, screw the back panel to the left-hand end panel. Also attach corner braces along the top edges of the drawer compartment to serve as mounting brackets for the cabinet top.

PHOTO H: The first step in machining the drawer joints is to cut a ¼ × ¼-in. dado into the drawer sides, ¼ in. from the ends.

PHOTO I: Cut ¼ × ¼-in. rabbets in the ends of the drawer fronts and backs to form matching tongues.

PHOTO J: Use countersunk 1-in. screws to fasten the bottoms to the drawers. If the bottoms are cut square, they can be used to square up the drawers by keeping the drawer box outer faces flush with the edges of the bottoms.

㉒ Cut the drawer front cores and door cores to size from ¾-in. particleboard. Cut plastic laminate to cover the cores, at least ¼ in. larger than the cores in each direction. Attach an auxiliary plywood fence to your table saw's rip fence when cutting the thin laminate to keep it from sliding under the rip fence.

㉓ Laminate the edges of the drawer fronts and the door first, then laminate the faces. Start by rolling contact cement on the vertical edges of the parts and their mating laminate edging strips. When the adhesive has dried so it's no longer tacky, apply the edging and roll it firmly with a J-roller. Trim overhanging laminate with a laminate trimmer and a piloted flush-trim bit. Repeat this procedure with the horizontal edging on all parts. Then laminate the back faces of the parts and finally the front faces, trimming the overhanging laminate each time with the laminate trimmer or router and flush-trim bit. File all laminate edges so they're flush, and soften any sharp edges.

㉔ Install the European hinges according to the manufacturer's instructions and hang the doors on the cabinet.

㉕ Slide the bottom drawer into the cabinet. Use double-sided tape to fit a drawer front onto the drawer box. It should be ½ in. from the door, with its bottom edge flush with the bottom of the door. Put the other drawer fronts in position similarly, with ½-in. spaces between them. Remove the drawers from the cabinet and drill pilot holes from inside the drawer boxes, then attach the drawer fronts permanently with pan-head screws (over-size the guide holes through the fronts of the drawer boxes slightly so the position of the drawer fronts can be adjusted). Drill holes and mount knobs on the drawer fronts and the door. Adjust the door and drawer fronts as necessary so they are straight and aligned properly.

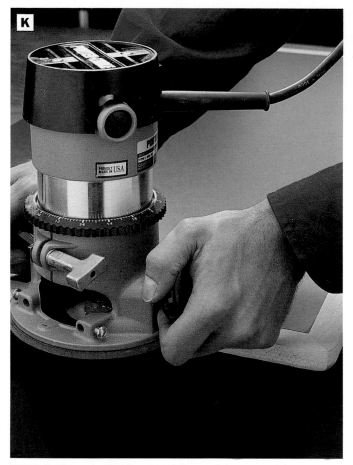

PHOTO K: After rounding the sharp corners of the top, round over the top and bottom edges of the wood all around with a ¼-in.-radius roundover bit in the router.

PHOTO L: After the finish has dried, rehang and adjust the door and the drawer fronts for proper alignment.

BUILD & MOUNT THE TOP

26 Cut the top core to size from ¾-in. particleboard. Cut a piece of plastic laminate slightly larger than the core. If it's more convenient than cutting on the table saw, you can cut laminate by scoring it against a steel straightedge and breaking it along the scored lines. Glue the laminate onto the top core as with the drawer and door cores, and trim the excess.

27 Cut the front and side edging to size from solid wood. Miter the front corners so the edging wraps around the core. Machine the edging and the edges of the top core for #20 biscuit joints, and glue the edges to the core. Remember to glue the edging miters.

28 Round the front corners of the top to a ¾-in. radius, using a belt sander. Then run a router with a ¼-in.-radius roundover bit around the top and bottom edges **(See Photo K)**.

29 Mount the top on the cabinet and center it so the overhang is even all around. Attach it to the internal cabinet with countersunk screws driven up from inside the cabinet. Drive them in only until the heads are flush with the surface. Attach the left side of the top to the cabinet with the metal corner braces in the top of the door compartment.

FINISHING TOUCHES

30 Remove hardware and finish-sand all surfaces. Apply finish of your choice. We used clear satin polyurethane.

31 When the finish has fully cured, reassemble and rehang the door and drawers **(See Photo L)**. Install the knobs. Attach bumpers to the back faces of the drawer fronts and the door. Insert the shelf pins and install the adjustable shelves.

Entry Bench

This Shaker-inspired slat-back bench offers perfect occasional seating in any room. Made from a single sheet of plywood, the project comfortably seats three adults, yet it is light enough for one person to carry or move with ease.

Entry Bench: Step-by-step

The unique feature of this bench is that the stretcher and legs are notched where they join together to form half-lap joints. Half-lap joints help keep the legs from racking once the bench is assembled and allow the stretcher to pass through the legs in essentially one piece.

MAKE THE LEGS & SEAT

❶ Cut the legs to rough size. In order to build the bench from one sheet of plywood, it is necessary to lay out two legs along the length of the plywood sheet and one leg across the width. Make one leg by cutting an 18-in.-wide, 48-in.-long strip from the short end of the sheet. Then rip-cut another 18-in.-wide strip along the length of the remaining sheet for the other two legs.

❷ Lay out the three legs. Follow the *Leg Layout* drawing to draw the leg profiles, half-lap notches and round bottom cut-outs. Scribe the 4¼-in.-radius cut-outs with a compass **(See Photo A).**

❸ Cut the three legs to shape with a jig saw: To cut out the square-bottomed half-lap notches, drill

PHOTO A: Lay out the three leg shapes on 18-in.-wide sections of plywood. Draw the curved bottom cut-outs that form the bench "feet" with a compass set to a 4¼-in. radius.

⅜-in.-dia. pilot holes in the corners of the notches first. This will allow room for turning the jig saw at the bottom of the notch. Cut out the notches. Square-off the bottom of each notch with a narrow file and sandpaper.

❹ Cut the seat panel to size.

Entry Bench

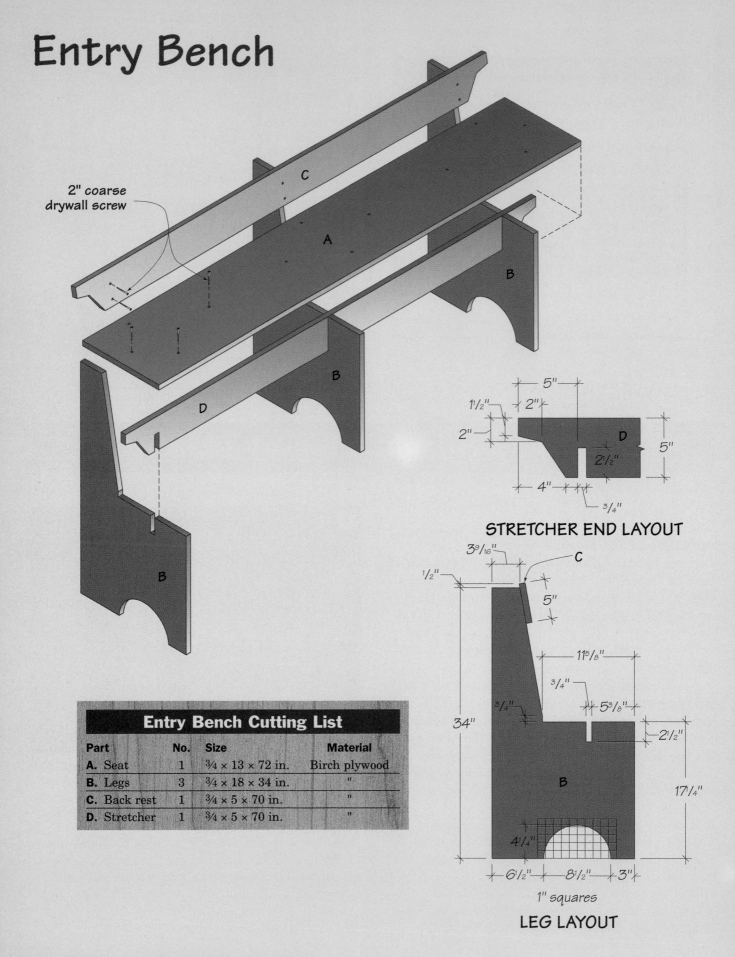

2" coarse drywall screw

C

A

B

B

D

B

STRETCHER END LAYOUT

5"
1¹/₂"
2"
2"
D
5"
2¹/₂"
4"
³/₄"

LEG LAYOUT

3⁹/₁₆"
C
¹/₂"
5"
11⁵/₈"
³/₄"
5³/₈"
³/₄"
34"
³/₄"
2¹/₂"
B
17¹/₄"
4¹/₄"
6¹/₂"
8¹/₂"
3"
1" squares

Entry Bench Cutting List

Part	No.	Size	Material
A. Seat	1	³/₄ × 13 × 72 in.	Birch plywood
B. Legs	3	³/₄ × 18 × 34 in.	"
C. Back rest	1	³/₄ × 5 × 70 in.	"
D. Stretcher	1	³/₄ × 5 × 70 in.	"

MAKE THE BACKREST & STRETCHER

5 Cut stretcher and back rest to size.

6 Since the end profiles of the stretcher and backrest match, follow the *Stretcher End Layout* drawing to mark the ends of both workpieces with the angled cutting profile. Trim the ends of the parts to shape with a jig saw.

7 Mark the stretcher with three half-lap notches, two spaced 5 in. from the ends and one centered on its length. Cut out the stretcher half-lap notches as you cut the legs, first drilling out clearance holes in the bottom corners of the notches, then removing the waste with a jig saw. File the notch corners square **(See Photo B).**

8 Test-fit the half-lap joints by slipping the stretcher over the bench legs so the notches between the parts interlock **(See Photo C).** You'll know you've got a correct fit if the top edge of the stretcher is flush with the top (seat) edges of the legs. A poor fit can be remedied by either widening or deepening the notches slightly with a file.

ASSEMBLE THE BENCH

9 Spread glue into the half-lap notches on the stretcher and legs and assemble these parts.

10 Set the seat in place on the legs and adjust it so the seat overhangs the ends of the stretcher by 1 in. Mark this position on the bottom face of the seat. Mark stretcher and leg centerlines on the top face of the seat as well, for locating screws. Spread glue on the legs where the seat will go. Reposition the seat on the legs and fasten it in place with 2-in. countersunk drywall screws.

11 Clamp the backrest on the upper ends of the legs so it overhangs 5 in. on each end and ½ in. above the tops of the legs. Mark the backrest for driving pairs of screws at each leg. Spread glue on the edges of the legs in the backrest areas, clamp the backrest in place and fasten it to the legs with 2-in. countersunk drywall screws.

FINISHING TOUCHES

12 Fill recessed screwheads and plywood voids with wood putty and sand the entire bench smooth. Brush or roll on a coat of primer and two coats of paint.

PHOTO B: Cut the three half-lap notches in the stretcher with a jig saw. Drill ⅜-in.-dia. clearance holes in the bottom corners of the notches first, so you can turn the saw to cut the square bottoms.

PHOTO C: Slip the seat and stretcher notches together to check the fit of the half-lap joints. File the notches wider or deeper, a little at a time, to improve the fit, if necessary.

PHOTO D: Install the seat and the backrest on the leg assembly with glue and 2-in. drywall screws, driven into countersunk pilot holes.

Entry Bench 279

Nesting Tables

Store three tables in the space you need for one by building these nesting tables. Our cherrywood tables are sized appropriately to fit beside sofas and chairs or could be the perfect display stands for plants or pottery. Set your table trio in the family room and they'll be at the ready for your next gameboard tournament.

Vital Statistics: Nesting Tables

TYPE: Nesting tables

OVERALL SIZE: Large: 24W by 24D by 24H

Medium: 19W by 19D by 20¾H

Small: 14W by 14D by 17½H

MATERIAL: Cherry, cherry plywood

JOINERY: Dowel, miter and butt joints

CONSTRUCTION DETAILS:

· Plywood tabletops with solid-wood edging
· Legs taper on two sides
· Dowel joints between the legs and aprons
· Tabletops secure with simple corner blocks

FINISHING OPTIONS: Danish oil; topcoat with three coats of satin polyurethane varnish if your tables will be subject to moisture

Building time

PREPARING STOCK
1-2 hours

LAYOUT
2-3 hours

CUTTING PARTS
2-3 hours

ASSEMBLY
2-3 hours

FINISHING
3-4 hours

TOTAL: 10-15 hours

Tools you'll use

· Jointer
· Table saw
· Random-orbit sander
· Drill/driver
· Tapering jig
· Doweling jig
· Japanese-style pull saw or fine-toothed back saw
· Bar or pipe clamps
· C-clamps

Shopping list

☐ (1) ¾ in. × 4 ft. × 4 ft. cherry plywood

☐ (3) 8/4 × 8/4 in. × 8 ft. cherry

☐ (1) ¾ × 8 in. × 8 ft. cherry

☐ (1) ⅜ in. × 6 ft. hardwood dowel

☐ #8 × 1¼ in. panhead wood screws

☐ Wood glue

☐ Finishing materials

Nesting Tables

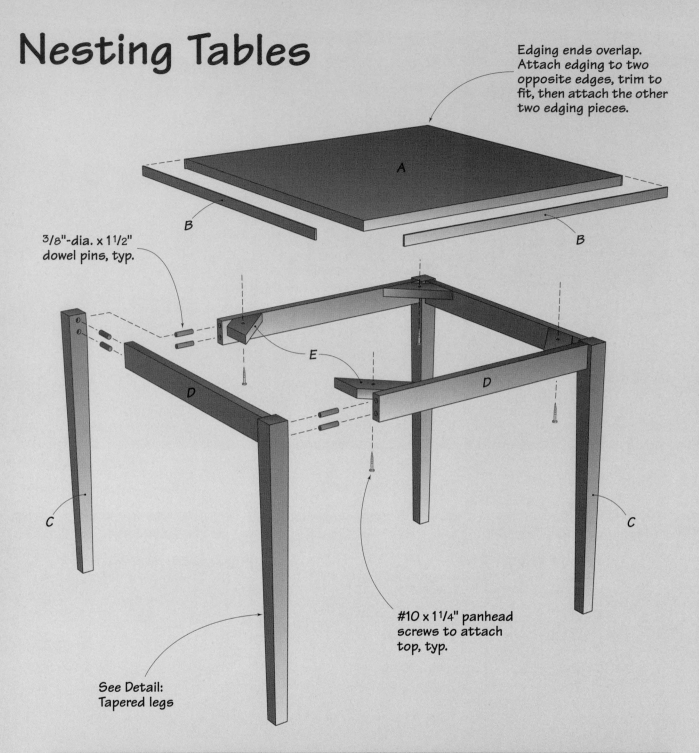

Edging ends overlap. Attach edging to two opposite edges, trim to fit, then attach the other two edging pieces.

³⁄₈"-dia. x 1¹⁄₂" dowel pins, typ.

See Detail: Tapered legs

#10 x 1¹⁄₄" panhead screws to attach top, typ.

Nesting Tables Cutting List

Part	No.	Size (Large)	Size (Medium)	Size (Small)	Material
A. Top	1	³⁄₄ × 23³⁄₄ × 23³⁄₄ in.	³⁄₄ × 18³⁄₄ × 18³⁄₄ in.	³⁄₄ × 13³⁄₄ × 13³⁄₄ in.	Cherry plywood
B. Edging	4	¹⁄₈ × ¹³⁄₁₆ × *	¹⁄₈ × ¹³⁄₁₆ × *	¹⁄₈ × ¹³⁄₁₆ × *	Cherry
C. Legs	4	1¹⁄₂ × 1¹⁄₂ × 23¹⁄₄ in.	1¹⁄₂ × 1¹⁄₂ × 20 in.	1¹⁄₂ × 1¹⁄₂ × 16³⁄₄ in.	"
D. Aprons	4	³⁄₄ × 2 × 20 in.	³⁄₄ × 2 × 15 in.	³⁄₄ × 2 × 10 in.	"
E. Corner blocks	4	³⁄₄ × 2 × 6 in.	³⁄₄ × 2 × 6 in.	³⁄₄ × 2 × 6 in.	"

Part quantities are given for one table only.   * Cut to fit

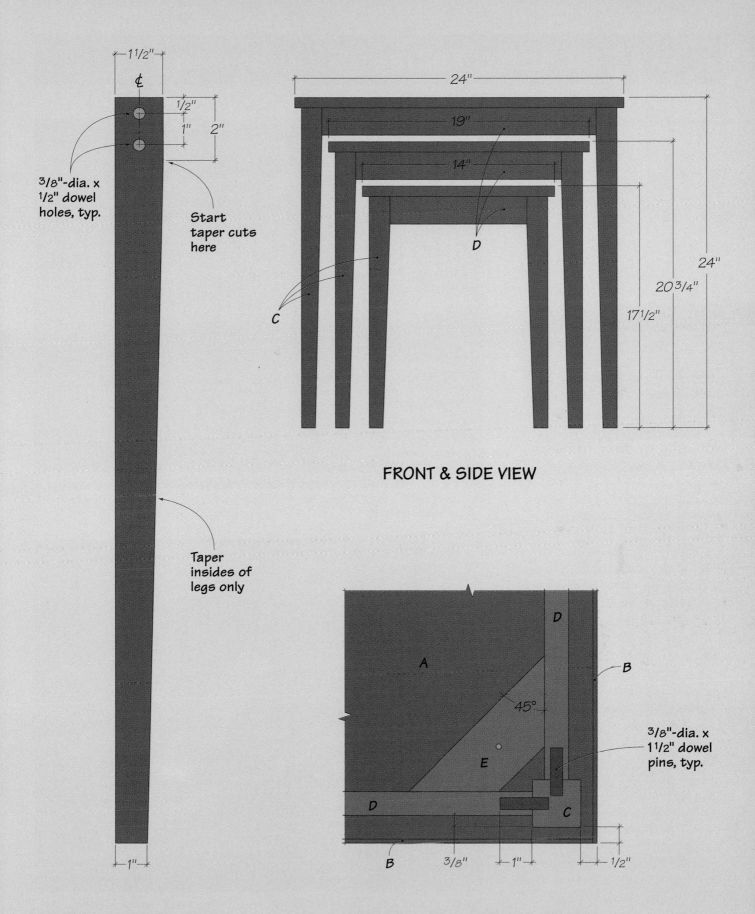

1¹/²"

¢

³/₈"-dia. x
¹/₂" dowel
holes, typ.

¹/₂"
1"
2"

Start
taper cuts
here

24"

19"

14"

D

C

24"

20³/₄"

17¹/₂"

FRONT & SIDE VIEW

Taper
insides of
legs only

1"

A

D

B

45°

E

D

C

B

³/₈"-dia. x
1¹/₂" dowel
pins, typ.

³/₈"

1"

¹/₂"

DETAIL: TAPERED LEGS

SECTION VIEW: CORNER OF TOP

PHOTO A: Glue edging strips to two opposite sides of the plywood tabletop panel, using electrical tape to hold the strips in place. Tape the edging near the center of the panel first, then work outward toward the ends.

The construction steps to assemble these tables are the same for all three; the only differences are in the part sizes. Depending on how you work best, you could either build the tables one at a time, as separate projects, or mass-produce them all at once.

MAKE THE TOP

❶ Cut the plywood tabletop panel to size.

❷ Cut the four ⅛-in.-thick tabletop edging strips to size. Select a piece of solid cherry for the edging at least 1³⁄₁₆ in. thick. Run one edge of the stock through the jointer. Then rip-cut ⅛-in.-thick strips on the band saw with the jointed edge against the saw fence.

❸ Cross-cut the four edging strips about 2 in. longer than listed in the *Cutting List*. The edging strips conceal the laminations and voids in the plywood.

❹ Glue edging strips to two opposite edges of the tabletop. Select a face of the tabletop that will become the top, and position the edging so it lines up with the bottom face of the plywood and extends slightly above the top face. You'll sand the edging flush with the top face later. Spread glue evenly along both mating surfaces of the joints, and use

PHOTO B: Trim the excess edging flush with the edges of the plywood. We used a Japanese-style saw, but any fine-tooth hand saw will also work. Clamp the workpiece to your workbench to hold the panel steady as you cut.

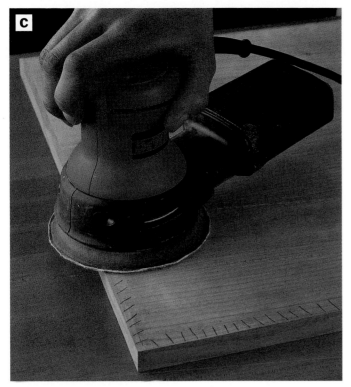

PHOTO C: Sand the tabletop edging so it's flush with the plywood top. Draw short pencil marks across the top of the edging, then sand just until the pencil marks disappear.

Tapering jig

PHOTO D: Cut the leg tapers—we used a tapering jig on the table saw. Cut tapers on two adjacent edges of each leg. Guide the workpiece with a pushstick.

strips of electrical tape spaced about 4 in. apart to "clamp" the edging strips onto the plywood **(See Photo A).** Let the glue dry and remove the tape.

5 Trim the overhanging ends of the attached edging strips flush with the exposed edges of the plywood **(See Photo B).** Use a fine-tooth back saw or hand saw (we used a Japanese-style saw). Then flush the overhangs with a few strokes of a small hand plane.

6 Attach the remaining two edging strips to the other two uncovered edges of the plywood so their ends overhang the edging already glued in place. When the glue dries, remove the tape and trim the overhanging ends of the edging flush.

7 Sand the top edges of the edging flush with the tabletop. To keep from oversanding, draw pencil marks across the edging and sand the edging just until the pencil lines disappear **(See Photo C).**

CUT THE LEG TAPERS

8 Cut the legs to length from stock that's at least 1½ in. square. Joint the edges of the legs flat.

9 Lay out tapers along two adjacent edges of each leg. The tapers start 2 in. down from the top of the

leg and extend to the bottom of the leg, reducing it to 1 in. square **(See Photo D).** We used a table saw with an adjustable tapering jig to make the leg tapers. For more information on using a tapering jig, see below. Sand the tapered edges smooth.

CUTTING TAPERS WITH A TAPERING JIG

Draw the desired taper on the work-piece and set the workpiece in the jig with the jig against the saw fence. Adjust the jig angle and the saw fence until the blade will follow the layout taper line. Lock the jig angle. Then push the jig along the fence, keeping the workpiece held tightly against the jig, to cut the taper. Guide the workpiece with a pushstick.

PHOTO E: Drill holes for the dowel joints between the aprons and legs. We used a doweling jig. For best results, drill the holes in the aprons first. Wrap masking tape around your drill bit to mark the hole depth. Drill dowel holes in all the aprons, then mark and drill the leg holes.

PHOTO F: Glue and clamp the apron together. Start by gluing and clamping a rail between pairs of legs. Once these glued-up assemblies dry, finish the apron by gluing the remaining two rails to the leg assemblies, inserting dowels into the joints.

MAKE THE TABLE BASE

10 Rip- and cross-cut the aprons to size, according to the dimensions given in the *Cutting List*, and sand them smooth.

11 The legs are joined to the aprons with dowel joints. For accuracy, we used a purchased doweling jig that allows you to clamp the jig to the workpiece and drill perfectly perpendicular holes. Lay out and drill ⅜-in.-dia. dowel holes in the legs and aprons using a doweling jig **(See Photo E).** Drill the dowel holes in the aprons first. Center the holes on the thickness of the aprons (See *Detail: Tapered Legs* for hole placement). Drill two ½-in.-deep holes in the ends of each apron.

12 Drill pairs of 1-in.-deep dowel holes in the legs near the tops on the edges with the tapers to correspond with the holes you drilled in the aprons. The holes in the legs should be 1 in. deep.

13 Cut hardwood doweling to connect the legs to the aprons. Chamfer the ends of each dowel by rubbing the dowel edges off with sandpaper. Chamfered ends will make inserting the dowels into the leg and apron holes easier during glue-up.

14 Join the legs to the aprons. First, glue two legs to an apron, inserting dowels into the dowel holes. Clamp up the leg/apron assembly, using scrapwood pads between the clamp jaws to keep from marring the workpieces. Then glue up and clamp the other two legs to another apron in the same fashion. Let both apron assemblies dry and remove the clamps.

15 Glue and clamp the two leg/apron assemblies to the two remaining aprons, inserting dowels into the dowel holes **(See Photo F).** Check the resulting base assembly for square by measuring diagonally between the inside corners of each leg. Adjust the clamps until the diagonal measurements are equal to square the base assembly.

ATTACH THE TABLETOP

16 Cut four corner blocks from a length of 2-in.-wide maple stock, miter-cutting the ends of each corner block at 45° (See *Section View: Corner of Top* for proper miter orientation). The corner blocks will provide a way to fasten the tabletop to the base with screws.

17 Drill a ⅛-in.-dia. pilot hole through each corner block. Center the hole across the width and length of each corner block. You'll attach the tabletop to the apron with screws through these holes later. Spread glue along the mitered edges of the corner blocks and position the blocks in the corners of the table base, flush with the top of the assembly. Clamp the blocks in place. NOTE: *You may need to create notched clamp pads to fit over the outer corner of each leg, in order to clamp the corner blocks in place. Otherwise, clamp the corner blocks with clamps that are outfitted with soft pads on the jaws to keep the jaws from marring the legs.*

⓴ Finish-sand the tabletop and the base assembly, then apply the finish of your choice. We used Danish oil and topcoated with three coats of polyurethane varnish **(See Photo G)**. *TIP: When you finish the tabletop, slip spacer blocks underneath the workpiece to keep the finish from bonding with the drop cloth or newspaper underneath.* Finish both faces of the tabletop, as well as the edges and all surfaces of the base.

⓳ Fasten the tabletop to the base. Lay the tabletop facedown on your workbench and position the base on it so the tabletop overhangs the apron evenly on all sides. Drill pilot holes into the tabletop for #8 × 1¼-in. panhead screws, using the corner block holes as references. NOTE: *Wrap a strip of masking tape around your drill bit first and use it as a depth stop to keep from drilling all the way through the tabletop.* Drive the screws **(See Photo H).**

PHOTO G: Apply the finish to the tabletop and the base before attaching the two. We used Danish oil and topcoated with three coats of polyurethane varnish.

PHOTO H: Attach the tabletop to the base by screwing through the four corner blocks with #8 × 1¼-in. panhead wood screws.

Nesting Tables 287

Formal Bookcase

Built with walnut-veneer plywood and a solid walnut face frame, this bookcase has a rich, formal appearance. The design is highlighted by walnut shelf-edge trim with an ogee profile. Decorative appliques accent the contours of the top face frame rail. This is a simple project with fine-furniture appeal.

Vital Statistics: Formal Bookcase

TYPE: Bookcase

OVERALL SIZE: 31½W by 60¾H by 10¾D

MATERIAL: Walnut and walnut plywood

JOINERY: Rabbet and dado joints, dowel joints in face frame

CONSTRUCTION DETAILS:
- Fixed center shelf fits into stopped dadoes in standards
- Three adjustable shelves
- Shelf-edge is profiled with ogee router bit
- Decorative birch appliques treated with walnut stain

FINISHING OPTIONS: Clear coat with tung oil varnish. For more even color, apply light walnut stain to darken plywood.

Building time

 PREPARING STOCK
1 hour

 LAYOUT
1-2 hours

 CUTTING PARTS
3-5 hours

 ASSEMBLY
2-4 hours

 FINISHING
1-2 hours

TOTAL: 8-14 hours

Tools you'll use

- Circular saw with plywood cutting blade
- Straightedge cutting guide
- C-clamps
- Router table with piloted ¾-in. ogee bit
- Router with ¾-in. straight bit and ⅜-in. rabbet bit
- Tape measure
- 36-in. or longer bar or pipe clamps (6)
- Jig saw, band saw or scroll saw
- Hammer and tack hammer
- Combination square
- Doweling jig
- Drill/driver
- Nailset
- Stopped dado jig
- Pegboard drilling guide

Shopping list

- ☐ (1) ¾ × 4 ft. × 8 ft. sheet veneer-core walnut plywood
- ☐ (1) ¼ × 4 ft. × 8 ft. sheet plywood (walnut or other) for back panel
- ☐ (1) ¾ × 4 in. × 8 ft. walnut for face frame and shelf-edge strips
- ☐ Decorative appliques for top rail
- ☐ (1) ⅜-in.-dia. wood dowel for shelf pins
- ☐ Finishing materials
- ☐ 1-in. wire brads, 4d finish nails
- ☐ Wood glue

Formal Bookcase

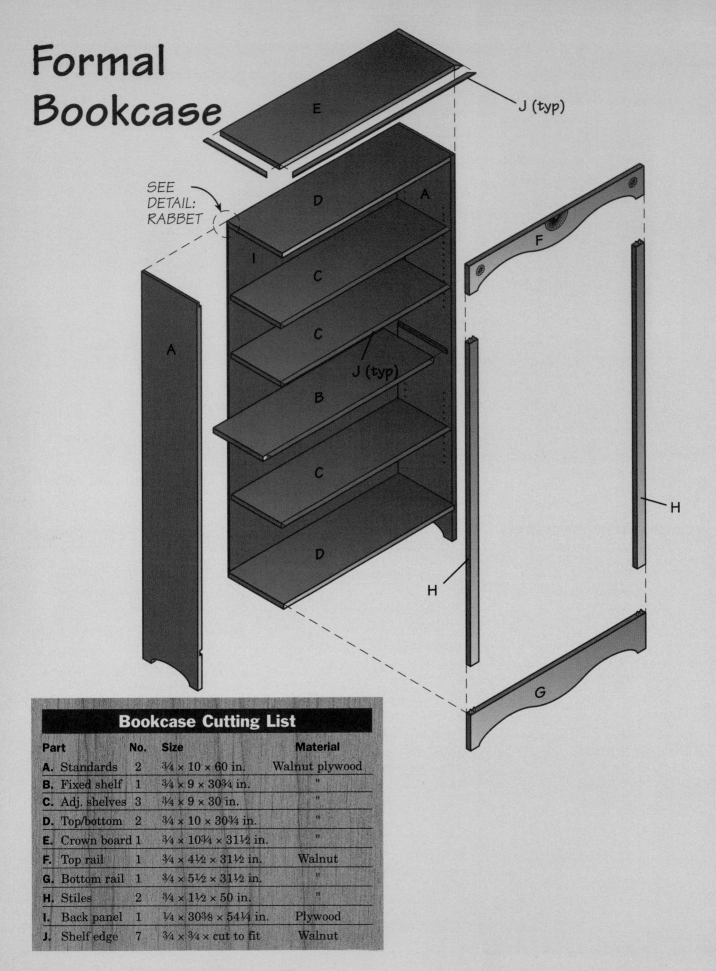

J (typ)

SEE DETAIL: RABBET

E

D

A

I

C

C

J (typ)

B

C

D

A

F

H

H

H

G

Bookcase Cutting List

Part	No.	Size	Material
A. Standards	2	¾ × 10 × 60 in.	Walnut plywood
B. Fixed shelf	1	¾ × 9 × 30¾ in.	"
C. Adj. shelves	3	¾ × 9 × 30 in.	"
D. Top/bottom	2	¾ × 10 × 30¾ in.	"
E. Crown board	1	¾ × 10¾ × 31½ in.	"
F. Top rail	1	¾ × 4½ × 31½ in.	Walnut
G. Bottom rail	1	¾ × 5½ × 31½ in.	"
H. Stiles	2	¾ × 1½ × 50 in.	"
I. Back panel	1	¼ × 30⅜ × 54¼ in.	Plywood
J. Shelf edge	7	¾ × ¾ × cut to fit	Walnut

Each square equals 1"

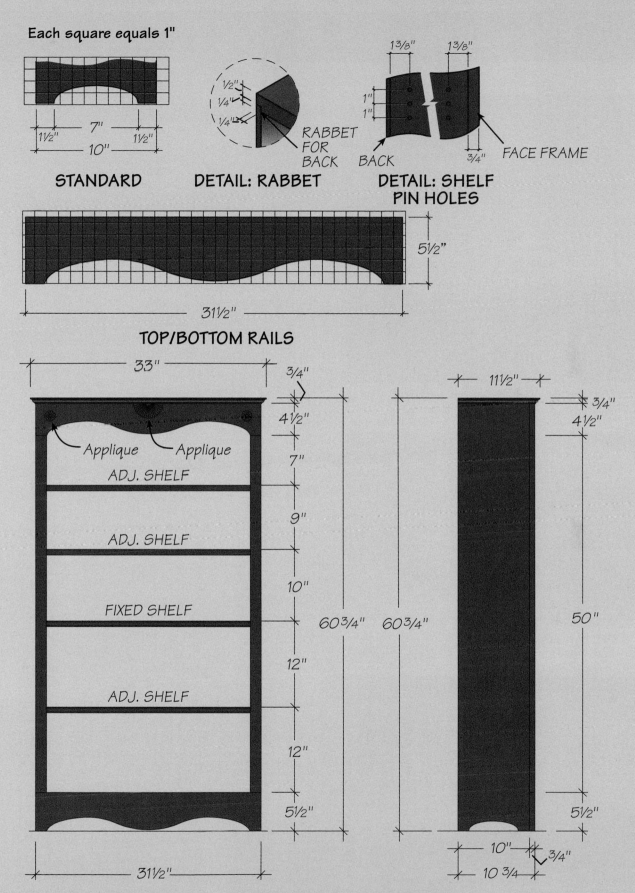

STANDARD

DETAIL: RABBET

1/2"
1/4"
1/4"

RABBET
FOR
BACK

DETAIL: SHELF
PIN HOLES

1³/₈"   1³/₈"

1"
1"

3/4"

BACK

FACE FRAME

5½"

31½"

TOP/BOTTOM RAILS

33"

3/4"

4½"

7"

Applique   Applique

ADJ. SHELF

9"

ADJ. SHELF

10"

FIXED SHELF

12"

ADJ. SHELF

12"

5½"

60³/4"

31½"

11½"

3/4"

4½"

60³/4"

50"

5½"

10"

3/4"

10 3/4"

ELEVATIONS (SIDE & FRONT)

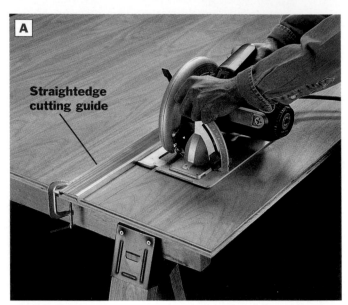

PHOTO A: Cut the plywood parts using a circular saw and straightedge cutting guide. The plywood should be good-face-down.

PHOTO B: Profile the jointed edge of a strip of walnut, using an ogee bit mounted in your router table. Rip the profiled edge to ¾ in. wide.

PHOTO C: Make a jig for cutting the stopped dadoes in the standards. An L-shaped jig like the one above provides a straight edge for the router base to follow and also creates a stopping point.

CUT THE PLYWOOD PARTS

All the plywood parts for this bookcase (except the ¼-in.-thick back panel) are cut from a single piece of ¾-in. plywood. Because we wanted to achieve a rich, formal appearance, we used walnut-veneer plywood and trimmed it with a solid walnut face frame. Walnut plywood is available at most lumberyards (you likely won't find it at a general building center), but it is among the most expensive plywood types. For economy, you could use oak plywood with oak trim and still end up with a very attractive bookcase. Whichever type of plywood you use, make sure the sheet you purchase is created with cabinet-grade veneer on both faces. *Tip: For economy, sketch a cutting diagram before you start cutting the parts.*

❶ Begin by rip-cutting two 9-in.-wide strips from the plywood sheet to make the fixed shelf and the three adjustable shelves **(See Photo A).** Rip-cut 10 in.-wide-strips for the top, the bottom and the two standards (the bookcase sides). Cut the crown board to 10¾ in. wide. Then cross-cut all parts to length according to the *Cutting list.*

MAKE THE SHELVES

We used strips of shelf-edge trim to conceal the edges of the plywood shelves. The shelf-edge is made by profiling walnut boards on a router table, then ripping them to width. If you prefer, you can simply rip-cut ¾-in.-wide strips of solid wood and round over or chamfer the edges. If you're building your bookcase with oak or pine, you may be able to find premilled shelf-edge at a lumberyard.

❷ Mount a piloted profiling bit with a ½-in. shank into your router table—we used a ¾-in. ogee bit. Joint one edge of a ¾-in.-thick walnut board, then pass the jointed edge over the router bit to create the profile **(See Photo B).** Rip-cut a ¾-in.-wide strip from the profiled edge of the board, using a table saw. Continue profiling and ripping edge strips until you have enough shelf-edge for all the shelves and for the front and sides of the crown board (about 16 lineal ft.).

❸ Cut four strips of shelf-edge to 30 in. long for the shelves (the shelf-edge is inset ⅜ in. from each end of the fixed shelf). Attach the shelf-edge with glue and 1 in. wire nails driven through pilot holes at 8- to 10-in. intervals. Do not attach the shelf-edge for the crown board yet.

MAKE THE STANDARDS

❹ Transfer the *Grid pattern* for the cutouts on the bottoms of the standards to the standard workpieces. *Tip: Use a white colored pencil to draw cutting lines on dark wood like walnut.* Use a band saw, jig saw or scroll saw to cut out the shape (for uniform results, gang the standards together). Cut just to the waste side of each line. Use a rasp, file or sandpaper wrapped around a dowel to smooth the contours.

❺ Cut a ¾-in.-wide × ⅜-in.-deep stopped dado in each standard for the fixed shelf. The tops of the dadoes should be 29½ in. up from the bottom of each standard. Stop the dadoes ¾ in. from the front edge of each standard and square them off with a chisel **(See Photo C).** Cutting stopped dadoes with a router and straight bit requires a stopblock. We made an L-shaped jig that is clamped to the workpiece, as seen in **Photo C**. The jig is sized for the setback distance of the router bit from the edge of the router foot. When positioned properly, it ensures that the router follows a straight cutting line, as well as provides a stopping point for the cut. Make the cuts in at least two passes, increasing the cutting depth with each pass.

❻ With your router and straight bit (or on a table saw), cut a ¾-in.-wide × ⅜-in.-deep dado on the inside face of each standard for the bottom of the bookcase. Locate the top of each dado 5½ in. up from the bottom of each standard.

❼ Cut a ¾-in.-wide × ⅜-in.-deep rabbet at the top of each standard to accept the top.

ASSEMBLE THE CARCASE

❽ Dry-assemble the bookcase carcase, with the top, bottom, and fixed shelf in place. This is an important step that allows you to make any adjustments necessary in the joints so the fit is right. It also is your opportunity to make sure your planned clamping

PHOTO D: Measure the diagonals between corners of the carcase to check for square. Adjust the clamps until the diagonals are equal.

PHOTO E: Cut a ¼ × ¼-in. rabbet groove all the way around the back inside edge of the carcase to provide a recess for the back panel. Square off the cuts at the corners with a chisel.

technique will work. As you disassemble the setup, keep the clamps at the same settings and close at hand. Lay out the parts and spread glue evenly into the dadoes and rabbets. Clamp the carcase up, using ¾ in. cauls to protect the wood and spread the clamping pressure across the sides. After all the clamps are on, measure the diagonals of the bookcase to see if it's square **(See Photo D).** Adjust the carcase by shifting the clamps until the diagonal measurements are equal. Remove glue squeeze-out with an old chisel after a film has formed on the glue. Leave the clamps on until the glue is cured.

❾ Lay the bookcase down on its front edge and rabbet the back inside edge of the carcase to accept the back **(See Photo E).** Use a router with a piloted ¼-in. rabbet bit to rout a ¼- × ¼-in. rabbet all the

PHOTO F: Tack profiled shelf-edge around the front and sides of the crown board, mitering the corners.

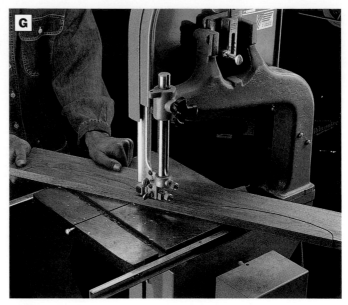

PHOTO G: Cut the decorative contours in the top and bottom face frame rails on your band saw, or with a jig saw.

way around. Rest the router base on the back edge of the carcase and carefully hold the router straight and plumb as you run it along with the pilot bearing riding against the inside of the plywood. The bearing will stop in the corners, leaving a rounded, partially cut rabbet. You'll need to square off the corners of the rabbet with a chisel, as well as finish the rabbet cut next to the fixed shelf (the shelf will obstruct the router bit as you make the rabbet cut).

⑩ Measure the overall dimensions of the rabbeted opening and cut the ¼ in.-plywood back panel to fit. If you're using non-walnut plywood (cheaper maple plywood is shown here), stain the front face to match the walnut plywood. When the stain is dry, install the panel using 1-in. wire brads—no glue. Nail carefully into the rabbet, angling the brads toward the outside so they don't break through the inside face of the carcase. Mark a line on the back panel, centered over the fixed shelf. Drive brads through the back and into the fixed shelf along the line.

⑪ Drill holes for the adjustable shelf pins. A drilling guide made from perforated tempered hardboard (pegboard) makes drilling evenly spaced holes easy. Cut a strip of pegboard to fit into the top and bottom sides of the bookcase. Rip one edge so it's 1⅜ in. from the centerline of a row of holes. Measure 6 in. up from the bottom and 6 in. down from the top and start marking drilling points through the holes in the pegboard. Drill your holes using a depth marker (like masking tape) set to ⅜ in. on your drill bit.

Keep the drill as close to perpendicular as you can.

ATTACH THE CROWN BOARD

⑫ Test the fit of the crown board, then attach it to the top of the bookcase carcase with glue and 4d finish nails. It should be flush with the outside and back edges of the carcase and overhang the front by ¾ in. Miter-cut three pieces of shelf-edge to frame the crown board and attach them with glue and 4d finish nails **(See Photo F)**.

MAKE & ATTACH THE FACE FRAME

⑬ Rip two strips of ¾-in. walnut to 1½ in. wide × 50 in. long for the face frame stiles. Cut a 4½- × 31½-in. top rail and a 5½- × 31½-in. bottom rail (be sure to check your measurements against the actual size of the bookcase for an accurate fit).

⑭ Transfer the contour shown in the *Grid pattern* onto the top rail, starting 1½ in. in from each end. Cut the profile using a band saw or jig saw and sand or file the edges smooth **(See Photo G)**.

⑮ Using the top rail as a template, draw the contour onto the bottom rail. Cut out the shape on the bottom rail and sand the profile smooth.

⑯ The face frame should be assembled separately, then attached to the carcase. We used dowels to reinforce the butt joints at the corners of the face frame. Biscuits, splines, pocket screws or even finish nails could be used instead. To make the dowel joints, use

PHOTO H: Reinforce the corner joints on the face frame. We used a doweling jig to make dowel joints.

PHOTO I: Set all exposed nail heads with a nailset, then fill the nail holes with walnut-tinted wood putty. Sand all wood surfaces with 150-then 180-grit sandpaper.

a doweling jig and drill two dowel holes in each joint between the rails and stiles **(See Photo H).** Assemble the face frame using glue and clamps. Check with a framing square or by measuring the diagonals to make sure the face frame is square.

⑰ Attach the face frame to the bookcase carcase with glue and 4d finish nails. Be sure to drill pilot holes before nailing to avoid splitting the wood. You can use a small drill bit, or just cut off the head of one of the finish nails and chuck it in the drill. Sink the nails with a nailset **(See Photo I).**

APPLY FINISHING TOUCHES

Decorative wood appliques on the top rail add interest and give this bookcase a more formal appearance. You can buy unfinished wood appliques at most woodworking stores or craft stores, and from woodworking supply catalogs. The birch appliques we used are stock numbers WC3040 and WC3001 from *Constantine's Woodworker's Catalog.*

⑱ Stain the appliques to match the color of the face frame material—we used a light walnut stain. After the stain dries, lay the appliques on the top rail and adjust them until you're satisfied with their location. Make small reference marks around the appliques with a white pencil or with pieces of tape **(See Photo J).** Glue them in place using your marks to guide you in positioning, and secure them with padded clamps or a heavy object until the glue dries.

PHOTO J: Use tape or a white pencil to mark reference lines for the appliques, then glue the appliques to the top rail.

⑲ Fill all nail holes with walnut-tinted wood putty. Finish-sand all surfaces, including the adjustable shelves, with 150-grit sandpaper, then 180-grit. Wipe the surfaces with a tack cloth. Apply the finish of your choice to all parts according to the manufacturer's directions. We mixed our own blend of 1/3 turpentine, 1/3 linseed oil, and 1/3 varnish and applied three coats.

⑳ Insert shelf pins (either brass or wood dowels) into the shelf pin holes at the desired heights and install the adjustable shelves.

Walnut Writing Desk

Create a dedicated space for keeping up on your correspondence when you build this Shaker-inspired writing desk. It's an attractive furnishing for the library, den or any other room in your home. The table's clean, understated styling and rich walnut wood tones give it the look and feel of solid hardwood construction—but here's the secret: Our table is built almost entirely of veneered plywood and MDF at a considerable savings over building with solid walnut. The table's legs taper on two faces and can be removed from the table, should the table need to be moved or stored.

Add more storage space to this desk project by building the matching desktop console.

Vital Statistics: Walnut Writing Desk

TYPE: Writing desk with drawer

OVERALL SIZE: 30W x 48L x 30H

MATERIAL: Walnut-veneer plywood, walnut veneer, solid walnut, birch plywood, MDF

JOINERY: Biscuit joints, face-glued laminated joints, tongue-&-groove corner joints, miter joints

CONSTRUCTION DETAILS:

· Legs are face-glued MDF, tapered and veneered

· Metal corner brackets attach legs to aprons

· Walnut plywood is cut so that grain matches across front aprons & drawer front

· Iron-on veneer edging tape

· Plywood drawer fitted with flush-fitting drawer front; tongue-and-groove construction

FINISH: Two coats of satin polyurethane varnish

Building time

PREPARING STOCK
2 hours

LAYOUT
2-4 hours

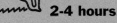
CUTTING PARTS
2-4 hours

ASSEMBLY
2-3 hours

FINISHING
2-3 hours

TOTAL: 10-16 hours

Tools you'll use

· Table saw
· Tapering jig
· Clamps
· Band saw
· Jointer
· Biscuit joiner
· Drill/driver
· Right-angle drilling guide or drill press
· Pocket-screw jig
· Router with ⅜-in. roundover bit

Shopping list

☐ (1) ¾ × 48 × 48 in. walnut plywood

☐ (1) ¾ × 48 × 48 in. MDF

☐ ½ × 18 × 48 in. birch plywood

☐ ¼ × 24 × 24 in. birch plywood

☐ ¹⁄₆₄ × 10 × 48 in. walnut veneer

☐ (4) ¾ × 1½ in. × 4 ft. walnut

☐ (1) ¹³⁄₁₆ in. × 8 ft. walnut veneer edge banding

☐ (4) metal leg corner brackets

☐ (8) ¼ × 2 in. hanger bolts, washers & wing nuts

☐ (2) 20 in. full-extension drawer slides

☐ (8) 1 in. brass L-braces

☐ #20 biscuits

☐ #8 × 1¼ in. flathead wood screws

Walnut Writing Desk

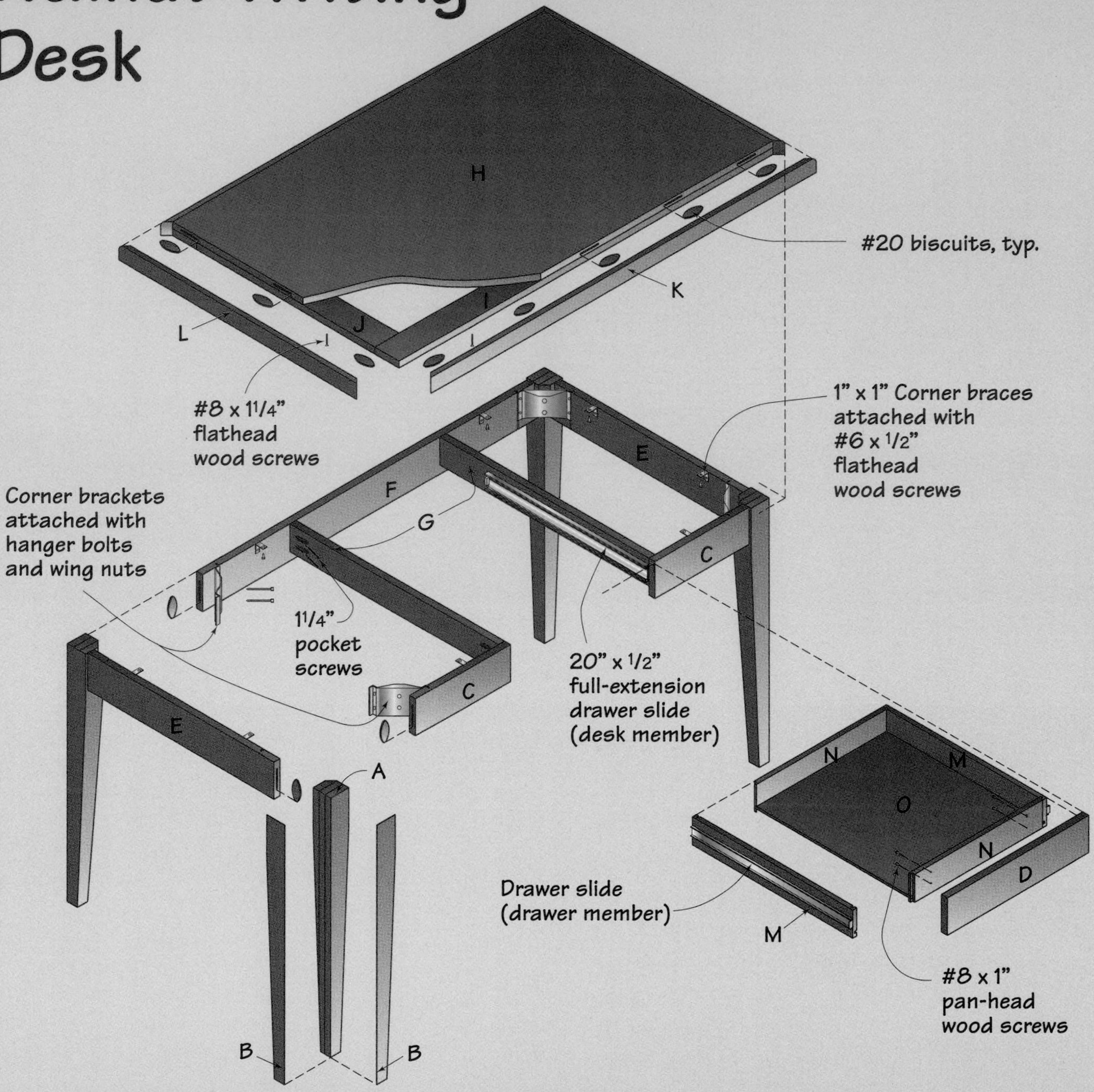
H
#20 biscuits, typ.
K
I
J
L
I
#8 x 1 1/4" flathead wood screws
1" x 1" Corner braces attached with #6 x 1/2" flathead wood screws
E
F
G
C
Corner brackets attached with hanger bolts and wing nuts
1 1/4" pocket screws
C
E
20" x 1/2" full-extension drawer slide (desk member)
A
N
M
O
N
D
Drawer slide (drawer member)
M
#8 x 1" pan-head wood screws
B
B

Walnut Writing Desk Cutting List

Part	No.	Size	Material
A. Leg blanks	12	¾ × 2½ × 29 in.	MDF
B. Leg veneer	16	1⁄64 × 2½ × 29 in.	Walnut veneer
C. Front apron	2	¾ × 4 × 11¾ in.	Walnut plywood
D. Drawer front	1	¾ × 3⅞ × 17 11⁄16 in.	"
E. Side apron	2	¾ × 4 × 23½ in.	"
F. Back apron	1	¾ × 4 × 41½ in.	"
G. Spreader	2	¾ × 3 × 26 in.	"
H. Tabletop	1	¾ × 28½ × 46½ in.	"
I. Front/back build-up	2	¾ × 3 × 46½ in.	MDF
J. Side build-up	2	¾ × 3 × 22½ in.	"
K. Front/back edge	2	¾ × 1½ × 48 in.	Solid walnut
L. Side edge	2	¾ × 1½ × 30 in.	"
M. Drawer side	2	½ × 3 × 20 in.	Birch plywood
N. Drawer front/back	2	½ × 3 × 16½ in.	"
O. Drawer bottom	1	¼ × 19½ × 16½ in.	"

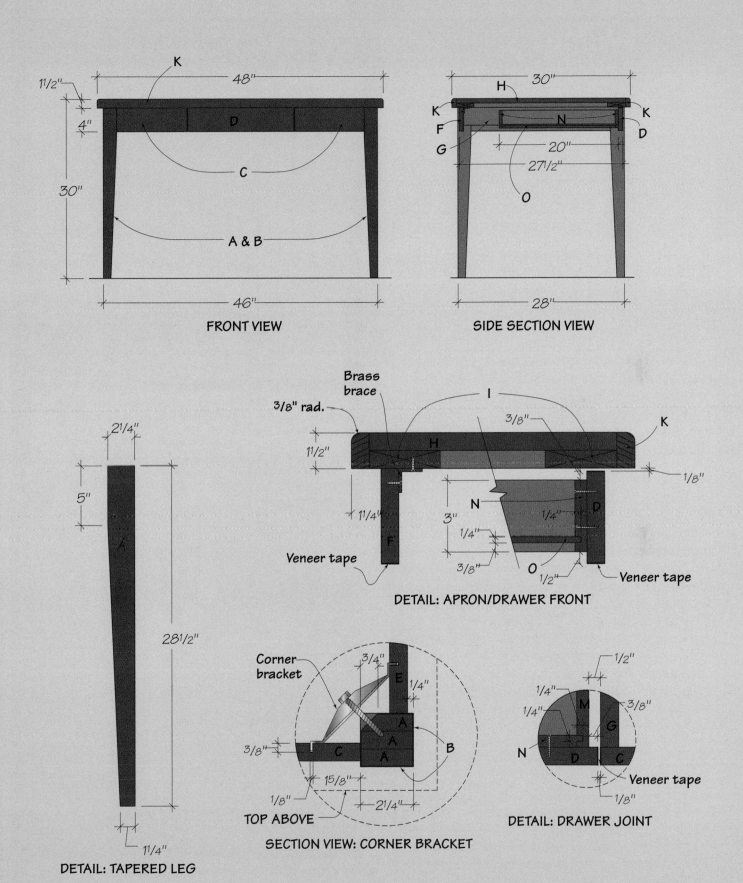

K

1 1/2"
4"
30"

48"

D

C

A & B

46"

FRONT VIEW

H
30"

K
F
G

N

20"
27 1/2"

K
D

O

28"

SIDE SECTION VIEW

2 1/4"

5"

28 1/2"

A

1 1/4"

DETAIL: TAPERED LEG

Brass brace

3/8" rad.

1 1/2"

1 1/4"

F

Veneer tape

I

H

3/8"

K

1/8"

N

D

3"

1/4"

Veneer tape

1/4"
3/8"

1/2"

O

DETAIL: APRON/DRAWER FRONT

Corner bracket

3/4"

E
1/4"

A

3/8"

C

A

A

B

15/8"
1/8"
2 1/4"

TOP ABOVE

SECTION VIEW: CORNER BRACKET

1/2"

1/4"

M
3/8"

1/4"

G

N

D
C

Veneer tape

1/8"

DETAIL: DRAWER JOINT

PHOTO A: Cut tapers on two adjacent sides of each leg using a table saw and tapering jig. When cutting MDF, wear a particle mask—sawing MDF generates fine sawdust.

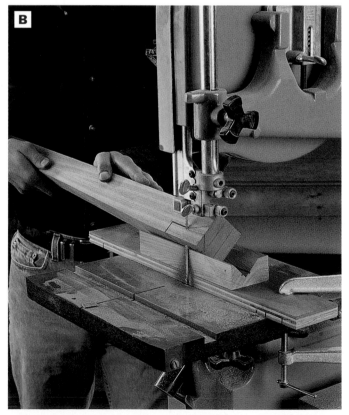

PHOTO B: Use a band saw and a shop-made V-block support cradle to cut a stopped chamfer on the top inside corner of each leg. Make the long chamfer cuts first, then swivel the jig 90° to cut the wastepieces free, creating recesses for the leg hardware.

MAKE THE LEGS

1 Cut 12 leg blanks to size from ¾-in. MDF. The blanks are oversized so the legs can be cut to size after they are face-glued into four, three-board assemblies. Spread glue on the faces of the blanks and clamp up a stack of three blanks for each leg. Use plenty of evenly spaced clamps spaced about 6 in. apart to hold the glue joints closed. After the glue dries, scrape off glue squeeze-out with a paint scraper (wear safety glasses to protect your eyes from flying glue chips).

2 Rip-cut the legs to a finished width of 2¼ in. and cross-cut each leg to 28½ in.

3 Taper two adjacent faces of each leg. The taper starts 5 in. down from the top of the leg and extends to the bottom of the leg, reducing it to 1¼ in. square. Draw layout lines to mark the tapers and use a tapering jig on the table saw to cut the tapers. Adjust the jig's angle and the saw's rip fence so the blade will follow the marked taper line as the jig and leg are pushed together along the rip fence. Cut the tapers, holding each leg tightly against the tapering jig with a push stick **(See Photo A)**. Once you've cut the first taper, turn the leg in the jig so the taper side faces up and taper a second leg face. Sand away any surface unevenness left by the sawblade.

4 Cover the leg faces with walnut veneer. Use a veneer saw or a utility knife to cut strips of walnut veneer for the four faces of each leg. When cutting the veneer, guide your veneer saw or knife blade against a straightedge, especially when slicing in the direction of the grain, as blades have a tendency to follow and split the grain. Cut the veneer strips about ¼ in. oversize in width and length to overhang the leg faces. Spread a thin layer of glue evenly over two opposite leg faces (not on the veneer), and clamp the

PHOTO C: Cut the front apron pieces and the drawer front from one piece of walnut plywood so the grain will match on all three parts.

Lag screw side   Bolt side

PHOTO D: Tighten two nuts against each other on the "bolt" side of the hanger bolts to serve as a "head." Use a wrench to twist the "lag screw" side of each hanger into its hole in the legs. Then remove the nuts.

veneer in place, using scrap wood cauls between the clamp jaws and the veneer. The cauls should cover the veneer on the leg faces completely to press the entire sheets of veneer flat. NOTE: *Line the cauls with wax paper to keep any glue that migrates through the veneer from bonding the cauls to the veneer.* The tapered faces of the legs will need two separate cauls—one for the leg portion above the taper and the other to cover the taper. After the glue dries, trim off excess veneer carefully with a router and flush-trimming bit, a block plane or a sharp chisel. Try to cut with the grain rather than against it, so any grain that splits will fracture away from, rather than into, the veneer covering the leg face. Then veneer the remaining two faces of each leg in the same way.

❺ Cut a stopped chamfer along the top inside corner of each leg (the corner that separates the tapered faces of the legs). The chamfers provide clearance for metal corner braces that will be used to attach the legs and table aprons. To lay out the chamfers, draw a pair of 3-in.-long layout lines ¾ in. from, and parallel to, the inside leg corner along the adjacent leg faces. Cut the chamfers on a band saw using a "V-block" cradle to hold the leg at a 45° angle to the blade (**See Photo B**). To make the cradle jig, joint the edges and faces of a 2 × 4 straight and square. On the table saw, make two passes with the blade set to 45° to cut a 1-in.-deep, V-shaped notch along the face of the 2 × 4.

Make your bevel cuts so the V-notch is positioned next to a long edge. Attach the cradle to a piece of plywood long enough to clamp to the saw table and flush with one edge of the plywood. Set a leg in the V-notch so the chamfer layout extends beyond the edge of the plywood and lines up with the saw blade. Clamp the jig in place on the saw table. Slide all four legs along the cradle, cutting the chamfer up to the chamfer stop line. Then unclamp the cradle setup, swivel it perpendicular to the blade and use it to support the legs in order to crosscut the chamfer wastepieces free.

ASSEMBLE THE LEGS & APRON

❻ Cut the front apron, drawer front, side aprons, back apron and stretchers to size from ¾-in. walnut plywood. Cut the front apron pieces and the drawer front from one long, 4-in.-wide strip of plywood so the grain on the parts will match all the way across the front of the table (**See Photo C**). Trim ⅛ in. off the top long edge of the drawer front to allow for edge-banding and clearance space under the tabletop.

❼ Cut #20 biscuit slots into both ends of the back and side aprons and the ends of the front aprons opposite the drawer front. Center the slots on the apron ends. Inserting biscuits at these locations will help align the aprons with the legs during assembly. Then cut a #20 biscuit slot into both chamfered faces of each leg but not in the chamfered areas. Position

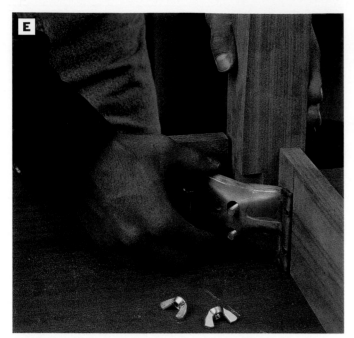

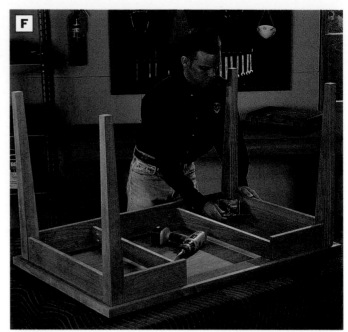

PHOTO E: Assemble the legs and apron parts by attaching the legs to the corner brackets and aprons with wing nuts. Tighten the wing nuts to close the joints—no glue is required.

PHOTO F: Attach the tabletop to the apron assembly with brass L-braces and ½-in. screws. Adjust the brackets so the screws pull the tabletop snugly against the apron assembly.

these slots 9⁄16 in. from the edge opposite the chamfer, and center the slots 2 in. below the top of the leg. This way, you'll create a ¼-in. decorative reveal between the legs and aprons. Glue biscuits into the slots in the ends of the aprons and clean off excess glue.

8 Fit the aprons and legs together upside-down on the workbench and set the corner brackets in place in the leg chamfers. Mark bracket hanger bolt hole locations on the legs in the chamfered areas. Also mark the insides of the aprons where grooves will need to be cut to receive the metal "lips" on either end of each bracket. Disassemble the apron. Drill straight holes for the hanger bolts into each leg using a right-angle drilling guide or by clamping the V-block to the drill press table. Install the hanger bolts by threading two nuts onto the bolt and tightening the nuts against one another. Then grip the top nut with a wrench and screw the bolt into the wood **(See Photo D)**. Remove the nuts.

9 Cut ¼-in.-deep grooves following your bracket layout lines to house the bracket lips. Apply iron-on walnut veneer edge tape to the bottom edges of the back, side and front aprons. Edge-band the ends of the front aprons that will face the drawer, as well as all four edges of the drawer front. For more information on applying edge banding.

10 Reassemble the apron parts on the workbench and square up the assembly by measuring diagonally between the legs. Use wing nuts to fasten the legs to the corner brackets and aprons **(See Photo E)**. NOTE: *It isn't necessary to glue the apron biscuits into the leg slots for strength. The corner brackets will hold the legs securely and make leg removal easy in the future, should you need to disassemble the table for transport.*

11 Cut the spreaders to size. Drill holes for pocket screws on the ends of the spreaders and screw them to the front and back aprons. Position each spreader 11 in. from the closer leg pair, and be sure that the top edges of the spreaders are flush with the tops of the aprons.

CONSTRUCT & ATTACH THE TABLETOP
12 Cut the tabletop to size from ¾-in. walnut plywood. Cut the front, back and side buildups from ¾-in. MDF. Attach the buildups to the underside of the tabletop with glue and countersunk 1¼-in. flathead wood screws, keeping the build-up edges flush with the outside edges of the tabletop.

13 Cut the front, back and side tabletop edging from ¾-in. solid walnut, leaving the ends long. Miter-cut the ends of the edging so the pieces fit snugly around the tabletop. Cut #20 biscuit slots about every 12 in. to aid in aligning the edging. Spread glue on the

PHOTO G: Glue and clamp up the drawer parts with the drawer bottom captured in its groove. Use short wood cauls to apply clamping pressure along the whole wood joint.

PHOTO H: With the drawer mounted in place on metal slides, clamp the drawer front temporarily in position with spring clamps. Then attach the drawer front to the drawer box with screws.

mating surfaces and the mitered corners and clamp the edging in place. Use pads between the clamp jaws to protect the edging. After the glue dries, remove the clamps and rout a roundover around the top edge of the tabletop using a ⅜-in.-dia. roundover bit.

14 Center the apron assembly on the bottom of the tabletop and attach the aprons to the tabletop build-ups with brass L-braces. Screw two braces to each apron, fastening them in place with ½-in. screws **(See Photo F)**. Position the braces on the front aprons near the spreaders to anchor the spreaders and aprons where they bear the weight of the drawer. Since the metal L-braces are slotted to allow for adjustment, position them slightly below the top edge of each apron. This way, when you fasten each bracket to the tabletop buildups, the screws will pull the tabletop tight against the apron.

BUILD THE DRAWER

15 Cut the drawer front, back and sides to size from ½-in. birch plywood. Cut the drawer bottom from ¼-in. birch plywood. Use a table saw and dado-blade set or a router table and straight bit to construct inter-locking ¼ × ¼-in. rabbet joints on the ends and edges of the drawer parts. (See *Detail: Drawer Joints* to con-figure the joints). Cut a ¼ × ¼-in. groove along the inside faces of all four drawer parts, ⅜ in. up from the bottom edges, to capture the drawer bottom. Finish-sand the interior faces of all drawer parts. Apply glue

to the joint rabbets (use no glue in the drawer bottom groove), slide the drawer bottom into place and secure the drawer box parts with clamps and cauls **(See Photo G)**. Wipe away any excess glue with a damp cloth. Check the drawer for squareness by measuring across the diagonals, and reposition the clamps as needed to correct for square.

FINISHING TOUCHES

16 Finish-sand all table parts and apply the finish of your choice. We used two coats of satin polyurethane varnish, rubbing between each dry coat with 0000-fine steel wool. If you like, you can stain the birch drawer parts to match the rest of the walnut before applying the varnish.

17 Attach metal drawer slide hardware to the table spreaders and drawer box according to the manufac-turer's instructions. Center the drawer in the opening so the bottom edges of the front aprons and the drawer face align.

18 Slide the drawer into the apron and attach the drawer front to the drawer box. Adjust the position evenly beneath the tabletop and the front aprons using small spring clamps to temporarily hold the drawer front in place from below. Once you are satis-fied with the position of the drawer front, drill pilot holes and install 1-in. panhead screws from inside the drawer box **(See Photo H)**.

Walnut Writing Desk & Console 303

Desktop Console

Add a new dimension to a desk or tabletop by building this handsome desktop storage console. Designed to match the walnut writing desk, this simple project converts little-used space into useful storage with five cubbies and an upper shelf. The project can be built from one sheet of walnut plywood in less than a day's time.

Vital Statistics: Desktop Console

TYPE: Desk console

OVERALL SIZE: 13D × 46L × 18H

MATERIAL: Walnut plywood

JOINERY: Butt joints

CONSTRUCTION DETAILS:
- Simple butt joints reinforced with biscuits & nails
- Plywood edges taped with iron-on veneer

FINISH: Two coats of satin polyurethane varnish; match your finish to the walnut writing desk if you are building this project as a companion piece

Building time

 PREPARING STOCK
2 hours

 LAYOUT
1 hour

 CUTTING PARTS
2-3 hours

 ASSEMBLY
2-3 hours

 FINISHING
1 hour

TOTAL: 8-10 hours

Tools you'll use

- Combination square
- Bevel gauge
- Jig saw
- Straightedge
- Biscuit joiner
- Clamps
- Deep clamp extenders (optional)
- Hammer
- Nailset

Shopping list

- ☐ (1) 3/4 in. × 4 ft. × 8 ft. walnut plywood
- ☐ Walnut edge banding
- ☐ #20 biscuits
- ☐ 2 in. finish nails
- ☐ Wood glue
- ☐ Finishing materials

Desktop Console

2" finish nails

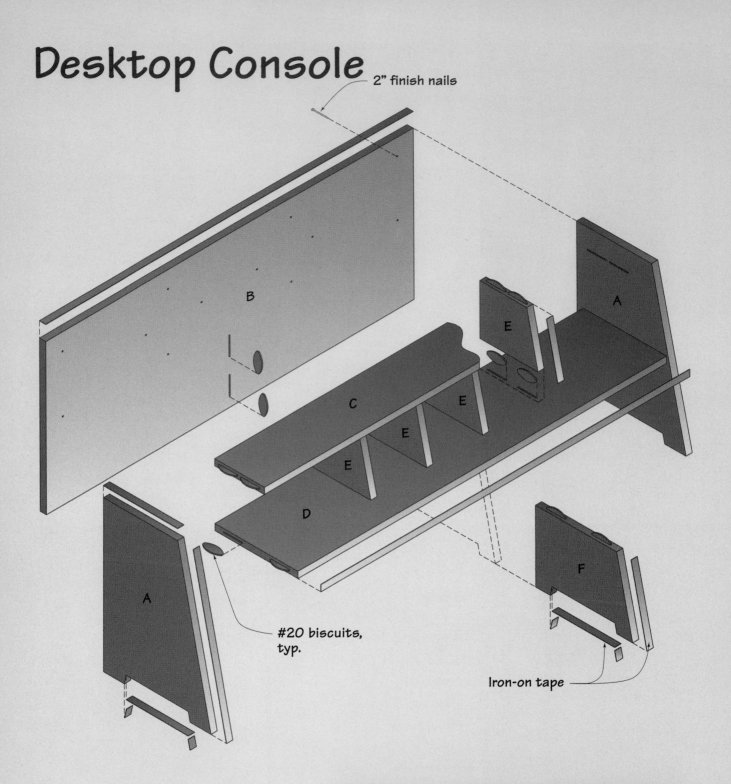

B

A

E

E

E

C

E

D

E

#20 biscuits, typ.

A

F

Iron-on tape

Desktop Console Cutting List			
Part	**No.**	**Size**	**Material**
A. End	2	¾ × 13 × 18 in.	Walnut plywood
B. Back	1	¾ × 44½ × 18 in.	"
C. Top shelf	1	¾ × 6 × 44½ in.	"
D. Bottom shelf	1	¾ × 10 × 44½ in.	"
E. Middle divider	4	¾ × 7 × 6 in.	"
F. Bottom divider	1	¾ × 11⅝ × 8½ in.	"

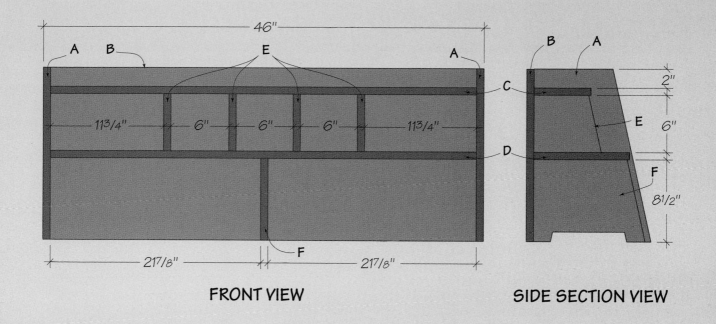

FRONT VIEW

SIDE SECTION VIEW

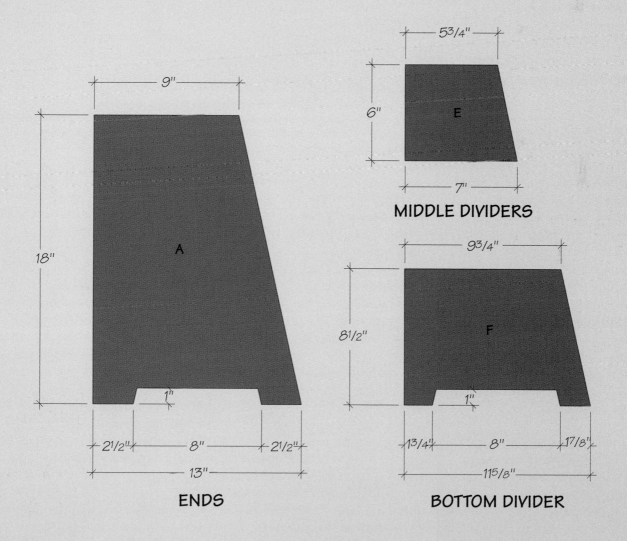

MIDDLE DIVIDERS

ENDS

BOTTOM DIVIDER

PHOTO A: Lay out the front angle on the end pieces by making a mark 9 in. out from the back along the top edge and connecting the mark with the bottom front corner. Use a bevel gauge set to this angle to lay out the ends of the bottom cutout, and a combination square to lay out the depth of the cutout. Make the cuts with a jig saw against a straightedge guide.

MAKE THE ENDS & DIVIDERS

❶ Rip and crosscut the console ends to size from ¾-in. walnut plywood. Along the top edge of one of the end pieces, measure over 9 in. from the back edge and make a reference mark. Use a straightedge to draw a line connecting this point with the lower front corner of the end piece to establish the angled profile along the console's front edge.

❷ Lay out the bottom cutout on the same end piece you marked in Step 1. Mark a pair of reference points 2½ in. from the front and back corners along the bottom edge. Set the rule on a combination square to 1 in. and butt the head of the square against the bottom edge of the end piece. Hold a pencil against the end of the rule and slide the square along the bottom edge to draw the top edge of the cutout. Set a bevel gauge to match the angle on the front edge of the end piece and use this setting to lay out the angled ends of the cutout (**See Photo A**).

❸ Cut the console end pieces to shape. To do this, clamp the piece you just marked on top of the other end piece, aligining the edges. Gang-cut both end pieces. First, remove material in the cutout area with a jig saw, using a fine-toothed jig saw blade to minimize chipping the surface veneer. (These sawn edges need to be smooth; you'll cover them with walnut veneer later.) Then clamp a straightedge in place to guide the jig saw when cutting the angled profile along the front edge of each end piece. Smooth all cut edges with sandpaper.

❹ Lay out and cut the bottom divider to size. The cutout area and the angled front edge of the bottom divider should match the profile of the end pieces. Lay out the cutout on the bottom divider the same way you did for the end pieces, this time measuring in 1⅞ in. from the front and back corners. Use one of the console ends as a pattern for drawing the cutout and establishing the angled front edge profile. Complete the cutout and front profile cuts with a jig saw.

❺ Measure and cut four middle dividers using the *Middle Divider* illustration as a layout guide. The angled profile on the front edge of each middle divider should match those cut in the end pieces and bottom divider.

❻ Conceal the front and top edges of the console ends with iron-on walnut veneer edge tape. Apply veneer tape to the front edges of the dividers as well. Then cover each of the three edges of the bottom cutouts on the end pieces and bottom divider with veneer tape. When veneering the cutouts, apply veneer tape to the long sections first, then install the short end pieces of tape, butting the tape into the cutout corners. TIP: *The veneer tape will fit more tightly in the cutout corners if you first cut a small bevel along the ends of the tape with a sharp chisel.* Trim off any overhanging tape with a chisel, edge-banding trimmer or utility knife.

CUT THE SHELVES & BACK

❼ Cut the console back and top and bottom shelves from ¾-in. walnut plywood. Apply veneer tape to the top edge of the console back and the front edges of the shelves. The rest of the edges on the shelves and back can be left untaped—they'll be concealed when you assemble the console.

CUT THE BISCUIT SLOTS

Since the desktop console bears little weight, we used #20 biscuit slots and glue for assembling all the console parts. TIP: *When cutting biscuit joints, lay one part face-up on the workbench and clamp the mating part flat on top of it, aligning the layout lines of both halves of the joint. With the fence set at 90°, butt the biscuit joiner base against the end of the mating part to cut the joint. Then flip the biscuit joiner around with its base flat against the face of the first part to cut the joint in the end of the mating part.*

❽ Start by marking slot locations for the middle dividers on the appropriate faces of the top and bottom shelves (See *Front View*). With the back edges of the dividers and the shelves flush, lay out biscuit joints in these parts and cut the slots. Mark lines for the bottom divider location on the lower surface of the bottom shelf,

PHOTO B: Lay out and cut biscuit slots in all console parts. Mark the joint locations with chalk to make them easier to see. Use one of the workpieces as a straightedge to align the fence of the joiner when cutting slots on the face sides of parts. Where possible, cut both slots for a joint one after the next to keep part orientation clear.

PHOTO C: Protect the mating surfaces with tape, then brush on finish to all the interior surfaces. The cubby holes in the console would be difficult to finish thoroughly if the console were assembled first.

and cut two biscuit slots in each part.

9 Mark and cut slots for biscuits that will join the shelves to the console end pieces **(See Photo B)**. The bottom edge of the bottom shelf is 8½ in. up from the bottom edges of the end pieces. The top edge of the top shelf is 2 in. down from the top edges of the ends. Since the back panel fits between the end pieces, be sure to account for the thickness of the back panel when positioning slots for the shelves.

10 Cut slots for a joint along the back edge of the bottom divider and the front face of the back panel. Assemble all console parts without glue to check the fit, then disassemble the parts for further preparation.

FINISH INTERIOR SURFACES
11 Once the console is glued up, the cubby areas and inside corners are difficult to reach for applying finish. Instead, finish all the interior surfaces of the console parts before assembly. Sand smooth all surfaces that will face into the console and ease sharp edges where the veneer edging meets the faces of the plywood. Remove all sanding dust with a brush, followed by a careful rubdown with a tack cloth. Cover joint areas with strips of masking tape to keep the biscuit slots dry. Lay out all parts and apply your desired finish, being careful not to get finish on any exposed, biscuited ends **(See Photo C)**. We used two coats of satin polyurethane varnish.

ASSEMBLE THE CONSOLE
12 Start by gluing and clamping the middle dividers between the top and bottom shelves **(See Photo D)**. Use cauls or deep

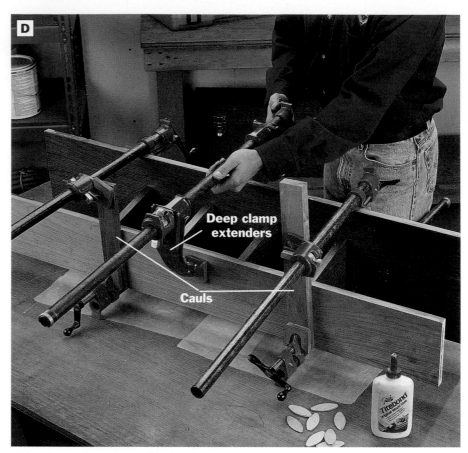

PHOTO D: Glue the middle dividers to the top and bottom shelves. Use scrap wood cauls or deep clamp extenders to apply even clamping pressure across the joints. We used both homemade scrap wood cauls and store-bought clamp extenders.

PHOTO E: Glue and clamp the ends to the shelves and back panel. Drive finish nails through the back into the shelves and the middle dividers, and use a nailset to sink the nailheads below the surface.

clamp extenders to spread clamping pressure evenly across the biscuit joints. Be sure the back edges of the dividers and shelves remain flush as you clamp. The biscuit slots will allow some play between the parts if you need to make minor adjustments. Use wax paper to protect the benchtop and keep from inadvertently gluing the console assembly to the bench. Clean up any glue squeeze-out with a damp rag.

13 Use a combination square and tape measure to draw lines on the outside of the back panel, marking locations for the dividers and shelves. These lines will guide you when nailing the back in place. The centerline of the top shelf is 2⅜ in. from the top edge of the back. The centerline of the bottom shelf is 8⅞ in. from the bottom edge.

14 After the glue has dried on the first assembly, glue and clamp the shelves and back in place between the ends, keeping the top edge of the back flush with the top edges of the ends. Drive finish nails through the back into the shelves and middle dividers, using the reference lines you drew to position the nails **(See Photo E)**. Set the nailheads below the surface with a nailset.

15 Attach the bottom divider to the back panel and the underside of the bottom shelf using biscuits. Clamp the bottom divider in place **(See Photo F)**.

16 Sand the outside surfaces of the console, and ease any remaining sharp edges. Apply finish to all remaining surfaces.

PHOTO F: Attach the bottom divider to the bottom shelf and the back with glue and biscuits, clamping it in place. Use scrap blocks to pad the clamps. Make sure the front of the bottom divider Is square to the shelf.

Attaching the desktop console to a desk

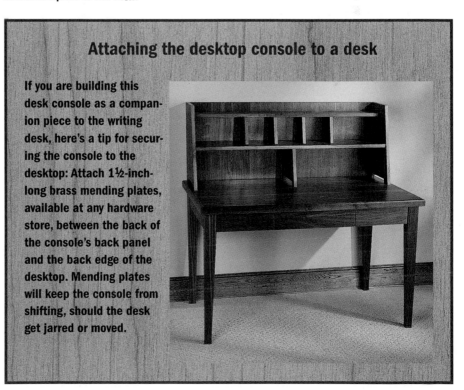

If you are building this desk console as a companion piece to the writing desk, here's a tip for securing the console to the desktop: Attach 1½-inch-long brass mending plates, available at any hardware store, between the back of the console's back panel and the back edge of the desktop. Mending plates will keep the console from shifting, should the desk get jarred or moved.

Arts & Crafts Bookcase

The popular Arts and Crafts furniture style (similar to the Mission style) is reflected in this attractive oak bookcase. Simple yet elegant, it will blend into just about any room. And because it's made mostly of oak plywood, the cost is relatively low.

Vital Statistics: Arts & Crafts Bookcase

TYPE: Bookcase

OVERALL SIZE: 30W by 48H by 13D

MATERIAL: White oak, white oak plywood

JOINERY: Biscuit, dado, half-lap, miter, butt joints

CONSTRUCTION DETAILS:
- Decorative arched cutouts on the base
- Glass lite panels are flush-mounted in doors against half-lap muntins
- Decorative cabinet top features chamfered solid oak edging
- Exposed plywood edges on carcase are concealed with iron-on veneer edge tape

FINISHING OPTIONS: For a traditional Arts and Crafts finish, apply a dark wood stain such as medium or dark walnut, followed by a satin-finish topcoat (we used tung oil). For a more contemporary look, use lighter wood stain, or topcoat only.

Building time

PREPARING STOCK
2-3 hours

LAYOUT
2-3 hours

CUTTING PARTS
3-4 hours

ASSEMBLY
2-3 hours

FINISHING
1-2 hours

TOTAL: 10-15 hours

Tools you'll use

- Jointer
- Table saw
- Planer
- Router with piloted ⅛-in. rabbet bit, ½-in. straight bit, ¾-in. straight bit, ⅜-in. rabbet bit
- Jig saw, band saw or scroll saw
- Biscuit joiner
- Bar, pipe, C-clamps
- Miter saw (power or hand)
- Drill press
- Drill/driver
- Right-angle drilling guide
- ¾-in. Forstner bit

Shopping list

- ☐ (1) ¾ in. × 4 ft. × 8 ft. white oak plywood (preferably quartersawn)
- ☐ (1) ¼ in. × 4 ft. × 4 ft. plywood for back panel (birch plywood)
- ☐ (5) 4/4 × 4 in. × 8 ft. white oak
- ☐ (6) 1⅜ × 2½ in. brass butt hinges
- ☐ (2) 1⅛ × 1⅛ in. wooden door pulls
- ☐ (20) Glass retainer pads
- ☐ Shelf support pins
- ☐ #6 × 1¼ in. flathead wood screws
- ☐ #20 biscuits
- ☐ ⅛-in. tempered glass (for door panels; cut to fit)
- ☐ Finishing materials

Arts & Crafts Bookcase

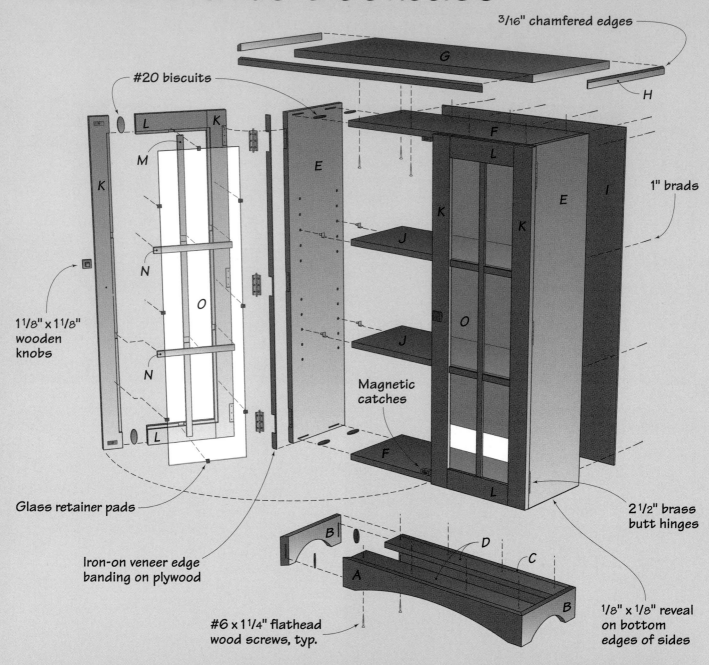

3/16" chamfered edges

#20 biscuits

1" brads

1 1/8" x 1 1/8" wooden knobs

Magnetic catches

Glass retainer pads

2 1/2" brass butt hinges

Iron-on veneer edge banding on plywood

1/8" x 1/8" reveal on bottom edges of sides

#6 x 1 1/4" flathead wood screws, typ.

Arts & Crafts Bookcase Cutting List

Part	No.	Size	Material	Part	No.	Size	Material
A. Base front	1	3/4 × 4 × 28 1/2 in.	White oak	**I.** Back	1	1/4 × 27 3/4 × 42 1/2 in.	Oak plywood
B. Base sides	2	3/4 × 4 × 11 1/4 in.	"	**J.** Shelves	2	3/4 × 9 7/8 × 26 3/4 in.	"
C. Base back	1	3/4 × 4 × 27 in.	Scrap	**K.** Stiles	4	3/4 × 2 1/2 × 43 in.	White oak
D. Stretchers	2	3/4 × 3 × 27 in.	"	**L.** Rails	4	3/4 × 2 1/2 × 9 3/16 in.	"
E. Sides	2	3/4 × 10 7/16 × 43 1/4 in.	Oak plywood	**M.** Muntins (vert.)	2	1/4 × 3/4 × 38 3/4 in.	"
F. Top/bottom	2	3/4 × 10 7/16 × 27 in.	"	**N.** Muntins (hor.)	4	1/4 × 3/4 × 9 15/16 in.	"
G. Cabinet top	1	3/4 × 12 3/4 × 29 1/2 in.	"	**O.** Lites	2	1/8 × 9 7/8 × 38 11/16 in.	Glass
H. Edging	3	1/4 × 7/8 × *	White oak	* Cut to fit			

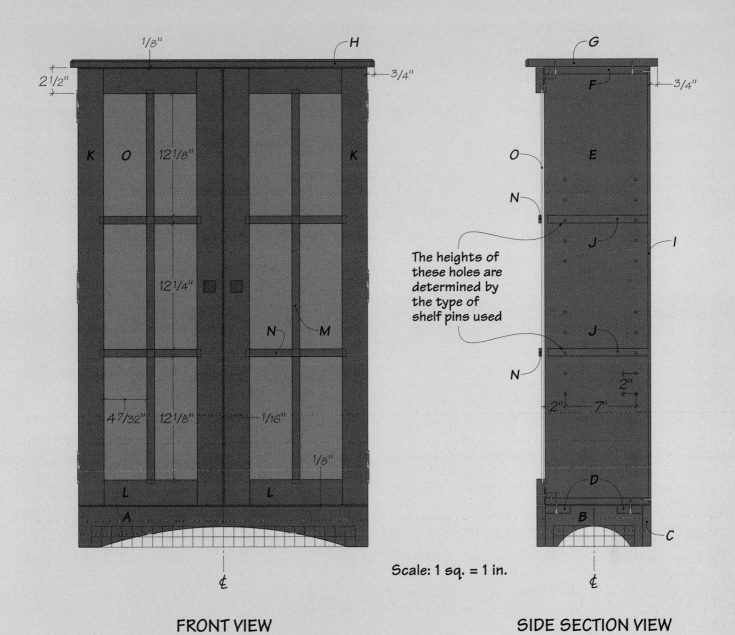

FRONT VIEW

1/8"

H

2 1/2"

3/4"

K   O   12 1/8"   K

12 1/4"

N   M

4 7/32"   12 1/8"   1/16"

1/8"

L   L

A

¢

Scale: 1 sq. = 1 in.

SIDE SECTION VIEW

G

F

3/4"

O

E

N

J   I

The heights of
these holes are
determined by
the type of
shelf pins used

J

N

2"

2"   7"

D

B

C

¢

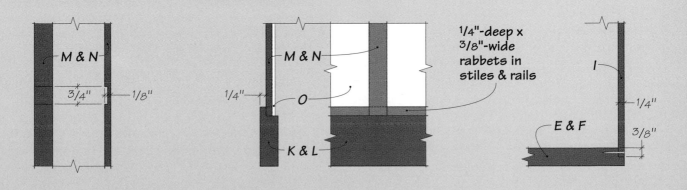

M & N

3/4"   1/8"

MUNTIN HALF-LAP JOINTS

M & N

1/4"

O

K & L

DOOR STILES & RAILS

1/4"-deep x
3/8"-wide
rabbets in
stiles & rails

I

1/4"

E & F   3/8"

RABBETS FOR BACK

PHOTO A: Apply iron-on veneer edge tape to the front edges of the sides, top, bottom and shelves.

MAKE THE CARCASE

The carcase for this bookcase is made with ¾-in. white oak plywood (if it's available and you're willing to spend a few extra dollars, use plywood with quartersawn white oak veneer). As with any plywood used for furnituremaking, you'll want to conceal the visible edges. To accomplish this, there are two options: you can attach thin strips of solid wood edging (as we do for the decorative cabinet top), or you can apply iron-on veneer edge strips.

❶ Cut the carcase sides, top/bottom, shelves and cabinet top to size from ¾-in. oak plywood. To minimize splintering, use a fine-toothed plywood-cutting blade in your table saw.

❷ Cut strips of iron-on veneer edge tape to cover the front edges of the sides, top/bottom, and shelves (we ordered a 50-ft. roll of 13⁄16-in.-thick white oak edge tape from a woodworkers' supply catalog). Use a pair of scissors to cut strips that are about an inch longer than the edge you're covering. There are special irons used to activate the adhesive backing on veneer edge tape, but an old household iron will work fine in most cases. We covered the face of the iron with foil to protect it from the adhesive and to distribute the heat a little more evenly. Turn the iron on to medium setting. Make sure the plywood edges are clean and free of debris, then clamp the workpiece panel in your bench vise, edge-up. Lay the strip of veneer tape along the edge (remove the protective backing strip, if it has one) and adjust it so the tape overhangs both the top and bottom edges. Touch the iron to the tape lightly in a few spots to tack it down. Then, starting at one end, hold the iron on the wood for a few seconds, covering as much surface area as possible. You'll see the adhesive start to melt. Remove the iron and immediately burnish the tape down to seat it, using a small wooden roller or a small block of

PHOTO B: Trim off the overhanging veneer edge tape so the tape is flush with the top and bottom of each workpiece. We used a hand trimmer with a blade that cuts flush to the panel.

wood. Work your way along the edge to the end of the panel (**See Photo A**).

❸ When the veneer strip is bonded and the adhesive has cooled, trim the overhang flush to the panel faces and ends. We used a special veneer tape trimmer (**See Photo B**). If you're careful and use a straightedge, you can trim the excess with a utility knife or sharp chisel instead.

4 Drill two rows of holes (front and back) in each side for the shelf support pins **(See Photo C).** Use a strip of perforated hardboard (Peg Board) cut to the panel width as a drilling template. Spacing the holes at every other pegboard hole should be adequate. Circle the desired holes on the template with a permanent marker before drilling, and clamp the template onto each side at the identical height from its bottom edge so the holes will be at the same level on both sides. Drill holes the correct size and depth for your shelf support pins. *TIP: If you've got a pretty good idea where you want the shelves to be, drill only two or three holes near the planned location for each shelf end—this will save time and avoid creating rows of unsightly holes on the cabinet interior.*

5 Cut a ⅛ × ⅛-in. rabbet along the bottom, outer edge of each side panel. This will create a ⅛-in. reveal under the carcase to visually coincide with the ⅛-in. gap under the doors. We used a router and ⅛-in. piloted rabbeting bit to cut the rabbets.

6 Cut biscuit slots at the joints between the sides, top and bottom to prepare them for assembly.

7 Cut ⅜ × ¼-in. rabbets along the back inside edges of the top, bottom and sides to create a recess for the back panel **(See Photo D).**

8 Dry-fit the carcase members, then finish-sand all the parts up to 150-grit. Use a light touch when sanding the veneer-taped edges to avoid sanding through.

9 Glue the biscuit joints and clamp up the carcase **(See Photo**

PHOTO C: Drill holes for shelf-support pins in both sides, using a perforated hardboard drilling template and a right-angle drilling guide.

Rabbeting bit

PHOTO D: Cut a ¼ × ⅜-in. rabbet in the back edges of the top, bottom and sides to accommodate the back panel, using a router and a piloted ⅜-in. rabbeting bit (See inset photo).

E). Make sure to align the front edges of all the parts before applying clamping pressure. Measure the diagonals on the frame to make sure it's square, and adjust as needed. Use scrapwood clamping cauls to pad the clamp jaws and distribute pressure across the joints. Clean up any glue squeeze-out with a wet rag.

10 Cut the back panel to size from ¼-in. plywood (we used inexpensive birch plywood because it can be stained to match just about any type of hardwood, including white oak). To keep the cabinet square, make sure the back is cut square and fits tightly in its rabbet. Finish-sand the interior face of the back, then install it in the carcase and secure it with 1-in. brads (do not use glue).

11 The decorative top panel that is attached to the carcase top is trimmed with solid oak edging before it's attached. Using your band saw or table saw to resaw thicker stock, cut about 60 lineal inches of ¼ × ⅞-in. white oak edging. Cut the pieces to length, miter the front corners and wrap them around the cabinet top. Glue the edging onto the front and sides of the panel, using clamps and full-length cauls. Try to install the edging so it's flush with the top surface of the cabinet top. If not, when the glue is dry you can flush up the edging to the plywood surfaces using a sharp hand plane or cabinet scraper.

PHOTO E: Assemble the carcase, using glue and biscuits. Measure across the diagonals to make sure the carcase is square, and adjust the clamps as necessary.

PHOTO F: Rout a ³⁄₁₆-in. chamfer around the front and side edges of the cabinet top.

12 Rout a ³⁄₁₆-in. chamfer at the top of the edging strips **(See Photo F)**. Finish-sand the cabinet top, and attach it to the carcase with #6 × 1¼-in. flathead wood screws, driven up through countersunk pilot holes in the underside of the carcase top. The cabinet top should overhang the carcase by ¾ in. on the sides and back.

MAKE THE DOORS

13 Cut the stiles and rails for the door frames to size from solid white oak. *TIP: To assure that the door parts will fit properly, careful jointing and planing of the stock is important. After jointing one face of the rough lumber flat, remove stock equally off both faces with the planer. Joint and plane it halfway down and let it sit overnight with narrow plywood strips, or stickers, in between the boards to allow air to flow all around them. Then, joint the stock flat again and plane it to final thickness. Be sure to joint one edge before rip-cutting the parts to width.*

14 Cut biscuit joints to join the rails to the stiles, and glue and clamp the door frames together **(See Photo G)**. Make sure the frames are absolutely square by measuring the diagonals and make corrections as necessary. When the glue is dry, unclamp the frames and smooth the joints with a scraper.

15 To create recesses for the glass lite panels, cut a ¼-in.-deep × ⅜-in.-wide rabbet around the inside edges of the door frames. Square off the corners of the recesses with a wood chisel.

PHOTO G: Clamp the door frames together, using glue and biscuited butt joints.

16 We added decorative wood strips (called muntins) to the door frames to create a multi-lite panel effect (a standard treatment with glass doors in Arts and Crafts designs). The muntins fit together with half-lap joints, with the ends set into small mortises in the glass-recess rabbets on the inside edges of the door frames. To cut the mortises, begin by marking centerpoints along the inside edges of the glass recess rabbets (See *Front View* for spacing). We used a ¾-in. Forstner bit in the drill press to drill out the ¼-in.-deep mortises, then squared up the edges with a wood chisel **(See Photo H).** A ½-in.-thick piece of scrap clamped next to the inside frame edge provides a drilling surface where the bit extends past the edge of the frame.

17 Resaw strips of white oak to ¼ in. thick and ¾ in. wide to make the muntins. A band saw is the safest tool for cutting small, thin workpieces like the muntin strips. Cross-cut the strips to fit inside the door frames.

18 The vertical and horizontal muntins are joined using half-lap joints. Lay out the joints, and cut the ⅛-in.-deep × ¾-in.-wide laps with a router and a ¾-in. straight bit **(See Photo I).** Clamp the two verticals together and rout dadoes into the back faces of both at once. Clamp the four horizontals together and rout a dado through the center of all the front faces at once. Use a clamped-on straightedge to guide the cuts and a scrap backer board to prevent tearout.

19 Apply glue to the half-lap joints and clamp the muntins together, making sure the assemblies are square. Finish-sand both faces of the door frames and the muntins, then fit the muntin assemblies into the doors and glue and clamp them in place **(See Photo J).**

CONSTRUCT THE BASE

20 Joint and plane white oak stock to ¾ in. thick, and rip-cut the base front and sides to 4 in. wide. Cut the parts to length, with 45° mitered ends for the front corner joints (the backs of the sides are square).

21 Draw the endpoints and tops of the arched cutouts on the base front and sides, using the grid pattern as a guide. Place each workpiece facedown on a piece of scrap plywood. Tack a long finish nail into the plywood next to the wood at the marked points along its lower edge. Then, tack another nail into the workpiece, ⅛ in. down from the top mark. Cut a strip

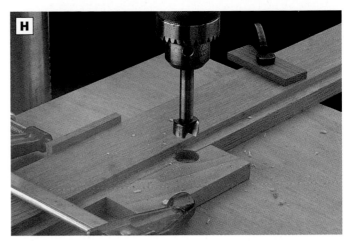

PHOTO H: Use a ¾-in. Forstner bit to remove the waste material from the ¼-in.-deep mortises for the ends of the muntins. A scrap board clamped to the workpiece provides a surface for the drill bit.

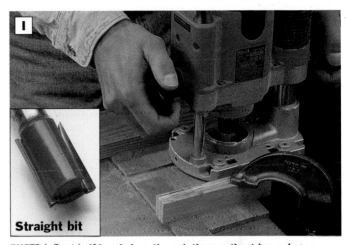

Straight bit

PHOTO I: Rout half-lap dadoes through the muntin strips, using a straightedge guide and a router with a ¾-in. straight bit. Gang the muntins together before routing.

PHOTO J: Glue the muntin assemblies together, then glue the assemblies into the mortises in the door frames.

PHOTO K: Flex a piece of ⅛-in. tempered hardboard to create a smooth arc for tracing the cut profiles onto the base front and sides.

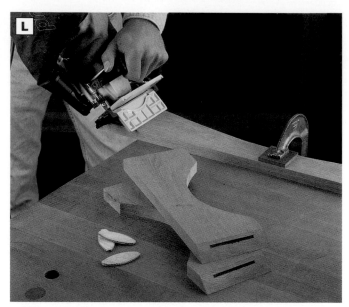

PHOTO L: Cut biscuit slots in the base parts. Adjust the biscuit joiner fence to 45° for the front mitered joints. The rear joints and the stretchers have straight 90° biscuited butt joints.

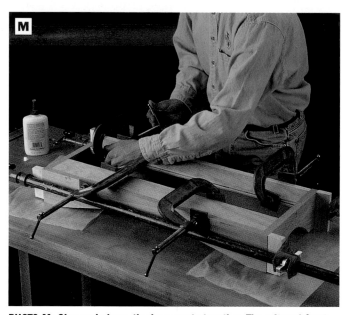

PHOTO M: Glue and clamp the base parts together. The mitered front joints should be clamped in both directions.

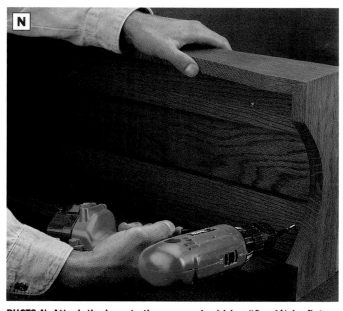

PHOTO N: Attach the base to the carcase by driving #6 × 1¼-in. flat-head wood screws up through the base stretchers and into the bottom of the carcase.

of ⅛-in.-thick tempered hardboard to 1 in. wide and about 32 in. long. Slip the strip over the top nail, with the ends behind the endpoint nails so it bends evenly. Trace along the top edge to draw the cutout profiles in the workpieces (See Photo K).

㉒ Cut the base back and the two stretchers to size from ¾-in. scrap hardwood or plywood. Cut slots for #20 biscuits at the joints between base parts (See Photo L).

㉓ Dry-fit the base assembly and test to make sure it's flush with back and sides of the carcase, and extends ¾ in. past the front edge of the carcase. Adjust as needed, then glue and clamp the assembly together, reinforcing with #20 biscuits (See Photo M). When dry, make sure all the glue is removed and finish-sand the base.

HANG THE DOORS

24 Cut mortises for butt hinges in the door frames and carcase sides, using a sharp chisel. We used three 1⅜ × 2½-in. brass butt hinges per door. Install the hinges and hang the doors to make sure they open and close properly.

25 Remove the doors and hinges, then apply a wood finish to the project. We used dark walnut wood stain with three coats of tung oil for a traditional, dark Arts and Crafts finish. Be sure to finish-sand thoroughly and wipe all surfaces with a tack cloth before applying the finish. To prevent warping, finish the back of the bookcase the same way as the rest of the bookcase.

26 After the finish dries, attach the base assembly to the bottom of the bookcase carcase with #6 × 1¼-in. flathead wood screws **(See Photo N)**.

27 Install the glass lites in the door frames. We had two pieces of ⅛-in.-thick tempered glass cut to size at a local hardware store for the project. Tempered glass is less prone to breaking than ordinary window glass. But we waited until we'd finished and hung the door before ordering the glass, just in case the dimensions came out differently than those listed in the *Cutting List*. To install the glass, set each panel into a door frame recess, then install glass retainer pads behind the glass panels in the door frame to hold the panes in place **(See Photo O)**.

28 Drill holes through the inner door stiles for attaching the door pulls. We used 1⅛-in.-square wooden knobs.

PHOTO O: Secure the glass in the door frames with glass retainer pads that are screwed to the rails and stiles to hold the glass against the rabbets and the muntins. Use 10 pads per door.

PHOTO P: Screw the hinges into their mortises and hang the bookcase doors. Make sure they operate properly and adjust the hinges if necessary.

29 Reattach the doors, handling them with care to avoid breaking the glass **(See Photo P)**.

30 Install magnetic door catches at the top and bottom of the bookcase, following the manufacturer's instructions.

31 Install the shelf pins and insert the shelves at the desired height—they'll look best if they align with the horizontal muntins.

Corner Cupboard

Turn an unused corner of your kitchen or dining room into a display area with this reproduction of a Colonial-style corner cupboard. Made from dimensional pine, our cupboard features a contoured face frame, three open shelf areas for display purposes and hangs on the walls by way of hidden French cleats.

Vital Statistics: Corner Cupboard

TYPE: Corner cupboard

OVERALL SIZE: 34W by 42¾H by 13D

MATERIAL: Pine

JOINERY: Biscuit joints on face frame; reinforced butt joints on carcase

CONSTRUCTION DETAILS:
· Curved face frame details accentuate Colonial styling
· Space-saving corner design creates ample display area
· Painted pine makes this an economical project to build
· Cabinet hangs on wall with hidden French cleats

FINISHING OPTIONS: Primer and paint or dark stain with clear topcoat

Building time

PREPARING STOCK
2 hours

LAYOUT
2-4 hours

CUTTING PARTS
2-4 hours

ASSEMBLY
2-3 hours

FINISHING
1-2 hours

TOTAL: 9-15 hours

Tools you'll use

· Jointer
· Table saw
· Power miter saw
· Circular saw with edge guide
· Router with piloted ⁵⁄₃₂-in. ogee bit, ½-in.-rad. cove bit
· Biscuit joiner
· Bar or pipe clamps
· Jig saw
· Back saw or Japanese-style pull saw
· Hammer and nailset
· Drill/driver
· Drill press drum sander or spindle sander

Shopping list

☐ (5) ¾ × 5¼ in. × 10 ft. pine (nominal 1 × 6)

☐ (1) ¾ × 9¼ in. × 8 ft. pine (nominal 1 × 10)

☐ #20 biscuits

☐ Wood glue

☐ #8 flathead wood screws (1-, 1½-, 2½-in.)

☐ Finish nails (3d, 4d, 6d)

☐ Finishing materials

☐ Heavy-duty wall anchors and screws

Corner Cupboard

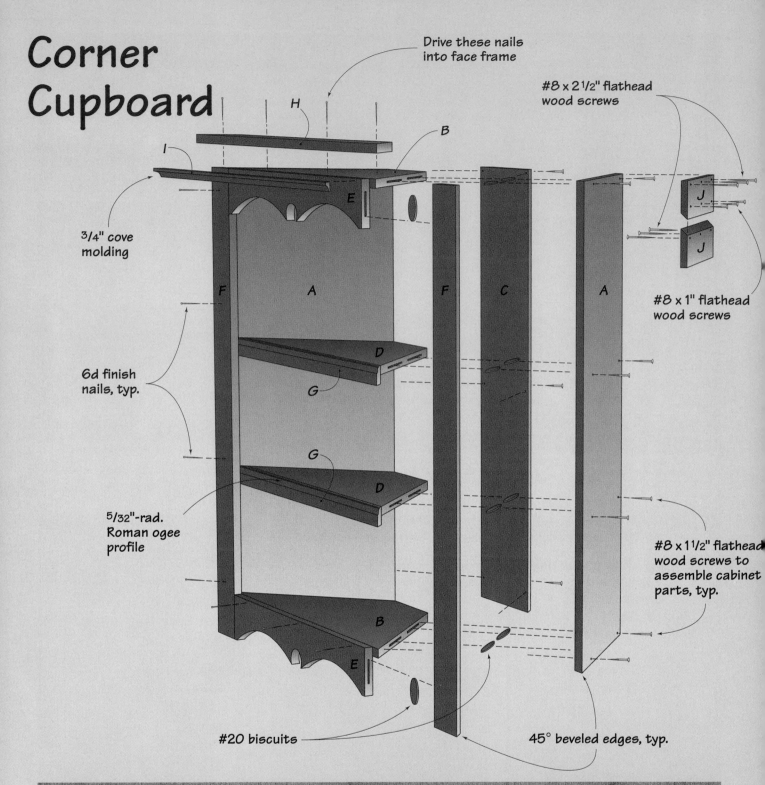

Drive these nails into face frame

#8 x 2½" flathead wood screws

H

B

I

E

¾" cove molding

F

A

F

C

A

J

J

#8 x 1" flathead wood screws

6d finish nails, typ.

D

G

G

D

#8 x 1½" flathead wood screws to assemble cabinet parts, typ.

5/32"-rad. Roman ogee profile

B

E

#20 biscuits

45° beveled edges, typ.

Corner Cupboard Cutting List								
Part	**No.**	**Size**	**Material**		**Part**	**No.**	**Size**	**Material**
A. Sides	2	¾ × 15⅝ × 38¾ in.	Pine		**F.** Face frame stiles	2	¾ × 3½ × 42 in.	Pine
B. Top, Bottom	2	¾ × 10½ × 27 in.	"		**G.** Shelf edge	2	¾ × 1½ × 27 in.	"
C. Back	1	¾ × 8 × 38¾ in.	"		**H.** Crown	1	¾ × 3 × 34 in.	"
D. Fixed shelves	2	¾ × 9¾ × 25½ in.	"		**I.** Cove molding	1	¾ × ¾ × 34 in.	"
E. Face frame rails	2	¾ × 4 × 25 in.	"		**J.** French cleats	4	½ × 3 × 12 in.	"

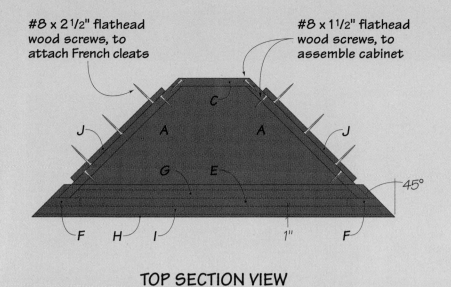

#8 x 2½" flathead wood screws, to attach French cleats

#8 x 1½" flathead wood screws, to assemble cabinet

C

J   A   A   J

G   E

45°

F   H   I   1"   F

TOP SECTION VIEW

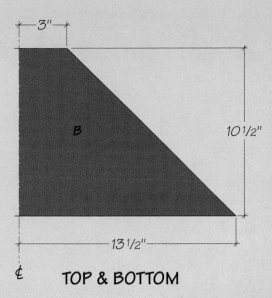

3"

B

10½"

13½"

TOP & BOTTOM

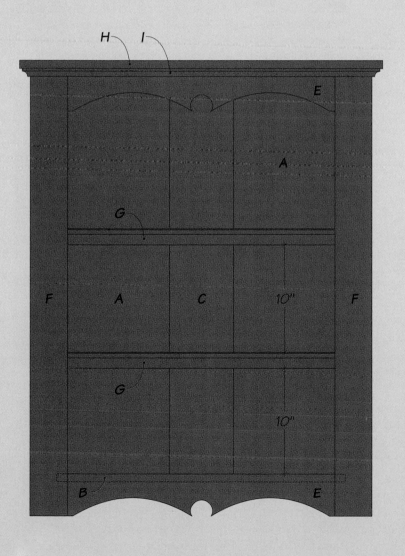

H   I

E

A

G

F   A   C   10"   F

G

10"

B   E

FRONT VIEW

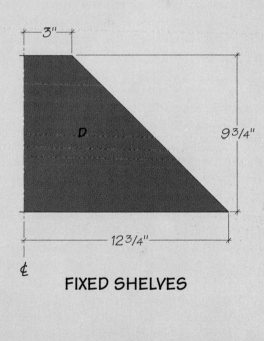

3"

D

9¾"

12¾"

FIXED SHELVES

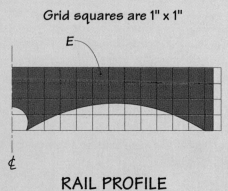

Grid squares are 1" x 1"

E

RAIL PROFILE

ASSEMBLE THE CARCASE

1 Edge-glue panels to use for the cabinet sides, top and bottom. We used 1 × 6 pine. Make sure to joint all edges first. The panels should be at least 1 in. longer and wider than the finished sizes of the parts. After the glue has dried, smooth the faces of the panels with a hand plane or cabinet scraper and a random-orbit sander.

2 Bevel-rip one edge of each carcase side panel at 45°. Then make a parallel bevel cut on the opposite edge to rip the panel to width **(See Photo A).** Cross-cut the sides to length.

3 Lay out the carcase top, bottom and fixed shelves. Since the top and bottom of the carcase are the same size, as are the fixed shelves, stack the glued-up panels on top of one another for similar-sized carcase parts, and draw the layout lines on the top panel. Then screw the panels together in the waste areas (away from where the saw blade will run). Use a circular saw and a straightedge cutting guide to gang-cut the angled edges in the workpieces **(See Photo B).** *TIP: You can make an edge guide for your saw by screwing a scrap of edge-jointed 1 × 4 to a strip of ¼-in.-thick hardboard, then running the saw along the 1× to trim the hardboard, creating a blade reference edge.* Align and clamp the cutting guide to one of the ganged stacks and cut both carcase parts at the same time. Then gang-cut the other parts.

4 Mark the locations for the carcase top and bottom and fixed shelves on the cabinet sides. The carcase top and bottom are flush with the ends of the carcase sides. The fixed shelves are spaced 11½ in. and 23 in. from the top face of the carcase bottom. Make reference marks for #20 biscuits on the shelves, top and bottom and sides, and use four biscuits per joint **(See Photo C).** Cut biscuit slots in the mating parts of each joint.

Blade guard removed for clarity

PHOTO A: Bevel-rip the glued-up panels on both edges to make the cabinet sides. The 45° bevels should be parallel. Clamp featherboards to the saw table and fence to hold the panels securely as you cut.

Shop-made edge guide

PHOTO B: Gang-cut the carcase top and bottom panels to size, then gang-cut the fixed shelves. Use an edge guide clamped to the workpiece and your workbench to ensure straight cuts.

5 Rip-cut and cross-cut the two shelf edge strips to size. Use a piloted 5⁄32-in.-radius Roman ogee bit to cut profiles in the shelf edge strips. We used a router table to cut the profiles, but a hand-held router would also work **(See Photo D).**

PHOTO C: Lay out all the carcase parts and draw alignment marks for biscuit joints. Be sure to keep the orientation of the side panel bevels in mind when you lay out and mark the parts.

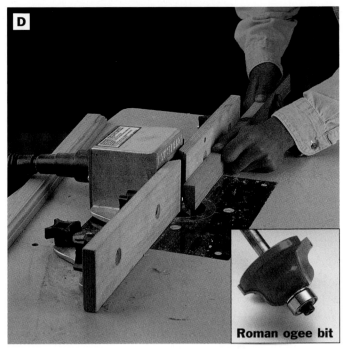

Roman ogee bit

PHOTO D: Rout an ogee profile along one edge of both shelf edge strips with a piloted 5⁄32-in.-radius Roman ogee bit (See inset). The edging is oversize at this stage to keep your fingers clear of the bit.

6 Glue the shelf edging to the front edges of the fixed shelves so the profiled edge is flush with the top of each shelf. Use masking tape to hold the edging in place while the glue dries. The edging is oversize and should overhang the shelves on both ends. Let the glue dry and remove the tape.

7 Trim the overhanging shelf edging to continue the lines of the angled sides of the shelves, using a back saw or fine-toothed Japanese-style pull saw. Clamp the shelves to your workbench for easier cutting **(See Photo E).** Work carefully to avoid splintering the edges of the edging as you make the cuts.

8 Rip the carcase back to width from 1 × 10 stock, and bevel both long edges at 45° on the table saw. The bevels should face in opposite directions from one another. Then cross-cut the back panel to length.

9 Finish-sand the carcase parts and assemble the carcase with biscuits in place, to check the fit of all the parts. You'll attach the sides to the top, bottom and fixed shelves first, then attach the back to the sides. Drill countersunk pilot holes first, then fasten the carcase parts together using 1½-in. flathead wood screws. Screw the carcase sides to the shelves, then drill angled pilot holes through the back and into the sides, slide the back into place, and attach it with screws **(See Photo F).**

PHOTO E: Clamp the fixed shelves to your workbench and trim the profiled shelf edging to match the angled ends of the shelves. We used a fine-toothed Japanese-style pull saw to make the cuts.

ATTACH THE FACE FRAME

10 Rip- and cross-cut the face frame stiles to size. Bevel one edge of each stile to 45° on the table saw.

11 Rip- and cross-cut the face frame rails to size according to the *Cutting List*. Enlarge the grid pattern to full size on paper for the rail profile, then glue it to a piece of scrap plywood. Cut the plywood to shape, creating a half template for the rail profile.

PHOTO F: Assemble the carcase parts using #8 × 1½-in. flathead wood screws to reinforce the joints. Attach the cupboard back by driving the screws at an angle through the back and into the sides.

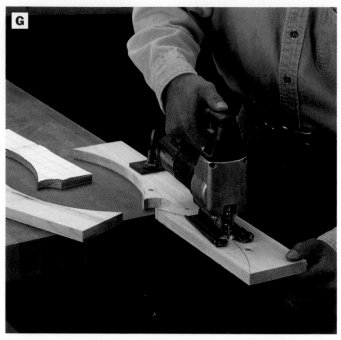

PHOTO G: Make a template of the face-frame rail profile and use it to lay out the curves on the rails. Cut the profiles using a jig saw, band saw or scroll saw.

Trace the outlines of the template onto a rail, then flip the template over and finish the outline by tracing the mirror image on the rest of the rail. Outline the second rail. Cut out the rail profiles with a jig saw, band saw or scroll saw and smooth the cut edges **(See Photo G)**. *TIP: A drum sander in the drill press or a spindle sander is a great way to smooth up all the curved sawn edges.*

⓬ Arrange the face frame parts together. The ends of the rails should butt against the flat edges of the stiles; position the beveled edges of the stiles so they taper toward the back of the cupboard. Cut biscuit slots for #20 biscuits to join the ends of the face frame rails to the stiles, one biscuit per joint. Then glue up and clamp the face frame on a flat surface. NOTE: *You may need to fashion notched clamping pads for the clamp jaws so they'll fit over the beveled edges of the stiles, to keep the clamp jaws from marring the stile bevels.*

⓭ Align the face frame with the front of the carcase so the top edge of the face-frame top rail is even with the top of the carcase and the stiles overhang the carcase sides evenly. Attach the face frame with wood glue and 4d finish nails. Set the nails below the surface of the face frame with a nailset **(See Photo H).** Fill the nail holes with wood putty and finish-sand the face frame smooth with 180-grit sandpaper.

ATTACH THE CROWN ASSEMBLY

⓮ Cut the crown strip to rough size (about 36 in. long), then miter the ends at 45° to continue the angled lines of the face frame. Use a table saw or a power miter saw to cut the miters in the workpiece. Finish-sand the front edge of the crown, then attach it to the carcase top and face frame with glue and 4d finish nails. The crown should overhang the face-frame top rail by 1 in.

⓯ Cut a strip of molding to fit the gap between the crown strip and the face frame. We routed a Roman ogee profile into a strip of stock, then ripped the molding to width on the table saw **(See Photo I).** You could use milled cove molding instead. Miter-cut the molding to length, making sure the ends will follow the lines of the crown and the edges of the face frame. Attach with glue and 3d finish nails.

FINISHING TOUCHES

We painted the cabinet front before attaching the French cleats used to hang it. Because pine is a soft-wood, we primed the surfaces first, then applied two coats of satin paint. (We chose periwinkle blue because it's similar in tone to the blue milk paint often used to finish Colonial-style furnishings).

⓰ Cut the French cleats to size from scrap pine, and bevel one edge of each cleat to 45°. Glue and screw one cleat to each side of the cabinet along its top edge, so the beveled edges of the cleats face down and in toward the cabinet. Use three #8 × 1-in. flathead wood screws per cleat (**See Photo J**).

17 To hang the cupboard, attach the two remaining French cleats to the two walls bevel-side up so the bevels face the walls. Level the cleats to one another on the walls and space them 7 in. from the corner. Drive #8 × 2½-in. flathead wood screws through the cleats and into the wall, making sure to hit wall studs. Since the cleats will support the full weight of the cupboard and its contents, use wall anchors and appropriate screws if you cannot attach the cleats to wall studs.

18 Hang the cupboard on the wall so the French cleats interlock. The cleat bevels will force the cabinet tight against the wall. Tack the cabinet to the wall with one screw through each side and cleat.

PHOTO H: Attach the face frame to the cupboard carcase with glue and 4d finish nails. Drive the nailheads below the face frame surface with a nailset.

Blade guard removed for clarity

PHOTO I: Rip the cove molding for the cupboard crown to width on the table saw. Use a featherboard and pushstick.

Cleat bevel faces down and in toward carcase sides

PHOTO J: Attach French cleats to the sides of the cabinet, flush with the top of the carcase. The cleat bevels face down and into the sides.

Mission Rocker

Truly a classic woodworking project, this handsome rocking chair features all the characteristics that make Mission furniture one of the most popular and enduring styles. Featuring the rich beauty of quartersawn oak, simple, elegant lines, and rock-solid pinned mortise-and-tenon joints, this rocker is an heirloom quality showpiece to be built and used with great pride.

Vital Statistics: Mission Rocker

TYPE: Rocking chair

OVERALL SIZE: 26W by 36H by 28D

MATERIAL: White oak

JOINERY: Pinned mortise-and-tenons, screw joints

CONSTRUCTION DETAILS:
- Rockers made from laminated strips of ¼-in. oak
- Tenoned back slats fit into mortises in rails
- Peak on crest rail for decorative touch
- Upholstered, padded seat

FINISHING OPTIONS: Medium to dark walnut stain with protective topcoat. Should have a darker, antique appearance.

Building time

PREPARING STOCK
3-4 hours

LAYOUT
3-4 hours

CUTTING PARTS
14-18 hours

ASSEMBLY
4-6 hours

FINISHING
4-6 hours

TOTAL: 28-38 hours

Tools you'll use

- Band saw
- Table saw
- Drill press
- Power miter saw
- Drill/driver
- Hand trim saw
- 40-in. or longer bar or pipe clamps (8)
- Wood mallet
- Wood chisel (¼-in.)
- File
- Power sander
- Combination square/ marking gauge
- Doweling jig
- Portable drill guide
- 2-in.-dia. hole saw
- Resawing guide
- Tenoning jig
- Stapler (electric or pneumatic)

Shopping list

- ☐ (1) 6/4 × 5½ in. × 8 ft. plain-sawn white oak
- ☐ (1) 6/4 × 3½ in. × 8 ft. plain-sawn white oak
- ☐ (2) ¾ × 6 in. × 8 ft. quartersawn white oak
- ☐ (1) ¾ × 4 in. × 8 ft. quartersawn white oak
- ☐ ¾-in. plywood scraps
- ☐ Finishing materials
- ☐ #10 × 2½-in. wood screws
- ☐ Wallboard screws (1¼, 2 in.)
- ☐ Upholstery fabric (36 × 36 in.)
- ☐ 4 × 16 × 19-in. foam
- ☐ ⅜-in.-dia. white oak plugs
- ☐ ¼-in.-dia. walnut doweling

Mission Rocker

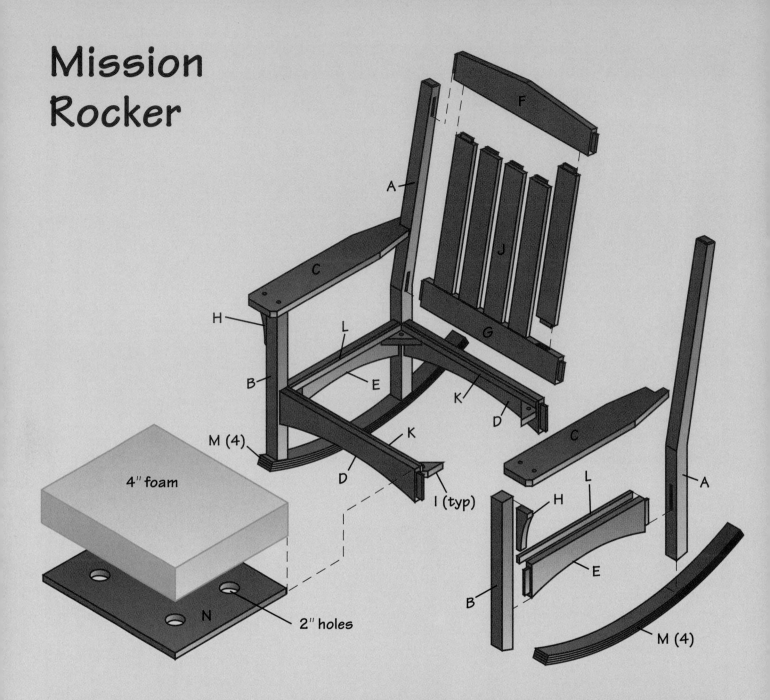

4" foam

M (4)

2" holes

Rocking Chair Cutting List

Part	No.	Size	Material	Part	No.	Size	Material
A. Back legs	2	1½ × 5½ × 36 in.	White oak	**H.** Corbels	2	¾ × 1½ × 5 in.	White oak (QS)
B. Front legs	2	1½ × 1½ × 19 in.	"	**I.** Corner blocks	4	¾ × 1½ × 4 in.	White oak
C. Arms	2	¾ × 4 × 21 in.	White oak (QS)	**J.** Back slats	5	½ × 2½ × 18 in.	White oak (QS)
D. Seat rails (front/back)	2	¾ × 4 × 20½ in.	"	**K.** Filler strips (front/back)	2	⅜ × ¾ × 19 in.	White oak
E. Seat rails (side)	2	¾ × 4 × 17½ in.	"	**L.** Filler strips (side)	2	⅜ × ¾ × 16 in.	"
F. Crest rail	1	¾ × 4 × 20 in.	"	**M.** Rocker plies	8	¼ × 2¼ × 32 in.	White oak (PS)
G. Lower back rail	1	¾ × 3 × 20½ in.	"	**N.** Seat board	1	¾ × 15⅝ × 18⅝ in.	Plywood

KEY: QS= quartersawn; PS= plain (face) sawn

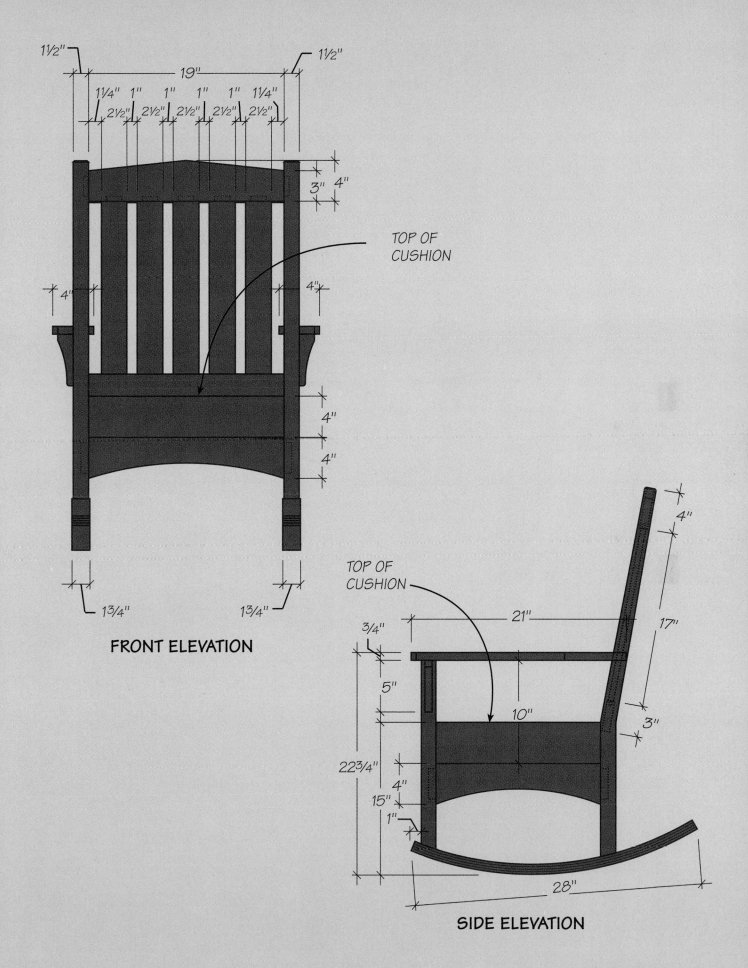

FRONT ELEVATION

SIDE ELEVATION

TOP OF CUSHION

TOP OF CUSHION

1½" 1½"
19"
1¼" 1" 1" 1" 1" 1¼"
2½" 2½" 2½" 2½" 2½"
3" 4"
4" 4"
4"
4"
1¾" 1¾"

¾"
5"
21"
17"
4"
10"
3"
22¾"
4"
15"
1"
28"

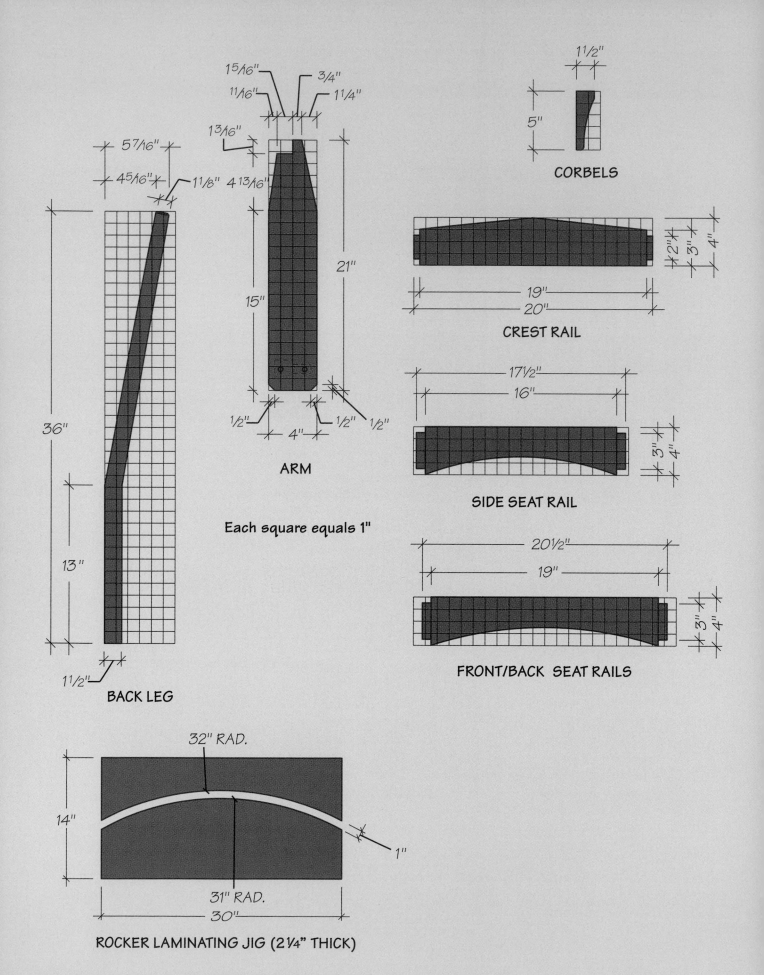

1½"

CORBELS

1⁵⁄₁₆"   3/4"
1¹⁄₁₆"   1¼"

13⁄16"

5⁷⁄₁₆"
4⁵⁄₁₆"   1¹⁄₈" 4¹³⁄₁₆"

21"

15"

CREST RAIL

2"
3"
4"

19"
20"

ARM

Each square equals 1"

½"   ½"
4"   ½"

17½"
16"

3"
4"

SIDE SEAT RAIL

36"

13"

20½"
19"

3"
4"

1½"

BACK LEG

FRONT/BACK SEAT RAILS

32" RAD.

14"

1"

31" RAD.

30"

ROCKER LAMINATING JIG (2¼" THICK)

334 The Complete Book of Woodworking

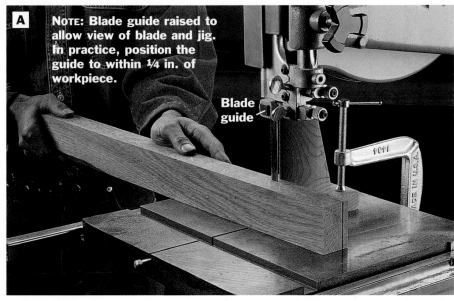

NOTE: Blade guide raised to allow view of blade and jig. In practice, position the guide to within ¼ in. of workpiece.

Blade guide

PHOTO A: Use a band saw with a resawing guide to cut thin oak strips for the back slats and the lamination plies used to make the rockers.

PREPARE THE STOCK

In addition to routine squaring and planing of stock you'd do for any woodworking project, you'll need to resaw lumber into thin strips to build this rocker. You can purchase oak milled to ½ in. thick for the back slats and ¼ in. thick for the plies used to make the laminated rockers, but generally it's more economical to resaw thicker stock yourself. We used a band saw with a "pivot point" resawing jig to cut the thin strips.

❶ Select plain-sawn oak stock for resawing the ¼-in.-thick plies used to make the laminated rockers (using plain-sawn stock, where the grain runs parallel to the plies, allows it to conform to the curve of the rockers). Joint one edge of each board, then rip-cut to 2¼ in. wide and cross-cut to 32 in. long.

❷ Resaw the strips to ¼ in. thick, using a band saw and resawing jig (See Tip, right), or a table saw and rip fence. We used a ½-in.-wide, 4 tooth-per-inch, skip-tooth blade for the task. When resawing, cut the board slightly thicker then the finished width, since you'll need to plane it smooth after the cut is made. Lay the stock on the saw table with the jointed edge down, to ensure a square cut. Feed the stock into the blade, and angle the board as nec-

essary to keep it tight against the resawing guide (See Photo A). Feed the stock slowly enough that the blade isn't stressed, but not so slowly that it burns the wood. Cut enough stock to make all eight rocker plies, then plane the plies down to ¼ in. thick with your surface planer.

❸ Select stock for the ½-in.-thick back slats. We used quartersawn oak for the high-visibility parts of the chair, including the back slats. Due to the nature of the milling process, quartersawn lumber is most readily available in thinner dimensions. We chose ¾-in.-thick stock to make the back slats, removing ³⁄₁₆ in. by resawing, then planing the boards to ½ in. thick.

❹ Plane, joint and rip-cut stock for the rest of the chair parts, according to the thicknesses and widths listed in the Cutting list. Observe the notations made regarding grain pattern.

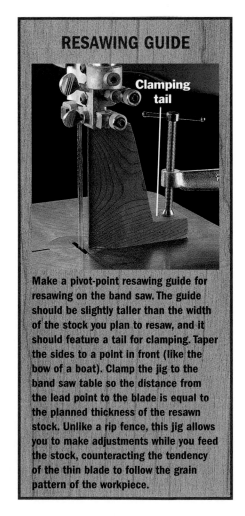

RESAWING GUIDE

Clamping tail

Make a pivot-point resawing guide for resawing on the band saw. The guide should be slightly taller than the width of the stock you plan to resaw, and it should feature a tail for clamping. Taper the sides to a point in front (like the bow of a boat). Clamp the jig to the band saw table so the distance from the lead point to the blade is equal to the planned thickness of the resawn stock. Unlike a rip fence, this jig allows you to make adjustments while you feed the stock, counteracting the tendency of the thin blade to follow the grain pattern of the workpiece.

PHOTO B: Square off and clean up the mortises with a ¼-in. wood chisel. Use a drill press and ¼-in. brad-point bit or a router and ¼-in. straight bit to remove the wood in the mortise area.

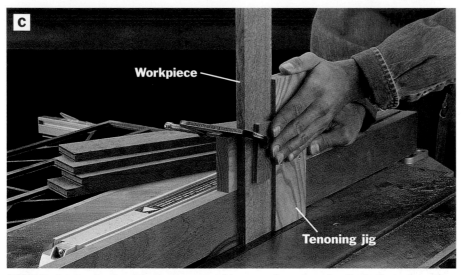

Workpiece

Tenoning jig

PHOTO C: Cut the cheeks of the tenons on a table saw, using a tenoning jig that's sized so the horizontal member rides on top of the saw fence and the vertical member is flat on the table.

PHOTO D: After all cheek cuts are made, trim off the sides of the tenons, using the tenoning jig. Set the saw fence to remove ½ in. of wood from each side.

CUT & MACHINE THE PARTS

Because it's easier to cut tenons on square stock, do not make contour cuts on the seat rails and crest rails until after the tenons have been cut. As a general rule, cut the mortises first, then lay out and cut the tenons to fit.

5 Cut the 1½ × 5½ × 36-in.-long blanks for the back legs. Lay out the shapes of the legs on the blanks before cutting the rest of the chair parts to size—you should be able to cut several parts, including the front legs, from the waste areas left over after the back legs are cut. Use the *Grid pattern* as a reference for plotting the back leg shape onto one of the blanks. Cut out the leg along the cutting lines, using a band saw or jig saw. Sand the back leg to its final shape and to smooth out any unevenness in the cut, then use the leg as a template for laying out the second back leg.

6 Cut out the second leg and the remaining chair parts, according to the dimensions given in the *Cutting list*. Sand the second leg to match the first.

7 Use a router with a chamfering bit, a stationary disc sander or a file to make four chamfers on the tops of the back legs.

8 Lay out and cut all the mortises in the legs and the crest rail and lower back rail. All mortises should be ¼ in. thick. Mortises for the back slats and the crest rail are ½ in. deep, and those for the tenons in the lower back rail and seat rails should be ¾ in. deep. The length of each mortise is 1 in. shorter than the width of the part it accepts (½ in. per side). Use a marking gauge to scribe the outline for each mortise, then remove the wood in the mortise area with a ¼-in-dia. brad-point bit, or with a router and ¼-in. straight bit. Square off the ends and sides of each mortise with a sharp ¼-in. wood chisel **(See Photo B).**

9 Lay out and cut the tenons in the ends of the seat slats, the crest rails, the lower back rail and the seat rails. Use a tenoning jig for your table saw to make the tenon cuts. Begin by making the ½- and ¾-in. deep cheek cuts **(See Photo C),** resetting the blade height and distance from the fence as needed. Then clamp the parts to the jig so the edges are against the fence and make cheek cuts for the sides of the tenons **(See Photo D).** Finish by cutting the tenon shoulders using your miter gauge to feed each piece through the blade. Clamp a relief block on the infeed side of the blade to set up the cuts **(See Photo E).** Test the fit of each tenon in the mating mortise, and trim the tenons with a chisel if they're too large.

10 Lay out and cut the arches in the lower edges of the seat rails, using the *Grid patterns* as references. Also lay out and cut the peak on the crest rail. The basic shape for the arms can be cut at this point also, although you'll need to transfer the angle of the back leg to bevel the front of the notch cut in the arms after the chair is assembled.

ASSEMBLE THE CHAIR

11 Finish-sand all exposed part surfaces and ease sharp edges. Don't sand tenons or any surfaces that will be joined together.

12 Dry-fit the parts for the back—the crest rail, the lower back rail, and the five slats. Then apply glue

PHOTO E: Cut the tenon shoulders, using a miter gauge to feed the workpieces over the blade. Clamp a relief block to the infeed side of the blade and use it to set up the cuts. Be sure to reset the blade height as needed to cut just up to each tenon.

PHOTO F: Assemble the back. Glue the back slats into the lower back rail first, then glue on the crest rail and clamp up the assembly, using clamp pads to protect the wood.

PHOTO G: Miter-cut the ends of the seat rail tenons so they'll meet to form clean miter joints inside the mortises in the legs. We used a sliding compound miter saw, but it could also be done on a table saw.

to the mortises and tenons and clamp up the assembly **(See Photo F).** Square-up the back by measuring the diagonals and adjusting the clamps as necessary.

13 The tenons of the seat rails are designed to meet inside the mortises in the legs. Cut a 45° miter at the ends of each tenon so they'll fit together neatly inside

the legs. We used a power miter saw to make the miter cuts **(See Photo G).**

14 Glue and clamp the back assembly and the back seat rail into their joints between the two back legs. Also glue up the front seat rail to the front legs and clamp **(See Photo H).**

PHOTO H: Glue up the chair in stages to keep control of the work. Here, the front seat rail is attached between the front legs.

PHOTO I: Glue the side rails into the back legs, then attach the front assembly to the side rails. Clamp up the whole framework, checking the diagonals to make sure it's square.

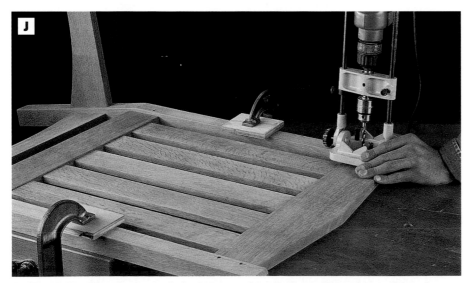

PHOTO J: Drill guide holes for the ¼-in. dowels used to pin the mortise-and-tenon joints. A portable drill guide ensures perpendicular holes drilled to the correct depth.

⑮ Now glue and clamp the front assembly to the back, with the side seat rails between them (**See Photo I**). Check to make sure all parts are square to one another and adjust the clamping pressure, if needed, before the glue sets.

⑯ Lay out and drill holes for the ¼-in.-dia. dowels used to pin the tenons that fit into the front and back legs. We used walnut doweling for a dramatic, contrasting appearance. Use two pins for each joint, taking care to align the dowel guide holes. We used a portable drill guide to ensure that the dowel holes are perpendicular and deep enough to extend all the way through the tenon and into the wood on the opposite side of each mortise (**See Photo J**). Beyond their ornamental aspect, these also serve to lock the tenon joints. Apply glue to the end of each pin and drive it home with a wood mallet. Trim the top of the pin flush after the glue cures.

⑰ Glue and clamp the four seat filler strips to the insides of the seat rails. Their top edges should be flush with the top edges of the rails. The filler strips create a square opening for the seat board.

⑱ Drill a countersunk screw hole through the underside of each corner block, to be used to screw the seat down. Drill countersunk screw holes to attach the corner blocks to the seat rails, just below the filler strips. Glue and screw them in place with 1¼-in. wallboard screws (**See Photo K**).

ATTACH THE ARMS
⑲ Glue and clamp the corbels to the front legs. They should be centered on the legs and flush with the leg tops.

PHOTO K: Apply glue, then screw the corner blocks in place just below the filler strips, using 1¼-in. wallboard screws.

PHOTO L: With the arm level and resting on the front leg, trace the angle of the back leg creating a bevel line to cut the arm notch.

PHOTO M: Glue and screw the arms to the chair frame. Drive two screws into the leg/corbel support and one into the back leg.

20 Lay each arm in place, resting on the front leg and corbel. Keeping the arm level, hold the back end against the back leg. Mark the angle of the back leg onto the edge of each arm, starting at the end of the notch at the top **(See Photo L).** Remove the arms and use a small hand trim or back saw to bevel the notches along the cutting line.

21 Fit the arms in place and center them on the front leg/corbel assembly. Drill and counterbore screw holes so the screws can be plugged, then screw the arms down with two 2-in. wallboard screws each **(See Photo M).** Drive one screw to attach each arm to its back leg.

22 Plug the screw holes with ⅜-in.-dia. white oak plugs and sand the plugs flush.

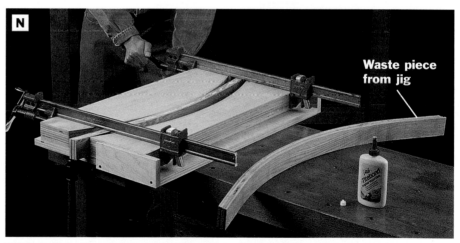

Waste piece from jig

PHOTO N: Press the oak plies together in a laminating jig to face-glue the blanks for the rockers. The plywood base and the short sides help keep the two halves of the jig aligned during the glue up. Let the glue dry overnight before removing each glued-up rocker blank.

MAKE THE ROCKERS

23 Make the bending jig (See *Rocker jig illustration*) from three layers of scrap plywood or particleboard, glued up to make a 2¼ × 14 × 30-in. blank.

24 Draw the two different radius curves 1 in. apart on the blank, and cut them out with a band saw. Cut a 30-in.-sq. piece of plywood

for a jig base and screw ½ of the jig form to it. Attach short strips of plywood to the edges of the base at the top of the jig (these will help keep the moveable half of the jig aligned with the fixed half when the rocker plies are clamped between them). Wax the curved surfaces of the jig to keep the glue from sticking.

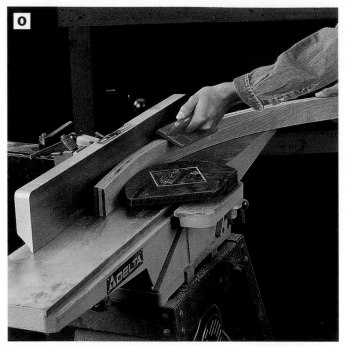

PHOTO O: After laminating, joint one edge of each rocker flat and square. Keep the outer face against the fence and carefully feed the rocker along its curve, using push blocks to guide the workpiece.

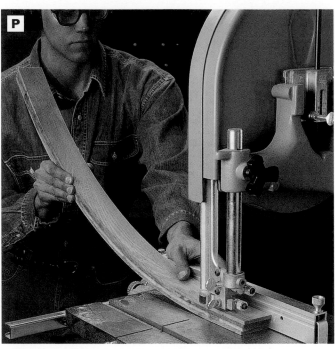

PHOTO P: Use the rip fence of your band saw as a guide to rip-cut the rockers to 1¾ in. wide. Keep the jointed edge against the fence. If you don't have a rip fence, clamp a straightedge to the table.

PHOTO Q: Scribe the arc of the rockers onto the leg bottoms by holding the rockers in proper position against the legs and marking with a pencil. Trim the bottoms of the legs to follow the curved cutting lines, using a hand saw to remove most of the wood. Smooth out the cuts with a sander or file.

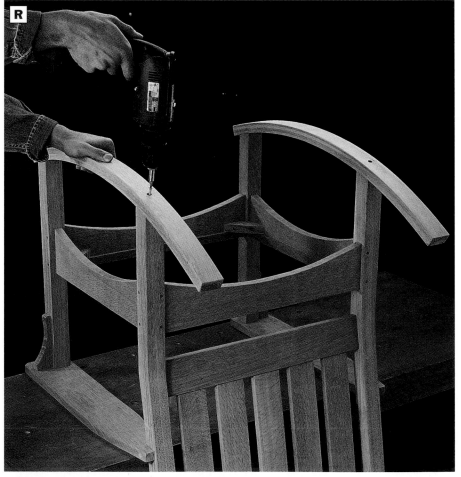

PHOTO R: Attach the rockers to the legs with glue and one #10 × 2½-in. wood screw driven through a counterbored pilot hole. Plug the counterbores with ⅜-in.-dia. wood plugs.

㉕ Spread glue on the mating surfaces of four of the ¼-in.-thick plies and stack them together face to face.

㉖ Position the glued-up plies between the two halves of the laminating jig and begin tightening clamps at each end, adjusting the glue-up to keep it centered in the jig and to keep the edges of the plies aligned (See Photo N). Tighten the clamps a little at a time, alternating between ends, until the plies are pressed together tightly. Add another clamp in the middle.

㉗ Leave the rocker in the jig overnight. Then remove it and glue up the other rocker.

㉘ Scrape as much of the dried glue as you can from one edge of each rocker with a paint scraper. Then clean up and square the edge by flattening it on a jointer, keeping the outer face of the glue-up against the fence (See Photo O).

㉙ Rip-cut the rockers to 1¾ in. wide, using a band saw with a rip fence (See Photo P).

㉚ Cut the ends of the rockers square to the curve. You can square a line and cut the ends on a band saw or make the cuts on a table saw, chop saw, or with a back saw in a miter box. The finished length of the rockers should be 28 in., measured in a straight line from end to end.

㉛ Hold each rocker in place against the front and back legs and scribe the line of the curve on the bottoms of the legs. Start the curves at the inside, bottom edges of the legs (See Photo Q). Use a hand saw to remove the waste, then smooth out the cuts with a file or sander.

㉜ Finish-sand the rockers. Lay the chair upside down on its arms and rest the rockers on the leg bottoms. Center the legs on the rockers, and adjust the rockers so their front ends protrude 1 in. in front of the front legs. Drill countersunk pilot holes, then attach the rockers with glue and one #10 × 2½-in. screw per leg (See Photo R). Plug the counterbores with white oak plugs.

FINISHING TOUCHES

㉝ Touch up any rough areas with sandpaper. Apply your desired finish. We used walnut-tinted Danish oil with a tung oil topcoat.

㉞ Cut the seat board to size from scrap ¾-in. plywood. Use a hole saw to drill four 2-in.-dia. vent holes in the seat board.

㉟ Cut a piece of 4-in.-thick high-density foam the same dimensions as the seat board, then center the foam on the underside of a 36-in.-sq. piece of upholstery fabric. Neatly tuck the upholstery around the corners and tack it to the bottom of the seat board with a pneumatic stapler or upholstery tacks (See Photo S). You may want to hire an upholsterer to make the seat, especially if you cover it with leather.

㊱ Attach the upholstered seat with 1¼-in. wallboard screws driven up through the pilot holes in the corner blocks (See Photo T).

PHOTO S: You can upholster the chair seat yourself by using a pneumatic or electric stapler to tack a 36-in.-sq. piece of upholstery fabric over 4-in. foam. Work carefully when making the corners.

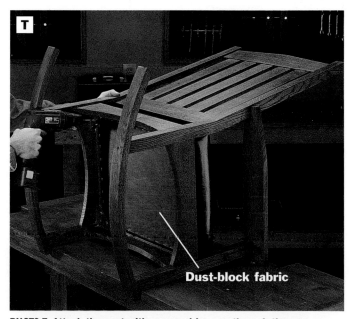

Dust-block fabric

PHOTO T: Attach the seat with screws driven up through the corner blocks and into the seat board.

OUTDOOR PROJECTS

Page 404

Page 374

Page 398

Page 412

Page 344

Page 356

Page 382

Page 422

Page
432

Page
364

Page 392

Patio Tea Table

Whether you're enjoying coffee and the morning paper or a cool afternoon beverage, spend more of your leisure time outside with the help of this attractive patio table. You'll find many uses for its spacious top and lower shelf: from serving a crew of thirsty kids to hosting a casual game of cards. Our table is made of cedar, an inexpensive wood that is naturally weather resistant and easy to work with.

Vital Statistics

TYPE: Patio table

OVERALL SIZE: 29½ dia. by 18⅞H

MATERIAL: Cedar

JOINERY: Butt joints reinforced with screws

CONSTRUCTION DETAILS:
· Round top cut to shape with a jig saw guided by a shop-made circle-cutting jig
· Both shelf and top slats held apart with spacers during installation to promote water drainage

FINISH: Clear deck sealer or none

BUILDING TIME: 6-8 hours

Shopping List

☐ (3) 1 × 4 in. × 8 ft. cedar
☐ (2) 2 × 2 in. × 8 ft. cedar
☐ Deck screws (1½, 2½ in.)
☐ Finishing materials

Patio Tea Table: Step-by-step

PHOTO A: Clamp the four shelf frame members together so the ends of one pair overlap the ends of the other pair, then attach the frame parts with a single deck screw at each joint. Insert clamp pads between the clamp jaws and the frame to keep from marring the soft cedar.

ASSEMBLE THE SHELF

❶ Crosscut the shelf frame pieces and four slats to length, according to the *Cutting List*.

❷ Assemble the shelf frame: Arrange the frame pieces so that one pair overlaps the ends of the other pair. Clamp the frame members in place, using clamp pads to keep from marring the soft cedar. Drill one pilot hole at each corner and attach the frame pieces to one another with 2½-in. deck screws **(See Photo A).**

Patio Tea Table

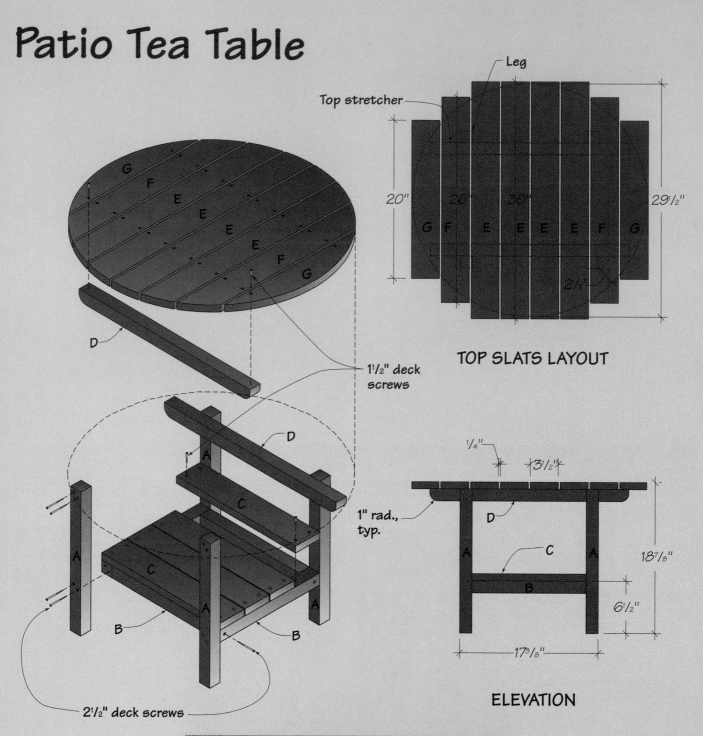

Leg

Top stretcher

20" 26" 30" 29½"

G F E E E E F G

2½"

TOP SLATS LAYOUT

G
F
E
E
E
E
F
G

D

1½" deck screws

D

A
C
A
C
A
B
B

2½" deck screws

¼" 3½"

D

1" rad., typ.

A C A
B

18⅞"

6½"

17⅜"

ELEVATION

Patio Tea Table Cutting List			
Part	**No.**	**Size**	**Material**
A. Legs	4	1½ × 1½ × 18 in.	Cedar
B. Shelf frames	4	1½ × 1½ × 14⅜ in.	"
C. Shelf slats	4	⅞ × 4 × 17⅜ in.	"
D. Stretchers	2	1½ × 1½ × 25 in.	"
E. Top slats (long)	4	⅞ × 4 × 30 in.	"
F. Top slats (medium)	2	⅞ × 4 × 26 in.	"
G. Top slats (short)	2	⅞ × 4 × 20 in.	"

3 Attach the shelf slats. Begin by placing one slat so it is flush with one long side of the frame. Attach this slat with four countersunk 1½-in. deck screws. Then lay out the remaining three slats on the frame so the fourth slat is flush with the opposite side of the shelf frame. Adjust the two middle slats so there is an even spacing between all of the slats (about ¼ in., although this spacing may vary, depending on the actual width of the cedar stock you buy). Locate a pair of scrap spacers that match the slat spacing width you've determined. Then drill pilot holes and install the remaining slats, one at a time, with the spacers inserted **(See Photo B).**

MAKE THE LEG ASSEMBLIES

4 Crosscut the legs and stretchers to length, then scribe a 1-in. radius on both ends of the two stretchers with a compass.

5 Round over the stretcher ends with a jig saw **(See Photo C).**

6 Attach the legs to the stretchers: Position a pair of legs on each stretcher so the top ends of the legs are flush with the top (flat) edge of the stretchers. NOTE: *The rounded corners of the stretchers should face the bottoms of the legs.* Inset the legs 3¾ in. from the ends of each stretcher. Drill two pilot holes through each leg into the stretcher, and attach the parts with 2½-in. deck screws **(See Photo D).**

JOIN THE SHELF TO THE LEG ASSEMBLIES

7 Fasten the leg assemblies to the shelf: First cut four 5-in.-long 2 × 4 scrap blocks to support the shelf when joining it to the leg assemblies. Set the shelf on top of the scrap blocks set on-end.

PHOTO B: Attach one slat flush to one long side of the shelf frame. Position the remaining slats evenly across the frame with temporary spacers inserted in between. The ends and edges of the slats should not overlap the frame.

PHOTO C: Mark the bottom corners of the stretchers with a 1-in. radius curve, then trim the corners to shape with a jig saw. Be sure to secure the workpiece with clamps before you cut.

D

Spacers

PHOTO D: Fasten the legs to the stretchers so the top ends of the legs align with the top (flat) edges of the stretchers. Scrap 2 × 4 spacers provide level support for the legs while you attach them to the stretchers with countersunk screws.

Position the leg assemblies, one on each long side of the shelf, so the stretchers face inward and the outside edges of the legs are flush with the ends of the shelf frame. Drive two countersunk 2½-in. deck screws through each leg and into the shelf frame (**See Photo E**). Position the screws carefully so they do not hit the shelf frame assembly screws.

INSTALL & SHAPE THE TOP

8 Lay out and attach the top slats to the stretchers. Be aware that the slats vary in length according to their position on the table. Position the two shortest slats at the ends of the stretchers, followed by the medium slats. The four long slats make up the middle of the table. The space between the two long center slats should mark the center of the stretchers. Insert spacer scraps between the

E

PHOTO E: Elevate the shelf to its proper height in relation to the legs with four 5-in.-long 2 × 4 scraps. Position a leg assembly against each long edge of the shelf, with the stretchers facing inward. Drill offset pilot holes through the legs, and secure the legs to the shelf frame with 2½-in. deck screws.

F

PHOTO F: Arrange and fasten the top slats across the stretchers. The shortest slats should overhang the ends of the stretchers, followed by the medium and long slats. Hold the slats evenly apart with scrap spacers. Work outward from the center to the ends, inserting spacers as you go, and fasten the slats with countersunk 1½-in. deck screws.

slats to keep them separated evenly. Attach the slats to the stretchers with 1½-in. deck screws, driving two screws per joint (**See Photo F**).

❾ Cut the tabletop to shape with a jig saw: We used a simple circle-cutting jig, which consists of a 3-ft. strip of plywood outfitted on one end with a frame to hold the jig saw base. A hole cut in the blade area inside the frame provides clearance for the blade. The jig pivots around a nail tacked at the center of the circle. The distance from the blade to the nail establishes the circle's radius. If you choose to use this jig rather than cut freehand, locate the tabletop centerpoint to determine the position of the jig's pivot nail. Since the center of this tabletop lands on a space between two slats, tack a scrap piece of thin material (we used a piece of ⅛-in.-thick hardboard) to the tabletop to provide a nailing surface for the pivot nail. Set the distance from the pivot point to the blade to 14¾ in. and tack the pivot nail into place. It's a good idea to insert a pencil into the blade hole and lay out the full circumference of the circle before starting to cut; this way you can monitor how the blade tracks the layout line as you cut. Then insert the saw in the jig and trim the top to shape, starting as close as possible to the edge of one of the short top slats (**See Photo G**).

FINISHING TOUCHES

❿ Give the project a thorough sanding, particularly around the curved edge of the table to ease all sharp edges and corners.

⓫ Topcoat the project with several coats of clear deck sealer, if you wish, to help preserve the cedar wood tones (**See Photo H**).

Pivot nail

PHOTO G: A circle-cutting jig saw jig makes easy, accurate work of cutting the tabletop to shape. Since the middle of the circle falls between slats, you'll need to tack a thin scrap to the tabletop to provide a stable anchor for the pivot nail. Use the jig to mark a cutting line with a pencil first. Then insert the saw and pivot the jig around the nail to cut the tabletop to shape.

PHOTO H: Sand the project to remove splinters and to break the edges. Then brush on several coats of clear deck sealer to help protect the wood from the elements.

Cedar Birdhouse

You'll think the birds are singing your praises when a couple of feathered friends take up residence in this project. Our cedar birdhouse is easy to build, and a hinged panel on the side makes it a snap to clean out for next season once the birds fly south.

Vital Statistics

TYPE: Birdhouse

OVERALL SIZE: 9½D by 8½W by 10H

MATERIAL: Cedar

JOINERY: Butt joints reinforced with glue and nails

CONSTRUCTION DETAILS:
· Beveled edges of roof parts can be cut with a jig saw

FINISH: None or clear deck sealer

BUILDING TIME: 2 hours

Shopping List

☐ (1) 1 × 6 in. × 6 ft. cedar

☐ (2) 1 in. brass or galvanized butt hinges

☐ (2) ¾ in. dia. eye hooks (optional)

☐ (1) Threaded "L" hook

☐ 2 in. galvanized finish nails

☐ Moisture-resistant wood glue

☐ Finishing materials (optional)

Cedar Birdhouse: Step-by-step

MAKE THE HOUSE PARTS

❶ Cut the bottom, front, back, side and door to length.

❷ Crosscut a 5¾-in.-long blank for the door stop, then rip-cut the stop to its 2-in. width.

❸ Label the parts with strips of masking tape and their *Cutting List* letter labels to identify them.

❹ Mark the roof angles on the front and back workpieces **(See Photo A).** Cut the roof angles.

❺ Drill the drain holes in the bottom: Mark the bottom for four drain holes, spaced 1½ in. in from the ends and the edges of

PHOTO A: Cut workpieces for the front, back, bottom, side and door stop. Label the parts so you won't confuse them. Lay out the roof angles on the front and back, and cut out the roof profile on these parts with a jig saw.

Cedar Birdhouse

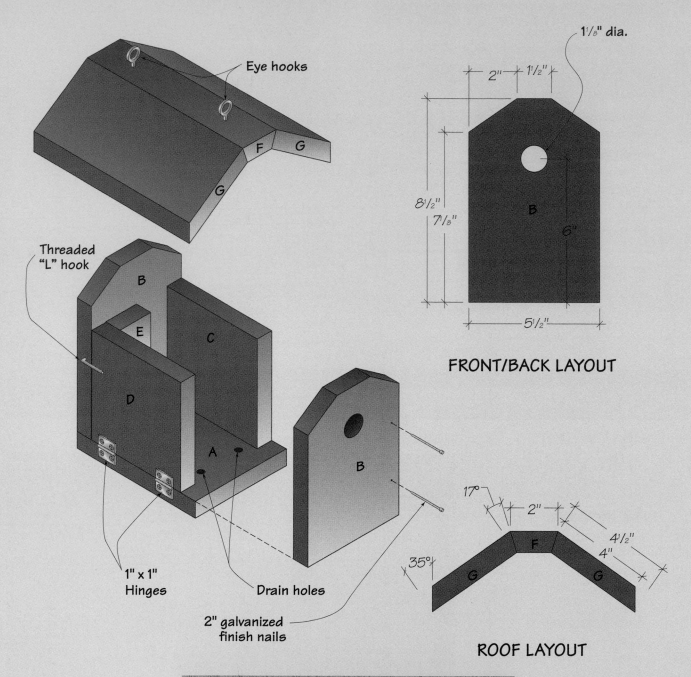

Eye hooks

1⅛" dia.

2" 1½"

8½"

7⅛"

B

6"

5½"

FRONT/BACK LAYOUT

Threaded "L" hook

B

E

C

D

B

A

1" x 1" Hinges

Drain holes

2" galvanized finish nails

17"

2"

F

4½"

4"

35"

G

G

ROOF LAYOUT

Cedar Birdhouse Cutting List			
Part	**No.**	**Size**	**Material**
A. Bottom	1	⅞ × 5½ × 7 in.	Cedar
B. Front/back	2	⅞ × 5½ × 8½ in.	"
C. Side	1	⅞ × 5½ × 5¾ in.	"
D. Door	1	⅞ × 5½ × 5¾ in.	"
E. Door stop	1	⅞ × 2 × 5¾ in.	"
F. Roof peak	1	⅞ × 2 × 9½ in.	"
G. Roof sections	2	⅞ × 4½ × 9½ in.	"

the bottom panel. Bore the holes with a ⅜-in.-dia. drill bit.

6 Drill the bird entry hole in the front panel: Mark the centerpoint of the entry hole 6 in. up from the bottom of the front panel, centered on the width of the workpiece. Drill the hole with a spade bit **(See Photo B)**. NOTE: *See the tint box, below, for entry hole sizes that are appropriate for specific kinds of birds.*

ASSEMBLE THE HOUSE

7 Arrange the front, back, side and bottom together so the house is upside down on your worksurface. Check the fit of the parts. The bottom panel overlaps the bottom ends of the front, back and side. The side fits in between the front and back.

8 Spread moisture-resistant glue on the mating surfaces of the parts, and clamp them together in the same orientation as Step 7. Slip the door in place without glue so it can serve as a spacer. Reinforce the glue joints with 2-in. galvanized finish nails, but do not nail into the door **(See Photo C)**.

9 Install the door. First, check the fit of the door on the house assembly. If it fits so tightly that it binds against the front and back panels, sand the door edges until it moves freely in its opening. Otherwise the wood may swell once it's exposed to the elements and the door may not open. Fasten the door to the house bottom with two hinges, spaced about ½ in. in from the edges of the door **(See Photo D)**.

10 Glue the door stop to the birdhouse back so it is flush against the back of the door.

PHOTO B: Mark the centerpoint of the bird access hole on the birdhouse front, and drill the hole with a spade bit. Clamp a backer board beneath the bird house front before you drill the hole to keep the bit from tearing out as it exits.

PHOTO C: Assemble the front, back, side and bottom with glue and clamps. Insert the door (without glue) to serve as a spacer. Nail the glued parts together and recess the nailheads.

Suggested entry hole sizes by species

The size of the entry hole you drill on your birdhouse will influence the species of birds that may take up residence there. Here are some recommended hole sizes for attracting different birds:

1⅛-in. hole
Chickadee, Prothonotary Warbler

1¼-in. hole
Titmouse, Red-breasted Nuthatch, Downy Woodpecker, House Wren

1⅜-in. hole
White-breasted Nuthatch, Tree & Violet-Green Swallows

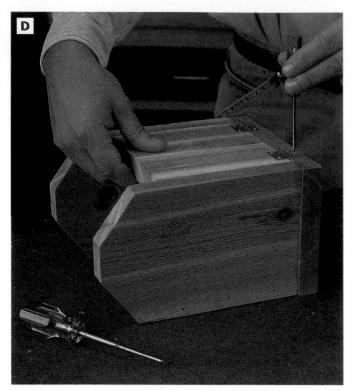

PHOTO D: Attach the door to the birdhouse bottom with two hinges. Mark pilot holes for the hinge screws first with a scratch awl.

BUILD & INSTALL THE ROOF

⑪ Make the roof peak: Crosscut a 9½-in.-long section of 1 × 6 first, so you'll have ample extra material for supporting the saw base when you cut the narrow peak to width. Lay out the long beveled edges of the peak so they taper from 2 in. on its top face to 1½ in. on its bottom face.

⑫ Bevel-rip the peak to shape with a jig saw: Set a bevel gauge to match the peak bevel angles, and use the gauge to adjust the saw base and blade to the same angle **(See Photo E)**. Cut the peak bevels.

⑬ Crosscut two boards for the roof sections: Lay out the beveled edges of each roof section according to the angles given in the *Roof Layout* drawing. Use a protractor to determine and mark the 17° and 35° beveled edges on the roof section boards, then set the saw base accordingly to bevel-rip the edges **(See Photo F)**.

⑭ Dry-fit the roof parts on the birdhouse to check the fit of the bevel joints. Sand or file the beveled edges to improve the fit and close the joints.

PHOTO E: Transfer bevel angles you've marked on the roof parts to your jig saw for setting up the cuts. A bevel gauge makes this process easy.

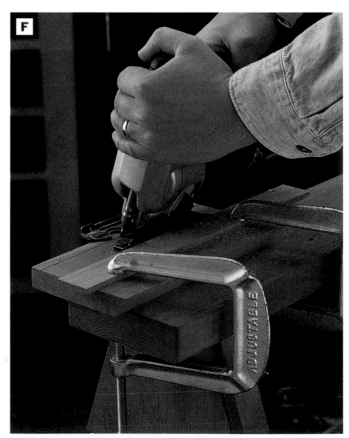

PHOTO F: Bevel-cut the edges of the roof sections and peak with a jig saw guided against a straightedge. Clamp the workpiece and straightedge to your worksurface to hold it steady while you cut.

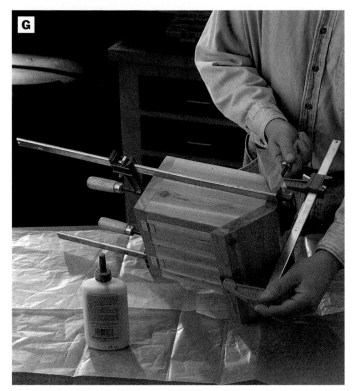

PHOTO G: Glue and clamp the roof parts together on the house assembly, then attach the roof with galvanized finish nails.

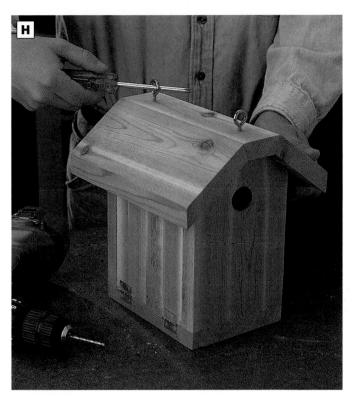

PHOTO H: Twist threaded eye hooks into pilot holes in the roof peak to prepare for hanging the project. Use a screwdriver to make turning the hooks easier.

15 Install the roof: Spread glue liberally on the mating edges of the roof parts as well as the top edges of the house front and back. Clamp the roof on the house so the roof overhangs the house evenly front to back (**See Photo G**). Drive 2-in. finish nails down through the roof parts into the house front and back to further secure the parts.

FINISHING TOUCHES

16 If you plan to hang the birdhouse, thread a pair of eye hooks into pilot holes in the roof peak, about 1½ in. in from the ends (**See Photo H**).

17 Form a "turnbuckle style" door latch by screwing a threaded "L" hook into an edge of the birdhouse back next to the door. Position the "L" hook so it holds the door closed when swivelled over the door.

18 Apply a protective topcoat of clear deck sealer, if you wish, to preserve the cedar's natural wood color.

HANGING INSTRUCTIONS

19 Hang the birdhouse from a sturdy tree limb, eave or other support at least 6 ft. from the ground. The house should be sheltered from prevailing winds.

Mounting option

If you'd rather mount this birdhouse to a post than hang it, drill pilot holes down through the bottom panel, and drive galvanized nails or a few screws into the post from inside the house. Another option is to attach the birdhouse to a post with small galvanized or brass angle brackets.

Basic Garden Bench

Garden benches come in many varieties, from rustic and casual to refined and formal. This casual bench is built from cedar, employing exposed screws in a construction style that's surely within the range of most weekend woodworkers. Like many of our plans, this project can be easily adapted. By simply changing the finish to bright paint or modifying the profile of the back, you'll have the perfect project to suit your personal taste or setting. It's a piece of furniture that can withstand the elements year-round and, after weathering outdoors for a bit, will look as natural in your garden as the primroses and petunias.

Vital Statistics: Basic Garden Bench

TYPE: Garden bench

OVERALL SIZE: 24½D by 59½L by 36H

MATERIAL: Cedar

JOINERY: Butt joints reinforced with galvanized deck screws

CONSTRUCTION DETAILS:
- Wide seat and modestly angled back ensure comfort
- Gentle contoured design on the back slats can be easily adapted to other shapes
- Exposed screws enhance rustic, outdoor appearance
- Assembly of three substructures—back, seat and leg/arm assemblies—simplifies construction

FINISHING OPTIONS: Penetrating UV protectant sealer or leave unfinished to weather naturally to gray

Building time

 PREPARING STOCK
0 hours

 LAYOUT
2-4 hours

 CUTTING PARTS
2-4 hours

 ASSEMBLY
4-6 hours

 FINISHING
2-3 hours

TOTAL: 10-17 hours

Tools you'll use

- Circular saw or power miter saw
- Jig saw
- Drill/driver
- Clamps
- Combination square
- Carpenter's square

Shopping list

- ☐ (1) 2 × 6 in. × 4 ft. cedar
- ☐ (5) 2 × 4 in. × 8 ft. cedar
- ☐ (1) 2 × 2 in. × 4 ft. cedar
- ☐ (1) 1 × 8 in. × 4 ft. cedar
- ☐ (2) 1 × 6 in. × 8 ft. cedar
- ☐ (1) 1 × 6 in. × 6 ft. cedar
- ☐ (3) 1 × 4 in. × 8 ft. cedar
- ☐ Galvanized deck screws (1½-, 2½-, 3-in.)
- ☐ UV protectant sealer

Basic Garden Bench

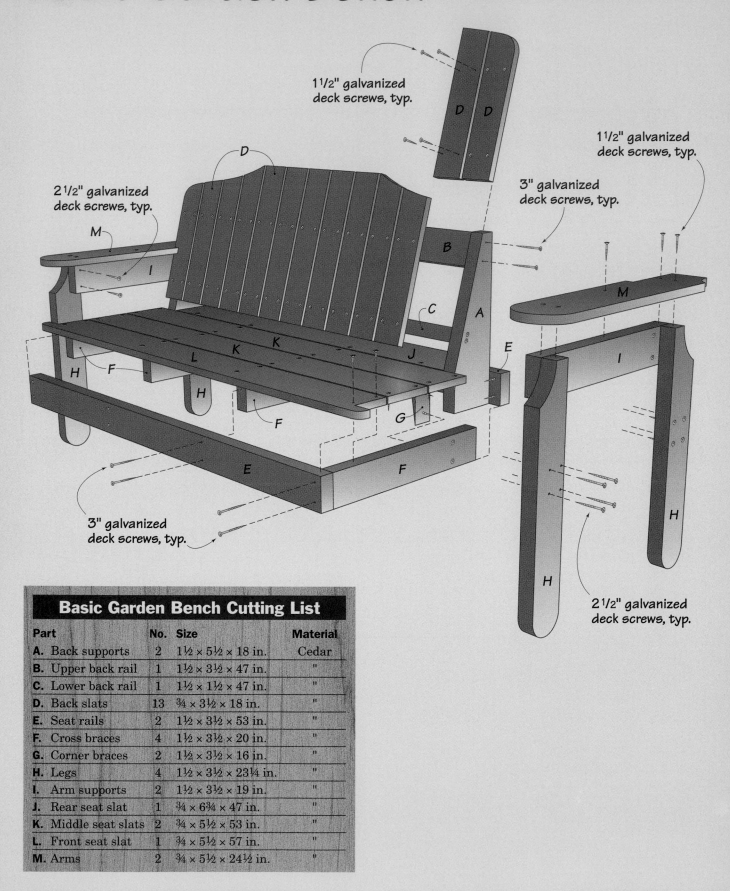

1½" galvanized deck screws, typ.

2½" galvanized deck screws, typ.

1½" galvanized deck screws, typ.

3" galvanized deck screws, typ.

3" galvanized deck screws, typ.

2½" galvanized deck screws, typ.

Basic Garden Bench Cutting List			
Part	**No.**	**Size**	**Material**
A. Back supports	2	1½ × 5½ × 18 in.	Cedar
B. Upper back rail	1	1½ × 3½ × 47 in.	"
C. Lower back rail	1	1½ × 1½ × 47 in.	"
D. Back slats	13	¾ × 3½ × 18 in.	"
E. Seat rails	2	1½ × 3½ × 53 in.	"
F. Cross braces	4	1½ × 3½ × 20 in.	"
G. Corner braces	2	1½ × 3½ × 16 in.	"
H. Legs	4	1½ × 3½ × 23¼ in.	"
I. Arm supports	2	1½ × 3½ × 19 in.	"
J. Rear seat slat	1	¾ × 6¾ × 47 in.	"
K. Middle seat slats	2	¾ × 5½ × 53 in.	"
L. Front seat slat	1	¾ × 5½ × 57 in.	"
M. Arms	2	¾ × 5½ × 24½ in.	"

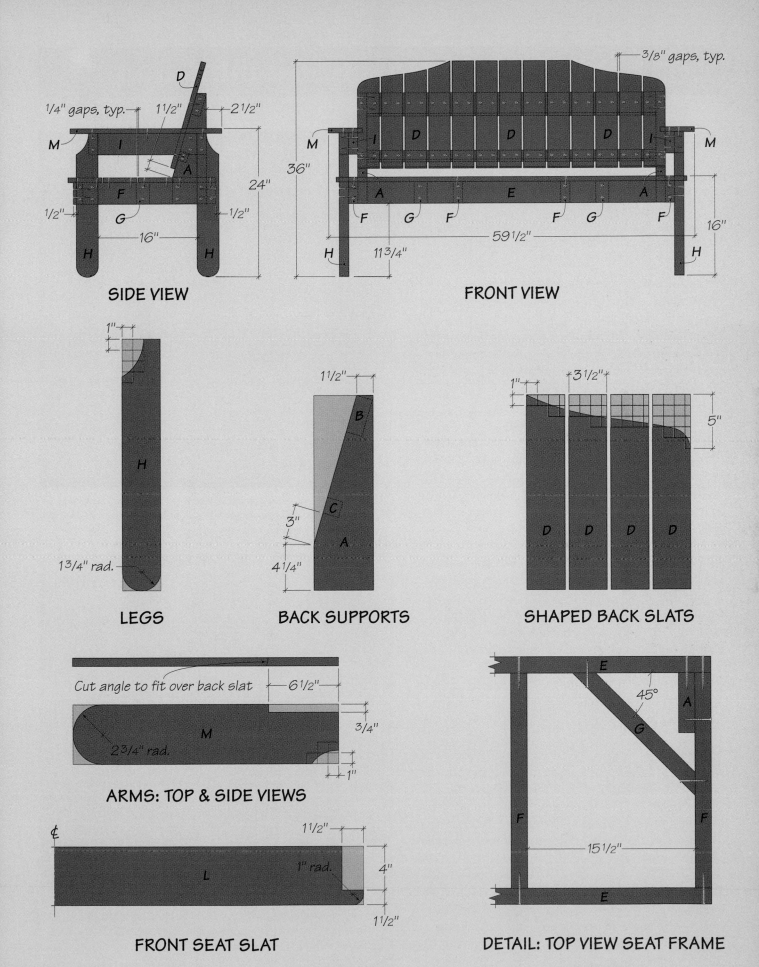

SIDE VIEW

1/4" gaps, typ.
1 1/2"
2 1/2"
24"
1/2"
1/2"
16"
M
I
D
A
F
G
H
H

FRONT VIEW

3/8" gaps, typ.
36"
59 1/2"
16"
11 3/4"
M
I
D
D
D
I
M
A
E
A
F
G
F
F
G
F
H
H

LEGS

1"
H
1 3/4" rad.

BACK SUPPORTS

1 1/2"
B
3"
C
A
4 1/4"

SHAPED BACK SLATS

1"
3 1/2"
5"
D
D
D
D

ARMS: TOP & SIDE VIEWS

Cut angle to fit over back slat
6 1/2"
M
3/4"
2 3/4" rad.
1"

DETAIL: TOP VIEW SEAT FRAME

E
45°
A
G
F
F
15 1/2"
E

FRONT SEAT SLAT

¢
1 1/2"
L
1" rad.
4"
1 1/2"

PHOTO A: Cut the back supports to length and lay out the angled edge on both supports. Clamp the supports to your worksurface and cut along the angled layout lines with a jig saw.

The styling of this bench is largely determined by the profiles of the shaped pieces—the back, arms and legs. With a little thought and planning, it's possible to change all these contours without affecting the basic construction methods or dimensions of the parts. Want to express yourself with something more whimsical? Let this be your chance.

BUILD THE BACK

1 Make the angled back supports. Cut the blanks to length from 2 × 6 cedar stock. Refer to the measurements on the *Back Supports* drawing, and mark the angles onto the back rests. Clamp each blank to your worksurface, and cut the angles with a jig saw **(See Photo A)**.

2 Install the upper and lower back rails on the back supports. Cut the upper and lower back rails to length. Clamp the rails between the back supports flush with their angled edges. The bottom rail is located 3 in. up from the bottom corner of the angled portion, and the upper rail aligns with the top angle corner. Use long clamps to hold the rails in place between the back supports while you drill countersunk pilot holes. Attach the parts with 3-in. galvanized deck screws.

3 Make the back slats. Cut the slats to length from 1 × 4 stock. Lay one slat in position on the back frame and mark the center of both back rails on the slat. These marks will serve as reference points for locating the screws. Line up all the slats next to one another and extend the rail reference marks across the faces of all the slats.

4 Attach the back slats. Position the two end slats, holding their outer edges flush with the outer faces of the back supports, and attach them with countersunk 1½-in. galvanized deck screws. Clamp a straightedge

PHOTO B: Establish slat positions by attaching the end slats flush to the outer edges of the back supports, then clamping a straightedge across the bottom. Use a long ⅜-in.-thick spacer to position the intermediate slats as you fasten them in place.

across the lower ends of the two slats to align the ends of the remaining slats. Use a long ⅜-in. spacer to establish consistent gaps between the slats, and fasten the slats to the rails with galvanized deck screws **(See Photo B)**.

5 Cut the profile on the back slats. You can create your own unique contour for the back, or create a hardboard template of the pattern provided in the *Shaped Back Slats* drawing. After drawing your profile along the top edge of the back slats, clamp the back assembly to your worksurface and cut the profile with a jig saw **(See Photo C)**. Sand the cut edges smooth.

BUILD & ATTACH THE SEAT FRAME

6 Cut the two seat rails and the four cross braces to length from 2 × 4 stock.

7 Assemble the seat frame. Clamp the cross braces in place between the rails, with the inner braces spaced 15½ in. from the end braces. Drill countersunk pilot holes and fasten the rails to the braces with 3-in. galvanized deck screws **(See Photo D)**.

8 Cut and attach the two corner braces. Cut the braces to length and miter-cut the ends to 45° **(See Photo E)**. Position the braces inside the back corners of the seat frame, drill countersunk pilot holes near the ends of the braces and attach the corner braces with 2½-in. galvanized deck screws.

9 Fasten the back assembly to the seat frame. Stand the back assembly upright and inside the seat frame so the back supports butt against the back corners of the seat frame. Drill countersunk

PHOTO C: Once you've marked the profile (either your own design or the one we've provided in the drawings) on the back slat assembly, trim along the profile lines and smooth the cut edges.

PHOTO D: Begin assembling the seat by clamping the end cross braces between the seat rails and positioning the inner two braces 15½ in. from the end braces. Fasten the rails to the braces with 3-in. galvanized deck screws.

PHOTO E: After cutting the two corner braces to length, miter-cut the ends to 45°. The corner braces will fit inside the seat frames between the rails and the end cross braces.

PHOTO F: Stand the back assembly inside the seat frame behind the corner braces. Drill countersunk holes through the end cross braces and attach the back to the seat frame with countersunk deck screws.

PHOTO G: Use a compass to lay out the rounded bottom ends of the legs. Make a small hardboard template to mark the top leg profile on all four legs. Then cut the leg profiles to shape.

PHOTO H: Clamp the leg assemblies to the seat/back assembly. The bottom edge of the seat frame should be 11¾ in. up from the bottoms of the legs and extend ½ in. beyond the front legs.

pilot holes through the outer cross braces into the supports. Attach the seat frame to the back supports with 2½-in. galvanized deck screws (**See Photo F**).

BUILD & ATTACH THE LEG ASSEMBLIES

🔟 Make the legs. Cut the legs to length, then lay out the leg profiles (**See Photo G**) following either the *Legs* pattern provided or your own personal design. Cut the legs to shape with your jig saw and sand the cut edges smooth.

⓫ Crosscut the arm supports to length and clamp them between the legs (be sure to orient the upper leg contours correctly). Drill countersunk pilot holes and attach the supports to the legs with 2½-in. galvanized deck screws. When you fasten these parts together, check the assemblies with a carpenter's square to be sure that the legs are perpendicular to the arm supports and are parallel with one another.

⓬ Fasten the leg assemblies to the seat frame. Clamp each leg assembly in place against the ends of the seat frame, so the bottom of the seat is 11¾ in. from the bottoms of the legs, and the front edges of the front legs are held back ½ in. from the front of the seat frame. The arm supports should be positioned on the inside, so they rest against the outside face of the back supports. Drill countersunk pilot holes and fasten the leg assemblies in place with 2½-in. galvanized deck screws driven through the legs into the seat frame (**See Photo H**) and through the arm supports into the back supports.

ATTACH THE SEAT SLATS & ARMS

13 Make and attach the seat slats. Rip the rear seat slat to width from 1 × 8 stock and cut it to length. Cut the middle slats to length from 1 × 6 stock. Cut the front seat slat to length, and notch the ends to fit around the front legs, as shown in the *Front Seat Slat* drawing. Sand the cut edges smooth. Lay the slats in position on the seat frame. The outside edge of the back seat slat should be flush with the back of the seat frame. Set the front slat so it notches around the front legs. Then space the two middle slats evenly between the outside slats. Drill countersunk pilot holes and attach the slats with 1½-in. galvanized deck screws (**See Photo I**).

14 Make and attach the arms. Cut the arms to length. Lay out the arm profiles and shape them with your jig saw. Note that you'll need to bevel-cut a portion of the arm rest notch at an angle to match the angle of the seat back. Sand the cut edges smooth. Position the arms on the tops of the leg assemblies, drill countersunk pilot holes, and fasten the arms with 1½-in. galvanized deck screws (**See Photo J**).

FINISHING TOUCHES

15 Sand all edges and surfaces well, and apply the finish of your choice—stain, paint or clear UV protectant sealer.

PHOTO I: Once the seat slats have been cut to length and, in the case of the rear slat, ripped to width, sand the slats smooth. Then drill countersunk holes and secure the slats to the seat frame with deck screws. The front slat will need to be notched and shaped before it is installed.

PHOTO J: Cut the arms to size and shape and fasten them to the arm supports with countersunk screws. You'll need to cut a small beveled notch on the back inside edges of the arms so the arms can butt tightly against the outermost back slats.

Formal Garden Bench

Here is an attractive interpretation of the classic mahogany garden bench you've possibly seen in formal gardens and city parks throughout the world. Its simple lines are elegant and restrained, its proportions are comfortable, and its construction is sturdy enough to last for generations. Due to the hidden-dowel joinery and plugged screws, this stately bench has no exposed metal to cause unsightly mineral streaks or to heat up in the sun. All you see and feel is the subtle beauty of natural wood.

Vital Statistics: Formal Garden Bench

TYPE: Garden bench

OVERALL SIZE: 23¼D by 58¼L by 35H

MATERIAL: Honduras mahogany

JOINERY: Butt joints reinforced with dowels or wood screws

CONSTRUCTION DETAILS:

· Concealed joints and fasteners refine traditional outdoor bench design

· Back slats and spacers fit into dado grooves in the back rails

· Seat supports and braces contoured to make seat slats a more comfortable surface on which to sit

FINISHING OPTIONS: Penetrating UV protectant sealer or leave unfinished and allow to weather naturally to gray

Building time

PREPARING STOCK
1-2 hours

LAYOUT
3-4 hours

CUTTING PARTS
4-6 hours

ASSEMBLY
6-8 hours

FINISHING
1-2 hours

TOTAL: 15-22 hours

Tools you'll use

· Table saw outfitted with a dado blade

· Band saw

· Power miter saw

· Drill press

· Doweling jig

· Drill/driver

· Router with ¼-in. roundover bit

· Flush-trimming saw

· Wooden mallet

· Pneumatic nail gun or hammer and nailset

· Clamps

· Combination square

· Trammel points or string compass

· Tape measure

Shopping list

☐ (1) 1¾ × 6 in. × 6 ft. Honduras mahogany

☐ (2) 1¾ × 2¾ in. × 8 ft. Honduras mahogany

☐ (2) 1¾ × 2 in. × 8 ft. Honduras mahogany

☐ (1) 1½ × 1½ in. × 4 ft. Honduras mahogany

☐ (1) ¾ × 2¾ in. × 4 ft. Honduras mahogany

☐ (7) ¾ × 2½ in. × 6 ft. Honduras mahogany

☐ (3) ¾ × 1¼ in. × 8 ft. Honduras mahogany

☐ Fluted dowels (⅜ × 2-in. and 5⁄16 × 1½-in.)

☐ Moisture-resistant wood glue

☐ Flathead wood screws (1½-in.)

Formal Garden Bench

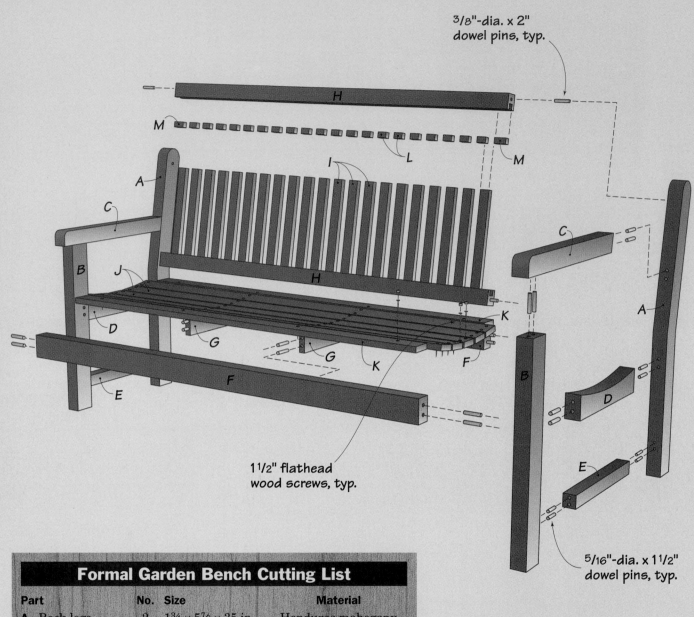

3/8"-dia. x 2" dowel pins, typ.

1¹/₂" flathead wood screws, typ.

5/16"-dia. x 1¹/₂" dowel pins, typ.

Formal Garden Bench Cutting List

Part	No.	Size	Material
A. Back legs	2	1¾ × 5⅞ × 35 in.	Honduras mahogany
B. Front legs	2	1¾ × 2¾ × 23¼ in.	"
C. Arm rests	2	1¾ × 2 × 20 in.	"
D. Seat supports	2	1¾ × 2¾ × 14½ in.	"
E. End stretchers	2	1½ × 1½ × 14½ in.	"
F. Stretchers	2	1¾ × 2¾ × 54½ in.	"
G. Braces	2	¾ × 2¾ × 14½ in.	"
H. Back rails	2	1¾ × 2 × 54½ in.	"
I. Back slats	21	¾ × 1¼ × 13¼ in.	"
J. Inner seat slats	5	¾ × 2½ × 58 in.	"
K. Outer seat slats	2	¾ × 2½ × 54½ in.	"
L. Short spacers	40	¾ × ¾ × 1¼ in.	"
M. Long spacers	4	¾ × ¾ × 1⅝ in.	"

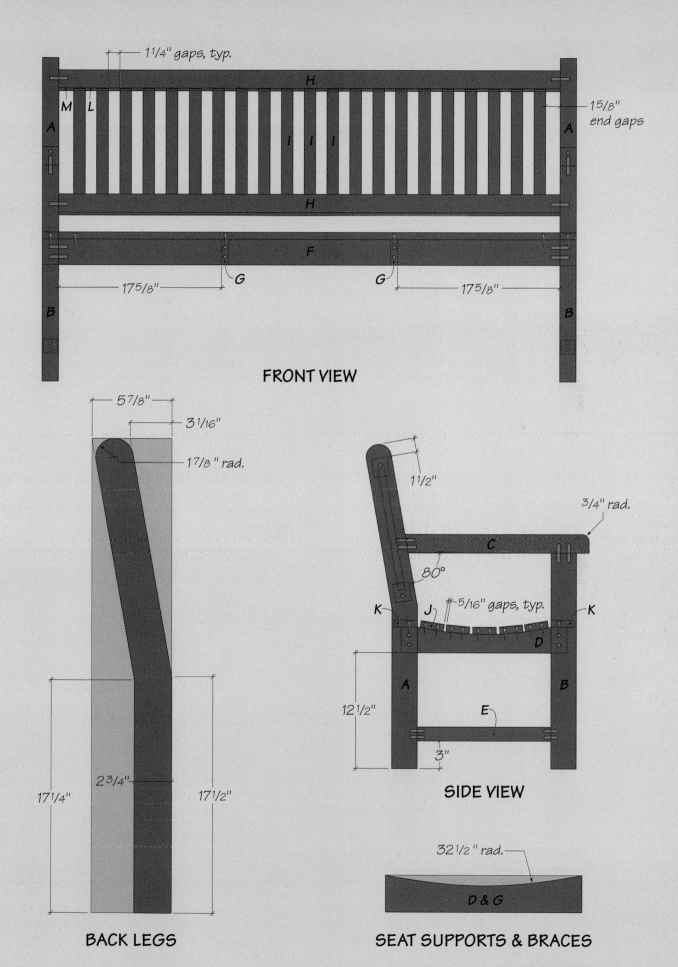

1 1/4" gaps, typ.

H

M L

A

1 5/8" end gaps

A

H

F

G   G

17 5/8"   17 5/8"

B   B

FRONT VIEW

5 7/8"

3 1/16"

1 7/8" rad.

1 1/2"

3/4" rad.

C

80°

K   5/16" gaps, typ.   K

J   D

A   B

12 1/2"   E

3"

2 3/4"

17 1/4"   17 1/2"

SIDE VIEW

BACK LEGS

32 1/2" rad.

D & G

SEAT SUPPORTS & BRACES

This bench is built entirely of Honduras mahogany, a very dense, finely-grained wood that has excellent natural durability in out-door settings and needs no finish. In order to get 1¾-in.-thick stock for this project, you'll likely have to buy 8/4 (2-in.) stock and plane it down to final thickness.

BUILD THE LEG ASSEMBLIES

1 Make the back legs. Refer to the *Back Legs* drawing to draw the back leg profiles onto 1¾-in. mahogany stock. Cut out the legs on your band saw **(See Photo A)**. Sand the cut edges.

2 Make the arm rests. Cut blanks to length and width. Bevel-cut the back ends to 10° and cut the top front corners to a ¾-in. radius. Rout a ¼-in. roundover on the top edges of the arms using a router and roundover bit.

3 Make the seat supports. Again, cut the blanks to length and width from 1¾-in. stock. Then mark the 32½-in.-radius arc on the top of the blanks with trammel points or a string compass, and cut out the profiles on a band saw.

4 Cut the front legs and end stretchers to length and width.

5 Mark the dowel locations. Lay the parts for the leg assemblies in

PHOTO A: Lay out and cut the back legs. A band saw works best for making uniform cuts in thick stock, like this mahogany. Feed the workpieces slowly through the blade, steering from both the side and the back to follow your layout lines.

PHOTO B: When all the pieces of the leg assemblies have been cut, shaped and sanded, position the parts and dry-clamp them together. Draw pairs of short lines across each joint to mark for drilling dowel holes.

place on a worksurface and clamp them together. Mark pairs of dowel hole locations across each joint to use as drilling references **(See Photo B)**.

6 Drill the dowel holes. Note that the dowels in the end stretchers are smaller than the others (5⁄16 × 1½ in.), because the proportions of these stretchers are smaller. Use a doweling jig as a guide **(See Photo C)**, and drill the holes ⅛ in. deeper than necessary in order to provide a little clearspace in the ends of the holes for glue.

7 Build the leg assemblies. Set aside the arms, which will be attached later. Insert glue-coated fluted dowels into the ends of the seat supports and the end stretchers. Drop a generous spot of glue into the dowel holes in the legs, and spread a thin layer of glue onto the mating surfaces of the wood. Clamp-up both leg assemblies **(See Photo D)**, using wood cauls to protect the leg surfaces from being marred by the clamps.

BUILD THE SEAT ASSEMBLY

8 Make the stretchers and braces. Cut all the pieces to length, then mark the 32½-in.-radius arc profiles on the braces and cut with a band saw. Sand the cuts smooth.

9 Mark and drill the ⅜-in.-dia. dowel holes. On the stretchers, mark the centerlines of the brace positions using the *Front View* drawing. Mark centerlines on the ends of the braces as well, from edge to edge. Mark matching dowel locations on the ends of the braces and the inside faces of the stretchers. Use a doweling jig to drill the pilot holes.

PHOTO C: Disassemble the clamped-up leg assemblies and extend the dowel reference lines across the ends of the workpieces. Drill holes with a doweling jig. Mark the bit depth with tape.

PHOTO D: Insert glue-covered dowels into the seat supports and stretchers, then coat the ends of the mating parts with glue and assemble the leg assemblies. Pull the joints tight with clamps.

PHOTO E: With the dowel joints of the braces and stretchers glued up, clamp the seat assembly and check for square by measuring the diagonals. Adjust as needed by repositioning the clamps.

PHOTO F: With a ¾-in.-wide dado blade installed on your table saw, set the height to ¾ in. and machine a groove, end to end, into one edge of both back rails. These will be the channels that accept the back slats and spacer blocks.

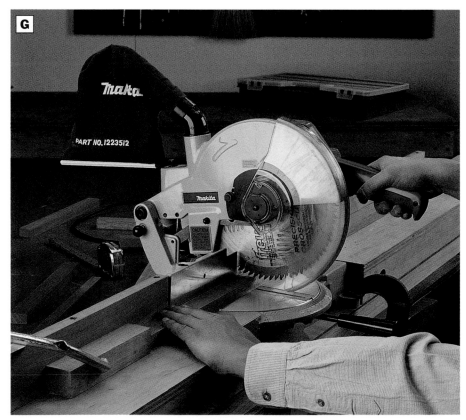

PHOTO G: A power miter saw makes quick work of cutting the back slats to a consistent length. Clamp a stopblock to the saw fence 13¼ in. from the blade, and cut the slats.

⑩ Build the seat assembly. Spread glue on the dowels and insert them into the braces. Spread glue onto the mating wood surfaces as well. Fit the stretchers and braces together, and clamp up the assembly. Before the glue sets, check the seat for square (**See Photo E**) by measuring corner-to-corner. If the diagonals are not equal, the assembly is out of square. Realign the parts by adjusting the clamps.

BUILD THE BACK ASSEMBLY
⑪ Make the back rails. Cut the rails to length from 1¾-in. stock. Set up your table saw with a dado blade, and cut a ¾ × ¾-in. groove down the center of one edge of both rails (**See Photo F**) to accept the back slats and spacers.

⑫ Make the back slats. Rip the slat stock to width on the table saw. Then clamp a stopblock to the fence of a power miter saw and use it as an index to crosscut all the slats to exactly the same length (**See Photo G**).

⑬ Make the short spacers. Rip a piece of ¾ × ¾-in. stock at least 6 ft. long. Crosscut the short spacers to length on the miter saw.

⑭ Install the slats and spacers in the bottom rail. It works best to start with the center slat and work toward the ends; this way, even if there are slight discrepancies in lengths of spacers or widths of slats, the end spaces will be equal and the slats will be accurately centered in the completed back assembly. Begin by measuring and marking the centerlines on the faces of the top and bottom rails. Stand the bottom rail on its edge, and lay a bead of wood glue along the bottom and sides of the groove. Apply a light coat of glue around the end of the center slat, and insert it into the groove at the center of the rail. Apply glue to the surfaces of two spacers, position one on each side of the first slat, and tack them in position with pin nails or finish nails. If you hammer the nails rather than install them with a pneumatic nail gun, recess the nailheads with a nailset. Install the remaining slats and spacers similarly (**See Photo H**). When you come to the end of the rails, measure, cut and insert the four long spacers.

⓯ Install the top rail. Lay a bead of glue onto the bottom and sides of the rail's groove. Position the rail over the ends of the slats and clamp lightly in place so you can still adjust the slats slightly if needed. Apply glue to the spacers and insert them between the slats (**See Photo I**), tacking them in place with nails. After all the spacers have been installed, check the back assembly for square. Clamp the assembly until the glue dries.

⓰ Clean up any dried glue that squeezed out of the joints with a sharp chisel.

ASSEMBLE THE BENCH
⓱ Drill dowel holes for connecting the three sub-assemblies—legs, seat and back. Refer to the *Side View* drawing for orienting the back and seat on the leg assemblies. Drill pairs of ⅜-in.-dia. holes for dowels to connect the back rails and seat stretchers to the bench legs. Dry-fit the bench together with dowels to check the fit of the parts. Then disassemble the sub-assemblies.

⓲ Make the seat slats. Cut the inner and outer slats to length, and ease the edges on one face of each slat with a router and ¼-in.

PHOTO H: Locate the position of the center seat slat in the bottom rail. Working from the middle toward each end, secure the slats and short spacers in the bottom rail with glue. Nail the spacers in place. We used a pneumatic nail gun and pin nails.

PHOTO I: Attach the top rail to the back assembly by applying glue along the three inside faces of the rail's groove and clamping. Install spacer blocks between the slats on this rail as well.

Formal Garden Bench 371

PHOTO J: After the rear seat slat has been attached, lay a leg assembly on the floor and set the back and seat into position. Then set the other leg assembly in place. Use glue and dowels in all the joints.

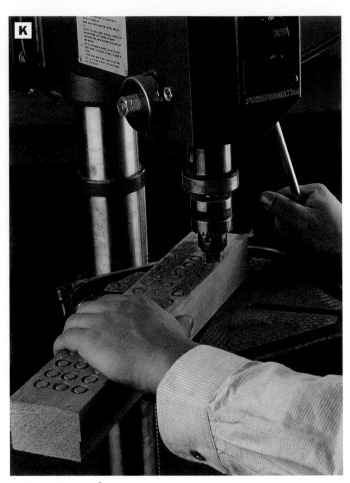

PHOTO K: Mount a ⅜-in. plug cutter in your drill press to cut wood plugs for the screws. Cut about 56 plugs into the face grain of a length of mahogany. Bore the plug cutter ½ in. deep into the wood.

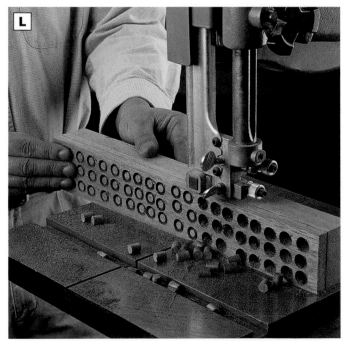

PHOTO L: Trim all the plugs to ⅞₆ in. long in one operation by cutting along the face of the plug area using a band saw. Doing so will release the plugs.

roundover bit. Measure and mark the centerlines of the attachment screws. Drill pilot holes along the guidelines that are counterbored ⅜ in., in order to install wood plugs above the screw heads.

⑲ Attach the rear slat to the back stretcher of the seat assembly. Install it so the front edge of the slat is flush with the inside edge of the back seat stretcher. This slat needs to be fastened now before the back assembly is installed. Otherwise the back will obstruct drill/driver access to drill and install screws.

⑳ Assemble the bench. Lay one end assembly on the floor. Put a spot of glue in the dowel holes. Insert glue-coated, fluted dowels into the ends of the back rails and seat stretchers, spread a thin layer of glue onto the mating surfaces of the joints, and position the back and seat on the end assembly. Apply glue to the remaining dowels and insert them into the other end of the rails and stretchers. Slip the other end assembly in place (**See Photo J**), and clamp the bench structure together.

㉑ Attach the remaining seat slats. Fasten the slats in place with countersunk 1½-in. flathead wood screws. Use a ⁵⁄₁₆-in. spacer to ensure uniform gaps between the inner slats.

㉒ Cut the screw plugs. You'll need approximately 56 wood plugs. Make them by mounting a plug cutter in your drill press and boring into the face grain of a single piece of mahogany stock (**See Photo K**). After boring for the plugs, cut along the mahogany slab ⁷⁄₁₆ in. in from the board's face with a band saw to cut the plugs free (**See Photo L**).

㉓ Install the plugs with glue, using a small brush. Insert plugs into the counterbores and seat them by tapping gently with a wooden mallet. When the glue dries, trim the plugs with a flush-cutting saw (**See Photo M**) and sand the plug areas smooth.

㉔ Attach the arm rest to the arm assembly. Insert glue-coated dowels into the arm rest, apply a thin layer of glue to the mating surfaces of the wood, and install the arm rests (**See Photo N**).

FINISHING TOUCHES

㉕ Go over the entire bench with sandpaper to smooth all surfaces.

㉖ You may apply UV-protectant sealer if desired. However, Honduras mahogany is usually left unfinished, as it weathers to a soft gray color that blends with natural garden settings.

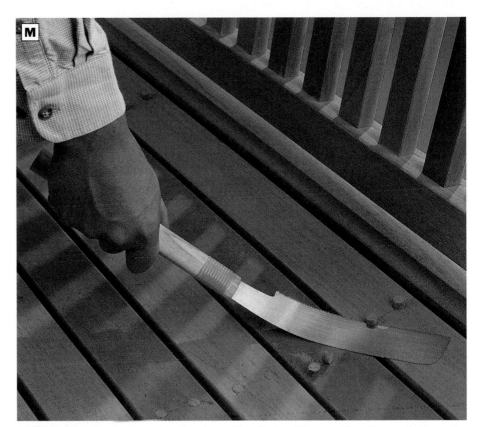

PHOTO M: After the glue dries, trim the plugs with a flush-cutting saw. Given the cup in the seat, use a flexible blade saw that can adjust to the contour of the slats. Be careful not to mar the seat slats as you trim against them.

PHOTO N: Glue dowels into holes drilled previously in the arm rest. Coat the mating surfaces with glue, then attach the arm rests to the end assemblies and tap into place with a wooden mallet.

Patio Table & Chairs

This patio table and chair set is significantly more formal than the traditional picnic table and benches, yet it is very easy to build. Made entirely of cedar for all-weather durability and beauty, this table will be the centerpiece of many memorable summer meals for you and your family. And if you need a table that is slightly larger, it's a simple matter to expand the table length and build a couple more chairs.

Vital Statistics: Patio Table & Chairs

TYPE: Patio table and chairs

OVERALL SIZE: Table: 48W by 48L by 30H
Chairs: 18W by 23L by 36½H

MATERIAL: Cedar

JOINERY: Butt joints reinforced with
galvanized deck screws

CONSTRUCTION DETAILS:
- Many parts on both the table and chairs are chamfered to minimize sharp edges
- Table aprons reinforced with corner braces to strengthen leg joints

FINISHING OPTIONS: Penetrating UV protectant sealer or leave unfinished to weather naturally to gray

Building time

 PREPARING STOCK
0 hours

 LAYOUT
3-4 hours

 CUTTING PARTS
2-3 hours

 ASSEMBLY
6-8 hours

 FINISHING
2-4 hours

TOTAL: 13-19 hours

Tools you'll use

- Table saw
- Power miter saw
- Router table and piloted chamfering bit
- Drill/driver
- Clamps
- Combination square

Shopping list

- ☐ (2) 4 × 4 in. × 6 ft. or (1) 4 × 4 in. × 10 ft. cedar
- ☐ (3) 2 × 8 in. × 10 ft. cedar
- ☐ (5) 2 × 6 in. × 8 ft. cedar
- ☐ (4) 2 × 4 in. × 8 ft. cedar
- ☐ (9) 1 × 4 in. × 8 ft. cedar
- ☐ (4) 1 × 2 in. × 6 ft. cedar
- ☐ Galvanized deck screws (2-, 2½-in.)
- ☐ Finishing materials

Patio Table & Chairs

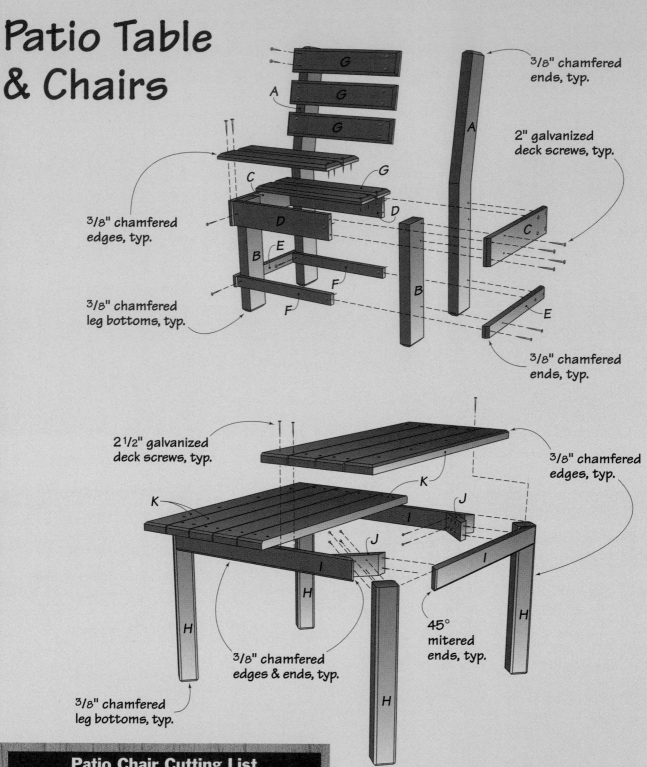

3/8" chamfered ends, typ.

2" galvanized deck screws, typ.

3/8" chamfered edges, typ.

3/8" chamfered leg bottoms, typ.

3/8" chamfered ends, typ.

2 1/2" galvanized deck screws, typ.

3/8" chamfered edges, typ.

3/8" chamfered edges & ends, typ.

45° mitered ends, typ.

3/8" chamfered leg bottoms, typ.

Patio Chair Cutting List

Part		No.	Size	Material
A.	Back legs	2	1½ × 7¼ × 36½ in.	Cedar
B.	Front legs	2	1½ × 3½ × 16½ in.	"
C.	Upper frame sides	2	¾ × 3½ × 17½ in.	"
D.	Upper frame ends	2	¾ × 3½ × 16 in.	"
E.	Lower frame sides	2	¾ × 1½ × 17½ in.	"
F.	Lower frame ends	2	¾ × 1½ × 16 in.	"
G.	Slats	7	¾ x 3½ × 18 in.	"

Patio Table Cutting List

Part		No.	Size	Material
H.	Legs	4	3½ × 3½ × 28½ in.	Cedar
I.	Aprons	4	1½ × 3½ × 38 in.	"
J.	Braces	4	1½ × 3½ × 9⅛ in.	"
K.	Top slats	9	1½ × 5⅛ × 48 in.	"

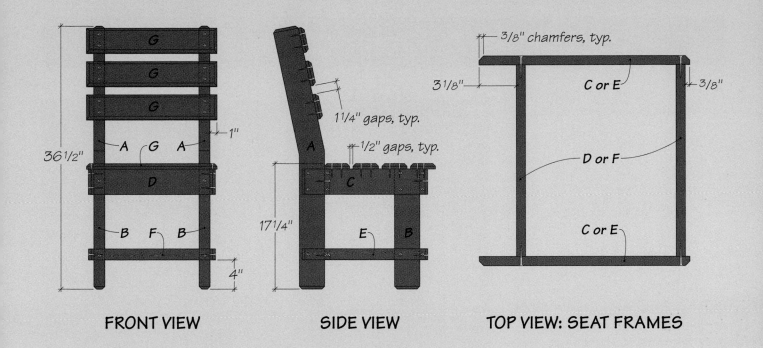

FRONT VIEW

SIDE VIEW

TOP VIEW: SEAT FRAMES

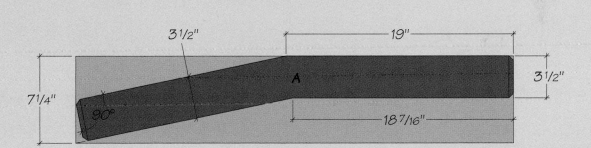

BACK LEGS

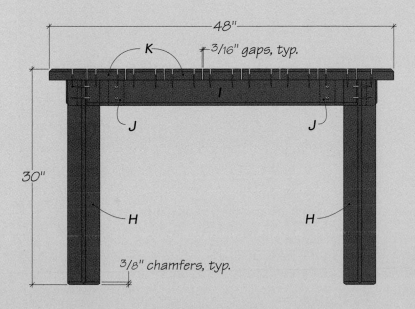

FRONT VIEW

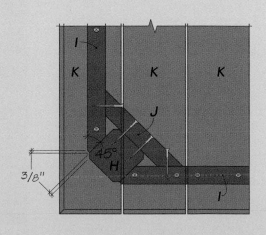

TOP VIEW: CORNER DETAIL

BUILD THE CHAIRS

Since you're building four identical chairs, cut parts for all the chairs and build them simultaneously. In this situation, make sure your measurements are accurate before cutting all the pieces.

❶ Make the back legs. Cut blanks to length from 2 × 8 stock, and lay out the legs **(See Photo A)** following the measurements in the *Back Legs* drawing. Cut out the back legs with a jig saw. After cutting the legs to shape, chamfer the top and bottom ends of the legs, using a router table with a piloted chamfering bit set to ⅜ in.

❷ Build the upper and lower seat frames. The construction of both frames is identical, but the width of the parts is different. Cut the upper and lower side and end pieces to size for both frames. Rout ⅜-in. chamfers along the outside ends of the side pieces. Clamp each frame together using the *Top View: Seat Frames* drawing as a guide for positioning the parts. Drill countersunk pilot holes through the sides, and fasten the frames together with 2-in. galvanized deck screws **(See Photo B)**.

❸ Make the front legs. Cut the legs to length from 2 × 4 stock, and chamfer all four edges of the bottom ends of each leg.

PHOTO A: Lay out and cut eight back chair legs to shape. Use the *Back Legs* drawing to establish reference points for drawing the leg shapes. Connect the points with a straightedge.

PHOTO B: Build an upper and lower frame for each chair. Note that the end pieces of each frame are inset ⅜ in. and 3⅛ in. from the ends of the side pieces. Clamp the frame parts together, and drive 2-in. galvanized deck screws through the sides and into the ends to make the frames.

4 Screw the legs and frames together. Attach the frames to the back legs first, with the top edge of the upper frame 16½ in. above the leg bottom. Place the bottom frame 4 in. from the leg bottom. Then clamp the front legs in position inside the front corners of both frames, and fasten with galvanized deck screws **(See Photo C)**.

5 Make the slats. All the slats are the same length and shape, but the position of the attachment screws is different between the back slats and the seat slats. Cut the slats to length from 1 × 4 stock, and chamfer all four edges of one side. Designate 12 slats (three per chair) as back slats, and mark centerlines for the attachment screws. These back slats will attach to the back legs. Next, measure and mark centerlines for the attachment screws in the seat slats. These slats fasten to the upper frame sides. Drill countersunk pilot holes along the lines in all the slats, two screws per joint.

6 Attach the slats. Align the top edge of the uppermost back slat as shown in the *Front* and *Side View* drawings, and leave 1¼-in. spaces between the slats. Leave ½-in. spaces between the seat slats, with the rear seat slat held tight against the back legs. Fasten the slats with countersunk galvanized deck screws **(See Photo D)**.

BUILD THE TABLE

All visible corners and ends of the table legs, aprons and slats are chamfered. Although you can use a hand-held router and a piloted chamfering bit, a router table makes the task quicker and easier. Chamfers for all parts are cut at the same ⅜-in. height setting.

PHOTO C: Attach the upper and lower frames to the back and front legs with countersunk screws.

Spacer

PHOTO D: To create uniform slat spacing, use a ³⁄₁₆-in. spacer for positioning the seat slats and a 1¼-in. spacer for the back slats. Start the back slats at the bottom of the back leg angle. Install the seat slats so the back seat slat butts against the back legs.

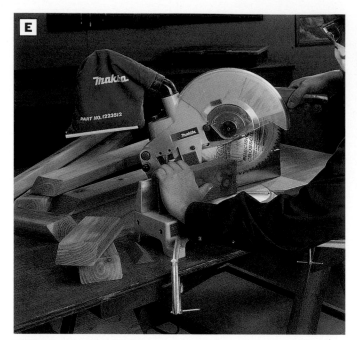

PHOTO E: Miter-cut the ends of the leg braces and table aprons to 45°. The safest way to make these cuts, particularly on the short leg braces, is to use a power miter saw or table saw rather than a circular saw.

PHOTO F: The bottom edge and both ends of each apron piece are chamfered. Make these cuts at the router table, using a piloted chamfering bit set to a height of ⅜ in.

PHOTO G: Assemble the table legs, aprons and corner braces. Attach the parts by driving 2½-in. galvanized deck screws through countersunk pilot holes in the leg braces. Fasten the brace to each apron with a pair of screws driven in at an angle into the aprons, and use four screws for securing the leg. Be sure the legs are tight against the aprons and braces as you drive the screws.

7 Make the legs. Cut the legs to length from 4 × 4 stock. Chamfer all four long edges and the edges of the leg bottoms.

8 Make the aprons and braces. Cut the aprons and braces to length, and miter-cut the ends at 45° (**See Photo E**). When mitering these parts, use extra care to cut accurately.

9 Chamfer one edge and both ends on one face of each apron (**See Photo F**). Since the apron ends are mitered, there is less surface to guide against the router table fence when chamfering. One solution is to clamp the aprons together with the ends flush and rout all the ends in one pass. NOTE: *If you are using a hand-held router, the mitered ends don't provide a surface for the chamfer bit bearing to guide against. Clamp the aprons together on your worksurface, with the ends flush. Position and clamp a straightedge across the aprons to use as a guide for the router base before making the cuts.*

⑩ Assemble the table legs, aprons and braces. First drill six countersunk pilot holes in the braces—four holes for attaching the leg and two holes angled at each end for the aprons, as shown in the *Top View: Corner Detail* drawing. Stand the legs upside down on the floor or your worksurface, position the aprons and braces around each leg, and attach the parts with galvanized deck screws **(See Photo G)**.

⑪ Make the nine top slats. Cut the slats to length, and rip them to width on the table saw **(See Photo H)**. Chamfer the outer edge of the two end slats on your router table. Chamfer the top edges of the ends of the slats.

⑫ Drill pilot holes in the slats. Lay a slat across the table structure, with an equal overhang on both ends. Mark the centerpoint of the aprons on the edge of the slat and transfer these marks to the face of the slat. Use this first slat as a guide to mark screw locations on all the slats. Drill countersunk pilot holes along the guidelines on all the slats, two holes per joint.

⑬ Attach the slats. Determine the centerline of the table and install the center slat over this line. Use two $3/16$-in.-thick spacers to establish the slat gaps. Install slats out from the center slat, fastening each with galvanized deck screws **(See Photo I)**.

FINISHING TOUCHES

⑭ Sand the table and chairs well to smooth the surfaces and edges. Make sure all screws are countersunk below the surface of the wood.

⑮ Apply a clear UV protectant sealer or leave unfinished to weather naturally to gray.

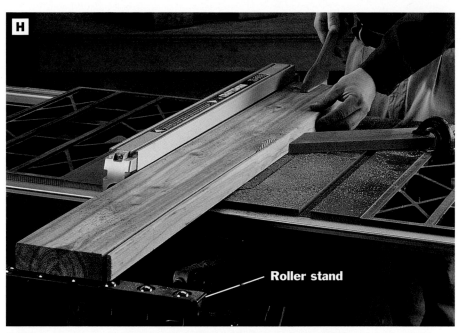

PHOTO H: Rip-cut 2 × 6 stock down to a width of 5⅛ in. to form the tabletop slats. You could make these cuts with a circular saw and straightedge guide, but a better choice is to use the table saw and rip fence. Support workpieces with a roller stand as they leave the saw table.

PHOTO I: Attach the top slats to the aprons with 2½-in. deck screws. Fasten the center slat first, then work outward. This way, the overhang will be consistent on both ends of the table, and the slats will be evenly positioned. Use a pair of 3/16-in. spacers to create uniform gaps between the slats.

Tile-Top BBQ Center

Can't you just smell the charcoal already? Outdoor cooking is often the centerpiece of summer gatherings, and when you get together with family and friends for barbecued ribs, grilled steaks or juicy burgers, this attractive outdoor grilling accessory will make the chef's job so efficient that he or she will be able to enjoy the conversation as well. Then, if the conversation lags, you can casually let people know that you built this versatile cart yourself, in just a weekend's worth of time. Impression guaranteed.

Vital Statistics: Tile-Top BBQ Center

TYPE: Tile-top BBQ center

OVERALL SIZE: 26⅞W by 44¼L by 35½H

MATERIAL: Cedar, ceramic tile

JOINERY: Butt joints reinforced with galvanized screws

CONSTRUCTION DETAILS:
- Ceramic tiles laid on exterior plywood subbase
- Integral handle and wheels for easy moving
- Recessed condiment shelf

FINISHING OPTIONS: Penetrating UV protectant sealer, exterior paint or leave unfinished and allow to weather naturally to gray

Building time

PREPARING STOCK
0 hours

LAYOUT
1-2 hours

CUTTING PARTS
2-3 hours

ASSEMBLY
5-6 hours

FINISHING
2-3 hours

TOTAL: 10-14 hours

Tools you'll use

- Circular saw
- Power miter saw
- Compass
- Jig saw
- Drill/driver
- Clamps
- Hammer, nailset
- Combination square
- Tiling tools (¼-in. notched trowel, grout float, sponge)
- Hack saw

Shopping list

- ☐ (1) ¾-in. × 4 × 4 ft. exterior plywood
- ☐ (1) ¾-dia. × 24-in. hardwood dowel
- ☐ (2) 2 × 6 in. × 8 ft. cedar
- ☐ (1) 2 × 4 in. × 6 ft. cedar
- ☐ (2) 1 × 6 in. × 8 ft. cedar
- ☐ (2) 1 × 6 in. × 6 ft. cedar
- ☐ Galvanized deck screws (2-, 3-in.)
- ☐ 6d galvanized finish nails
- ☐ (48) 4¼ × 4¼ in. glazed ceramic tiles
- ☐ Thin-set mortar, tile grout
- ☐ (2) 6-in.-dia. wheels; ½-in.-dia. × 24-in. steel rod, washers, cotter pins
- ☐ UV protectant sealer

Tile-Top BBQ Center

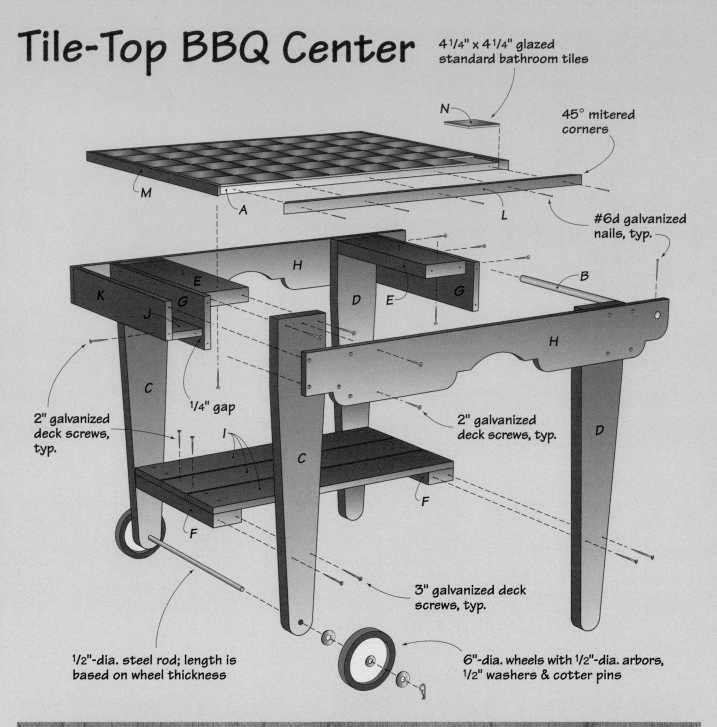

4 1/4" x 4 1/4" glazed standard bathroom tiles

45° mitered corners

#6d galvanized nails, typ.

N

M

A

L

E

H

K

J

G

C

D

E

G

H

B

D

2" galvanized deck screws, typ.

1/4" gap

I

C

F

2" galvanized deck screws, typ.

F

3" galvanized deck screws, typ.

1/2"-dia. steel rod; length is based on wheel thickness

6"-dia. wheels with 1/2"-dia. arbors, 1/2" washers & cotter pins

Tile-Top BBQ Center Cutting List

Part	No.	Size	Material	Part	No.	Size	Material
A. Plywood subtop	1	¾ × 26⅛ × 34⅞ in.	Exterior plywood	G. End aprons	2	¾ × 5½ × 20 in.	Cedar
B. Handle	1	¾ dia. × 21½ in.	Hardwood dowel	H. Side aprons	2	¾ × 5½ × 44¼ in.	"
C. Front legs	2	1½ × 5½ × 32⅞ in.	Cedar	I. Shelf slats	3	¾ × 5½ × 31¾ in.	"
D. Back legs	2	1½ × 5½ × 34½ in.	"	J. Condiment shelf	1	¾ × 3½ × 20 in.	"
E. Upper crosspieces	2	1½ × 5½ × 17 in.	"	K. Condiment front	1	¾ × 4 × 20 in.	"
F. Lower crosspieces	2	1½ × 3½ × 17 in.	"	L. Top side edging	2	¾ × 1 × 36⅜ in.	"
				M. Top end edging	2	¾ × 1 × 27⅝ in.	"
				N. Tiles	48	¼ × 4¼ × 4¼ in.	Glazed bathroom tile

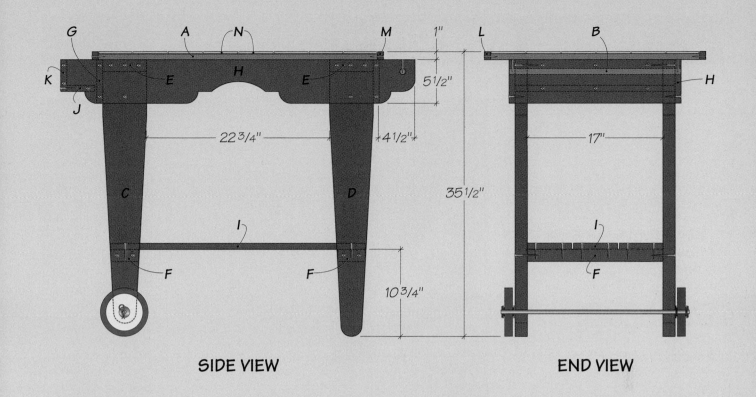

SIDE VIEW

END VIEW

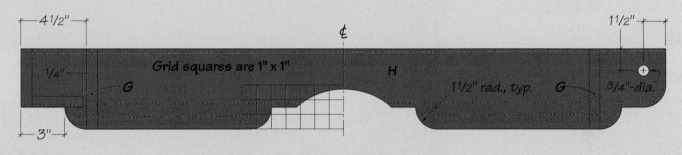

Grid squares are 1" x 1"

SIDE APRONS

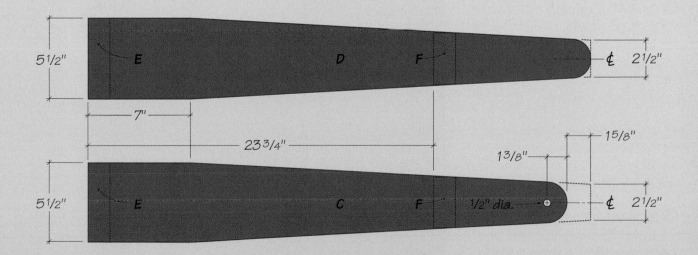

FRONT & BACK LEGS

PHOTO A: Once you've cut the leg tapers and shortened the front legs, mark and cut the rounded feet with a jig saw. Clamp each leg to your workbench to make sawing the feet easier.

BUILD THE LEG ASSEMBLIES

1 Crosscut the legs to size. Cut identical blanks for all four legs, even though the front legs will eventually be shortened to allow clearance for the wheels.

2 Measure and mark the location of the lower crosspieces on the inside faces of the legs. Position the upper face of the crosspieces 10¾ in. from the bottom of the legs. Extend the marks across the legs with a combination square.

3 Cut identical tapers on all four legs (See *Front & Back Legs* drawings). The tapers begin 7 in. from the tops of the legs and reduce them to 2½ in. at the bottom. Draw the foot radius on the two back legs with a compass.

4 Cut 1⅝ in. off the bottom ends of the front legs, then mark for the 1⅜-in. foot radius. When you draw the foot radii, the pivot point for the compass marks the center-point of the wheel axle.

5 Clamp each leg to your work-surface and cut the curved foot profiles on all four legs with a jig saw **(See Photo A)**.

6 Bore the ½-in.-dia. axle hole in the front legs. You may want to mount your drill in a right-angle drilling guide to ensure that these axle holes are straight.

PHOTO B: Fasten the legs to the upper and lower crosspieces with deck screws. Position the upper faces of the lower crosspieces so they are 10¾ in. from the bottoms of the legs.

❼ Cut the upper and lower cross-pieces to length. Set the cross-pieces between the legs, and hold the parts in place with clamps. Drill countersunk pilot holes through the legs into the cross-pieces, and attach the legs to the crosspieces with 3-in. galvanized deck screws **(See Photo B)**.

CUT THE REMAINING PARTS

Cedar is commonly sold smooth on one side and rough on the other. For the 1× apron, slat and condiment parts, you could choose to have the rough side facing out or in, depending upon the surface appearance you prefer. Building the cart with workpieces facing smooth-side out will lead to fewer splinters later and will be easier to keep clean.

❽ Make the side aprons. Cut the two apron blanks to length. Transfer the side apron profile (See *Side Aprons* drawing) to one of the blanks, and mark the centerpoint of the handle dowel hole. Stack the marked blank on top of the unmarked one with the edges aligned, and clamp the blanks together on your worksurface. Gang-cut the profile on both aprons at once with your jig saw. Sand the cut edges smooth.

❾ Bore the ¾-in.-dia. handle dowel holes while the side aprons are still clamped together.

❿ Cut the end aprons, shelf slats, and handle dowel to length.

⓫ Cut the condiment shelf and front to size. First rip 1 × 6 stock to width (See *Cutting List*), then cut the pieces to length.

PHOTO C: Attach the end aprons to the legs, then turn the leg assemblies upside-down and fasten the side aprons in place. Hold the parts in position with clamps while you drive the screws.

PHOTO D: Fasten the shelf slats in position, then attach the condiment shelf and front to the side aprons. Leave a ¼-in. gap between the condiment shelf and the end apron (See *Side Aprons* drawing) to allow for water drainage. Use 2-in. galvanized deck screws on these parts.

PHOTO E: Arrange rows of tiles to determine the length and width of the tile top. NOTE: *You may need to space the tiles to allow for grout lines if your tiles don't have self-spacing nubs on the edges.* The overall dimensions will establish the size of the plywood subtop.

PHOTO F: Spread a layer of thin-set mortar over the subtop using a ¼-in. notched trowel. Press the tiles into the mortar in a systematic fashion, working out from one corner both lengthwise and widthwise. Keep watch on your tile spacing to ensure that all the tiles will fit on the subtop.

ASSEMBLE THE WORKSTATION

⓬ Attach the end aprons to the leg assemblies with 2-in. galvanized deck screws. Fasten the parts by screwing through the end aprons and into the upper crosspieces and legs. NOTE: *Make sure that the longer back legs are at the same end of the aprons as the handle dowel holes.*

⓭ Fasten the side aprons to the leg assemblies. Stand leg assemblies upside-down on your work surface with the end aprons facing out. Clamp the side aprons in place so they extend 4½ in. beyond the the end aprons on both ends of the cart. Drill countersunk pilot holes, and attach the side aprons to the leg assemblies with 2-in. screws, four screws per joint (**See Photo C**).

⓮ Install the shelf slats. Stand the workstation right-side-up on the floor. Put a 1½-in.-thick board under the shorter front legs to hold the workstation approximately level. Position the shelf slats so their ends are flush with the outer edges of the lower crossbraces and there are equal gaps between the slats. Drill countersunk pilot holes through the slats and into the lower crosspieces, and fasten the slats in place.

⓯ Attach the condiment shelf and front pieces. Start by drilling countersunk pilot holes in the side aprons on the end opposite the cart handle. Position the shelf ¾ in. from the ends of the side aprons to allow space for attaching the condiment front. Make sure there is about a ¼-in. gap between the shelf and the end apron to allow for water drainage. Fasten the shelf between the side aprons with 2-in. screws. Install the front by attaching it to the side aprons and the shelf with 2-in. screws **(See Photo D)**.

BUILD THE TOP

The sizes of the plywood top and edging are based on the assumption that the tiles are 4¼ in. square and grout lines between the tiles are all ⅛ in. We did not leave a distinct grout line between the tile and the edging because this is an outdoor project, and the wood edging will expand and contract with changes in humidity. If you use a different size tile, you will need to modify the overall size of the top. Be sure to also factor in the space needed for grout lines.

16 Determine the plywood top size by laying out lines of tiles to mark the length and width of the workstation top **(See Photo E)**. Cut the plywood subtop to size, taking care that it is square.

17 Fasten the top to the workstation. Position the subtop so there is an even overhang all around, and attach it with 2-in. screws driven through the upper crosspieces from below (attaching the top from below allows you the option of removing the top later on without destroying the tile).

18 Apply an even layer of thin-set mortar to the subtop with a ¼-in. notched trowel. Be sure to wear gloves when working with mortar or grout.

19 Set the tiles into the mortar **(See Photo F)**. If you are not an experienced tile setter and your tiles are not self-spacing, we recommend starting at one corner of the top and setting one line of tile across the width and one line across the length. This allows you to verify the exact size of the grout lines, since it will be easier to

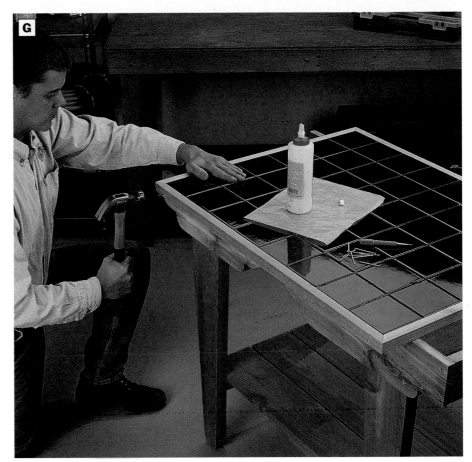

PHOTO G: Wrap the tile top with ¾ × 1-in. cedar edging, mitering the corners. Fasten the edging pieces with wood glue and 6d galvanized finish nails, nailing into the plywood subtop. Then recess the nailheads with a nailset.

adjust the positioning of these first few guide tiles, if need be, than to reposition the whole top-full of tiles. Press the tiles firmly into the thin-set mortar to ensure that they seat fully and will not come loose. Allow the mortar to dry thoroughly before continuing to finish the top.

20 Make and install the edging. Rip ¾ × 1-in. strips from 1 × 6 stock, and crosscut the edging to length. Miter-cut the ends to 45°. Drill pilot holes, and attach the edging to the edges of the subtop with glue and #6d galvanized finish nails **(See Photo G)**. Recess the nailheads with a nailset.

21 Apply the grout. Select a grout color that complements your tile; generally speaking, darker grout

shows spotting and stains much less than lighter-colored grout. Mix powdered grout according to the manufacturer's instructions to produce a relatively dry mixture that retains its shape when you ball it in your hand. Protect the top surface of the wood edging with masking tape.

22 Spread grout across the tiles and into the joints, using a grout float **(See Photo H)**. Work diagonally across the tabletop to avoid digging the grout out of some joints as you fill others.

23 Wipe away the excess grout. Again working with diagonal strokes, use a sponge to remove the excess grout from the tile surface **(See Photo I)**. Rinse the sponge frequently and get the top

PHOTO H: Press grout into the gaps between the tiles using a grout float. Work diagonally across the surface, pulling the float toward you as you go. Working diagonally helps to minimize the chances of accidentally pulling grout out of the gaps you've already filled.

PHOTO I: Remove excess grout and smooth the grout lines with a water-dampened sponge. Again, work diagonally. Continue wiping the tiles, rinsing the sponge and wringing it out until the tiles are clean. Wipe away haze left by the grout with a soft cloth.

clean before the grout has a chance to fully set. As the grout dries, any grout residue will appear as a hazy film on the tiles. Wipe them clean with a soft, dry cloth.

INSTALL THE WHEELS

㉔ Cut the ½-in.-dia. axle rod to length with a hack saw. To accommodate the washers and cotter pins, the axles must extend beyond the legs ¾-in. plus the thickness of the wheel hub on each side. Wheel hub dimensions will vary. Thus, if your wheel hubs are 1-in. thick, the axles need to be at least 23½-in. long.

㉕ Drill holes in the axle for the cotter pins. To do this easily, make a wooden cradle by cutting a V-shaped groove into the face of a 8- to 12-in. piece of 2 × 4 with two passes of your saw set at a 45° angle. Fasten the grooved 2 × 4 to a slightly larger piece of ¾-in.

scrap. Clamp the cradle to your drill press table to support the axle while you drill it. Set the axle in the groove and drill a ⅛-in. hole through the axle near (verify the exact position) each end of the rod **(See Photo J)**. TIP: *Use a slow speed setting on the drill press and lubricate the bit with a drop of light machine oil to keep the bit from overheating.*

26 Install the wheels. Slide the axle into place on the legs, slip washers onto the axle next to the legs to serve as spacers, slide the wheels and another set of washers onto the axle, and insert the cotter pins to lock the wheels in place **(See Photo K)**.

FINISHING TOUCHES

27 Check that all nailheads are set and all screw heads are countersunk slightly below the surface of the wood. You can either fill nail- and screw head recesses with wood putty or simply leave the heads exposed for a more rustic appearance.

28 Sand all exposed surfaces and edges, then apply the finish of your choice. We used a clear penetrating exterior wood sealer with good UV protection in order to retain and highlight the natural beauty of the wood. Depending on the tile you've selected for your top, you could elect to paint the workstation for a more dramatic look. Or, as with any cedar furniture, you may leave it unfinished and let it weather to a silvery gray.

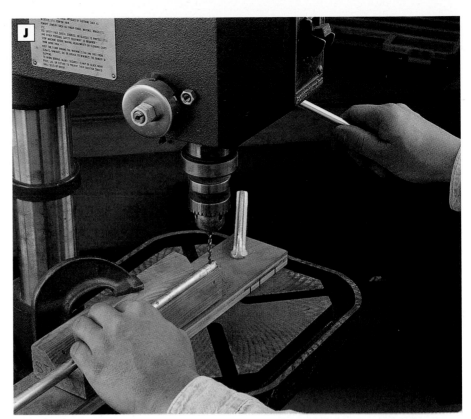

PHOTO J: Cut a V-shaped notch in a scrap of 2 × 4 to help steady the axle as you drill holes for cotter pins. Fasten the notched cradle to another scrap, and clamp the jig to the drill press table. Drill through the rod using a slow speed setting and firm—but not excessive—force on the bit.

PHOTO K: Insert the axle through the holes in the front legs, then install washers, wheels and cotter pins to secure the wheels. The washers next to the cotter pins keep the wheels from rubbing against the cotter pins as the wheels turn.

Kid-Size Picnic Table

Children are sure to enjoy this piece of picnic furniture built especially for them. Made of cedar, the project is sized so four children can sit comfortably. Whether you put the table outdoors or bring it inside, it may well become the kids' favorite spot for lunch and dinner. And with no sharp corners or free-standing, tippy benches to cause injuries, you can rest easily, too.

Kid-Size Picnic Table: Step-by-step

LAY OUT & CUT THE FRAME PARTS

1 Crosscut the legs, top and seat stringers and stretcher to length. Cedar is easy to cut with a jig saw, but you'll get straighter cuts using a circular saw.

2 Lay out the legs: Refer to the *Leg Layout* drawing to mark one end of each leg for cutting the top angle. To mark the legs for curved feet, set your compass to a 1¾-in. radius, and determine the center-point of the arc on all four legs. Draw the curved feet.

PHOTO A: Lay out the legs and stringers. Scribe the curved end of the legs and the curves on the stringers with a compass, set to the radii given in the technical drawings.

Kid-Size Picnic Table

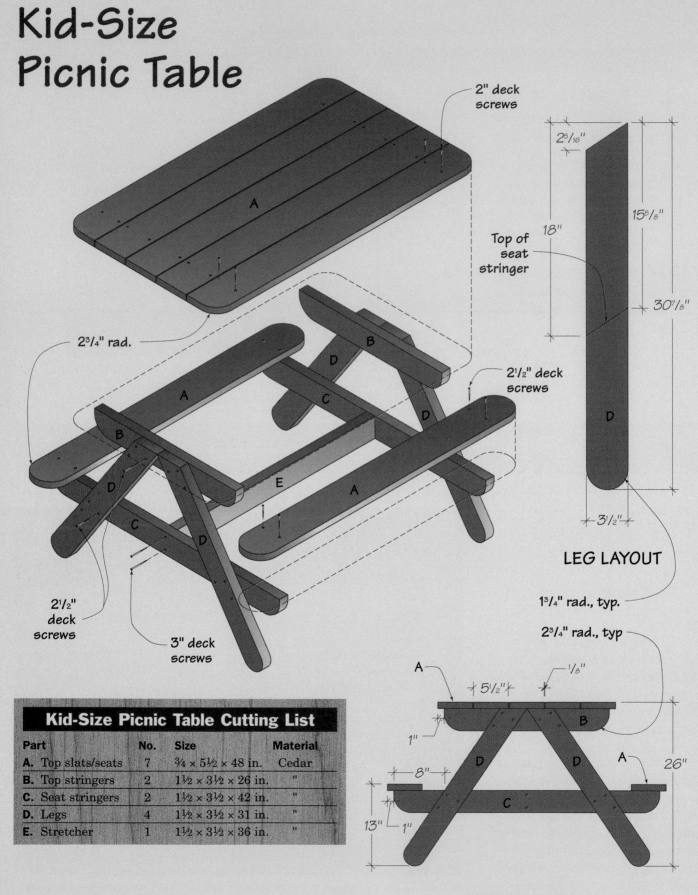

2" deck screws

2⁵⁄₁₆"

18"

15⁵⁄₈"

Top of seat stringer

30⁷⁄₈"

2¾" rad.

2½" deck screws

A

B

D

C

D

A

B

D

E

A

D

D

3½"

LEG LAYOUT

2½" deck screws

3" deck screws

1¾" rad., typ.

2¾" rad, typ

A

⅛"

5½"

B

1"

D   D

A

26"

8"

13"

1"

C

SIDE ELEVATION

Kid-Size Picnic Table Cutting List			
Part	No.	Size	Material
A. Top slats/seats	7	¾ × 5½ × 48 in.	Cedar
B. Top stringers	2	1½ × 3½ × 26 in.	"
C. Seat stringers	2	1½ × 3½ × 42 in.	"
D. Legs	4	1½ × 3½ × 31 in.	"
E. Stretcher	1	1½ × 3½ × 36 in.	"

3 Lay out the top stringers and seat stringers. Like the legs, these pieces also receive rounded ends. However, only the bottom corners of the stringers are curved—the top corners remain flat to support either the seats or the top slats. Reset your compass to draw a 2¾-in. radius, and scribe the curves on the stringers **(See Photo A).**

4 Cut the legs and stringers to shape with a jig saw. Guide the saw against a clamped straight-edge to cut the leg angles.

ASSEMBLE THE FRAME

5 Connect the top stringers and legs. First, find the center along the length of each top stringer, and mark this point on the top flat edge. Then arrange the legs in pairs on your worksurface with the top angled ends forming a straight line and the legs splaying apart in a "V" configuration. Set a top stringer in place on each pair of legs so the top edges of the stringers are flush with the top ends of the legs. Tack the stringer to each leg with a single counter-sunk 2½-in. deck screw. (You'll drive additional screws into these joints once the seat stringers are positioned and fastened.)

6 Install the seat stringers on the leg assemblies: Mark the seat stringer locations on the legs, according to the *Leg Layout* draw-ing. Set the seat stringers on the leg assemblies so the top edges of the stringers align with the leg reference lines. Pivot the legs in or out slightly so the dis-tance from the outside edges of the legs to each end of the seat stringers is 8 in. Secure the top and seat stringers with counter-sunk 2½-in. deck screws, four screws per joint **(See Photo B).**

PHOTO B: Set pairs of legs on your worksurface so they splay outward with their angled ends aligned. Attach the top stringers flush to the tops of the legs, and install the seat stringers so they overhang the legs by 8 in. on each end. Fasten the parts with countersunk 2½-in. deck screws to form two leg assemblies.

PHOTO C: Stand the leg assemblies top-down to attach the stretcher between them. Hold the stretcher in place with clamps so it is centered on the length of the seat stringers. Drive coun-tersunk 3-in. screws through the seat stringers and into the ends of the stretcher.

PHOTO D: Set the frame upright on the floor to secure the seats into position. The ends of the seats should overhang the seat stringers by about 4½ in. Make the outside edges of the seats overhang the ends of the seat stringers by 1 in.

PHOTO E: After setting the slats into position on the top stretchers and marking alignment lines for screw holes, insert spacers between the slats—we used ¼-in.-thick hardboard. Clamp the top slats together to keep them aligned, and fasten them to the top stringers with countersunk 2-in. deck screws.

❼ Complete the frame by joining the leg assemblies to the stretcher: Stand the leg assemblies upside down on your worksurface, and clamp the stretcher to the seat stringers so it's centered on their lengths. Drive pairs of 3-in. countersunk deck screws through the seat stringers and into the ends of the stretcher to fasten the parts **(See Photo C).**

PREPARE & ATTACH THE SEATS
❽ Crosscut the seats to length.

❾ Scribe the rounded ends on the seats with a compass set to draw a 2¾-in. radius.

❿ Cut the rounds ends of the seat boards with a jig saw. Smooth the curves with a file.

⓫ Attach the seats to the frame: The ends of the seats should extend past the seat stringers equal amounts on both sides (about 4½ in.). Let the outside edges of the seat boards overhang the ends of the seat stringers by 1 in. With the seats in position, fasten the parts with countersunk 2½-in. deck screws driven through the seats and into the seat stringers **(See Photo D).**

INSTALL THE TOP SLATS
⓬ Cut the five top slats to length and set them in place on the two top stringers so they overhang the stringers evenly. Don't worry about spacing between the slats yet. With a straightedge, draw lines for screw holes across the slats to mark the centerlines of the top stringers.

⓭ Fasten the slats to the top stringers: Insert scrap spacers between the slats first to provide for even spacing (we used ¼-in. hardboard for spacers). Because not all dimensional lumber is precisely the same width, you may need to determine the spacing between your slats according to the boards you're using. Clamp the top slats together to hold them in place. Drill pairs of countersunk pilot holes through the slats along the stringer marks, and install the slats with 2-in. deck screws **(See Photo E)**.

⑭ Set your compass for a 2¾-in. radius, and scribe curves onto the outer four corners of the table top. Cut the corner curves, and file the cut edges smooth **(See Photo F)**.

FINISHING TOUCHES

⑮ Sand all exposed project surfaces with a random-orbit sander and 150-grit sandpaper **(See Photo G)**.

EDITOR'S NOTE: *We left this project bare rather than finishing with an exterior topcoat, because most of these products aren't safe for use on eating surfaces.*

PHOTO F: Mark a 2¾-in. radius on each of the four corners of the tabletop, and trim the corners with a jig saw.

PHOTO G: Since cedar is prone to splintering, you'll want to give the table a good sanding to break the edges and smooth the parts. A random-orbit sander is the best tool for the job. It's a good idea to wear a dust mask when sanding cedar; the dust can be a respiratory irritant.

Frame-Style Sandbox

Turn off your TV and put away those video games. Instead, get out the old spatulas and pans and cars and trucks. Here's a simple project to build that will give your children or grandchildren hours of fun. And, if you're lucky, they'll even let you play with them. Built completely from 2 × 4s, this project can easily be completed—even with little helpers—in a weekend. If you elect to use cedar rather than treated lumber and not paint it, the sandbox can easily be completed in an afternoon. Got a big family? Simply lengthen the side boards to make the sandbox whatever size works best for you.

Vital Statistics: Frame-Style Sandbox

TYPE: Sandbox

OVERALL SIZE: 51W by 51L by 12H

MATERIAL: Treated lumber

JOINERY: Butt joints reinforced with galvanized deck screws

CONSTRUCTION DETAILS:
- Design is easily expandable
- Corner braces double as children's benches
- Corner joints alternate from tier to tier for strength
- Straightforward joinery speeds construction

FINISHING OPTIONS: Exterior latex primer and paint

Building time

PREPARING STOCK
0 hours

LAYOUT
1-2 hours

CUTTING PARTS
1-2 hours

ASSEMBLY
1-2 hours

FINISHING
2-4 hours

TOTAL: 5-10 hours

Tools you'll use

- Power miter saw or circular saw
- Drill/driver
- Combination square

Shopping list

- ☐ (9) 2 × 4 in. × 8 ft. treated lumber
- ☐ Galvanized deck screws (2½-, 3-in.)
- ☐ Latex primer
- ☐ Exterior latex paint

Frame-Style Sandbox

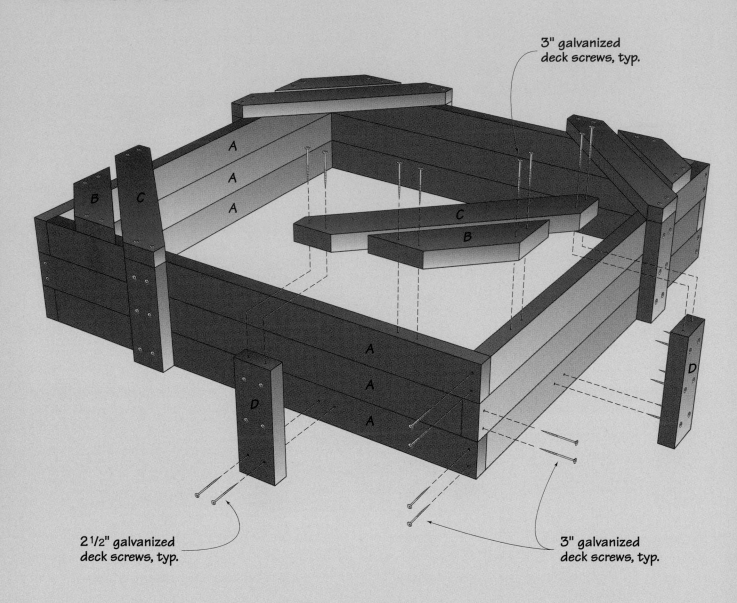

3" galvanized deck screws, typ.

2 1/2" galvanized deck screws, typ.

3" galvanized deck screws, typ.

Sandbox Cutting List			
Part	No.	Size	Material
A. Side tiers	12	1½ × 3½ × 46½ in.	Treated lumber
B. Short seats	4	1½ × 3½ × 14½ in.	"
C. Long seats	4	1½ × 3½ × 25 in.	"
D. Braces	8	1½ × 3½ × 10½ in.	"

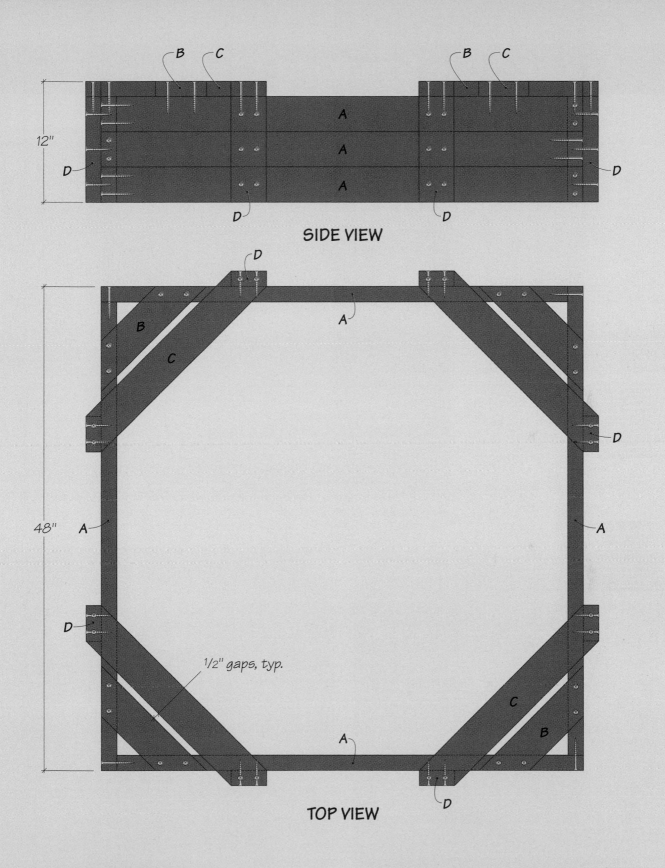

SIDE VIEW

12"

48"

1/2" gaps, typ.

TOP VIEW

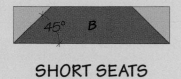

45° B

SHORT SEATS

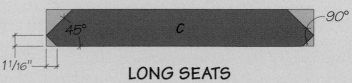

45° C 90°

1 1/16"

LONG SEATS

① Cut the 12 side tier pieces to length from 2 × 4 stock.

② Make the three tiers. Align the side pieces of each tier. Form the four butt joints on the tiers so that one end of each side piece overlaps the next side piece, while the other end is overlapped by the side piece before it. Assemble each tier, using countersunk 3-in. galvanized deck screws **(See Photo A).**

③ Make the long seats. Cut the blanks to length, then measure

PHOTO A: Place the parts that compose each tier in position on your worksurface, alternating the orientation of the butt joints around the tier. Attach the parts with countersunk 3-in. galvanized deck screws. It's a good idea to wear gloves when working with treated lumber.

PHOTO B: Saw the long and short seat pieces to length, then miter-cut the ends to shape. A power miter saw makes this task easy.

PHOTO C: Set a long seat on top of two braces, and drill countersunk pilot holes through the ends of the seat piece into the braces. Use 3-in. galvanized deck screws to secure the parts.

and mark the shape of the ends according to the *Long Seats* drawing. Cut the ends to shape with a power miter saw.

4 Make the short seats. Cut the blanks to length, then miter-cut the ends **(See Photo B)** to 45°.

5 Cut the eight braces to length.

6 Build four seat assemblies. Drill two countersunk pilot holes through the ends of each long seat, and fasten braces to the ends of the long seats with 3-in. galvanized deck screws **(See Photo C).**

7 Assemble the sandbox. Stack the completed tiers on top of each other, alternating the direction of the corner joints. Position the seat assemblies over the tier corners. Drill countersunk pilot holes through the braces, and fasten the braces to all three tiers by driving 2½-in. galvanized deck screws through the braces and into each tier **(See Photo D).**

8 Attach the short seats. Hold the ends flush with the outer face of the top tier. Drill countersunk pilot holes along the angled ends of the short seats, and fasten the seats with 3-in. deck screws.

FINISHING TOUCHES
9 Smooth the surfaces and ease corners and edges thoroughly with sandpaper, especially on and around the seats.

10 Finish the sandbox with latex primer and two coats of paint **(See Photo E).**

11 Position the sandbox. Line with landscape fabric to deter growth of unwanted vegetation. Fill the box with sand. TIP: *You'll need about 8 cubic ft. of sand.*

PHOTO D: Stack the three tiers with their corner joints alternating before installing the long seat assemblies. Secure the braces to the tiers with countersunk screws driven at every tier.

PHOTO E: Apply latex primer to all exposed surfaces of the sandbox, then follow up with two coats of exterior latex paint. We covered the whole box in a single color, but you could also create a multi-colored paint scheme instead.

Adirondack Chair

This lively interpretation of the classic Adirondack chair emphasizes curves and comfort. Both the seat and the back are shaped to welcome you as you nestle in for a little reading or relaxation. Its high back slats have gently radiused ends, and the generously proportioned arms provide ample room for resting a snack or a cool drink. Building this piece of furniture takes a little time and skill, but the results are worth the effort.

Vital Statistics: Adirondack Chair

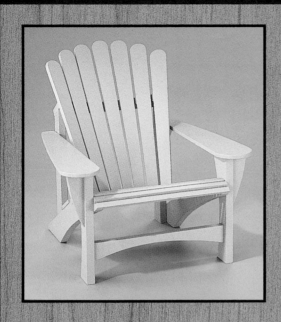

TYPE: Adirondack chair

OVERALL SIZE: 37¼W by 39¼L by 37¾H

MATERIAL: Pine

JOINERY: Butt joints reinforced with galvanized deck screws

CONSTRUCTION DETAILS:
· Chair parts are primed before assembly
· Seat and back assemblies are contoured
· Screws are countersunk, with the holes filled and sanded

FINISHING OPTIONS: Exterior latex primer and paint

Building time

 PREPARING STOCK
0 hours

 LAYOUT
3-4 hours

 CUTTING PARTS
4-6 hours

 ASSEMBLY
6-8 hours

 FINISHING
3-4 hours

TOTAL: 16-22 hours

Tools you'll use

· Circular saw
· Table saw (optional)
· Power miter saw (optional)
· Jig saw
· Compass (nail and string) or trammel points
· Drill/driver
· Clamps
· Combination square

Shopping list

☐ (2) 2 × 6 in. × 8 ft. pine
☐ (1) 2 × 4 in. × 6 ft. pine
☐ (1) 1 × 8 in. × 8 ft. pine
☐ (1) 1 × 6 in. × 6 ft. pine
☐ (5) 1 × 4 in. × 8 ft. pine
☐ Galvanized deck screws (1½-, 2-, 2½-in.)
☐ Wood or auto body filler
☐ Latex primer
☐ Exterior latex paint

Adirondack Chair

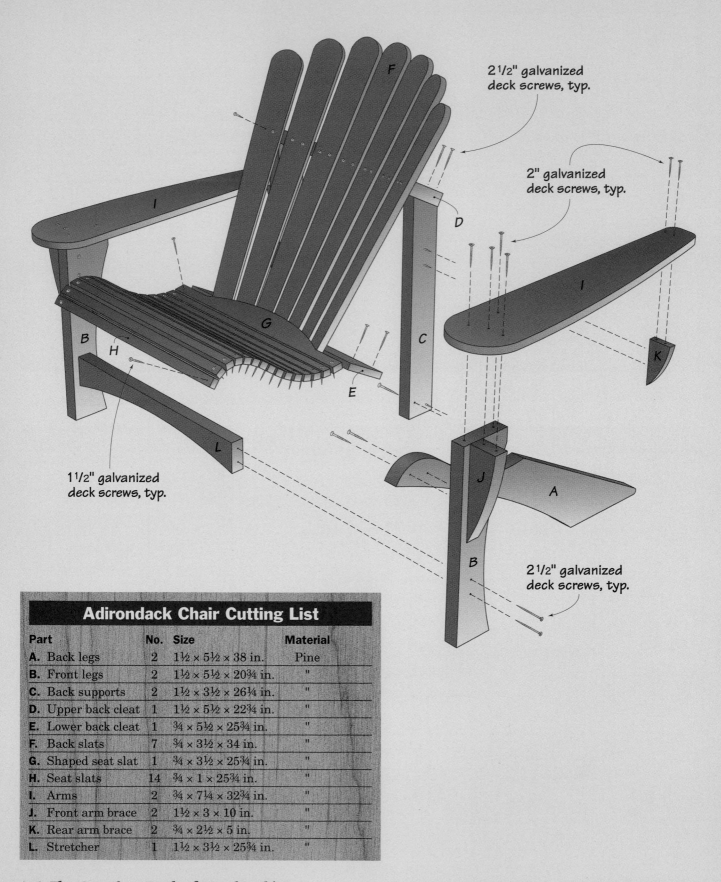

2¹/₂" galvanized deck screws, typ.

2" galvanized deck screws, typ.

F

I

D

C

E

B

H

G

L

K

J

A

B

I

1¹/₂" galvanized deck screws, typ.

2¹/₂" galvanized deck screws, typ.

Adirondack Chair Cutting List			
Part	No.	Size	Material
A. Back legs	2	1½ × 5½ × 38 in.	Pine
B. Front legs	2	1½ × 5½ × 20¾ in.	"
C. Back supports	2	1½ × 3½ × 26¼ in.	"
D. Upper back cleat	1	1½ × 5½ × 22¾ in.	"
E. Lower back cleat	1	¾ × 5½ × 25¾ in.	"
F. Back slats	7	¾ × 3½ × 34 in.	"
G. Shaped seat slat	1	¾ × 3½ × 25¾ in.	"
H. Seat slats	14	¾ × 1 × 25¾ in.	"
I. Arms	2	¾ × 7¼ × 32¾ in.	"
J. Front arm brace	2	1½ × 3 × 10 in.	"
K. Rear arm brace	2	¾ × 2½ × 5 in.	"
L. Stretcher	1	1½ × 3½ × 25¾ in.	"

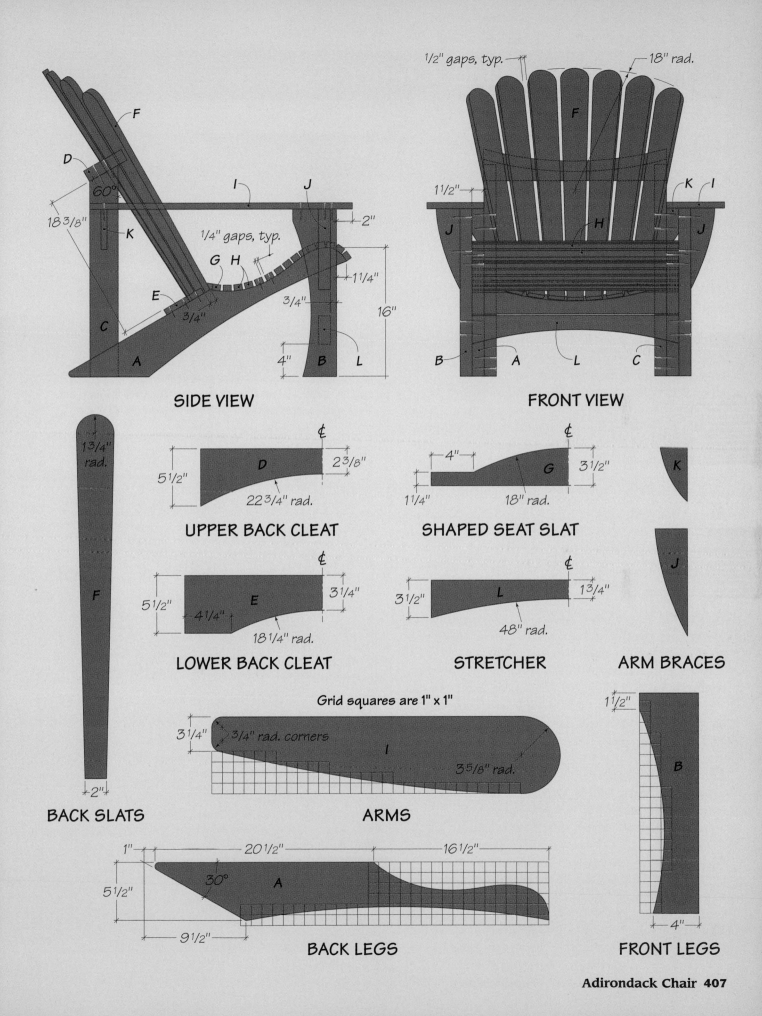

½" gaps, typ.

18" rad.

F

F

1½"

D

60°

18³⁄₈"

I

J

K

I

K

2"

J

H

J

¼" gaps, typ.

G H

1¼"

E

¾"

C

¾"

16"

A

B

L

4"

B

A

L

C

SIDE VIEW

FRONT VIEW

1¾" rad.

5½"

D

2³⁄₈"

¢

22³⁄₄" rad.

4"

G

3½"

¢

1¼"

18" rad.

K

UPPER BACK CLEAT

SHAPED SEAT SLAT

5½"

E

3¼"

¢

4¼"

18¼" rad.

3½"

L

1³⁄₄"

¢

48" rad.

J

LOWER BACK CLEAT

STRETCHER

ARM BRACES

F

Grid squares are 1" x 1"

3¼"

¾" rad. corners

I

3⁵⁄₈" rad.

1½"

B

BACK SLATS

ARMS

1"

20½"

16½"

5½"

30°

A

9½"

4"

BACK LEGS

FRONT LEGS

PHOTO A: Make templates for the arms and legs, trace the parts onto blanks for the workpieces and cut the parts with a jig saw.

CUT OUT THE ARMS & LEGS

1 Cut pairs of blanks to length for the arms, front legs and back legs as specified on the *Cutting List*.

2 Refer to the drawings to construct full-sized templates for the arms, front legs and back legs. Stiff cardboard will work if you plan to build only one of these chairs, but ¼-in. hardboard is a better choice because the template can be reused again and again. Bend a piece of flexible hardboard to help form the gradual curved profiles when you draw them on the templates. Cut the templates to shape, and smooth the edges as needed.

3 Lay the templates on the arm and leg workpieces, draw the shapes and cut out the arms and legs with a jig saw **(See Photo A).**

MAKE THE BACK SLATS

The chair's back slats taper on both edges along their full length. You could shape the slats by first making a template from ¼-in. hardboard, tracing the profiles on the slat blanks, and then using a jig saw to cut out the slats. An alternate method is to build a simple clamping jig (See *Clamping Taper Jig*, right), to cut the tapered back slats on the table saw instead. The jig will allow you to make the tapered cuts quickly and produce smooth, flat edges on the slats.

4 Cut seven blanks for the back slats to length from 1 × 4 stock. NOTE: *All the slats start out the same length at this stage, but six of the seven will be trimmed to actual length later during chair assembly.*

5 Lay out the end radius and draw the tapered edges on the slat blanks, using the *Back Slats* drawing.

6 Cut the tapered edges on the back slats. If you use the table saw and jig method for making these cuts,

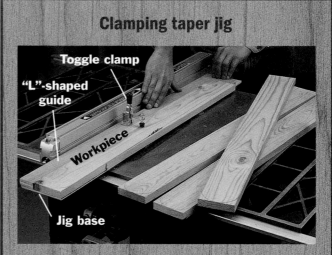

Clamping taper jig

Toggle clamp
"L"-shaped guide
Workpiece
Jig base

This clamping jig allows you to make tapered cuts on the table saw using the saw's rip fence as your guide. Build the jig by fastening a piece of ¾-in. "L"-shaped scrap to a length of ¼-in. plywood. The thin plywood serves as a base to support the workpieces, and the "L"-shaped piece guides the slats at an angle through the blade. Select the jig base from a piece of plywood longer than your back-slat workpieces. Cut the ¾-in. stock into an "L" shape, so the long inside edge of the "L" matches the taper angles you'll cut on the back slats. Fasten the jig parts so the back slats rest in the "L" guide, and one cutting line on the slat workpieces lines up with the edge of the jig base. Attach a toggle clamp to the jig to hold the workpieces in place as you cut. Slide the jig along the rip fence with the workpiece clamped in place to make the cuts. Once you cut the first taper, save the angled wastepiece—you'll need it to serve as a spacer for making the tapered cut along the opposite long edge of each slat.

cut one tapered edge on each slat first. To do this, adjust the rip fence on the table saw so the jig rests against the rip fence, and the outside edge of the jig base is flush with the blade. Set the slats into the jig and clamp securely. Slide the jig and workpiece past the blade to make the first taper cuts.

7 Cut the second tapered edge on the back slats. Set one of the scrap wastepieces you made in Step 6 into the crook of the "L" on the jig, and flip each slat over in the jig so the tapered edge you just cut on the slats rests against the "L". This configuration should align the second taper cutting line on each workpiece with the edge of the jig base for making the second taper cuts. Clamp the slats in the jig and make the taper cuts (**See Photo B**).

8 Cut the radiused ends of the slats with your jig saw. Sand the cuts smooth.

CUT THE REMAINING PROFILED PARTS

9 Cut the front and rear arm braces to size and shape. The exact curvature of the profiles on these parts isn't critical, but like parts should match.

10 Cut the upper back cleat, the lower back cleat, the shaped seat slat and the stretcher to size and shape. The profiles on these parts are simple arcs of various circles, and the radiuses are specified in the drawings. To establish the radiuses, first rip- and crosscut blanks for the parts. Clamp each workpiece to your benchtop. Find the centerline of the workpiece and extend the line onto the bench. Measure from the workpiece along the centerline the distance of the radius to establish the centerpoint for drawing the arc. Fashion a large compass by driving a nail into the worksurface at the centerpoint. Attach a string to the nail, and loop a pencil to the string at the appropriate radius. Mark arcs on the workpieces, and cut out the parts.

MAKE THE BACK SUPPORTS & SEAT SLATS

11 Crosscut the back supports to length, and trim the top ends to a 60° angle, as shown in the *Side View* drawing.

12 Cut the 14 seat slats to size. Rip ¾-in. stock to 1 in. wide on the table saw or with a circular saw. Cut the slats to length. Crosscutting the slats is quick to do with a power miter saw if you clamp a stop to the saw fence. Or you could also use a circular saw.

PHOTO B: Cut tapered edges on the back slats. We used a table saw jig for making these angled cuts. Once you've cut the first tapered edge, flip the slats over in the jig and cut the second tapered edge.

PHOTO C: Sand the chair parts smooth, and prime all surfaces with exterior latex primer. Primer will seal the wood and provide an even bonding surface for topcoating with paint.

PRIME THE PARTS

Because this chair is intended to remain outside in all kinds of weather and needs to be well sealed, it's a good idea to prime the surfaces of all the parts at this stage before you begin assembly. Also, since the chair will be assembled with screws but no glue, priming now will not affect glue bonds.

13 Sand and smooth the all chair parts. Prime the parts with latex-based primer (**See Photo C**).

BUILD THE ARM ASSEMBLIES

14 Attach the front arm braces to the outside of the front legs, with the top edges flush. The braces should set back ¾ in. from the front edges of the front legs.

PHOTO D: Attach the arms to the arm braces on the front legs and back supports. Drive screws though the arms and down into the front legs as well. Drill countersunk pilot holes before you install the screws.

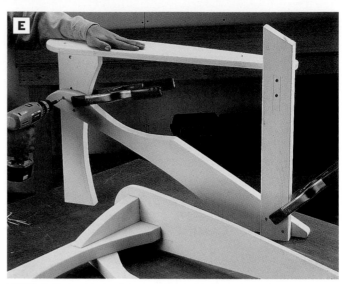

PHOTO E: Fasten the back legs to the inside face of the front legs and the outside face of the back supports with screws. Hold the parts in position with spring clamps to keep the parts from shifting.

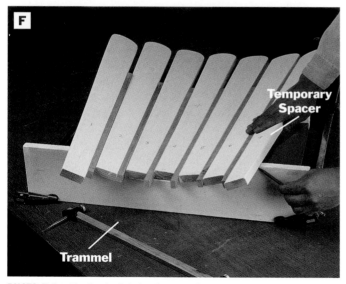

PHOTO F: Lay the back slats in place on the upper and lower back cleats. The tops of the back slats should follow the curve of an 18-in. radius. Mark the centerpoint of this radius on the center slat, and use a trammel or simple string compass to position the rest of the slats. Mark the slats for trimming where they intersect the lower back cleat.

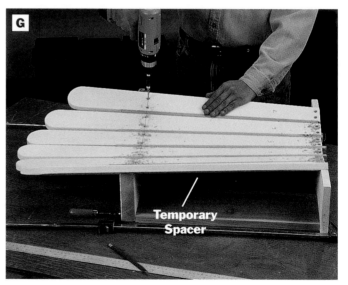

PHOTO G: Drill countersunk pilot holes for attaching the back slats to the upper and lower cleats. You may want to draw a reference line across the slats first to help establish screw placement on the upper back cleat. Attach the parts and remove the temporary spacer.

15 Attach the rear arm braces to the outside faces of the back supports, with the top edges of the braces set 20¾ in. from the bottom ends of the supports.

16 Attach the arms to the front legs and back supports with 2-in. galvanized deck screws (**See Photo D**). Refer to the *Side View* and *Front View* drawings for more information about exact placement of the arms.

17 Attach the back legs to the inner faces of the front legs and the outer faces of the back supports. Position the back legs so that the front tip of the back leg over-hangs the front leg by 1¼ in. Adjust the parts until the measurement from the front edge of the front leg to the front edge of the back support is 27¼ in. Clamp the assemblies, drill countersunk pilot holes and attach the parts with 2½-in. galvanized deck screws (**See Photo E**).

BUILD THE BACK ASSEMBLY

18 Cut two temporary spacers to hold the upper and lower back cleats in position while you attach the back slats. Cut the spacers 18⅜ in. long.

⑲ Stand the upper and lower back cleats on their flat back edges, and clamp the temporary spacers from Step 18 between the cleats. Lay the back slats into the curves on the cleats. Insert ½-in. spacers between the back slats to hold them evenly apart. Adjust the center back slat so it is even with the bottom face of the lower back cleat. Arrange the rest of the slats on the cleats so their top curved ends follow an 18-in.-radius arc. The easiest way to lay out this arc is to make a mark 18 in. from the top of the center slat and use this as the centerpoint for a trammel or string compass when you swing an arc. Adjust the back slats so the curved ends intersect with the end of the compass. Draw a line on the back slats where they cross the lower back cleat **(See Photo F)**.

⑳ Remove the back slats and trim the bottom ends.

㉑ Reposition the slats on the back cleats, drill countersunk pilot holes and fasten the slats to the cleats with 2-in. galvanized deck screws **(See Photo G)**.

ASSEMBLE THE CHAIR

㉒ Clamp the back assembly in position between the arm assemblies, with the lower back cleat held back ¾ in. from the point where the curved seat profile begins on the top edge of the back legs. The upper back cleat should rest on the back supports.

㉓ Install the stretcher between the front legs; this will keep the structure rigid while you attach the back assembly. Fasten the stretcher 4 in. up from the bottoms of the front legs.

㉔ Attach the back assembly. Fasten the lower cleat to the back legs with 2-in. galvanized deck screws and the upper back cleats into the back supports with 2½-in. deck screws **(See Photo H)**.

㉕ Attach the seat slats. Remove the arms temporarily, for easier access to the screws. Attach the shaped seat slat first. Space the remaining seat slats evenly so they follow the full length of the curved profile on the back legs. Fasten the slats with countersunk 2-in. deck screws **(See Photo I)**. Reattach the arms.

FINISHING TOUCHES

㉖ Fill all of the recessed screw holes with wood or auto body filler. Let the filler dry and sand smooth. Spot prime the filled screw heads.

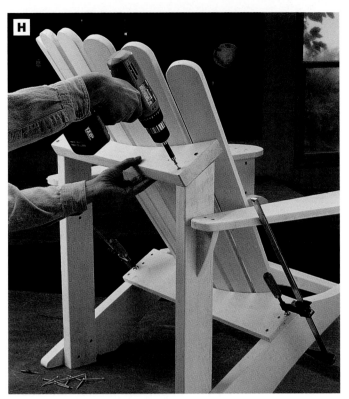

PHOTO H: Set the back assembly in place between the two arm assemblies and clamp the parts together. Drive screws through the upper and lower cleats into the back supports and back legs.

PHOTO I: Remove the arm pieces to provide clearance for attaching the seat slats. Install the seat slats along the profiled areas of the back legs starting with the shaped seat slat. Space the slats evenly apart along the back leg. A ¼-in.-thick scrap spacer will help keep the slat spacing uniform as you install the slats.

Sun Lounger

Y ou'll find this handsome lounge chair perfect for relaxing outdoors, whether your preference is lying in the sun and working on your tan or enjoying shady summer breezes with the company of a good book. The back adjusts to four positions, so you're sure to be able to find the one that suits your mood and activity. The foot section also is adjustable for even greater versatility and comfort.

Vital Statistics: Sun Lounger

TYPE: Lounge chair

OVERALL SIZE: 24W by 80¾L by 14½H (38H with the back raised)

MATERIAL: Cedar, hardwood dowel

JOINERY: Butt joints reinforced with galvanized deck screws, stainless-steel bolts, washers and nuts

CONSTRUCTION DETAILS:
· Back rest adjusts to four positions by means of a pivoting back brace
· Foot rest is adjustable or removable

FINISHING OPTIONS: Penetrating UV protectant sealer, exterior paint or leave unfinished to weather naturally to gray

Building time

PREPARING STOCK
0 hours

LAYOUT
2-3 hours

CUTTING PARTS
3-4 hours

ASSEMBLY
3-5 hours

FINISHING
2-3 hours

TOTAL: 10-15 hours

Tools you'll use

· Circular saw, power miter saw or radial arm saw
· Router with ½-in. roundover bit, ¾-in. core box bit
· Jig saw
· Drill/driver
· Clamps
· Sockets
· Combination square
· Bevel gauge

Shopping list

☐ (11) 2 × 4 in. × 8 ft. cedar

☐ (2) 1-in.-dia. × 3-ft. hardwood dowels

☐ (1) ¾-in.-dia. × 3-ft. hardwood dowels

☐ (4) ⅜ × 3½-in. stainless-steel bolts (12 washers, 8 nuts)

☐ Galvanized deck screws (2½-, 3-in.)

☐ Galvanized nails (#6d, #4d)

☐ UV protectant sealer

Sun Lounger

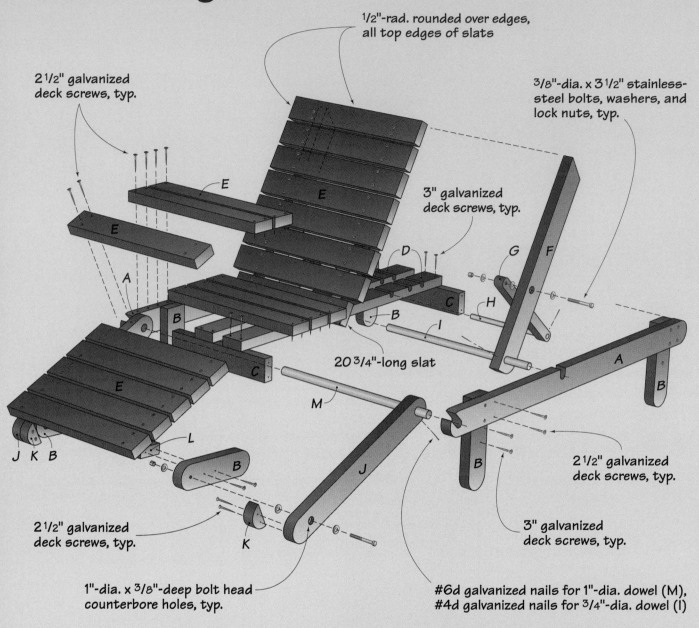

1/2"-rad. rounded over edges, all top edges of slats

2 1/2" galvanized deck screws, typ.

3/8"-dia. x 3 1/2" stainless-steel bolts, washers, and lock nuts, typ.

3" galvanized deck screws, typ.

20 3/4"-long slat

2 1/2" galvanized deck screws, typ.

3" galvanized deck screws, typ.

2 1/2" galvanized deck screws, typ.

1"-dia. x 3/8"-deep bolt head counterbore holes, typ.

#6d galvanized nails for 1"-dia. dowel (M), #4d galvanized nails for 3/4"-dia. dowel (I)

E E E A B C E J K B L D C B M J K G F H I A B B

Sun Lounger Cutting List

Part	No.	Size	Material	Part	No.	Size	Material
A. Seat rails	2	1½ × 3½ × 56¼ in.	Cedar	**H.** Adjustment dowel	1	¾ in. dia. × 13¾ in.	Hardwood
B. Legs	6	1½ × 3½ × 13 in.	"	**I.** Back rest dowel	1	1 in. dia. × 24½ in.	"
C. Seat stretchers	2	1½ × 3½ × 18 in.	"	**J.** Foot rest rails	2	1½ × 3½ × 27½ in.	Cedar
D. Back supports	2	1½ × 3½ × 46 in.	"	**K.** Leg stops	2	1½ × 3½ × 1¾ in.	"
E. Slats	19	1½ × 3½ × 24 in.	"	**L.** Foot rest stretcher	1	1½ × 3½ × 14⅞ in.	"
F. Back rails	2	1½ × 3½ × 31 in.	"	**M.** Foot rest dowel	1	1 in. dia. × 24½ in.	Hardwood
G. Adjustment braces	2	1½ × 1½ × 16½ in.	"				

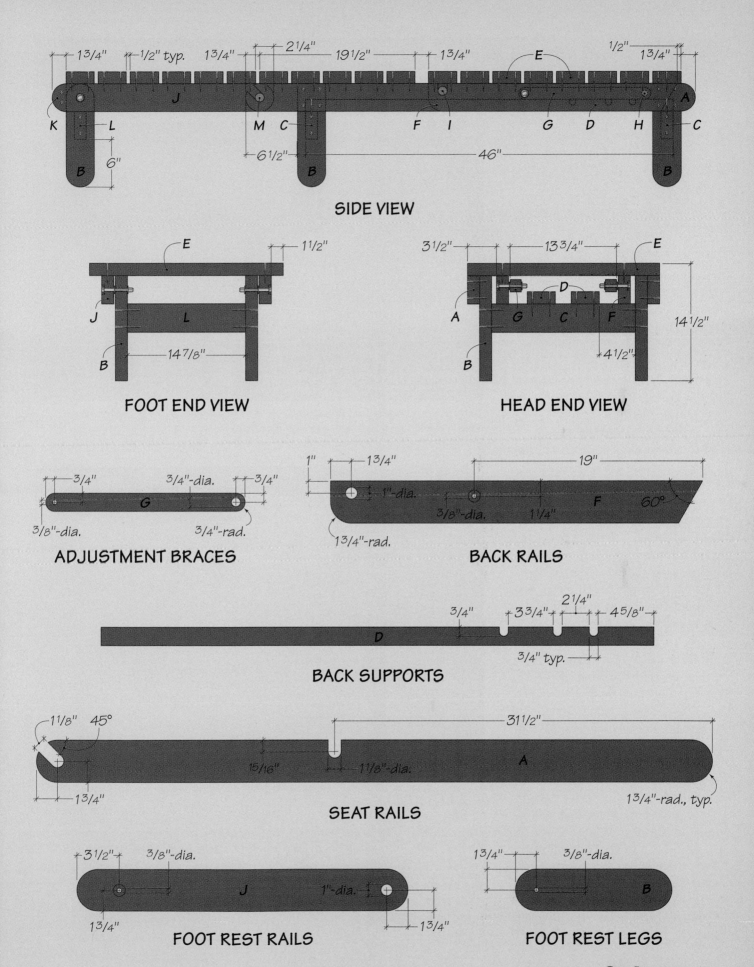

SIDE VIEW

FOOT END VIEW

HEAD END VIEW

ADJUSTMENT BRACES

BACK RAILS

BACK SUPPORTS

SEAT RAILS

FOOT REST RAILS

FOOT REST LEGS

The lounge chair is made up of three sections: a stationary seat, an adjustable back rest and an adjustable foot rest. The seat section provides the basic structure and is built first. All the parts, except for the dowels, are made from cedar 2 × 4s.

SHAPE THE SEAT RAILS

❶ Crosscut the long seat rails to length. Draw a 1¾-in. radius on both ends of each rail. Find the centerpoint of each radius by using a combination square and marking a 45° line from both corners at each end. Position your compass at the intersection of these lines and draw the radius. Cut out the curves with a jig saw, and sand the cut edges smooth.

❷ Cut notches for the foot rest dowel and the back rest dowel. The notches are made by first boring 1⅛-in.-dia. holes, then cutting a slot from these holes to the top edge of each rail. Start with the foot rest dowel notches. Using the centerpoint you established on the ends of the rails in Step 1, bore a 1⅛-in.-dia. hole. Draw two 45° lines to connect the hole to the top corner of the rails. Cut along these lines to form the foot rest notches **(See Photo A)**. Form the back rest notches by measuring 31½ in. from the ends of the rails opposite the foot rest notches. The center-

PHOTO A: Cut notches in the seat rails for back rest and foot rest dowels by boring 1-in.-dia. holes in the rails first, then cutting through the rails to the holes to form the notches. The foot rest notch (shown) is angled 45° on the seat rail, while the back rest notches are perpendicular.

PHOTO B: Fasten the leg assemblies to the seat rails with 2½-in. galvanized deck screws. Be sure the foot rest notches on the seat rails face down on your worksurface when you fasten the legs to the rails. Check the leg assemblies with a square to be sure they are perpendicular to the rails before driving the screws.

point for the 1⅛-in.-dia. hole is ¹⁵⁄₁₆ in. from the top edge of the rails. Drill the holes, then form the notches by drawing a pair of lines from each hole perpendicular to the top edge of the rails. Cut along the lines to form the two notches.

BUILD & ATTACH THE LEG ASSEMBLIES TO THE SEAT RAILS

❸ Cut six legs to length. Draw and cut 1¾-in. radiuses on both ends of the two foot rest legs and on one end of the four seat section legs.

4 Cut the seat stretchers to length. Mark the stretcher locations on the inside faces of the four seat section legs. Center the stretchers on the width of the legs. The top edges of the stretchers are 3½ in. down from the square ends of the legs. Clamp the parts together and fasten the legs to the seat stretchers with countersunk 3-in. galvanized deck screws.

5 Attach the leg assemblies to the seat rails. Fasten one leg assembly 6½ in. from the ends of the rails with the foot rest notches using 2½-in. deck screws. Attach the second leg assembly so the span between the outside faces of the seat stretchers is 46 in. **(See Photo B)**.

INSTALL THE BACK SUPPORTS

6 Measure and cut the two back supports to length.

7 Rout the three back rest grooves in each back support. Refer to the measurements on the *Back Supports* drawing to determine the groove locations. Clamp the back supports side by side so you can mark and gang-cut slots on both supports at one time. Then rout the grooves with a ¾-in. core box bit. Cut the slots in multiple passes to keep from overloading the router bit **(See Photo C)**.

8 Attach the back supports to the tops of the seat stretchers. Leave a 4½-in. space between the supports and the legs (See *Head End View*) to allow ample room for the back rails and adjustment braces. Align the ends of the back supports so they are flush with the outside faces of the seat stretchers. Drill pilot holes, and fasten the parts with 3-in. galvanized deck screws **(See Photo D)**.

Straightedge jig

PHOTO C: Gang-rout notches in the back supports to ensure that the notches will line up perfectly on both pieces. Use a ¾-in. core box bit, and cut the notches in several passes of increasing depth. We clamped a short T-square style straightedge jig to guide the router when cutting.

PHOTO D: Fasten the back supports to the seat stretchers. Leave 4½-in. spaces between the back supports and the legs to provide clearance for the chair back rails and adjustment braces.

PHOTO E: Cut the 19 seat slats to length, and ease the top edges and ends of each slat with a ½-in. roundover bit in the router. We used a plywood jig clamped to the benchtop to "frame" each slat on all sides and hold it steady while routing. This way, the slats require no further clamping.

PHOTO F: Screw the five seat slats to the seat rails. Determine and mark the positions of the end slats first, then space the remaining three slats evenly between the end slats. If the slat space is consistent on your chair, use a scrap spacer to make spacing easy when fastening the parts.

PHOTO G: Bore a 1-in.-dia. hole through each back rail for the back rest dowel and a ⅜-in.-deep counterbore for the heads and washers of the adjustment brace pivot bolts.

CUT & ATTACH THE SLATS

9 Cut all the slats to length. Cut one slat 3¼ in. shorter than the others so it can fit between the seat rails when the back rest is inclined.

10 Rout a ½-in. roundover on the face edges of the slats. We made a plywood jig and clamped it to our worksurface to hold each slat steady for routing (**See Photo E**).

11 Attach the five slats that make up the fixed seat of the chair to the seat rails. First mark the positions of the two end slats. Locate the edge of the slat closest to the foot rest notch by measuring 1¾ in. from the foot end of the seat rails and marking a line. Then measure 19½ in. from this line to locate the edge closest to the back rest notch. Space the remaining three slats evenly between the end slats. NOTE: *The spacing between the slats will vary, depending upon the width of your slat stock. What is most important is that all the slats fit between the marks you've just drawn on the seat rails.* Fasten the slats to the rails with 2½-in. deck screws (**See Photo F**).

BUILD THE BACK REST

12 Rip and crosscut the two adjustment braces to size, and cut ¾-in. radiuses on both ends of each part. Drill one end for a ⅜-in.-dia. pivot bolt and the other end for the ¾-in.-dia. adjustment dowel. Bore the holes at the centerpoints you established for marking the end radiuses.

13 Cut the back rails to length, then miter-cut one end at a 60° angle. Cut a 1¾-in. radius on one corner of the other end of the rails with a jig saw as shown in the *Back Rails* drawing.

14 Bore holes in the back rails for the back rest dowel and adjustment brace pivot bolts. Refer to the *Back Rails* drawing for locating these hole positions. Clamp each rail to your worksurface. Bore a 1-in.-dia. hole through the radiused ends of the rails for the back rest dowel. Using the same bit, drill a ⅜-in. deep counterbore for the pivot bolt head and washer (**See Photo G**).

15 Drill a ⅜-in.-dia. hole through the back rails for the adjustment brace pivot bolts in the center of the counterbores you drilled in Step 14 (**See Photo H**).

16 Install the adjustment dowel in the adjustment braces. Cut the ¾-in.-dia. dowel to length, and fasten the dowel into the holes in the adjustment braces with 4d galvanized finish nails.

17 Attach the slats to the back rails. On the seven full-length slats, drill a line of countersunk pilot holes 4¼ in. from each end. On the short slat, drill the pilot holes 1⅛ in. from each end. Attach the end slats first. Align the short slat so it is even with the radiused ends of the back rails, and overhang the upper slat ½ in. beyond the angled ends. Make sure these two slats are square with the rails and that the inside faces of the rails are 14 in. apart. Screw these first two slats in place. Then space and attach the six intermediate slats evenly between the end slats.

18 Cut the 1-in.-dia. back rest dowel to length. Slide it through the holes in the back rails, overhang the ends evenly and fasten the dowel in place with a 6d galvanized nail at each end (**See Photo I**). Drill pilot holes to keep the nails from splitting the dowels.

PHOTO H: Drill ⅜-in.-dia. holes through the back rails, centered on the 1-in.-dia. counterbore holes. These holes will house pivot bolts for the adjustment brace that supports the chair back and holds it in one of three positions.

PHOTO I: Tack the back rest dowel in place on the back rest rails with #6d galvanized finish nails. Drive the nails through the rails and into the dowels. To keep the dowels from splitting, drill a pilot hole for the nails first.

PHOTO J: Install the adjustment brace to the back rest with bolts, washers and nuts. Place a washer on either side of each adjustment brace. Thread two nuts on each bolt and tighten the nuts against one another to lock them together, yet allow the adjustment brace to swing freely.

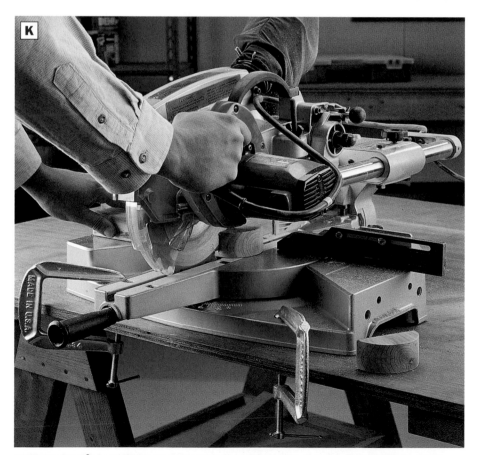

PHOTO K: Cut 1¾-in. radiuses on either end of a section of 2 × 4 cedar. Cut off these curved ends with a power miter saw or radial arm saw. The pieces will serve as leg stops on the foot rest. Cutting short workpieces from longer stock keeps your hands a safe distance from the blade.

19 Secure the adjustment brace assembly to the back rest rails with bolts, washers, and double nuts (**See Photo J**). Leave enough play when tightening the nuts against one another so the brace assembly swings freely.

ASSEMBLE THE FOOT REST

20 Cut the foot rest rails to length, then round off both ends with 1¾-in. radiuses.

21 Bore holes through the foot rest rails for the foot rest dowel and the leg pivot bolts. Locate the centerpoints for the holes using the *Foot Rest Rails* drawing. Drill a 1-in.-dia. hole through one end for the foot rest dowel. Using the same bit, drill a ⅜-in.-deep counterbore in the other end for the pivot bolt head and washer.

22 Make and attach the two leg stops. Cut 1¾-in. radiuses on both ends of a piece of 2 × 4 cedar scrap, then cut off these two semi-circles (**See Photo K**). Fasten the leg stops to the pivot bolt ends of the foot rest rails with screws.

23 Drill the ⅜-in.-dia. holes for the pivot bolts. Clamp a foot rest leg in place beneath a rail on your work-surface. Drill a ⅜-in.-dia. hole through the center of the counter-bore in the rail and through the leg (**See Photo L**). Repeat the process for the other rail and leg.

24 Cut the foot rest stretcher to length and fasten it to the legs. Center the stretcher on the width of the legs, and position the bot-tom edge 6 in. from the bottoms of the legs. Drill countersunk pilot holes and fasten the parts with 2½-in. galvanized deck screws.

25 Attach six slats to the foot rest rails. Drill countersunk pilot holes

PHOTO L: Drill holes through the foot rest rails and the legs. The parts will attach with bolts so the legs can pivot on the rails.

2¼-in. from each end of the slats. Attach the end slats first. Locate one slat 1¾ in. from the leg ends of the short rails. Set the other end slat 2¼ in. from the dowel-hole ends of the rails. Make sure the framework is square. Then fasten the intermediate slats evenly between the end slats.

㉖ Cut and attach the foot rest dowel to the rails with 6d finish nails. The dowel should overhang the rails evenly on both sides.

㉗ Attach the leg assembly to the foot rest rails with ⅜-in.-dia. bolts, washers and double nuts (**See Photo M**).

FINISHING TOUCHES
㉘ Ease all chair edges thoroughly with sandpaper (**See Photo N**). Stain and/or seal as desired. We applied a clear exterior sealer to highlight the beauty of the cedar, but this project could be stained, painted or left unfinished.

PHOTO M: Attach the foot rest stretcher to the legs with 2½-in. deck screws, then join the leg assembly to the foot rest with bolts, washers and double nuts.

PHOTO N: Set the back and foot rests in place on the seat, and test the action of the parts. Then sand all exposed surfaces of the chair with medium-grit sandpaper. If you sand in an enclosed place, wear a particle mask. Cedar dust can be irritating to your nose and lungs.

Porch Swing

A cool breeze and a calming motion are the main returns you'll earn if you invest a little time and money in building this porch swing. Made of lightweight cedar (or any exterior wood), this swing will seat two adults comfortably while standing up to any abuse the elements can send its way.

Vital Statistics: Porch Swing

TYPE: Two-person outdoor swing

OVERALL SIZE: 58½W by 26H by 30D

MATERIAL: Cedar

JOINERY: Half-lap joints reinforced with glue and screws, butt joints reinforced with screws

CONSTRUCTION DETAILS:
· All parts cut from standard dimensional cedar
· Comfortable slope to seat and back rest
· Four eyebolts for hanging
· Three slat supports distribute weight evenly

FINISHING OPTIONS: Clear coat with UV-resistant wood sealer, stain with exterior stain or paint white or gray for a more formal appearance.

Building time

PREPARING STOCK
1 hour

LAYOUT
2-4 hours

CUTTING PARTS
3-5 hours

ASSEMBLY
2-4 hours

FINISHING
1-2 hours

TOTAL: 9-16 hours

Tools you'll use

· Table saw
· Band saw or jig saw
· Drill press
· C-clamps
· Router table with piloted ¼-in. roundover bit
· Tape measure
· Spring clamps
· Drill/driver
· Portable drill guide
· Dado-blade set for table saw

Shopping list

☐ (5) 2 × 6 in. × 8 ft. (nominal) cedar

☐ (4) 1 × 6 in. × 8 ft. (nominal) cedar

☐ (4) ⅜ × 4-in. eyebolts; ⅜-in. nuts and washers

☐ Galvanized deck screws (2-, 2½-, 3-in.)

☐ Finishing materials

☐ 30-40 ft. heavy rope (not cotton) or chain

☐ Weatherproof wood glue

Porch Swing

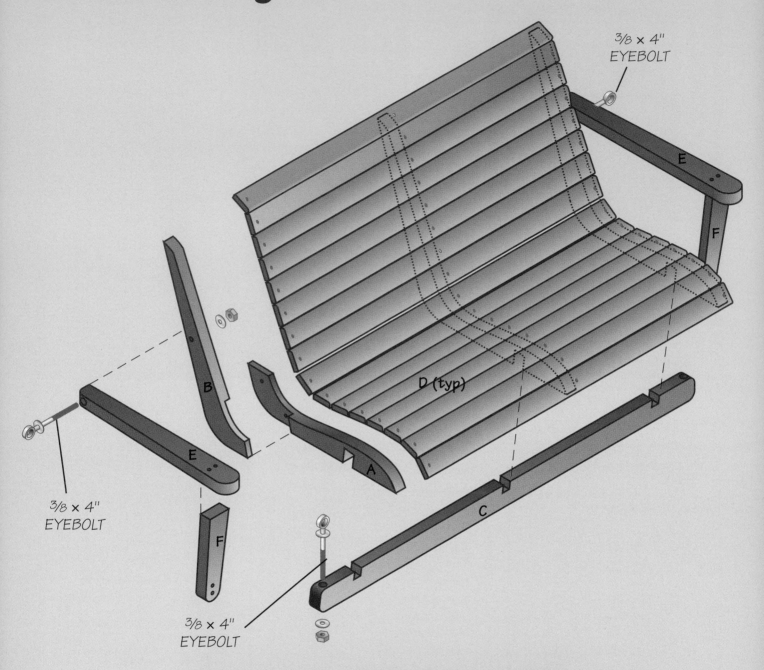

3/8 × 4"
EYEBOLT

E

F

D (typ)

A

B

E

F

3/8 × 4"
EYEBOLT

C

3/8 × 4"
EYEBOLT

Porch Swing Cutting List			
Part	**No.**	**Size**	**Material**
A. Seat supports	3	$1\frac{1}{2} \times 5\frac{1}{4}^* \times 24$ in.	Cedar
B. Back supports	3	$1\frac{1}{2} \times 5\frac{1}{4}^* \times 25\frac{1}{2}$ in.	"
C. Cross support	1	$1\frac{1}{2} \times 3 \times 58\frac{1}{2}$ in.	"
D. Slats	16	$\frac{3}{4} \times 2\frac{1}{2} \times 48$ in.	"
E. Arms	2	$1\frac{1}{2} \times 3 \times 25$ in.	"
F. Arm supports	2	$1\frac{1}{2} \times 3 \times 13$ in.	"
* Width of rough stock prior to finished cutting			

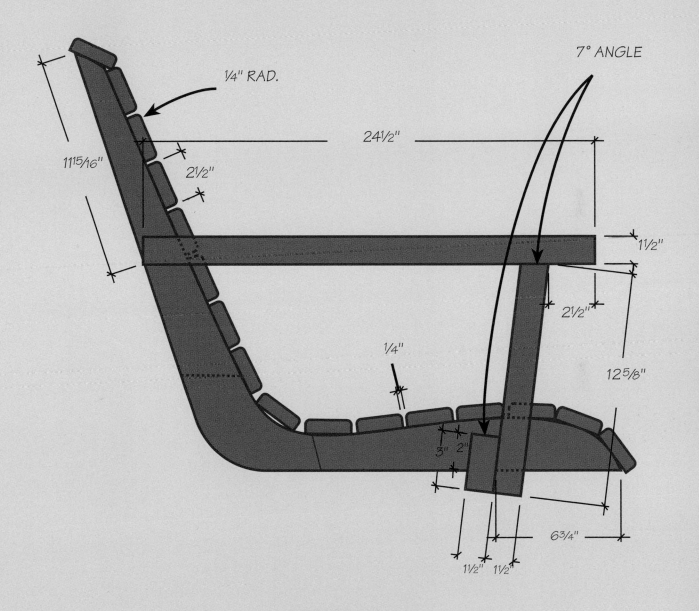

7° ANGLE

¼" RAD.

24½"

11¹⁵/₁₆"

2½"

1½"

2½"

¼"

12⁵/₈"

3" 2"

6¾"

1½" 1½"

SIDE ELEVATION

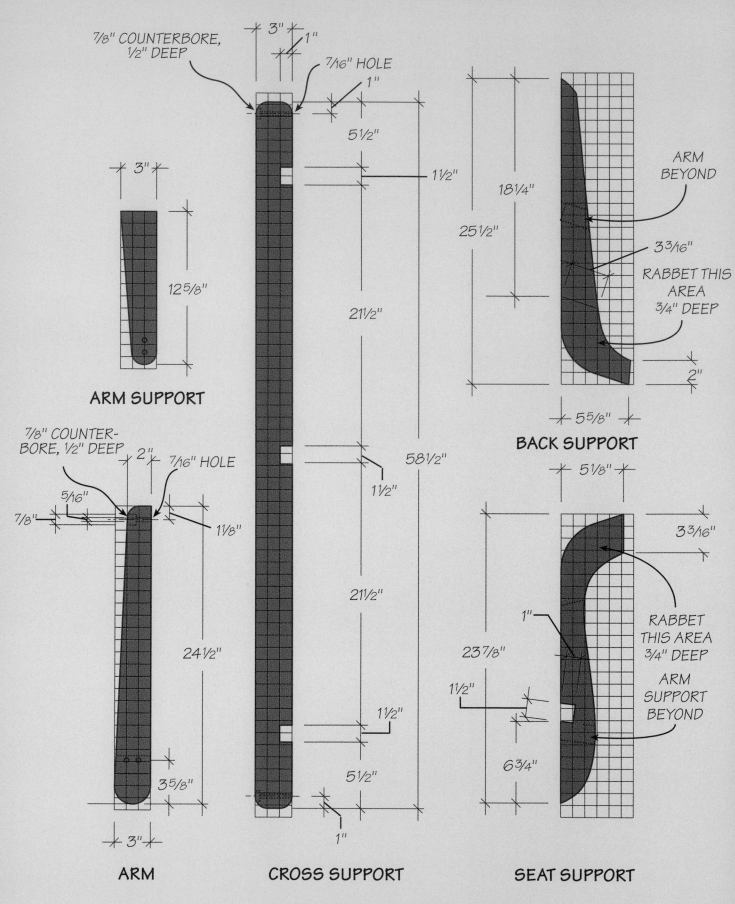

7/8" COUNTERBORE,
1/2" DEEP

3"

1"

7/16" HOLE

1"

5 1/2"

1 1/2"

3"

12 5/8"

ARM SUPPORT

21 1/2"

58 1/2"

1 1/2"

ARM
BEYOND

18 1/4"

25 1/2"

3 3/16"

RABBET THIS
AREA
3/4" DEEP

2"

5 5/8"

BACK SUPPORT

7/8" COUNTER-
BORE, 1/2" DEEP

2"

7/16" HOLE

5/16"

7/8"

1 1/8"

24 1/2"

21 1/2"

3 5/8"

1 1/2"

3"

5 1/8"

3 3/16"

1"

RABBET
THIS AREA
3/4" DEEP

ARM
SUPPORT
BEYOND

23 7/8"

1 1/2"

6 3/4"

5 1/2"

1"

ARM

CROSS SUPPORT

SEAT SUPPORT

Each square equals 1"

Porch Swing: Step-by-step

MAKE THE SUPPORT ASSEMBLY

The structural members of this porch swing consist of three L-shaped, two-part supports that are fitted over a thick horizontal cross support in front. To simplify the layout and construction of the two-part supports, we joined the parts together with half-lap joints before any of the contoured profiles were cut.

❶ Start by making a full-size template of the back support and seat supports shapes, using the *Grid patterns* as references. Either enlarge the patterns on a photocopier or draw a grid on the template paper and plot out the shapes.

❷ Cut 2 × 6 cedar blanks for the seat supports and back supports to the lengths listed in the *Cutting list*. Lay the blanks next to one another in pairs, in an "L" shape, on a flat surface. Overlap the seat support and back support templates so they join together at the half-lap joint lines indicated on the pattern. Lay the templates onto each pair of 2 × 6 blanks and mark the positions of the half-lap cuts onto the blanks.

❸ Cut the half-laps into the 2 × 6 blanks. Install a dado-blade set, set for its maximum cutting

PHOTO A: Cut the half-laps in the seat supports and back supports with a dado-blade set, making multiple overlapping passes. The final pass on each board should be right along the marked cutting line. Set the miter gauge to 65°. Making the half-lap joints prior to cutting the contours of the parts simplifies the layout of the contours.

PHOTO B: Set the cutting angle of the dado-blade set to 7° and cut 1-in.-deep notches for the seat supports into the bottom edges of the seat supports.

PHOTO C: Glue and clamp the half-laps of the seat supports and the back supports together to create L-shaped blanks for the three support structures. Use weatherproof glue.

PHOTO D: Use a template to transfer the patterns of the back supports and seat supports onto the glued-up blanks, and cut out the shapes with a band saw or jig saw.

width, in the table saw. Raise the dado-blade set to a ¾-in. cutting depth. Set the angle of the miter gauge to 65° (the angle of the half-laps). Keeping the wood pressed flat on the table and held firmly against the miter gauge fence, run the appropriate end of each blank over the dado blades to remove the wood in the half-lap area **(See Photo A).** Make multiple passes. The final pass should be right to the cutting line. Cut the half-laps in all three pairs of blanks.

❹ Use the same dado set to cut notches in the bottoms of the seat supports. Angle the blades to 7°, and reset the miter gauge to 90°. Raise the blades to give a 1-in. depth of cut at its highest point (use some scrap stock to make practice cuts in order to get the notch correct). Make two passes to cut the notch in each seat support **(See Photo B).** Clean out any roughness in the notches with a chisel if necessary.

❺ Spread exterior, weatherproof glue evenly across the face of the half-lap on one seat support and on the half-lap of a back support. Join the faces, aligning the joint shoulder of each member up tight against the other. Clamp the boards together in position until the glue is dry **(See Photo C).** Glue up all three assemblies.

❻ Use the joined seat support and back support templates to trace an outline of the contours onto the three assembled support structure blanks.

❼ Cut out the support structures with a band saw or a jig saw. Cut carefully along the waste side of the lines **(See Photo D).** File or sand the sawn edges smooth.

8 Rip-cut a piece of 2 × 6 cedar to 3 in. wide on the table saw and cross-cut it to 58½ in. to make the cross support.

9 Enlarge the pattern for the cross support to full size, and transfer it to the workpiece. This will give you the shape of each end and the location of the notches and the eyebolt holes.

10 Cut the seat support notches into the top of the cross support, using your table saw and dado-blade set. Start the end notches 5½ in. in from each end, and center the middle notch. All notches should be 1½ in. wide and 1 in. deep. Cut the notches in at least two passes, using the miter gauge to feed the workpieces (**See Photo E**).

11 With a drill press or a portable drill and a drilling guide, bore a hole through each end of the cross support for the 4-in. eyebolts. Drill from the underside and center the holes 1 in. in from the ends of the board. First, use a ⅞-in. Forstner or brad-point bit to drill ½-in.-deep counterbore holes for the nut and washer. Then drill a ⁷⁄₁₆-in.-dia. guide hole all the way through, locating the drill bit in the centerpoint recess left by the previous bit. To minimize tearout, use scrap wood to back up the exit side (top) when drilling clear through the cross support.

12 Cut the rounded ends of the cross support to shape with a jig saw or coping saw. Smooth the cuts with a sanding block.

13 Set the three L-shaped support structures seat-side down on a flat work surface, so the back support components point toward the floor. Set the cross supports on top of

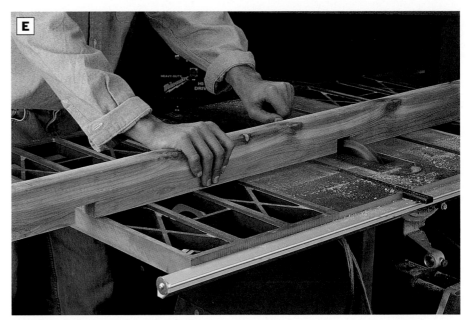

PHOTO E: Cut 1½-in.-wide notches on the top edge of the cross support. The notches fit together with the notches cut into the bottoms of the seat supports.

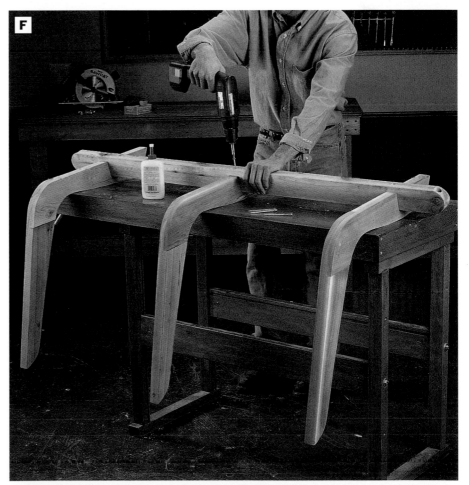

PHOTO F: Attach the support structures to the cross support with weatherproof glue and 3-in. galvanized deck screws. The notches match up to create lap joints.

them, matching up the notches. Drill a countersunk pilot hole at each joint (through the cross support and into each seat support). Attach the parts with waterproof glue and 3-in. galvanized deck screws **(See Photo F).**

INSTALL THE SEAT SLATS

14 Rip-cut and cross-cut 16, 2½ × 48-in. slats from cedar stock. We used 1 × 6 in. × 8-ft. boards (¾ in. thick actual).

15 Drill three countersunk screw holes into each slat. Clamp two scrap boards (a long and a short) in a right angle to create a reference fence in order to place the holes quickly and consistently **(See Photo G).** Measure from the corner, where the end of each slat will be, and mark off the distances of the three holes. The holes in the slats should be centered on the support structures, so you can get your distances by measuring the support assembly. Place each slat into the fence setup. Hold it tightly against the side and end fences and drill centered holes aligned with the marks on the fences.

16 Round over the top edges of each slat with a router and a ¼-in. piloted roundover bit.

17 Beginning at the front of the seat support, attach the slats with 2-in. galvanized deck screws. Butt the first three slats up against one another. From there, use a ¼-in. spacers between the slats **(See Photo H).** The ends of the seat slats should be flush with the sides of the supports.

MAKE & ATTACH THE ARMS

18 From 2 × 8 cedar stock, rip-cut and cross-cut two arm blanks to 3 × 24½ in., and cut two arm supports to 3 in. × 12⅝ in.

19 Make full-size templates for the arms and arm supports, using the *Grid drawings* as a reference. Use the templates to trace the appropriate shapes onto the corresponding workpieces. Mark the centerpoints for screw holes and the locations for the bolt holes on the arms.

20 Cut the parts out with a band saw or jig saw and smooth the edges and surfaces.

21 Drill ⁷⁄₁₆-in.-dia. guide holes with ⅞ in. dia. × ½ in. deep counterbores into the back, outside edge of each arm. The edge of each counterbore should be 1 in. back from the end of the arm **(See Photo I).**

PHOTO G: Drill countersunk screw holes into the seat slats. Use a fence setup with measured guide marks for quick and consistent drilling.

PHOTO H: Screw the slats to the back-and-seat support structures. Butt the first three slats together, then use a ¼-in.-thick spacer between the rest of the slats for consistent gaps. Keep the ends of the slats flush with the sides of the supports.

22 Set the table saw blade to 7° and use the miter gauge to cut a bevel on the top (wide) end of each arm support.

23 Position the arm supports against the faces of the cross supports, flush with the bottom of the cross supports and with the 7° bevels sloping from front to back. Clamp the arm supports in this position. Attach the arm supports with 2½-in. galvanized deck screws driven through countersunk pilot holes in the arm supports, and into the cross support.

24 Attach the arms: Rest each arm on the arm support so the screw hole centerpoints in the top of the arm are centered on the top of the arm support. Hold each arm against the outer back support, and extend the 7⁄16-in.-dia. guide hole through the back support **(See Photo J).**

25 Drill 7⁄8-in.-dia., ½-in.-deep counterbores on the inside faces of the back supports. Insert a 3⁄8-in.-dia. × 4-in.-long eyebolt into each arm and through the back support. Thread a nut and washer onto the other end and snug with a wrench. Attach the arms to the arms supports with two 3-in. deck screws driven at the centerpoint locations.

Finishing touches
26 Insert 4-in. eyebolts into the counterbored holes in the cross support. Thread nuts and washers onto them and tighten them with a wrench.

27 Apply a finish, then hang the swing with heavy rope or chain attached to the eyebolts. Be sure to anchor the ropes or chains with eyebolts into a ceiling joist that can bear the overall weight.

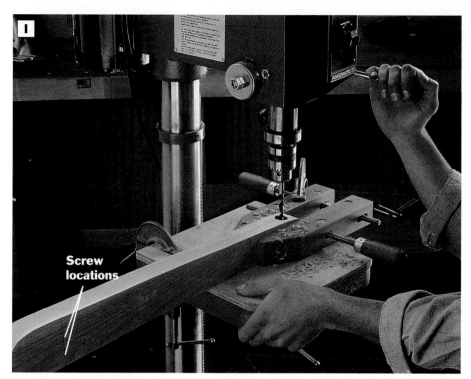

PHOTO I: Use a drill press with a Forstner or brad-point bit to drill counterbored guide holes in edges of the arms for the eyebolts.

PHOTO J: Extend the 7⁄16-in. eyebolt guide holes in the arms through the back supports, then attach the eyebolts with washers and nuts.

Picnic Table & Benches

This unusual picnic table and bench set combines the look of traditional picnic table styling with the space-efficiency of a round table. With the 58-in.-dia. top and four long benches, as many as eight adults can enjoy dining in the great outdoors using this lovely set.

Vital Statistics: Picnic Table & Benches

TYPE: Round cross-buck picnic table with curved benches

OVERALL SIZE: 58-in.-dia. by 30H (table)

17H by 41¾W by 12¾D (bench)

MATERIAL: Dimensional cedar

JOINERY: Half-lap joints and butt joints reinforced with carriage bolts and galvanized deck screws

CONSTRUCTION DETAILS:
· Spacious round tabletop seats up to eight adults
· Traditional cross-buck look on legs
· Alternating board width on tabletop and benchtop
· No planing or jointing required

FINISHING OPTIONS: Clear, UV-resistant topcoat (exterior wood stain optional), or leave untreated for natural gray look.

Building time (table)

PREPARING STOCK
1 hour

LAYOUT
2-3 hours

CUTTING PARTS
4-6 hours

ASSEMBLY
4-6 hours

FINISHING
1-2 hours

TOTAL: 12-18 hours

Tools you'll use

· Straightedge cutting guide
· C-clamps
· Router with ⅜-in. roundover bit
· Table saw with dado-blade set
· Tape measure
· 64-in. or longer bar or pipe clamps (2)
· Spring clamps
· Jig saw or band saw
· Combination square
· Framing (carpenter's) square
· Drill/driver

Shopping list

(for TABLE and ONE BENCH)

☐ (6) 2 × 6 in. × 8 ft. (nominal) cedar

☐ (6) 2 × 8 in. × 8 ft. (nominal) cedar

☐ (13) 2 × 4 in. × 8 ft. (nominal) cedar

☐ Carriage bolts with nuts and washers: (20) ⅜ × 3½ in.; (10) ⅜ × 3 in.

☐ #10 galvanized deck screws (2-, 2½-, 3-in. lengths)

☐ Finishing materials

Picnic Table & Benches

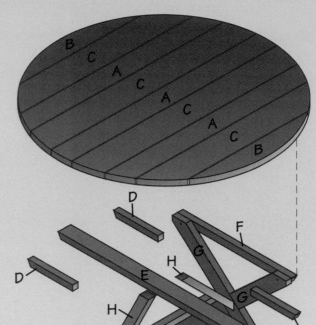

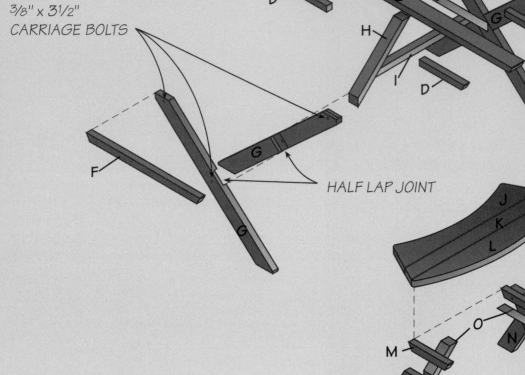

B
C
A
C
A
C
A
C
B
D
F
G
H
D
E
G
H
D
I
D
3/8" x 3 1/2"
CARRIAGE BOLTS
F
G
HALF LAP JOINT
G
J
K
L
M
O
M
N
N
N
N

Picnic Table Cutting List			
Part	**No.**	**Size**	**Material**
A. Top slat	3	1½ × 5½ × 60 in.	Cedar
B. Top slat	2	1½ × 5½ × 48 in.	"
C. Top slat	4	1½ × 7¼ × 60 in.	"
D. Batten	4	1½ × 1½ × 12½ in.	"
E. Batten	1	1½ × 3½ × 56 in.	"
F. Batten	2	1½ × 1¾ × 32 in.	"
G. Legs	4	1½ × 3½ × 43 in.	"
H. Buttress	2	1½ × 1¾ × 20¾ in.	"
I. Stretcher	1	1½ × 1¾ × 27 in.	"

Picnic Bench Cutting List (one bench)			
Part	**No.**	**Size**	**Material**
J. Top slat	1	1½ × 7¼ × 48 in.	Cedar
K. Top slat	1	1½ × 5½ × 48 in.	"
L. Top slat	1	1½ × 3½ × 48 in.	"
M. Batten	2	1½ × 1¾ × 11 in.	"
N. Legs	4	1½ × 3½ × 19⅝ in.	"
O. Buttress	2	1½ × 1¾ × 9¾ in.	"

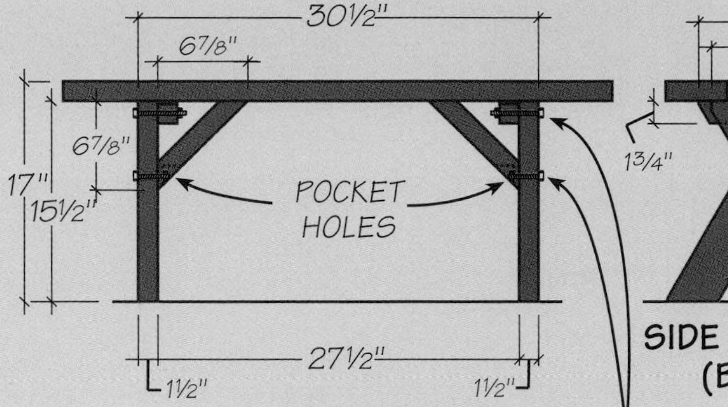
30½"
6⅞"
6⅞"
17"
15½"
POCKET HOLES
27½"
1½"
1½"
3/8" x 3½" CARRIAGE BOLTS

FRONT ELEVATION (BENCH)

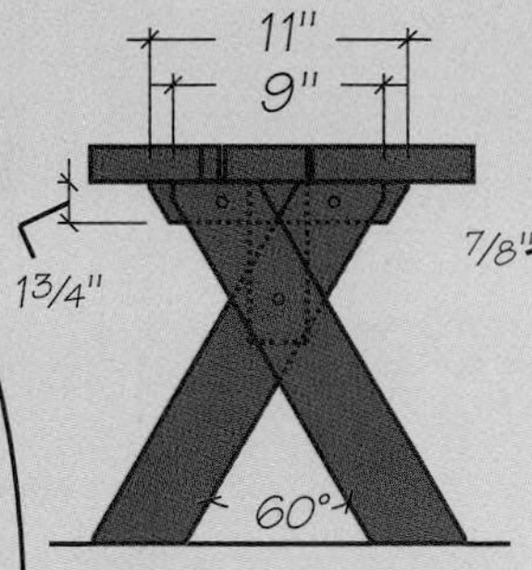
11"
9"
1¾"
60°

SIDE ELEVATION (BENCH)

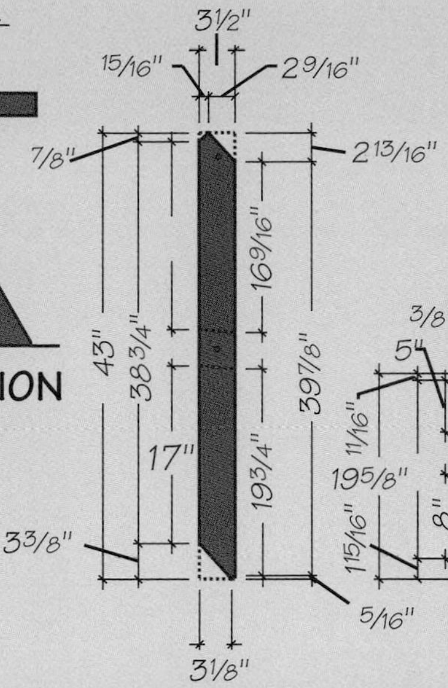
3½"
15/16"
2 9/16"
7/8"
2 13/16"
16 9/16"
43"
38¾"
39⅞"
17"
19¾"
3⅜"
5/16"
3⅛"

TABLE LEG

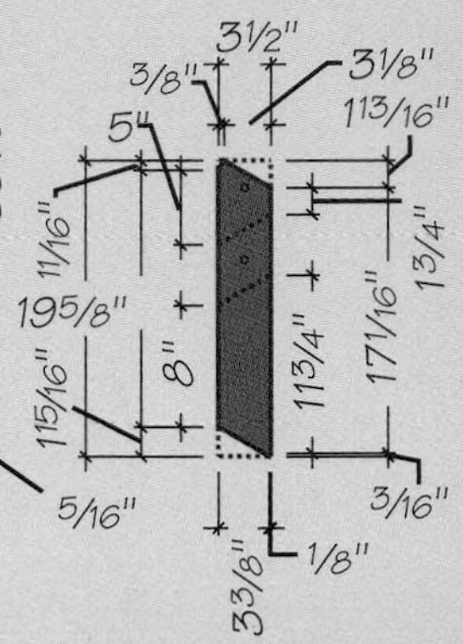
3½"
3/8"
3⅛"
1 13/16"
5"
11/16"
19⅝"
1 5/16"
8"
11¾"
17 1/16"
1¾"
3/16"
3⅜"
1/8"

BENCH LEG

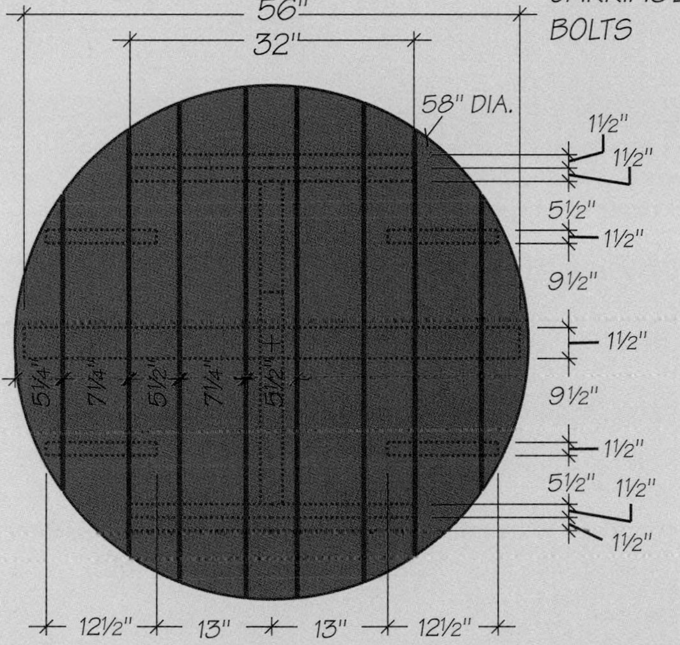
56"
32"
58" DIA.
1½"
1½"
5½"
1½"
9½"
1½"
9½"
1½"
5½"
1½"
1½"
5¼
7¼
5½
7¼
5½
12½"
13"
13"
12½"

TOP VIEW (TABLE)

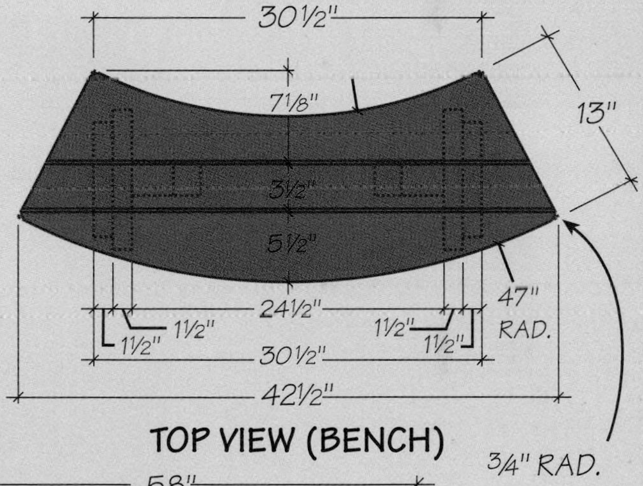
30½"
7⅛"
13"
3½"
5½"
47" RAD.
24½"
1½"
1½"
1½"
1½"
30½"
42½"
¾" RAD.

TOP VIEW (BENCH)

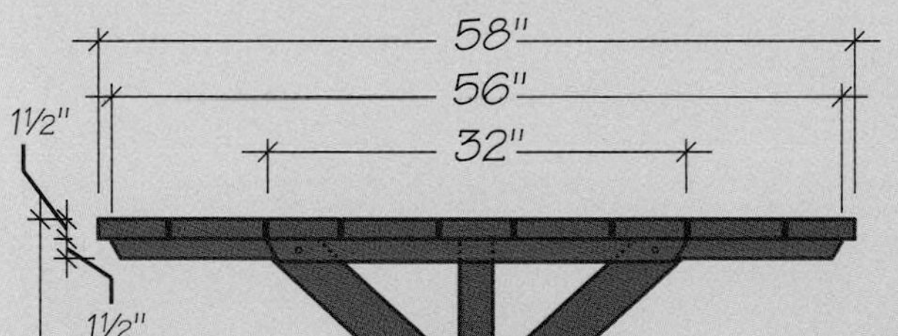
58"
56"
32"
1½"
1½"
29"

FRONT ELEVATION (TABLE)

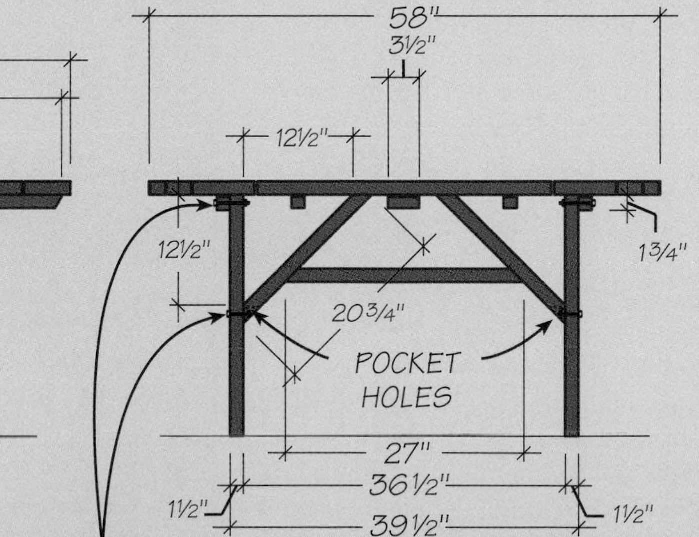
58"
3½"
12½"
12½"
1¾"
20¾"
POCKET HOLES
27"
36½"
1½"
1½"
39½"
3/8" x 3½" CARRIAGE BOLTS

SIDE ELEVATION (TABLE)

PHOTO A: Lay out the boards with the tabletop facing down. Separate the boards with ¼-in. spacers and clamp the setup together. Draw two perpendicular centerlines, and use a trammel to swing a 29-in.-radius circle from the point where the two lines intersect.

MAKE THE TABLETOP

The round top for this picnic table is cut from nine 2× cedar boards laid edge-to edge. The layout alternates between 5½-in.-wide boards (nominal 2 × 6) and 7¼ in.-wide boards (nominal 2 × 8) for an interesting pattern that, when added to the ¼-in. gap between boards, results in a tabletop that has a generous diameter of 58 in.

❶ Cut the nine boards for the tabletop to the lengths listed in the *Cutting list*. Select a 60-in.-long 2 × 6 and draw a centerline along the length of the board to mark the center of the tabletop. Use a combination square and pencil to draw the centerline. Lay out the boards in the order shown in *Top view (Table)*, positioning the board with the centerline in the middle of the layout. Insert spacers made from ¼-in.-thick scrap between the boards, then draw the boards together with a pipe clamp near each end of the layout.

❷ Draw a centerline perpendicular to the first centerline. Measure to find the midpoints of the two end boards to mark endpoints for the second centerline. Lay a straightedge across the boards to mark the line, but check with a framing square first to make sure the centerlines are perpendicular.

PHOTO B: Attach the battens to the underside of the tabletop using #10 × 2 in. galvanized deck screws for the short battens and the center batten. Use 2½-in. screws for the leg-side battens.

❸ Use the point where the two lines intersect as a centerpoint for scribing a 58-in.-dia. (29-in.-radius) circle onto the boards **(See Photo A).** We used a shop-built trammel made of hardboard to draw the circle.

❹ Cut the seven battens to size. Cross-cut the center batten to 56 in. from a 2 × 4, and cut the four short battens to 12½ in. long from 2 × 2 stock. Rip the leg-side battens to 1¾ in. wide from a 2 × 3 or 2 × 4, then cross-cut them to 32 in.

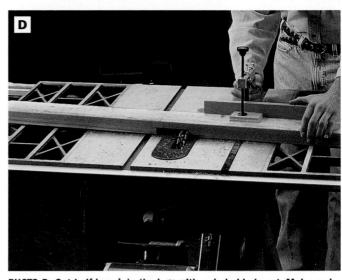

PHOTO C: Round over the top and bottom edges of the tabletop with a router and ⅜-in. roundover bit. Move clockwise around the tabletop.

PHOTO D: Cut half-laps into the legs with a dado-blade set. Make multiple passes, using a miter gauge set at 85° to guide the stock.

5 Make a 60° trim cut at the end of each batten, starting ¼ in. down from the face of the batten that will contact the underside of the table. The trim cuts serve to eliminate the sharp ends. Make the trim cuts on a power miter saw. *NOTE: The battens that attach to the legs are installed with the 1½ in. edge up against the tabletop, so be sure your trim cuts are on the correct faces.*

6 Mark the midpoint of the center batten's length, and square the line all around the board. Now measure 1¾ in. on either side of the second (cross-grain) centerline on the tabletop and lay the center batten on these marks, aligning the midpoint line on the batten with the centerline along the center board of the tabletop.

7 Drill countersunk pilot holes, then attach the center batten to the tabletop boards with #10 × 2-in. galvanized deck screws. Position the remaining battens on the underside of the tabletop, as shown in *Top view (Table)*, and attach with screws **(See Photo B).**

8 Cut out the circle along the waste side of the line with a jig saw. Smooth out any unevenness in the cut with a power sander.

9 Install a piloted ⅜-in. roundover bit (See *FYI*, right) in your router and round the top and bottom edges of the tabletop **(See Photo C).**

MAKE & ATTACH THE TABLE LEGS

10 Lay out and cut the four table legs from 2 × 4 cedar. Use the measurements shown in the drawing as a reference for scribing the layout lines. Cut the parallel, angled ends and the 90° tip cutoffs on the table saw or power miter saw.

11 Lay out the half-lap joints cut into the legs in the positions indicated on the drawing.

12 We used a dado-blade set mounted in our table saw to remove the wood in the half-lap joint areas. Set the blade to its widest cutting width, then raise it to a ¾-in. cutting depth. Set the miter gauge on your table saw to 85°, and feed each leg over the

ROUNDOVER BITS

Piloted roundover bits, like the ⅜-in. roundover bit shown above, cut smooth, even curves into edges of boards. Rounded edges increase safety and visual appeal. Other examples of edge-profiling bits are chamfer bits and ogee bits.

blade in multiple passes to remove the wood in the joint areas **(See Photo D).**

13 Put the half-laps together to assemble the legs. Clamp the joints temporarily to stabilize them. Then position the leg assemblies in place against the

PHOTO E: Clamp the legs together and drill clearance holes for carriage bolts through the battens and legs. Keep the drill level.

PHOTO F: Drill clearance holes for ⅜ × 3½-in. carriage bolts through the end of each buttress, then through the half-lap leg joint.

PHOTO G: Screw the buttresses to the tabletop. Use a square to maintain a perpendicular angle between the leg assembly and the tabletop.

leg-side battens. Align the ends of the leg tops flush with the ends of the battens.

⓮ Clamp the legs to the battens (along with a scrap backup board to prevent drilling tearout), and drill clearance holes for ⅜ × 3½-in. carriage bolts through the battens and the leg tops, in the positions shown **(See Photo E).**

⓯ Insert the 3½-in. carriage bolts from the outside, and secure the legs to the battens with washers and nuts fastened to the bolts.

INSTALL THE TABLE LEG SUPPORTS

The table legs receive lateral support from a pair of buttresses and a spreader that form a center brace assembly.

⓰ Rip-cut 2 × 4 or 2 × 3 stock to 1¾ in. wide. Cut the angled buttresses to length, making 45° miter cuts at the ends. The buttresses should be 20¾ in. long at their longest points. Cut the center stretcher to size, mitering the ends so it's 27 in. long at it's longest point.

⓱ Measure up 12½ in. from the underside of the tabletop and make a mark on the inside juncture of each leg assembly. Mark the center of the width on one end of each buttress. Measure across the juncture of the leg assembly and mark a midpoint, then extend it vertically with a carpenter's square. Hold a buttress in place against one of the leg assemblies, with the lower edge of its upper miter at the height mark, and the centerlines on the buttress and leg assemblies aligned. Drill a pocket hole into the buttress, then follow with a clearance hole for a carriage bolt, keeping the drill level **(See Photo F).** Bolt the buttress to the legs with ⅜ × 3½-in. carriage bolts. Repeat for the other side.

⓲ Drill countersunk pilot holes and screw the free ends of the buttresses to the underside of the tabletop **(See Photo G).** To make sure the buttresses are in the right position and the legs are perpendicular to the top, hold a carpenter's square up against each leg as you attach it.

⓳ Put the center stretcher in place across the buttresses. Place a level on the stretcher and adjust it until it's level. Then drill angled pilot holes and screw the stretcher to the buttresses with #10 × 2-in. deck screws **(See Photo H).**

BUILD THE BENCHES

The following instructions, the *Shopping List* and the *Cutting List* all provide information for building one bench only. If you want to build four of the curved benches to complete the outdoor dining set, multiply the quantities for the bench parts by four to calculate your shopping list. Much of the assembly sequence for the benches repeats techniques used to make the table. Refer to the above sections for more information if you're unsure about any steps in the bench-construction process.

20 Lay out the boards for the benchtop with ¼-in. spacers between them and stabilize the setup with clamps. Draw the outline of the benchtop shape onto the boards, using the measurements and arc radii shown in the illustrations. (If you're planning to build all four benches, it would be worth your while to make a template for the benchtops.)

21 Rip-cut one edge of the batten stock and cut the battens to length. Cut the angled ends the same as those on the table battens.

22 Screw the battens to the underside of the top, 24½ in. apart and positioned as shown in the illustration.

23 Cut the benchtop to shape with a jig saw **(See Photo I),** and round the corners with a ¾-in. radius, using your jig saw. Smooth the edges, then run a router with a ⅜-in. roundover bit around the edges as before.

24 Cut the legs and buttresses to size. Lay out and cut the leg half-laps using the same methods you did on the table legs, but use a 60° angle instead of 85°.

25 Assemble the leg structure as before. Follow the same steps for bolting the legs to the battens, and for attaching the buttresses **(See Photo J).**

26 Sand the wood lightly to smooth out any rough or splintered surfaces.

27 Use an exterior stain to seal and protect the wood. Alternatively it can be painted or left to age gracefully to an elegant silver-gray (cedar and redwood are highly weather-resistant).

PHOTO H: Attach the ends of the stretcher to the buttresses with two #10 × 2-in. deck screws at each joint. Make sure the stretcher is level.

PHOTO I: After the battens have been attached, cut out the shape of the benchtop with a jig saw.

PHOTO J: Attach the bench buttresses as you did the table buttresses, using a square to keep the legs perpendicular.

Picnic Table & Benches 439

WORKSHOP PROJECTS

Page
450

Page
446

Page
442

Page 468

Page 312

WORKSHOP PROJECTS

Sawhorses

Sawhorses may well be a handyman's most trusted companion. They create a durable worksurface wherever you need it, whether in the shop or in the field. This sturdy, shop-tested model, made of 2 × 4s and plywood, features a shelf beneath to keep necessary tools and supplies handy. Although one of these horses can be a great help, build a pair to create your own "work crew"—without paying them hourly wages!

Vital Statistics

TYPE: Sawhorses

OVERALL SIZE: 24W by 30H by 38L

MATERIAL: Pine, plywood

JOINERY: Butt joints reinforced with screws

CONSTRUCTION DETAILS:
- Legs are miter-cut near their top ends to form the A-shaped leg spread
- Plywood gussets reinforce the leg joints

FINISH: None or a clear protective topcoat

BUILDING TIME: 6-8 hours (for two)

Shopping List (for two)

- ☐ (2) ¾ × ¾ in. × 8 ft. quarter-round molding
- ☐ (4) 2 × 4 in. × 8 ft. pine
- ☐ (2) 2 × 6 in. × 8 ft. pine
- ☐ (1) ¾ in. × 2 × 4 ft. plywood
- ☐ Deck screws (2, 2½, 3 in.)
- ☐ 1¼ in. galvanized finish nails

Sawhorses: Step-by-step

PHOTO A: Assemble pairs of legs with a plywood gusset, keeping the gusset flush with the top and outside edges of the legs. Flip the assembly over and install the shelf support so the ends are flush with the outside edges of the legs (about 10 in. up from the leg bottoms).

CUT THE PARTS TO SIZE

❶ Crosscut the top plate, legs and shelf supports to length. Cut the plywood gussets and shelves to rough size. Miter-cut quarter-round shelf-lip pieces to length.

❷ Using the three layout drawings, draw the angles on the legs, shelf supports and gussets. Make these angle cuts with a jig saw or circular saw.

MAKE THE LEG ASSEMBLIES

❸ Arrange two legs and a gusset on your worksurface so the top miter cuts of the legs butt together and the angled edges of the gusset are flush with the outside edges of the legs. Join the gussets to the legs with 2-in. deck screws driven through countersunk pilot holes.

Sawhorses

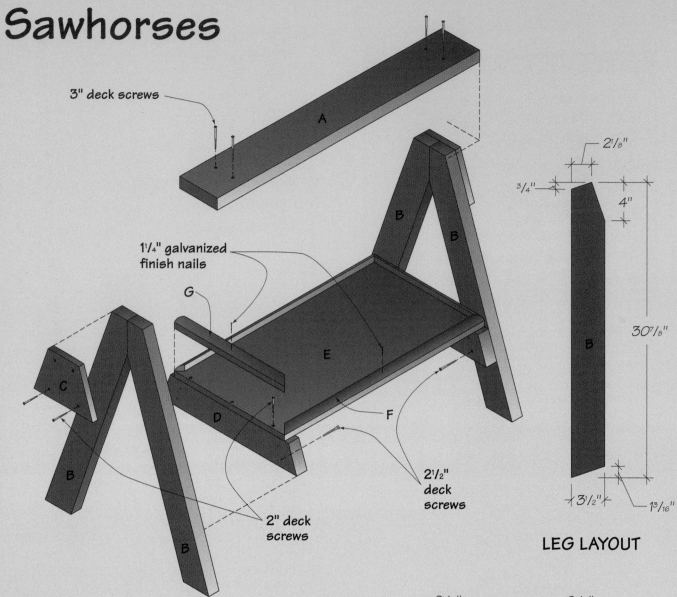

3" deck screws

1¼" galvanized
finish nails

3" deck screws

2" deck
screws

2½"
deck
screws

2" deck
screws

A

B

B

B

B

G

E

D

F

C

LEG LAYOUT

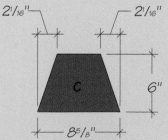

2⅛"

¾"

4"

30⅞"

B

3½"

1³⁄₁₆"

GUSSET LAYOUT

2¹⁄₁₆"

2¹⁄₁₆"

C

6"

8⅝"

SHELF SUPPORT LAYOUT

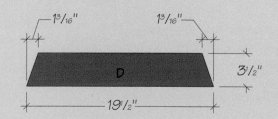

1³⁄₁₆"

1³⁄₁₆"

D

3½"

19½"

Sawhorses Cutting List (makes two)

Part	No.	Size	Material
A. Top plates	2	1½ × 5½ × 38 in.	Pine
B. Legs	8	1½ × 3½ × 31 in.	"
C. Gussets	4	¾ × 8⅝ × 6 in.	Plywood
D. Shelf supports	4	1½ × 3½ × 19½ in.	Pine
E. Shelves	2	¾ × 29 × 16 in.	Plywood
F. Shelf lips (long)	4	¾ × ¾ × 29 in.	Quarter-round molding
G. Shelf lips (short)	4	¾ × ¾ × 16 in.	"

4 Flip the leg assembly over to attach the shelf support. Align the angled ends of the shelf support so they're flush with the outside edges of the legs (this should place the shelf support about 10 in. up from the leg bottoms). Fasten the shelf supports to the legs with countersunk 2½-in. deck screws **(See Photo A).**

5 Repeat Steps 2 through 4 to build the other three leg assemblies.

ATTACH THE SHELF & TOP PLATE

6 Attach the shelf: Stand two leg assemblies upright on the floor so the shelf supports face inward. Set a shelf panel in place on the shelf supports. Hold the parts together with clamps. Fasten the shelf to the shelf supports with countersunk 2-in. deck screws. Do the same for the other sawhorse.

7 Install the top plate. Center the top plate over the leg assemblies. Drill countersunk pilot holes, and drive 3-in. deck screws down through the top plate into the top ends of the legs **(See Photo B).**

FINISHING TOUCHES

8 Attach the shelf lip pieces to the shelves to form a shallow tray. Start by nailing a short lip piece in place, and work your way around, matching up the mitered joints as you go. Avoid splitting the narrow quarter-round by drilling pilot holes for the finish nails. Use a nailset to set protruding nailheads **(See Photo C).**

EDITOR'S NOTE: *If you choose to topcoat these sawhorses, avoid using paint or stain; these finishes could mar other workpieces when the sawhorses are in use. Use a clear protective finish instead, like varnish or tung oil.*

PHOTO B: With the sawhorses standing upright, center each top plate over the legs so it overhangs evenly all around. Drill countersunk pilot holes and secure the top plates to the top ends of the legs with 3-in. deck screws.

PHOTO C: Attach the quarter-round shelf lips to the shelves with 1¼-in. finish nails. Start at a short side, driving the finish nails through pilot holes. Set the nailheads below the surface of the wood with a nailset.

2 × 4 Workbench

Agood workbench should be generously proportioned, yet small enough to fit into cramped working quarters. It should be solidly constructed, yet light enough to move around the shop. The best benches make use of the space below the top for shelving and storage. We took all of these considerations seriously when designing this workbench. Its reinforced hardboard top provides a smooth, sizable worksurface that's easy to replace. The laminated 2 × 4 legs will support even your heaviest projects. When you're done working, tuck the bench against a wall and use the bottom shelf for storage.

Vital Statistics

TYPE: Workbench

OVERALL SIZE: 24W by 36H by 60L

MATERIAL: Pine, plywood, hardboard

JOINERY: Butt joints reinforced with screws

CONSTRUCTION DETAILS:
- Legs are made of pairs of 2 × 4s face-glued and screwed together
- Hardboard worksurface is attached to plywood sub-top with finish nails only so it can be replaced when the surface wears out

FINISH: Clear protective topcoat or none

BUILDING TIME: 4-6 hours

Shopping List

- ☐ (1) ¼ in. × 4 × 8 ft. hardboard
- ☐ (7) 2 × 4 in. × 8 ft. pine
- ☐ (1) ¾ in. × 4 × 8 ft. plywood
- ☐ Deck screws (1¼, 2, 2½, 3 in.)
- ☐ 1½ in. finish nails
- ☐ Wood glue
- ☐ Finishing materials (optional)

2 × 4 Workbench: Step-by-step

PHOTO A: Attach the top and shelf rails to the legs with 3-in. deck screws to create two leg assemblies. The top rails should be flush with the tops of the legs. Fasten the shelf rails so their top edges are 11¾ in. up from the leg bottoms.

CUT THE PARTS

1 Cut the legs, stretchers, rails and crossbrace to length.

2 Cut the sub-top, shelf and work-surface parts to size.

MAKE THE LEG ASSEMBLIES

3 Build the legs by gluing and screwing pairs of leg pieces together. Be sure the edges and ends of the parts are flush, and stagger the screw pattern.

4 Join the legs and rails: Turn the legs over so the screwheads face down on your worksurface. Position a top rail so it's flush with the top ends of a pair of legs. Set the shelf rails so the top edges are 11¾ in. up from the leg bottoms. Attach the rails to the legs with 3-in. deck screws to form the leg assemblies **(See Photo A).**

2 × 4 Workbench

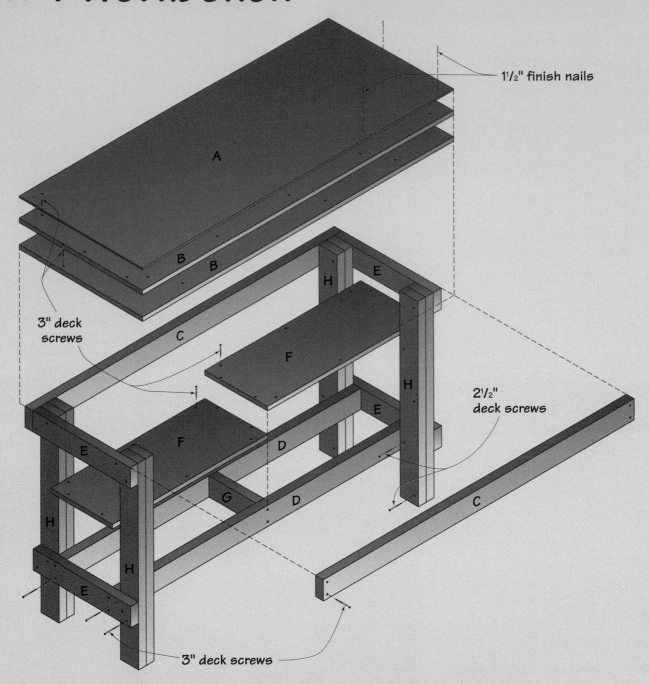

1¹/₂" finish nails

3" deck screws

2¹/₂" deck screws

3" deck screws

		2 × 4 Workbench Cutting List						
Part	**No.**	**Size**	**Material**		**Part**	**No.**	**Size**	**Material**
A. Worksurface	1	¼ × 24 × 60 in.	Hardboard		**E.** Top/shelf rails	4	1½ × 3½ × 19 in.	Pine
B. Sub-top	2	¾ × 24 × 60 in.	Plywood		**F.** Shelf sections	2	¾ × 12 × 30 in.	Plywood
C. Top stretchers	2	1½ × 3½ × 60 in.	Pine		**G.** Crossbrace	1	1½ × 3½ × 9 in.	Pine
D. Shelf stretchers	2	1½ × 3½ × 57 in.	"		**H.** Legs	8	1½ × 3½ × 34½ in.	"

PHOTO B: Build the shelf assembly by attaching the shelf stretchers to the crossbrace first, then clamp the shelf frame between the legs, even with the shelf rails. Drive 3-in. deck screws through the shelf rails into the ends of the shelf stretchers.

PHOTO C: Center the sub-top over the top stretchers, allowing for an even overhang, front to back. The ends of the sub-top are flush with the top rails. Secure the sub-top to the top stretchers and rails with 3-in. deck screws.

ASSEMBLE THE BENCH & SHELF FRAMES

Because of the size of the workbench, continue the assembly working on the floor.

❺ Set the leg assemblies on edge to attach the top stretchers. These stretchers should sit flush with the tops of the leg assemblies and overlap the ends of the top rails. Install the top stretchers with countersunk 3-in. deck screws driven into the ends of the top rails.

❻ Assemble the shelf stretchers and crossbrace according to the technical drawing. Position the crossbrace so it is centered on the shelf stretchers, and attach the parts with 3-in. deck screws.

❼ With the bench assembly on its side, install the shelf frame between the legs and shelf rails. Align the ends of the shelf stretchers with the shelf rails, and clamp the parts together. Fasten the shelf frame to the bench with 3-in. deck screws driven through the side rails (See Photo B).

ATTACH THE SHELF & TOP

❽ Screw the two shelf sections to the shelf stretchers, shelf rails and crossbrace. Use countersunk 2-in. deck screws.

❾ Laminate the two plywood sub-top pieces together with glue and 1¼-in. screws.

❿ Install the sub-top: Center the sub-top on the top stretchers and align the ends of the sub-top with the

outside faces of the top rails. Attach the parts by driving 3-in. countersunk deck screws through the sub-top into the stretchers and rails (See Photo C).

⓫ Attach the worksurface, aligning it evenly with the sub-top all around. Use 1½-in. finish nails, spaced evenly around the perimeter, to secure the hardboard to the sub-top (See Photo D). Recess the nailheads with a nailset.

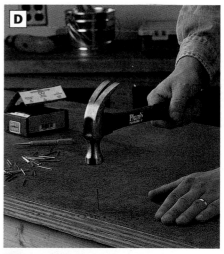

PHOTO D: Tack the hardboard worksurface to the sub-top with 1½-in. finish nails. Set the nailheads to create a flat bench surface.

FINISHING TOUCHES

⓬ Round over the corners of the worksurface and sub-top: Cut off the sharp corners with a jig saw or circular saw, then smooth the profiles with a coarse file and sandpaper until they're round and even.

⓭ Apply several coats of wood finish, if you wish, to help protect the bench from stains and abrasions. We brushed on two coats of Danish oil, but varnish also would be a good choice.

Sheet Goods Cart

Every shop can benefit by increasing storage and reducing clutter. If wall space is at a premium in your shop, our sheet goods cart is a clever alternative to permanent shelving. Made of inexpensive CDX plywood, the cart occupies only 12 square ft. of floor space, yet it provides ample storage for full-sized sheet stock, center shelves for longer boards and five bins of of various widths for shorter cutoffs and scrap. The top shelf is perfect for storing containers of hardware or smaller tools, and one end of the cart sports notched holders for pipe or bar clamps. Casters allow you to roll the cart right where it's needed or out of the way entirely.

Vital Statistics: Sheet Goods Cart

TYPE: Rolling storage cart

OVERALL SIZE: 53H x 72L x 24W at base

MATERIAL: CDX plywood

JOINERY: Dadoes, screwed butt joints

CONSTRUCTION DETAILS:
- Cart side that stores full sheets angled back 5° to keep sheets from tipping over
- Shelves between tall sides secured with dadoes and screws
- Storage bins separated by angled dividers
- Cart bottom reinforced with blocking to provide solid base for mounting casters
- Built-in clamp rack constructed from scrap CDX

FINISH: None

Building time

PREPARING STOCK
2 hours

LAYOUT
2-3 hours

CUTTING PARTS
3-4 hours

ASSEMBLY
2-3 hours

FINISHING
None

TOTAL: 9-12 hours

Tools you'll use

- Table saw
- Circular saw
- Drill/driver
- Sliding power miter saw (optional)
- Router and ¾-in. straight bit
- Jig saw
- Clamps
- Sockets

Shopping list

- ☐ (4) ¾ in. × 4 ft. × 8 ft. CDX plywood
- ☐ (16) ⅜ × 2-in. carriage bolts, nuts & washers
- ☐ (2) 4-in. straight casters
- ☐ (2) 4-in. swivelling casters with brakes
- ☐ #8 flathead wood screws (1¼-, 1½-, 2¼-in.)
- ☐ Wood glue

Sheet Goods Cart

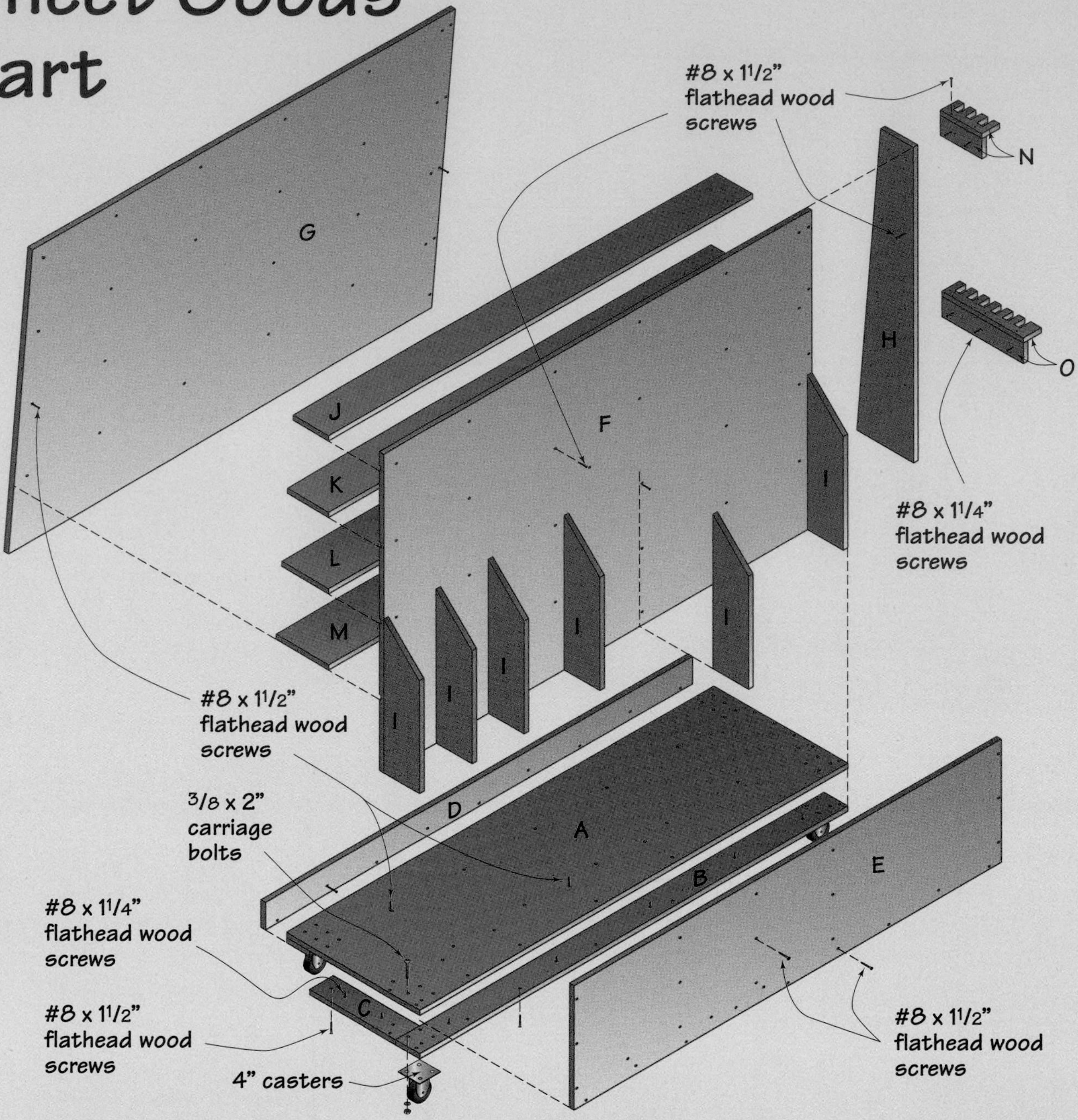

G
#8 x 1 1/2" flathead wood screws
N
J
F
H
O
K
L
M
I
#8 x 1 1/4" flathead wood screws
#8 x 1 1/2" flathead wood screws
3/8 x 2" carriage bolts
D
A
B
E
#8 x 1 1/4" flathead wood screws
C
#8 x 1 1/2" flathead wood screws
4" casters
#8 x 1 1/2" flathead wood screws

Sheet Goods Cart Cutting List

Part	No.	Size	Material	Part	No.	Size	Material
A. Base	1	¾ × 22½ × 72 in.	CDX plywood	**I.** Divider	6	¾ × 6 × 22½ in.	CDX plywood
B. Blocking (long)	2	¾ × 4 × 72 in.	"	**J.** Top shelf	1	¾ × 6³⁄₁₆ × 71¼ in.	"
C. Blocking (short)	2	¾ × 4 × 14½ in.	"	**K.** Shelf	1	¾ × 7³⁄₁₆ × 71¼ in.	"
D. Short edge	1	¾ × 4 × 72 in.	"	**L.** Shelf	1	¾ × 8⅛ × 71¼ in.	"
E. Tall edge	1	¾ × 18 × 72 in.	"	**M.** Shelf	1	¾ × 9⅛ × 71¼ in.	"
F. Vertical side	1	¾ × 46½ × 72 in.	"	**N.** Clamp holder	2	¾ × 3 × 7 in.	"
G. Angled side	1	¾ × 46¾ × 72 in.	"	**O.** Clamp holder	2	¾ × 3 × 13¾ in.	"
H. End	1	¾ × 9¾ × 46½ in.	"				

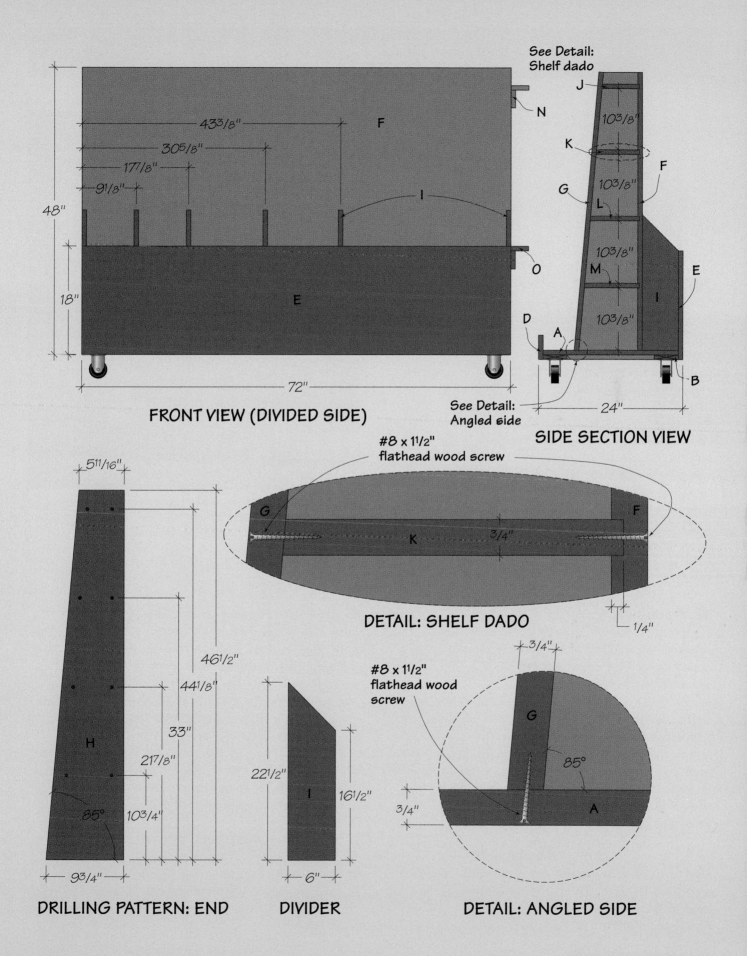

See Detail:
Shelf dado

FRONT VIEW (DIVIDED SIDE)

43³/₈"
30⁵/₈"
17⁷/₈"
9¹/₈"
48"
18"
72"

F
I
E
N
O

J
10³/₈"
K
10³/₈"
G
L
F
10³/₈"
M
10³/₈"
E
I
D
A
B
24"

See Detail:
Angled side

SIDE SECTION VIEW

#8 x 1¹/₂"
flathead wood screw

G
K
3/4"
F
1/4"

DETAIL: SHELF DADO

5¹¹/₁₆"
46¹/₂"
44¹/₈"
33"
21⁷/₈"
10³/₄"
85°
9³/₄"
H

DRILLING PATTERN: END

22¹/₂"
16¹/₂"
6"
I

DIVIDER

#8 x 1¹/₂"
flathead wood
screw

3/4"
G
85°
3/4"
A

DETAIL: ANGLED SIDE

PHOTO A: Attach the long and short blocking pieces to the bottom panel, flush around the perimeter, with glue and 1¼-in. flathead wood screws. Drill pilot holes for the screws first.

BUILD THE BASE

❶ Cut to size the base, bottom blocking and short and tall edge pieces from ¾-in. plywood. Use a circular saw and a straightedge guide for making the initial cuts to reduce full sheets to a more manageable size. (Remember to account for the offset between the blade and the saw foot as you line up the straightedge guide for your cuts.)

❷ Lay the base on a flat worksurface and attach the short and long blocking to it. The ends of the short blocking pieces fit in between the longer blocking. Use glue and 1¼-in. flathead wood screws to fasten the parts **(See Photo A)**. Mark two reference lines along the length of the base on the blocking side to serve as centerlines for attaching the tall side pieces later. Draw a line for the angled side 5⅝ in. from one edge, and draw another line for the vertical side 6⅜ in. from the other edge.

❸ Attach the short and tall edges to the base assembly using glue and 1½-in. flathead wood screws. Flip the base assembly over before attaching the edge pieces so the blocking faces down. Align the ends of the parts and make sure the bottoms of the edge pieces are flush with the bottoms of the blocking. Drill pilot holes first, spacing the screws about every 8 in. Alternate the screws between the base and blocking to increase the joint strength. Mark centerlines on the outside of the tall edge for fastening the dividers. See *Front View (Divided Side)* for locating the dividers. Position the outermost divider lines ⅜ in. from the ends of the tall edge.

INSTALL THE DIVIDERS

❹ Cut the six dividers to size. Follow the measurements given on the *Divider* diagram to mark the angled ends. We used a power miter saw to cut the dividers **(See Photo B)**, but you could also use a

circular saw, table saw or hand saw to make these cuts.

❺ Attach the dividers to the tall edge piece. The outer dividers are attached to the tall edge using glue and 1½-in. screws. Keep the outside faces of the outer dividers flush with the ends of the tall edge. Cut two scrap-plywood spacers, 8 and 12 in. wide, and insert a spacer between each pair of dividers as you attach the dividers with glue and screws **(See Photo C)**. Use the centerlines you drew on the outside of the tall edge for lining up the screws. Then, extend the divider centerlines down around the bottom blocking, and drive two 2¼-in. screws up through the cart base and into the bottom of each divider.

ASSEMBLE THE CENTER SECTION

❻ Rip- and cross-cut the angled side and the four shelves to size. For each of these parts, tilt the saw blade 5° to create a bevel along one long edge. Mark the beveled edges on the parts to keep the orientation clear later.

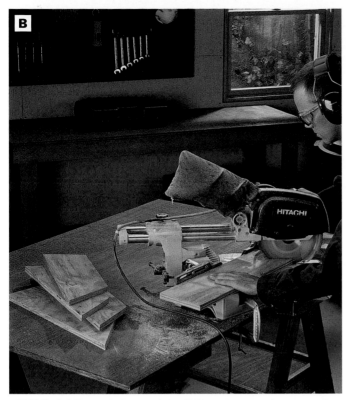

PHOTO B: Cut the angled ends of the dividers. A power miter saw makes this task quick and easy, once you've established the cutting angle. You can also make these cuts with a jig saw, table saw or circular saw.

Spacers

PHOTO C: Glue and screw the dividers to the tall edge with 1½-in. wood screws. Use scrap-wood spacers inserted between the dividers to establish divider spacing.

7 Cut the vertical side to size and rout the shelf dadoes into one face. The dadoes are ¾ in. wide and ¼ in. deep. Mark a set of long reference lines for each of the four dadoes using the *Side Section View* to place the dadoes. Then, extend dado centerlines to the other face of the vertical side to serve as screw guide lines. Cut the dadoes with a router and a ¾-in. straight bit **(See Photo D)**. Clamp a straight-edge on the vertical side to guide the router. To line up the guide, measure the distance from the edge of the router bit to the outer edge of the router base. This is the distance the straightedge must be offset from the closest marked dado line of each cut. Reset the straightedge for cutting each dado.

8 Attach the vertical side. Spread glue onto the edges of the dividers and clamp the vertical side in place so the dadoes face away from the dividers. Drive 1½-in. flathead wood screws through the vertical side into pilot holes in the two end dividers. Then, using your 8- and 12-in. spacers between the dividers as alignment aids, screw the vertical side to the inside dividers. Tip the cart assembly onto the face of the tall edge and drive 1½-in. screws along the vertical side reference line to attach the vertical side to the base.

PHOTO D: Cut shelf dadoes in the vertical side with a router and straightedge guide. Pull the router toward you as you make each cut, being careful to hold the router base tight against the straightedge as you work.

Sheet Goods Cart 455

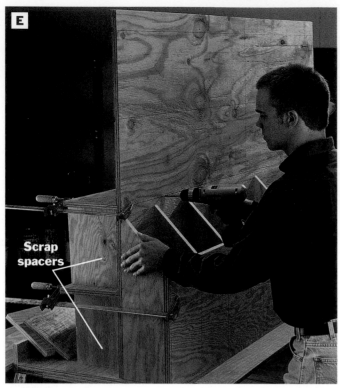

PHOTO E: Fasten the shelves to the vertical side with glue and screws. Support the shelves with scrap-wood spacers. Insert the square edge of the shelves into the dadoes, and keep the beveled edges facing up.

PHOTO F: Draw centerlines for the shelves on the angled side, then fasten the angled side to the shelves with glue and screws. Screw up through the bottom to attach the angled side from below.

9 Attach the shelves to the vertical side (**See Photo E**). Cut eight 10⅜-in.-long scrap spacers to support the ends of the shelves during assembly. Spread glue in the bottom dado and insert the square edge of the bottom shelf into the dado. With the divider side of the cart facing you, keep the end of the shelf flush with the left end of the vertical side. The dado joint for this bottom shelf will be fastened with glue only. Install this shelf so the beveled edge faces up (See *Detail: Shelf dado*) and clamp the shelf. Then, install the rest of the shelves into the dadoes with 1½-in. wood screws and glue. Arrange each shelf so the beveled edge faces up, and support the shelves with spacers. Make sure the left shelf ends are flush with the end of the vertical side.

10 Set the angled side against the shelves and clamp it in place temporarily. Draw shelf centerlines across the face of the angled side, then remove the shelf spacers. Glue and fasten the angled side to the shelves with 1½-in. screws (**See Photo F**). Screw the cart base to the angled side, following the angled side reference line you drew in Step 2.

11 Lay out and cut the end piece to size, using the measurements given in *Drilling Pattern-End.*

Mark the screw locations on the end piece. Set the end piece into position on the end of the cart where the shelves are set back from the ends of the side panels. Attach the end piece to the ends of the shelves with glue and 1½-in. wood screws. Fasten the end piece with 2¼-in. screws driven up through the base and blocking.

INSTALL THE CASTERS
12 Tip the cart on its side and install the four casters. Lay the base of each caster in place on the blocking pieces and use the caster base holes to mark locations for carriage bolts. Position the casters so that all four corners of each caster rest firmly on the bottom blocking. Also, be sure the caster holes will not interfere with screws attaching the bottom blocking or dividers. Drill ⅜-in. pilot holes for each caster. Install the two straight casters on one end and swivelling casters on the other end, with the washers and nuts facing the caster wheels (**See Photo G**).

FINISHING TOUCHES
Expand the storage possibilities of your cart by adding clamp holders to one end. We made ours out of scrap CDX left over from the project. The holder configuration you choose will depend on the number,

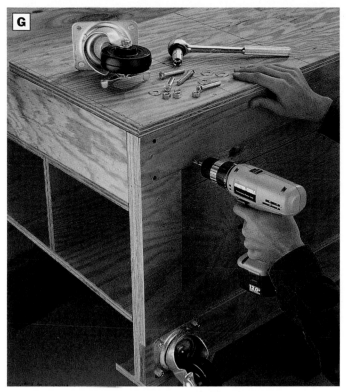

PHOTO G: Attach the casters. Mark bolt hole locations on the corners of the cart bottom, positioning the casters so they sit squarely on the bottom blocking. Drill the holes and bolt the casters in place, with the washers and nuts facing the cart bottom.

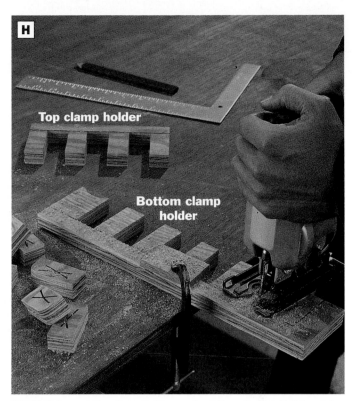

PHOTO H: Lay out the clamp holders and cut them to size. Notches 1 in. wide and 2 in. deep are a good size for holding standard pipe clamps. The bottom clamp holder can be made longer than the top, spanning across the end piece and the end divider.

style and length of clamps you have. We've designed the storage cart tall enough to hang several 4-ft.-long pipe or bar clamps without the clamps dragging on the floor. The bottom holder has additional cutouts for shorter clamps.

13 Make the clamp holders. Each clamp holder is composed of two parts that form an "L" when the parts are assembled. Mark cutouts on the top member of each holder and cut them out with a jig saw (**See Photo H**). For standard pipe clamps, 1-in.-wide cutouts 2 in. deep will hold each clamp securely. Assemble the holders with glue and 1½-in. screws. Then attach the holders to the closed end of the cart using glue and 1½-in. screws (**See Photo I**). Make sure to keep the top and bottom clamp holders aligned when fastening them to the cart so long clamps will hang straight.

14 Break all exposed sharp edges with sandpaper to minimize splinters. We chose not to apply any finish to our sheet goods cart, but you may prefer to dress yours up with a couple coats of enamel paint. If you plan to store veneered plywood sheets with finished faces on your cart, you may want to add strips of carpet to the face of the angled side to protect the veneer from scratches.

PHOTO I: Fasten the clamp holders to scrap blocking, and screw the blocking to the end of the cart with 1½-in. wood screws. Keep the slots aligned between the holders so the clamps will hang straight.

Sheet Goods Cart 457

Wall-Hung Utility Cabinet

Wouldn't it be great to get tools, paint and odds-and-ends off the garage floor and out of sight? This sturdy wall unit provides lots of secure, accessible storage space. It features shallow lipped shelves on both doors as well as deeper shelves in the cabinet itself. This cabinet has a place for everything, and with both doors fully opened, it's all right there at your fingertips. When not in use, your tools and hazardous materials can be securely protected behind lock and key.

Vital Statistics

TYPE: Wall-mounted locker

OVERALL SIZE: 48W by 48¾H by 18D

MATERIAL: Exterior plywood

JOINERY: Butt joints reinforced with glue and screws

CONSTRUCTION DETAILS:
- Efficiently built from just three sheets of plywood
- Designed without complex joinery in order to simplify construction
- Finished inside and out to withstand damp garage or basement environments
- Fastens to wall studs with lag screws

FINISH: Exterior primer and paint

Building time

PREPARING STOCK: 0 hours

LAYOUT: 1-2 hours

CUTTING PARTS: 2-4 hours

ASSEMBLY: 3-5 hours

FINISHING: 3-5 hours

TOTAL: 9-16 hours

Shopping List

- ☐ (3) ¾ in. × 4 × 8 ft. exterior plywood
- ☐ 2 in. deck screws
- ☐ (4) 4 in. flush-mounted butt hinges
- ☐ Hasp
- ☐ (6) ¼ × 3½ in. lag screws, washers
- ☐ #10 flathead machine screws, washers, nylon lock nuts (for mounting the hinges)
- ☐ (6) ¼ × 3½ in. lag screws, washers
- ☐ Moisture-resistant wood glue
- ☐ Finishing materials

Wall-Hung Utility Cabinet

4" flush-mounted steel hinges. Attach with #10 - 24 x 1 1/4" machine scews, washers & lock nuts, typ.

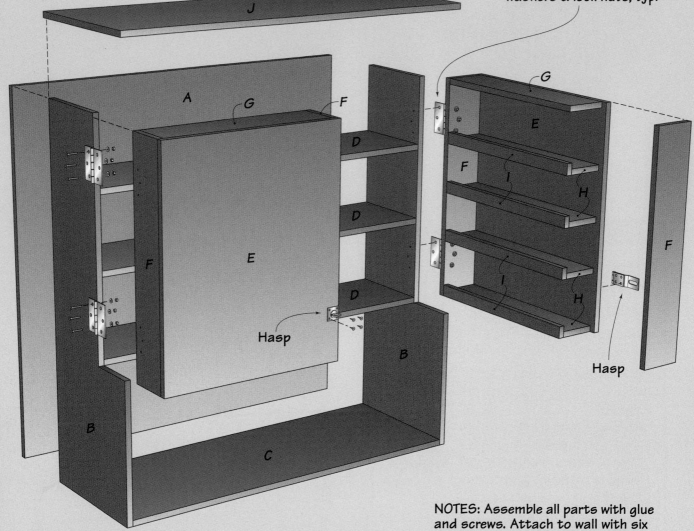

Hasp

Hasp

NOTES: Assemble all parts with glue and screws. Attach to wall with six 1/4" x 3 1/2" lag screws & washers. Drive lag screws into wall studs.

Wall-Hung Utility Cabinet Cutting List

Part	No.	Size	Material
A. Cabinet back	1	3/4 × 48 × 48 in.	Exterior plywood
B. Cabinet sides	2	3/4 × 16³/4 × 48 in.	"
C. Cabinet bottom	1	3/4 × 16³/4 × 46½ in.	"
D. Cabinet shelves	3	3/4 × 10⁵/8 × 46½ in.	"
E. Door backs	2	3/4 × 23³/4 × 29 in.	"
F. Door sides	4	3/4 × 5¼ × 29 in.	"
G. Door tops	2	3/4 × 5¼ × 22¼ in.	"
H. Door shelves	8	3/4 × 4½ × 22¼ in.	"
I. Door shelf lips	8	3/4 × 1½ × 22¼ in.	"
J. Cabinet top	1	3/4 × 18 × 48 in.	"

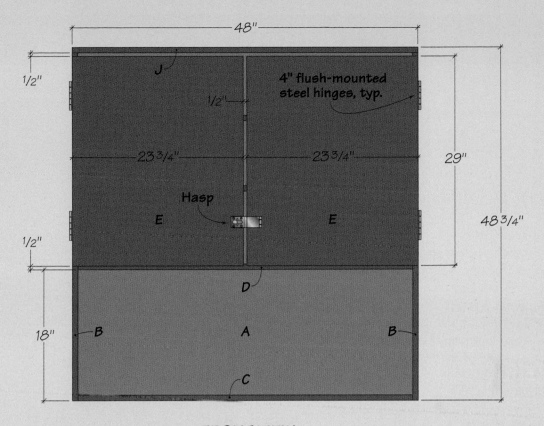

FRONT VIEW

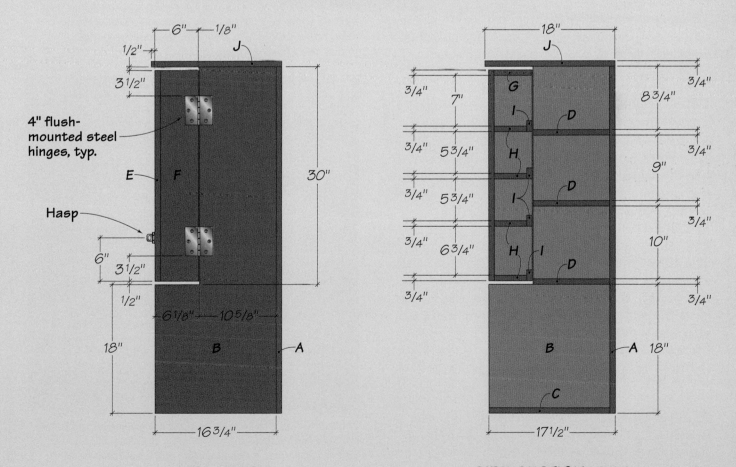

SIDE VIEW

SIDE SECTION VIEW

This heavy-duty utility locker is designed to be constructed entirely from three 4 × 8 sheets of ¾-in. exterior plywood. Before actually cutting any parts, we recommend laying out a cutting scheme to ensure that you'll be able to cut all the parts from the three sheets. Also, before you begin building, think about what you want to store in your cabinet; we have specified shelf positions that make efficient use of the interior space and facilitate storing many kinds of tools and supplies, but you may want to vary some of the shelf positions depending on your specific storage needs.

This project consists of three structures—the basic cabinet and two doors—which are built individually and then joined to form the completed cabinet.

BUILD THE CABINET

❶ Lay out and cut out the cabinet parts—the back, sides, bottom, shelves and top. The safest way to cut down full-size plywood sheets is to use a circular saw guided along a clamped straightedge. When cutting the side pieces to their final "L" shape, make the primary cuts with a circular saw and finish the inside corners with a hand saw or jig saw.

❷ On the cabinet sides, mark center lines for drilling pilot holes for the screws that will attach the bottom and the shelves. Place the sides back-to-back on your worksurface with their ends aligned, measure and mark the screw hole locations, and use a framing square as a guide to extend reference lines across both plywood pieces at one time (**See Photo A**). See the *Side Section View* drawing for locating the cabinet shelf positions.

❸ Begin assembling the cabinet. Stand the side pieces on their back edges on your worksurface so your screw layout lines face outward. Spread an even layer of glue on the ends of the shelves and bottom.

PHOTO A: Mark reference lines on the cabinet sides for drilling pilot holes for screws that will attach the shelves and bottom. Lay the cabinet sides back to back. Draw both sets of reference lines at once with a framing square.

PHOTO B: Spread glue on the ends of the cabinet shelves and bottom, set these parts between the cabinet sides and clamp the assembly together. Reinforce the glue joints with countersunk screws, driven through the cabinet sides.

PHOTO C: Lay the cabinet face-down on a pair of sawhorses or another suitable worksurface. Spread glue along the back edges of the shelves and bottom. Clamp the back in place and drive countersunk screws through the back into the shelves and bottom.

PHOTO D: Glue a strip of shelf nosing along one long edge of each 8-ft. piece of shelving to form a long shelf blank. Clamp the nosing in place so one edge is flush with one of the shelf faces.

Clamp the shelves and bottom into position between the sides. Drill countersunk pilot holes along your reference lines, and fasten the pieces together with 2-in. deck screws **(See Photo B).** Remove the clamps.

4 Attach the cabinet back. Turn the cabinet over and apply glue to the back edges of the bottom, shelves and sides. Clamp the back in place, using it to square up the cabinet box. Draw reference lines across the back to mark the shelf positions for locating screws. Fasten the back to the cabinet with screws driven into countersunk pilot holes **(See Photo C).** Use plenty of screws when fastening the back to the sides, shelves and bottom—all the weight of the cabinet and its contents will be supported by the back when the cabinet hangs on the wall.

5 Install the cabinet top. Stand the cabinet right-side-up on the floor, apply glue to the top edges of the sides and back, then position the top so its back edge and ends are flush. Drill countersunk pilot holes and attach the top to the cabinet with screws.

BUILD THE DOORS
The doors are actually two small shelf units. The door shelves are lipped along the front edges to prevent items from sliding off when the doors swing.

6 Make the door shelf stock. Rip two pieces of ply-

wood 4½ in. wide × 96 in. long for the shelves. Rip two additional pieces 1½ in. wide × 96 in. long for the shelf nosing. Glue a nosing strip to the edge of each shelf strip, holding the pieces in place with clamps until the glue dries **(See Photo D).**

PHOTO E: Cut the door shelves to length. We used a power miter saw with a stopblock clamped to the fence so the shelf lengths would match. Incidentally, you can use the same stopblock setting for cutting the door tops to length.

PHOTO F: Glue and clamp the door sides, top and shelves together, then drive countersunk 2-in. screws through the door sides to reinforce all the door joints. Once the door frames are assembled, attach the door backs to the frames with glue and screws.

PHOTO G: Conceal all screwheads with wood filler, sand the entire cabinet and apply a coat of primer followed by two coats of paint. If moisture resistance or appearance aren't concerns for you, you could also leave the cabinet unfinished.

7 Cut the door shelves to length. Clamp a stopblock to the fence of a power miter saw to ensure that all the shelves will be exactly the same length (**See Photo E**). You could also cut the shelves with a circular saw or a table saw. However you make these cuts, be sure the shelf lengths are equal.

8 Cut the remaining door parts— the backs, sides and tops—to size.

9 On the door sides, mark screw-hole centerlines for attaching the shelves and the tops. Assuming the shelf positions are identical for both door units, the door sides can be quickly and accurately gang-marked by laying the parts side by side with their ends aligned.

10 Assemble the door parts. Spread glue on the ends of the shelves and top, and clamp them in place between the pairs of sides. Drill countersunk pilot holes along the centerlines, and fasten the parts together with deck screws (**See Photo F**).

11 Attach the door backs. Measure and mark screw hole centerlines on the door backs. Apply glue to the back edges of the sides, shelves and top. Set the door backs into place, using them to square up the door frames. Drill countersunk pilot holes and attach the backs to the door frames with screws.

FINISH THE CABINET & DOORS

12 Fill the screw holes and any voids in the plywood edges with wood filler. Once the filler dries, sand all surfaces and edges. Apply primer and two coats of exterior paint (**See Photo G**).

MOUNT THE DOORS

Since the doors are heavy, the hinges attach to the doors and cabinet with #10 machine screws, washers and nylon lock nuts.

⓭ Install the doors. Lay the cabinet on it's back and use ⅛-in.-thick shims for spacing the doors out from the cabinet. Position the doors top-to-bottom and left-to-right. Use the *Side View* drawing for locating the four corner holes of each hinge on the cabinet. Fasten the hinges temporarily with wood screws. Drill the remaining hinge holes to accept the machine screws, and install the screws with washers and lock nuts **(See Photo H)**. Remove the wood screws and replace them with machine screws, washers and nylon lock nuts.

⓮ Position and attach the hasp to the door backs using the screws provided with the hasp.

INSTALL THE CABINET

When positioning the cabinet on the garage wall, consider three factors: A) The height of the cabinet off the floor—is there enough space for whatever you want to store below it? B) The overall width of the cabinet with the doors open—is there enough room for full access to the cabinet? C) Sufficient support; try to position the cabinet so you can fasten it to three studs if possible, and definitely to no fewer than two.

⓯ Prop the cabinet securely in place against the wall and level it. Drill ¼-in. pilot holes through the cabinet back into the wall studs, and attach the cabinet to the wall with 3½-in. lag screws and washers **(See Photo I)**.

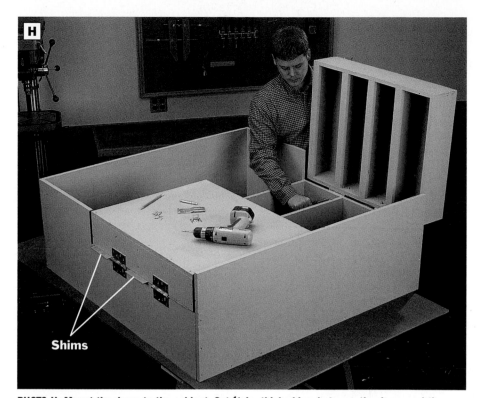

Shims

PHOTO H: Mount the doors to the cabinet. Set ⅛-in.-thick shims between the doors and the cabinet first, locate the hinge positions and attach the hinges temporarily with a few wood screws. Drill pilot holes for machine screws that will attach the hinges to the cabinet parts. Then install the machine screws with washers and nylon lock nuts to ensure strong connections.

PHOTO I: Select a spot for the cabinet that allows you to open the doors fully while providing at least two wall studs for mounting purposes. Position and level the cabinet on the wall. Then drive ¼ × 3½-in. lag screws through the cabinet back and into the wall studs.

Woodworking Workbench

Your workbench sets the tone for your workshop. From a discarded kitchen table or an old door laid across a pair of rickety sawhorses, to a gleaming oak masterpiece that looks too fancy to dine on, much less work on, there are just about as many styles of benches as there are woodworkers. The maple workbench built in this chapter is stylish enough for showing off, but it's designed to be used—and used hard. The design is simple enough that you can easily modify it to meet your special needs or tastes.

Vital Statistics: Workbench

TYPE: Workbench

OVERALL SIZE: 60W by 36H by 24D

MATERIAL: Hard maple

JOINERY: Butt joints reinforced with lag screws, and dowel joints

CONSTRUCTION DETAILS:
- Solid maple, butcher-block style benchtop with 1,440 sq. in. of worksurface
- Storage shelf
- Adjustable bench dogs
- Comfortable 36-in. working height
- Permanent woodworking vises

FINISHING OPTIONS: Danish oil (one coat only) or other clear topcoat that can be refreshed easily, such as linseed oil.

Building time

PREPARING STOCK
4-6 hours

LAYOUT
2-4 hours

CUTTING PARTS
4-6 hours

ASSEMBLY
4-6 hours

FINISHING
1-2 hours

TOTAL: 15-24 hours

Tools you'll use

- Surface planer
- Jointer
- Table saw
- Band saw or jig saw
- Circular saw
- Straightedge cutting guide
- Bar or pipe clamps
- Drill
- Belt sander or hand plane
- Combination square
- Doweling jig
- Drill guide
- Socket wrench and sockets

Shopping list

- ☐ (4) 6/4 × 6 in. × 12 ft. hard maple boards
- ☐ (3) 6/4 × 4 in. × 8 ft. hard maple boards
- ☐ (2) 4/4 × 4 in. × 6 ft. hard maple boards
- ☐ (1 or 2) woodworker's bench vises
- ☐ (4-6) 3/4-in.-dia. brass bench dogs with square tops
- ☐ Wood glue
- ☐ #10 × 1½-in. wood screws
- ☐ 3/8 in. lag screws (1½ in., 2 in., 3 in.) with washers
- ☐ ½ × 2-in. fluted dowel pins
- ☐ Finishing materials

Woodworking Workbench

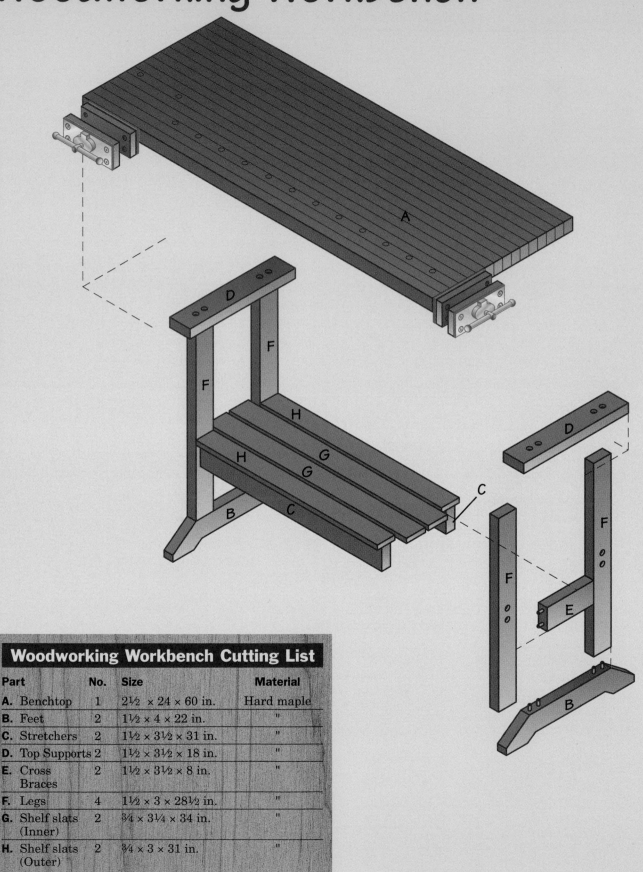

Woodworking Workbench Cutting List

Part	No.	Size	Material
A. Benchtop	1	2½ × 24 × 60 in.	Hard maple
B. Feet	2	1½ × 4 × 22 in.	"
C. Stretchers	2	1½ × 3½ × 31 in.	"
D. Top Supports	2	1½ × 3½ × 18 in.	"
E. Cross Braces	2	1½ × 3½ × 8 in.	"
F. Legs	4	1½ × 3 × 28½ in.	"
G. Shelf slats (Inner)	2	¾ × 3¼ × 34 in.	"
H. Shelf slats (Outer)	2	¾ × 3 × 31 in.	"

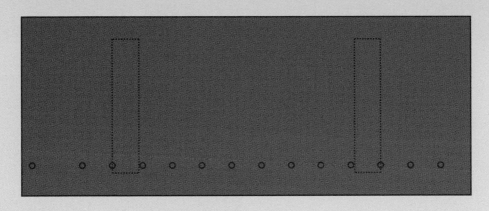

TOP VIEW

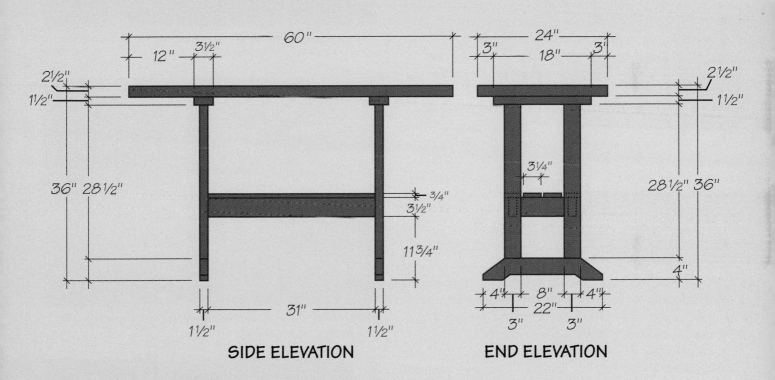

60"

12" 3½"

2½"
1½"

36" 28½"

¾"
3½"

11¾"

31"

1½" 1½"

SIDE ELEVATION

3" 24" 3"
18"

2½"
1½"

3¼"

28½" 36"

4"

4" 8" 4"
22"

3" 3"

END ELEVATION

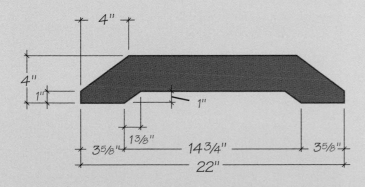

4"

4"
1"

1"

3⅝" 1⅜" 14¾" 3⅝"
22"

FOOT LAYOUT

PHOTO A: Face-glue the benchtop in sections of four or five boards, then face-glue the sections together.

MAKE THE LAMINATED BENCHTOP

Butcher-block style, face-laminated benchtops made from hardwood have several advantages: they are exceptionally stable from side to side and end to end; the worksurface itself consists of edge grain (or, in some cases, end grain), which is highly dent resistant and can be resurfaced easily after extended wear; and, because most hardwoods are very dense, the sheer weight of a solid hardwood benchtop results in a very sturdy worksurface. *Tip: The workbench project shown here has a 2½-in.-thick benchtop that was designed to accommodate a vise with 2½-in.-tall jaws. Because jaw size varies widely, it's a good idea to purchase your vise or vises before building the benchtop and modify the thickness of the top, if needed, to fit the particular vise you buy.*

1 Face-joint 6/4 hard maple stock to create smooth surfaces on both faces. This will result in boards not quite 1½ in. thick, but it's far more economical (and less time-consuming) than reducing 8/4 stock to 1½ in. thick. You can use a surface planer to smooth the boards, but it's important to joint the faces as well, since a planer will not square the stock. Prepare enough stock for 16, 62-in.-long × 2½-in.-wide boards.

2 Joint one edge of each board, then rip-cut them into 2½-in.-wide strips. Cross-cut the boards to 62 in. long (you'll trim off the excess length after the glue-up is completed). Lay out the wood strips side-by-side, 2½ in. high, on a flat worksurface. Clamp the strips together with a bar or pipe clamp, making sure the edges are all flush on the top surface of the benchtop. Draw reference lines 8 to 10 in. apart across the top, perpendicular to the joints, and number the boards in sequence.

3 Unclamp the boards and divide them into groups of four or five boards (for glue-ups involving more

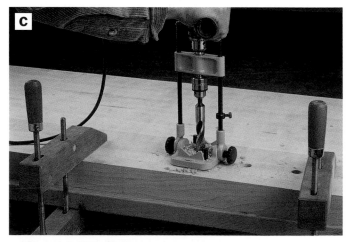

PHOTO B: Flatten the top and bottom surfaces of the benchtop, using a belt sander or a hand plane.

PHOTO C: Drill holes for the bench dogs at approximately 6-in. intervals, using a portable drill guide to keep the holes straight.

PHOTO D: Use fluted, ½ × 2-In. dowel pins to reinforce the joints between the legs and the cross braces.

PHOTO E: Use pipe clamps to draw the feet tightly against the bottoms of the legs.

than four or five pieces of stock, it's easier to break up the project into smaller sections, then glue those sections together). Apply glue to the mating wood faces and glue up each section. Use bar or pipe clamps to draw the boards together, and keep the edges of the boards flush (the ends can stagger slightly, since they'll be trimmed square later).

❹ After the glue on the benchtop sections has cured, glue the sections together to create the benchtop **(See Photo A).** Take care to keep the edges flush at the top and bottom of the benchtop—wood cauls clamped above and below the benchtop are helpful for this purpose. Alternate bar or pipe clamps above and below the glue-up to equalize clamping pressure. Only tighten the clamps until the joints are tight; don't overtighten or you can squeeze the joints dry of glue. Leave the clamps on until the glue cures.

❺ Scrape the dried glue from both sides, and level the top and bottom surfaces using a belt sander or hand plane. If using a belt sander, avoid sanding belts coarser than 100-grit, and make initial sanding passes diagonally across the glue joints **(See Photo B).** If using a hand plane, plane diagonally across the grain until the surface is flat, then plane with the grain. Finish smoothing with a cabinet scraper or sandpaper. Run a long straightedge over the surfaces to test for flatness. A perfectly flat worksurface is very important to successful woodworking, so it's worth investing some time and energy into achieving a perfectly flat top.

❻ Use a circular saw with a straightedge cutting guide fence to trim the ends of the benchtop so it's 60 in. long. Trim some stock from both ends, making sure the ends are square to the edges of the top.

❼ Mark a layout line for drilling guide holes for the bench dogs. We used a ¾-in.-dia. brad-point bit to drill the guide holes for the ¾-in.-dia. dogs we purchased. If the vise you'll be installing on the end of your bench has a pop-up bench dog, draw the layout line so it's aligned with the center of the vise dog after the vise is installed. Otherwise, center the line with the midpoint of the vise jaw. We drilled guide holes every 6 in. Use a portable drill guide to ensure that the holes are exactly vertical **(See Photo C).**

BUILD THE BASE

❽ Rip four 1½-in.-thick boards to 3 in. wide, then cross-cut them to 28½ in. to make the legs. Rip the two 1½-in.-thick leg cross braces to 3½ in. wide, then cut them to a length of 8 in.

❾ Draw square lines across the inside edges of the legs for the placement of the cross braces. The lower lines should be 7¾ in. up from the bottoms of the legs, and the upper lines should be 3½ in. above the lower lines. Lay out holes for two ½ × 2-in. fluted dowels per joint and drill holes with a dowel drilling guide. Glue the dowels and joints and clamp up two legs to a cross support, padding the clamps to protect the wood **(See Photo D).** Check the squareness by measuring to make sure the distance between the

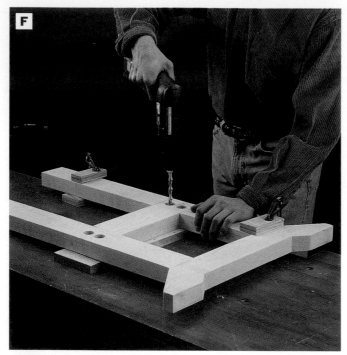

PHOTO F: Drill counterbore holes for the lag screw heads and washers, and drill clearance holes and pilot holes for the shanks of the screws.

PHOTO G: After pilot holes are drilled, assemble the base with lag screws and washers driven with a socket wrench.

tops of the legs and the bottoms is the same. Make both side assemblies.

10 Cut the feet to 4 × 22 in. Lay out the angled cutting lines by marking out the measurements shown in the *Foot layout drawing*. Use a straightedge to draw lines connecting these marks. Cut out the shape of the feet with a band saw or jig saw. Sand the sawn edges smooth.

11 Lay out and drill dowel holes connecting the ends of the legs to the tops of the feet. Glue and clamp the feet to the legs **(See Photo E)**.

12 Rip the two leg stretchers and the two leg top supports to 3½ in. wide from 1½ in. stock. Cross-cut the stretchers to 31 in. and the supports to 18 in.

13 Continue the cross support layout lines already on the legs, squaring them across the faces of the legs to serve as placement lines for the leg stretchers. Mark lines for the thickness of the stretchers, centered on the legs. Mark centerpoints for two lag-screw pilot holes at each joint. Drill ¾-in.-dia. × ⅜-in.-deep counterbores for each hole, then drill ¼-in. pilots through the center of each counterbored hole **(See Photo F)**.

14 Position the stretchers between the side assemblies and assemble the base temporarily by clamping across the leg cross supports. Line the stretchers up with their marks and drill pilot holes through the lag holes into the ends of the stretchers. Drill counterbored holes in the top supports, then center the top supports on the legs and drill pilot holes into the tops of the legs. Also drill guide holes for the lag screws that attach the top supports to the underside of the benchtop.

15 Attach the legs to the ends of the leg stretchers with ⅜ × 3-in. lag screws fitted with ⅜-in. washers **(See Photo G)**. Bolt the leg top supports to the tops of the legs with the same size lag screws.

INSTALL THE SHELF

16 Plane 4/4 maple down to ¾ in. thick to make the shelf slats. Rip-cut and cross-cut the inner and outer slats to size.

17 Lay the outside shelf slats onto the stretchers, with their edges flush with the sides of the legs. Drill a countersunk pilot hole for a #10 × 1½-in. flathead wood screw near each end of each outer slat, centered over the stretcher below.

18 Place the inside shelf slats on the leg cross braces with their ends flush with the braces. Use ½-in.

PHOTO H: Screw the inner and outer slats to the stretchers and cross braces to create a storage shelf.

PHOTO I: Center the base on the underside of the benchtop, then attach it with lag screws driven through the top supports.

spacer blocks between slats to ensure even gaps. Drill a pair of countersunk pilot holes at the end of each inner slat, centered over the cross brace below. Drive two #10 × 1½-in. flathead wood screws at each end **(See Photo H).**

ATTACH THE BENCHTOP

⑲ Sand all parts to 150-grit and ease all sharp edges.

⑳ Lay the benchtop upside-down and center the base on the underside of the top. Drill counterbored pilot holes into the top and attach the leg top supports to the underside of the top with washers and ⅜ × 3-in. lag screws **(See Photo I).**

APPLY FINISHING TOUCHES

㉑ Read the manufacturer's instructions for installing your bench vises. Cut hardwood jaw plates and screw them to the metal jaws through the jaw holes on the vise. Make up the appropriate filler blocks to shim each vise so the top edges of the jaws are flush with the benchtop. The vises we selected for our bench are installed with ⅜ × 2-in. lag screws driven up through the underside of the vise and into the benchtop **(See Photo J).**

㉒ Apply a protective finish to the workbench. We used a single coat of Danish oil. Do not apply more

PHOTO J: Install the vise or vises according to the manufacturer's installation instructions (they may differ from model to model).

than one coat of finishing material, since multiple layers make the surface more slippery. Every other year or so, depending on wear, remove the oil finish with mineral spirits, sand the surface, and apply a fresh finish.

Index